POISONING THE PRESS

POISONING
THE PRESS

RICHARD NIXON, JACK ANDERSON,

AND THE RISE OF WASHINGTON'S

SCANDAL CULTURE

MARK FELDSTEIN

FARRAR, STRAUS AND GIROUX   NEW YORK

Farrar, Straus and Giroux
18 West 18th Street, New York 10011

Distributed in Canada by D&M Publishers, Inc.
Printed in the United States of America
First edition, 2010

Library of Congress Cataloging-in-Publication Data
Feldstein, Mark Avrom.
     Poisoning the press : Richard Nixon, Jack Anderson, and the rise of
Washington's scandal culture / Mark Feldstein. — 1st ed.
        p.   cm.
     Includes bibliographical references and index.
     ISBN 978-0-374-23530-7
     1. Nixon, Richard M. (Richard Milhous), 1913–1994—Relations with
journalists.   2. Anderson, Jack, 1922–2005.   3. Press and politics United
States—History—20th century.   4. Presidents—United States—Press coverage—
Case studies.   5. United States—Politics and government—1969–1974.
6. Political corruption—United States—History— 20th century.   7. Political
culture—United States—History—20th century.   8. Political culture—
Washington (D.C.)—History—20th century.   9. Presidents—United States—
Biography.   10. Journalists—United States—Biography.   I. Title.

     E856.F45 2010
     973.924092—dc22

                                                            2010010272

Designed by Jonathan D. Lippincott

www.fsgbooks.com

1   3   5   7   9   10   8   6   4   2

For Beth and Robbie,
my unconditional pride
and everlasting joy

One day we'll get them—we'll get them on the ground where we want them. And we'll stick our heels in, step on them hard, and twist.

—Richard Nixon

Nothing produces such exhilaration, zest for daily life, and all-around gratification as a protracted, ugly, bitter-end vendetta that rages for years and exhausts both sides, often bringing one to ruin.

—Jack Anderson

CONTENTS

POISONING
THE PRESS

PROLOGUE

It seemed an unlikely spot to plan an assassination. After all, the Hay-Adams was once one of Washington's most venerable old mansions, adorned with plush leather chairs, rich walnut paneling, and ornate oil paintings, located on Lafayette Square directly across the street from the White House. But on a chilly afternoon in March 1972, in one of the most bizarre and overlooked chapters of American political history, the luxury hotel did indeed serve as a launching pad for a murder conspiracy. More surprising still was the target of this assassination scheme, syndicated columnist Jack Anderson, then the most famous investigative reporter in the United States, whose exposés had plagued President Richard Nixon since he had first entered politics more than two decades earlier. Most astonishing of all, the men who plotted to execute the journalist were covert Nixon operatives dispatched after the President himself darkly informed aides that Anderson was "a thorn in [his] side" and that "we've got to do something with this son of a bitch."

The conspirators included former agents of the FBI and CIA who had been trained in a variety of clandestine techniques, including assassinations, and who would later go to prison for their notorious break-in at Democratic Party headquarters in the Watergate building. According to their own testimony, the men weighed various methods of eliminating the columnist: by spiking one of his drinks or his aspirin bottle with a special poison that would go undetected in an autopsy, or by putting LSD on his steering wheel so that he would absorb it through his skin while driving and die in a hallucination-crazed auto crash.

In one sense, the White House plot to poison a newsman was unprecedented. Certainly no other president in American history had ever been suspected of ordering a Mafia-style hit to silence a journalistic critic. Yet it was also an extreme and literal example of a larger conspiracy to contaminate the rest of the media as well, a metaphor for what would become a generation of toxic conflict between the press and the politicians they covered. It was not just that Nixon's administration wiretapped journalists, put them on enemies lists, audited their tax returns, censored their newspapers, and moved to revoke their broadcasting licenses. It was, more lastingly, that Nixon and his staff pioneered the modern White House propaganda machine, using mass-market advertising techniques to manipulate its message in ways that all subsequent administrations would be forced to emulate. Nixon simultaneously introduced the notion of liberal media bias even as he launched a host of spinmeisters who assembled a network of conservative news outlets that would drive the political agenda into the twenty-first century. At the same time, Nixon and subsequent presidents effectively bought off news corporations by deregulating them, allowing them to gorge themselves on a noxious diet of sensationalism and trivialities that reaped record profits while debasing public discourse.

How did all of this come to pass? In many ways, the rise of Washington's modern scandal culture began with Richard Nixon and Jack Anderson, and their blistering twenty-five-year battle symbolized and accelerated the growing conflict between the presidency and the press in the Cold War era. This bitter struggle between the most embattled politician and reviled investigative reporter of their time would lead to bribery and blackmail, forgery and burglary, sexual smears and secret surveillance—as well as the assassination plot. Their story reveals not only how one president sabotaged the press, but also how this rancorous relationship continues to the present day. It was Richard Nixon's ultimate revenge.

It was this very lust for revenge—Nixon's obsession with enemies—that would destroy him in the end. In the President's eyes, his antagonists in what he called the "Eastern establishment" were legion: liberals, activists, intellectuals, members of Congress, the federal bureaucracy. But none was more roundly despised than the news media, and none in the media more than Jack Anderson, a bulldog of a reporter who pounded out his blunt accusations on the green keys of an old brown manual typewriter in an office three blocks from the White House. Although largely forgotten today, Anderson was once the most widely read and feared newsman in the United States, a self-proclaimed Paul Revere of journalism with a confrontational style that matched his beefy physique. Part freedom fighter, part carnival huckster, part righteous rogue, the flamboyant columnist was the last descendant of the crusading muckrakers of the early twentieth century. He held their lonely banner aloft in the conformist decades afterward, when deference to authority characterized American journalism and politics alike.

At his peak, Anderson reached an audience approaching seventy million people—nearly the entire voting populace—in radio and television broadcasts, magazines, newsletters, books, and speeches. But it was his daily 750-word exposé, the "Washington Merry-Go-Round," that was the primary source of his power; published in nearly one thousand newspapers, it became the longest-running and most popular syndicated column in the nation. Anderson's exposés—acquired by eavesdropping, rifling through garbage, and swiping classified documents—sent politicians to prison and led targets to commit suicide. He epitomized everything that Richard Nixon abhorred.

The President had always believed the press was out to get him, and in Anderson he found confirmation of his deepest anxieties. The newsman had a hand in virtually every key slash-and-burn attack on Nixon during his career, from the young congressman's earliest Red-baiting in the 1940s to his financial impropriety in the White House during the 1970s. Even Nixon's most intimate psychiatric secrets were fodder for Anderson's column. The battle between the two men lasted a generation, triggered by differences of politics and personality, centered on the most inflammatory Washington scandals of their era. In the beginning, Anderson's relentless reporting helped plant the first seeds of Nixonian press paranoia. In the end, Anderson's disclosures led to criminal convictions of senior presidential advisors and portions of articles of impeachment against the Chief Executive himself. The columnist both exposed and fueled the worst abuses of the Nixon White

House, which eventually reached their apogee in the Watergate scandal that ended his presidency in disgrace.

Surprisingly, the story of the Nixon-Anderson blood feud is little known, in part because the muckraker's checkered reputation made him an unsympathetic hero to contemporaries and in part because he was overshadowed by other reporters during the Watergate scandal. In addition, the Nixon cover-up continues even from the grave, as his estate and federal agencies block access to many historical records. Still, a wealth of fresh material—oral history interviews, once-classified government documents, and previously secret White House tape recordings— shed new light on this fascinating tale of intrigue.

The struggle between Nixon and Anderson personified a larger story of political scandal in the nation's capital during the decades after World War II and involved a virtual Who's Who of Washington's most powerful players: Joseph McCarthy, J. Edgar Hoover, Martin Luther King, George Wallace, Henry Kissinger, Ronald Reagan, and all three Kennedy brothers, John, Robert, and Teddy. Anderson's vilification of Nixon, a blend of courageous reporting and cheap shots, focused on his private as well as his public life and helped usher in what another beleaguered president, Bill Clinton, would call "the politics of personal destruction." It was a supreme irony that Nixon triggered a renaissance of the very investigative reporting he so passionately reviled, and it turned out to be one of his most lasting legacies.

In turn, the President's fierce campaign against Anderson proved to be the forerunner of the modern White House political attack machine. Not only did Nixon set the combative tone that would resonate in the "war rooms" of future election campaigns and administrations, he also helped launch the careers of many powerful personalities— Dick Cheney, Donald Rumsfeld, Patrick Buchanan, Karl Rove, Roger Ailes, Lucianne Goldberg—who would achieve notoriety for their own abilities to manipulate the media on behalf of Nixon's presidential successors. While Anderson's tireless muckraking of Nixon was exceptional, the vitriol it spawned would become standard fare in the nation's capital for the next generation.

To be sure, Anderson was just one in a legion of Nixonian enemies, just as Nixon was only one of Anderson's many antagonists; in no sense was the relationship between the President and the columnist one of equals. It is not surprising that the two men had only a handful of face-to-face encounters over the years: Nixon kept his distance from most reporters, even sympathetic ones, and Anderson rarely spent much time with his prey. Still, "as a target of ugly thoughts," the President's legal counsel said, the investigative columnist eclipsed all of Nixon's other adversaries. "At the White House," another senior advisor recalled, "we considered him our arch nemesis."

For a variety of reasons, Anderson posed the greatest threat of any newsman: because he was willing to publish derogatory information that more mainstream journalists eschewed; because his syndicated column allowed independence from censorship by any single editor or publisher; and because he was unencumbered by any pretense of objectivity. Indeed, Anderson unabashedly thrust himself into the fray, gleefully passing out classified documents to other reporters and righteously testifying before congressional committees and grand juries that would invariably be convened in the wake of his disclosures. In the secret office of Nixon's White House operatives, Anderson's name was posted on the wall as a kind of public enemy number one, inspiring them against their foe. According to one presidential aide, Nixon's enmity was so great that "he will fight, bleed and die before he will admit to Jack Anderson that he's wrong or that he's made a mistake."

The warfare between the two was intermittent, punctuated by an occasional truce born of expediency or exhaustion or some greater enemy looming temporarily on the horizon. With each attack came a counterattack, until it became nearly impossible to determine who struck first or who was really at fault. While Anderson hounded Nixon in the full glare of the media spotlight, the President's assaults were launched in secret and designed to remain hidden.

In their determination to vanquish each other—and in their larger quest for power—Nixon and Anderson did not hesitate to use ruthless tactics. The President's transgressions, of course, were criminal, and included obstruction of justice by paying hush money to cover up the Watergate break-in, and other acts of political sabotage and abuse of power. Anderson's infractions were less infamous but also glaring. Years before Watergate, he was linked to bugging and break-ins, and he came perilously close to exposure for bribery and extortion of his news sources. Both men rationalized their duplicitous means in the belief that their ultimate ends were pure. Neither seemed to appreciate the inherent moral contradiction in what they did, or the similarities between their own calculating opportunism. Although both were propelled by a sense of personal virtue, they would be remembered above all for their dirty tricks.

In the end, Nixon and Anderson both learned the hard way the true, coarse price of power, brazenly grasped through fleeting alliances of convenience and a myriad of compromises great and small. "Few reach the political pinnacles without selling what they do not own and promising what is not theirs to give," Anderson wrote, for "it is easy to forget that power belongs not to those who possess it for the moment, but to the nation and its people." Yet this was as true for journalists like Jack Anderson as it was for politicians like Richard Nixon. In utterly different ways, these utterly different men both played crucial parts in poisoning government and the press.

Of course, predatory politics did not begin with Richard Nixon, and America's scandal-obsessed media long predates Jack Anderson. In the earliest days of the Republic, vilification of the press was standard fare. The normally controlled George Washington was "much inflamed" by the "personal abuse which had been bestowed on him" by journalists, said his secretary of state, Thomas Jefferson; the first president was enraged when newspapers published confidential Cabinet minutes, which may have been leaked by Jefferson himself in an effort to influence administration policy. Through the press, Jefferson supporters also exposed a sex scandal involving his rival, Treasury Secretary Alexander Hamilton, a character assassination that became quite literal when it culminated in Hamilton's fatal duel with Jefferson's vice president, Aaron Burr. But using the media as an instrument of political warfare worked both ways, and venomous editors savaged Jefferson with equal bile; one newspaper claimed that the Chief Executive kept "as his concubine, one of his slaves" and with "this wench Sally, our president has had several children." It would be nearly two centuries before DNA testing corroborated this sexposé, which lived on for posterity thanks to the free press that Jefferson championed. No wonder the father of the First Amendment ultimately lamented "the putrid state into which our newspapers have passed."

In Jefferson's time, most publications were funded not by advertising, as they are today, but by political parties, which used the press as a weapon of propaganda. In the nation's capital, favored printers received lucrative federal contracts to transcribe congressional debates, making Washington journalism an unsavory blend of stenography and partisanship that has persisted to the present. Still, as media outlets evolved from party organs to profit-making businesses, the most vicious forms of journalistic invective began to fade away. The commercialization of news led papers to try to maximize circulation and avoid alienating readers by not choosing sides between one party or the other. Politicians and the press formed symbiotic relationships, linked by professional and financial self-interest; many Washington reporters secretly moonlighted on the side for officials they covered. Journalistic and governmental corruption became particularly rampant in the late nineteenth century, when the soaring profits of the industrial revolution led politicians to sell their votes and reporters to prostitute their pens to the highest bidder. When the *Philadelphia Inquirer's* Washington bureau chief uncovered massive bribery of members of Congress, for example, instead of exposing the corruption he extorted payoffs to cover it up. Other newsmen used their connections to arrange federal appointments or leak inside information to financial speculators in exchange for bribes.

By the early twentieth century, the most flagrant corruptions of politics and press had ceased, but generally each still found cooperation more advantageous than conflict. Gentlemen reporters politely vied to be called upon at presidential news conferences and socialized after hours with Washington's ruling class. The vituperation that characterized coverage in the early years of the Republic largely disappeared.

In the modern era, however, predatory politics and merciless media returned with a vengeance. Policy differences effectively became criminalized as partisans used the investigative machinery of government and the press to wage political battle. In the same way that war was diplomacy by other means, so attack journalism became politics by other means, and the news media became the crucial vehicle by which this guerrilla combat was waged.

This confrontation between politics and the press paralleled the coming of age of Richard Nixon and Jack Anderson. The most hated politician and reporter of their time rose to power through unremitting attacks on their opponents: Nixon, the vociferous anti-Communist congressman of the 1940s and '50s, skillfully shifted to the politics of resentment as a way to divide and conquer in the 1960s and '70s. And Jack Anderson, the take-no-prisoners muckraking scandalmonger, published secrets that respectable journalists only whispered in their private Georgetown drawing rooms to trusted confidants. Yet in a few short years, mainstream media began to imitate Anderson, thriving on the very exposé coverage it had once so fervently disdained.

For better and for worse, Washington's modern scandal culture had begun.

PART I
BEGINNINGS

I

THE QUAKER AND
THE MORMON

They were born barely thirty miles from each other, in the dry air and open skies of the early-twentieth-century West, before asphalt and strip malls conquered the soil and spirit of the southern California desert. Although Richard Nixon and Jack Anderson would ultimately become fierce antagonists, what is most striking about their early years is not their differences but their similarities. The politician and the reporter both were raised in small Western towns, sons of the struggling working class during the Great Depression of the 1930s. Both men had strict religious upbringings and devout fundamentalist Christian parents. Both signed up for sea duty in the Pacific during World War II and headed afterward to Washington, D.C., to realize their large ambitions. And both would spend the next three decades in the nation's capital, embroiled in some of the most ferocious political and journalistic brawls of their time.

Yet despite their similar beginnings, the two men had fundamentally different dispositions and responded in wholly different ways to their parallel backgrounds. The effect would produce a clash of personalities and professions that would transcend the usual adversarial relationship between politicians and journalists.

For Richard Milhous Nixon, it began in Yorba Linda, California, a farming village forty miles southeast of Los Angeles. "It wasn't a town," a resident recalled. "It was turkey mullein, cactus, rattlesnakes, tumbleweeds and tracks." And it was there, in his parents' tiny stove-heated bungalow in January 1913, that the future president was born.

Nixon descended from a long line of Quakers, so named because their religious devotion led them to "tremble at the word of the Lord." With a heavy emphasis on silence and simplicity, traditional Quakers austerely rejected dancing and other frivolities. But unlike more progressive Friends from back East, whose history of political activism championed pacifism, the Nixon family belonged to a fundamentalist strain that engaged in evangelical revivals. Nixon's parents "ground into me with the aid of the church," he later said, "their strictest interpretation" of the "infallibility and literal correctness of the Bible." Young Richard—his parents eschewed the more familiar "Dick"—went to church four times on Sunday, from morning until evening; he also read from the Bible before going to bed at night: "We never had a meal without grace. Usually it was silent. Sometimes each of us would recite a verse of scripture." At age thirteen, Richard publicly declared his "personal commitment to Christ and Christian service."

Richard grew up in Whittier, an insular Quaker town of harsh piety and rigid conformity, devoid of bars, liquor stores, or movie theaters, where village elders instructed female teachers not to go to dances or talk to men on the street. The Nixon family "practiced a stout, unquestioned tribal closeness," one biographer wrote. "It was a plain, exacting life." Along with religious orthodoxy, Nixon imbibed something of the Quakers' interest in politics, though he was less concerned with the social gospel than with political rectitude. At age twelve, Richard read newspaper accounts of the Teapot Dome political scandal in Washington and reportedly vowed, "When I grow up, I'm going to be an honest lawyer so things like that can't happen." He won speech contests by extolling patriotic themes and wanted to "enter politics for an occupation so that I might be of some good to the people." A debating opponent from high school said that Richard "would have made a wonderful missionary, because he was always right, he knew everything. God was on his side."

Richard was the second of five sons fathered by Francis Nixon, an industrious but often itinerant worker whose success never measured up to his dreams. Orphaned as a child, with only a fourth-grade education, Frank Nixon bounced from job to job—carpenter, butcher, painter, brick-maker, potter, streetcar operator, lemon farmer, grocer— but never let failure dampen his work ethic. "To him playing was day-dreaming," one of his brothers said. Frank's childhood was undeniably harsh and troubled: his mother died of tuberculosis when he was eight years old; his stepmother beat him; schoolmates bullied him. The result was a volatile personality given to unpredictable rages. "My father was a scrappy, belligerent fighter," Richard remembered, "a strict and stern disciplinarian." Others were less polite: "Quarrelsome," said one of Frank's siblings. "Nasty," recalled a niece. "Explosive," stated a baby-sitter. "A collector of resentments, a chronic shouter," a family friend wrote. "Hard . . . beastly . . . like an animal," according to an acquaintance. Nixon's father hit his sons with rulers and straps. "I still remember Uncle Frank . . . beating [Richard's older brother] so hard his hollering could be heard all up and down" the block, an onlooker marveled decades later.

Richard's mother, Hannah Milhous Nixon, was more even-tempered than her rough-hewn husband. "She was considered in Yorba Linda a cultured, refined, educated person from a rather superior family in comparison to Mr. [Frank] Nixon," a neighbor said. Raised in a pious Quaker family, Hannah pushed her promising second son to work hard, trust in God, and dutifully practice the piano. "Richard was clearly his mother's favorite," a contemporary remembered. The future president returned the adulation. "My mother was a saint," he said tearfully on his last day in the White House. "She will have no books written about her. But she was a saint." Others considered Hannah Nixon less angelic. "She was a hard character," one friend of the family said; another called her "cranky and puritanical." Richard was just seven years old when a classmate saw him with his mother: "She was sitting on the piano bench with a switch in her hand while he was practicing." Unlike her husband, Hannah usually spared the rod, but she substituted stern lectures that Richard "dreaded far more than my father's hand." Nixon reportedly said of his mother, "In her whole life, I never heard her say to me or anyone else 'I love you.'" His doctor, psychotherapist Arnold Hutschnecker, believed that Hannah's chilly, conditional love failed to nurture her son even while she "completely smothered" him with demands: "A saint is someone who you cannot pray enough to, improve enough for, beg enough to," the physician pointed out. "The image of the saintly but stern face of his mother defeated him more than any other factor . . . He wanted his mother to believe him perfect. That was his problem."

Nixon's quiet need to be thought perfect was reinforced by the tragic early deaths of two brothers. Seven-year-old Arthur Nixon died unexpectedly when Richard was twelve. The future president "sat staring into space, silent and dry-eyed," his mother remembered. "He sank into a deep impenetrable silence." Richard cried about the loss every day for weeks. Two years later, his older brother, Harold, contracted tuberculosis, a painful and lingering disease made worse because Frank Nixon wouldn't allow treatment at the county TB ward for fear of "taking charity." Ultimately, Hannah took Harold to Arizona for care and was separated from the rest of her family off and on for five years until he died in 1933. "From that time on, it seemed Richard was trying to be three sons in one, striving even harder than before to make up to his father and me for our loss," Hannah said. "Unconsciously, too, I think that Richard may have felt a kind of guilt that Harold and Arthur were dead and that he was alive."

Despite the searing deaths, Hannah and Frank continued to be uncompromising with their three surviving sons. "They were very strict parents and expected them to do right in everything," a neighbor recalled. From an early age, Richard learned to satisfy his demanding mother and appease or avoid his hot-tempered father. The boy's strategy for maneuvering around his dad was simple: "I tried to follow my mother's example of not crossing him when he was in a bad mood." He advised his brothers, "Just don't argue with him. You'll have a better chance of getting what you want out of him in the long run." Such family dynamics—an explosive father who had to be manipulated, an ambitious mother who demanded perfection—pushed Richard to strive for success without being open about it. "He offended some of his Quaker teachers by his willingness to justify bad means by the ends," a schoolmate remembered. Yet Richard could also be kind and compassionate: he looked after a student crippled by polio and often strained to carry his friend's paralyzed body up steep stairs.

From the time he was a baby, an older playmate said, Nixon was "a very serious child, not lots of fun." His first-grade teacher noticed that he "kept mostly to himself" and "rarely ever smiled or laughed." Unathletic and bookish, Richard seldom played with other children, who nicknamed him "Gloomy Gus." He studied hard and got good grades, but his peers viewed him as a grind. "He once said he didn't like to ride the school bus because the other children didn't smell good," his cousin recalled. Nixon was an "oddball" with a "'holier than thou' attitude," a contemporary stated. "Let's face it," another exclaimed, "he was stuffy!" He wore a starched shirt to class. "Dick was a very tense person, always," a classmate said. Ill at ease with himself, Nixon tried to compensate by projecting an artificial friendliness that came across as false and insincere. Underneath the smile, fellow students remembered, he "had a nasty temper" and was "slightly paranoid." His debate coach thought "there was something mean in him, mean in the way he put his questions [and] argued his points."

It was no way to win friends of either sex. By high school, Richard had a well-deserved reputation as a shy loner who shunned school dances and girls. "I never could get up the nerve to ask them for dates," he admitted. Nixon "didn't know how to be personable or sexy with girls," said a schoolmate. "He didn't seem to have a sense of fun." By his senior year, Richard acquired a steady girlfriend, the daughter of the local police chief, but he clung to her as he once had to his mother, in an awkward mix of insecurity and aggressiveness. According to his sweetheart, Ola Florence Welch, Nixon would often "be harsh and I'd cry. Then we'd make up." Ola believed that Richard's problem was that he "didn't know how to mix. He had no real boy friends. And he didn't like my girl friends. He would stalk out of the room where they were, his head high." Nixon repeatedly asked Ola to marry him but she put him off. Ola felt sorry for him: "He seemed so lonely and so solemn . . . I think he was unsure of himself, deep down."

Still, Richard inherited his father's determination to succeed. At age eleven, he sent the *Los Angeles Times* a letter offering to work for "any pay offered . . . Hoping that you will accept me for your service, I am, Yours Truly, Richard M. Nixon." A few years later, he played the piano in his father's grocery store while staging mock radio shows with commercials touting goods for sale. With railroad tracks only a mile from his home, Nixon often said, he watched the trains go by during the day and woke up to their whistles in the night, dreaming of "far-off places."

In the midst of the Depression, Richard could not afford to attend Harvard or Yale, despite encouraging signals from the prestigious schools. Instead, he enrolled in his mother's hometown Quaker alma mater, Whittier College, which offered a full-tuition scholarship. After his sophomore year, Richard purchased a Model A Ford and traveled with his college debate team to San Francisco, where he tasted hard liquor for the first time at a Prohibition-era speakeasy. But he had to work hard for everything he got. Nixon became physically nauseated— "sixteen weeks of misery," he called it—toiling as a sweeper in a lemon packinghouse in Yorba Linda. He was equally unhappy picking green beans on nearby farms. "We would work twelve long hard hours to earn that one dollar," he recalled many years later. "I still hate the sight of string beans."

In 1934, Richard enrolled at Duke University Law School. He rented a room for five dollars a month until he discovered a cheaper "clapboard shack without heating or inside plumbing." Nixon once again studied dutifully, and graduated third out of his class of twenty-six. But lacking proper connections or social graces, he was turned down by every prestigious New York law firm to which he applied. It was the beginning of a lifetime of resentment against the Eastern establishment. "What starts the process, really, are laughs and slights and snubs when you are a kid," he later confided to an aide. "But if you are reasonably intelligent and if your anger is deep enough and strong enough, you learn that you can change those attitudes by excellence, personal gut performance, while those who have everything are sitting on their fat butts."

After law school, Richard returned to Whittier in 1937 and joined one of the two small legal firms in his hometown. He handled wills, taxes, and divorces, and began to be exposed for the first time to the larger world. (Nixon "turned fifteen colors of the rainbow," he recalled, when a beautiful female divorce client gave a "personal confession" of her intimate marital problems.) In an attempt to make contacts in the community and drum up legal business, the shy young attorney took a small acting role in Whittier's community theater. There, he met twenty-six-year-old Thelma Catherine Ryan. "For me it was a case of love at first sight," Richard recalled. But not for the Whittier High school-teacher and cheerleading coach, who was nicknamed Pat because she was born on the eve of St. Patrick's Day. Pat repeatedly spurned Nixon's advances, refusing to answer the door when he unexpectedly dropped by, accepting his masochistic offers to drive her to dates with other men. "Don't laugh!" he told her. "Some day I'm going to marry you!" At first, "I thought he was nuts," she recalled. "I just looked at him. I couldn't imagine anyone saying anything like that so suddenly." But eventually she succumbed to his persistence and they were married in 1940. Richard's pursuit of Pat, who smoked cigarettes, drank alcohol, and was not a Quaker, was perhaps his first open rebellion against his narrow upbringing.

Two years later, in another assertion of independence, Nixon voluntarily joined the navy even though his religion entitled him to a deferment. He was at his physical prime: five feet, eleven inches tall, slender, with brown wavy hair, equally dark deep-set eyes, and heavy eyebrows. He had not yet formed the scowl lines and heavy jowls that would become fodder for future political cartoonists, but his familiar rounded shoulders and ski-slope nose were already present. The navy sent him to the Pacific, where the young lieutenant won two battle stars but saw no real military action. Instead, Richard learned to smoke cigars, play poker, and curse like the sailor that he had become.

After World War II, Nixon returned to Whittier and decided to make his first try at political office as a Republican. In a divisive race in which he campaigned wearing his navy uniform to emphasize his patriotism, Nixon accused the incumbent congressman of being soft on communism. On Election Day, the upstart challenger won a stunning victory. In January 1947, at the age of thirty-three, Congressman-elect Richard Nixon moved to Washington, D.C.

Also relocating to the nation's capital that year was another naval veteran returning from the Pacific—an aspiring journalist named Jack Anderson.

.

A decade after Richard Nixon's birth, just thirty miles away, Jack Northman Anderson was born in October 1922. Like his future adversary, Anderson grew up with a volatile, authoritarian father and a strict, unbending religious orthodoxy: the Church of Jesus Christ of Latter-Day Saints, more commonly known as Mormons. Often persecuted for its beliefs, which at one time included polygamy, the sect settled in the remote Utah desert to practice its religion freely. Nils Anderson, Jack's paternal grandfather, was the patriarch of the family. A huge, imposing brick-maker with a stern visage and a long Old Testament beard, he was converted by Mormon missionaries in his native Sweden and moved to Utah in 1876. With four (serial) wives, he fathered seventeen children. The eleventh was Jack's father, Orlando.

Jack's dad was an angry, irritable army veteran who seemingly never recovered from shell shock suffered in the trenches of World War I. Orlando Anderson returned home with ambitions of becoming a famous actor. But like Nixon's father before him, he ended up instead holding a series of temporary menial jobs—in a beet factory, a laundry, a woolen mill, a restaurant, a power plant, and a veterans' hospital. He married a Danish immigrant and fellow Mormon, Agnes Mortensen. Jack described his mother as "a patient and persevering woman with a steely side." She brought Orlando to live with her mother in Long Beach, California, where Jack was soon born. After two years, the family returned to Utah, settling on the outskirts of Salt Lake City in a town called Cottonwood. Orlando landed a stable but low-level nighttime job as a postal clerk. Two more sons followed.

Like the Nixons, family life for the Andersons centered on their religion. Jack prayed daily, attended church every Sunday, and was inculcated with traditional Mormon strictures against alcohol, tobacco, caffeine, and cursing. He studied the Book of Mormon, which preached that America was a chosen land, and absorbed his religion's conservative values of discipline, self-reliance, and moral obligation. The Andersons tithed 10 percent of their annual income to the church and opened their home to the needy. A homeless man lived with them for more than a year.

Jack's father developed a stubborn austerity excessive even by Depression-era standards. While the rest of the family took the train to visit relatives in California, Orlando saved money by riding his bicycle there from Utah, through seven hundred miles of rough desert terrain. Jack's father bought a large Tudor house on four wooded acres in a prosperous neighborhood overlooking Mount Olympus—but then rented it out to make extra money, forcing his family to live in the cellar, without indoor plumbing. Jack had to bathe in a laundry tub, which was heated by a nearby coal stove. "We would take craps in the outhouse," he recalled with distaste. Orlando insisted on keeping the temperature in Jack's bedroom cold because "it is better for my health" and "saves on the heat," he wrote in a school essay. "I plunge into the icy room, scramble into my clothes, and dash for the nearest stove . . . with my teeth chattering." Jack was convinced that his family didn't need to make such sacrifices but that his father had a "martyr complex" that made him "glory in his poverty."

Orlando Anderson also possessed a violent temper. "A smoldering volcano," Jack called him. "He was shouting all the time . . . He somehow felt that any dictums that he issued would be more effective if he ran up the volume." Decades later, Jack's boyhood friend, Darwin Knudsen, still shook his head recalling Orlando's harsh punishment of Jack's noisy five-year-old brother: "His father opened his fingers and pinched his nose till the tears just streamed down his face." Periodically, Orlando's eruptions became so explosive that he would abandon his family for weeks at a time, heading off suddenly to Alaska or other parts unknown. Unlike young Richard Nixon, who mostly placated or maneuvered around his hot-tempered father, Jack was openly defiant: he simply refused to do the never-ending set of household chores assigned to him. "If I did everything my father yelled at me to do," Jack later explained, "he would have me spinning . . . the whole day long."

Like Frank Nixon, Orlando Anderson tried to build his son's character by imposing outdoor manual labor, though instead of picking beans, twelve-year-old Jack was forced to thin beets in the scorching summer sun. "Atop the rock-hard Utah soil, on hands and knees, I swatted at beet greens with a sawed-off hoe," Jack later wrote. After two weeks, his knees raw with scars and "cooked" from the desert heat, "I abruptly quit, pedaled my bike over to the nearest newspaper, the *Murray Eagle*, and talked my way into a reporting job." It was a pivotal decision in Anderson's life, both personally and professionally. "Jack psychologically escaped from his father when he took that job," said his friend Knudsen. "And I think one of the driving forces in Jack's behavior was to escape from this rigid discipline." The driving force to escape—and to triumph over arbitrary authority—would last the rest of his life.

Jack proved a natural reporter and his new job earned seven dollars a week, a sizable sum for a twelve-year-old. He used the money to buy a typewriter, then took typing lessons and learned shorthand. "Jack rode his bicycle to every fire and every accident he could pedal his way to," a classmate recalled. His first exposé, about a dangerously narrow bridge where a local paperboy had broken his jaw in an accident, led authorities to widen the overpass—and gave the cub reporter his first real taste of the power of the press. Jack's world began opening up. He visited Utah's lone left-wing bookstore and overheard the local Communist Party leader discuss overthrowing the U.S. government. No news story resulted, but Jack contacted the FBI, which created the first of what would become more than fifty files on Anderson, whom the agency initially assigned the moniker "Informant 42." In a back alley of Salt Lake City, Jack also tracked down an opium den and a bordello. "A big black madam came to the door and brought us in," remembered a friend of Jack's who tagged along. "She brought us three girls to choose from. Jack took one look at the girls and said, 'Is that the best you got?' The madam chased us out of the apartment."

In addition to journalism, Jack starred in school plays, was elected student body president, and became an Eagle Scout. Unlike the young Nixon, Anderson was a popular boy. He pored over his school yearbook looking for pictures of the prettiest girls to ask out on dates. "I used to get on at the bus stop and there would be a group of cute girls crowded around him," a classmate remembered. His father disliked all of it. Jack was "uppity-up," Orlando recalled resentfully decades later. "He was very much for himself. I thought he should have been more common. He wanted to be in the limelight." Orlando feared that Jack's success might make his two younger brothers feel inadequate, so he boycotted Jack's high school graduation ceremony, where his son was valedictorian. "He, in his inappropriate and foolish way, was trying to say, 'Jack's getting too many honors, so I won't go,'" Anderson explained.

Jack's brother Warren believed that their father's disapproval had a simple cause: jealousy. Jack's aspirations were a reminder of the dreams Orlando once held but had not achieved. Worse, beginning even in childhood, Jack was succeeding where his father had failed. "All these high ambitions he's got," Orlando snorted angrily as his son left home after high school. "He'll be slapped back, because he's not that smart." But his father's efforts to put Jack in his place only seemed to have the opposite effect. "In trying to restrain his son's ambition," a fellow journalist later wrote, "Orlando unleashed it a hundredfold."

Jack began reporting for the *Salt Lake Tribune* while he was still in high school. It was the leading newspaper in the state, and he continued working there full-time while also taking classes at the University of Utah. But the lure of the library was no match for the excitement of the city desk; within a year, he dropped out of college because "it seemed like a waste of time."

He decided to expose a secret polygamous Mormon sect by going undercover to infiltrate it. Without telling his father, Jack borrowed Orlando's 1936 Plymouth to attend polygamy meetings, pretending that he wanted to join. Soon, the car was spotted in suspicious locations, and church elders summoned Orlando and demanded an explanation. Jack's father came home "in a towering rage" to relate the "unspeakable" accusation that had been lodged against him. Jack fessed up, he remembered with a chuckle, but his father responded with "steam, fire, brimstone! I don't think he ever forgave me." The subconscious hostility of his act never seemed to occur to Jack, whose only real lament was that his cover was blown on the story.

The Mormon church was no more amused than Orlando. Suddenly, nineteen-year-old Jack was told that it was time for him to begin his required two-year religious proselytizing "mission" even though he had not yet reached the customary age of twenty-one. "They wanted me out of that story," Jack recalled. The young reporter was not happy to interrupt his up-and-coming journalistic career but knew it would "break my parents' heart if I didn't go." After all, to forsake his mission would be tantamount to renouncing Mormonism. Jack's mother began driving a taxicab to finance his journey. He was assigned to win converts in the rural South. In late 1941, at the Salt Lake City train station, a throng of admiring girls from his church turned out to say goodbye.

It proved to be quite an adventure. As a lay minister, Jack criss-crossed the country in an old jalopy, journeying to the courthouse squares of small towns in Mississippi, Alabama, Florida, Georgia, and South Carolina, literally standing on a wooden soapbox to preach the gospel of the Book of Mormon at street meetings designed to drum up converts among unbelievers. Sometimes his only audience was the town drunk. Jack would start by singing a religious hymn, then offer a prayer, before launching into his sermon. He learned to think quickly on his feet and make his voice heard above the din and indifference of the crowd. Jack developed an old-fashioned evangelist's pitch that had been used successfully for generations in revivalist tent meetings throughout the South. "He had a tendency to grab an audience by the throat and never relax his grip until he sat down," a missionary who served with Jack recalled. "The colorful anecdotes he used and the dramatic gyrations he employed would remain with a listener long after the talk ended." To keep his audience keyed up, Jack would alter his orations from a scolding shout to a breathless whisper to a righteous roar, a technique he would later repeat on the lecture circuit when he became famous. Jack also went door-to-door knocking on homes in what he called "the moss-covered woods . . . working with the country folk," dressed in the proselytizer's classic uniform: white shirt with black suit, shoes, and tie. "It was an assignment that taught pluck, faith, persistence, and the value of a thick skin to ward off the rebuffs of your fellow man," one observer noted.

It was a spartan existence. Jack lived in a renovated chicken coop and rose before the sun at four a.m. His mattress had bedbugs, his diet was filled with lard, and he contracted hepatitis. Like all Mormon missionaries, Jack was prohibited from dating local girls. Yet sinful temptations were everywhere, and acting as a lay preacher among the heathen flock proved to be an eye-opening experience for the sheltered young Mormon. "Suddenly I am asked to advise couples, married couples who are having domestic problems of the sort that I didn't think existed," Jack marveled. "Oh, believe me, I learned a lot about human nature." Jack's own rebellious nature remained unchanged. In Florida, offended by the racial segregation of Jim Crow, he deliberately walked to the back of the bus to sit with African American passengers. Church elders, wary of insulting local authorities, "hauled me up front and gave me a stern lecture," Jack recalled. He also clashed with his mission's "hard-headed" president—he was "as bad as my father," Jack complained—and retaliated by correcting his superior's ungrammatical English.

Above all, Jack's mission showed him how to reach across the divides of race, class, and religion. It expanded the horizons of his constricted Utah upbringing, and trained him to win the trust of strangers with whom he otherwise had little in common. "My missionary experience had taught me that deep in the souls of most people lurks a compulsion to talk about themselves," Anderson later wrote, "to confide in someone their darkest secrets, to spill what they know—against their own interests, even against their fears. It is as though by retelling their experiences to an appreciative listener, they are showing an otherwise indifferent world that they, too, have trod the earth, have coped, have counted." It was a critical lesson for the budding muckraker, one he would use time and again in the future as he persuaded reluctant sources to divulge their most intimate secrets.

After his stint as a missionary, Jack faced the World War II draft. A military physical showed that he was in excellent health; he stood five feet, ten inches tall and weighed 185 pounds, with brown hair, blue eyes, and a handsomely ruddy complexion. But Jack admitted that he "didn't relish the thought of hand-to-hand combat with some Nazi in Germany." He persuaded a friend from the Boy Scouts who was working for Utah's influential senator Elbert Thomas to finagle an appointment for him to the navy's merchant marine officers program. It was, Jack freely acknowledged, a "boondoggle" for the privileged, to try to shield them from combat. But it worked. Jack's assignment kept him safe until the war was over.

In the fall of 1944, Jack shipped out to sea in the South Pacific. His job was a modest one, to safeguard lifeboats and provisions. But Jack soon grew as weary of military routines as he once did of thinning beets—and with similar results. In the spring of 1945, as the war wound down, he defected from duty and simply walked away from his station. Jack once again got his friend on Senator Thomas's staff to intervene, this time so that he could leave the navy and instead file dispatches from Asia as a journalist. "I can serve my country better . . . as a reporter than sailing as an ordinary seaman," he argued in a letter home, because his news stories "carry a high morale value, both for the boys about whom they are written and their friends who read about them at home." But Jack's local draft board was not persuaded; it forwarded his name to the FBI for investigation. Jack's father was similarly unconvinced and wrote a characteristically intemperate letter to Senator Thomas, accusing him of helping Jack avoid the draft. Jack's friend denied any favoritism, but warned Orlando that because Jack had already jumped ship "the possibility of his [criminal] indictment seemed pretty serious." Fortunately, the staffer said, Senator Thomas was able "to clear up an apparent misunderstanding so that he would not be prosecuted" for draft-dodging.

Jack's efforts to outwit his draft board would later be used against him by wounded targets of his political exposés. The incident also foreshadowed the reporter's willingness to cut corners if it proved expedient, to ignore the rules applied to lesser mortals, to act first on instinct and ask questions later—if at all. Jack was a young man in a hurry. "My father worked really hard to get away from being raised poor and to show his dad," Jack's daughter Laurie said later. Although he did not quite cross the line into illegal draft-dodging, he demonstrated an early and telling ability to push the limits of what he could get away with and then wiggle his way out of trouble. This, too, would become a hallmark of Anderson's later investigative career in Washington.

Meanwhile, Jack made his way to China and began freelancing as a reporter. His sojourn there as a war correspondent put him in greater danger than if he had stayed in the enclave of his navy officers program. For six weeks, Jack recalled, he was "the only white man" traveling with Chinese guerrillas as they battled for territory "along the Jap-controlled border." In Chongqing, he met and befriended Communist leader Chou En-lai, who would later become China's premier, in a dingy building whose windows were "covered with greased brown paper" and located in a "maze of slime-slick alleys that gave off an overpowering stench—a blend of odors rising from open gutters and wafting from a thousand Chinese cooking pots." Jack's journalistic connections to the guerrillas attracted the notice of American intelligence officers, who persuaded him to spy on his news sources for the U.S. government. He submitted unsigned reports on "Soviet activity in China" and "Communist influence & morale breakdowns" among GIs.

Eventually, the Selective Service caught up with Jack and assigned him to serve out the rest of his term in the army. He managed to stay in China by wrangling an assignment in Shanghai, writing for the military newspaper *Stars and Stripes*. "It is hardly like being in the army at all," he wrote home happily, although he promised "to keep my eyes open for any loopholes that will let me out" altogether. Jack also began freelancing for the Associated Press, using the name "Jack Northman" as a byline. "I do that chiefly to avoid trouble from the army[,] which is fussy about the stuff which its enlisted men write," he told his parents; "it is too much trouble to submit every little thing for censorship."

Jack loved being a foreign correspondent. "Working for *Stars and Stripes* is the next best thing to being a civilian," he wrote a friend. His letters home described exotic sights, and he enjoyed shocking his family by telling them more than they needed to know about his treatment for sore feet at the Red Cross: "Our room adjoins the VD ward which is populated with colorful characters who describe their exploits in loud and picturesque language." When General Dwight Eisenhower visited, Jack "chatted breezily with him, while an assembly of colonels and generals hung timidly in the background, watching eagerly for a smile or nod." Best of all, Jack had "become a minor celebrity" in Shanghai as a news broadcaster for the best English-language radio station in town: "Wherever I go now, people inquire reverently: 'Are you the Jack Anderson who broadcasts the news?'" he wrote his parents. "Once I got an anonymous phone call, sponsored by a number of girls who giggled at the other end. The spokesman admitted that she couldn't love me until she met me, but she was willing to take a chance on my looks."

Jack was less popular with his military superiors. A colonel "who hates newsmen in general and Anderson in particular" tried to stop his journalistic road trips, Jack told his family. So he threatened his commanding officer: "I reminded him firmly that I was still an accredited

correspondent and would cause trouble for him in Washington" if necessary. Six months later, Jack's reporting led navy brass to try to get
him suspended after General George Marshall "wired a terse message
from Washington, wanting to know how [my] story got out," he wrote
his parents. But *Stars and Stripes* backed Anderson up and "I steadfastly refused to tell where I learned the story on the grounds that a
newsman's sources are a newsman's secret. Admirals and Generals
sputtered and sweated under their collars. But no order to shoot me at
sunrise has yet been posted."

None was. In November 1946, Jack received an honorable discharge
from the military. He soon headed home, and then on to Washington
to begin his career as a muckraker.

Jack Anderson's successful clashes with military superiors reinforced
his instinctive rebelliousness and his desire to use journalism to challenge authority. But his religion also influenced his crusading career,
which he regarded as a "calling" from God. Mormon theology preaches
that life is an eternal struggle between good and evil, and this
black-and-white view of the world would be reflected in Anderson's
reporting, which often divided the world into villains and victims,
saints and sinners. Anderson also shared the traditional Mormon suspicion of government, which had so often persecuted his ancestors;
this, too, would become a critical theme of his exposés. Indeed, Anderson's syndicated column would reflect the puritanical belief that power
was inherently contaminated by a kind of original sin: political leaders
especially were prone to corruption and needed to be vigilantly watched
to ensure they did not abuse their position. Because the Mormon faith
holds that God inspired the U.S. Constitution, including the First
Amendment, Anderson sincerely believed that his muckraking fur-
thered the Lord's work.

Jack's journalism was strongly influenced by secular concerns as
well. Anderson's childhood deprivations led to an unabashed populist
style that reflexively championed the little guy. His later ostracism from
Washington's elite circles further fueled his iconoclastic reporting and
his imperviousness to outside hostility. "On numerous occasions I have

thanked my pragmatic parents, who taught me not to put too much stock in the accolades of men," Anderson wrote in his memoirs. "I would have folded fifty years ago had I worried about winning popularity contests."

Perhaps most of all, Jack's open defiance of his father's iron will hardened his own drive and antipathy to abuse of power by those in authority. "Over the years, he came to see his work as a heroic candle lit against the darkness of political corruption, greed and arrogance," one journalist wrote. "About this he is undeniably sincere. But deep inside Jack Anderson—in the intimate, painful place where boundless ambition must reside—a little machine also runs constantly, always has, propelling him ahead in private rebellion and indignation." As Anderson would soon discover, politics in the nation's capital would sharpen his well-honed sense of righteousness.

When he was thirteen, Richard Nixon hung a portrait of Abraham Lincoln over his bed, along with an inscription from the poet Henry Wadsworth Longfellow:

> *Lives of great men all remind us*
> *We can make our lives sublime,*
> *And, departing, leave behind us*
> *Footprints on the sands of time . . .*

Jack Anderson hung no such inspirational lyrics over his bed when he was a boy. For him, what was sublime was not leaving behind footprints but humbling those who presumed to foist their imprint on others in the first place.

And so Nixon and Anderson were both unmistakably shaped by their parallel backgrounds even as they reacted in strikingly different ways to them. While Nixon mollified his despotic father, Anderson defied his; while Nixon was a dutiful conformist, Anderson became a rebellious contrarian; while Nixon learned to seek power, Anderson chose to subvert it. Partly, of course, it was the nature of their temperaments: Nixon, the withdrawn loner, anxious and insecure; Anderson, the gregarious leader, stubbornly impish and outrageous. By whatever combination of genetics and environment, the two became polar opposites: On the outside, Nixon was a modest, pious Quaker; on the inside, he was grasping and self-aggrandizing. On the outside, Anderson was righteous and evangelical; on the inside, he was an irreverent rascal. But each was immeasurably driven to prove himself, and each would learn to use merciless means to achieve his ends.

In the aftermath of World War II, the politician and the journalist would find a wider canvas for their ambitions in the nation's capital. And in the years ahead, their conflict would come to symbolize a larger clash between the institutions they represented: politics and the press.

PART II

RISE TO POWER

2

WASHINGTON WHIRL

When Richard Nixon and Jack Anderson moved to Washington after World War II, the nation's capital—like the two young men themselves—faced extraordinary change. For more than a century, Washington had been a sleepy Southern town, and reporters there adopted the attitudes—political, social, sartorial—of its leaders. Officials "wore white linen suits in the summer, with Panama hats and black-and-white wing-tip shoes," commentator David Brinkley recalled, and journalists were "still affecting spats, canes, pince-nez glasses and Homburg hats. To the younger newsmen they looked like European foreign secretaries on their way to an international conference to sell out some innocent and unsuspecting country." But by the mid-1940s, Washington was a metropolis on the move. The Great Depression and the world war that followed had greatly expanded the government, and the city had trouble keeping up. Trolley cars could hold only a fraction of federal employees commuting to work; rooms to rent were so scarce that civil servants streaming into the capital crowded around newspaper pressrooms to grab first editions and get a jump on housing ads. While Europe struggled to rebuild itself from the devastation of the most destructive war in history, Washington emerged unscathed, the booming capital of the world's only atomic superpower.

In November 1946, the Republican Party gained fifty-six seats in the House and thirteen in the Senate, the GOP's first victory since Franklin Roosevelt's Democratic coalition had taken over Washington fourteen years earlier. The newly elected Eightieth Congress was the most conservative in decades, determined to roll back the liberal social and foreign policies of the New Deal. Freshman congressman Richard Nixon would join and eventually help lead the feisty Republican chorus.

Jack Anderson's concerns were considerably more modest. After finally satisfying his draft board, the twenty-four-year-old journalist headed to Washington to land a job because the nation's capital was clearly "the news center of the world" and as such "the best place for [me] to get established," Jack wrote his family. "The best newspapermen in the world are here, and I want to ease into their society." First, Jack needed a place to live. At three dollars a night, his hotel was too expensive to stay in for long, yet the city's postwar housing shortage left little alternative. (It did not help that local banks refused to cash Jack's out-of-state checks.) Eventually, with the help of a local Mormon church, he found a small attic room in a pink stucco house near the Washington zoo, furnished with "a narrow hospital trundle bed which fits me as far as the ankles . . . I hang my clothes on a sawed-off broomstick, suspended from the ceiling by string . . . The most attractive feature," Jack told his parents, "is the price: only $15 per month."

Finding work as a reporter proved more difficult, so Anderson enrolled as a part-time student in the evening program at Georgetown University. "It is a fusty, old-fogey Catholic university," he wrote his family, "straggled with ivy on the outside and mental cobwebs on the inside. The lectures are dry, dull, profound. The books are thick, involved, wearisome." After covering war and revolution abroad, Jack longed to be back in the action. He soon abandoned his studies. Anderson considered writing a book about his adventures as a foreign correspondent but feared his ordinary-sounding name was a handicap. There are "a million other Jack Andersons," he complained; he needed a "distinctive, unusual name." Since he had already begun using Northman, his middle name, as his byline in Asia—ostensibly to avoid getting in trouble with the military when he filed dispatches for the Associated Press—he decided to adopt it as his permanent nom de plume. His father was furious. Jack had renounced the Anderson side of the family, Orlando believed, and was clearly ashamed of him; obviously, he had failed as a father. Jack replied in letters home that he meant "nothing personal" by the name change; it "was a simple expedi-ent" made "for cold professional reasons only." Jack seemed blind to the hurt he caused and scolded Orlando for "indulging in self pity far be-yond what is good for you." He told his father: "Quell your explosive disposition, swallow some of your intolerance and crawl out of the pit of worry and pity that you have dug for yourself." But in the end, Jack decided to revert to the Anderson name after all.

In May 1947, Jack got the break that would launch his career. He was hired as a researcher by syndicated columnist Drew Pearson. It would prove to be the single most important event in Jack's profes-sional life; all that he would become in the next half century grew out of his apprenticeship under the tutelage of the most controversial in-vestigative reporter of his era. "The name Drew Pearson evoked the image of the ubiquitous, hyperactive news hawk," Anderson recalled, "with open collar, clipped mustache, the inevitable reporter's hat set back on his head, fast-talking into a mike." *Time* magazine called Pear-son "the most intensely feared and hated man in Washington" thanks to his "ruthless, theatrical, crusading, high-voltage, hypodermic jour-nalism." Pearson's syndicated column ran in more newspapers than any other in the country, with an audience of forty million; another twenty million listened to him religiously on his weekly radio news broadcast. "In a career spanning nine presidents," one writer observed, "his millions of words reached more Americans regularly than those of any other journalist, novelist, entertainer, preacher or politician."

Pearson was an unabashed liberal, a combative Quaker who used journalism to crusade for global peace—and smite those who got in his way. He started his column, the "Washington Merry-Go-Round," in 1932, as an antidote what he called the "trivial, reactionary and subservi-ent" newspapers of the day, which were overwhelmingly conservative and Republican. Pearson wrote in a folksy colloquial style, sprinkling his column with such stock subheads as "Washington Whispers" and "Wash-ington Whirl," literally awarding favored politicians a brass ring "good for one free ride on the 'Washington Merry-Go-Round.'" It was a kind of cross between the reformist muckraking of Lincoln Steffens and the broadcast tattletale of Walter Winchell, an unusual hybrid that Jack An-derson would imitate and extend into the early twenty-first century.

Pearson was best known for his lacerating attacks on public officials, which earned him the nickname "the Scorpion on the Potomac." During World War II, he exposed General George Patton for hitting a shivering soldier who had been hospitalized for shell shock. Pearson also helped turn public opinion against Father Charles Coughlin, the right-wing radio priest, by revealing that the man of the cloth had paid $68,000 as compensation for "alienating the affections" of a physician's wife. Douglas MacArthur, another bellicose general attacked by Pearson, filed a libel lawsuit against the newsman—only to back down after Pearson threatened to make public embarrassing love letters the middle-aged general had written his teenage mistress. Tangling with Pearson could literally be fatal. After reading a "Merry-Go-Round" account of how he used his office to profit from a secret investment in cotton futures, one U.S. senator dropped dead from a stroke. And President Truman's defense secretary, James Forrestal, committed suicide after the columnist let loose a series of attacks that were widely blamed for his death.

On the surface, Pearson seemed an unlikely character assassin. "The polecat in his lair was disarmingly mild," Anderson remembered. "He had an impressive, high forehead under thinning light-brown hair, and a general look of learnedness that made him seem too dignified and elegant for the rough-and-tumble he in fact relished." But underneath Pearson's aristocratic demeanor was a Machiavellian toughness that did not shrink at using blackmail and bribery to further his goals. He put eavesdropping waiters and chauffeurs on his payroll, bribed a navy clerk to leak classified data, and ordered an assistant to break into the desk of a prominent Washington attorney to search for incriminating financial records. He stymied World War II censors, foiled government eavesdroppers, and outwitted federal agents who tailed him—although on at least one occasion agents managed to penetrate his office and "extract" documents from his locked files. All of this foreshadowed the White House attacks that Richard Nixon would one day unleash on Pearson's successor, Jack Anderson.

In all, Anderson's mentor was a man of fierce contradictions: gentle in private but ferocious in public; a pacifist who waged unconditional war on his enemies; a wealthy elitist who championed the common man; an intellectual who wrote with down-to-earth simplicity. Pearson used cynical tricks for idealistic purposes, told lies to uncover truth, and employed unsavory means to advance noble ends. He was, Anderson concluded, "a man of great principle in spite of some of the unprincipled things he did." The same could one day be said of Anderson himself, for no one would do more to shape the cub reporter's worldview and professional future.

Ironically, it was Anderson's future adversary, FBI director J. Edgar Hoover, who launched the young journalist on his national career. In the spring of 1947, Hoover phoned to warn Pearson that one of his staff members had been a member of the Communist Party. Pearson's liberalism notwithstanding, he couldn't afford to be considered sympathetic to communism. "That's not compatible with my beliefs," the columnist informed his left-wing reporter. "You'll have to leave." Soon after, Anderson had the good fortune to walk through Pearson's door looking for work. He "was overly impressed with the fact that I was a war correspondent," Anderson remembered, "which I advertised by wearing my uniform" to the job interview. Jack offered to work for Pearson on a trial basis for free. A few days later, Pearson theatrically sent a telegram across town to announce his decision: Anderson was hired. His new title: "legman," an anachronistic newspaper term for an assistant who gathered information on foot. Anderson's salary was fifty dollars a week. He reported for duty, one chronicler wrote, "a fresh-faced youth in baggy clothes, his hair parted just off center and pomaded, like a small-town salesman."

Anderson's office was housed in Pearson's mansion, a yellow-brick Federal-style home with polished brass, located on a quiet tree-lined street in Georgetown. A residential wing housed the master's family and servants; an office wing contained four secretaries and four legmen, including a onetime undercover government sleuth from Prohibition days. It was "a combination newsroom and spy cell," Anderson recalled, noisy "from the clacking of a news ticker, the clattering of typewriters turning out copy, the continual ringing of ten telephones through the day and far into the night." Above all, there was the "atmosphere of the clandestine: anonymous phone callers; the mumbo-jumbo of an elementary code we often used because of our assumption that our phones were tapped; the thirty-odd file cabinets that protected our derogatory treasures, standing against the walls locked and portentous."

The source of the muckrakers' power was not just their words but also the vehicle that delivered their message: the syndicated column, which made it impossible for any one newspaper to censor their exposés. While an individual paper might occasionally spike the "Merry-Go-Round," or, like *The Washington Post*, relegate it to the comics page, hundreds of other outlets could be counted on to give prominent display to their articles. The syndicated column offered editorial independence and a nationwide platform unequaled by any mere newspaper reporter.

In his first few months on the job, Anderson helped expose the secret Ku Klux Klan ties of a congressman and then testified before a Senate committee about what he had dug up. For the greenhorn reporter from Utah, it was heady—and intimidating. "I couldn't ask for a better job, but it will keep me fluttering for some time," Anderson wrote his parents. "Snooping for scoops isn't easy." Still, "I certainly am learning a great deal about inside Washington. Several of the Senators already call me by my first name." After a dinner party at Pearson's country estate, Anderson confided in a letter home, the "other guests were a bit out of my class [and] talked about fox hunts and topics [to which] I could hardly contribute much enlightened conversation."

Anderson's unfamiliarity with foxhunts was the least of the obstacles that he encountered in Washington. "I was a laughably naïve Sherlock Holmes to be let loose on the nation's capital," he later wrote, "a Mormon in Gomorrah." The young reporter discovered that Capitol Hill was filled with alcoholism, lechery, and financial corruption. "I did not know what to make of all this, confounding as it did my boyhood visions of heroic figures in marble halls," Anderson remembered. "I had been brought up to regard the Constitution as a divinely inspired document, literally, and to look upon its protectors—as I assumed presidents and senators to be—with the same reverence that was due the Apostles of my Church." But "shabbiness in things small and large was so widespread, so confidently strident, that the majority was resigned to it."

The political education of Jack Anderson was under way.

•

Richard Nixon was also new to Washington that year and was also embarking upon his own political education as a freshman member of the House of Representatives. By the end of his first term, as a member of the House Un-American Activities Committee, he catapulted to nationwide attention investigating allegations of Soviet espionage by former State Department official Alger Hiss. It was the formative experience of Nixon's career, a model of how to use the apparatus of government and the press to undermine political adversaries. The junior congressman performed brilliantly in the case, outmaneuvering his opponents while stoking anti-Communist hysteria for maximum publicity. "We won the Hiss case in the papers," Nixon later said. "I had to leak stuff all over the place." He was assisted by a coterie of seasoned FBI agents and congressional investigators assigned to his Capitol Hill office, one of whom would later be dispatched to spy upon Jack Anderson. "Nixon entered and employed, as few politicians ever do, a shadowy world of operators and fixers," one writer observed, "as marginally but distinguishably apart from conventional politics as the seamy Los Angeles private eyes of the 1930s and 1940s stood apart from the upstairs, smoky, glass-doored law offices that sometimes employed them. He would strike the alliance and bargain from the beginning—and it was there, an underlying curse of Watergate, at the bitter end."

Nixon discovered that his quickest route to fame was by attacking—and creating—opponents. A small-town boy who wanted to be accepted by others, he accepted this Faustian pact, but it came at a heavy psychic cost. Nixon's emotional wounds would never fully heal, no matter how much he tried to persuade himself that he would rather be respected than loved. Jack Anderson was also a small-town boy who achieved renown in Washington by assailing others. Anderson's new status as a pariah took genuine adjustment; he had been accustomed since childhood to being well liked. But his more resilient personality made him happier to trade popularity for prominence. When a congressman physically attacked the legman soon after he arrived in Washington, Anderson laughed off the incident and enjoyed the publicity it brought him. Yet during the same time, Nixon brooded about even the modest criticism he received while sending Alger Hiss to prison.

Throughout his life, Nixon continually returned to the Hiss case as a seminal event, one that provided enduring lessons for his many crises to follow. In particular, Nixon fixated on one of the more bizarre side-bars of the affair: homosexuality. Real or imagined, there was no more virulent accusation that could be hurled at an opponent in the ho-mophobic era of postwar America. It was the ultimate in smears, a kind of sexual nuclear weapon used as a last (usually fatal) resort. Over the next generation, it would become a recurring if veiled leitmotif for both Nixon and Anderson in their wars against their enemies, includ-ing each other.

In the Hiss case, it turned out that Nixon's key witness, a former Communist named Whittaker Chambers, was, in the indelicate words of J. Edgar Hoover, "an admitted pervert." Hiss claimed that Chambers framed him as a spy because he was a "spurned homosexual" who formed "some obscure kind of love attachment" to Hiss and sought revenge "out of jealousy and resentment" after his advances were re-buffed. That Chambers was gay is not disputed, but whether he impli-cated Hiss as sexual retribution is pure speculation. Nixon, however, became convinced that Chambers and Hiss had been lovers and that this was the Rosetta stone that explained their covert alliance. Decades later, as president, the homophobic Nixon would often draw parallels to the Hiss case and assert, without any evidence, that Vietnam-era figures who made classified documents public—including Jack Anderson—must also have done so because of homosexuality. Anderson shared Nixon's homophobia and would level the same libel at his own targets of opportunity, including Nixon's White House aides. Ultimately, both Nixon and Anderson were products of the same sexual paranoia and promulgators of its slander.

In a strange twist of fate, Richard Nixon's rapid rise was helped im-measurably by an accidental ally: Jack Anderson. As the congressional probe of Alger Hiss heated up, Anderson exposed Nixon's chief com-petitor on the House Un-American Activities Committee, Chairman

J. Parnell Thomas. Anderson discovered that Congressman Thomas—bald, heavy and pink-fleshed—was an improbable lothario who not only cheated on his wife but was two-timing his longtime secretary with a younger female receptionist who also worked in his Capitol Hill office. The scorned secretary decided to get revenge and turned over paperwork to Anderson showing that Thomas collected illegal kick-backs by putting phantom employees on his congressional payroll—including his daughter-in-law, his wife's elderly aunt, and his secretary's maid. "The man at the head of a committee [that is] supposed to be an example of good Americanism practices cheap, tawdry and illegal Americanism," Anderson and Pearson wrote in the "Merry-Go-Round." They scoffed at Thomas's "amazing capabilities for brazenly feeding at the public trough" and—to satisfy Anderson's source, the jilted secretary—mentioned that "Congressman Thomas usually lunches in his private office with a bottle of premixed martinis" while accompanied by the nubile rival who had replaced the secretary in the chairman's affections.

Anderson not only exposed the corruption of Nixon's rival, the newsman also maneuvered behind the scenes to force prosecutors to file criminal charges against Thomas. When top Justice Department officials claimed they could not indict the congressman because of a supposed lack of proof, Anderson hand-delivered the hard evidence, including photostats of canceled checks and names of eyewitnesses. Pearson "believed that to get the job done he must intrude during all phases of the battle," his legman explained. "Not only would he expose the abuse, he would hound the tribunal until it investigated, instruct witnesses on their testimony, propagandize the galleries, help draft the remedial legislation, and write a popular history of the affair." The strategy meant being more than just a reporter covering events; he was also a "maximum politico—part intelligence sleuth, part commentator, part lobbyist, part propagandist, part conspirator, part caucus-master." Thomas served nine months in prison.

Meanwhile, Nixon took advantage of the chairman's absence to grab for himself the whirlwind of publicity from the Hiss case. If not for Anderson's timely exposé, history might have unfolded very differently. Indeed, without this unintentional assistance from his future enemy Jack Anderson, Richard Nixon might never have come to national attention in the first place.

Three weeks after Alger Hiss was convicted of perjury, Senator Joseph McCarthy waved a sheet of paper in the air at a gathering of the Republican faithful and claimed that it contained a list of 205 American diplomats who were members of the Communist Party. McCarthy's incendiary remarks were partly plagiarized from an address Congressman Nixon had recently delivered on the House floor but mostly were invented in an impulsive burst of bombast. "Here I was making this speech," McCarthy sheepishly confided to J. Edgar Hoover. "I was getting a lot of applause and I got carried away. So I reached into my pocket and I pulled out a laundry slip" and "made it appear like I was really reading from the laundry slip" even though "there was nothing on it. I don't have any such names." Nevertheless, the fiercely anti-Communist Hoover leaked classified documents to McCarthy anyway to try to help him back up his manufactured charges.

So did a youthful news reporter whom McCarthy had befriended, Jack Anderson. At the time, McCarthy "was a pal of mine," Anderson remembered, "irresponsible to be sure, but a fellow bachelor of vast amiability and an excellent source of inside dope on the Hill." The freshman senator confessed to Anderson that he was in a jam: "I don't have a thing. I shot off my mouth. Now I gotta back it up . . . Can you help me? Do *you* have any facts?" But instead of exposing McCarthy for his demagoguery, Anderson, too, dug into his files to try to find evidence to support the senator's unverified accusations. "For one thing, I owed him" for all his previous leaks and hoped to get more, the legman later explained; besides, Anderson shared McCarthy's hostility to communism, which the patriotic Mormon viewed as "an across-the-board onslaught on all the basic beliefs I had been raised in."

McCarthy also contacted Congressman Nixon and asked if he had any "ammunition" in his files. By chance, Anderson happened to be in McCarthy's office when Nixon returned the senator's call: "For ten minutes, he worked on Congressman Nixon. Repeatedly, McCarthy pressed the theme that he was on the spot, the *cause* was on the spot, and he needed all the help as he could get. As nearly as I could judge from the McCarthy end of the conversation, Nixon became a back-room collaborator." Congressman Nixon shared not only his own confidential files but also a hard-won lesson from the Alger Hiss case—to use only vague generalities when accusing the administration of harboring Reds: "You will be in an untenable position if you claim that there are umpteen, or however many, card-carrying Communists in the State Department because you cannot prove that."

So Nixon and Anderson were in on the Big Lie from the very beginning, and each did what he could to prop it up. If either man had done otherwise and publicly revealed McCarthy's deliberate falsehoods, his witch-hunting might have been stopped at the outset. Instead, Nixon and Anderson both expediently put their own short-term advantage above the truth, helping poison American politics for years to come.

Meanwhile, buoyed by his fame from the Hiss affair, Nixon launched a campaign for the Senate against Democratic congresswoman Helen Gahagan Douglas. The contest drew national notice for its viciousness as Nixon publicly accused Douglas of being "pink down to her underwear" and reinforced his smear by publishing a flyer on pink paper attacking her supposedly subversive voting record. "Don't vote the Red ticket," Nixon ads proclaimed, "vote the Red, White, and Blue ticket. Be an American, vote for Nixon."

The acrimonious race brought the first glimmers of Nixon's dark side to the fore. After hearing "somewhat unflattering" comments about him by Congresswoman Douglas, Nixon vowed to an aide, "I'll castrate her." In the stress of the campaign, Nixon was even nastier to his wife. In a five-minute obscenity-filled tirade, Nixon lashed out in fury at Pat Nixon, calling his wife a "lousy cunt" and "fucking stupid bitch"—before realizing, to his horror, that a reporter for *Time* magazine was within earshot. The incident was hushed up but those closest to the Republican politician were discovering what the rest of the country would learn a generation later: that behind Nixon's straitlaced and sanctimonious façade lurked a foul-mouthed rage that could explode under pressure. Nonetheless, in November 1950, at the age of thirty-seven, he was elected with more votes than any other Senate candidate in the nation.

•

Less than two years later, in the summer of 1952, Senator Nixon became the Republican Party's vice presidential nominee, the running mate of the popular military hero at the head of the ticket, General Dwight Eisenhower. But at the same time, Drew Pearson and Jack Anderson discovered that Nixon was the beneficiary of a secret personal slush fund that supplemented his government salary with donations from wealthy California businessmen. The cash, Nixon backers privately acknowledged, was not for his campaign but for the senator himself. One donor said that the purpose was to "see that Dick was denied none of the things that a senator's station in life required." Another remembered being "appealed to on the ground that the Nixon family needed a larger home." In all, Nixon collected more than $18,000—significantly more than his annual salary and the contemporary equivalent of more than $160,000—from real estate, finance, manufacturing, and oil interests, many with substantial federal contracts or pending regulatory issues before the government.

Worse still, Nixon allegedly used his position in Congress to benefit his patrons. These facts could be devastating, Pearson and Anderson believed, because of Nixon's self-righteous attacks on corruption in the Truman administration. Still, the slush fund revelation could easily be lost in the midst of the noisy presidential race. The reporters "needed time," Anderson realized, "time for the campaign to be further evolved and Nixon to emerge an inextricable part of it, time to button down the story beyond wriggling out and to trace the favors received from government by the various contributors to the Nixon fund—for *this* was the half of the story that could change the fund from a civic enterprise to a criminal conspiracy."

As Anderson and Pearson began to dig further, Nixon learned of their investigation. "With considerable care, the vice presidential nominee chose the threat best calculated to deter Drew," Anderson recalled, "and the ambassador best suited to deliver it." Nixon's messenger was his advisor William Rogers, Pearson's onetime lawyer who would later become President Nixon's secretary of state. "Dick tells me that Drew is working on [the slush fund] story," Rogers warned Anderson. "This would be very damaging to him at this time and Dick wanted me to pass on the message that if he's going to work on that story—it's one thing for Joe McCarthy to call him a Communist, Joe McCarthy is discredited with a lot of people, but if Richard Nixon joins in on the campaign, it could be very damaging to Drew." Anderson was taken aback: "Bill, are you sure you want me to deliver that message?" Rogers insisted that he did. "I'll change my story on Nixon," Pearson responded defiantly. "I'll make it stronger."

But in September, while Anderson and Pearson were still working to nail down their facts, they were scooped by Nixon himself, whose aides leaked a sanitized and self-serving version of events in an effort to try to spin the forthcoming scandal. The candidate followed up with his infamously overwrought "Checkers" speech, in which he declared himself innocent of wrongdoing, engaged in selective financial disclosure, and vowed to keep the gift of a black-and-white cocker spaniel named Checkers that had been given to his daughters: "And you know the kids love the dog and I just want to say this right now, that regardless of what they say about it, we're going to keep it." Nixon's prime-time performance, broadcast live to the largest audience that had ever tuned in for a political speech, solidified his hard-core conservative Republican base, securing his place on the ticket and his continuation in public life.

For Pearson and Anderson, the injury of being scooped on their own story only added to the insult of Nixon's threatened Communist smear. The reporters were determined to even the score. Anderson checked Nixon's Senate record "from beginning to end," the legman told his boss, but the results were disappointing: besides a few sanctimonious quotes about Truman administration corruption that could be embarrassingly juxtaposed against his slush fund scandal, "Nixon's voting record was pretty much what you might expect, though not as extreme as some of the Republican reactionaries." Nonetheless, during the remaining six weeks of the campaign, Anderson and Pearson churned out more than two dozen stinging attacks on Nixon. On ABC Radio and in the "Merry-Go-Round" column, the muckrakers "unearthed a slew of thinly substantiated reports about Nixon's shady transactions," one historian wrote, "which they fired at Nixon like grapeshot." They charged that Nixon had illegally hired a Swedish maid; played up his supposed conflicts with the popular Eisenhower; quoted Democrats who made fun of Nixon; and rehashed details about his finances long after his "Checkers" speech had defused the issue with the rest of the press.

In a frenzy to attack Nixon on the eve of the election, the newsmen falsely reported that the senator and his wife were so eager to save fifty dollars on property taxes that they lied about their assets in a "sworn statement" to California officials. In fact, it was a different couple, also named Richard and Pat Nixon, who signed the tax form in question. Nixon's attorney demanded a retraction of the "false, fraudulent, un-founded . . . malicious, defamatory and libelous" column. Their own lawyer privately warned Pearson and Anderson that they did not stand "on very strong ground," but they waited until nineteen days after the election to issue a correction. (Pearson hated to retract a story, Anderson later acknowledged, and "seldom gave targets the benefit of the doubt, 'maximizing' his material on the assumption that they were already covering up far worse shenanigans than he would ever get wind of.")

The muckrakers were more successful with other exposés. They reported that Nixon had successfully "interceded" with the federal government to try to help a millionaire Romanian exile named Nicolae Malaxa get a large tax break despite "considerable controversy as to whether he is pro-communist." According to U.S. intelligence agencies, not only was Malaxa embraced by the Communist regime of Romania, he had also been a business partner of Nazi war criminal Hermann Goering's brother and helped finance the Romanian equivalent of the SS. Yet, as Anderson and Pearson disclosed, after the disreputable Romanian hired Nixon's old Whittier law firm to represent him, the senator personally wrote a letter to federal officials to try to get Malaxa "a tax reduction of sixty percent." The story posed much graver risk to Nixon than a casual reader could have understood at the time. Pearson and Anderson received an anonymous tip that Nixon pocketed "$100,000 as a political campaign contribution from Malaxa," a secret infusion of cash equivalent to nearly $900,000 today. The reporters could not confirm the allegation and did not publish it, but decades later, a retired CIA officer stated that the intelligence agency had indeed obtained a copy of a $100,000 check from Malaxa that was deposited in Nixon's Whittier bank account as a payoff for Nixon's support of the Romanian exile. Clearly, the potential threat even from the more limited "Merry-Go-Round" story about Malaxa must have generated alarm at the highest levels of the Nixon campaign.

In the final days of the race, in repeated attacks on the air and in their column, Anderson and Pearson laid out the case that Nixon used his office to benefit donors to his slush fund and exploited it to enrich himself. Less than a week before Election Day, the muckrakers revealed that Nixon's public statements about his finances contradicted his confidential tax forms, which the vice presidential nominee had refused to make public; this suggested that Nixon had lied about his fund to the public or to the government—potential fraud. More disturbing, as far as Nixon was concerned, was that the column, "characteristically teeming with innuendo and loose facts, included information from my tax returns. Partisans in the Bureau of Internal Revenue had obviously leaked them." Twenty years later, President Nixon would cite this leak in an attempt to excuse his own use of the IRS to target political enemies.

On November 2, just two days before the election, Pearson and Anderson reminded their large broadcasting audience that Nixon "said that he had never pulled any wires on behalf of the men who contributed to his fund." But in fact, the newsmen reported, the senator introduced a bill to help two of his donors "get the inside track" on a federal oil lease and lobbied on behalf of his slush fund's lawyer. Nixon was enraged and fired off an angry telegram demanding IMMEDIATE RETRACTION of this LIBELOUS . . . MALICIOUS MISREPRESENTATION OF FACTS. When ABC Radio offered Nixon equal time to respond, the candidate brushed off the compromise and escalated his pressure: UNLESS A FORMAL RETRACTION IS MADE IN ACCORDANCE WITH MY REQUEST OF LAST NIGHT, ABC MUST ASSUME THE LEGAL CONSEQUENCES.

Nixon never made good on his threat to sue. In fact, a lawsuit with its protracted legal discovery posed greater risk than benefit to the politician precisely because so many of the reporters' allegations contained more truth than even they realized at the time. In the end, Anderson concluded, "it was a case of premature exposure, as Nixon's classic escape quickly demonstrated. Had we been ready, as we soon were, with our stories about Nixon's reciprocal services [to help his donors], I doubt that the vice presidential nominee would have been able to sell his Boy Scout version of the fund. But Richard Nixon had already won the battle of public opinion by the time we brought up our reserves."

By Election Day, historian David Greenberg wrote, the column's "once powerful cannonades faded into background noise" and "no hard proof of corruption emerged to tarnish Nixon irreparably." Yet despite his political victory, "an air of venality [now] hovered around him, casting suspicion on his every move thereafter." The new vice president blamed the media in general, and the "Merry-Go-Round" in particular, for serving up a menu of "half-truth" and "smear" against him. This "character assassination," Nixon later wrote, "permanently and powerfully affected my attitude toward the press" and left "a deep scar which was never to heal completely."

Still, while Anderson and Pearson relentlessly hectored Nixon, their reports were frequently censored or watered down by their newspaper outlets. More important, the rest of the media gave only modest attention to their charges and endorsed Nixon's candidacy by a margin of eight to one. But that didn't mollify the future president. In spite of his "largely admiring press," one author noted, Nixon "nonetheless nursed his disillusionment," developing a "smoldering presumption that the 'press' was now largely, almost naturally and inevitably against him."

Throughout the 1950s, Jack Anderson and Drew Pearson continued to stoke Richard Nixon's paranoia about the press. Barely a month after the Vice President's election, before he could even take the oath of office, the newsmen reported that "Washington is buzzing" about a potentially devastating corruption scandal involving Nixon "and the oil industry." The journalists neglected to mention that they themselves were the primary cause of the buzz and had begun lobbying allies on Capitol Hill to begin a formal investigation. "We have dug up some pretty depressing information on our next Vice President," Anderson wrote to his parents. The evidence included a damaging letter from the Union Oil Company acknowledging that it paid Nixon "more than $52,000 in the course of this year"—the contemporary equivalent of nearly $500,000—so that the senator would be "serving our whole industry" by providing "anything [we] need in Washington." The correspondence seemed proof that Nixon was receiving payoffs from powerful oil conglomerates.

To keep from being sued, Anderson and Pearson avoided specific details in their report: they did not mention Union Oil by name, let alone openly accuse Nixon of bribery. Still, the vice president–elect pronounced the story a "libel" and "forgery" leaked by Democrats "to malign my character and integrity." That was "highly unlikely," Anderson believed, but he began "double-checking on the remote possibility that the letter could be a phony." Pearson circulated a copy of the document to Democrats on Capitol Hill in an effort to foment congressional hearings, which would then allow the "Merry-Go-Round" to report the charges more fully while lessening the risk of a lawsuit from Nixon.

But the vice president–elect insisted he was innocent and endorsed the idea of an official Senate probe. Staff investigators questioned witnesses and gathered more than five hundred pages of evidence, including testimony from the oil industry executive to whom the incriminating correspondence was addressed, who swore that he never received "that purported letter." In February 1953, a bipartisan Senate subcommittee unanimously concluded that the Pearson-Anderson document was indeed forged and that there was no evidence of any wrongdoing by Nixon. The panel traced the fake letter to the Democratic National Committee, which passed it on to the "Merry-Go-Round." Nixon was vindicated not only in his claim that the story was a hoax but also that it had been disseminated by his enemies to besmirch his reputation. The Vice President's sense of grievance, already acute, intensified.

Apparently chastened by their embarrassing mistake, Anderson and Pearson took only minor potshots at Nixon for the next two years. Instead, they focused their firepower on his ally, Joe McCarthy. Ashamed of his earlier collaboration with the senator, Anderson helped attack McCarthy in more than four hundred "Merry-Go-Round" columns and innumerable radio broadcasts. Their friendship came to an abrupt end. When Anderson ran into McCarthy in the halls of Congress, the senator refused to let the reporter near him: "You wait for the next elevator, Jack. I don't want you stinking up this one." The insult was tame compared to McCarthy's retaliation against Pearson, whom he literally beat up at a Washington dinner party. It was Nixon who broke up the fight. "There was Joe McCarthy with his big, thick hands around Pearson's neck," Nixon recalled. "Pearson was struggling wildly to get some air. When McCarthy spotted me, he drew his arm back and slapped Pearson so hard that his head snapped back. 'That one was for you, Dick,' he said." Three days later, McCarthy took advantage of the Constitution's protection of congressional speech by using the libel-proof Senate floor to denounce Anderson's boss as a "Moscow-directed character assassin" and "diabolically clever voice of international communism."

Pearson and Anderson fought back with escalating attacks in their column, eventually unleashing their ultimate weapon of destruction: the homosexual smear. The muckrakers compiled an extensive dossier filled with unsubstantiated allegations that McCarthy engaged in sexual liaisons with men and leaked the information to Democrats on Capitol Hill and to other newsmen. But homosexuality was so taboo in the 1950s that virtually no politician or journalist dared speak its name in public. So Anderson persuaded a friendly attorney to bring up the sordid rumors in a Nevada court trial, creating legal protection for the charges, thus allowing the "Merry-Go-Round" to safely quote the accusation that McCarthy was "a disreputable pervert." Anderson and Pearson followed up with innuendo-laced columns on McCarthy's gay but closeted chief counsel, Roy Cohn, whom they noted was "unusually preoccupied with investigating alleged homosexuals." The "supposedly fearless McCarthy is deathly afraid of pint-sized" Cohn, the reporters wrote suggestively, because "Cohn knew all the secrets" about the senator, including "extraordinary allegations" involving McCarthy's "personal life which cannot be repeated here." By 1954, the rest of the media that had for so long abetted McCarthy by giving him stenographic coverage finally turned on him. So did the Senate itself, which formally condemned McCarthy, ending his four-year rampage.

Vindicated at last, Anderson and Pearson resumed their attacks on McCarthy's old collaborator Richard Nixon. As the 1956 election approached, the muckrakers promoted a "Dump Nixon" movement to get President Eisenhower to pick a different running mate in his reelection bid. The "Merry-Go-Round" reported that Nixon's renomination would create an "almost certain" rift in GOP ranks because opponents would "wage their entire campaign against the vulnerable Californian."

Actually, that was already the strategy of Democrats, who had begun targeting Nixon's hard-nosed operative Murray Chotiner as a way to sully the Vice President. Loud, fat, and rumpled, Chotiner was a notorious wheeler-dealer whose reputation was as oily as his dark, wavy hair.

A onetime lawyer for California gangsters, Chotiner had coached Nixon through his slush fund scandal and Red-baiting election campaigns, and was known to brag about his closeness to the Vice President. He was the perfect foil for the ambitious and crusading thirty-one-year-old Senate counsel Robert F. Kennedy, brother of the Democratic senator who was positioning himself to become Nixon's presidential opponent four years later. Kennedy subpoenaed Chotiner's financial and legal records and cross-examined him under oath in an unsuccessful effort to tarnish Nixon. RFK also leaked to Anderson and Pearson, who in turn assailed Chotiner as an influence-peddler and mastermind of Nixon's "communist smear and guilt by association."

In the spring of 1956, the newsmen escalated their attacks on the Vice President, reporting that Chotiner was Nixon's "contact man" with the Mafia and had used a Los Angeles gangster named Mickey Cohen to "collect campaign money" for Nixon "from the underworld." Unlike the muckrakers' other recent salvos, this latest accusation was potentially ruinous: no politician with national ambitions could survive if the public discovered he was subsidized by organized crime. A short, moon-faced mobster who got his start in Chicago with Al Capone, Cohen was notorious for controlling the Mob's narcotics and gambling operations in California; he had been arrested more than thirty times, including for murder. "I've killed no one that in the first place didn't deserve killing," the husky-voiced hoodlum declared. It was not a philosophy that Richard Nixon wanted to defend on the campaign trail.

Cohen would later admit that he raised more than $25,000—the contemporary equivalent of nearly a quarter million dollars—for Nixon from Mafia associates, which he funneled through Chotiner. But at the time, Nixon's consigliere was able to cover it all up. Chotiner mounted a furious counterattack against the Pearson-Anderson exposé, sending letters to more than a hundred news outlets demanding a correction and apology for their "slanderous" report. In response, the newsmen lobbied Robert Kennedy to launch a new Senate probe and helpfully provided a four-page list of barbed questions to ask Chotiner under oath. But "Bob Kennedy flatly refused to discuss the Chotiner case with me," Anderson lamented to his boss, and Republicans were able to "bulldoze" further investigation, most likely because congressional

Democrats had their own links to the Mob as well. Although Pearson and Anderson refused to retract their story, their damning allegations were widely dismissed in the mistaken belief that they were once again crying wolf.

None of these attacks inflicted any immediate damage on the Vice President, who was overwhelmingly reelected in November. Still, the secret of Nixon's Mafia money would hang over his future like a toxic cloud, threatening to destroy everything he had worked for. Nursing his sense of victimization, he would not forget or forgive the reporters who were stalking him.

In January 1957, forty-four-year-old Richard Nixon became the youngest vice president in history to be sworn in for a second term. Just ten years after arriving in Washington, he was now his party's heir apparent, the uncontested front-runner for the next Republican presidential nomination.

Jack Anderson also celebrated his tenth anniversary in the nation's capital that year. His professional success was nowhere near as meteoric as Nixon's, but at the age of thirty-five he had solidified his position as the top reporter for Washington's top columnist and had begun raising a family. Jack met his future wife, an FBI clerk named Olivia "Libby" Farley, in their local Mormon church. "When I saw her, I was immediately struck," he recalled. "She was a very pretty girl with big dark eyes and dark hair." Ever the investigative reporter, Jack decided first to do a background check and took one of her relatives to lunch to pump for information. "It was a dirty trick," he later admitted, "but when you're in this job you pick up bad habits." Libby passed Jack's screening test, but then he had to pass hers. At first he tried to impress her by taking her to fancy restaurants and dropping important Washington names, but soon gave up after realizing it didn't work. A coal miner's daughter from West Virginia, she had little patience for pretense. "After he stopped trying to be debonair," Libby decided, "he was all right."

Six months later, Jack introduced his girlfriend to his mother, who was visiting Washington. Libby survived the inspection. As his mom traveled back to Utah, Jack mailed his dad money he owed him and a short note: "The only news is that I have at last decided to get married.

I am engaged to a lovely girl, whom Mother met . . . She's a member of the Church, of course . . . Mother seemed to like her." Jack and Libby wed in a Mormon temple two hundred miles north of Salt Lake City. Jack's mother attended the ceremony; his father, as always on chilly terms with his son, did not. Afterward, Libby returned to her job at the FBI, where her supervisors now kept a close watch to make sure she didn't leak any sensitive information to her new husband.

Two years later, Libby became pregnant and quit her job to stay home raising children. Five boys and four girls would be born over the next sixteen years. "We have had children by every conceivable means of birth control," Jack laughed. On his meager $130-a-week salary, finances were tight. "We wore mostly hand-me-downs," daughter Laurie remembered. "Mom mowed the lawn herself." Drew Pearson gave out hundred-dollar bonuses to employees who had babies but stopped after the second Anderson child was born; the boss's generosity was limited by his belief in family planning. Pearson seemed to take pride in his parsimony. He liked to point out that his employees' office wing was once the slave quarters of the old Georgetown mansion in which his family lived.

Unfortunately, Pearson was as stingy with praise as he was with money. Although Anderson broke many of the column's biggest scoops, Pearson "wouldn't say anything," Jack complained. "He would just go on to the next story. It was what he expected me to do. It would have been gracious if he had said a nice word. But he never did." It reminded Jack of his disapproving father, who was born the same year as Pearson. It wasn't just age that separated the columnist from his underling; it was also class. "Jack was very unsophisticated," Pearson's stepson Tyler Abell remembered. "He wore the most God-awful neckties I think I had ever seen . . . Drew certainly didn't regard him as a member of the family."

In 1954, the underpaid legmen who toiled for Pearson in anonymity staged a revolt. Despite his resentments, Jack did not join them—until the dissidents brandished paperwork filched from Pearson's desk showing that their employer was secretly grooming another reporter as heir to the column. Jack confronted his boss, who admitted the uncomfortable truth. Anderson quit on the spot. He was soon hired as the Washington bureau chief for *Parade* magazine, a widely read and lucrative if noninvestigative supplement to Sunday newspapers. But within days, Pearson had a change of heart and offered to make Anderson his successor after all. Instead of a raise, Pearson gave Anderson permission to double-dip on the side at *Parade*. The new arrangement more than tripled Jack's salary, although it required him to juggle two jobs at once. But the work at *Parade* was much less time-consuming and its extra money enabled Jack to hire a staff of his own to do legwork for him. He left Pearson's "slave quarters" and rented an office closer to the action in downtown Washington. Anderson was literally moving away from Pearson's turf and coming into his own.

Jack hired Opal Ginn, a secretary in Pearson's office, to manage his new office. It proved to be a pivotal decision that would shape much of Anderson's career for the next three decades. A busty, raw-boned redhead from rural Georgia, Opal was a party animal who served as Jack's eyes and ears on the Washington social circuit, which the teetotaling Mormon avoided. Ferociously devoted to her boss, she hosted secret meetings in her apartment with confidential informants and reportedly donned a disguise to pose as a cleaning lady on Capitol Hill to swipe incriminating documents from a corrupt senator. Often, Opal's lovers doubled as sources, from high-level elected officials and military officers to prominent newsmen and lobbyists, both married and single. But her heart belonged elsewhere. "It was obvious to everyone that she was in love with Jack," Anderson's legman Marc Smolonsky observed. "She just worshipped him." Opal viewed Anderson as a surrogate husband, her sister remembered, and confided that she turned down a suitor's marriage proposal because of Jack's objections. But although "she was madly in love with my dad," his daughter Laurie said, "Opal respected him too much to ever let him know. He was oblivious to it."

But not Jack's wife. It didn't help that Opal deliberately scheduled Jack for out-of-town trips on Libby's birthday and the couple's wedding anniversary, or that Opal cooked Jack elaborate lunches and babysat his children. "I used to think that Opal was Jack's Mormon polygamous 'other' wife," Anderson's reporter James Grady recalled, but like the rest of the "Merry-Go-Round" staff, he eventually became convinced otherwise: "Despite all those kids, sex was never something Jack cared about or was comfortable with and such a liaison would have undercut Jack's power over Opal and made him vulnerable to her." The domestic book-ends in Jack's life, Opal and Libby shared more than just their love of the same man. Both were country girls who fled their limited upbringings to come to the nation's capital during World War II to work for the federal government. They were part of an unsung legion of women—pre-feminist, post-suffragette—who supported their much-heralded "Greatest Generation" of men.

Richard Nixon also hired as his secretary a redheaded "government girl" who came to Washington during World War II. Like Opal Ginn, Rose Mary Woods was fiercely dedicated to her boss and would work for him for decades. Neither woman ever married. "These thick-ankled babes were called secretaries but were a lot more than that," observed Nixon operative Lucianne Goldberg, who knew them both. "They were office wives in every way except sexually, they knew where the bodies were buried, and their loyalty was unquestioning." In an era when the term *career girl* was a virtual oxymoron if not an epithet, Woods and Ginn considered themselves married to their jobs. Although each dated important men, none were as powerful as their employers; and the invisible influence these two women wielded behind their desks was enormous. Nixon and Anderson were among the most hated men of their era, and yet their secretaries loved them with an intensity that became the subject of gossip. Both women were so protective, they would take their bosses' secrets with them to the grave.

3

BUGGING AND BURGLARY

Richard Nixon's long climb to the White House began with an attempt to soften his polarizing image. His handlers began promoting what they touted as "the New Nixon." Most of the press accepted this reinvented persona at face value. Not Jack Anderson and Drew Pearson. Although the publisher of *The Washington Post* began playing golf with the Vice President and "seems to think he is getting more human," Pearson noted in his diary, the columnist wasn't persuaded; he went out of his way to duck social events with Nixon and dispatched Anderson to dig up more dirt on him. The newsmen tried to discover how the Vice President had acquired the money to buy a fancy new nine-thousand-square-foot English Tudor house in Washington, complete with eight bedrooms, six bathrooms, a library, a butler's pantry, and a solarium. Nixon reportedly confided to a friend that he could not have made the down payment on his new house without his controversial slush fund, but Anderson could find no financial records to prove it—although it was not for want of looking.

The next year, in June 1958, Anderson revealed that President Eisenhower's chief of staff had collected bribes from a disreputable Boston businessman. Although Nixon was not implicated in the corruption, he helped spearhead the administration's counterattack by drafting rebuttals to newspapers carrying the "Merry-Go-Round" and having his staff investigate who was leaking to Anderson. Despite the Vice President's attempts at damage control, however, Anderson's exposé dominated the news for weeks. Behind the scenes, the legman helped orchestrate House hearings and planted "potent questions" with Democratic congressmen to sharpen their interrogation of witnesses.

Anderson later acknowledged that his crusade was designed to strike "a mighty blow" at the respectable "façade that Richard Nixon was about to inherit" from Eisenhower and "redeem at one last roll our blunted offensives" against the Republicans. Anderson and Pearson tried to link Nixon to the scandal by drawing a connection between the lavish presents White House chief of staff Sherman Adams had received as payoffs and those the Vice President acquired on his many trips abroad. The "Nixon home is studded with gifts from foreign governments," the journalists wrote, including "a teakwood chest inlaid with mother-of-pearl" and so many expensive Oriental rugs "in their new 22-room house overlooking Rock Creek Park that they even put them outside on the veranda." Unlike Adams's booty, Nixon's was perfectly legal because no special favors were performed in return. But the muckrakers argued that the Vice President's spoils came "indirectly from the American taxpayers" because Nixon's benefactors "are heavy recipients of American aid . . . So when you see old Sherm [Adams] squirming over his gifts, you have to remember that he has precedent in very high places."

Nixon and the Republicans were soon able to change the topic by implicating Anderson in a scandal of his own. In July, the newsman and a Democratic congressional investigator were caught with bugging equipment in Washington's Sheraton-Carlton Hotel while clandestinely recording the Boston businessman who had bribed Adams. Police were called to the scene and newspapers across the country plastered Anderson's photo on the front page below banner headlines. *The Washington Post*, which had heavily promoted the reporter's recent scoops, now published an editorial expressing "revulsion amounting to disgust" at his surreptitious newsgathering. The *New York Journal-American* denounced the bugging as "grotesque" and "offensive to the American sense of fair play." Despite pressure to fire Anderson, Pearson stood by his legman, but the columnist confided in his diary that it was a "very embarrassing situation" made worse because "Jack had registered in the [hotel] room under an assumed name."

The White House immediately seized on the incident to divert attention from its own corruption scandal. Vice President Nixon instructed his staff to "get a congressman or senator"—later modified to the Republican National Committee—to ask leading journalistic organizations "whether they approve of Pearson's 'bugging' technique as a means of acquiring news." Nixon aides also dispatched two GOP congressmen to "raise question of violation of federal law," including the "false registry of Anderson" at the hotel. In turn, a senior Republican congressman obligingly blasted the "disgraceful" conduct of "snooper" Anderson and demanded a grand jury investigation. The Vice President's staff informed Nixon that it had planted "letters to editors of all newspapers handling Pearson columns as a follow-up to the attack here." Anderson was publicly vilified as a "Peeping Tom."

At the same time, the White House began pressuring the Justice Department, led by the Vice President's close political ally, Attorney General William Rogers, to launch a criminal probe of Anderson. The reporter soon received a subpoena to appear before a grand jury. Anderson's sworn testimony was marred by so many convenient bouts of memory loss that a prominent opposing counsel labeled it "the greatest morass of concealment, dissemblance and demonstrable perjury to which I have ever been exposed in a courtroom." Indeed, Anderson later admitted that he deliberately feigned amnesia on the witness stand to protect his sources. "Everybody knew I was lying," the reporter cheerfully recalled, "but I knew I could get away with saying 'I don't remember.'" According to a confidential FBI informant, Anderson also paid off a key witness in the case with "four or five $50 bills" plus another thousand dollars for expenses.

Meanwhile, Pearson began an aggressive counteroffensive, thundering in his column against "the uneven-handed justice now being meted out by the Justice Department," which had "ignored" Sherman Adams's bribery but "called a special grand jury to indict" Anderson and his sources who uncovered the corruption in the first place. This "political investigation" was the result of "pressure from the White House," Pearson charged, and should be the subject of public hearings by Congress. Clearly, the administration could prosecute Anderson only at its own political peril. Authorities dropped their investigation of the newsman and his informants.

It was a close call, but Anderson escaped the noose that had been prepared for him. At the time, he thought "getting caught was the most embarrassing thing that ever happened to me." But he eventually decided it "didn't hurt me at all" because "it proved we were getting [exclusive] keyhole evidence." The scandal toughened the young legman, preparing him for the retaliatory strikes that inevitably followed his reporting. "What comes back to me with greatest pungency from those years," he later reflected, "is the atmosphere of combat, of shooting and being shot at, of exposing villainies and being despised for it."

Ultimately, Anderson's narrow escape reinforced his most brazen instincts, rewarding rather than punishing his rash excess. Now that he was quoted by NBC News anchorman David Brinkley and profiled in *The Washington Post* and other national publications, the legman relished the publicity that at long last allowed him to step out from Pearson's shadow. After all, in Anderson's eyes notoriety was better than anonymity, and although he admitted that "deep down" he wanted the approval of his journalistic peers, he also recognized that he and Pearson would always be "pariahs, and that there was no point in pretending we weren't." Above all else, Anderson learned the need to be fearless under attack, to respond ferociously when challenged, even to use bribery and blackmail if necessary when all else failed. It was an indelible lesson that Anderson would draw upon in the years ahead in multiple battles with adversaries.

Vice President Nixon would draw his own conclusions from the bugging affair. He would repeatedly bring it up as evidence of Anderson's dastardly tactics, and it would shape his conviction that electronic eavesdropping was standard fare in the nation's capital. It was a rationale that would eventually lead to Watergate and forever stain his place in history.

In the summer of 1960, the Republican Party nominated Richard Nixon for president. It was an extraordinary triumph for the Quaker boy from Whittier. By dint of hard work, discipline, and perseverance, he had elevated himself from nowhere to become the front-runner for the most powerful office in the land. Nixon's deft maneuvering had led to steady advances from the House to the Senate to the vice presidency, and his vociferous anticommunism had earned the undying support of a hard-core base of Republican conservatives even while permanently antagonizing Democratic liberals. Although he had suffered several narrow misses at the hands of foes like Jack Anderson, Nixon managed to survive and go on to greater glory. Indeed, his steady rise underscored the lesser import of his journalistic critics, who achieved prominence only by splattering mud on the successful politician. For the undeniable reality was that the Vice President had overcome a harsh childhood, vitriolic political campaigns, and innumerable scandals without a single electoral defeat—and now seemed poised for his ultimate victory.

Nixon's opponent was Democratic senator John F. Kennedy, whose more modest political experience was offset by greater glamour, money, and media support. In particular, Anderson had been friendly with the Massachusetts politician for more than a dozen years, ever since the two first moved to Washington after World War II. "Since we were both young bachelors at the time, it was suggested on occasion that we go out together on double dates," Anderson recalled. But the straitlaced Mormon cautiously ducked the social opening: "Though I was sorely tempted to see how a Kennedy recreated himself, I was even more apprehensive that my frugal, abstemious, church-ridden manner of courting might have a depressing effect on the jet-set sophisticate and make an incongruous botch of the evening, so I would demur, a decision which no doubt contributed to the longevity of our cordial if episodic relationship."

Early on, Anderson learned of JFK's womanizing, complete with some titillating if circumstantial photographic evidence of the embarrassed senator leaving a young female aide's Georgetown apartment in the middle of the night while trying to hide his face with a handkerchief. But like virtually all journalists of the time, Anderson had "no intention of tattling" about Kennedy's marital infidelity, believing that "an office holder should answer to a Higher Power than a muckraker for what he or she does in the privacy of the bedroom." The Democratic nominee trusted Anderson enough to solicit his political advice, and in turn, Anderson pushed his boss, Drew Pearson, to crusade on Kennedy's behalf. The battle against Nixon gave "Drew that which energized him above all else—a menace to combat," Anderson later wrote. "Our columns and broadcasts were soon discovering Kennedy's virtues and rediscovering Nixon's old sins" as they "jumped into the fray on Kennedy's side, rounding on Nixon from day to day with our routine ammunition while searching for the reporter's desideratum— the exposé that would make a difference." In the last two weeks before the election, Anderson and Pearson ended up publishing just such an exposé, one that would end up haunting Nixon for the rest of his political life.

The muckrakers' story would become known as the Howard Hughes loan scandal, named after the eccentric billionaire who secretly funneled money Nixon's way in the latest instance of financial irregularity by the politician whose career had been shadowed by such impropriety from the beginning. Rightly or wrongly, the Vice President and his advisors would come to believe that the "Merry-Go-Round" exposé— unleashed on the eve of the 1960 election—cost them the White House. Indeed, the dirty tricks behind the revelation eerily presaged and in many ways helped sow the seeds of the Watergate scandal that would eventually topple Nixon's own presidency fourteen years later.

It all began in December 1956, just a month after Nixon had safely been reelected as Vice President, when his ne'er-do-well younger brother, Donald, suddenly received a $205,000 "loan" from the wealthy Hughes, whose far-flung business empire was heavily dependent on government contracts and connections. The billionaire was a "manipulative recluse," Anderson recognized, "known for his nonplatonic relationships with politicians" of both parties. One month after Hughes signed off on the $205,000 payment to the Nixon family, the Vice President bought his elegant new house in Washington. Decades later, after Nixon was dead, one of his best friends admitted that while the Hughes money was channeled through his brother Donald, it "was really for Richard, to help him live. He was a relatively poor man."

Hughes's investment was ostensibly to help Nixon's brother finance a Los Angeles drive-in restaurant whose main attraction was a unique triple-decker menu offering called "Nixonburgers." But the business venture proved to have as little popular appeal, as its main culinary dish and the eatery was soon on the verge of bankruptcy. Citing his brother's financial woes, the Vice President approached Hughes's lawyer, an old family acquaintance, to ask for help. According to the billionaire's top lieutenant, Noah Dietrich, Nixon refused to take no for an answer. The Vice President "needs some cash," Dietrich was informed. "Actually, he needs two hundred and five thousand dollars." The Hughes executive literally let out "a whistle of astonishment." The money would be equivalent to more than $1.6 million today. It made the Nixon slush fund that had nearly destroyed his career four years earlier seem puny in comparison.

Dietrich asked Hughes about the audacious request and learned that his boss had already spoken directly with the Vice President about the payment. "I don't give a darn about the size of it," the billionaire told his aide, "because it's a chance to cement a relationship." Dietrich knew that Hughes frequently lavished money on politicians but felt that this time he "was going too far" because disguising the transaction as a loan through Nixon's brother was so obviously "fishy." The industrialist was unperturbed. "I want the Nixons to have the money," Hughes instructed. "Let 'em have it."

The Nixon "loan" was unorthodox in many respects. To begin with, it was not really a loan: the paperwork Donald Nixon signed explicitly exempted him from personal liability and did not require that he ever pay the money back. He never did. In effect, the Hughes money ended up being a gift to the Nixons. Equally suspicious was the elaborate secrecy surrounding the payment. The money was funneled through various middlemen to hide the source of the cash. The Vice President's name was deliberately kept off the paperwork, which referred to him only by a code name—"the Eastern division" of the California-based company—to conceal his role in the affair. As one writer observed, "This is perhaps the only instance in history when a secret code has been invoked in communications devoted to the affairs of a drive-in restaurant."

What Hughes received in exchange has long been debated. Less than three months after Nixon's family received the money, the IRS reversed its earlier position and granted tax-exempt status to a Hughes offshoot, a ruling said to be worth tens of millions of dollars to the tycoon. In addition, the Pentagon awarded a defense contract to the Hughes Aircraft Company, the Justice Department agreed to settle a lawsuit against Hughes, and the Civil Aeronautics Board granted lucrative new routes to Hughes's Trans World Airlines. But it was never proved that the Vice President was responsible for any of this government largesse nor that he intervened to influence the process. Reports of an explicit quid pro quo between Nixon and his financial benefactor "were impossible to verify," one reporter who covered the story later wrote, but "politics rarely works that way" because the "exercise of political influence is more subtle; one uses one's money to make friends and then waits hopefully for the functioning of gratitude." At the time, there was no hard evidence that the Vice President himself personally pocketed any of the mogul's money or even that he solicited the cash payment in the first place; such testimony would come only decades later, after Nixon was dead. Still, even at the time, it was obvious that Hughes "was definitely not a philanthropist," as his aide Dietrich put it. "In the back of his mind, there was no question [the money] was to put the vice president of the United States under his obligation." Indeed, Hughes bragged to intimates that Nixon was "eating out of his hand."

The Vice President's elaborate secrecy kept the payment hidden for nearly four years. But in 1960, one of the middlemen who had been used to conceal Nixon's role in the deal, a Los Angeles accountant named Phillip Reiner, had a falling-out with his Hughes-backed partners. Reiner, it turned out, was a Democrat. He and his lawyer contacted Robert Kennedy, manager of his brother's presidential campaign, who enthusiastically referred the accountant to Washington attorney James McInerney, the man who ran what Jack Anderson called the "clandestine investigative arm" of the Kennedy machine. Nixon's top political enemies now learned about one of his most sensitive secrets.

But there was a problem: Reiner had no proof to back up what he knew. His thick file on the case—stuffed with letters, memos, court records, and other documentation—was in the hands of his estranged partners, who were still in Nixon's camp. As the last few weeks of the neck-and-neck campaign began closing in, what happened next is a matter of dispute. According to Reiner, someone in his old office mistakenly sent the bulky Nixon-Hughes file to him at home in a fortuitous accident. According to one of the accountant's former partners, however, someone broke into the office and stole the precious file in an act of political sabotage that resembled the Watergate break-in a dozen years later. In fact, Reiner's ex-partner filed a burglary report with the police, but no one was ever charged with the crime. Years later, the partner's widow suggested that the accountant himself "purloined" his file to sell to the Kennedys, who did indeed pay Reiner the contemporary equivalent of more than $100,000 for the paperwork. Still, at this point the accountant was unwilling to go public and balked when Democrats tried to get him to sign an affidavit about the scandal.

Soon, another bizarre twist occurred: twenty-eight-year-old Teddy Kennedy, campaigning on behalf of his brother, received a phone call from an anonymous attorney who said he had something "hot" that could swing the election. The lawyer would not discuss details over the telephone, but the youngest Kennedy brother agreed to meet the mysterious informant a few days later. The future senator flew to the Los Angeles airport, where he was handed a one-page contract to be signed by Robert F. Kennedy stating that "I and my father Joseph Kennedy" would pay $500,000 in exchange for paperwork documenting how Vice President Nixon "secretly negotiated and obtained $205,000.00 from someone engaged in multimillion-dollar contracts with the United States Government. The transaction was feebly disguised as a 'loan.'" Uncertain what to make of it all, and undoubtedly suspicious of a set-up, Teddy Kennedy mumbled, "I don't know whether we would use this or not" and quickly departed. "I never heard another word from him or anybody else," the attorney later said. "No one signed the agreement so of course no one paid me anything." But the lawyer reportedly held more than one secret meeting with Democrats to discuss selling the documents.

In any case, word of this strange shakedown quickly reached Reiner. "It bowled me over," the accountant recalled. "There I was in the middle of this loan and suddenly a guy is trying to peddle something about it for $500,000. I decided that if this story was going to blow, I wanted the whole thing told." Reiner agreed to go public and Kennedy attorney McInerney put together a package of incriminating paperwork for dissemination to the news media. In early October, he delivered his hot file to *St. Louis Post-Dispatch* reporter Richard Dudman, who had aggressively covered Nixon's slush fund scandal eight years earlier but had never even met the Democratic operative before. The startled newsman couldn't believe his good fortune. "We had a terrific scoop," Dudman recalled, "a red-hot story." He raced to verify the report and (in an era before copying machines) hired a photographer to shoot pictures of the documents. But Dudman accidentally left his briefcase filled with the records behind, and by the time he realized his mistake, a scavenging employee of the photographic studio evidently realized there was money to be made peddling the damaging paperwork to the media.

Within forty-eight hours, an enterprising private eye approached *Time* magazine and offered to sell the Nixon-Hughes file for "a large sum." *Time* said no but immediately assigned five reporters to investigate. One of them, Frank McCulloch, was friends with former Hughes aide Noah Dietrich, whose recent falling-out with his ex-boss led him not only to confirm the story verbally but also to provide key documentary evidence to back it up. *Time*, too, was now in striking distance of exposing the scandal.

An alarmed Hughes called his aide Robert Maheu and asked him to "save Nixon's neck." The billionaire realized that if the transaction "came out in public, the loan could cause Richard Nixon tremendous embarrassment, and possibly the election." Maheu lobbied news outlets to kill the story. "Fortunately, those were the days when you could count on the press to have a heart, and they printed not a word," Maheu later said. The journalists who worked on the story were unhappy but they were also accustomed to having their scoops spiked for political reasons. "I pushed for it like hell," McCulloch recalled, but *Time*'s pro-Nixon editors decided that it would be unfair to publish such an explosive article just three weeks before the election. Other journalists had similar concerns. None dared run the story.

Except, as usual, for Jack Anderson and Drew Pearson.

As Election Day neared, the Kennedy camp told Pearson about the Nixon-Hughes deal. The columnist eagerly summoned Anderson to his Georgetown office. "Jack, this time we may have Nixon," Pearson declared. "Of course," he quickly added, "Nixon is still the great contortionist, and this is just the hour to be hung with a hoax. Before this is over, he may have *us*." While Anderson took notes, his boss explained the complicated loan. "On the face of it, this looks like a thinly disguised gift," Pearson observed. Anderson agreed and began digging into the story. But he realized that at such a late date in the campaign, his proof would have to be ironclad to avoid backfiring: "If the public did not perceive the story as legitimate, its effect would be to create sympathy and votes for Nixon, the more so given his genius for tear-inspiring self defense."

Because public records carefully concealed Nixon's link to Howard Hughes, Anderson returned with only circumstantial evidence that was too flimsy to torpedo the Republican nominee. Pearson was disappointed: "The trouble with all this is that [Hughes] is always winning [airline] routes and contracts and settlements from the government. Unless we catch Nixon directly intervening, you can't put your finger on any of them and say 'this is a pay-off.'" Without disclosing the identity of his source, Pearson suggested that Anderson contact James McInerney: "I've called Jim and he's been looking into it for me. Jim has the resources to crack this for us in a hurry. I suggest you see what he's come up with, and then get back to me." Anderson hurried to see the Kennedy operative. "On my way to McInerney's office," the newsman recalled, "I mulled over his presence among us." Anderson knew that McInerney "was helping the Kennedy campaign in some murky way having to do with intelligence" and recognized that it was "something of a journalistic atrocity for Drew, near the climax of the campaign, to enlist the Kennedy hawkshaws to help us get the goods on their opponent." But Anderson's appetite was whetted by the story's undeniable potential, "evocative of semisleeping perceptions of Nixon the sharpster, the corner-cutter, the huckster whose personal ethics were less than presidential."

McInerney greeted Anderson with a truculence that the reporter attributed to "a reluctance to reveal any details that might further implicate the Kennedy campaign as a helpmate to this exposé." But with "a pride that only the diligent investigator can know, he presented a neatly arranged packet which I devoured unceremoniously, in the reflexive manner of a vagrant who has been offered a bottle he fears might be reclaimed at any moment." The paperwork included internal documents indisputably linking Nixon's money to Hughes and corroborating affidavits put together by the Kennedy gumshoes.

But Pearson surprised Anderson by expressing reluctance to publish the story. "It's late," Pearson told his legman, "awfully late, to lob something ugly like this into a presidential campaign." The columnist worried that the loan was not really "relevant" to Nixon's fitness for office and would needlessly "distract" voters. "Distract?" Anderson was incredulous as he felt his scoop slipping away. "What is more relevant than whether a candidate is on the take?" Pearson quietly reminded Anderson of the backlash their previous election-eve mistakes had produced: "People never forgive you for something like this. Editors don't. Maybe we should hold it till after election day."

"What good will it do to footnote it *after* the election?" Anderson retorted. "It's what voters know *before* that counts." The reporter argued it was their "duty" to make the information public, especially because the rest of the press was afraid to.

"Jack, believe me, when you have one of these things in front of you there's no way to know for sure what's the right thing to do . . . I don't want the column to be identified mainly with eleventh-hour campaign assassinations of politicians we're known to be against. It undermines all the things we're trying to do."

"I was sick," Anderson recalled. "I had not yet learned to let go of any story, let alone one of this size and personal significance . . . I feared that by pressing hard I would push him over the edge of a 'no' decision, yet I knew how important it was to contest what he said, to get in a last word . . . I said, as softly as I could manage, 'Drew, this is just the kind of story, at just the kind of time, that our column exists for.'"

A few days later, Pearson came up with a Machiavellian ploy that, as Anderson put it, would eliminate the "onus of starting such a brawl while making it more likely . . . that people will perceive it as a proper dispute rather than a last-minute smear job." Although Anderson and Pearson usually avoided tipping off targets of an ongoing investigation, this time they deliberately contacted Nixon and Hughes in a manner designed to "alarm them" that they were "about to pounce" but falsely "reassure them as to the rudimentary nature" of what they knew, dribbling out just "fragments of the story" as if they had learned only of the sanitized documents that were already in the public record but nothing else. Their goal was to "agitate the Nixon antennae . . . to provoke Nixon's fears and then his counterattack." The muckrakers' response would depend on the Vice President. "If Nixon bites and tells anything near the truth, Drew will leave it alone," Anderson explained. "If," however, "Nixon bites and lies, to expose him will be proper, for a calculated lie in a presidential candidate on a question of personal honesty should be made known to the voters no matter how late the campaign hour." If Anderson and Pearson were lucky, the candidate and his staff "might yet [try to] lie their way out of it, at least for two weeks. If they opted for this course, we had them."

Nixon fell headlong into the trap that Pearson and Anderson set for him. According to the Vice President's press secretary, Herbert Klein, Nixon learned that the "Merry-Go-Round" was "about to unload some kind of 'blockbuster' regarding the loan." In response, "Nixon decided that the best way to defuse such a story" was to leak "the Nixon side of the case" to a friendly reporter "rather than sit back and wait for a column to put us on the defensive." The Republican nominee realized that he was taking a "gamble," Klein said, because "the election was close and no one actually knew what Pearson might write, if anything." Still, Nixon "put out a story knowing it was negative, but feeling we could better protect our side of the story" if we "scooped" the muckraking columnists.

The Vice President turned to a conservative journalist for Scripps Howard who had written positively about the candidate in 1952 when he successfully used the same tactic to neutralize the "Merry-Go-Round" exposé of the notorious Nixon slush fund. Under a headline that implied Nixonian forthrightness—VP BARES STORY OF KIN'S "DEALS"—the story was framed as if it had been written by the Republican nominee himself. According to Scripps Howard, the Vice President had learned that the Democrats were investigating his brother to try to embarrass him just before the election: "In an attempt to offset any such move, the Nixon headquarters here in Washington has made available to this reporter a full explanation of all relevant facts in the record, to get the story out in the open and end the gossip." But the account ignored the two most important names in the financial deal: Richard Nixon and Howard Hughes. The Vice President's pivotal role in arranging the transaction was not reported, and Hughes's name was not mentioned once. Instead, the article included only the names of the obscure middlemen as if they, not the billionaire, were behind the payment. "To call it unbelievable was being kind," one Hughes aide involved in the scandal admitted years later. "I counted many outright lies in the story." The Nixon campaign simply "lost their heads" and "panicked" at the possibility of another exposé by Anderson and Pearson, Hughes's lawyer explained, and "put out a cock-and-bull story."

Nixon's disinformation gave the muckrakers precisely the excuse they had been looking for to unload their election-eve stink bomb, which could now be righteously defended on the grounds that they were merely correcting the Vice President's falsehoods. The day after the Scripps Howard article appeared, on October 25, Pearson and Anderson announced in their column that they, too, had been digging into the same story "but hesitated to write" about it "chiefly because it was late in the election campaign and any revelation regarding another conflict-of-interest case involving Mr. Nixon was certain to bring charges of 'smear.'" But now that the campaign had issued "a completely distorted version of the facts, the public is entitled to know all of them."

For the first time, the newsmen publicly revealed that Hughes, not his middlemen, bestowed the money "with the approval and knowledge of the Vice President." Pearson and Anderson also exposed the secrecy designed to conceal the payment, including the code name used to refer to the Vice President and the "dummy owner" used to hide Hughes's involvement. They pointed out that the billionaire "had various important matters before the government at the time" and that "many of these problems"—which they detailed—"got better treatment after the loan." While there was "no evidence that the Hughes loan was connected with any government favors given Hughes," Anderson explained that "the reason for conflict of interest laws is because of this very fact—namely that it is difficult, if not impossible, to prove favoritism in high places." Which is why, the muckrakers argued, the deal was unethical even if there was no conclusive proof that it was a payoff.

Headlines trumpeted the "Merry-Go-Round" revelations around the country. Nixon's press secretary refused to allow journalists to question the Vice President directly, and the middlemen who had supposedly put up the money for the loan suddenly could not be located. Public suspicion intensified. In response, Nixon's campaign manager, Robert Finch, publicly announced that the Vice President was not involved in any way with the payment; the story was just another Pearson-Anderson "smear" and there was "no basis for any claim" that the money "came from Hughes." This final lie ultimately proved to be fatal because it could be so easily refuted. "Drew did not want the story to come to a head too quickly," Anderson recalled, "so he turned the Nixon camp slowly on the spit. Referring mysteriously to correspondence in his possession . . . he issued a challenge: 'I should be delighted to produce photostats of the secret deeds, transfers and other documents pertaining to the Howard Hughes loan, and show them on television with Don Nixon or Howard Hughes or Robert Finch present to deny them.'" Not surprisingly, the offer was declined.

The Vice President began an abrupt retreat. Nixon's campaign manager was forced to admit that he could "not make a flat statement" about whether Hughes was behind the loan "because I was not privy to the transaction." Aides said they would need another week to gather "all the documents together" to answer reporters' questions. "Now fearing the worst," Anderson recalled, "the Nixon camp had to go into reverse gear and back off, a fatal shift once a dispute has reached the headline state . . . The telltale aura of culpability hovered over the sweating evasions of public relations men." The candidate's silence, Anderson realized, "conveyed a sense of the sinister" and "the announcement that 'the Nixon family' was to be suddenly thrust out front to do the talking from now on seemed to presage that there remained no defense but bathos."

Indeed, on October 31, just eight days before the election, Donald Nixon for the first time issued a public statement pronouncing himself "deeply grieved" that Pearson and Anderson have "attempted to smear my brother by detailing my unsuccessful business ventures." He invoked every family member but his brother's dog Checkers: "Those were humiliating times for my wife, my children and my mother. The scars they left are deep." Obviously, the muckrakers were only bringing it up now "in the hope that somehow they would embarrass my brother" and "influence the outcome of the presidential election." But after all the self-pitying rhetoric, Donald finally acknowledged that Hughes was in fact the source of the loan, contrary to the Nixon campaign's previous denials.

News accounts trumpeted the Vice President's about-face. LOAN ADMITTED BY NIXON KIN was one of many banner headlines across the nation. In a report picked up by hundreds of newspapers, the Associated Press stated that "Donald Nixon, the Vice President's brother, now admits that the controversial $205,000 loan came from industrialist Howard Hughes" even though "the Vice President's personal campaign manager denied this last week." Meanwhile, Anderson and Pearson convincingly refuted the Vice President's claim that he knew nothing of the deal by citing documents showing that he was a stockholder in his brother's company. Other legal paperwork revealed that the transaction was notarized in Nixon's Capitol Hill office building. Even the conservative Scripps Howard journalist who had defended the Vice President admitted, "They made a sucker out of me."

The following day, accountant Reiner went public and further demolished the California politician's version of events. Contrary to Nixon's claims, Reiner revealed, "all major decisions" involving the Hughes money "were cleared" in advance with the Vice President himself, who even flew from Washington to Los Angeles to plot how to shield the payment from taxes on capital gains. Nixon and his financial angel Hughes were so determined to hide the deal, the accountant added, that he was instructed to use pseudonyms, backdate legal papers, and make sure key documents were never filed in court. CODE NAME HID DICK NIXON'S ROLE, blared the *New York Post*, which denounced "the fantastic attempt of the Nixon organization to conceal and distort the facts."

A day later—less than a week before the election—former president Harry Truman joked that Nixon needed "a bigger dog," a sarcastic reference to Checkers. Hecklers greeted the Vice President on the campaign trail with derisive signs. "Nixon and Hughes," rhymed one, "You're going to lose." "Henceforth," Anderson recalled, "the Nixon camp hunkered down on its past statements and retreated into silence." Silence, however, was not what Anderson and Pearson had in mind.

They milked their scoop for six separate columns in the last days before the election, taking care not to let subtlety get in their way. "Mr. Nixon has been talking about experience," Pearson declared in an election-eve broadcast. "It now develops that his experience, which began with an $18,000 personal expense fund, has progressed to a $205,000 loan, which later became a gift . . . This is the kind of experience the American people can do without."

The muckrakers also began a drumroll to get Congress to hold public hearings on the scandal. They drafted a statement for their friend Senator Lyndon Johnson, the Democratic vice presidential nominee, requesting that "a special Senate committee be convened at once to investigate" Nixon's financial dealings, complete with subpoenas and sworn testimony. "The charges are too serious to be brushed aside or dismissed as a political smear," the newsmen wrote in their statement for LBJ. "Nixon owes the voters an explanation." The reporters used the same tactic with Democratic congressman Jack Brooks, wiring him a telegram headlined: SUGGEST PRESS STATEMENT SOMEWHAT ALONG THESE LINES. Brooks parroted the Pearson-Anderson statement virtually word for word to the rest of the media: "Because of the seriousness of the charges, and the right of the American people to know the facts," Brooks announced, his House subcommittee would "conduct a thorough investigation at the earliest opportunity." Senator Estes Kefauver, another friend of Anderson and Pearson, also called for a federal inquiry into the Nixon loan, which the Tennessee Democrat declared was directly related "to the integrity of our government and the leadership of the political party which is asking for a mandate by the American people less than two weeks from now."

It is no exaggeration to say that Pearson and Anderson flawlessly executed a brilliant and chillingly ruthless political hit, flushing out Nixon's secret financial transaction just days before the election in a manner calculated to inflict maximum damage in the closely fought race. Still, the muckrakers' blockbuster exposé did not necessarily play the pivotal role its authors intended. Despite their best efforts, the majority of the news media failed to follow the column's aggressive lead. "Because Pearson was a persistent critic of Nixon," one reporter who covered the story wrote, "and because the story broke at the eleventh hour in the campaign, few newspapers picked it up. Those that did reported it in such a fragmentary and cautious manner that readers could make little sense of it." Most publishers remained overwhelmingly Republican and backed Nixon on both their editorial and news pages, just as they had eight years earlier during his slush fund scandal.

In the end, Nixon lost to Kennedy by less than one-tenth of one percent in what was then the closest presidential contest ever in American history. The impact of the Hughes exposé was impossible to calculate. It "came too late in the campaign, and the case was too complex, to have a major effect," one historian concluded. Besides the more sweeping economic, political, and social currents that influenced voters, a host of other factors shaped the outcome as well: the televised debates between the candidates, Eisenhower's tepid support for his vice president, vote fraud in Texas and Illinois, and Kennedy's last-minute support for the jailed civil rights leader Martin Luther King, among others. In a race so close, defeat as well as victory had a thousand fathers.

The day after Nixon conceded the contest, Donald Nixon approached his brother. "I hope I haven't been responsible for your losing the election," he said. The Vice President graciously reassured his sibling. But in the years to come, Nixon and his closest advisors privately confided that they believed the Hughes scandal had indeed cost them the White House. Robert Kennedy agreed, saying the "Merry-Go-Round" exposé was a "decisive factor" in Nixon's defeat. Accurate or not, this perception would haunt Republicans for years.

Richard Nixon always believed he was the true winner of the 1960 campaign. He blamed not only Anderson and Pearson for their election-eve "smear" but also the Kennedys, whom Nixon called "the most ruthless group of political operators ever mobilized" who "approached campaign dirty tricks with a roguish relish" that "overcame the critical faculties of many reporters." Just as Anderson's eavesdropping escapade helped shape the Vice President's belief that electronic bugging was commonplace in Washington, so the break-in to recover his incriminating financial documents convinced him that burglary was standard practice in national politics. Nixon vowed that he would never be caught unprepared again, and he would ultimately establish his own corps of hard-nosed operatives to carry out such espionage and sabotage.

In the end, of course, Nixon's cutthroat tactics would become not his salvation but his ruin. "What lost Nixon [the 1960] election," wrote one reporter who covered it, "was the same mind-set that did him in later in the Watergate scandal . . . His handling of Watergate paralleled his mishandling of the Hughes loan with such exactitude that it appeared that the loan fiasco was a rehearsal of his final disaster. In both instances there was the initial denial that anything was amiss . . . the same behind-the-scenes cover-up, the demeaning of the motives of his critics, the misuse of his own colleagues, the self-pitying portrayal of himself as victim, not offender . . . even a reemergence of covert money from Howard Hughes."

Once again, it would be exposed by Jack Anderson.

4

COMEBACK

On the surface at least, Richard Nixon was all smiles as he stood on the Capitol's inaugural platform in January 1961 and watched his rival John F. Kennedy sworn in as Chief Executive. Despite allegations of ballot box stuffing, Nixon had not publicly challenged the results. "What if I demanded a recount and it turned out that despite the vote fraud Kennedy had still won?" he later wrote. "Charges of 'sore loser' would follow me throughout history and remove any possibility of a further career." At the relatively young age of forty-seven, Nixon hoped that a magnanimous concession would keep his political prospects alive for the future.

A few months later, the defeated politician moved with his family back to California and began planning a comeback by running for governor in his home state. Once again his staff promoted the notion of a "New Nixon" but this time fewer journalists were persuaded. His campaign tactics against Democratic governor Edmund Brown closely resembled those of the Old Nixon. "Is Brown Pink?" bumper stickers asked. Pamphlets denounced Nixon's opponent as a "Red appeaser" and showed a doctored photo of Brown bowing to Soviet leader Nikita Khrushchev.

But Nixon's Red-baiting proved less effective in 1962 than it had a dozen years earlier. Voters wanted a governor who would fix potholes and improve schools, not make grand pronouncements on foreign policy. Nixon was widely viewed as wanting to be governor merely as a stepping-stone to the White House. This impression was bolstered when the former vice president denounced rural voters as "fucking local yokels" and refused to meet with regional reporters by saying he "wouldn't give them the sweat off my balls"—although the comments were too crude for the press to report publicly.

Jack Anderson and Drew Pearson had no intention of allowing Nixon to return to power. In the six months leading up to the gubernatorial election, they ran twenty-five negative columns on their longtime antagonist, rehashing their top anti-Nixon hits over the years. They also embarked on a campaign to persuade gangster Mickey Cohen to go public about funneling Mafia money to Nixon's congressional campaigns. Pearson took the mobster and his wife to dinner, wrote letters of recommendation to help his nephew get into medical school, and marketed the racketeer to talent agencies as a motivational speaker. The "Merry-Go-Round" even championed the cause of Cohen's mistress, urging a pardon for the prostitute-turned-porn-star who was jailed after police found drugs hidden in her brassiere. ("I'm inclined to get on my white steed and go charging off for various lost causes," Pearson admitted in his diary, "but this is one which I don't enthuse over.") Still, despite the wooing, Cohen was not ready to accuse Nixon publicly. So the newsmen focused instead on "the dynamite-laden" Howard Hughes loan, the Nixons' "family skeleton." Although Pearson and Anderson uncovered no new information, they managed to turn their two-year-old exposé into one of the single biggest issues in the race. "I must have answered the question about the Hughes loan at least a hundred times," Nixon complained. "The media loved the story and played it up big—both because it made such tantalizing copy and because it was so damaging to me."

On Election Day, Nixon lost the gubernatorial race by five percentage points. Afterward, he delivered his famously embittered attack on "all the members of the press [who] are so delighted that I have lost." He thrust his clenched fist at reporters: "For sixteen years, ever since the Hiss case, you've had a lot of fun—a lot of fun—that you've had an opportunity to attack me." Scowling fiercely, lips tight, Nixon glared: "But as I leave you I want you to know—just think how much you're going to be missing." An artificial smile: "You won't have Nixon to kick around anymore, because, gentlemen, this is my last press conference."

Yet while Nixon blamed a biased media for his defeat, the reality once again was that, except for Anderson and Pearson, journalistic invective during campaign was actually quite tame. "The press mainly reported what was said by the two candidates—and, with [few] exception[s], little more," Nixon's top PR man acknowledged; "the election was not decided by press coverage." The politician's departing outburst was widely regarded as an act of professional suicide that forever tagged Nixon with the "sore loser" label he had so assiduously avoided by graciously congratulating Kennedy on his victory two years earlier. ABC News broadcast what it called "The Political Obituary of Richard Nixon." James Reston of *The New York Times* concluded, "No public figure of our time has ever studied the reporters so much, or understood them so little."

Nixon was defiantly unapologetic. "I gave it to them right in the ass," he told an aide. "It had to be said, goddammit." Many Americans agreed. In fact, by whipping up right-wing fury at the mainstream media in his "last" news conference, Nixon launched not a final exit but the opening salvo of his political comeback, the foundation for the antipress attack machine he would one day command from the White House.

For the previous decade, more than any other journalist in the nation, Jack Anderson had devoted himself to exposing Richard Nixon's financial misconduct. Yet the investigative reporter himself also abused his own position for private gain. With nine young children to feed and a parsimonious boss, Anderson secretly began taking money from Washington news sources whom he covered. Anderson moonlighted for at least one senator by ghostwriting speeches for him, even as he penned positive articles about his congressional patron in the "Merry-Go-Round." Anderson also accepted free stock from a wealthy entrepreneur and complimentary airplane travel while plugging these benefactors in his column. In addition, according to declassified FBI records, Anderson received thousands of dollars in "loans" from a prominent Washington attorney to whom Anderson referred clients. Although the unwritten rules of journalistic ethics were more lax in that era than today—other reporters also accepted money and gifts from those they wrote about—Anderson's graft clearly undercut the moral high ground that he claimed for his muckraking mission.

Anderson's most notorious financial angel was a Washington fixer named Irv Davidson, a mobbed-up arms broker and lobbyist who peddled influence (and prostitutes) to his shady friends. Davidson's clients included Mafia don Carlos Marcello, Teamsters Union boss Jimmy Hoffa, Cuban dictator Fulgencio Batista, and Nicaraguan strongman Anastasio Somoza. Dubbed the "Handy Andy of behind-the-scenes Washington," Davidson looked the part, with gold cuff links, pinky rings, and perfectly manicured nails. "His wardrobe featured sleek, well-tailored suits and alligator shoes," one of Anderson's assistants remembered. "He always seemed to be carrying large sums of cash." Davidson handed out tens of thousands of dollars to Anderson and his family, picking up the reporter's expenses for office rental and hotels, giving him inside stock tips, even bribing an important news source so that Anderson could gain inside intelligence without technically compromising his integrity.

Davidson's largesse to Anderson was no more philanthropic than Howard Hughes's was to Richard Nixon. "The only thing I ever tried to do was to get Jack to do good stories on my friends," Davidson later said. "I wanted Jack to keep away from my friends, and he never did any bad articles on them." Indeed, Anderson duly wrote a number of positive articles about the lobbyist's notorious sponsors, which Davidson saved in a special file and proudly showed off to visitors. The Washington fixer believed he got his money's worth because Anderson was "writing articles favorable to [my] clients."

How could Anderson justify such a blatant conflict of interest? After all, he relentlessly exposed the same kind of corruption when it involved Richard Nixon and other public officials. But somehow the righteous reporter managed to rationalize comparable behavior when it involved himself. In his eternal balancing of ends and means, the newsman simply believed it was worth the trade-off, that he gained more from the money and inside information that Davidson and other sources provided than he lost by the compromises he had to make in exchange. Certain of his own rectitude, the moralistic Mormon persuaded himself that he was too incorruptible to allow outside business deals with sources to taint the truth of his reporting. "Remember, God had redeemed Jack already, his place in Heaven was assured," Anderson's legman James Grady explained. "He could make mistakes but not do wrong because he was doing God's work and therefore all was forgiven—indeed, ordained and perhaps mandated."

Anderson's financial ties to Davidson were never publicly disclosed during his lifetime. But they nearly destroyed the reporter's career in 1963, when congressional investigators stumbled onto them as part of a wider probe of foreign lobbying in Washington. Senator J. William Fulbright's Foreign Relations Committee targeted several suspicious operatives, including Davidson, whose brazen influence-peddling on behalf of his disreputable clients was documented in embarrassing correspondence and bank records subpoenaed by Senate investigators. Fulbright's staff, led by a young aide named Walter Pincus—who would one day become a leading investigative reporter for *The Washington Post*—discovered that Davidson not only lavished money and gifts on lawmakers but also on members of the press.

The worst journalistic offender was Jack Anderson. Senate investigators uncovered six checks totaling the contemporary equivalent of $15,000 that Davidson issued to Anderson and his secretary from the bank account of the Somoza regime in Nicaragua; the subpoenaed paperwork also showed that the lobbyist paid the newsman's out-of-town hotel expenses. This was just a tiny fraction of the money that Davidson bestowed upon Anderson over the years, but it was damning enough all by itself to threaten the reporter with exposure and ruin. Authorities also discovered that Davidson arranged to hire the son of an Anderson friend, a maneuver the lobbyist acknowledged was "expedient" but which let him "take advantage of this favor to get some good P.R." from the newsman. According to a Senate aide, the "facts relating to the 'loans' between Anderson and Davidson and the 'favors' each did for the other, if released publicly, could seriously jeopardize the public 'image' of Anderson." The muckraker reached a similar conclusion and told authorities that "there are a lot of people who are out to get him, and he was very fearful this material would leak." The irony of an investigative reporter who specialized in leaks trying to squelch one in which he was personally implicated did not seem to occur to Anderson.

In March 1963, Davidson was forced to testify under oath in a secret congressional hearing. Senators excoriated the lobbyist for being an "influence peddler" but targeted his wheeling-and-dealing with the government, not the news media. The only mention of Anderson was a brief reference to a Los Angeles hotel bill that Davidson paid for the reporter. Senators carefully avoided any discussion of subpoenaed bank records that documented numerous other business transactions between Anderson and the lobbyist. Why? The panel was not afraid to expose the newsman's financial misconduct, an investigator later explained, but the focus was political, not journalistic, corruption. Once again, Anderson narrowly managed to escape professional destruction.

Coincidentally, Richard Nixon was also put at risk by the Senate probe. Davidson confided to intimates that he personally delivered a $5,000 cash payoff to the then vice president on behalf of the Somoza dictatorship. Davidson told Anderson about it but the reporter had no way to corroborate the story, so he disguised the identities of the participants and published a cursory description of the transaction:

> Not long ago, two urbane, well-dressed men met briefly in a San Francisco hotel room. Their conversation was so guarded as to be meaningless to anyone else. Then one held out a roll of bills. The other took the money, grinned sheepishly and said: "My fingers are sticky." This scene, described to me by the one with the wad of money, concluded [a] deal to influence U.S. policy. The money which changed hands was a $5,000 "campaign contribution" to a prominent, widely respected politician from an agent for a Latin American dictator.

Davidson's claim that he bribed Nixon was never proved and, except for Anderson's veiled account, never reported publicly. But it is no wonder that the muckraker's relentless stalking over the previous decade led the former vice president to despise the newsman with a fear that bordered on the obsessive.

The irony was inescapable: Nixon and Anderson, two pillars of sanctimonious rectitude, were both purportedly on the take from the same influence peddler. Neither could expose the other without risking disclosure of his own impropriety. Each saw his ugliest reflection in his enemy's likeness.

In the aftermath of his defeat and humiliating "last" press conference, Nixon turned inward, withdrawing from public life, brooding with self-pity. In private, he lashed out at onetime friends and allies, denouncing former president Eisenhower as a "senile old bastard," giving free rein to the dark side of his personality, which, at least in public, he had mostly managed to keep in check. Nixon was "a sad, depressed man, as pathetic a national figure as I had ever seen," a witness recalled. "He was drinking heavily, and my heart went out to his family." By one account, Nixon's fury led him to hit his wife; another report claimed that Pat Nixon talked of divorcing her husband. "There was a sadness," his daughter Tricia Nixon remembered, "and the sadness went on for years."

To try to end this despair, the Nixon family left California for New York City. The former vice president joined one of Manhattan's leading law firms and for the first time began earning a substantial salary. Still, his heart was in politics, not law, and by 1964 he started making preliminary moves to position himself once again as a possible presidential candidate. Nixon began giving speeches around the country and traveling abroad, holding press conferences and making pronouncements on foreign and domestic policy. He also reached out to the news media he had so recently scorned: "My friends in the press—if I have any," he joked at a stag dinner of the Washington press corps' Gridiron Club. "If I haven't any, maybe it is more my fault than theirs. I hope a man can lose his temper once in sixteen years and be forgiven for it."

Nixon's conciliatory comments and increased visibility produced results. Without actively campaigning, he received more than fifteen thousand write-in votes during New Hampshire's presidential primary. But in the end, the Republican Party nominated conservative senator Barry Goldwater of Arizona. Nixon introduced Goldwater to thunderous applause at the GOP convention, then piled up a raft of political IOUs by making more than 150 campaign appearances for Republican candidates in thirty-six states. After President Lyndon Johnson crushed

Goldwater in the November election, Nixon carefully positioned himself as one of his party's future presidential possibilities.

Two years later, during the 1966 midterm elections, Nixon repeated and enhanced his performance. This time, he spoke before more than four hundred Republican groups in forty states, raising money and helping revive the party's base after the Goldwater debacle. Once again, journalists began writing about a "New Nixon," whom columnist Walter Lippmann now called "a maturer, mellower man who is no longer clawing his way to the top" and had "outgrown the ruthless politics of his early days." According to Nixon aide Len Garment, "The press, lulled by the idea that Nixon had been defanged, cooperated in sounding the theme of his transformation." When Republicans made significant gains in the midterm election, Nixon received credit for his party's resurgence.

The GOP's success also ushered in a new presidential competitor: California governor-elect Ronald Reagan, a smooth and handsome Hollywood actor beloved by the party's hard-core activist base. According to *The New York Times*, "Without a day in public office, [Reagan] is already the favorite Presidential candidate of Republican conservatives." But in a strange twist, Nixon's fiercest journalistic antagonists inadvertently—but immeasurably—advanced Nixon's comeback.

In October 1967, Jack Anderson and Drew Pearson charged in their column that "a homosexual ring has been operating" on the staff of Governor Ronald Reagan, whose security detail "came up with a tape recording of a sex orgy" involving eight men at a Lake Tahoe cabin leased by gubernatorial aides. Furthermore, the newsmen reported, Reagan "did not move to clean up his office" by firing the advisors until six months after he first learned of the scandal: "It will be very interesting to note what effect the incident has on the Governor's zooming chances to be president of the United States."

The lurid "Merry-Go-Round" account of a gay sex ring ultimately turned out to be exaggerated. "It wasn't much of a 'ring,'" Anderson later admitted. "Only two of the eight [men] had current ties to the Reagan gubernatorial administration." But the essence of the report, that Reagan's staff included gays, was accurate. Two months earlier, the governor had quietly replaced his chief of staff, "a natty dresser with dark good looks and a receding hairline," and his younger scheduling assistant after being informed by other aides that the two men were "practicing homosexuals." Reagan's advisors Edwin Meese, William French Smith, William P. Clark, Stuart Spencer, and Lyn Nofziger, all of whom would later become powerful during Reagan's presidency, provided their boss with explicit descriptions of sexual acts allegedly committed by the two gubernatorial advisors in various hotel rooms throughout California. In an internal investigation that Nofziger later acknowledged "made the Keystone Cops [sic] look good," the governor's loyal if incompetent homosexual-hunters tried—but failed—to tape record the "daisy chain" in flagrante delicto. "I wanted [Reagan] to be elected president," Nofziger explained, "and I was certain it would hurt his chances if the voters, especially conservatives, who were his base, thought he had surrounded himself with 'queers.' Because he came out of the Hollywood scene, where homosexuality was almost the norm, I also feared that rumors would insinuate that he, too, was one."

Most newspapers in California, and many around the country, refused to publish the sexually charged "Merry-Go-Round" column, even though the muckrakers had carefully omitted the names of the gay gubernatorial aides. But the day after the article was released, Reagan unwittingly spread the story during an extraordinary news conference in which he baldly denied the allegations: "Rumors are rumors and . . . I just don't know what you're talking about, really." Reporters pressed Reagan on specifics. "In your investigations, have you ever uncovered or discovered a homosexual?" a journalist asked. "No," the governor falsely replied. Pearson and Anderson were simply "lying," their report was "scurrilous . . . vicious and dishonest . . . I myself wonder how respectable newspapers can continue to carry the column." Reagan added that the muckrakers "shouldn't be using a typewriter and paper" but "a pencil on outbuilding walls." According to Nofziger, Reagan "was determined not to give [the column] credibility, even if he had to lie. And lie he did."

But the governor's move backfired and focused additional attention on the affair. REAGAN DENIES "HOMO" RUMOR, the *San Francisco Ex-*

aminer blared above its page-one masthead. As the scandal refused to recede, Reagan held another news conference and acknowledged that he might have developed a "credibility gap" but only because he refused to "destroy human beings" who had been caught up in the scandal. When reporters pressed the would-be president further, Reagan again exploded: "I just can't believe that you fellows want to pursue this question. I told you a few days ago I'd made my last statement on this . . . [The] subject, as far as I'm concerned, is closed. Now do we want to have a press conference or do we want to just stand here with me refusing to talk?" Reagan's public outburst—and his admission that he had not told the truth before—made clear that he was not yet ready for prime time. He "greatly diminished [his] credibility, a priceless political possession nearly impossible to regain once lost," columnist Robert Novak wrote; it was "the first truly serious error of his political career with potentially deep national implications," Novak predicted.

Amazingly, the original source of the embarrassing publicity turned out to be Reagan's press secretary Nofziger, who had previously blabbed to several reporters about the "aberrant sexual behavior" in the governor's office. "I was talking too much in the naïve belief that no one would write the story," Nofziger later admitted, but Pearson "did what I thought no reporter or columnist would do in those days, because nobody that I knew of had—he wrote about a homosexual scandal. A real ground-breaker for one of the great scandalmongers of our times." Actually, the Reagan sex scandal was no ground-breaker for the muckrakers; fairly or unfairly, Anderson and Pearson had outed political figures before and would continue to do so again. For Pearson, the rationale was simple: all was fair in the heat of journalistic battle. For Anderson, however, the calculus was different: he viewed politicians' bedroom behavior as a private matter unless it affected their public actions. "It could be argued that the public had a right to read this story," Anderson later wrote, but he also understood that the column's "harsh language was reserved for politicians Drew opposed." Pearson viewed journalism "essentially as a tool for the advancement of higher causes," Anderson realized, in which words were "weapons in a just war, with the truth as their only acknowledged restriction—and truth was often a subjective matter. I would raise misgivings with him about a particular tactic, but I was much too bound to him, too largely in agreement with him, to let these misgivings become a cause of personal division."

The politician who most benefited from the scandal that Anderson and Pearson exposed was their longtime enemy Richard Nixon, who now emerged as the Republican Party's presidential front-runner. It was a quirk of fate that Nixon could not have missed as the enemy of his enemy now unintentionally became his friend. After all, each blast from the "Merry-Go-Round," and each response from Reagan, further fueled the story, diverting attention as Reagan traveled around the country to raise money and test the waters for his presidential bid. Not even the Machiavellian Nixon could have devised a more insidious way to tarnish his rival than to embroil Reagan in a controversy involving homosexuality; but the former vice president made sure to capitalize on it by personally drafting a statement that opportunistically fanned the scandal's flames even while self-righteously pretending to do the opposite. "Mr. Nixon," the press release said, "never dignifies a Pearson column with comment."

After tangling with Pearson and Anderson, Reagan's undeclared presidential campaign came to an end. Pearson claimed that his "Reagan piece on homosexuals . . . pretty well knocked Reagan out of the box as a Republican candidate" and stopped "an attempt by the far right to take over the Republican Party—and the United States." That, of course, proved to be wishful thinking: Reagan's time would eventually come, but not for another dozen years, only when the embers from the "Merry-Go-Round" sexposé had finally cooled. For now, Republicans would return to Richard Nixon.

Nixon began his comeback campaign in the state with the nation's first presidential primary. "Gentlemen," he announced in New Hampshire with a smile, "this is *not* my last press conference." He won 79 percent of the state's Republican vote and went on to other overwhelming victories in what proved to be a steady march to his party's nomination. By the summer of 1968, when the GOP convention met in Miami Beach, Nixon had a commanding majority of delegates and was preparing for a regal coronation. His campaign paid top dollar to reserve the luxurious Hilton Hotel as its convention headquarters. "To prevent incursion by the press," Nixon aide John Ehrlichman said, "we took stringent security measures, including fencing off the fire escapes" to guard the floors where Nixon and his advisors plotted strategy. But Ehrlichman encountered a nasty surprise when the hotel informed him at the last minute that it was "preempting our reservation" because two rooms had previously been promised to two journalists.

"Who?" Ehrlichman demanded to know.

"Drew Pearson and Jack Anderson."

"No!" Ehrlichman yelled. "Of all reporters in the world, not those two!"

It turned out that the hotel was owned by the Teamsters Union, which wanted to curry favor with the investigative columnists by providing them choice accommodations. No doubt Anderson's pal Irv Davidson, the Teamsters lobbyist who had given the newsmen free lodging at other political conventions, was behind the deal.

Ehrlichman knew all too well that the "Merry-Go-Round" journalists were Nixon's "deadliest foes." Nixon had a particular "phobia about Anderson," Ehrlichman recognized, and allowing the reporter—with his history of bugging targets in hotel rooms—into the bosom of the Nixon command center risked potential disaster. Even if nothing untoward occurred, Ehrlichman feared that when the high-strung Nixon discovered Anderson's presence, the candidate "would have a stroke on the very eve of his nomination." Eventually the Hilton backed down and surrendered the two rooms to the Nixon campaign, but Ehrlichman continued to worry about "the look on Nixon's face if he had happened to run into Pearson and Anderson in the Hilton elevator one day."

Ultimately, Ehrlichman's fear proved misplaced. In August 1968, the Republican Party once again nominated Richard Nixon for president. Maryland governor Spiro T. Agnew was selected to be his running mate. Richard Nixon's political exile was over at last.

Ronald Reagan wasn't the only Nixon rival wounded by a sex scandal unearthed by Drew Pearson and Jack Anderson during the 1968 campaign. So, too, was Senator Robert F. Kennedy, brother of the slain president, who was now running for president as well. The affair disclosed by the "Merry-Go-Round" did not involve RFK's own love life or that of his late libertine brother. Rather, Anderson and Pearson revealed Robert Kennedy's role snooping on the bedroom activities of civil rights leader Martin Luther King. In the end, the sordid spying by the government would nearly be matched by the tawdry tactics of the muckrakers who uncovered it.

The origin of this scandal, like so many others, could be traced to FBI director J. Edgar Hoover, Washington's obsessive collector of sexual gossip, who wielded his secret dossiers as a weapon to blackmail presidents and congressmen into political submission. A backroom bureaucratic brawler without parallel who had become an unchecked institution in the nation's capital, Hoover was a rabid anti-Communist and right-wing racist who believed blacks genetically inferior to whites. Publicly puritanical and privately voyeuristic, Hoover was also known to harbor a perverse fetish about interracial sex.

All of these compulsions—racial, sexual, political—converged in Hoover's hatred of Martin Luther King, whom the FBI director targeted as his unofficial public enemy number one. Convinced that King was conspiring with Communist agitators, Hoover pushed for authority to bug the civil rights leader. Robert Kennedy, then attorney general, was reluctant to authorize wiretaps because he was skeptical that King posed a threat to national security and worried that such spying could create a public scandal. But Kennedy feared Hoover's wrath even more because the FBI director had amassed a voluminous file on the sexual peccadilloes of his presidential brother. So RFK authorized Hoover to tap King even though the administration had no court order to do so. Federal agents, working with local police, conducted round-the-clock surveillance of the civil rights leader, taking surreptitious photos and planting listening devices in King's home, office, and hotel rooms.

The FBI wiretaps unearthed nothing that impugned King's patriotism. Quite the opposite: instead of disclosing secret links with Communists, the eavesdropping documented his unwavering commitment to nonviolence in his crusade to end segregation. But the wiretaps also revealed King's womanizing, which Hoover and his minions greeted with undisguised glee. More than a dozen large tape reels were rushed to the FBI laboratory to enhance the audio so that Hoover could personally listen to King's ribald jokes and the sounds and sighs of group sex. "King is a 'tom cat' with obsessive degenerate sexual urges," Hoover declared after one briefing on the minister's love life. After another, Hoover said of the King tapes: "They will destroy the burrhead."

To "destroy the burrhead," the FBI distributed documents quoting some of the most salacious portions of the King tapes throughout Washington, from the White House and federal bureaucracy to members of Congress and the press. As the FBI listened in, the civil rights leader was heard justifying his adultery based on his heavy travel schedule and stressful work. "Fucking is a form of anxiety reduction," King explained. The minister reportedly described one of his lovers, a curvaceous young blond schoolteacher, as "a piece of tail who can go all night long." Jack Anderson received a memo alleging that FBI bugs had recorded King "making it with a couple of white girls" while "physical surveillance picked up a picture of King entering a lodging place with a woman of ill repute (show girl or whore) . . . in Las Vegas." Witnesses who listened to the FBI tapes even recalled hearing a sex orgy in which a voice that sounded like King's proclaimed rapturously that "I'm fucking for God!" and "I am the best pussy-eater in the world." The FBI also spread word that King "was loaded"—drunk—when he received the Nobel Peace Prize in Norway and was seen "running naked through [his] Oslo hotel . . . after some babe."

The FBI accounts of King's sexual antics turned out to be embellished, although exactly what the civil rights leader said and did while bugged is impossible to know for certain: in the mid-1970s, a federal judge ordered the evidence sealed for fifty years. In any case, despite Hoover's best efforts to leak the dirty details all over town, the Washington press corps did not report King's marital infidelity; in the mid-1960s, such sensational gossipmongering was still anathema to the mainstream media. Still, no journalists had the courage to reveal the FBI's witch hunt against King, either; news executives feared crossing Hoover no less than politicians did. (By one account, Hoover blocked a critical magazine story by circulating photos of the publisher's wife performing fellatio on her black chauffeur.)

King's assassination by a white supremacist in April 1968 didn't stop Hoover's vilification of the minister. Instead, the worldwide grief over King's murder made Hoover more determined than ever to spread the salacious stories about the martyr's sex life. The FBI director dispatched his deputy Deke DeLoach to meet with Jack Anderson, who had obsequiously tried to ingratiate himself with the FBI by making the preposterous claim that Hoover "would go down in history for the protection of civil rights." As a reward, DeLoach told Anderson that the FBI believed that King may have been murdered by a jealous husband, an African American dentist from Los Angeles whose wife was allegedly one of King's lovers. King may have even fathered the woman's child, Anderson was informed. DeLoach "told me that I could have the story exclusively, he wasn't going to pass it on to anybody else," Anderson recalled, "so I caught the first plane to L.A." Anderson was "afraid the dentist wouldn't want to talk to newsmen. So my subterfuge when he answered the door was, 'We're from Washington.' He thought we were from the FBI." But the reporter quickly ascertained that the mild-mannered dentist played no role in King's murder. Anderson returned home to Washington empty-handed.

For the next month, Anderson debated what to do with the information the FBI had leaked about King's affair. Despite his support for civil rights, Pearson wanted to find a way to publish the juicy story "to show that King was not superhuman." On the other hand, exposing King's infidelity was no more newsworthy at that point than when the FBI had first begun leaking details of King's womanizing four years earlier. Indeed, if anything, King's assassination made the tale even more squalid than before.

But the resourceful columnists soon found a way to tell the story by centering it not on adultery by Martin Luther King—too sleazy—nor on the smear tactics of J. Edgar Hoover—too dangerous—but on the role of Robert F. Kennedy, who had approved the King wiretaps yet was now running for president on a strong civil rights platform. No matter that RFK had virtually been blackmailed by Hoover into authorizing the spying. The indisputable fact was that it was Kennedy himself who signed the paperwork permitting warrantless eavesdropping on King.

In May, as the presidential primaries approached their climax, the "Merry-Go-Round" revealed Kennedy's previously secret role in spying on King, whose assassination the previous month was still a fresh, deep wound in the African American community. Anderson and Pearson cited classified documents to explain how Kennedy's decision gave the FBI license to snoop on the sex life of the civil rights leader. King "has been having an illicit love affair with the wife of a prominent Negro dentist in Los Angeles since 1962," the columnists quoted FBI memos as saying. "King calls this woman every Wednesday and meets her in various cities throughout the country." Because RFK denied any role in spying on King, Pearson and Anderson declared, the FBI documents were "very important in gauging Kennedy's qualifications to be President and whether he is telling the truth" since "the public has a right to know all of his record before voting."

The columns created a furor, making public for the first time both King's adultery and the FBI spying that unearthed it. As Kennedy barnstormed the country invoking King's mantle as a defender of the poor and the powerless, the candidate suddenly stood exposed as a hypocritical conspirator in one of the sleaziest governmental abuses of power of the 1960s. The disclosure threatened to destroy Kennedy's support among black and liberal white voters as he was trying to shed his image as a ruthless backroom operator by championing the plight of minorities and the underprivileged.

In the wake of the muckrakers' revelations, RFK was defeated in Oregon's presidential primary, the first time a member of the golden Kennedy clan had ever lost an election. Worse still, California's pivotal contest, with its huge block of minority voters, was just one week away. RFK's campaign feared that the "Merry-Go-Round" columns would be passed out to voters in black neighborhoods. Kennedy told his staff that he wanted to duck televised debates because he might be asked about the embarrassing facts; after changing his mind, he carefully rehearsed his answer with aides so he could be prepared for the inevitable questions.

Once again, the "Merry-Go-Round" columns were political hits designed to inflict maximum damage. "Of course it was timed," Anderson later admitted. "Drew got it from [President] Lyndon" Johnson, RFK's bitter enemy, and then "got me to confirm it with the FBI." White

House logs corroborate that LBJ personally met with Pearson six days before his bugging revelations were published. Attorney General Ramsey Clark also suspected that the President was responsible for the leak and wrote Hoover that he was "deeply troubled by the Drew Pearson–Jack Anderson column," which "must come from secret documents . . . known to only a very few people" in the government. Clark authorized the FBI director to conduct "whatever investigation you deem feasible to determine how . . . such sensitive information . . . [was] disseminated outside of these offices" in "such a breach of integrity." But Hoover had only to look in the mirror to spot the culprit because he himself had dispatched his trusted deputy Deke DeLoach to leak the key documentary evidence in the first place. It was Anderson who arranged a lunch with DeLoach at Pearson's Georgetown mansion, where Hoover's messenger gave the columnists a copy of RFK's secret order to bug King, complete with Kennedy's incriminating signature. DeLoach not only cleared his actions ahead of time with Hoover but spoke directly with President Johnson the day before the "Merry-Go-Round" revelations were published.

It was a surprising leak in one sense because Hoover disliked Pearson and Anderson almost as much as he hated King and Kennedy. The FBI director had previously called Pearson a "rat" and "a mental case" and termed Anderson "a flea-ridden dog" who was "lower than the regurgitated filth of vultures." But Hoover's loathing of King and Kennedy bordered on the pathological and trumped his distaste for the "Merry-Go-Round" columnists. Besides, by divulging RFK's role in spying on King's sex life, Hoover was simultaneously able to wound Kennedy's presidential campaign and besmirch the martyred civil rights leader's moral character.

Instead of following Attorney General Clark's instructions to investigate the leak, Hoover engaged in a skillful cover-up to conceal his own culpability. With the help of his underling DeLoach, the veteran Washington bureaucrats created a paper trail that pointed blame elsewhere. "Jack Anderson called and stated he wanted to speak in confidence" about the King wiretaps, DeLoach wrote in one memo. "I told him if it concerned an official matter I could not agree with this stipulation." DeLoach conveniently omitted the fact that he had already given secret documents to Anderson at their recent lunch. Hoover, who had personally approved the leak, jokingly asked DeLoach, "How did Jack Anderson get that information?" DeLoach laughed as he recounted his reply: Anderson is "an excellent investigative reporter as far as I know." But Hoover's carefully concocted paper trail allowed him to falsely assure Attorney General Clark that the information given to Anderson and Pearson "did not originate from representatives of this Bureau." Indeed, Hoover added that "it is inconceivable that any FBI employee having access to such data would volunteer information of this nature to these columnists" given "the unjustified criticism that has been leveled at the FBI over the years by Messrs. Pearson and Anderson." The choice of the dreaded muckrakers as recipients of Hoover's broadside was now used to shore up FBI deniability.

Grateful for their scoop, Pearson and Anderson uncritically parroted the FBI's false claim that Kennedy, not Hoover, was the driving force behind the King spying. Eventually, Anderson concluded that the leak was a "deliberate bum steer" by the FBI to derail RFK's presidential campaign and involve King in "a posthumous scandal, to turn even his death into a sordid affair." The columnist would eventually correct the record, but only years later, after Hoover was safely dead, long after Anderson had allowed himself to be used to further the FBI director's slanderous ends.

Despite it all, Robert Kennedy won the California presidential primary on June 4. That night, after finishing his victory speech, he was gunned down by an assassin and died twenty-five hours later. Yet another roadblock between Richard Nixon and the White House disappeared.

In August 1968, Democrats chose Vice President Hubert Humphrey to oppose Nixon in the November election. But the party's Chicago convention was overshadowed by student protests and police violence. In the bloody aftermath of the King and Kennedy assassinations, the country seemed under siege. Meanwhile, Nixon vowed to restore law and order to America's streets. He campaigned against permissiveness and harked back to the more tranquil Eisenhower era, pledging to end the war in Vietnam through "peace with honor." To counter his slippery public image, Nixon initiated a strategy called Operation Candor and began sprinkling his conversation with phrases designed to suggest frankness, such as "Let me make myself perfectly clear."

Nixon was determined to avoid the mistakes of his last presidential campaign. He ducked television appearances with opponents and instead hired PR professionals who put together carefully controlled infomercials in which he answered puffball questions served up by preselected supporters. Roger Ailes, the campaign's twenty-eight-year-old TV producer, was blunt about his approach. "Let's face it," the future founder of the right-wing Fox News Channel explained, "a lot of people think Nixon . . . is a bore. They look at him as the kind of kid who [would] always have his homework done and he'd never let you copy. Now you put him on television, you've got a problem right away. He's a funny-looking guy. He looks like somebody hung him in a closet overnight and he jumps out in the morning with his suit all bunched up and starts running around saying, 'I want to be President.' I mean, this is how he strikes some people. That's why these shows are important. To make them forget all that." The commercials Ailes designed for Nixon were the first widespread adaptation of Madison Avenue advertising techniques to presidential politics. Their success would forever change election campaigns and force Nixon's successors to imitate the same manipulative tactics.

Nixon also played hardball, using attack ads and a "Southern strategy" that played to racist sentiments though code words while carefully giving the candidate deniability. For example, Ailes deliberately cast a "good, mean" bigoted cabdriver in a TV commercial to give angry working-class white voters someone to identify with; the cabbie's role was to use semiveiled language to ask Nixon, as Ailes put it, "Awright, mac, what about these niggers?" Meantime, the candidate assiduously avoided reporters. Convinced that his previous criticism of the news media had created "a guilt complex" that made the press "more respectful," Nixon's underlying contempt for journalists continued unabated. "They had responded with much kinder treatment than in the old days," campaign strategist H. R. Haldeman said. "But this never fooled Nixon. He knew they were still the enemy and they could not be trusted."

Jack Anderson and Drew Pearson were appalled by Nixon's resurgence. "For eight years following the Kennedy-Nixon election," Anderson wrote, Pearson "took satisfaction from the notion that, whichever of his objectives in life had gone awry, he had at least had a hand in keeping down Richard Nixon. But suddenly there he was again, revived, rehabilitated and leading Hubert Humphrey in the polls." The "Merry-Go-Round" column's response was predictable. "We upheld Humphrey, of course," Anderson recalled, "and smote Nixon with standard fare about how the special interests represented by his New York law firm would be in the saddle if the Republican won." The newsmen recycled their old and familiar Nixon skeletons: his history of Red-baiting, his senatorial slush fund, and the Hughes loan. If elected president, the columnists added, Nixon would "revert to type," create "dossiers on all potential rivals," "purge innocent[s]," and command "personal goons" to carry out his orders. The claim seemed grotesquely exaggerated at the time but in fact would prove disturbingly prescient.

As the campaign moved into its fall finale, Anderson and Pearson tried one last time to persuade gangster Mickey Cohen, now in prison for his various crimes, to link Nixon publicly to the Mafia. Pearson even promised the mobster that Democrats would give him a medical parole if he would help defeat the Republican nominee. This time, with nothing to lose, Cohen agreed to cooperate. He gave the muck-rakers a signed statement detailing how he had raised Mob money for Nixon's 1950 Senate campaign. "I invited approximately two-hundred fifty persons who were working with me in the gambling fraternity" to a fund-raiser at Hollywood's Knickerbocker Hotel, Cohen said, naming specific hoodlums who were present: "It was all gamblers from Vegas, all gambling money, there wasn't a legitimate person in the room." After Nixon delivered a short speech, Cohen recalled, the Mafia men collected more than $17,000 in cash "but this did not meet the quota set by Nixon and [his aide Murray] Chotiner and the group was informed they would stay until the quota was met." Cohen's thugs barred the doors to prevent any escape until a total of $26,000—"a considerable piece of money for those days," worth a quarter of a million dollars today—was handed over.

Less than a week before the election, Pearson and Anderson unleashed their story, reporting for the first time that they had now "secured a statement from Mickey Cohen" detailing how the gangster had collected cash for Nixon from organized crime. "Nixon and Chotiner were putting the squeeze on the leading gamblers of Southern California," the newsmen wrote. "Obviously the gamblers had a right to expect something in return." Not surprisingly, the Republican nominee denounced the charges, thus enabling Anderson and Pearson to produce a follow-up story the next day. "Nixon's press secretary got into a great dither and sent about 400 telegrams to newspapers all over the United States denying everything," Pearson said happily. Still, the mobster's belated confession was viewed with suspicion, not only because of his criminal background, but also because it was promoted by the ardently anti-Nixon "Merry-Go-Round." The column was largely dismissed by the rest of the media and lost amid the end-of-the-campaign hoopla.

In the final days of the race, Humphrey came from behind to pull nearly even with Nixon in the polls, thanks in part to the independent presidential candidacy of segregationist governor George Wallace of Alabama, who was draining votes from Nixon's right-wing flank. With Humphrey now in striking distance of victory, Pearson and Anderson made one last, desperate attempt to defeat Nixon by unleashing yet another election-eve exposé, this time questioning his mental stability.

Richard Nixon had always been tightly wound, anxious, brooding, and socially awkward. He was "a very odd man, an unpleasant man," his advisor Henry Kissinger later said. "He didn't enjoy people. What I never understood is why he went into politics." Despite his undeniable tenacity and cunning, Nixon was otherwise ill suited to the rough-and-tumble of public life. Nixon "never really healed" from the slashing attacks that he generated and inspired in turn, his aide Len Garment believed. "Each layer of scar tissue formed over the last" as Nixon "entered, exited, and re-entered" the national arena, fueled by "a boundless, almost inhuman determination to even the score." Jack Anderson believed that Nixon suffered from a kind of split personality: shy and thin-skinned in private, harsh and aggressive in public. Nixon referred to his political persona "in the third person as if he were a separate being," Anderson observed. "It was always that other Nixon, the politician in the spotlight, who did the attacking. But it was the sensitive, private Nixon who was battered by the answering bombardments."

During the 1950s, to try to cope with this stress, then-senator Nixon sought out Dr. Arnold Hutschnecker, a German-trained internist who ran a psychotherapy practice in New York City. From Washington, Nixon made numerous visits to see Hutschnecker in his Manhattan office and stayed in touch with the doctor in the years that followed. Nixon particularly leaned on Hutschnecker during his greatest political crises but eventually stopped visiting him out of fear that the stigma of psychotherapy would produce a scandal. "It is safer for a politician to go to a whorehouse than to see a psychiatrist," Hutschnecker later explained.

Still, rumors about "Nixon's shrink" leaked out. Neighbors and other patients spotted the vice president in Hutschnecker's Park Avenue office and the psychotherapist himself was less than discreet about his famous client. In 1960, operatives for the Kennedy campaign put together a dossier on Nixon's mental treatment. Frank Sinatra, then a Kennedy intimate, reportedly peddled a private investigator's report on Nixon and Hutschnecker to gossip columnist Walter Winchell, who published a snide though veiled reference to it. But JFK, whose own medical skeletons outnumbered Nixon's, decided not to risk making Nixon's psychiatric history a public issue in the 1960 race.

Decades later, after Nixon's death, more substantive evidence came out about his mental health difficulties. One intimate acknowledged secretly supplying antianxiety medication to his friend. Another, Len Garment, said that Nixon suffered from "pseudo-ulcers and pseudo-colon problems" that were "characteristic of people who have immense anxieties" and were caused "by stress, by aggressive feelings that have to be mastered and controlled." Dr. Hutschnecker himself revealed that he had diagnosed Nixon's "neurotic symptoms" and "deep-seated inhibitions" from his "emotionally deprived" childhood, which caused Nixon to regard "love and physical closeness as a diversion that would drain him, deplete him, make him less manly." Nixon's "deep depression," Garment believed, "might have been quite different if he'd had access to antidepressant" drugs developed in later years, when the stigma for such treatment had diminished. Instead, the sad and poignant truth was that the politician felt forced to hide his debilitating condition and never really received proper treatment that might have alleviated it. Hutschnecker later said that Nixon insisted on secrecy out of fear that if voters learned about his counseling sessions, they would believe he "must be cuckoo."

In October 1968, in the final lap of the close presidential race, Anderson and Pearson learned about Nixon's secret visits to his psychotherapist. One of Hutschnecker's friends sent the muckrakers an "urgent & confidential" letter stating that the doctor had "concern[s about] Nixon's instability" and "may be willing to speak freely" about it "in view of the horrible prospect of a Nixon/Agnew victory." On the morning of October 29, Pearson called Hutschnecker for comment. The columnist informed the physician that he knew about Hutschnecker's "psychiatric treatment" of Nixon and wondered whether his former patient was "the right man to have his finger on the nuclear trigger." Surprised by the question, the doctor acknowledged that Nixon had been a patient but said it was a "delicate matter" that he was "reluctant to talk about." Hutschnecker asked Pearson to call back later that afternoon after he had finished counseling his other patients.

That was enough for Pearson, who immediately drafted a special column to send out that evening. "Reports that Richard Nixon has been under psychiatric care in the past have been confirmed by Dr. Arnold Hutschnecker, prominent New York psychiatrist," the story announced. Voters are "entitled to a full report on the health of the presidential candidates" because a "presidential prospect's mental health, even more than his physical fitness, is a matter of national concern" since the chief executive "must be one who at no time needs a psychiatric crutch."

Meanwhile, Anderson sought comment from the Nixon camp. Not surprisingly, the candidate denied the alarming allegation but braced for the inevitable eleventh-hour assault by the columnists. "Given the history of the Nixon-Pearson relationship" and the fact that Pearson and Anderson "had tangled with Nixon in almost every campaign since 1946," Nixon advisor Herb Klein said, "we expected such a thing just before the election." Klein and Murray Chotiner urgently contacted Hutschnecker, who claimed he had acknowledged only that Nixon had been a patient, not a *psychiatric* patient. Because the physician's practice had once included internal medicine as well as psychotherapy, Nixon's men suggested that Hutschnecker's comments had been misconstrued. The doctor hurriedly called the "Merry-Go-Round" office to clarify that he had treated Nixon "only for problems involving internal medicine," and then only "for a brief period" during the 1950s.

Pearson complained that Hutschnecker had "changed his story completely." The columnist didn't believe the doctor's new, sanitized version. "It seemed to me strange that Nixon should go all the way to New York to consult a well-known Park Avenue psychotherapy specialist concerning his internal medical problems," Pearson observed, "when some of the best internists in the United States are located [nearby] at Walter Reed Hospital and Bethesda Naval Hospital where Nixon as Vice President could have had their services on the cuff." Anderson was unfazed by the psychotherapist's denial. "Dr. Hutschnecker could not be expected to reveal confidences about Nixon's condition, and would be in violation of his code if he did," the reporter recognized. "On the contrary, he could be expected, like all previous doctors of presidential-level patients, to minimize the implications of Nixon's problem, whatever it was, and he did. But the very fact that Nixon had been under the care of a psychiatrist, whatever the explanation, would probably galvanize the sleeping concern of many that Nixon had emotional problems."

Unlike eight years earlier, when the Nixon campaign's false denial of the Hughes loan gave Anderson and Pearson an excuse to launch their election-eve bombshell, Nixon's team now kept silent, allowing Hutschnecker to speak for them. "Our position was that any public statement by us in advance would increase interest in a Pearson column and perhaps offer authenticity," Klein explained. Instead, Nixon's staff readied its list of newspapers carrying the "Merry-Go-Round" in preparation for lobbying them to suppress the exposé. Still, Klein realized that many papers would publish the story anyway "and thus one damaging column could have tipped the close election."

But at the last minute, Pearson decided to pull the plug on his piece. "KILL NIXON STORY," he wrote at the bottom of the column he had drafted. According to Anderson, Pearson "seemed torn by concerns that a few years before would not have finally inhibited him,"

including the fact that "Nixon would be victimized by the public's igno-
rant fear of things psychiatric" and that the column "would be thought
incorrigibly partisan and venal" for launching yet another last-minute
campaign smear. Nixon's spokesman later said that Pearson and Anderson "deserve credit" for spiking the story, which "probably would
have changed the results of the election."

Five nights later, on November 5, 1968, Richard Nixon was elected
president with 43 percent of the popular vote, a margin of less than one
percent over Hubert Humphrey. With nearly 14 percent of the ballots,
independent George Wallace almost cost Nixon the election. But it
was enough: Richard Nixon—battered and bruised but at long last
victorious—was finally headed to the White House.

Any possible truce between the president-elect and the "Merry-Go-
Round" columnists would prove short-lived. Just nine days after Nixon's
election, Drew Pearson struck again, publicly announcing at a press
conference what he had chosen not to publish in his column: that
Nixon had "psychiatric problems." In a speech to reporters at the National
Press Club in Washington, Pearson stated not only that Dr. Hutschnecker had provided psychotherapy treatments to Nixon but also that
the doctor had expressed concern that his onetime patient had problems "standing up under great pressure." As one chronicler put it, "Correspondents who had previously deemed the rumor unfit to print [now]
had an excuse to pursue the story—which they immediately did." It
was the beginning of a trend that would continue for the next generation in which the Washington press corps would exploit the titillation
of political scandal while pretending to do otherwise by dressing it up
as reporting on how other media outlets covered the story.

Nixon was furious. His press secretary declared, "I simply will not
comment in any way on a Pearson speech, utterance or anything else.
It's totally untrue, of course. Most of his columns are." Hutschnecker
told reporters that Pearson's remarks were "absolutely false." Even *The
Washington Post* blasted its columnist for the "decision to bring the
report to public attention now without offering any evidence to sustain
it . . . It was a serious disservice to air a rumor of such vaporous char-

acter." For his part, Pearson tried to fend off criticism by feigning admiration for his longtime enemy: "Personally I sympathize with Nixon and the mental strain under which he has labored. He deserves credit for getting help with his problems of stress and strain."

The president-elect did not appreciate Pearson's ostentatious display of compassion. At Nixon's direction, his communications director Herb Klein sent telegrams to hundreds of newspaper editors in an attempt to kill coverage of the columnist's remarks. "Obviously," Klein said, "Pearson had volunteered the rumor story before the press club as a vitriolic punch at the President-elect he had openly expressed dislike for on many public occasions over a twenty-year period." Undoubtedly true. On the other hand, for once Pearson had refrained from uncorking his poison just before the election and instead waited until voters had already made their choice before spreading the noxious fumes. Jack Anderson, for one, was disappointed; he believed Nixon's psychotherapy was a "legitimate story" that should have been published before Election Day. Unlike the more urbane Pearson, Anderson viewed psychiatrists as quacks and was automatically suspicious of anyone who sought their help.

In any case, in the aftermath of Nixon's election, the muckrakers received an anguished letter from the prison cell of Mickey Cohen. "I wonder if you can possibly imagine the shock that I sit here under tonight?" the mobster wrote. "In my wildest dreams [never] could I ever have visualized or imagined 17 or 18 years ago that the likes of Richard Nixon could possibly become the President of the United States . . . Let's hope that he isn't the same guy that I knew as a rough hustler [when he was] a goddamn small-time ward politician. Let's hope this guy's thinking has changed, and let's hope it's for the betterment of our country."

But it was not to be.

In the past, Nixon's capacity to strike back at his adversaries was restrained by the limits of his office. But with his election as president, he became the most powerful man on the planet, his retaliatory might second to none. Another man might have spent his time savoring his triumphal elevation to the White House. Not Nixon. "This was an ego finely tuned to believe that it was nothing unless it was everything," author Rick Perlstein noted, "one for which winning wasn't everything, it was the only thing—but which even victory could never fully satisfy."

Indeed, the month after his election, the president-elect instructed his staff to dredge through old newspaper columns in search of "smears of Richard Nixon back through the years," especially "the more vicious press comments." A month later, on the eve of his inauguration, he took time out to remind aides "to see that someone is assigned to read the Pearson columns for the purpose of determining whether anyone in the Administration has violated my counsel for them not to talk to his people."

At what should have been the crowning pinnacle of his career, Nixon was still obsessed by past wrongs. "Enemies had always been essential to him, they fueled his drive, he had always, in some deep psychic way, needed them, as some people need to bite against a sore tooth," journalist David Halberstam wrote. "Now, now that he was President, he would make them pay; he would not coopt them, that was too easy. Rather he would cut them off, crush them."

Richard Nixon was ready to begin his presidency.

PART III

POWER

5

THE PRESIDENT AND
THE COLUMNIST

Inauguration day—January 20, 1969—dawned chilly and gray in Washington. Hundreds of demonstrators lined the streets to protest the Vietnam War, chanting obscenities, burning American flags, throwing stones at the new president's motorcade. In victory as in defeat, Richard Nixon remained beleaguered, a polarizing figure in polarizing times.

Six months later, the Nixon White House was shaken by its first domestic scandal. Once again, the troublemaker was Jack Anderson. As before, the investigative reporter's focus was fueled by homophobia, this time physically centered in the Watergate building, which would eventually become the eternal symbol of Nixonian notoriety. The fancy new apartment complex, overlooking the Potomac River just a mile from the White House, was now home to the new president's top advisors: Attorney General John Mitchell and other Cabinet members, Chief of Staff H. R. Haldeman, and long-standing Nixon loyalists Rose Mary Woods and Murray Chotiner. These Watergate residences, no less than the White House itself, now became the site of intrigue and infighting among the President's staff. In particular, Nixon veterans Woods and Chotiner had been pushed to the sidelines by Haldeman and the President's other top aide of Germanic descent, John Ehrlichman. Relative newcomers, Haldeman and Ehrlichman were collectively—and unaffectionately—known as the "Berlin Wall" because they blocked access to Nixon. Indeed, when Woods was informed that she had been exiled to a basement room far from the Oval Office, she yelled at the president-elect with uncharacteristic profanity: "Go fuck yourself!" Chotiner also was "too old and too much a reminder of the rough-stuff origins of the early Nixon to be up front as top staff dog," Anderson noted. But rather than shout obscenities at the President, Chotiner was more typically devious in the way he handled being frozen out of power. Just weeks after Nixon's inauguration, the President's old political guru retaliated by setting in motion a chain of events that led to fabricated charges of a gay White House sex ring.

Chotiner's revenge began with an approach to the dreaded Jack Anderson through their mutual friend, the ubiquitous Washington lobbyist Irv Davidson. Chotiner and Davidson had much in common: both had been raised in Pittsburgh's close-knit Jewish community; both had transformed themselves into wealthy Washington influence-peddlers by representing mobbed-up clients; and both had befriended Nixon years before he became president. At Chotiner's request, Davidson put out a feeler to Anderson, who assured his friend that he would not rebuff a White House overture. Chotiner then phoned Anderson to suggest that he "drop by to pay a courtesy call and talk a little business." The muckraker was puzzled but curious: "What could he possibly want with me?" Anderson wondered. "At every juncture of Nixon's rise, every campaign, every crisis, our column had been Nixon's avowed enemy." But Anderson had always taken care to keep relations with Chotiner personally cordial despite their professional differences. The White House consigliere soon visited the newsman's office. "In the flesh, Chotiner was not much of an ogre," Anderson wrote in an unpublished manuscript. "Short of stature, he was almost avuncular, a mellowed elder statesman of jugular politics."

"Jack," Chotiner told the reporter, "I'm speaking for the President when I say that we would like to let bygones be bygones and start off fresh with you fellows." Anderson amiably returned the gesture, responding that he and Drew Pearson believed that "every new President was entitled to a period of neutrality and the benefit of the doubt." "We can be of help to you," Chotiner continued. "We know the need you have for information about what's going on and the President has authorized me to offer you our help. Whenever you want to know something that you're having a hard time getting at, call me and we'll see that you get it." Anderson replied that he was happy to hear that. The two men shook hands and parted. "I could not see a very long life for the Chotiner alliance," Anderson decided, figuring that "it was only a matter of time before we'd be at sword's point." The veteran newsman was astute enough to recognize the "danger that I would be used by the Nixon White House as a vehicle for dubious information it was trying to propagate for its own interests. But this troubled me little; give me the information, I told myself cock-surely, and I'll happily be the judge of whether it checks out and of who is using whom."

Before long, Chotiner presented Anderson with a story tip that was at once sensationalistic, self-serving, and false: that Chotiner's White House rivals Haldeman and Ehrlichman were gay lovers. Chotiner told Anderson that the two pillars of the "Berlin Wall," along with Haldeman's handsome twenty-eight-year-old assistant Dwight Chapin, regularly "engaged in homosexual and perverted activities" early in the morning before reporting to work at the White House. Chotiner claimed the homosexual trysts took place in Haldeman's Watergate apartment and across the street at the Howard Johnson's Motor Lodge, where the White House trio was often joined by "a Naval officer who is a notorious homosexual." Chotiner said that Ehrlichman had been spotted at the Watergate picking up Haldeman and the sailor in a Mustang sports car.

It was a patently ludicrous charge—Nixon's senior aides were straight-arrow husbands with children—but it was a measure of the era's homophobia that even the threat of such false gossipmongering could pack such a political punch. Anderson tried to verify the lurid allegations by dispatching his staff to conduct surveillance outside Haldeman's Watergate residence and at the motel across the street. Every day for six weeks, legman Joe Trento and a photographer staked out the premises, beginning at four a.m., trying to look as inconspicuous as possible while keeping an eye on the two locations. If necessary, Trento said, Anderson wanted them to break in and photograph the White House aides in flagrante delicto. "I thought it was insane," Trento remembered. "It was just bizarre." Trento saw Haldeman entering and exiting the Watergate but never spotted Ehrlichman, Chapin, the navy officer, or the Mustang, let alone any sexual encounters between the presidential advisors. "Jack was convinced the story was true," Trento recalled, "and was angry that we weren't finding anything." Trento concluded that "Murray Chotiner was just jealous of this new Nazi crowd [Ehrlichman and Haldeman] that Nixon had brought in to the White House" and was merely trying to undermine the competition. But Anderson wanted to keep Chotiner happy and decided to escalate his investigation.

On June 11, 1969, Anderson dropped by unannounced at the office of his old source Deke DeLoach, the deputy FBI director who had previously leaked dirt on Martin Luther King's sex life. Anderson laid out what he called the "very damaging information" he had received from an "absolutely reliable" but unnamed Nixon advisor about a gay sex ring in the White House. Flabbergasted, DeLoach told Anderson that the FBI "could not sit on a story of this nature" and would have to report it to President Nixon. Anderson said he had no objection but "wanted his name to be kept out of it."

DeLoach immediately contacted his boss, J. Edgar Hoover, and wrote an official memo about Anderson's inflammatory charge. Hoover seized on the accusation and passed it on to the President through Rose Mary Woods, Chotiner's Watergate neighbor and compatriot, who was also smoldering from being pushed out of Nixon's inner circle. "Nothing could grab Nixon's attention faster" than an allegation about "a coterie of homosexuals at the highest levels of the White House," Ehrlichman recalled, and the President "immediately called Hoover for the details." The director was only too happy to oblige his new boss. "There is a ring of homosexualists at the highest levels of the White House," Hoover gravely announced. He made certain that Attorney General Mitchell and National Security Advisor Henry Kissinger were also briefed about the FBI's sensitive new investigation of presidential "deviates."

Mitchell was assigned the unenviable task of informing Haldeman and Ehrlichman. After dinner with the two aides and Nixon on the presidential yacht *Sequoia*, the attorney general gave the White House advisors a ride home in his limousine. "Mitchell got out of the car, walked us away so the driver wouldn't hear and told us Hoover had come up with this homosexual report," Haldeman remembered. Mitchell informed the men that there was corroborating evidence in the form of photos showing them "going in and out of each others' villas late at night" at the presidential compound in Key Biscayne, Florida. The explanation was perfectly innocent—they met each other to watch a movie together after work—but Chapin realized that because they were unaccompanied by their wives, "anyone with a sinister motive" could cause "immense" damage. "Jack Anderson's column would've been the one place" in the mainstream media capable of publishing such an incendiary story, Chapin recognized, and that would be enough to "send the wolves off." The White House communications director begged Anderson for mercy, asking "what we could do to disprove" the allegation and prevent it from being published.

Meantime, with the President next door in the Oval Office, Hoover personally cross-examined Nixon's men under oath in the White House Cabinet room to discover if there was "any sexual contact" between them or any other "gay cell" in the White House. The FBI director also dispatched his trusted assistant W. Mark Felt—later revealed to be the famous secret source called "Deep Throat"—along with a stenotypist to transcribe testimony. All three aides asserted their heterosexual innocence and began keeping careful logs of their whereabouts, day and night, to fend off any further allegations. "I had good alibis for the dates alleged," Ehrlichman recalled. "I was elsewhere with other people, including a satisfactory number of women. I answered all Felt's questions under oath . . . But I was not sure I had convinced him of my sexual orientation. He was coolly non-committal."

Hoover worried that the homosexual rumor had been "dumped" in his lap so that Anderson could report that the FBI had launched an official investigation, thereby transforming the unsubstantiated rumor into a newsworthy story. Worse, Hoover feared that if he now failed to look into Anderson's bogus charge, the muckraker could accuse the FBI of a cover-up. Hoover's solution was to execute an act of bureaucratic jujitsu that would simultaneously protect his hind flank while strengthening his position with the new president: he locked up the evidence exonerating Nixon's aides in his personal safe, the better to suppress the allegations from publicity but protect the FBI if Anderson ever accused Hoover of failing to follow up on them.

Hoover then pronounced himself satisfied with the denials of the President's staff and passed word to Anderson that he had been "misinformed" about the gay sex ring. At the time, White House aides felt "appreciation" and "gratitude." But they ultimately realized that they had been had. "Mitchell's conclusion was that this was an attempt by Hoover to lay a threat across our path," Haldeman said later, "to keep us in line, remind us of his potential." Ehrlichman, too, "came to think that Hoover did this to show his claws or ingratiate himself to Nixon— probably both. It was my early introduction to the way the game was played." None of the White House advisors were savvy enough to real- ize that it was the devious Chotiner who had instigated the furor in the first place as payback for freezing out the old-time Nixon stalwart.

Anderson never wrote about the trumped-up scandal in his column, but his complicity in spreading word about it to the FBI was crucial to Chotiner's designs. It is doubtful that Chotiner confided his true inten- tions to Anderson, but the seasoned newsman may well have deciphered Chotiner's underlying motives and chosen to become an accomplice anyway to pave the way for more legitimate leaks in the future. Indeed, Anderson later said he "didn't believe for a minute that the [homosexu- ality] reports were true," but "bounced the rumor off" the FBI "hoping to shake loose" another story, "something less scandalous and more newsworthy." But of course that was not what the bluffing muckraker told the FBI, according to its report: "Anderson stated that this story would of course be quite a bombshell if it appeared in his and Pearson's column. He stated that Pearson wanted to print it; however, he, Ander- son, was against printing the story until he had further evidence."

Hoover was not fooled by the columnists' familiar Good Cop/Bad Cop technique, "which is the way they work," he noted disdainfully. The FBI director reminded Nixon's men that Pearson and Anderson "were the first ones who spotted" homosexuality on the staff of Gover- nor Reagan nineteen months earlier and asserted that the journalistic duo were masters of using "innuendo . . . in such a way that it is not libel, but near it." Hoover tried to conceal his veiled blackmail by feign- ing indignation: "My reaction was of such outrage and disgust that I did not want to dignify it," he told the White House. "This thing is so absurd and typical of Pearson and this fellow Anderson to spread that kind of stuff, but they say it of everybody they don't like." Of course, the same was no less true of Hoover himself.

Only decades later, when he obtained his FBI file, did Anderson learn that his casual bluff had "stirred up a minor panic in the White House and the FBI." While Anderson's deliberate disinformation campaign may have helped his source Chotiner by impugning Haldeman and Ehrlichman, the more lasting effect was to strengthen the clout of Hoover, to whom Nixon now felt indebted for derailing a potentially damaging sex scandal. Perhaps it was poetic justice that Anderson himself would become the victim of an equally ludicrous homosexual smear campaign initiated by the President himself. But that would not take place for another two and a half years, only when Nixon began turning to more nefarious means to silence his critics. In the meantime, the episode further fueled White House fear and loathing of its journalistic bête noire.

Anderson understood the source of the President's paranoia: "Other presidents looked out the windows of the White House and saw the world. Richard Nixon looked out those windows and saw his own troubled reflection staring back at him." It did not seem to occur to the muckraker that he was at least partly responsible for the President's siege mentality.

Jack Anderson's offer to wipe Nixon's slate clean and start anew may have been a temporary ploy, but it wasn't an outright lie. In the weeks after his inauguration, most "Merry-Go-Round" references to the new president were positive or neutral; and of the few negative stories, almost all were mild editorial comments, not hard-hitting exposés. "During the first months of the Nixon Administration, the column was uncharacteristically observant of the honeymoon tradition," Anderson wrote. "At the six-month mark, Drew called his staff together to discuss whether or not the time had come to call off the truce and go on the attack. Most of us favored opening up. But Drew decided to give President Nixon more time to reveal his direction. 'Nixon was working for his ambition until he became president,' he said. 'Now he is working for the history books.'"

It was the last staff meeting Pearson ever held. In September 1969, the seventy-one-year-old columnist had a heart attack and died. As "a

descendant of the tradition made feared and famous by such earlier prac-
titioners as Lincoln Steffens and Upton Sinclair," *The New York Times*
editorialized, Pearson "adapted the untiring and often merciless skill of
investigative political reporting . . . to the modern idiom of the insider's
gossip." He "had the conscience of a Quaker and the touch of a steve-
dore," *The Washington Post* eulogized, "robust, free-swinging, sometimes
very wild." One thousand people attended a memorial service at the
Washington Cathedral, where Pearson was extolled by the capital's liberal elite. His ashes were buried on his farm along the Potomac.

The first hours after Pearson's death left Anderson in a dreamlike
blur. Stunned and upset by his mentor's death, Anderson paid tribute
to his fallen partner in the "Merry-Go-Round" and in a series of interviews with television crews that descended on his home. "I was overwhelmed with grief and suffocated by the challenge of carrying on
without him," Anderson recalled. But his anguish was also tempered
by long-simmering resentment over his subordinate role as Pearson's
underpaid workhorse and uncertainty about his future and that of the
column. The aristocratic Pearson had always viewed the middlebrow
Anderson not as a social equal but as a hired hand, like his cook and
butler. "Jack really resented it," Anderson's legman Joe Trento recalled.
"Jack railed about how Drew mistreated him, how he had nine children
to support and Drew never gave him enough money." At the time of his
death, Pearson paid Anderson just $255 a week. Now, even that mod-
est salary was in doubt.

Could the "Washington Merry-Go-Round" survive the demise of
its legendary founder? Most syndicated columns were idiosyncratic
one-man operations that inevitably died with their authors. Although
Pearson had been the most prominent columnist in America, carried
by nearly twice as many newspapers as any other, thirty-six papers
abruptly canceled the column in the wake of his death, including the
important *Los Angeles Times.* If the "Merry-Go-Round" managed to
survive, would it ever again wield the muckraking might that had made
it the scourge of Washington officialdom?

Even the simple issue of who was in charge was ambiguous. Anderson insisted that Pearson had promised that he would inherit the column but he had nothing in writing to prove it, and Pearson's stepson,

Tyler Abell, "served notice on me that he was taking over the column himself," Anderson said. Abell's qualifications were dubious—he was a lawyer, not a reporter, who later frankly acknowledged he lacked the requisite ability to run such a demanding venture—but Anderson was still vulnerable. "Jack was in an absolute panic," a friend recalled, "incoherent with confusion." The undeniable reality was that he remained as unknown as Pearson had been famous, despite the fact that the junior partner's byline had been added to the column four years earlier as a reward for the tireless digging that had produced many of Washington's most important scoops over the past two decades. Compared to his flamboyant mentor, Anderson seemed, as one journalist put it, "sort of a pastel character" incapable of generating the requisite charisma and controversy essential for captivating a nationwide audience.

Fortunately for Anderson, the Bell-McClure Syndicate, which distributed the "Merry-Go-Round" column, felt equally vulnerable and rushed to lock him in as Pearson's successor. Anderson was so eager to seal the deal—and eliminate any possible competition—that he signed the syndicate's legal contract without even reading it. Pearson's stepson denounced the arrangement as "inappropriate" and "totally without authorization" but was powerless to stop it. Pearson's widow was more accepting and agreed to Anderson's offer of a thousand dollars a month for use of the "Merry-Go-Round" name. At the age of forty-six, Jack Anderson, the onetime apprentice, was now in charge of the top newspaper column in the nation.

It was a long way from Cottonwood, Utah. The young Mormon hayseed who headed East after World War II had grown from a callow fact-checker who merely chased Pearson's leads to the most aggressive and enterprising investigative reporter in Washington. He had supplied the factual firepower that allowed his boss to carry on his high-profile journalistic crusades and then outmaneuvered his rivals to take over the column for himself. After years of subordinating his ego, he was now positioned to make his own mark as he saw fit.

For both Jack Anderson and Richard Nixon, 1969 would prove to be a watershed year. Twenty-two years after moving to the nation's capital, both had ascended to the very top of their professions. Despite their change in status, the underlying adversarial nature of their relationship continued as before, dominated by animosity, punctuated by short-lived periods of rapprochement. What was different this time was the clout each man now had at his disposal, and with this greater influence came an escalation of their conflict. As their power increased, so did the stakes of their battles; and what began as little more than a game of "gotcha," of winning and losing, would eventually involve matters of life and death, war and peace.

In the fall of 1969, Jack Anderson's first priority was stabilizing his new business. Some of Drew Pearson's dozen-person staff quit rather than work for their new, younger boss; others were so burned out that Anderson eased them out the door. Besides the "Merry-Go-Round," Anderson inherited Pearson's outstanding bills and unfulfilled lecture and broadcasting commitments, which the overworked new columnist now raced to fulfill. He also needed to find some new reporters to replace the ones who had left, especially a strong second-in-command. Lobbyist Irv Davidson tried to persuade Anderson to hire a newsman named Seymour Freidin, who was secretly moonlighting on the side as a paid operative of both the CIA and President Nixon and undoubtedly would have spied on Anderson as well; the muckraker did not know about this espionage but decided not to bring Freidin aboard anyway. Instead, Anderson chose forty-one-year-old Les Whitten, a veteran of *The Washington Post* and the Hearst newspaper chain, described by one magazine as "a man of boyish movie star good looks" whose Renaissance-man erudition concealed a tough and hard-bitten contempt for authority. Whitten admired Anderson as a fellow "swashbuckler" who wouldn't back down in a fight. The new hire became the chief legman for the "Merry-Go-Round," Anderson's Anderson.

The next task was breaking some big stories. "Jack was afraid he'd lose as much as a third of the papers after Drew died," Whitten remembered. The new columnist "was fighting for his journalistic life," one magazine reported. "By his own admission Anderson called every friend he had in town . . . to beg and borrow enough stories to stay afloat." His new team quickly got to work. Their first victims turned out to be top Democratic politicians: in part because they were the most immediate targets of opportunity, in part because Anderson wanted to distinguish himself from Pearson by demonstrating his political independence, and in part because of covert help he received from his new Nixon White House ally, Murray Chotiner.

In October 1969, Anderson began a series of columns exposing corruption in the office of House Speaker John McCormack, a Democrat from Massachusetts. By planting an undercover intern in the congressman's Capitol Hill office, Anderson learned that the Speaker's closest advisor regularly fixed cases on behalf of reputed Mafia figures by impersonating his boss's distinctive Boston accent in telephone calls to federal agencies. The aide's "mimicry" of McCormack's voice, Anderson reported, was "almost perfect" and once "even fooled" President Lyndon Johnson. After Anderson's columns were published, the Speaker announced that he would retire from Congress and his advisor was sentenced to three years in prison for influence-peddling.

With the help of Republican sources, Anderson also took aim at Senator Edward Kennedy, the last surviving brother and heir to the political dynasty whose ambitions threatened the President's reelection. Nixon "wanted to be rid of the Kennedys, once and for all," one biographer wrote, a wish that essentially came true in July 1969, when the senator drove off a bridge on the Massachusetts island of Chappaquiddick, drowning his passenger, twenty-eight-year-old Mary Jo Kopechne. The crash became an instant scandal not only because of suspicion that the married Kennedy had been frolicking with the unmarried younger secretary but, more important, because he failed to call in rescuers who might have saved her life in what appeared to be an attempt to shirk responsibility for the tragedy. "It marks the end of Teddy," the President predicted, and he instructed his staff to "check it out and get it properly exploited." The White House dispatched its own private eye to the scene. "It'll be hard to hush this one up," Nixon enthused. "Too many reporters want to win a Pulitzer Prize."

Jack Anderson was particularly hungry to prove himself and soon began publishing sealed deposition transcripts of the secret inquest into the crash. The columnist got these leaks not only from anti-Kennedy Republicans but also by bribing another reporter to filch *Time* magazine's in-house memos about the accident. Anderson gathered additional intelligence by provoking Kennedy intimates with deliberately outrageous assertions, playing them off against one another and taking advantage of internal divisions that deepened as the senator's handlers tried to cope with the disaster. ("One of the perversities of the informant is that he is generally more willing to give you information if he thinks you already have it," Anderson later explained. "If the word is already out, he is less responsible and identifiable as a source, and besides, if Anderson already knows, what's the harm in a little elaboration?")

In a series of columns, Anderson charged that Kennedy "didn't tell the whole truth" about how he "invited pretty, young Mary Jo to join him for a midnight swim" and then "set out on a nocturnal adventure." After crashing his car, Anderson reported, Kennedy "conceived a preposterous, absurd idea" to have his cousin "take the rap" by pretending he had driven the auto. "Kennedy felt it was too late to save Mary Jo," the newsman wrote, "but it might be possible to save his presidential dream" by "establish[ing] an alibi" for his whereabouts at the time of the accident. Kennedy publicly denied Anderson's "innuendoes and falsehoods" but declined to discuss specifics. "I wouldn't make any comment other than it's untrue," he told CBS News anchorman Walter Cronkite. Other journalists, unable to verify Anderson's scoops, dismissed them. "The Anderson reconstruction of the Chappaquiddick incident," *Time* reported, "is regarded as largely fictional." But in subsequent years, in-depth investigations by other news organizations corroborated much of the columnist's reporting.

The National Enquirer didn't wait for history to render its verdict. The owner of the supermarket tabloid, an old friend of Drew Pearson, offered to buy Anderson's secret transcripts of the Chappaquiddick inquest. "Drew's death had left the office finances in limbo, and I had no money to make payroll," Anderson recalled. "I paused only to draw a deep breath before I said, 'How much?' The offer was $12,500—a huge sum in those days—and I took it."

Thanks to the tabloid money, Anderson could afford to hire another legman: twenty-six-year-old Brit Hume, a lanky, long-haired reporter for United Press International who would later catapult to fame as the leading anchorman for the right-leaning Fox News Channel. At his job interview, Hume recalled, Anderson came across as "boastful," with "a certain severity both in his voice and his expression." His "hair, once parted near the middle, was now combed forward and across the front, apparently to conceal a receding hairline," but he could not hide an "ample waistline and a certain over-all fleshiness." Anderson "dressed like a man who never noticed the passing of the early 1950s," Hume added, with "baggy, pleated pants that drooped over his shoe tops, faded white shirts with narrow, non-descript neckties, and brightly colored socks." This unpretentious bearing was a striking contrast to the patrician Pearson. Anderson "frequently padded around the office" without shoes "and sometimes he would remove his socks to rub his feet or pick at his toes," Hume remembered. "He also occasionally picked his ear with a paper clip and would emerge from even the most elegant restaurants with a toothpick in his mouth."

All of this was more than just a matter of etiquette or pedigree; it also reflected Anderson's more populist approach to journalism. "He would rather go to a movie than a state dinner, which was fortunate because he was never invited to any," *The New York Times* observed. When Pearson's widow hosted a dinner party with leading senators and Supreme Court justices to help give the new columnist a boost, Anderson was pleasant but never pursued the social entrée it offered. Hume, who attended the elegant gathering, remembers the witheringly sarcastic reaction from a doyen of Washington's media establishment upon learning that he worked for Anderson: "Have you considered going into journalism?" Hume was stung by the putdown: "You have to remember, at that time being an investigative reporter was like being a janitor—it was necessary but you didn't get much respect for doing it."

Anderson long ago grew accustomed to such snobbery and liked to say that he aimed his column at the average milkman in Kansas City, not the intelligentsia of the Ivy League. "The style is a trifle primitive," one journalist said of Anderson's writing, "gauche, aggressive, maudlin . . . it speaks in pungent slang [and] casts a jaundiced eye on the elite . . . Written for the proverbial 'Kansas City milkman,' the column has never lost its innocent vision of a nation run by scalawags and stuffed shirts whose gloss of sophistication cannot conceal the inherent probability that they are, in one way or another, inferior to the milkman."

Anderson's new staff learned to imitate the master's folksy style. "In the 'Merry-Go-Round,' people rarely paid for anything, they 'footed the bill,'" Hume explained. "No big shot ever had just an apartment, he had a 'plush' apartment." Leaked transcripts of secret congressional hearings "were the stuff of many 'ready-made'" columns because "they could usually be written from the documents themselves with little other reporting," except for embellishing with "imaginary descriptions of how the congressmen 'stormed' or 'demanded' or 'snorted,' while the witness 'squirmed,' 'admitted sheepishly' and 'insisted angrily.'" Anderson advised Hume that to get such transcripts from congressmen, "you've got to con them a little. Pretend you know all about whatever they're doing, even if you don't . . . If you just get them talking, they'll sometimes mention things that are of great significance without realizing it."

Anderson's approach began paying off. Six months after he took over the column, thirty-two additional newspapers signed on as clients, almost as many as canceled immediately after Pearson's death. The Aberdeen, South Dakota, *American News* was typical: its readers urged the paper to keep publishing the "Merry-Go-Round" by a margin of fifty-nine to one. "Just what other columnist enlightens the public as much as Mr. Anderson regarding the activities of our congressmen?" one reader asked. Another wrote, "We need and want Jack Anderson. We, the public, want the truth about our elected and appointed officials."

For Anderson, the worst was now over. An additional three hundred newspapers would syndicate his work over the next decade, giving him more readers than any other columnist in the nation. With adjustments that reflected the personality of its new leader, the "Merry-Go-Round" continued whirling into the future.

President Nixon took note of the column's transformation, especially its aggressive new pursuit of Democratic politicians. "I had no intention of selling out to the new Nixon administration," Anderson said, but he didn't mind conveying the opposite impression if it would provide access to White House intelligence. His strategy seemed to work. Six weeks after Pearson's death, the President expressed agreement with an aide that Anderson had begun to take the column "out of the pacifist, leftist" orbit it once occupied and thus "might be well worth working with, despite unpleasant relations in the past." Unaware that Murray Chotiner had already established a secret back channel to Anderson, Nixon suggested that his advisor John Ehrlichman "be the first one to try" normalizing relations with the muckraker, but the White House aide was afraid to do so.

Anderson reinforced administration suspicions when he published a false story that targeted thirty-seven-year-old Donald Rumsfeld, the future defense secretary then working as a White House staffer. As Nixon's "anti-poverty czar," Anderson wrote, Rumsfeld "has wielded an economic ax on programs for the poor" even while he "used some of the savings to give his own executive suite a more luxurious look, thus reducing the poverty in his immediate surroundings." The columnist charged that Rumsfeld added a bedroom and private bathroom to his office, along with "expensive lamps [to] give a soft, restful glow to the walls." As another journalist put it, Anderson had exposed the "head of the poverty program living in sybaritic luxury even as millions of America's teeming poor did without food and shelter." The only problem was that the story was not true: Anderson had not even bothered to visit the premises before publishing his column. Rumsfeld invited the newsman to his office to see for himself. Accompanied by his twenty-eight-year-old assistant Dick Cheney, the future vice president, Rumsfeld gave Anderson a tour and the columnist apologized for his error. But no retraction was ever published in the "Merry-Go-Round."

Anderson's mistake gave him only momentary pause. In an odd way, his checkered reputation could even be a tactical asset. "You call up some guy and he thinks, It's that crazy Jack Anderson, he'll print anything, so I better explain," Brit Hume said. "The guy thinks he's explaining, but as far as we're concerned he's confessing." Anderson's staff was reckless "in the best sense of the word," legman Les Whitten maintained. "We did the story and then we worried about it later . . . If it wasn't true, we'd apologize for it" afterward and hope to get out of trouble. It was not the way reporting was taught in journalism schools, but the fear it generated could be surprisingly useful. On Capitol Hill, "congressional leaders would greet Jack like he was the Pope,"

Anderson's reporter Marc Smolonsky recalled. "They slapped his back and treated him as if he was their best friend." Even senators who loathed the columnist reached out to him, passing on dirt about their enemies and trying to curry favor in the hope of gaining immunity in case Anderson later discovered their own misdeeds. Such "fear kept them honest," Whitten said, and "made them think that if they did anything wrong, Jack would find out."

Murray Chotiner knew better. After two decades of combat with Anderson, Nixon's counselor realized that the newsman was only as good as his sources and that leaking to him might be a more effective way to control him than attacking him. Despite the reservations of others in the White House, Chotiner's clandestine negotiations with Anderson soon produced dividends for both the new President and the new columnist—and led to felonies that would eventually result in a proposed article of impeachment against the Chief Executive.

George Wallace, the short, oily-haired Alabama governor whose feisty way of jutting out his jaw and curling his lip led writers to compare him to a bantam rooster, had nearly cost Richard Nixon the presidency. An unabashedly racist demagogue who in the early 1960s physically blocked two young black students from integrating the University of Alabama, Wallace had defiantly proclaimed, "Segregation now, segregation tomorrow, segregation forever!" In 1968, his independent presidential bid received nearly 14 percent of the vote, mostly from working-class Southern whites who otherwise would have supported Nixon. Because the President's margin of victory had been less than one percent, he justifiably viewed Wallace as his single greatest threat to reelection four years later. After Nixon's inauguration, Wallace further fueled White House fears by planning another presidential bid and warning that Republicans "cannot win without the South in the next election." In response, the President and his aides engineered a secret plan to neutralize Wallace that they dubbed the "Alabama Project."

The White House plot to derail Wallace used both bribery and blackmail—as well as Jack Anderson—in one of the Nixon administration's earliest use of the dirty tricks that would come to full flowering during the Watergate scandal three years later. At the President's direction, his personal lawyer secretly delivered $400,000 in cash—bundled in stacks of hundred-dollar bills and stuffed into manila envelopes—to bankroll the campaign of Wallace's gubernatorial rival in Alabama's Democratic primary. Nixon hoped that embarrassing Wallace in his backyard would limit his ability to drain away conservative votes in the next presidential race.

At the same time, the administration targeted Wallace for criminal prosecution based on evidence of corruption that Anderson had uncovered sixteen months earlier. The reporter alleged that Wallace received "kickbacks under the table" from state-licensed liquor distributors and "misused state funds for his own political purposes." In addition, Anderson reported that the law firm Wallace shared with his brother Gerald—"a weasel-like, underweight man with sunken cheeks and cadaverous complexion" widely known as the governor's "bagman"—had been "raking in large fees from clients interested in influence with the state." Anderson's assertions were backed up by "a bundle of cancelled checks, a wad of bank statements and a sheaf of brokerage bills and correspondence." Lest there be any doubt, the muckraker proclaimed, "We will be happy to assist [authorities] by furnishing documents or testimony." For good measure, Anderson contacted Internal Revenue Service commissioner Sheldon Cohen, a Democrat appointed to office by President Johnson. "I laid before him everything I could prove, and everything I had information on but could not prove," the columnist wrote in an unpublished manuscript. "Cohen took it all in, seemed impressed, and assured me that the IRS would certainly look into these matters."

By early 1970, the leads Anderson provided to the government had grown into a full-blown criminal investigation of the Wallace brothers. But details of the sensitive inquiry were tightly held by Nixon's new command in the IRS, which no longer included Anderson's old source, Commissioner Cohen. As a result, Anderson complained, "I would not be given squatters' rights and cut in on" the probe. "Which meant I would have to go higher" in the administration to learn what was happening. After months of currying favor with Murray Chotiner, Anderson decided "the time had come to put the Chotiner connection to the acid test" and "twisted his arm to get me a report on what the IRS had found out" about Wallace. "This won't be easy, Jack," Chotiner replied, "but will do."

In fact, deliberately leaking classified tax records was a felony under federal law. But doing so in the Wallace case would undermine the President's key adversary and was in Nixon's interest as well as Anderson's, as the reporter fully understood before he made the request. Chotiner scurried to the White House to pass on Anderson's proposal. The initial reaction was not one of horror at breaking the law but amazement that Chotiner had befriended Nixon's journalistic nemesis. "You went to Jack Anderson?" White House chief of staff Haldeman asked incredulously. "I did," Chotiner replied. "You must have the balls of a brass monkey!" Haldeman exclaimed.

The irony of using an old enemy to vanquish another could not have been lost on the President. "I remembered the IRS leaks of my tax returns to Drew Pearson in the 1952 campaign," Nixon later wrote in his memoirs. "We at least owed it to ourselves in self-defense to initiate some investigations" of Democrats. Chotiner put together a list of White House adversaries to be targeted for tax audits and demanded a copy of the government's confidential tax file on Wallace. White House aide Clark Mollenhoff, a gruff former newsman who thought Chotiner a "scoundrel," balked at this blatantly political maneuver. But Chief of Staff Haldeman overruled Mollenhoff and ordered the classified records delivered to Chotiner "at the request of the President" himself.

A few days later, Chotiner invited Anderson to stop by his suite in the Watergate apartments. "There, spread out on a table, was the full report from the IRS to President Nixon on the Wallace case," Anderson marveled. According to the columnist's unpublished manuscript, Chotiner "directed me to the chair" in front of the table on which the Wallace file was propped open:

He said he'd rejoin me in about forty-five minutes. The unspoken ground-rules were that I could look and copy but was on my honor not to lift anything from the file. There was a reason for this. With so little time to go through so much complicated data, a reporter could hope only to assimilate the highlights and scribble down a quote here and a fact there. He would miss things, misconstrue things, the quotes would be a little off. All of which was good for the leaker because . . . [the resulting story] would not look like it necessarily was based on possession of a classified document; if it had been it would have been more exact, more complete . . . This uncertainty provided the necessary bit of fog that official leakers needed to veil their movements.

In April 1970, Anderson went public with the sensitive tax data provided by the Nixon White House. SWARM OF AGENTS INVESTIGATE WALLACE, Anderson headlined. Citing "confidential findings" from the IRS and "confidential field reports, made available to this column," Anderson reported the exact amount of taxable income of Gerald Wallace, who "has fallen into sudden wealth since his famous brother became governor" and now "lives the life of a rich country squire" on a new "lush, 315-acre cattle farm" with "a private swimming pool, scenic lake and wooden dock with an elegant, many-sided gazebo" and "special quarters for his hunting dogs and their attendant." The White House file also corroborated the corruption allegations that Anderson had first disclosed a year and a half earlier, including kickbacks funneled through the Wallace law firm that were allegedly used to fund the governor's presidential campaign.

Anderson's exposé created a political firestorm. Gerald Wallace issued a statement accusing the muckraker of "trying to convict me by implications, misleading statements and without a trial." Attorney General Mitchell privately gloated that Wallace was now in a "peck of trouble." "Boy, that's good news," presidential aide Charles Colson replied, "because that'll get him out of the way for 1972." With Alabama's Democratic primary less than a month away, reprints of the "Merry-Go-Round" column blanketed the state. "Suddenly Wallace, who had regarded the gubernatorial race as a push-over on his way to the big race for the Presidency two years hence" was "on the edge of political extinction," Anderson wrote. The Wallace campaign realized that Nixon's men were behind the columns. "Why did they wait until three weeks before the election to publish them?" Gerald Wallace asked. "The reason is obvious—politics of the dirtiest sort." The Alabama governor responded in kind. UNLESS WHITES VOTE, a Wallace ad declared, BLACKS WILL CONTROL THE STATE. On Election Day, the governor brazenly told voters, "Now don't let them niggers beat us, you hear?" Despite the best efforts of both the White House and Jack Anderson, Wallace was reelected and once again positioned with a public platform to challenge Nixon for the presidency.

In Washington, tax officials were enraged by the Anderson leak. An assistant IRS commissioner began "screaming" that Anderson's column "carried information which exactly paralleled" a confidential memo to the President about the Wallace audit; another assistant commissioner stated flatly that Nixon's "memorandum was clearly the source of the Jack Anderson column." The muckraker's story led to a "furious and noisy" meeting of presidential advisors, White House aide Mollenhoff said, which "disintegrated into sheer bedlam" filled with "snarling" attempts to assign blame. Nixon's advisors could not escape the unpleasant fact that, as one put it, Murray Chotiner was the "Number One suspect" in the illegal leak—and that he was undoubtedly acting on behalf of the President. The IRS now launched a criminal investigation focusing on top White House officials. "Haldeman and Ehrlichman acknowledged that they were aware of the Jack Anderson column," an IRS counsel reported, "but they did not acknowledge that they had ever seen the memo with the tax information" that Anderson published. Instead, Nixon's "Berlin Wall" disingenuously offered to "look into the matter" and "prepare a memo for the staff cautioning them not to leak information." But of course they had no desire to uncover the culprits because doing so risked directly implicating the Chief Executive himself in the crime.

No criminal charges were ever filed over the leak to Anderson. But four years later, Nixon's role in the scandal became the focus of Watergate prosecutors and led to a proposed article of impeachment against the President. Investigators obtained testimony from top administration officials that the breach of privacy "constituted a criminal act" that "occurred at the highest White House level." Whether Nixon personally gave Wallace's classified file to his alter ego Chotiner or the President instructed his obedient aide Haldeman to do so for him, Nixon clearly must have known about and authorized the illegal disclosure.

Although Anderson had allowed himself to be used by the Nixon White House, his exclusive reporting on Wallace's corruption was an uncontested journalistic coup. More remarkable still, the newsman had turned his longtime foe, now the President of the United States, into a secret informant willing to commit a federal crime to slip him classified information. Anderson returned the favor by rising to Nixon's defense when the White House was first accused of leaking the Wallace tax file. "We owe it to the president to set the record straight," Anderson announced. "He didn't start the investigation into Wallace's tax records. We did." The columnist pointed out that the Wallace probe began before Nixon was in the White House and that he "merely inherited" the case: "To the president's credit, he refused to kill the investigation despite the political embarrassment it could cause him." Anderson was disingenuous at best. While it was technically true that the Wallace inquiry began two months before Nixon was inaugurated, it did not become a serious, full-fledged investigation until after he took office. The journalist's false assertion that the President had bravely taken a political risk was a misleading attempt to both conceal and reward Nixon's role as Anderson's source. The reality in the Wallace case, as the muckraker knew better than anyone, was that far from setting aside politics to follow the law, Nixon broke the law to advance his political interests.

Throughout 1971, a federal grand jury gathered additional evidence of corruption by Wallace's men and prepared to indict the governor's brother and more than a dozen co-conspirators. But in January 1972, the Nixon Justice Department unexpectedly issued a statement announcing that it was dropping the probe. The very next day, Governor Wallace held a press conference to declare that he would run for president as a Democrat rather than an independent, thus dividing the Democratic Party and immeasurably strengthening Nixon's chances for reelection. The timing seemed more than mere coincidence: by one account, the President and the governor reached a quid pro quo deal during a lunch on the presidential jet Air Force One. "Whether an explicit agreement was made or not," a biographer observed, "Wallace's decision to abandon his third-party affiliation was an act of extraordinary importance for the Nixon re-election campaign strategy. No longer would they have to worry about responding to Wallace; he was the Democrats' problem." As one White House aide correctly predicted,

Wallace would now "move through the Democratic primaries like a pyromaniac in the middle of a fireworks factory, leaving the party in shambles." Thanks to Jack Anderson, Richard Nixon's first major dirty trick of the 1972 campaign was off to a smashing start.

In an unpublished manuscript, Anderson later acknowledged that his collusion with the Nixon White House would have troubled him "back in the early mists of my career, when I would have regarded such plottings as evidence of a deplorable cynicism." But after more than two decades in Washington, Anderson recognized that "Chotiner and I were both big boys who knew that our association, like a treaty between governments, would last only so long as it did not conflict with our larger interests." Anderson preserved his integrity in his own way by adhering to an unconventional ethos: "I had come to believe that the ordinary-life virtues of loyalty, compassion, gratitude and unambiguousness should have a distinctly subordinate place in relations between a muckraker and an official. Each knows what the other is about, or ought to. Often the very basis of their association is the potential it offers for using one another. My duty was to see to it that I was not the one used, except when being used served the larger ends of exposure." Thus as long as Anderson's alliances were temporary, not permanent—as long as the greater good of the public ultimately received higher priority than the protection of nefarious sources—Anderson's conscience remained clean.

Sure enough, in the aftermath of the Wallace exposés, the columnist once again began writing stories that were critical of President Nixon. Anderson received a "plaintive" call from Chotiner: "Jeez, we did this great favor for you, and you're writing stories like that?" Nixon's advisor accused the newsman of violating their arrangement. "What arrangement?" Anderson asked. "I made no agreement. I thought you guys just wanted to be helpful." In response, the White House "olive branch was abruptly withdrawn." Unburdened by any lingering loyalty to the White House, Anderson revealed how Nixon's men "use[d] our column" to leak Wallace's confidential file, bringing "pressure on him through a tax investigation" to "eliminate" the "threat to President Nixon's re-election." Having already availed himself of the illegal White House leak, Anderson effectively outed his own source—but only once the flow of information had dried up for good.

None of it troubled the seasoned reporter. Informants who provided inside information often harbored an "unspoken hope of gaining personal immunity," Anderson recognized, but this "neither deterred me or bound me. I was usually willing to trade up for a better story, and was often unwilling to alienate a good source over a minor crime, but I was careful to avoid making overt suggestions of general immunity." Thus "the double game of seeking a man's help today in pursuing one crime while planning secretly to expose him tomorrow for another" was tolerable "until it reached a certain level of treachery." In the case of the Nixon White House, Anderson wrote in his unpublished manuscript, there

> was the question of whether it was unacceptably deceitful to seek White House help during a tactical truce knowing that the day would come when I'd be dumping on my collaborators. The operative word here was "unacceptably." Sure it was deceitful, on both sides. Deceitful for them to offer scoops with the unspoken but obvious intention of silencing an oft-damaging critic. Deceitful for me [to] accept the offer, all the while plotting to soon enough bite the hand that was feeding me news. But deceit is a constant companion in the quest for secret information about high officials, whether that questing is done by intelligence operatives to inform governments or by newspapermen to inform the public.

That, of course, was not how the White House viewed it. Instead, Nixon's men saw Anderson's longtime animosity now compounded by betrayal. It was bad enough for the newsman to be an implacable if predictable adversary, but to worm his way into the bosom of the White House by posing as an ally and then bite the breast that nursed him was a perfidy made more dangerous by Anderson's new, intimate knowledge of presidential crimes—and the muckraker's potential for blackmailing the powerful sources that once succored him. Clearly, Jack Anderson would have to be dealt with. So, for that matter, would the rest of the news media.

6

REVENGE

Truth will become the hallmark of the Nixon administration," White House communications director Herb Klein announced at the start of the President's term. But Richard Nixon had other ideas. "The press is the enemy," the Chief Executive repeatedly told his staff, not once but dozens if not hundreds of times. When Nixon used the word *enemy*, his speechwriter William Safire said, he "was saying exactly what he meant," that the news media should be "hated and beaten." Safire later admitted that White House aides engaged in a "conspiracy" to "discredit and malign the press" and "defame and intimidate" journalists. This "anti-media campaign" was "encouraged, directed and urged on by the president himself," Safire wrote, "and in that vein of vengeance . . . lay Nixon's greatest personal and political weakness and the cause of his downfall."

As president, Nixon began each day by reading a lengthy summary of the news coverage he received during the previous twenty-four hours, followed by presidential instructions to his staff on how to respond. "Nixon spent hours, every day, studying the press, manipulating the press, warning his associates about the press, threatening the press," one biographer noted. "Nixon's war with the press went back to the Hiss case, but it was in his Presidency, from the first day, that it reached levels of vengeance and vindictiveness previously unimagined, and stayed there right on through to his last day in the White House."

A telling sign of the President's contempt for the Washington press corps was his choice of White House spokesman: a twenty-nine-year-old adman and former Disneyland tour guide named Ronald Ziegler.

"Nixon was able to program Ziegler," a coworker said. "He would go out and say *exactly* what Nixon said, with *exactly* the tone Nixon wanted . . . like Charlie McCarthy," the wooden ventriloquist's dummy of 1940s showbiz fame. Guided by polling data and the President's personal input, Nixon's advisors met at 9:15 every morning to manufacture their "line-of-the-day," the first-ever White House propaganda effort orchestrated solely to shape the news media's daily message.

The President's spin doctors called themselves the "attack group," and they lived up to their name. Just months after taking office, Vice President Spiro Agnew launched a public assault on what he called the "small and unelected elite" of the national news media, which Agnew declared held a "concentration of power over American public opinion unknown in history." The Vice President's speech was written by White House aide Patrick Buchanan and approved word-for-word by the President himself. "This really flicks the scab off, doesn't it?" Nixon enthused. A week later, Agnew launched another broadside against the press. "The day when the network commentators and even gentlemen of the *New York Times* enjoyed a form of diplomatic immunity from comment and criticism of what they said—that day is over," Agnew proclaimed. Six weeks later, a business partner of Nixon's best friend filed paperwork with the Federal Communications Commission challenging the license renewal of a television station owned by the liberal *Washington Post*.

White House operatives did not try to conceal their attempts to harass the news media. On the contrary, they publicized them in the belief that their hardball tactics would be more effective that way. Echoing the lesson he learned from his angry "last" news conference seven years earlier, Nixon advised his aides that it "is good politics for us to kick the press around." The President invited top broadcasting executives to the White House and informed them that "your reporters just can't stand the fact that I am in this office. They have opposed me for twenty-five years [and] they'll continue to oppose me." Nixon's staff was even more explicit. Press Secretary Ziegler declared that all of the television networks were "anti-Nixon" and would "have to pay for that, sooner or later, one way or another." Presidential advisor Charles Colson told the head of CBS News that the White House would "bring you to your knees" as punishment for refusing to "play ball . . . We'll break your network."

The threats were not idle ones. The otherwise pro-business Nixon Justice Department filed antitrust charges against the three networks, accusing them of monopolistic practices. Federal prosecutors also drafted legislation to make it a felony for journalists to receive unauthorized leaks. "Almost every president of the United States has fought [the press] in his own way," one scholar wrote. But the "administration of Richard Nixon differed in the speed with which it moved to attack the media at many levels and in the intensity and scope of its well-orchestrated activities. From the Nixon White House there emanated, for the first time, attacks intended to damage the credibility not of a single journalist but of whole classes of them; to intimidate publishers and broadcast ownerships; and, almost unthinkably, to establish in American jurisprudence the legality of censorship."

While his administration denounced the media in public, the President also worked in private to undermine reporters. Nixon instructed J. Edgar Hoover to compile "a run down on the homosexuals known and suspected in the Washington press corps." The President also sent his staff "urgent" requests to use "nut cutters" in a "brutal" assault on journalists who were "out to get us." Nixon told aides to "pick the twenty most vicious Washington reporters" and leak derogatory information about them: "Just kill the sons of bitches." Jack Anderson's name was first on an official White House enemies list that eventually swelled to more than two hundred foes; these adversaries, presidential counsel John Dean declared, would be targeted for retaliation by tax audits, government lawsuits, and criminal prosecution as part of a strategy to "use the available federal machinery to screw our political enemies."

Most ominous of all, the President approved illegal wiretaps, without court-ordered warrants, on newsmen who criticized the administration. Unfriendly reporters even experienced mysterious burglaries in their homes in which no valuables were stolen but reporters' notes were rifled. Only later, after the Watergate break-in, would they suspect a connection to Nixon's men. And only later would the full extent of the President's war on the news media come to light. Those "who had hoped that his ascension to the highest office in the land would ease his insecurities, would give him confidence and temper his anger, were bound to be disappointed," journalist David Halberstam wrote. "It did not lessen his anger, he seemed if anything to demand more vengeance than ever against his old opponents . . . His grievances were a source of inner strength to him. The people who had belittled him and snubbed him made him, in some terrible dark way, more resilient." Fueled by his hatred, the President would eventually draw up special forms of revenge for his most enduring press enemy, Jack Anderson.

Anderson's willingness to bite the hand that leaked to him angered not only President Nixon and his wizard of the dark arts, Murray Chotiner, but also another sometime White House source, Vice President Spiro Agnew. Before his high-decibel attacks on the press made him the public face of Nixon's war on the media, Agnew had tried to cultivate the muckraker by providing small news tips and limited access to the new administration. The Vice President's press secretary encouraged the strategy in the belief that "the words 'Jack Anderson calling' were among the most dreaded in official Washington." But soon enough, the columnist wrote a story that criticized Agnew. The Vice President "let me know through a mutual friend that he felt I betrayed our friendship," Anderson said. Agnew failed "to grasp Anderson's cardinal rule," another journalist explained: "Friends and sources are only protected when the information they provide is much juicier than their own transgressions." Indeed, by letting Anderson know that he would not receive any further leaks, the Vice President gave the newsman little reason to hold back from going after Agnew in future columns.

In September 1970, Anderson returned to his homophobic leitmotif after a tip that the Vice President's twenty-four-year-old son, Randy, was, as Brit Hume put it, "a fag." Anderson assigned his legman to investigate. "Agnew's been lecturing the nation about child-rearing," the columnist told Hume, "and that makes [the subject] legitimate." Indeed, the Vice President had publicly denounced "permissive" parents who "threw discipline out the window" and held up his own marriage and children as examples of proper family values. The long-haired Hume tracked Randy Agnew down and persuaded him to give an interview, deliberately concealing the fact that he worked for Anderson. Hume made up a "lurid" tale claiming he had been told that the Vice President's son was living in "a hippie crash pad with lots of wild parties going on and drugs being used." The bluff worked. Although Randy denied any impropriety, he provided enough information for Anderson to put together a "Merry-Go-Round" column.

Five days later, newspapers around the country published Anderson's report that "Vice President Spiro Agnew is deeply troubled about his son Randy, who has broken up with his wife and has been living for the past month with a male hairdresser." The story did not explicitly state that Randy Agnew was gay but, as Anderson later acknowledged, was deliberately "weighty with double entendre" and "euphemisms . . . of implied homosexuality." Randy was described as "a weightlifting instructor" who "came to the door, barefoot, in white slacks and [an] open neck, striped shirt." The column referred to Agnew's male roommate as "a pleasant, dark-haired man of 27 with a moustache and goatee" who operated a "beauty parlor" with his mother. The Vice President's son publicly denied Anderson's homosexual "implications" and numerous newspapers spiked the column. Hume discovered that many Washington journalists were "surprised and disappointed we had published it. They considered it a cheap shot, unworthy of serious reporters." Hume decided that these critics were right: "We had no idea whether . . . the kid was gay [or whether] gayness had anything to do with the rift with his family." Ultimately, Anderson came to the same point of view. "I jumped into the Randy Agnew story encumbered by the prejudices of the day and driven by my enthusiasm for a scoop," the columnist later admitted. "We went after the kid to expose the father. It was not fair."

Surprisingly, Anderson missed the one truly significant story about the Vice President: his financial corruption, which would force his resignation in disgrace in 1973. Two years earlier, some state contractors admitted to Anderson that they had funneled kickbacks to Agnew while he was the governor of Maryland. But these witnesses had no corroboration for their allegations and the Vice President denied the charges when Anderson asked about them. Because it was "difficult to define precisely" when a gift or campaign contribution "becomes a bribe,"

Anderson explained later, he didn't pursue the story further. As a result, he never discovered that Agnew continued to receive payoffs as Vice President, using the money to fund extramarital affairs, including gifts of expensive jewelry and a foreign sports car that he lavished on a "well-endowed" brunette on his staff who was "the age of one of Agnew's daughters."

After the Vice President resigned, he defended his graft in part by saying he was no worse than Jack Anderson. Why? Because both men regularly received "freebies" of meat and produce from the same large grocery chain. "The media had a field day" reporting Agnew's "greediness and venality" in accepting "gifts of hams and turkeys [as] 'CARE packages,'" the ex–vice president complained, but "every time" the supermarket truck stopped "to drop off a food gift for the Agnews, the next scheduled stop for another CARE package was the home of columnist Jack Anderson . . . The Anderson gifts continued long after I left office. So much for sanctimony."

Agnew accused Anderson of financial hypocrisy just as Anderson accused Agnew of sexual hypocrisy. Neither man seemed to realize that they were both right.

Although most of Jack Anderson's earliest scoops about the Nixon administration were minor, he relished taunting the White House about them. In early 1971, the newsman appeared on the popular Dick Cavett TV talk show and bragged that he regularly received copies of the President's private memos and confidential minutes. "I can assure you that if the President knew who was leaking," Anderson declared, "he would be fired tomorrow." It was a challenge calculated to inflame the White House, and it worked. "I believe him," Nixon said of Anderson's boast. "What are we going to do about it?"

At the President's direction, his staff analyzed nearly one hundred recent "Merry-Go-Round" columns. "Anderson does, indeed, have access to intelligence digests," a federal investigator concluded, "and he proves it on a daily basis . . . An overt firing of a person directly connected with a leak would go a long way towards making the ability of the Andersons of the world to gain White House information both difficult and hazardous." A week later, the muckraker responded in his column by poking fun at the President's attempt "to intimidate our sources who, unhappily for White House security, have continued to smuggle out newsworthy memos." Just to drive the point home, Anderson then published another secret document. Eight days later, he again ridiculed the President's men by quoting more "confidential comments at the White House," this time about how Republican leaders did not like to be "quoted in this column." One senator "was miffed," Anderson wrote, "when we reported what he had said at a secret White House leadership meeting." The newsman stated that another congressman complained that "if everything that goes on at these meetings is going to wind up in Jack Anderson's column, there's no use holding any more meetings." Still failing to see the humor, a presidential advisor warned about "the latest in a long series of Jack Anderson columns" filled with details of sensitive White House deliberations. Anderson's "stories are always accurate," the aide wrote, and "this matter has been brought up several times without resolution . . . I hope you will alert the President once again to be on guard . . . Do you have any suggestions as to how we can uncover the culprit??? Are you satisfied the room is not bugged???" (A dozen years after being caught in the act, Anderson's reputation for eavesdropping continued to worry Nixon's men—even though it was the President himself who was secretly bugging the Oval Office.)

The overreaction of the administration to Anderson's minor scoops was telling, for it reflected the petty and controlling anxieties of the President himself. At the White House, Nixon's men issued a stream of directives in an effort to deconstruct the columnist's sources on even his least important stories. Anderson learned of the President's attempts to stop the leaks and made sport of it: "Anyone who was caught should have his or her head hoisted on a spike, as a warning to others who talked out of school."

Nixon would have been better off if he had followed the press strategy of his defense secretary, Melvin Laird. Anderson attacked the Pentagon chief as "the most chauffeured man in Washington . . . who not only keeps a gleaming Cadillac at the ready but also demands another rented limousine as a backup car." Anderson added that Laird used his "fabulously expensive, 24-hour chauffeur service for . . . delivering packages of Christmas cheese to friends and associates of the big cheese himself." But instead of getting angry, the defense secretary won Anderson over with humor. "Laird got the best-looking marine babe he could find, with big boobs, and told her to open up her shirt so the cleavage would show," a friend remembered. "She got in a big limousine and took a box of cheese over for Jack Anderson." The attractive marine handed Anderson a gift-wrapped box of cheddar, showed him her fancy Pentagon auto, and delivered a handwritten note from Laird:

Dear Jack,
  I'm sorry I left you off the list this year.
                    The Big Cheese

Anderson roared with laughter at Laird's practical joke. After that, an administration official observed, the crusading columnist "rarely wrote anything about [Laird] again that was negative."

Meanwhile, the President held another needlessly secret meeting that Anderson would reveal. Four days before Christmas, while visiting Washington, rock-and-roll legend Elvis Presley sent Nixon a barely legible handwritten note to offer his assistance in the administration's war on drugs. "I have done an in-depth study of drug abuse," the pill-popping singer wrote, "and I am right in the middle of the whole thing where I can and will do the most good." Nixon's taciturn chief of staff, H. R. Haldeman, had a four-word response: "You must be kidding." But even Haldeman realized that a private jam session with the popular entertainer could produce political dividends. The "opportunity for the President to have a shot at reaching young people through a certifiable rock star" was impossible to pass up, thirty-one-year-old White House aide Egil "Bud" Krogh pointed out, especially if it produced "a rock musical with a 'Get High on Life' theme." Advisors hurriedly cleared Nixon's schedule so he could meet with Presley in the Oval Office that very afternoon.

The result was one of the most bizarre encounters in the history of presidential summitry. Nixon, ill at ease as usual, was dressed in a conservative gray suit and white shirt with an American flag pin on his lapel. Elvis was "wearing tight-fitting dark velvet pants, a white silky shirt with very high collars and open to below his chest, a dark purple velvet cape, a gold medallion, and heavy silver-plated amber-tinted designer sunglasses with 'EP' built into the nose bridge," Krogh wrote. "Around his waist was a belt with a huge four-inch by six-inch gold belt buckle with a complex design . . . His hair was almost brittle from hair spray."

"It's very good to meet you, Mr. Presley," the President said awkwardly. "I appreciate your offer to help us on the drug problem." Elvis took the opening to attack his musical competition: "The Beatles, I think, are kind of anti-American," he told Nixon. The pop idol pulled up his sleeves to show the President his cuff links. Nixon feigned interest in Elvis's jewelry but that was not enough to sustain the conversation, which continued haltingly, filled with clumsy silences. Finally, the Chief Executive fell back on an old standby: White House trinkets with the presidential seal. "Here are some tie clasps," Nixon said, thrusting them at the glassy-eyed performer.

The two men posed for what would become an iconic photo, the most-requested National Archives picture in U.S. history. It was, a chronicler noted, a "deliciously bizarre image" of "hilarious incongruity: the epitome of Republican squareness forcing a smile with a bloated, over-the-hill, and quite possibly stoned rock star who was petitioning the president to join the war on drugs." Presley left Washington with an official badge from the U.S. Department of Justice certifying that "ELVIS PRESLEY, whose signature and photograph appear below, is duly appointed as SPECIAL ASSISTANT in THE BUREAU OF NARCOTICS AND DANGEROUS DRUGS and is authorized by the Bureau to perform such duties consistent with his special advisory position."

Presley asked to keep the meeting quiet so he wouldn't alienate left-leaning music fans, but Nixon's aide Krogh feared that would be impossible "given the nature of the White House with reporters all over the place." But as happened so often, the rest of the press corps missed the story and Jack Anderson ended up breaking it. "By presidential dictum," Anderson reported, "Elvis Presley, the swivel-hipped singer, has been issued a federal narcotics badge. The emotional Presley was so overwhelmed at getting his own genuine, gold-plated badge that tears sprang from his eyes and he grabbed President Nixon in a Hollywood bear hug." Until Anderson found out about it, Krogh said, the meeting between the King and the President "enjoyed more secrecy than most of the 'Top Secret' information floating around the White House those days."

Krogh was later assigned to spy on Anderson and went to prison for his Watergate crimes. Three years later, Presley died of a drug overdose at the age of forty-two.

For decades, whispers about John Edgar Hoover's sexuality filled Washington. In the early 1930s, a journalist noted the FBI director's "mincing" walk and "fastidious" attire "with Eleanor blue as the favored color for the matched shades of tie, handkerchief and socks." The lifelong bachelor who lived alone with his mother and was rarely seen in the company of women also had a voyeuristic fascination with sex and an unusual relationship with his top aide Clyde Tolson, an athletic younger FBI agent whom Hoover plucked out of obscurity and quickly promoted through the ranks to associate director. The two men became inseparable companions, driving to work together in the morning, sharing lunch in the afternoon and dinner in the evening, and vacationing together on their time off. "Johnny and Clyde," as the pair were called behind their backs, had a relationship that one biographer labeled "spousal," one that was, if not physically consummated, "so close, so enduring, and so affectionate that it took the place of marriage for both bachelors."

Jack Anderson was just one of many Washington journalists who ran across the ubiquitous rumor of Hoover's homosexuality. A police inspector advised the columnist that waiters at Washington restaurants "would tell stories about Hoover and Tolson holding hands under the table . . . and rub[bing] knees." Unlike most reporters of his era, Anderson was actually willing to report about homosexuality, as Spiro Agnew, Ronald Reagan, and Joe McCarthy all learned the hard way. Anderson and Hoover had also tangled before; over the years, Hoover had labeled the newsman a "dog," a "vulture," a "stinking . . . skunk," and "a rat of the worst type"—although the aesthetically minded lawman noted that Anderson "is a rather nice looking fellow." Nonetheless, even Anderson dared not question Hoover's sexuality during the height of his power. "So different were the times and so powerful was the mystique of the FBI chief, that it would have been considered almost an act of treason to expose him," Anderson later wrote.

But in January 1971, as the seventy-six-year-old director's influence began to wane, Anderson decided to take on Hoover, declaring in his column that "it was time someone pried into his personal life in the FBI manner and reported the excess of the man behind the myth." Anderson dispatched Les Whitten to tail Hoover and Tolson. The legman spied on the couple as they met at Washington's Mayflower Hotel for the director's daily lunch of grapefruit and cottage cheese, but the reporter saw no evidence of physical contact between the two men. Neither did other Anderson assistants who staked out Hoover's home. "Everybody that we knew and talked to about the relationship said it was homosexual," a frustrated Anderson recalled, "but we couldn't get any evidence." So the columnist fell back on his old tactic of hinting at it. "Edgar and Clyde . . . appear to take turns eating dinner at one another's homes," Anderson wrote. Hoover's "closest confidant and constant companion" also traveled with him to the same hotel "each summer to attend the races" at a California horse track.

In search of more conclusive evidence, another Anderson legman, Chuck Elliott, literally went digging for dirt by picking through Hoover's rubbish in garbage cans behind his home. "Chuck was relentless," Anderson recalled, "going back day after day to lurk in the alley waiting for the household help to bring out the trash." Finally, Hoover's African American butler caught Anderson's reporter in the act. "You can get arrested for that," the servant warned. "He put his trash out to be collected and I'm collecting it," Anderson's assistant retorted, and then quickly drove away.

The columnist pored through the debris culled from Hoover's garbage but discovered nothing to suggest homosexuality. Instead, there were only empty bottles of liquor and Gelusil heartburn medicine. On FBI letterhead, in the director's shaky handwriting, Anderson also found precise menu instructions for his cook: crab bisque soup, spaghetti and meatballs with asparagus, and peppermint stick ice cream topped with strawberries. "I can see why he needs the Gelusil," the reporter laughed.

In March 1971, under the headline HOOVER'S TRASH SHOWS HE'S HUMAN, Anderson made sport of the fearsome FBI director. "It's unsettling to think of a living legend like the great Hoover having gas pains," the columnist wrote. "But the evidence seems indisputable." Such satire appears modest in hindsight, but at the time, it seemed practically subversive, a direct challenge to Hoover's authority. Anderson defended his tactics by pointing out that FBI agents also perused the trash of their targets. "The only difference between the way we operated and the FBI operated was we did it in broad daylight," the newsman argued.

Over the next two months, Anderson broadened his assault on the FBI director, reporting that America's "tireless guardian of the nation's morals" pocketed royalties from books ghostwritten by FBI employees. "This is an offense, if it had been committed by some other government official, that the FBI might have been asked to investigate," the muckraker taunted. "For the money rightfully should have gone to the taxpayers, who paid the salaries of the FBI researchers and writers." Unaccustomed to criticism, Hoover denounced Anderson as "a venomous and vicious liar" and "jackal" who likes to "feed on carrion." But Anderson refused to back down and continued to make veiled hints about Hoover's sexuality. The FBI director and "his faithful companion Clyde Tolson, both bachelors . . . ran up a total tab of over $15,000" on vacation together, the columnist wrote, but they "never paid their bills, which were picked up" by a millionaire friend. In addition, there was "startling evidence" that Hoover "consulted" a "distinguished psychiatrist" named Dr. Marshall de G. Ruffin, "whose patients include some of Washington's high and mighty." Anderson did not explicitly state that Hoover was treated for homosexuality but many readers undoubtedly inferred it. (Nearly twenty years later, Dr. Ruffin's widow reportedly confirmed that her husband had diagnosed Hoover as "very paranoid about anyone finding out he was a homosexual.")

By rifling through Hoover's trash, questioning his masculinity, impugning his financial integrity, and mocking his flatulence, Anderson enraged the FBI director. Hoover "would explode every time Anderson mentioned him and the F.B.I. in a column," the director's gay friend

Roy Cohn said. Hoover beefed up his contingent of bodyguards and ordered an FBI investigation, including surveillance, of Anderson and his staff. "I want to assure you," Hoover told a television news crew, "that I do not have heartburn or gastric acidity—except when I read a certain man's column." In a speech to the American Newspaper Women's Club, Hoover declared that Anderson was "not a reporter, he's a scavenger. He's the top scavenger among the columnists." In another address a few weeks later, Hoover complained that one of his "more virulent critics—his name escapes me for the moment—has apparently fallen off his merry-go-round once too often [and] spent considerable time sifting through my garbage." The result, Hoover declared, is that Anderson "is becoming increasingly confused between the trash he examines and the trash he writes." To prevent future embarrassments, aides presented Hoover with a trash compactor at a party celebrating his forty-seventh year as FBI director. "Those of us who attended [the ceremony] tried to keep a straight face," Deputy Director Deke DeLoach remembered, "but it was hard." Anderson had reduced America's top cop to a laughingstock even among his loyal staff.

President Nixon invited Hoover to breakfast and commiserated about the ridicule he had endured from Anderson and other critics. The FBI director acted unfazed: "The tougher the attacks get, the tougher I get," Hoover asserted. But in fact the growing criticism made him more cautious and he began rejecting White House requests to conduct illegal break-ins, wiretaps, and infiltration that the FBI had routinely provided other presidents in the past. For the first time in decades, Hoover felt vulnerable.

Not Jack Anderson. Emboldened by his growing success, he would now move from uncovering sexual peccadilloes to matters of war and peace, striking at the heart of the President's most secret foreign policy operations.

7

VIETNAM

The Vietnam War offered no peace, and certainly no honor, to the President who had been elected promising both. Richard Nixon's pledge for ending American involvement in Vietnam proved to be an impossible contradiction in terms: achieving peace by admitting defeat and withdrawing more than half a million American troops did not fulfill Nixon's definition of honor, and peace by military victory in a massive all-out offensive was no longer possible because of resistance by both Vietnamese fighters and U.S. public opinion. In the end, after five more years of bloodshed—including the slaughter of an additional twenty thousand American troops and hundreds of thousands of Vietnamese—the administration would eventually be forced to pull out unilaterally anyway. The U.S.-backed regime in Saigon, too brutal and corrupt to inspire support from its populace, would collapse to Communist troops in a humiliating rout.

Before the fall, however, Nixon searched for a nonexistent middle ground that he dubbed "Vietnamization," in which local anti-Communist soldiers would take over from departing U.S. forces. Shaped by his experience as Eisenhower's vice president during the Korean War, Nixon wrongly believed that Vietnam's civil war could similarly be settled through diplomacy by permanently partitioning the country into a Communist north and non-Communist south, and he erroneously believed that he could negotiate such an agreement with Hanoi's more powerful Communist allies, China and the Soviet Union. When this attempt at a face-saving compromise proved impossible, the frustrated President alternated erratically between his two true options: pulling out American troops on the one hand and expanding the war on the other. So, to mollify the war-weary American public, Nixon announced periodic U.S. troop withdrawals—even while intensifying aerial bombardments and greatly increasing civilian casualties. It was a strategy destined to fail under the weight of its own inconsistency. "There are at least two words no one can use to characterize the outcome of the two-faced policy," Admiral Elmo Zumwalt conceded. "One is 'peace.' The other is 'honor.'"

The President's attempt to hide his escalation did not fool anyone in Southeast Asia as they saw their villages burn and their countrymen perish. Only the American people remained unaware of the destruction unleashed in their name. But this public ignorance would not last long. Four months after Nixon's inauguration, *The New York Times* exposed covert U.S. bombing of Communist sanctuaries in Cambodia, a neutral neighbor of Vietnam. Not only had Nixon widened the war without the consent of Congress or the electorate; he had also deliberately concealed the bombing from his own Cabinet, which opposed it. The President was enraged by what he called "this cock-sucking story" and instructed aides to "find out who leaked it, and fire him." With the enthusiastic support of his national security advisor, Henry Kissinger, Nixon ordered the FBI to wiretap journalists and administration officials suspected of revealing the secret bombing.

The President followed up in the spring of 1970 by ordering U.S. ground troops to invade Cambodia. American B-52s dropped more than a hundred thousand tons of aerial explosives, destabilizing the Cambodian government and ultimately ushering in the genocidal Khmer Rouge regime, which killed an additional two million people. In the end, while supposedly winding down the war, the Nixon administration unleashed more bombs, and killed more civilians, than the Johnson administration, which had so expanded the conflict in the first place. LBJ's war had now become Nixon's. "Peace with honor," historian Garry Wills noted darkly, "meant, in context, peace with war." Antiwar demonstrators took to the streets in massive protests around the country; college campuses were paralyzed with strikes; and six students were killed in clashes with law enforcement authorities at Kent State University and Jackson State College.

The President felt besieged. He publicly called demonstrators "bums" and privately accused them of practicing "revolutionary terrorism." Unable to sleep, Nixon made a bizarre impromptu middle-of-the-night visit to the Lincoln Memorial, where he baffled antiwar protesters by trying to make small talk about football. The President turned to alcohol in an attempt to relax and summoned his longtime psychotherapist, Dr. Arnold Hutschnecker, who concealed the purpose of his visits by signing in with false destinations on White House logs. To steel his resolve, Nixon repeatedly watched the movie *Patton*, which glorified the bellicose World War II general, and vowed to emulate his example in Vietnam: "We're gonna level that goddamn country!"

Nixon's belligerent deceit forced dissenting government officials to turn to the news media to try to stop the carnage, and Jack Anderson was soon at the forefront exposing the administration's clandestine policies. "Anderson was the most consistently bedeviling of the press corps," Defense Secretary Melvin Laird complained; his deputy confided in his diary that military leaders braced themselves before turning to the "Merry-Go-Round" every day at breakfast. Pentagon officials even erected their own Jack Anderson dartboard.

In early 1971, the columnist and his legman Brit Hume persuaded a disillusioned army sergeant named Stephen Linger to become a whistleblower against the war. Deeply religious, Linger had volunteered to fight communism in Vietnam and was subsequently promoted to Washington, where he handled top-secret back channel communications for the Defense Intelligence Agency. His job provided access to classified White House teletypes, which the twenty-four-year-old read with growing disenchantment. "I was stunned," Linger later wrote. "How could my Country be so 'two-faced' . . . in Vietnam when men my age were dying for what they believed to be a just war? . . . What I learned and believed in as a Christian and as an American was completely contradicted by the facts I read." Linger began gathering all the encrypted Pentagon cables that he could get his hands on. "I wanted out," he recalled. "The more I learned and [understood], the more I wanted to do something about it." He decided that somebody should tell the public what was really going on and contacted Anderson, whom he respected as an upright Christian, "the only guy" in Washington he trusted to tell the truth about the administration's expansion of the war. Linger met Hume outside a car dealership near the Pentagon and poured out his story for several hours. He then "spilled my guts out" to Anderson in the columnist's suburban house and produced a sheaf of paperwork revealing numerous administration secrets.

That spring, based on the classified records that Linger had smuggled out of the Defense Department, Anderson began a series of eighteen columns exposing the military's covert operations in Vietnam. On March 18, the newsman quoted "top secret" reports disclosing that a "hush-hush project" had seeded clouds to increase rainfall over the Ho Chi Minh Trail, interfering with North Vietnamese supply routes and washing out villages in the process. It was the first known use of weather warfare in military history and would lead to international condemnation because of its unpredictable and uncontrollable destructive potential. One admiral involved in the "very sensitive" operation warned his military colleagues that Anderson's "article was accurate . . . but until now [the project] has never been mentioned publicly" because details were safeguarded in a "vaulted area" of the Pentagon and "protected by [a special] cypher lock system." Anderson gloried in his breach of official secrecy. "Only those with top security clearance" knew about the operation, the muckraker boasted in his column, "until now."

Four days later, Anderson exposed the sham of U.S. peace talks with North Vietnam by revealing how the White House had deliberately restricted American diplomats in Paris from receiving ongoing intelligence about the war—the war whose end they were supposedly negotiating. Two days afterward, the columnist published what one author called Anderson's "most explosive story" yet, revealing American plans to bomb Hanoi and mine its harbor in Haiphong—an eerily accurate forecast of precisely the tactics the military would use the following year. The muckraker warned that some U.S. advisors feared this "would be a dangerous escalation of the war, endangering Soviet shipping in the busy harbor," and could "compel the Kremlin to retaliate."

The next week, Anderson continued to draw on his cache of classified documents to reveal repeated instances of administration duplicity: claiming minimal casualties in Laos despite a "secret" report that showed otherwise; misleading the public about the intent of a previous

Cambodian invasion; and denying the existence of more recent cross-border raids, whose secret military code names Anderson published. In other columns that month, Anderson cited "intelligence reports" and "confidential communiqués from Saigon" suggesting the administration believed it could win a military victory in Vietnam, contrary to White House claims to be winding down the war.

By the end of March, Anderson's detailed revelations created an uproar among the President's men. Although the columnist's disclosures "attracted little attention from other journalists," author Seymour Hersh wrote, they "threw the White House and [Pentagon] into a panic." According to top-secret minutes, Defense Secretary Laird told his staff that "there must be a bad leak" from inside because "Jack Anderson seems to get back-channel messages sooner than [even] Laird does." National Security Advisor Henry Kissinger's staff culled Anderson's columns, numbering and highlighting in yellow all classified quotes, which officials then tried to match to particular government documents, searching for patterns that could explain how Anderson got his information. At the same time, Attorney General John Mitchell ordered an "extensive investigation" by the Justice Department, including "interrogations" of all enlisted men who could have leaked the sensitive data.

But Anderson continued publishing classified documents throughout the spring of 1971. On April 9, the columnist quoted from "intercepted enemy messages" to reveal that "Hanoi had advance knowledge of both the Cambodian and Laos invasions" by the United States. According to a "secret message to the Pentagon," Anderson reported, "faulty" American intelligence had "caused heavy casualties." Furthermore, the newsman wrote, North Vietnam had been "alerted in advance of B-52 raids," thus allowing the North Vietnamese to "move their trucks off the Ho Chi Minh trails before the big bombers arrived." Anderson disclosed that Hanoi received this valuable heads-up by bribing American GIs with marijuana and heroin.

On April 30, yet another Anderson bombshell: the Nixon administration was secretly spying on its ally, South Vietnamese president Nguyen Van Thieu, intercepting his "private messages" and decoding them in a clandestine project "identified by the code name 'Gout.'"

According to the columnist, U.S. intelligence agents regularly rushed Thieu's personal communiqués "by teletype to the White House marked 'Exclusive for Dr. Henry A. Kissinger/White House.'" Anderson's revelation that the United States was spying on its partner in the war was "particularly distressing" because it was "accurate and very embarrassing," one presidential advisor warned. "Furthermore, the knowledge of this collection operation has been very tightly held."

A Pentagon investigator claimed that Anderson's Vietnam disclosures "really hurt" national security, "causing the compromise of codes, code names, and operations" that were "believed to be of significant interest to our enemies abroad." But the reality was that these leaks were more politically embarrassing than militarily dangerous, and the newsman insisted that the administration's attempt to deceive citizens about the secret escalation of the war deserved coverage. "The price for these intelligence goofs has been paid in blood," Anderson declared in one column. "Should those who were responsible be allowed to remain in their shadowy world safe from public exposure?"

Not surprisingly, President Nixon held a different view. He privately railed at the "cocksuckers" in the media who are "trying to kill us" and vowed that he would "not let the goddamn war be decided in the press." CIA records show that the spy agency began reviewing its old files on Anderson in an unsuccessful attempt "to show [that] JACK ANDERSON is a perjurer [about] his military obligation"—the old and discredited charge that Anderson evaded the draft during World War II. Intelligence officials "are becoming increasingly perturbed over information appearing in Jack Anderson's column," a White House advisor stated in a memo. "Although there are some who would like to see Anderson put to trial and hung, in either order, I believe that the sensible solution would be to identify and neutralize the source or sources of the information." The aide suggested that "a common thread" seemed to run through Anderson's columns, "possibly indicating a single, low level, but well placed source."

That conjecture was accurate, for Anderson's source was precisely such a low-level but well-placed informant. Yet Stephen Linger was never caught, even though Pentagon investigators interviewed him—and nearly two hundred other suspects—as part of their massive effort to stop the Anderson disclosures. The Defense Department investigation was led by W. Donald Stewart, a beefy and pugnacious former FBI agent who launched eleven separate probes in pursuit of Anderson, who "just about drove us crazy with leaks," Stewart recalled. "All doors were opened for us. If we needed planes, ships or donkeys, we had them. That was the hysteria created by the Jack Anderson columns."

But it still wasn't enough to locate Anderson's source. According to the Pentagon's investigation, Linger (falsely) told agents that he "had no direct knowledge of Jack Anderson or his staff. He also denied having been contacted by Anderson or having knowledge of individuals who might have been." Instead, Linger pointed blame elsewhere, telling agents about an army coworker "who seemed to 'snoop' into the message traffic" and another who "lived in a 'hippie house' and was in complete accord with Jane Fonda and her beliefs." Linger also identified two other servicemen who were "indebted financially" and thus might have a motive to sell documents to Anderson. Investigators were so persuaded by Linger's denial—and his helpful suggestions of other possible suspects—that they did not bother to interview him again, let alone administer a polygraph exam as they did with other, seemingly more suspicious candidates.

In classic bureaucratic fashion, Defense Department investigators determined that blame for the Anderson disclosures lay elsewhere in the federal government. After analyzing one "Merry-Go-Round" column, Pentagon agents erroneously deduced that "Anderson's information probably came from a State Department source because State is upset over the lack of intelligence information it is receiving" from the Defense Department. Another Anderson column, Pentagon sleuths incorrectly decided, "undoubtedly" came from the National Weather Service because one of its employees was "a fellow parishioner" in Anderson's church. In the end, federal agents came up empty-handed. "Investigation failed to identify Jack Anderson's source(s) for Subject articles," a final report concluded. "Due to the lack of any productive leads to pursue relative to the Jack Anderson articles, instant investigation is hereby terminated."

All of it provided only further fodder for the columnist, who publicly mocked the administration's attempt to "scare off our news sources by unleashing its bloodhounds to find out where we get our information. The bloodhounds are now loose again, searching up and down Pentagon corridors for our trail, growling menacingly at anyone who might have been seen talking to us . . . The brass would dearly like to find out who blabbed." As agent Stewart put it, "While we were conducting our investigations, [Anderson] was writing columns making us look like Keystone Kops."

Paradoxically, the impact of the Anderson revelations was both dramatic and disappointing. "Anderson's columns that spring and summer were to stagger Washington—and Henry Kissinger and Richard Nixon," Seymour Hersh wrote. At the same time, however, "all were ignored by the rest of the press." It was not that Anderson's columns were unimportant; on the contrary, Hersh observed, "Anderson's information was recycled by other reporters in stories years later, and invariably each was treated as major news." But "the failure of the press to follow up on his reports tells a little about Anderson's ambivalent status among his peers and a great deal about the Nixon Administration's ability to control events." Indeed, when a Democratic senator followed up on the Anderson disclosures by demanding an explanation from the Pentagon, officials refused to answer questions on the grounds that doing so would threaten national security; that was enough to make the problem go away.

Anderson was understandably exasperated that his important Vietnam exposés were ignored by Washington's media elite, but he was hardly surprised. After all, the capital's journalistic establishment had been dismissing his work for decades. "We were ahead of everybody" in reporting on Nixon's deceptions in Southeast Asia, the columnist complained. "We were frustrated all the time." Anderson's Vietnam scoops were some of the most important and groundbreaking of his career, based on top-secret documents that exposed in real time the administration's mendacity in foreign policy. Yet, as was often the case, the muckraker was hobbled by his own checkered reputation for accuracy, which gave his competitors the excuse they sought to ignore even his most significant revelations. At what might have been the apogee of his career, Anderson's remarkable disclosures remained buried on the comics pages of *The Washington Post*, ignored by the rest of the press and the public even as they spread panic inside the White House. Like Nixon himself, Anderson somehow always seemed unable to realize his full potential.

At the same time, Anderson was also thwarted by a lack of tangible evidence to corroborate his reporting. Because the President's men publicly denied the columnist's Vietnam stories, and because Anderson's anonymous source was so deeply buried in the bureaucracy, other members of the press corps could not confirm his information. Indeed, journalistic competitors had an incentive to minimize Anderson's disclosures rather than acknowledge their own inability to match his scoops or cultivate comparable sources. "In retrospect," Hersh wrote, "Linger's leaking failed to change American policy because Linger did not take the step of actually giving Anderson top secret documents" for publication. The muckraker would soon be forced to change tactics.

In the spring of 1971, as the Nixon administration unsuccessfully tried to catch Anderson's informant, another whistleblower stepped forward to expose White House deceit by leaking classified material to the press. Daniel Ellsberg's release of the Pentagon Papers—a secret seven-thousand-page Defense Department study that documented U.S. duplicity in Vietnam during three previous administrations—would lead to an unprecedented battle between the government and the news media. A year earlier, Jack Anderson had learned about the still-secret records from one of his sources on Capitol Hill but had "made no effort to get them," he said, "because they were described to me as an *historical study*" and "I was interested in what's going on in Vietnam *now* [not] in digging up past history." It was, Anderson later admitted, a serious "error in news judgment." Instead, Ellsberg approached *New York Times* reporter Neil Sheehan, to whom he had leaked information a few years earlier when both men were in Vietnam.

On June 13, 1971, the *Times* filled four entire pages in its first installment of what would become a series of extensive articles about the Pentagon Papers. At first, President Nixon dismissed the story because it uncovered misconduct only by previous, mostly Democratic administrations. Publication of the papers "doesn't hurt us," he told his staff, so "the key is for us to *keep out of it*." But two hours later, General Alexander Haig, whom Nixon admired for his toughness, persuaded the President that the disclosures threatened national security. Nixon reversed course and decided that the leak was "unconscionable," a "treasonable action on the part of the bastards that put it out." The *Times* story "serves the enemy," the President declared, and "people have gotta be put to the torch for this sort of thing."

The next day, after another page-one article on the classified documents, Nixon erupted. "Neil Sheehan of the *Times* is a bastard," the President growled, a "cocksucker" and "left-wing Communist son of a bitch." Daniel Ellsberg was even worse, another Harvard-educated traitor like Alger Hiss; indeed, as in the Hiss case, Ellsberg had microfilmed the classified documents he purloined. It "gets back to the whole Hiss syndrome," Nixon told his staff, "the intellectuals because, basically, they have no morals . . . This is a bunch of goddamn left-wingers trying to destroy" the administration.

The President calculated how best to exploit the case to undermine his enemies. Nixon decided to "launch an attack on the *Times*," White House chief of staff H. R. Haldeman wrote in his diary, and the Chief Executive instructed aides to "find out what the statute of limitations" is for bringing criminal indictments so that the administration could "subpoena all these bastards" and "charge them" in court. Nixon ordered Attorney General Mitchell to send a telegram putting the newspaper on notice that its publication of the Pentagon Papers was a violation of the Espionage Act: "As far as the *Times* is concerned, hell, they're our enemies" anyway. According to White House counsel John Dean, "the old man"—the President—"wanted to know how he could put those bastards . . . at the *New York Times* in jail."

On June 15, the administration went to court to stop the *Times* from publishing more articles based on the classified documents. Government attorneys asserted that additional disclosures would cause "immediate and irreparable harm to the security of the United States." This was a grotesque exaggeration; even Nixon's own solicitor general later admitted that there was no evidence of "any trace of a threat to the national security from publication." Nevertheless, the administration quickly obtained a temporary restraining order prohibiting the *Times* from printing further excerpts from the papers. "For the first time since the very adoption of the Constitution," one legal scholar wrote, "the U.S. government [imposed] prior restraint with respect to the freedom of the press."

The President considered personally arguing the case before the Supreme Court "to indicate the importance" of the matter. Nixon told aides that this was "one of those fights" the administration "*had* to make, and by God, it's one I enjoy. These bastards have gone too far this time." The President directed Attorney General Mitchell to draft "strong" legal language—using terms such as *irresponsible* and *a massive breach of security*—to condemn the newspaper: "Use some really high flown adjectives." Nixon instructed his aide Charles Colson to "pour it on . . . the main thing is to cast it in terms of [the *Times*] doing something disloyal to the country" that "risks our men" and gives "aid and comfort to the enemy." The President's order to Haldeman was even more explicit: "Do everything we can to destroy the *Times*."

The federal injunction effectively gagged the nation's leading newspaper. But as its legal appeal wound its way through the courts, Ellsberg once again took matters into his own hands and began leaking the Pentagon Papers to other news outlets. First *The Washington Post*, then *The Boston Globe* and the *St. Louis Post-Dispatch*, then more than a dozen other newspapers began publishing the classified documents in a crescendo of defiant journalistic solidarity that made the administration's attempted censorship impossible to sustain. It was the single most concerted act of media resistance to the government in American history. "A newspaper industry that for thirty years and more had been living happily . . . on government handouts was suddenly in widespread revolt," Ellsberg marveled. "One paper after another was clamoring for its chance, not just to get a piece of a story but to step across the line into radical civil disobedience." On July 1, the Supreme Court ruled against the Nixon administration and for the press: publication of the Pentagon Papers could continue.

The dramatic events stoked both Nixonian rage and media righteousness, helping lay the foundation for the Watergate scandal that would force the President from office three years later. The Pentagon Papers "energized the press and endowed it with a new confidence and sense of legitimacy . . . as the people's paladin against the impersonal, devious forces of government," historian Stanley Kutler wrote. It also "heightened the Administration's already substantial suspicions of the media" and further "intensified the adversarial relationship" between the presidency and the press, "a relationship that was to deteriorate still more sharply" in the future.

The Supreme Court's rebuff incensed the President. He blamed not his own overreaching but the news outlets that had opposed him. "Those sons of bitches are killing me," he angrily told his staff. "We're up against an enemy, a conspiracy. They're using any means. *We are going to use any means.* Is that clear?" Nixon's Justice Department indicted Ellsberg for espionage, conspiracy, and theft; he faced life in prison if convicted. Day after day, the President pressured his staff to attack Ellsberg: "Kill him in the press . . . play it gloves off. Now, goddammit, get going on it." And "convict the son of a bitch *in the press. That's the way it's done.*" White House aide Colson duly complied by spreading word that Ellsberg was a spy who helped pass classified documents to the Soviet embassy; the false report was published by conservative columnist Victor Lasky, who was secretly on the Nixon campaign's payroll—"our man," as Colson called him.

Henry Kissinger also did his part to undermine Ellsberg. Nixon's national security advisor denounced his former Harvard colleague with calculated vehemence, telling presidential aides that Ellsberg was a bisexual drug-user who copulated with his wife in front of their children. "Henry had a problem because Ellsberg had been one of his 'boys,'" Haldeman observed. The President agreed: "Every one of these people that are involved in stealing the papers and then publishing them were either students of [Kissinger] or associates of his." Many, like Kissinger, were also Jews; and in the anti-Semitic atmosphere of the Nixon White House, Kissinger repeatedly turned on Jewish colleagues if he felt they might endanger his standing with the President. (The President already called Kissinger—behind his back and sometimes to his face—"my Jew boy." Nixon also referred to Ellsberg as "the Jew" and compared him to Soviet spy Julius Rosenberg: "The Jews are born spies. You notice how many of them are just in it up to their necks?" *The New York Times*, too, was filled with "those Jews," the President complained: "I just wanna cool it with those damn people because of their disloyalty to the country.")

Anti-Semitism aside, Nixon admitted being "a paranoiac or almost a basket case with regard to secrecy." Even J. Edgar Hoover was "not going after [Ellsberg] as strong as I'd like," the President complained. "If we can't get anyone in this damn government to do something," Nixon vowed, "then, by God, we'll do it ourselves." The President literally pounded his desk in frustration, his face red, as he bellowed his orders to his staff: "I don't give a damn how it's done, do whatever has to be done to stop these leaks and prevent further unauthorized disclosures. I don't want to be told why it can't be done . . . I don't want excuses. I want results. I want it done, whatever the cost."

The result would be one of the most fateful, and fatal, of Nixon's presidency: the creation of a special White House secret police force, a covert dirty tricks operation that would lead directly and inexorably to resignation and ruin. "The Plumbers"—so called because their original mission was to plug leaks—would enlarge their mandate to include burglary, forgery, wiretapping, and sabotage: "horrible things," the President told aides, "but they've got to be done."

Nixon wanted "somebody just as tough as I am" to run the venture, "a son of a bitch . . . who will work his butt off and do it dishonorably." Someone who "will know what he's doing and I want to know, too. And I'll direct him myself."

Charles Colson knew just the man for such an operation, someone "hard as nails."

"What's his name?" the President asked.

"His name is Howard Hunt," Colson replied. "He just got out of the CIA . . . Kind of a tiger." Hunt had already participated in surreptitious break-ins overseas, as a spy. "The beauty of this type of CIA guy," Haldeman explained, is that "he's working outside [so] we can just hire him as a consultant" to hide his connection to the administration. Nixon liked the idea: "Bring him over."

Hunt was paired with former FBI agent G. Gordon Liddy, who had also been trained in assassinations and illegal "black bag" jobs. Their office was housed in the Executive Office Building, across the street from the White House, and contained elaborate security measures: a fireproof safe to guard sensitive documents; "sterile" telephones that could not be traced; voice scramblers to foil wiretaps; and a ceiling device that emitted ultrasonic waves to thwart electronic bugging. Liddy, a devotee of Germanic culture, literally played Nazi songs as the Plumbers devised various forms of mayhem: forging documents to implicate Democrats in crimes; spying on Senator Edward Kennedy to try to catch him in extramarital liaisons; firebombing the Brookings Institution, a liberal Washington think tank, to capture information that would undermine Democrats; burglarizing the office of Ellsberg's psychiatrist in search of evidence to discredit the antiwar whistleblower; and, most infamously, the Watergate break-in, which would ultimately force Nixon to leave the White House in disgrace.

In retrospect, the fact that the Pentagon Papers proved to be the catalyst for these crimes—and ultimately for the President's downfall—was incongruous; after all, they were only historical records about Vietnam from previous administrations that were far less sensitive than the classified documents about Nixon's *ongoing* offenses that Jack Anderson had just disclosed a few weeks earlier. In any case, the muckraking columnist would soon expose a new batch of secret documents that would make the Pentagon Papers seem tepid in comparison, unleashing a scandal that would intensify the President's paranoia by revealing an espionage operation aimed at the White House itself.

8

THE ANDERSON PAPERS

President Nixon's needless prolonging of the Vietnam War may have been his most obvious foreign policy failure, but it was not his only one. In 1971, he secretly intervened in another Asian conflict, the India-Pakistan War, helping fuel bloodshed that would kill more than two million people. Once again, Jack Anderson played a crucial role in exposing the White House machinations behind the carnage.

The origins of this catastrophe were rooted in the global rivalry between the world's two atomic superpowers, the United States and the Soviet Union. In what was one of many Cold War proxy battles between the international giants, the United States supported Pakistan while the Russians backed India during their war. In the midst of it all, Anderson disclosed that President Nixon secretly staged "his own nuclear showdown" with the Soviets and "brought the United States to the edge of another world war." It was not the muckraker's usual hyperbole: Anderson had once more obtained top-secret contemporaneous government documents that verified his incendiary claims.

The crisis began in the spring of 1971, when impoverished Bengalis in eastern Pakistan, oppressed by the ruling elite of western Pakistan, started breaking away to form their own independent country. Pakistan's military dictator, General Agha Muhammad Yahya Khan, had a simple solution: "Kill three million of them," he declared, "and the rest will eat out of our hands." The general was as good as his vow, imposing martial law and unleashing his troops in a massive genocidal purge that methodically rounded up and executed not only Bengali soldiers and activists but also women, children, and the elderly. Neighboring India became deluged with desperate families pouring over the border to escape the butchery—a hundred thousand exiles a day, ten million total, one of the greatest sudden mass migrations of refugees in history.

President Nixon was unsympathetic. Partly, it was personal: he preferred Pakistan's military dictator, a short, fat, strutting, womanizing alcoholic who nonetheless showed Nixon proper deference, to India's haughty fifty-three-year-old prime minister, Indira Gandhi, whom Nixon privately called "an old witch" and "that bitch, that whore." Mostly, however, the President sided with Pakistan for reasons of geopolitical Realpolitik: he was trying to normalize relations with Pakistan's ally, the People's Republic of China, to counter the world's other Communist colossus, the Soviet Union. So Nixon supported Pakistan as it squared off with Soviet-backed India. "We don't really have any choice," National Security Advisor Henry Kissinger told the President. "We can't allow a friend of ours and China's to get screwed in a conflict with a friend of Russia's." As a result, Nixon refused to condemn Pakistan's atrocities or use his relationship with its ruler to stop the violence, which was carried out with the help of U.S.-supplied tanks and aircraft.

On December 3, 1971, after accusing India of stoking the Bengali rebellion, Pakistan launched a surprise attack against India. World opinion was almost universal in its condemnation of the Pakistani aggression, and Nixon informed congressional leaders that the U.S. would maintain "absolute neutrality" and would not become "physically involved in any way." In fact, however, the President secretly plotted to rush arms to Pakistan. To circumvent a congressional ban on aid to the warring countries, Kissinger came up with a scheme to have intermediaries— Iran, Jordan, Saudi Arabia, and Turkey—supply the weaponry, skirting the law and avoiding visible American fingerprints. "I like the idea," Nixon responded. "Have it done one step away" so that if the truth leaked out, "we can have it denied." State Department officials warned that such third-party transactions were illegal, but the President proceeded anyway, issuing a "directive" that provided Pakistan with covert shipments of U.S. fighter jets and other arms. Privately, Kissinger acknowledged the risk the White House was taking: "We are standing alone against our public opinion, against our whole bureaucracy at the very edge of legality."

Unbeknownst to Kissinger, one of the bureaucratic functionaries upset by his manipulations was an informant for Jack Anderson. Just days after Pakistan attacked India, Anderson's source—who, the columnist said, "could no longer abide the deception" of his bosses—used a prearranged telephone signal to set up a meeting with Anderson at a Dart drugstore near the White House. "Such Hollywood spy games are not my usual style," the newsman conceded, but his informant had "learned that telephone conversations were not always private" and was caught up in the urgency of the moment. As Anderson's source nervously stood in an aisle pretending to look over the season's Christmas card offerings, he whispered that the administration had just dispatched a navy armada to the India-Pakistan front in what could set off "a nuclear powder keg" between the United States and the Soviet Union.

Anderson's source was right. On December 10, just a week after Pakistan invaded India, the President ordered the navy's Seventh Fleet into the Bay of Bengal; a task force of eight warships carried one hundred fighter-bombers, two thousand Marines, and nuclear weapons. Two days later, at Nixon's behest, Kissinger leaked word to the press that the U.S. naval armada was intended for "a possible rescue of American citizens" in war-torn eastern Pakistan. A State Department diplomat later acknowledged that this was a "transparently false cover story" because such a powerful arsenal was not needed to evacuate the handful of Americans who remained in the area. The reality was that the American flotilla was a deliberate provocation in support of Pakistan—a "pure power play" to "get the word out in order to put a little pressure" on India, the President privately admitted. Kissinger agreed that this "show of force" was necessary to "give the Soviets a warning" and recommended that the administration "brazen it up" to make their "bluff" sound more convincing. While there was "a high possibility" that the aggressive American maneuvers would ultimately fail, Kissinger added, "at least we're coming off like men." Nixon boasted that the policy would show that "'the man in the White House' was tough."

Although revealing the location of military ships is normally a violation of national security, the government decided to publicize its gunboat diplomacy to try to scare its adversaries into backing down. The administration now ordered the Seventh Fleet to travel "as much . . . as possible in daylight . . . in other words, in full view of the world," recalled Admiral Elmo Zumwalt, chief of naval operations for the Joint Chiefs of Staff. The deployment received prominent coverage by all leading newspapers and television networks. "Pentagon sources deliberately obliged newsmen by providing daily 'backgrounders' on the location of the warships," a *New York Times* reporter wrote. "Nixon and Kissinger wanted New Delhi and Moscow to know exactly what the fleet was doing."

Meanwhile, Anderson "needled" his source to hand over classified files that would back up his assertion that the United States was recklessly risking war with the Soviets. "I can't even run the story without documentation," the columnist insisted to his informant. "I've got to see the papers." Anderson later recalled that he "wasted little time in soul searching over the issue of disclosing national security issues. The only thing holding me back was the need to get enough proof from my source so my word would not be questioned." Anderson explained that he needed incontrovertible evidence to write an exposé that could withstand the inevitable administration denials. The newsman invoked Daniel Ellsberg's recent leak of the Pentagon Papers and argued that only by documenting governmental deceit in a similar way could another U.S. war in Asia be prevented. When Anderson's contact in the bureaucracy hesitated, the muckraker gently chided him: "You've got to decide whether you work for the country or for Kissinger."

Anderson's source "reluctantly" agreed. The two arranged to meet in a downtown Washington alley at midnight, where several manila envelopes filled with top-secret records changed hands. The investigative reporter then interviewed other officials from the White House, Pentagon, and State Department to try to gather more intelligence— and cover the tracks of his secret source.

On December 13, as the war between India and Pakistan reached its peak, Anderson began the first in a series of articles based on his new cache of classified documents. But his initial story attracted little public attention, in part because he obscured its newsworthiness by gingerly backing into the column with an irrelevant birthday ode to his late mentor Drew Pearson. Anderson also repeated the mistake of his reporting on Vietnam a few months earlier by failing to ballyhoo the fact that he had actually obtained classified government files. It was not that the columnist lacked access to important and timely information: his hoard of paperwork on the India-Pakistan War included actual minutes of the secret deliberations by Kissinger and his advisors just days earlier that documented in detail the administration's rash and duplicitous foreign policy maneuvers. But as Anderson later acknowledged, he was "cautious, even timid" in what he reported because his documents "were held so closely to the vest by the [Pentagon] that I feared to quote from them lest I pinpoint my source, cost him his job, and maybe land him in jail." As a result, the newsman complained, his "story got about as much attention as yesterday's horoscope."

Except in the White House. There, the President and his advisors read Anderson's column with alarm. "It's very important to put Anderson" down, Nixon told his aides. "Say nothing. Don't give any credibility to the story. Deny it all. Say he's lying."

The President's strategy seemed to work and mainstream media outlets ignored the "Merry-Go-Round" column. Irritated by his story's lack of impact, Anderson called his chief reporter, Les Whitten, into his office. "I never saw so many classified documents in my whole life," Whitten marveled. "Jack had them sitting there in his office in a goddamned box. They were all there, the real McCoy." To try to generate publicity for the story, Anderson and Whitten considered challenging White House press secretary Ronald Ziegler at his daily news briefing to deny that Anderson's files were genuine. Under the plan, the columnist would publicly offer the President's spokesman a deal: if Ziegler could prove the documents were phony, Anderson would give up his column—but if Anderson's information was authentic, Ziegler would resign as Nixon's spokesman. In the end, the muckraker abandoned the idea because he felt it would have been too nakedly self-promotional.

Instead, Anderson decided to change tactics by sharpening his written attacks to make them "more sensational" and using extensive verbatim quotes from the top-secret records. "It will probably bore the Kansas City milkman," Anderson's legman Brit Hume predicted, "but it might stir some interest from Jack's colleagues." The result would be a "baptism by fire" for his source, Anderson realized, but it would be the only effective way to expose the President's foreign policy deceit.

On December 16, Anderson reported that although the "Nixon administration has rung down the censorship curtain" on its actions, "secret White House minutes" from "behind the guarded doors of the White House Situation Room" proved "Nixon's duplicity" in the India-Pakistan War. In a series of escalating attacks, Anderson charged that the President and his advisors "lied" by claiming that the United States was neutral. "The president does not want to be even handed," the newsman quoted Kissinger as saying. "I am getting hell every half hour from the president that we are not being tough enough on India . . . *He wants to tilt in favor of Pakistan.*" Anderson also revealed that the White House privately plotted to smuggle arms to Pakistan in violation of the congressional embargo.

Anderson followed up on his revelations of White House mendacity by exposing its even more serious military recklessness. By rushing the Seventh Fleet into the Bay of Bengal, the columnist wrote, the administration risked bringing the superpowers to the brink of armed confrontation. The escalating crisis was rapidly becoming as perilous as it was volatile. According to "secret diplomatic dispatches" that Anderson had obtained, Russia reassured India that a "Soviet fleet is now [nearby] in the Indian Ocean" and promised that the Russian navy "will not allow the [U.S.] Seventh Fleet to intervene." The muckraker even quoted classified cables stating that the Soviets promised to provoke "a diversionary action" against China if necessary. The "world stood on the edge of another world war," Anderson declared, "and the American people were never told about it."

Indeed, the Soviet Union had actually dispatched two naval convoys to the Indian Ocean, each armed with cruise missiles. "What do we do if the Soviets move against [China]?" Nixon wondered. "Start lobbing nuclear weapons in?" "If the Soviets move against them . . . and succeed," Kissinger replied, "that will be the final showdown . . . We will be finished. We'll be through."

Alone among the Washington press corps, Anderson recognized the danger. Now, instead of obscuring the sensitive nature of the government papers that he had obtained, the newsman began flaunting his access to these highly classified documents: "The papers bear a variety of stamps: 'Secret Sensitive,' 'Eyes Only' . . . and other classifications even more exotic," Anderson wrote in his column. "Yet astonishingly, the documents contain almost no information that could possibly jeopardize the national security. On the contrary, the security labels are used to hide the activities—and often the blunders—of our leaders." The muckraker compared his documents to the Pentagon Papers, which he said also "exposed, all too late, the miscalculations and misrepresentations that entangled the U.S. in a jungle war in faraway Vietnam."

This time, Anderson's strategy worked. On December 30, he received a call from *The New York Times* asking him to comment on Kissinger's claim that he had been quoted out of context in the "Merry-Go-Round." Anderson believed that Kissinger felt free to deny the story because he assumed "that I couldn't possibly have [actual hard copies of] the secret minutes." So the columnist "impulsively" decided to prove Kissinger wrong. "I'll show you the context," Anderson told the *Times* reporter. "Come on over and read the documents for yourself." The muckraker then gave the *Times* some of his classified papers, after first having his staff retype them "lest my copy might in some note or doodle betray my source."

The next day, beginning on page one, the *Times* published extensive excerpts from Anderson's documents. "Officials in the Administration conceded that Mr. Anderson's information appeared genuine," the newspaper of record reported. "Several said privately that they learned more about top-level intra-governmental policy discussions from the column than they would normally learn in the course of their official duties." One unnamed government official admitted that "we come in every morning just wondering what's going to hit us next. [Anderson has] got onto something and no one seems to know how to stop him." The *Times* imprimatur legitimized Anderson's exposé with the rest of the establishment media, which now began picking up the story. ANDERSON STRIKES AGAIN, the *Washington Star* headlined.

On January 3, on a flight to Nixon's vacation home in San Clemente, California, Kissinger repeated to a pool of traveling reporters his claim that Anderson had distorted his remarks by taking them out of context. That gave the columnist just the excuse he was looking for to release additional copies of the classified documents to other news outlets, beginning with *The Washington Post*, which gave the story prominent front-page coverage and filled more than a page of text inside the newspaper with verbatim excerpts. "Every major news organization in town now wanted its own set of papers," Hume remembered, and "the office was in a virtual state of siege . . . The phones rang continuously."

Anderson was delighted to oblige other journalists. "I don't think the public should have to take either my word or Dr. Kissinger's," the newsman declared. "I invite reporters to compare Dr. Kissinger's statements at the secret strategy sessions" with the public record. Television networks extensively interviewed Anderson, who "held up several of the documents and the camera moved in for titillating close-ups that showed the black security markings they bore," Hume said. Anderson explained his strategy to his young reporter: "You've got to stay on the attack. If they get you on the defensive, then you look bad. I'm going to keep pounding away."

News outlets around the world now followed Anderson's lead and published lengthy excerpts from his documents. "Mocking headlines flashed 'Tilt! Tilt! Tilt!' like an old-fashioned pinball machine," one journalist wrote. Another said that Anderson "turned Washington upside down" and "sent shock waves throughout the Administration and Capitol Hill." PRESIDENT'S ADVISERS LIED DURING CRISES, proclaimed "one of the starker head[line]s" that caught the White House's attention. *The Washington Post* called Anderson's release of the classified documents "a major challenge to the secrecy surrounding U.S. policy in the Indo-Pakistani war." Anderson was "an unguided journalistic missile with multiple warheads likely to strike anywhere," presidential chronicler Theodore H. White wrote. "The Anderson columns stripped bare the essential privacy of national-security planners as never before."

White House advisors tied up phone lines in the middle of the night, warning each other about what Anderson would reveal in the morning's newspapers. Unfortunately, one administration aide reported, Anderson's column "was again completely accurate." CIA director Richard Helms acknowledged that he was "jolted" by the "dramatic" release of "the detailed notes" in "the Jack Anderson papers . . . He obviously got hold of the documents themselves and we were all somewhat awed."

Anderson and his staff worried how the President would react. After all, just six months earlier, government attorneys fought all the way to the Supreme Court to try to censor the Pentagon Papers. "If the

Administration would [try] to suppress years-old material which did not even cover its own activities, what might it do to prevent publication of highly damaging material that was only a few days old and contained proof of the baldest sort of duplicity?" Hume wondered. "Anderson seemed to be in the midst of what might become a major new battle in the war over secrecy. If he handled it well, he might swing public opinion a long way toward the view that secrecy is dangerous. If he handled it poorly, the public might become persuaded that the news media posed the greater danger."

Sure enough, the White House changed its position from claiming that Anderson had distorted the documents to asserting that he endangered national security by publishing them. Kissinger now blamed the messenger, asserting that the "very serious leaks to Jack Anderson"—rather than the administration's secret tilt to Pakistan—"adversely affected our relations with India" and therefore "constituted a serious security risk to our government." The President went even further, charging that the Anderson revelations were "one of the most serious incidents" of the entire India-Pakistan War. "The leak came as a shock," Nixon said, because the classified documents were available "only [to] the highest-ranking members of the military intelligence organizations and the State Department . . . From a diplomatic point of view, the leak was embarrassing; from the point of view of national security, it was intolerable."

But that wasn't the view of career professionals in the Defense Department. Admiral Zumwalt thought that the only real effect of the leak was that Jack Anderson had "fun" with "Kissinger's increasing irritability, not to say fury" over "his failures" in policymaking. Although the Anderson papers "are even more vivid" than the Pentagon Papers and "record the crisis managers in action barely one month after the fact," *The New York Times* reported, "senior Pentagon sources said the disclosures primarily affected diplomatic sensitivity rather than military security." Indeed, according to *The Chicago Daily News*, "officials concede that a court challenge to publication would be futile because they are deprived of the danger-to-national-security argument."

In a public relations offensive, Anderson repeatedly argued that public safety was not the issue. "There's no security in these papers,"

the muckraker thundered. "It's job security and censorship for the bureaucrats, not national security that's involved." To underscore his
patriotism—and perhaps warn the administration to back off lest he
cause further trouble—Anderson opened up his briefcase to show
journalists that he possessed dozens of other, more sensitive documents that he had decided *not* to publish out of concern for America's
defense. He also pointed out that he had been careful to conceal rout-
ing numbers and other information in the classified files "just in case
they would be useful to cryptographers" from foreign countries.

Like the Mormon missionary he once was, Anderson preached that
the purpose of national security was to safeguard liberty and not the
other way around: "If this nation were ever to decide that the government should have the power to silence the press in the name of national security, we will have defeated the very purpose of national
security. For the reason we have a national defense and a foreign policy is so that no other nation may gain control of our government and
trample upon our freedoms." Again and again, Anderson compared his
documents to the Pentagon Papers: "If we had this type of information
leaking out challenging the official version of the Gulf of Tonkin incident in 1965, we might have saved some of the 50,000 lives and $80
billion we've sunk into the thankless war there." The columnist invited
Congress to examine his documents as part of an official investigation
of the India-Pakistan War and the government's "massive" overclassifi-
cation of secrets.

Anderson's crusade against the Nixon administration was soon
echoed by other journalists. *New York Times* bureau chief James Reston, dean of Washington's media establishment, compared "the Anderson Papers" to the Pentagon Papers: both tell a "story of damaging
decisions arrived at in secret; of subjective presidential orders imposed
on the objective analysis of the president's own principal advisers; of
official explanations which mislead the Congress and the American
people." CBS News commentator Eric Sevareid said Anderson's disclosures revealed an administration credibility gap "approaching the size
of the San Andreas fault." Columnist Tom Wicker praised Anderson's
"remarkable series" as "a public service of the first order" that "demon-
strates that publication is one of the few remaining checks on the foreign policy powers of the imperial presidency." *The New York Times*

editorialized that "one of the striking revelations of the Anderson transcripts" was the President's disdain for career professionals working for
him, a deliberate "isolation from the first-hand advice and argument of
the Government's own experts . . . discouraging doubting questions
even about minor tactics. A Chief Executive who fails to expose himself to the fullest information, free debate and the challenges of others
to his prejudices can hardly be protected from blunders." And *The
Washington Post* decried the administration's "cynicism" and concluded
that "we can all be grateful to Jack Anderson, who has brought to the
public's attention material essential to the public's understanding" and
"right to know."

Anderson's exposé also became fodder for late-night comedians.
Because the government "has stolen our dollars, privacy and dignity,"
60 Minutes commentator Nicholas von Hoffman joked, it was now a
"delightful switch" to have something stolen from the government.
Cartoonist Pat Oliphant drew Nixon and Kissinger, knee-deep in water,
unsuccessfully using their hands and feet to try to plug a dam named
"Secrecy." The leaks were labeled "Greetings—Jack Anderson," "Hi!
Jack Anderson," "Jack Anderson—1972," and "Anderson was here."

The columnist's disclosures threatened to become an issue in
the 1972 presidential campaign, which was already well under way.
Within days, three different congressional committees followed up on
Anderson's suggestion and announced that they would hold hearings.
The "move is part of a new Democratic strategy to use the alleged dis-
crepancy in policy to try to erode the president's credibility," one newsman wrote. "This is where leading Democratic presidential candidates . . .
believe the president is vulnerable." White House chief of staff Haldeman discovered that Senator Edmund Muskie, the Democratic front-
runner, was going "to make a major charge against the P[resident]
regarding the Anderson papers." Nixon worried about the political fallout. "Remember my good friend Joe McCarthy," who achieved success
by going on the attack, the President reminded his staff; if the Democrats did so now, Nixon feared, "that could be a fatal mistake for us, a
fatal mistake."

At the same time, the bureaucratic blame game over the Anderson
disclosures began. *The New York Times* quoted "reliable sources" saying that the White House was not at fault because it called in the FBI

more than four months earlier to investigate other leaks of classified material to the news media. Meanwhile, "sources close to" the U.S. ambassador to India told journalists that he was "not unhappy" about the Anderson reports, which vindicated the diplomat's opposition to the Pakistani tilt. In anonymous asides to the press, the State Department blamed the Pentagon, the Pentagon blamed the White House, and the White House pointed back to the State Department. Hobbled by its own bureaucratic divisions, the administration launched a response that was feeble at best. United Nations ambassador George H. W. Bush, the future forty-first president, publicly called on Anderson to reveal the identity of his source, but that was obviously a naïve nonstarter. Another Republican, Congressman John Ashbrook, demanded a House investigation of the "vandals" who leaked "state secrets" to Anderson, but that suggestion went nowhere either.

In mid-January, more than a month after the columnist began publishing the classified documents, White House press secretary Ronald Ziegler belatedly stated that the Anderson leak is "a matter of great concern to the President," who wants to "make sure it doesn't happen again." An investigation was now under way "at direct Presidential direction," Ziegler said. According to *The New York Times*, this was "the first official acknowledgment of the President's personal concern about the Anderson papers, as well as the first official acknowledgment that Mr. Nixon himself had ordered steps taken to insure tighter security." The President privately counseled his spokesman to say no more on the subject because "I don't want to heighten this story anymore."

But Anderson's revelations could not be ignored. The very next day, a White House aide noted that "the 'Anderson papers' story is not dying, and there seems a disposition to keep it alive. Anderson was on the [Dick] Cavett show the other night, acting like the Great Crusader."

The public official most directly damaged by the scandal was Henry Kissinger, whose "personal standing lessened with each Anderson revelation," one author wrote. The President "decided that Kissinger's inability to handle the press—one of Kissinger's great successes up to now—was now responsible for his problems with Anderson and the India-Pakistan war." The thin-skinned national security advisor was "devastated by [the] press attacks on his professional competence,"

Nixon aide John Ehrlichman said, especially because Kissinger could not "change the fact" that the minutes of his embarrassing comments were in Anderson's possession. To avoid such catastrophes in the future, a senior senator lectured Kissinger, "you ought to stop the meetings" from occurring in the first place "if you can't keep it from leaking out." Kissinger instructed his staff to tighten document security so that "nobody should worry what will happen to these minutes." The Bavarian-born Kissinger joked darkly that "from now on the official minutes are going to be kept in German—with the verbs left out." Kissinger deputies also put together a lengthy rebuttal of the Anderson columns, but of course the White House advisor's incriminating comments—already transcribed in the government minutes that Anderson published—were undeniable. The most an aide could do was recommend that "it is best to avoid going into detail with a man like Anderson who has no concern for substance and is interested only in debater's points." Instead, Kissinger's office drew up a statement filled with indignant generalities. "We have no intention of engaging in a public exchange," the press release stated. "The record is clear for all who have a serious interest in reviewing it."

Indeed, thanks to Anderson, the record was now embarrassingly clear, and that was precisely the problem. "My credibility as a briefer is destroyed," Kissinger fretted to the President, and "the press will never believe me again." "I think that's pure bullshit," Nixon told Press Secretary Ziegler, who agreed: "Anderson doesn't have that many people in the press that really respect him." Still, for the first time in his career, Kissinger was the object of sustained public attack for his two-faced hypocrisy. If "my moral integrity" was besmirched, Kissinger huffed to a White House colleague, then "there is no point in doing my job." Haldeman reported that Kissinger's "staff got him all cranked up on the basis that [Anderson's reporting] had totally destroyed Henry's credibility and there was nothing left for him to do but quit . . . Henry's now at a point where he's so emotional about the issue that he's not really thinking it through clearly."

Kissinger's paranoia, already considerable in the best of circumstances, deepened. He feared that "the Nixon palace guard had deliberately arranged" the leak to Anderson to undermine Kissinger's position and that it was "done with Presidential connivance." In truth, it made no sense for the White House to give embarrassing classified documents to its longtime journalistic enemy, but Kissinger so distrusted Haldeman and Ehrlichman—and, for that matter, the President himself—that he saw conspiracies everywhere. "I have been acting as a lion-tamer," Kissinger told an administration ally, "and now they smell blood." Former defense secretary Robert McNamara advised Kissinger to "cut off [the] head" of Anderson's source. Another friend urged Kissinger to "get the guys who are leaking and hang them by their thumbs from the Washington monument." Kissinger agreed.

The strain between the President and his top foreign policy advisor now reached the breaking point. Nixon already envied Kissinger's popularity with the Eastern establishment and shared the view that his high-maintenance aide was "deceitful, egoistical, arrogant and insulting." Angered by the negative publicity produced by Anderson's exposé, the President stopped meeting Kissinger or returning his phone calls. "I am out of favor," the White House staffer realized, and once again threatened to quit. But Nixon was tired of Kissinger's "tri-weekly demand to resign" and wanted to call his bluff: "Maybe we have to let him go," the President told his closest aides. "Henry's problem is a deep emotional insecurity. He is . . . a deeply emotionally disturbed man."

According to Ehrlichman, "Henry's mood swings" so troubled the President that "Nixon wondered aloud if Henry needed psychiatric care." Kissinger was legendary in the White House for verbally abusing subordinates even while brazenly flattering the President with what Kissinger himself admitted was "obsequious excess." Since his days as a graduate student at Harvard, he had been nicknamed "Henry Ass-Kissinger," and Oval Office tapes recorded his repeated, shameless fawning over Nixon: "Mr. President, without you this country would be dead"; "It has been an inspiration to see your fortitude in adversity"; "You are a man of tremendous moves"; "You were absolutely spectacular!" At the same time, Kissinger belittled Nixon behind his back, calling him "that madman," "the meatball mind," a "maniac," and "our drunken friend." Ehrlichman believed that Kissinger was "very insecure" and that behind "a protective façade that was part self-deprecating humor and part intellectual showboating" Kissinger "cared desperately what people wrote and said about him." After publication of the Anderson papers, Ehrlichman recalled, "I'd never seen fingernails bitten so close to the quick as Henry's were during that time."

The President, no stranger to psychological troubles, took note of how Kissinger "ranted and raved" and decided that he must have a "suicidal complex." Nixon recommended that his aide read a self-help book by the President's own psychotherapist, Dr. Arnold Hutschnecker. Nixon also directed Haldeman to "make extensive memoranda about K[issinger]'s mental processes for his files" and instructed Ehrlichman to tell Kissinger that he should get professional counseling. But Ehrlichman ducked the unpleasant task. "I could think of no way to talk to Henry about psychiatric care," Ehrlichman recalled. "I had no confidence that that was what would help Henry nor could I bring myself to confront Henry with the President's apparent lack of confidence in his mental ability."

Nixon also approached the national security advisor's top aide, Alexander Haig, in an effort to manage Kissinger. "He's personalizing this India thing," the President told Haig. "His judgment is so warped" because he was "too emotional and . . . he just starts to wear himself out and crack up." Nixon told Haig to "get Henry out of the press" and "keep him out of it . . . It's time to forget this bullshit!" The President was in no mood to indulge what he viewed as Kissinger's "childish tantrums." "Henry was full of the usual charges of nobody on the staff defends him," Haldeman wrote in his diary. "We jumped on him pretty hard on the point that he couldn't go out to the press and defend himself and his credibility" without making matters worse. Nixon "told him the same thing," Haldeman said, "not to do anything now and not to talk to the press." The President advised against "overreacting" to the "Anderson papers" and instructed Kissinger, "Do not expose yourself to any reporter, don't attack Anderson, lay off anything in this area." Even one of Kissinger's most loyal aides warned that his desire to "take the press on" was "very dangerous, especially in light of the fact that [we] knew Anderson had more" classified documents in his possession.

But Kissinger ignored this advice and solicited support from friends in the media, whom he had assiduously cultivated during the past three years. "Henry started calling journalists and putting his side out," one of Kissinger's aides recalled. "He was talking to people and threatening to resign. He would use that threat to get good coverage. He was extraordinary." Ehrlichman, too, marveled at Kissinger's success: "Henry massaged the press as no one else in the White House did," using "blandishments" and "shameless self-congratulation." Kissinger played "host to the reporters and columnists who were invited to his office in a steady parade . . . so many that Henry often took them three at a time . . . It surprised me that veteran journalists would let him get away with using them as they did. But [they] came and went, congratulating themselves on having been the guests and confidants of Kissinger."

It did not take long before these friendly media pundits began weighing in on Kissinger's behalf. Publisher Walter Annenberg's exchange with the national security advisor—transcribed by a White House secretary secretly listening in on the phone call—typified the fawning treatment Kissinger received in public and in private:

"Henry," Annenberg said, "you have worked as hard and as diligently with the President as anybody and I regret the journalistic abuse you have been subjected to recently."

"That means a lot to me, Walter," Kissinger replied.

"All you have to do," Annenberg added, "is look at Mr. Anderson on TV—and TV is very revealing in terms of character—there is a sneaky, sleazy rat who just deals in hate."

"Well," Kissinger said, "I have spared myself taking a look at him so I don't really know."

"I hope you're not going to let this upset you," Annenberg counseled.

Eventually, after more than a month of ignoring Kissinger, Nixon decided to normalize relations with his national security advisor. The President believed that his aide had finally learned a lesson in humility "because he took such a horrible beating from his erstwhile friends" in the media over "the Anderson Papers." The result, Nixon told Haldeman, was to "put Henry in his place a little more about leaks."

Fittingly enough, the President marked his rapprochement with Kissinger by using him to plant a story to undermine Jack Anderson. Nixon informed Kissinger that "it was a good time" to leak to "a competitor" of Anderson selected portions of classified CIA intelligence that buttressed the administration's actions during the recent India-

Pakistan War. Two days later, columnist Joseph Alsop, a Kissinger friend, cited "the CIA's daily reports to the White House" to justify the administration's covert support for Pakistan. "It can be stated on positive authority that the U.S. government had 'conclusive proof' of India's intention to crush" and "dismember" Pakistan, Alsop wrote. The columnist, who was frequently wrong but rarely in doubt, stated that this "unchallengeable" CIA intelligence virtually compelled the administration's tilt toward Pakistan.

In fact, this "unchallengeable . . . conclusive proof" turned out to be nothing more than propaganda supplied by an unreliable CIA informant named Moraji Desai, a right-wing Indian politician who was a bitter enemy of Prime Minister Gandhi and whose political and personal bias should have automatically rendered him suspect. Gandhi had fired Desai from her Cabinet two years earlier and he was now a member of her political opposition who retaliated against her by circulating disinformation calculated to undermine her rule. In exchange, the CIA paid him twenty thousand dollars a year. Career professionals in the CIA, Pentagon, and State Department discounted Desai's dire warnings as exaggerated. But not Nixon and Kissinger. The President believed that Desai's report was "one of the few really timely pieces of intelligence the CIA had ever given him" and Kissinger continued to praise Desai years later—even after his "intelligence" had proved false—as "a source whose reliability we had never had any reason to doubt and which I do not question today." Indeed, Kissinger said that "these reports of Indian deliberations" were "among the most important reasons for our policy." But according to a top diplomat involved in the case, "Nixon and Kissinger were virtually alone in the U.S. government in interpreting [this information] as they did."

As happened earlier in Vietnam and would later happen in Iraq, career professionals in the government were ignored or demoted for their dissent, while facts were shaped by politics rather than the other way around. The Desai "intelligence fitted right into a prejudice," one administration official explained. "It gave Henry [Kissinger] and Nixon a chance to do what they wanted to do." Meantime, leaks of classified material were orchestrated from the top when they buttressed administration policy—and condemned when they challenged it. As *The*

New York Times dryly noted, unlike the leak to Jack Anderson, "there was no indication . . . that a security investigation had been ordered to determine the source of the 'unchallengeable' information cited by Mr. Alsop."

Nonetheless, despite all of the administration's efforts—political, military, propagandistic—Pakistan's army was quickly overrun by India's vastly superior armed forces. Less than two weeks after instigating the war, Pakistan surrendered in a humiliating rout. Eastern Pakistan achieved independence as the nation of Bangladesh. General Yahya, who was in a drunken stupor throughout much of the fighting, resigned in disgrace and spent the next five years under house arrest. Military coups and political executions would continue to haunt Pakistan decades into the future.

History ultimately vindicated Anderson's warnings about the administration's recklessness during the India-Pakistan conflict. The President made a "decision to risk war in the triangular Soviet-Chinese-American relationship," Kissinger later acknowledged, and Nixon ultimately admitted that the United States had come "close to nuclear war." Both men defended their belligerence as essential for courting China as an ally. In fact, however, what motivated the Chinese to seek closer ties to the United States was not America's support of Pakistan but China's need to counter the Soviet Union. "Through their misreading of the crisis, and their pro-Pakistan bias, Richard Nixon and Henry Kissinger succeeded in needlessly transforming a regional dispute into one which threatened to become a great power showdown," one scholar wrote. "From any standpoint," another analyst concluded, "Nixon and Kissinger's policy" was "replete with error, misjudgment, emotionalism, and unnecessary risk-taking . . . No national interest remotely warranted the risks [they] ran."

After the confrontation ended, Nixon assured Kissinger that "the Indians will come around." They did—but not as the President hoped. "The American decision to send a nuclear aircraft carrier task-force to the Bay of Bengal," an advisor to Prime Minister Gandhi wrote, "led to an acceleration of the Indian nuclear programme and eventually to the testing of a nuclear device." Pakistan inevitably followed by developing its own atomic arsenal and then supplied nuclear weapons technology to Iran, Libya, and North Korea, rogue nations with ties to anti-American terrorists. The roots of this proliferation could be traced to the disastrous policies of the India-Pakistan War that Anderson had helped expose. "The Anderson Papers," one scholar concluded, "were an appropriate postscript to a sorry chapter in U.S. diplomacy."

But the Anderson papers also represented a victory—of the columnist over the President, of the news media over the government, of disclosure over deception. "It is not the function of a secrecy system to shield public officials from accountability for their tantrums, folly or mindlessness," historian Arthur M. Schlesinger, Jr., wrote. "By outlining the 'tilt' policy only behind locked doors, the Nixon Administration deprived Congress and the electorate of the opportunity—one might say the right—to discuss President Nixon's pro-Pakistan program on its merits. This was the unpardonable sin and some anonymous, disgusted and courageous bureaucrat, with the help of Jack Anderson, was trying to rectify the situation."

After years of covering others in relative anonymity, Anderson finally became a newsmaker himself, a celebrity who graced magazine covers and commanded soaring readership, lucrative lecture invitations, and lengthy profiles by other journalists. "Now, like the Pentagon, he has earned the distinction of having a sheaf of secret papers named after him," *The New Yorker* observed, "and he is unquestionably an institution in his own right." In the Oval Office, Kissinger complained to the President that "Anderson, who is a skunk, has become a hero." The reason for the columnist's success was simple, *Newsweek* reported: "Anderson has the largest and most varied network of sources in all of newspaperdom" and his latest "revelations capped a long series of blockbusters that have both infuriated and titillated the Washington Establishment." According to *The Washington Star*:

> Television networks are vying for him as a guest on early-morning and late-night talk programs; his name and current exploits are spread across the front pages of the nation's newspapers . . . Anderson's patience, determination and non-stop muckraking have paid off . . . prov[ing] him the rightful heir to the country's most popular syndicated newspaper column.

The acclaim was not universal. Anderson engaged in "a breach of trust, and a breach of security, of the most profound implications," conservative columnist James J. Kilpatrick fumed, one that "goes beyond disloyalty; it sails close to the windward edge of treason." Indeed, "Jack Anderson is not a journalist," Kilpatrick declared, but "a sewer pipe"—a statement that brought laughter from the President when Haldeman read it aloud to him. *Time* called Anderson "Washington's most persistent sensationalist [who] thrives on contention" and sometimes "takes cheap shots . . . Many of his fellow newsmen regard as frivolous his uneven mixture of muckraking and kiss-and-tell gossip." Even *The Washington Post*, which published the "Merry-Go-Round," mocked Anderson for being "bombastic, loud, [and] evangelical . . . The column, as we all know, shouts. It is abrasive, acerbic, dogmatic, didactic and sometimes a pain."

Still, as journalist Mary McGrory observed, Anderson had "surpassed his detractors in celebrity. More people read his secrets than their laments." The pariah of the press, noted the *National Observer*, was clearly "savoring what must be the supreme achievement for a veteran newsman always a bit suspicious of and suspected by the Establishment press: Jack Anderson was the most quoted source in Washington."

None of it humbled the muckraker. "I didn't get my information out of a Daniel Ellsberg, who belonged to another Administration and has been out of government two years," Anderson bragged publicly. "I got my information from some of Nixon's own boys." Now the President and his "boys" were more determined than ever to hunt down Anderson's source—and punish the newsman who had tormented them for so long.

9

SEX, SPIES, BLACKMAIL

The White House Plumbers were back in business, and they had Jack Anderson to thank for it. President Nixon's secret dirty tricks operation had lain dormant since the Labor Day weekend of 1971, when operatives broke into the office of Daniel Ellsberg's psychiatrist in an unsuccessful effort to find evidence of drug use and sexual perversion by the Pentagon whistleblower. After botching the job, the Plumbers had been given little to do for three months. But in the final days of the year, Anderson's publication of highly classified documents about the administration's secret tilt toward Pakistan led the President to try once again to plug embarrassing leaks. The order to bring the Plumbers back was issued at the highest levels of the White House.

The leak investigation began less than twenty-four hours after Anderson's first India-Pakistan column was published, when White House aide John Ehrlichman received an urgent phone call. The President and Henry Kissinger had learned of the Anderson exposé at an international summit and were "beside themselves with rage over the leak." According to Ehrlichman, Kissinger persuaded Nixon to "launch a full-scale investigation of Anderson's penetration" of their inner circle. It was not just that "Henry's quoted tirades were . . . intemperate and embarrassing," Ehrlichman explained. "Worse, this was evidence that someone had given Jack Anderson the secret minutes of the meeting[s]."

Ehrlichman delegated the critical assignment to Plumbers' co-chief David Young, who "is hounding this one for us," a White House aide reported the next day in a memo: "The Anderson article . . . reveals an incredible leak" and authorities are "making a mammouth [*sic*] effort to track down the culprit." Pentagon investigator W. Donald Stewart, who had unsuccessfully tried to unearth other Anderson informants, also joined the case. The likelihood of pinpointing the columnist's source seemed remote; a federal report estimated that more than three hundred officials in the State Department alone—as well as many more in the White House, Defense Department, and Central Intelligence Agency—"had access to the documents involved." The CIA blew up freeze-frame images from Anderson's televised interviews to try to trace the secret memos that the columnist waved at news conferences, but he had carefully removed from the papers any telltale signs that might expose his informant.

Nevertheless, investigators soon got a lucky break. It turned out that only five copies had been made of one of the classified memos quoted in the "Merry-Go-Round," and they could be easily traced. Instead of hundreds of possible culprits, the list of potential Anderson sources now narrowed to a handful. Investigators quickly settled on a chief suspect: Navy yeoman Charles Radford, a gangly twenty-seven-year-old typist-stenographer who turned out to be a fellow Mormon and social friend of Anderson, and who had recently been passed over for a promotion. Assigned to the sensitive liaison office between the National Security Council run by Kissinger and the Joint Chiefs of Staff, Radford had top-secret security clearance and shuttled back and forth between the White House and Pentagon with some of the most classified documents in the government, including all that Anderson had just published. In the words of Stewart, "no newsman could have ever hoped to have a single source more centrally located."

Exactly how many records Radford gave Anderson may never be known; terrified of criminal prosecution, the sailor steadfastly maintained his innocence even under oath. But the evidence against him was overwhelming. Radford was sympathetic to India because he had served there as both a Mormon missionary and as a clerk in the U.S. embassy, where he befriended many locals. The yeoman also met two visiting American tourists in New Delhi's Mormon church: Orlando and Agnes Anderson, Jack's parents. When Radford was transferred to Washington, the Andersons invited him to supper at their son's home. The reporter quickly discovered that his parents' new friend "had easy access to Kissinger's office. Suddenly I began to view our dinner guest as the main course." Jack began cultivating Radford, and their wives started taking shopping trips together, bonding over their mutual interest in tracing Mormon genealogy. The impressionable young sailor was dazzled by the muckraker's celebrity. Anderson gently coaxed the navy clerk into confiding his misgivings about the temperamental Kissinger, whose tantrums Radford regularly witnessed at work. The yeoman thought Kissinger had an "animus toward India" that was "irrational" and that the secret American tilt toward Pakistan was "very hypocritical, very two-faced." Radford was particularly concerned that rushing a nuclear naval fleet to the Bay of Bengal put the United States "on the verge of another war" in Asia—until, he said, "Jack's column stopped it dead. His one single act there was actually the finger in the dike that stopped the flood."

On December 12, the night before Anderson's first India-Pakistan column was published, Jack and Olivia Anderson treated Chuck and Tonne Radford to dinner at the Empress, a Chinese restaurant located just a few blocks from the White House. (The Empress also happened to be Henry Kissinger's favorite Washington eatery. Fortunately for Radford, the national security advisor did not catch him there with Anderson that night.) Less than twelve hours later, millions of copies of Anderson's first India-Pakistan exposé rolled off the printing presses of newspapers around the world. "Boy, the shit hit the fan," Radford recalled. "It was like somebody had just stirred up an ant's nest because people were scurrying all over trying to cover their tracks." An officemate who knew of Radford's friendship with Anderson urged the navy stenographer to sever his ties with the journalist. "If people don't trust me by now," Radford replied, "breaking off my relationship with Jack Anderson won't help." The yeoman was soon summoned for a private meeting with his commanding officer, Admiral Robert Welander.

"Radford, did you give my memo to Jack Anderson?" Welander asked.

"No, sir," Radford replied, "I didn't."

The yeoman's supervisor didn't believe him but kept a poker face so as not to alarm Radford further. The admiral wondered what other documents might also be published in the "Washington Merry-Go-Round." After all, he realized that his typist had access to papers "of ten times more consequence than anything that's been leaked out in the Anderson articles" so far. Welander reported his suspicions to his superiors, including Admiral Thomas Moorer, chairman of the Joint Chiefs of Staff, who believed that Radford "became a crusader against those who were attacking his beloved India and that Jack Anderson took advantage of and exploited his attitude." Overnight, Pentagon security guards changed the locks on thirteen file cabinets filled with classified documents in Radford's office. The next day, the yeoman was relieved of duty.

On December 16, investigators began several days of grueling interrogations of Radford, including four lengthy polygraph exams. "We decided we should talk generally to get him to relax and then jump around—creating a sense of tension and pressure and then backing off," White House aide David Young said. The sailor was cross-examined in detail about his relationship with Anderson and his whereabouts, hour by hour, during the previous week. "I was very suspicious" of the polygraph, Radford recalled, "but felt that I had no alternative and that I had to do it. I felt that if I refused, that would make me look even guiltier." The navy clerk denied providing documents to Anderson but displayed an "extreme amount of general nervous tension" and was "emotionally distraught" under questioning, investigators reported. "He was quite nervous, swallowed a bit hard at the beginning, and very, very seldom looked anyone in the eye." According to White House chief of staff H. R. Haldeman, Radford's "polygraph makes clear that he did it."

Pentagon investigator Stewart was convinced that at long last he had caught "the son of a bitch that's giving everything out to Anderson." The rough-hewn gumshoe repeatedly cursed at the stenographer and called Anderson a "bastard" and a "traitor." Stewart said that Radford and Anderson "could do time" for their "clear-cut violations" of the Espionage Act. The security agent also drew up elaborate contingency plans to arrest the two men if they tried to flee the country and suggested obtaining a search warrant to seize the columnist's notes and documents to use as evidence to prosecute him. "Anderson was taunt-ing us," Stewart raged, "flaunt[ing] stolen classified material in his pos-session on television, exhibiting classified stamps and reading excerpts from the material in an effort to ridicule the classified subject matter . . . Vital security matters were in Jack Anderson's hands and he had be-come the sole judge of what would be made public." The newsman "made the enemy aware" of U.S. military secrets, Stewart added, di-vulging "more devastating security information [than Daniel] Ellsberg could ever hope to do."

After his first, bruising interrogation, Radford returned home on the edge of a nervous breakdown. "I was afraid I was going straight to prison," he recalled. "I felt like I'd have a knock at the door and be whisked away in the middle of the night and I wouldn't see my family again." His wife called the Andersons, who then rushed over to the Radfords' house that evening. "We can't talk here," the journalist warned, because of the likelihood the government was listening. "Let's get in my car." In the dark, the two men used a flashlight to search Anderson's vehicle for eavesdropping equipment—"under the seats, under the dash-board, behind the steering wheel, in the trunk, underneath the car and around the gas tank," Radford remembered. Once the auto passed in-spection, the two climbed inside and Anderson drove the sailor around the streets of Washington, keeping a wary lookout to see if they were being followed.

The columnist listened quietly as Radford filled him in on the gov-ernment's ongoing probe. The yeoman feared his military career was now over and worried how he would make a living. Anderson reassured him, offering to use his connections to help Radford get a new job to support his family. More crucially, Anderson coached him to simply deny that he had leaked the classified documents in the first place. "I won't tell them anything," the reporter vowed, "so the only way they will know is if you tell them." As long as Radford stood firm, the gov-ernment could never demonstrate that he was Anderson's source, because there were no other witnesses. "The way they get you is to get you to confess small things and go from there," the muckraker warned. "Don't tell anyone anything. They can't prove it." Instead, Anderson advised, "at-tack the lie detector. Attack those who would attack you. Discredit *them*." The newsman recounted the hard-won knowledge that a quarter century of Washington combat had taught him: a good offense always makes the best defense.

In the days that followed, Anderson and his wife made repeated trips to visit the Radfords at their home. Grateful for the moral support, the stenographer calmed down. "Because of my talking with Jack, and actually knowing that I had somebody that was in my corner, I didn't feel as vulnerable," Radford said later. "Jack was very helpful with his comments and his direction."

The yeoman followed Anderson's advice and steadfastly denied leaking him classified files. During interviews with federal investigators, Radford claimed that he "could not recall what specifically precipitated Anderson's invitation" to dinner the day before his first India-Pakistan article was published but allowed that "it was rather funny that Anderson called on such short notice." Radford implausibly insisted that on the night after his first traumatic polygraph interrogation, he did not even bother to talk to the columnist, who drove more than forty miles round-trip to Radford's house around midnight—because, the yeoman claimed, it was past his bedtime and the discussion only involved Mormon genealogy. "You are going to hurt a lot of other people if you don't come clean and tell us why you gave these papers to Anderson," Agent Stewart growled. "I have nothing to add on my own," Radford replied. "I'll be glad to answer your questions."

The next day, the Pentagon investigator tried again: "I am a cop and I am going to get to the bottom of this, and we are going to find out what happened [so you better] tell us all that you know right now." Radford's response was nearly identical to his earlier one: "I will be glad to answer any questions which you might have, but I really don't have anything else to say." Stewart tried insulting the navy clerk: "Don't you realize that there is only one reason why Anderson has been friendly to you—to cultivate you as a source?" Radford replied, "I think I would know if I were being cultivated. I've been around long enough to realize that." Besides, he added, "all you have is circumstantial evidence." Stewart called the well-mannered typist "undoubtedly one of the cleverest individuals I have ever interviewed" and complained that he "was trying to 'out con' the investigators." The government sleuth correctly

Richard Nixon (*top*) and Jack Anderson (*bottom*) shared similar backgrounds. Both men served in the Pacific during World War II, had strict religious upbringings, and were raised in small middle-class towns in the West. In 1947, both moved to Washington, D.C., to realize their ambitions—Nixon as a crusading anti-Communist congressman and Anderson as a crusading investigative reporter. (Top, courtesy of the Anderson family; bottom, courtesy of Whittier College)

Both Anderson and Nixon were tutored in Washington's dark arts: the reporter by his boss, columnist Drew Pearson (*top*), and the politician by operatives investigating the "Pumpkin Papers" in the Alger Hiss perjury case (*bottom*). (Top, Walter Bennett/Time & Life Pictures/Getty Images; bottom, University of Southern California Special Collections)

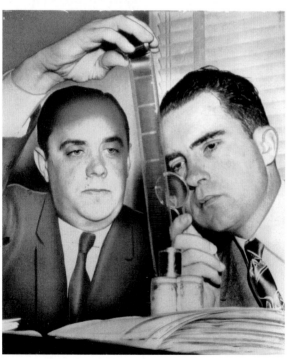

Even before Nixon entered the White House, Anderson's exposés were blamed for two of the politician's most humiliating moments: his mawkish Checkers speech in 1952 (*top*) and his angry "last" press conference ten years later (*bottom*). (Both: AP/Wide World Photos)

Anderson is a rat of the worst type	*Anderson is a malicious liar.*
a flea ridden dog	
a scavenger	*venomous & vicious*
lower than the regurgitated filth of vultures	*stinking*
Nothing he writes can be given any credence	*a skunk*
not to be given the time of day	*a jackal*

Anderson rifled through the trash of FBI director J. Edgar Hoover (*top*, with camera), searching for evidence of homosexual activity between Hoover and his top deputy and inseparable companion, Clyde Tolson (seated). Hoover was enraged by this and denounced Anderson in memos and handwritten notes to subordinates. (Top, AP/Wide World Photos; bottom, Freedom of Information Act request)

Homophobia plagued both Anderson and Nixon. The newsman attempted to "out" Senator Joseph McCarthy and his aide Roy Cohn (*top*), as well as Nixon White House advisors H. R. Haldeman and John Ehrlichman (*bottom*, seated). In turn, President Nixon ordered his staff to smear Anderson as gay. (Top, courtesy of D.C. Public Library, Star Collection, © Washington Post; bottom, National Archives)

Anderson unabashedly thrust himself into the political fray, flaunting top-secret government documents at news conferences (*top*) and testifying before Congress as an advocate (*bottom*, with his assistant Brit Hume). Anderson's exposés led to felony convictions of senior Nixon administration officials in what proved to be a dress rehearsal for the Watergate cover-up. (Top, AP/Wide World Photos; bottom, courtesy of D.C. Public Library, Star Collection, © Washington Post)

"And I demand to know the idiots who've been leaking those papers to Jack Anderson!"

By 1972, Anderson's revelations about President Nixon and his national security advisor, Henry Kissinger, had catapulted the columnist to nationwide prominence. (Top left, © Universal uclick; top right, © TIME, Inc.; bottom, © The Courier-Journal [Louisville, Ky.])

Nixon operatives G. Gordon Liddy (*top*) and E. Howard Hunt (*bottom*) plotted to assassinate Anderson. They conducted surveillance of the newsman's house to find the best way to break in and met with a CIA physician to find a poison that wouldn't be detected in an autopsy. Hunt said the order to eliminate Anderson came from White House counsel Charles Colson, whom Hunt believed to be operating under instructions from President Nixon. (Both: © Bettmann/Corbis)

surmised that "Anderson told him if he 'confessed' he would go to jail."

On the evening of December 21, President Nixon received a personal briefing on the Anderson investigation. The conversation was secretly recorded on Oval Office audiotapes.

Ehrlichman explained that investigators "were able to pinpoint that there was really only one place in the whole federal government where all of those documents" that Anderson published "were available. That was here in the Joint Chiefs of Staff liaison office" right inside the White House.

"Jesus Christ," the President exclaimed.

Ehrlichman went on to describe Radford's role in the operation over the past thirteen months: "He has access to everything from State, the Pentagon, National Security Council, everywhere else. And he just xeroxed this material for Anderson. There's no question."

"Can I ask how in the name of God do we have a yeoman having access to documents of that type?" the President inquired.

"Well, he's the key man," Ehrlichman replied. "He's the fellow that, that typed" up the secret memos in the first place, and as a result had access to "contingency plans, political agreements, troop movements, behind-the-scenes politics, security conferences going on between our government and foreign governments . . . This sailor is a veritable storehouse of information."

Nixon marveled at the betrayal: "If you can't trust a yeoman in the navy, I don't know goddamn who can you trust?"

Attorney General John Mitchell informed the President that "the yeoman served in India. He married his wife in India."

"Oh, he's pro-Indian?" Nixon asked. "Well, then, he did it."

The President added that "this young son of a bitch" must also have been Anderson's source of classified documents about Vietnam earlier in the year: "They had to *all* come from him! I don't mean just this but I mean previous" secret files as well. Ehrlichman assured the President that the Plumbers were "running down now all these columns for the last thirteen months to determine whether or not there's any relationship" to Radford.

But despite their certainty that Radford was Anderson's informant,

Nixon's advisors cautioned the President that the deceptively innocent-looking yeoman was proving a slippery target. "He handled his interrogation . . . just the way a pro[fessional] con man would," Mitchell noted, "very cool. [He said], 'Well, this is all circumstantial.'"

"Yes," Ehrlichman agreed, "he's very bright and very precise and [said] . . . 'I'm here to answer any questions you gentlemen have.' . . . This guy was trained." Obviously, by Jack Anderson himself.

It all reminded the President of Alger Hiss, whose testimony was also "too perfect," Nixon believed. The President paraphrased how Hiss tried to finesse his answers to investigators a quarter century earlier: " 'I can't, to the best of my recollection, recall.' 'To the best of my recollection, I do not remember.'" "This guy is exactly the same," Ehrlichman observed.

The next day, the President switched from worrying that Radford was another Hiss to a more contemporary foe. "He's another Ellsberg," Nixon feared. "That's the thing that concerns me." "Except that he probably knows a hell of a lot more than Ellsberg," Haldeman replied. "Yeah," the President concurred, "he *really* knows more . . . because he's been in on hard-core things . . . In terms of [other] documents that have been leaked . . . we can't be sure for the past thirteen months whether *this* son of a bitch didn't do it!"

The real problem, Nixon said, wasn't Radford but the columnist who had befriended him: "This son of a bitch Anderson really knows how to work us."

"He does," Ehrlichman agreed. "He's a master."

"He has more people around this government than, I guess, anybody has ever had," Mitchell said. "Far more than Drew Pearson ever had."

"Got more out of 'em," too, the President observed. "I think we better check everybody that Anderson knows and talks to."

"It's the hidden guys like this, who bootleg stuff to him, that we just stumble onto occasionally, that we've got to root out," Ehrlichman added.

The more Nixon thought about Anderson's source, the angrier he became. "That Radford," the President exclaimed, "the culprit who turned this crap over to Anderson . . . goddammit, leaking it, that son of a bitch should be shot! He has to be shot!"

The next day, Ehrlichman proposed a less violent way to handle the yeoman: dispatching a trusted high-ranking Mormon officer who worked at the Pentagon to try to extract a confession from Radford, including "whether Anderson has been blackmailing him or paying him." The designated Mormon official agreed to warn the sailor that his conduct was "gross in the eyes of the Church" and that he must "make a clean breast" of his sins and "cooperate fully" with the government. But Nixon vetoed the plan. "Those Mormons" who worked with Radford, the President decided, "are really turning out to be a bunch of scabs."

Initially, the President believed that Anderson must have bribed Radford to get him to leak classified documents. But Nixon soon came up with a more astounding explanation: homosexuality—a double-barreled blast that would simultaneously discredit both the obstreperous columnist and his source. The President concluded that "there is no apparent motive for this fellow turning these papers over to Anderson" unless they were gay lovers, Ehrlichman said.

It was a ludicrous notion on its face. Between them, Anderson and Radford had fathered seventeen children and each would remain married to the same wife for more than forty years. As members of the Mormon church—"one of the more puritanical religions on the planet," as Anderson put it—the two men were not only teetotalers, they did not smoke or even drink caffeine, let alone have homosexual trysts. "It's comical," Radford said later of Nixon's homosexual explanation. "It's embarrassing."

Nonetheless, on the evening of December 21, the President phoned Ehrlichman to inquire: "Is [the] yeoman [a] deviate?" Ehrlichman wrote the question down in his calendar, along with Nixon's recommendation: "Further interrogate." Nixon also contacted White House aide David Young to see "if there was any homosexual angle in Radford's relationship with Anderson." Young replied that "Radford was somewhat effeminate in his manner" and the President "directed that this be explored—especially in regard to Anderson." The next morning, in an Oval Office meeting with top advisors, Nixon announced that "after sleeping on it," he had decided to instruct investigators to find out whether the relationship between the columnist and the yeoman was, as Nixon indelicately put it, "sexual up the ass."

Attorney General Mitchell was carefully noncommittal, only mumbling, "Mm-hmm."

The President plunged ahead, once again harking back to the Hiss case, which was exposed by his gay accuser, Whittaker Chambers. "Hiss and Chambers, you know, nobody knows that, but that's a fact how that began," Nixon recalled. "They were both—that way."

"Mm-hmm," Mitchell mumbled once again.

"That relationship sometimes poisons a lot of these things," the President explained.

"Homosexuality destroyed" the Greeks and Romans, Nixon had lectured his aides a few months earlier: "Aristotle was a homo. We all know that. So was Socrates. You know what happened to the Romans? The last six Roman emperors were fags.

"Now, I think Anderson—I'm just guessing—but if there's any possibility of this, John, that can be key." After all, Radford "may be under blackmail" to Anderson.

Ehrlichman obediently offered to "slide into" the topic of homosexuality during the yeoman's next scheduled interrogation. "You never know what you're going to find," the President pointed out.

The next day, White House aide Young summoned Pentagon investigator Stewart to the Plumbers' office in the basement of the Executive Office Building. There, Stewart said, Young ordered him to interrogate Radford "at once" in order to "establish" that he had a "homosexual relationship with Anderson." Young "told me he wanted me to develop and prove that there was a homosexual relationship between Jack Anderson and Radford," Stewart recalled.

The Defense Department security agent was no friend of Anderson: for nearly a year, Stewart had relentlessly used interrogations and polygraphs in an effort to track down "traitor" Anderson's sources and stop that "bastard" from publishing classified information. Nevertheless, the Pentagon investigator refused the order to delve into Anderson's sex life. Stewart complained that the White House had instructed him "not to see what might be there, but to ensure that I found a homosexual relationship. When I said I wouldn't do it, Young got mad. 'Damn it, damn it, the President is jumping up and down and he wants this and we're always telling him everything can't be done. The President is mad at us and we're telling him it can't be done.'" Stewart said that Young was so upset that he, too, literally jumped up and down: "This came from the President. It's the President's order." But Stewart refused to budge and his Pentagon supervisors backed him up; Nixon's order to investigate "homosexual tendencies," said Stewart's boss, was just too "far out and ridiculous" to pursue.

Ehrlichman called Defense Secretary Melvin Laird to complain—and secretly recorded the conversation. The Pentagon chief pointed out that "there's nothing to indicate homosexuality" and argued that if Radford invoked his Fifth Amendment right against self-incrimination and "goes out and tells the press that that's what we're running here, I think we just get in a hell of a lot of—we blow the lid."

But Ehrlichman countered that the Chief Executive was adamant: "The President has instructed me to go on this."

"On the homosexuality?" Laird asked incredulously.

"Yes sir, he certainly did," Ehrlichman responded. "It was his idea."

Laird warned that "this will be an embarrassment for the President" and that it would be a public relations disaster "to break [in the media] on the basis of this guy refusing to answer questions on homosexuality."

"Mel, I see your point," Ehrlichman responded, "and I appreciate the hazard that you're suggesting and I will take it up with the President."

Nixon, however, would not back down. He quizzed aides about hooking up Radford to a polygraph "to check on a possible homosexual angle" and instructed Attorney General Mitchell to be sure investigators were "tailing Anderson" and "surveilling [Radford's] house to see whether Anderson's still calling." The fact that the reporter continued to meet with the sailor even "after he knew that [we] were onto him," Mitchell observed, "would indicate that Anderson has a pretty strong hold on this boy."

Two days later, Ehrlichman recommended "keeping [Radford] under surveillance in the hope of catching him in bed with Jack Anderson sometime." The President approved the plan.

So the Plumbers followed orders and doggedly investigated Anderson's sex life. Young interrogated Radford with "an obsessive line of questioning that had to do with homosexuality," according to a government official who saw the still-classified transcript: "I got the impression that, well, maybe they felt this would explain the kid's [motivation]."

Young and Ehrlichman also zeroed in on the subject of homosexuality while interrogating Radford's commanding officers, suggesting that the yeoman's "best friend" in the Pentagon was "quite effeminate" and that "Anderson might have a handle on him" because of "sexual deviation." One navy supervisor was astonished by the suggestion: "Homosexuality? Oh, absolutely not. And I think that after nearly 30 years in the navy of watching men at extremely close range that I could spot them." Said another of Radford's commanding officers: "Chuck is not the big manly type or anything, but nine-tenths of the navy yeomen are that way. Who else wants to be a typist?"

Finally, Defense Secretary Laird made a special trip to the White House to meet with the President and persuaded him to withdraw his written request for "one more polygraph" of Radford about "homosexual relations." But Nixon's staff continued to investigate whether "any homosexual activity" occurred between Anderson and the yeoman. The President's sexual obsession was "bullshit," Laird later said, but Nixon got "carried away" and "wanted heads to roll" no matter what.

In some ways, the Nixon administration's probe of Anderson's sex life was poetic justice. After all, over the years the muckraker himself had investigated allegations of homosexuality involving Haldeman and Ehrlichman, J. Edgar Hoover, Joe McCarthy, and aides of Ronald Reagan. Still, Anderson actually published only what he could document, and he lacked the coercive power of the state to wiretap, polygraph, or jail his targets.

In the end, of course, Nixon's men found no evidence of homosexuality by Anderson or his source. But the fact that the President himself had ordered government agents to investigate such intimacies demonstrated just how far Nixon was now willing to go in pursuit of his quarry. Indeed, in the basement office of the White House Plumbers, operatives posted the name Jack Anderson on a cork bulletin board to inspire them on against their foe, who had assumed the role of a kind of Nixonian public enemy number one.

Meanwhile, the interrogation of yeoman Radford continued. Ultimately, investigators did extract a confession, but not the one they expected. The navy clerk eventually admitted that he had been spying on the White House but claimed that he was doing so not for Jack Anderson but—amazingly—for the Pentagon's Joint Chiefs of Staff, which distrusted Nixon and Kissinger for their clandestine foreign policy initiatives. In all, Radford said, he stole more than five thousand pages of highly classified documents, secretly removing them at night from interoffice envelopes in the White House mailroom and from "burn bags," the contents of which were supposed to be destroyed. On one trip with Kissinger to New Delhi, the stenographer stated, he grabbed so many secret files that his suitcases could not hold them all, so he sent them back to Washington by diplomatic pouch, tightly sealing the envelopes and marking them on the outside with a concealed code to ensure that nobody tampered with them. Radford even admitted swiping documents from Kissinger's briefcase while they were flying together aboard the presidential airplane, Air Force One.

The yeoman insisted that he was operating at the behest of his supervisors in the Defense Department, to whom he turned over the purloined papers. He said Pentagon higher-ups repeatedly complimented him on his efforts and provided him with shopping lists of what records to steal next. The sailor also stated that his superiors showed him how to cover his tracks by removing telltale signs from the filched documents that might give away their espionage operation. "Be careful," Radford's commanding officer warned, "and don't get caught."

In the Oval Office, Ehrlichman informed the President and his top advisors of Radford's incendiary allegations. The yeoman "turned out to be, in effect, a reverse agent," Ehrlichman explained, working not only for Anderson but also "for the Pentagon inside" the White House. Ehrlichman reported that Radford admitted that he "has systematically stolen documents out of Henry's briefcase, [out of] people's desks—anyplace and everyplace in the [White House] he could get his hands on—and has duplicated them and turned them over to the Joint Chiefs."

The President was alarmed but also wondered if Radford had concocted the story to try to wiggle out of trouble for leaking to Anderson. Nixon instructed Ehrlichman to interview the yeoman's military superiors to see if his claim could be verified.

The next day, Radford's commanding officer, Admiral Robert Welander, was summoned to Ehrlichman's third-floor office in the West Wing of the White House, directly above the Oval Office. A bulky audio machine with a giant spool of tape sat on a coffee table between the two men, a large microphone sticking out from its stand to record the interview. Initially, the admiral tried to blame his typist for the spying. But under Ehrlichman's deft questioning, Welander corroborated and expanded upon Radford's "extraordinary account of his career as a thief in the employ of the nation's military commanders," as Ehrlichman later put it. The admiral confirmed that his assistant had "surreptitiously" pocketed "important and significant" paperwork—including crumpled rough drafts and discarded carbon copies—from trash bins and burn bags at the White House. Welander acknowledged that he not only knew about this pilfering but personally directed Radford to target sensitive records intended for the President's eyes only, such as confidential minutes about troop withdrawals from Vietnam and notes of Kissinger's clandestine meetings with Chinese premier Chou En-lai. Welander even admitted that he carefully hand-delivered these purloined files to his boss, Admiral Thomas Moorer, chairman of the Joint Chiefs, and then locked them in a special Pentagon safe outside Moorer's office. "I'm obviously not happy about having to relate that," Welander confessed, because it was "very personally embarrassing to me and I think it could be potentially embarrassing to Admiral Moorer."

Moorer's involvement greatly increased the gravity of the scandal. The chairman of the Joint Chiefs was a hard-liner who opposed Nixon's withdrawal of troops from Vietnam and disparaged Kissinger as being soft on Communism. Was Moorer's spying part of a larger military cabal to thwart the policies of America's civilian leaders?

Less than an hour after securing Welander's confession, Ehrlichman rushed to brief the President in the Executive Office Building. Moorer's deputy "confirms practically everything that the yeoman testified to," the White House aide announced. "I would say that there's no question that this yeoman was encouraged" to go through wastebaskets and fish out whatever documents he could find.

"And they knew that he was stealing from Kissinger?" the President asked.

"Oh, they *had* to!" Ehrlichman replied. "They had to."

"Jesus Christ!" Nixon exclaimed.

The President was especially aghast that Radford had taken documents out of Kissinger's briefcase during flights aboard Air Force One. "I've got stuff in my briefcases that are—that, that I don't think that [anyone] should ever see," Nixon said. "Never. All my notes and things, you know. Things you just think about and then discard . . . Oh my God."

The Chief Executive was incensed by Admiral Welander's betrayal: "Can him. Can him. Can him. Get him the hell out of here."

Nixon and his advisors now began to question who else was involved in this military spy ring. They were particularly suspicious of Admiral Elmo Zumwalt, the blunt-spoken naval commander of the Joint Chiefs, who had complained that his men were needlessly put at risk by the President's sudden decision to send a navy armada to the India-Pakistan front. "Zumwalt was the recipient of some documents" stolen by Radford, Ehrlichman informed Nixon, and Attorney General Mitchell agreed that "Zumwalt was involved" in the spying as well. The Joint Chiefs were all "a bunch of shits," the President decided, and Zumwalt was "the biggest shit of all."

Nixon also wondered about General Alexander Haig, who worked as Kissinger's deputy but who kept close ties with the Joint Chiefs. Widely regarded as the Pentagon's man in the White House, Haig was also known to inform his old military colleagues about sensitive matters that Kissinger tried to keep hidden. "I am afraid that Haig must have known about this operation," the President thought. "It seems unlikely he wouldn't, he wouldn't have known." Nixon pondered what to do. "Is Haig wiretapped?" the President asked. "Why not?" Haldeman responded, suggesting that a tap on Haig might be a good idea. "It's not going to hurt anyone at all," Mitchell agreed. "We can do that." "I would do that," Nixon instructed. Haig "knows damn well something's going on," the President realized. "The fact that we're not talking [to him about it], see, it's gonna worry him more [than a direct confrontation]. I think the strategy is to let it simmer [so] everybody [will] worry . . . Just let it rot."

Nixon concluded that the entire affair was "a federal offense of the highest order," nothing less than a Pentagon "espionage system" with the military "setting up their own Gestapo" and "spying on the President." Attorney General Mitchell agreed and thought it raised the "specter of [a] military takeover."

"If it was in a movie, you wouldn't believe it," Nixon marveled.

The President and his advisors wondered if the leak to Anderson originated with the military command itself.

They "*knew* he knew Jack Anderson," Ehrlichman pointed out.

"Who?" Nixon asked.

"Both [of Radford's navy superiors] knew that he had a social relationship with Jack Anderson" well before his exposés were published, Ehrlichman clarified.

"It's almost as if they, they meant to do something," Haldeman observed.

"That's what I fear," the President agreed.

"The Joint Chiefs," Haldeman said. "Think of that story."

Nixon thought about it and did not like the implications: "Now wait a minute. Now wait a minute. I'm suggesting that it was Moorer [who has responsibility for the] Anderson column. It's possible, right?"

But in the end, the President's men determined that Moorer had not authorized the leak to Anderson. After all, passing classified documents to the newsman would have needlessly jeopardized the Pentagon's espionage operation. Haldeman pointed out that any possible benefit from Anderson's exposés would have been "a poor substitute" for the unfettered access the navy clerk was already providing the Joint Chiefs.

Simply put, the military had "trained" Radford in "how to steal," White House aide Young concluded, "and he stole"—first for the Pentagon, then for Anderson—until it all spun "out of control." Ehrlichman decided that Radford's espionage for the Joint Chiefs had preconditioned the yeoman so that he likely "didn't feel too badly about turning this stuff over to Anderson because [he already] was a spy" and probably regarded "the morals involved in one [a]s about the same as the other." Thus "Anderson's cultivation of the boy" meant "that both the Joint Chiefs and Jack Anderson were beneficiaries of Radford's rummaging in Henry's files and wastebaskets."

Clearly, Moorer would have to be confronted about his culpability in the spying. Attorney General Mitchell volunteered for the delicate task. The nation's top law enforcement officer phoned the chairman of the Joint Chiefs and told him to "get his ass over to the Justice Department," as Mitchell later put it. Moorer duly showed up in the attorney general's office and did not deny that the spying took place but tried to blame his underlings for it. Mitchell concluded that "Moorer was up to his eyeballs" in the espionage.

But what should be done about it? One option, the President realized, would be to "use this as a device, of course, to clean out the Joint Chiefs." Nixon's Justice Department could even file criminal charges: "Prosecuting is a possibility for the Joint Chiefs," the President allowed. "Now I have to think about it." Yeoman Radford, "obviously, could be court-martialed" for his spying, Ehrlichman pointed out, or "given immunity" in exchange for his testimony against higher-ups. "Could we put him under some kind of arrest?" Haldeman asked. "We could," Attorney General Mitchell replied, but Ehrlichman interrupted: "This is a little bit like trying to catch a skunk." Nixon agreed: "That's right. Exactly right."

The President seemed more focused on going after Jack Anderson than after the military officers engaged in espionage. "Let me ask this first," Nixon said. "Is Anderson guilty of anything?"

"Yes," Mitchell stated.

"What?" the President wondered.

"He's guilty of possession of these documents."

"Can we really prosecute?" Nixon pressed.

"You can prosecute him—not for the publication but for the possession" of classified papers, the attorney general replied.

Haldeman was enthusiastic. "We certainly have Anderson," he declared.

The President ordered his staff to investigate what laws Anderson may have broken. Young put together a memo reporting that "our favorite columnist" could be charged with theft of government property. "For obvious political reasons, I am not advocating the above at this time," Young wrote; but if convicted, Anderson could be "imprisoned up to 10 years. The Statute of Limitations under this statute is 5 years."

Still, Nixon was not optimistic. "The only two guys who can prove it are the source and Anderson," the President told his advisors. While they could "bring Anderson in [to testify], I think everybody agrees that would be a fatal mistake—you can't bring a newsman in [without generating a media backlash]," Nixon said. The most likely way to nail Anderson, Nixon thought, was "to prosecute this bum [Radford]." If convicted, perhaps the yeoman would then implicate Anderson to avoid prison. But unless Radford confessed that he "stole the Anderson papers," any case against him would be strictly circumstantial. "We cannot prove it because we have no witness," the President recognized. "The only witness is Anderson"—who, of course, was far too savvy to incriminate himself or his source: "We know he did it. We know no one else could've done it. But that cannot convict a man in a court of law." To stop Anderson, Nixon instructed his aides, "you've gotta find something [else]" on him or "you just gotta invent something."

Vice President Agnew urged Nixon to introduce legislation to make it easier to imprison journalists who published classified documents. "One piece of information, revealed by a Jack Anderson" could "blow the cover of an important operative," Agnew argued. The President was sympathetic but worried about the political fallout: "We can't be in the business of prosecuting the press . . . prior to an election," Nixon told his Vice President. "I can definitely assure [you], though, that if we survive, it will be done." Agnew was glad to hear it. "Anderson [is] on television every day," the Vice President lamented. "We've gotten lambasted on this issue."

For his part, the columnist loudly welcomed prosecution by the administration. Anderson believed he would defeat any criminal charges brought against him, and that a legal ruling in his favor would expand press freedom. He also understood that asking to be indicted made good theater and helped keep his name in the headlines. Perhaps, too, the muckraker thought a little reverse psychology might persuade the White House to back off. If so, he was mistaken.

"I'd love to take that bastard Anderson" and prosecute him, the President reiterated.

"Well," Attorney General Mitchell replied, "if there's any way we could do it, we would."

"I would," Nixon emphasized.

"Not with this one" case, Mitchell added, "but—"

"Maybe find some others," the President suggested.

In the meantime, Haldeman argued, Anderson's source had to be stopped from inflicting further damage. "I can see you can't arrest him, you can't prosecute him, you can't take overt" action, Haldeman conceded, but "isn't [there] something you can do to bottle him up?" Nixon agreed that the yeoman should be kept "under wraps" to avoid a public scandal: "I think he's got to be told that a criminal offense hangs over him, that it's going to hang over him . . . to scare the son of a bitch to death!"

But the attorney general was concerned that "Jack Anderson and some of these friends that have gotten to Radford" are "telling him not to worry because he's got the upper hand with all the information he has [about] the Joint Chiefs participating in this." Indeed, the wily Anderson began using the news media to deliver precisely that message to the White House. "If my sources were identified, it would embarrass the administration more than it would me," Anderson told the *National Observer*. "It would make a very funny story." The columnist sent out similarly unmistakable threats during interviews with CBS News and the NBC *Today* show. "If the Government points a finger at my sources, they're pointing a finger at themselves," he warned *The Washington Post*. "If they want to finger them," he repeated to *The New York Times*, "they're going to wind up with bubble gum all over their faces."

In essence, Anderson was effectively blackmailing the President of the United States: if Nixon attempted to go after the newsman or his source for revealing the India-Pakistan papers, Anderson would reveal the far darker secret about the Pentagon espionage ring.

The President's men got the message. "Anderson would obviously know what [Radford] was doing, and how he was [spying on them]," the attorney general told the President. So "if you start opening up on Anderson—assuming you did make the case, turned [Radford], give him immunity and so forth—then Lord knows where this is going to lead to. . . . because he's going to come out with a story about the military espionage ring. Nixon concurred: such a story by Anderson "blows the Joint Chiefs right out of the Pentagon, through the roof of the Pentagon."

The President realized his options were limited. "The real sad thing is that the real culprit is Anderson," Haldeman said. "And we do not [do] a goddamn thing about him."

Ehrlichman proposed that Charles Colson, the hard-nosed White House aide, contact the columnist and "say to Anderson: 'Look, we've got the goods on you. You've printed top-secret material. You've suborned a yeoman to theft. There are violations of federal statutes. And we're [going to] forbear to prosecute you. But we just want you to know we know . . . You've made your fatal mistake and we've got you.'"

Nixon liked the idea but suggested that the threat be delivered instead by Murray Chotiner, his take-no-prisoners political advisor who had wrestled with Anderson for two decades. Haldeman thought Chotiner a good choice because he was now technically a private consultant and not directly on the administration payroll. That "keeps it" away from the White House but "would give Anderson the worry without the certainty" that the President was behind it. Ehrlichman amplified on his plan. "Just have Murray come in and say, 'Jack, I just think you ought to know—'"

"'—that they've got the goods on you,'" Haldeman interjected.

"'They've got the yeoman and—'" Ehrlichman added.

"'—he's confessed,'" Nixon embellished. "'He had a polygraph.'"

The Oval Office erupted in laughter at the thought of finally getting Jack Anderson. But then the President had second thoughts. "The son of a bitch, Anderson," Nixon realized, "he'll be very likely to write *that* story . . . that 'I was approached by Murray Chotiner and he tried to blackmail me.'" Which of course is exactly what Anderson would have done.

The White House plan to blackmail Anderson—in retaliation for Anderson's blackmailing the White House—was dropped.

In any case, the President still had other blackmailers to contend with. Admiral Welander, for one, was now threatening to blow the military espionage case "out of the water" by implicating higher-ups in the spying if he was charged with wrongdoing. Admiral Moorer was potentially even more dangerous. The chairman of the Joint Chiefs of Staff was an Alabama native and close friend of Governor George Wallace, whose presidential candidacy three years earlier had nearly cost

Nixon the White House. With November's election just ten months away, the President could not risk alienating right-wing voters by having a public falling-out with Moorer and Wallace.

Attorney General Mitchell, who managed Nixon's presidential campaign in 1968 and would do so again in 1972, warned his boss that "if you pursued it by way of prosecution of Moorer or even a public confrontation," it would directly pit "you against the Joint Chiefs." The law-and-order prosecutor unabashedly advised a cover-up: "I think that the important thing is to paper this thing over."

"Hmmph!" the President snorted.

But Nixon, always desirous of appearing tough, risked looking weak and ineffective if it came out that the Pentagon had spied on him. In an election year, the political fallout from such a public scandal could be devastating. In addition, disclosure of the military spy ring risked unraveling other administration scandals, especially the White House Plumbers' secret criminal activity.

The President pondered what to do. "If you go after Radford," Defense Secretary Melvin Laird argued, "you have to go after everyone else" in the Joint Chiefs of Staff who was involved in the spying as well, with wholesale court-martial proceedings and a huge national scandal. Ehrlichman agreed: "I lost more sleep [agonizing] on what to do with this guy. And I have finally come to the conclusion that you can't touch him."

Ultimately, Nixon came to the same conclusion: "The Joint Chiefs, the military [are] not to be viewed as our enemy. We cannot have it." The President decided his advisors were right to recommend covering up the scandal: "[We] can't let it get out." Not that Nixon was happy about it. "See, what we're doing here is, in effect, excusing a crime," the Chief Executive realized. "So it's a hell of a damn thing to do."

The final result, Haldeman wrote in his diary, was "a monumental hush-up all the way around" as the President's aides followed his orders to "sweep it under the rug." In effect, the military was able to cover up its espionage against the White House by blackmailing Nixon the same way Jack Anderson had.

At a news conference, the President announced, "We have a lot of circumstantial evidence" about Anderson's source, but it was not "ade-

quate to take to court. You can be sure that the investigation is continuing." In fact, it was just the opposite: no criminal investigation was
under way even though the evidence of criminality—by the military's
spies, not Jack Anderson—was substantial.

Kissinger, not surprisingly, was apoplectic: at the military's spying
on him, at the Anderson columns that exposed his duplicity, and at the
failure of the White House to punish those responsible. By his own account, the national security advisor was "beside myself . . . indignant . . .
[and] enraged" upon learning that the Pentagon had targeted him for
espionage. "Moorer should be in jail," Kissinger insisted. But Nixon
dismissed the idea out of hand; it is "the most ridiculous thing I can
think of," he said, "just *ridiculous!*" What mattered wasn't justice, the
President argued, but damage control: "The main thing is to keep it
under as close control as we can . . . We've really just got to keep the
lid on it." Kissinger literally stormed back and forth in the White House,
shouting in anger about Nixon and the Joint Chiefs: "They can spy on
him and spy on me and betray us and he won't fire them!"

The President tried to calm his volatile national security advisor.
"You see, ·Henry, if you were to throw Moorer out now," Nixon said,
"the shit's gonna hit the fan. And that's gonna hurt us. Nobody else.
We get blamed for it." Besides, the President pointed out, there were
also benefits to this strategy: "Henry, you gotta realize that for better or
worse, Moorer is still the chairman of the Chiefs. You gotta deal with
that. *He will carry out what you want.*"

In other words, Nixon and Kissinger could now blackmail Moorer
into supporting their policies just as he had effectively blackmailed
them into covering up his espionage operation. So the President let
Moorer know that "we had the goods" on him, Ehrlichman said. "After
this, the admiral was preshrunk." In subsequent weeks, the White
House took advantage of the scandal to wrest concessions from the
newly pliant chairman of the Joint Chiefs. Ironically, the Pentagon spying on the White House had boomeranged to Nixon's benefit.

Radford, too, had learned to wield blackmail to his advantage,
threatening to "get counsel and call their bluff." Federal investigators
feared that "if Radford got a lawyer, we were through." Defense Secretary Laird phoned the White House. "This damn yeoman [is] getting

cockier than hell," he warned. "Do you have a specific proposal for what to do with him?" Ehrlichman asked. "I'd send him someplace . . . where he'd be relatively innocuous," but where we "could keep an eye on him," Laird replied. Someplace where Radford would not have access to classified documents that could wind up in Jack Anderson's hands. Ehrlichman agreed: Radford should be told that for "national security reasons, you're not being prosecuted. But at the same time, you're going to be under constant surveillance, and the first minute you step out of line, the roof is going to fall in on you" because "the Anderson thing will send you up forever."

Three days later, Radford received a phone call from the Pentagon informing him that he was being transferred to a navy base in Oregon. His family was given just a few hours to pack their belongings, so little warning that the yeoman had to rush to burn any remaining incriminating paperwork before a moving van arrived at their home.

In the end, the President wrote in his memoirs, Radford was "a potential time bomb that might be triggered" at any moment and it was simply "too dangerous to prosecute the yeoman." Pentagon investigator Stewart put it more bluntly: Radford had Nixon "by the balls."

It was a Washington merry-go-round of blackmail: Radford, Anderson, Welander, and Moorer could each expose the military spy operation if Nixon tried to go after them. The President in turn could prosecute each of the men if they dared go public about the scandal. The end result was an uneasy balance of mutually assured destruction. Meanwhile, Nixon blackmailed the Joint Chiefs into supporting policies they would have otherwise opposed. "Finding out what you can and using it to your advantage," Radford said with disgust, "that's what that cesspool was all about. Washington was nothing but a big fester[ing] sore."

In a rare moment of self-awareness, the President realized that it was his own secret scheming that had started it all. "Damn, you know, I created this whole situation—this, this lesion," Nixon confessed. "It's just unbelievable. Unbelievable." But he soon reverted to blaming his adversaries for the problems of his own making. "There have been more back-channel games played in this administration than any in history," the President conceded, but only "[be]cause we couldn't trust the goddamn" bureaucracy.

"The thing that disgusts me about this," Ehrlichman said of the military spy ring, "if they'll do that—"

"What else are they doing?" Haldeman interjected.

"Yup, yup, yup, yup, yup," Nixon agreed.

"The worst thing about it," Haldeman pointed out the next day, "is that you start getting paranoid, and you start wondering about everything and everybody, and—"

"I know," the President affirmed.

"—you figure you can't—"

"But don't be too damn sure of anybody!" Nixon exclaimed. "Don't be too damn sure about anybody!"

10

CAT AND MOUSE

By January 1972, Jack Anderson's source had been exiled to a military base in Oregon with the threat of criminal charges hanging over his head. As a result, President Nixon boasted, "there were no further leaks" about India-Pakistan.

But Anderson continued his siege by publishing more classified government documents unrelated to India or Pakistan. On January 6, the newsman embarrassed the President while he met with Japan's prime minister by exposing secret White House briefing papers that warned of potential Japanese rearmament. HAVE CHECKED OUR FILES AND FIND THAT ANDERSON ARTICLE CONTAINED ACCURATE QUOTES, the U.S. ambassador in Tokyo cabled Washington. The Embassy was GREATLY DISTRESSED by the EXTENSIVE COVERAGE of Anderson's story and warned that diplomatic initiatives might be JEOPARDIZED. The next week, Anderson published columns revealing "secret cables" about American duplicity in Cambodia, "classified cable traffic" on bickering between Israel and the United Nations, and "secret" administration plans to cut troops in Europe. "Congress and the American people should not have to get their information on such important questions through the newspapers," Republican senator Clifford Case objected. According to a top CIA official, "If these security breaches continue, we will have to limit severely the distribution of sensitive intelligence information."

Still, Anderson's security breaches continued. He revealed "secret cables from Saigon," a "suppressed study" on wasted foreign aid, "classified reports" of global anti-Americanism, and "intelligence reports" about

U.S. battle failures. "I continue to get documents," Anderson announced, "and I'll continue to publish them because I believe that it is in the public interest to do so."

The public interest was not the muckraker's only motive. "I wanted to put out stuff from other sources to muddy the waters," Anderson later acknowledged, to camouflage the identity of his key informant, Yeoman Charles Radford. Legman Les Whitten spread word that the "Merry-Go-Round" now "had a great volume of material flowing in as a result of Anderson's notoriety," and a White House aide worried that "we might be in a for a real flood of disclosures of [a] damaging nature." But Pentagon investigator W. Donald Stewart carefully tracked the latest Anderson columns and found that they were based on old documents that had already passed through Radford's hands before he was transferred out of Washington. Stewart correctly concluded that the columnist was continuing "to publish data to make us believe we [had not caught] his source." Anderson "milked these leaks for about three months," Admiral Elmo Zumwalt said, "sometimes repeating quotes, sometimes fuzzing up that he had merged messages" from different records, to prevent the detection of his informant. Intelligence analysts meticulously dissected Anderson's reporting and traced seventy-three of his columns to classified documents that Radford had handled. CIA director Richard Helms assured fellow spies that he had "established where Anderson got this group of papers" and "action has been taken to see that it doesn't happen again . . . You [have my] assurance that this is not a running sore. It has been cauterized."

Once again, Anderson's columns were more politically embarrassing than militarily sensitive. But in one case, the Nixon administration charged that the newsman jeopardized an important covert operation by reporting that the United States bugged "the most private conversations of Kremlin and other world leaders." The columnist wrote that Pentagon eavesdropping established that Soviet premier Alexei Kosygin "is in poor health," that President Nikolai Podgorny was serviced by a masseuse named Olga, and that General Secretary Leonid Brezhnev "sometimes drinks too much vodka and suffers from hangovers." Anderson did not divulge that the American operation was code-named Gamma Gupy or, more important, that the information was gleaned from mobile Russian limousine phones: "For obvious security reasons," he wrote in his column, "we can't give a clue as to how it's done."

Nonetheless, the Nixon administration publicly asserted that Anderson "blew our best intelligence source in the Soviet Union." The muckraker insisted that the Russians already knew their phone conversations were monitored and the Justice Department soon publicly confirmed that fact. But CIA director Helms told Anderson that Soviet leaders sometimes seemed to forget about the eavesdropping and had resumed talking on their car phones; as a result, the columnist agreed not to publish any more articles that might remind the Kremlin about the bugging. Still, despite Anderson's cooperation, Nixon's men continued to claim that the reporter endangered national security, and embellished the details over time. "As the direct result of an Anderson story," Nixon operative G. Gordon Liddy charged, "a top U.S. intelligence source abroad" was tortured or killed. No evidence was ever produced to support such an outlandish assertion. But it would soon become the rationale for a White House plot to assassinate Anderson.

Meanwhile, the President worried what other secrets the muckraker might reveal. Her father "had been shaken" by Anderson's classified disclosures, Julie Nixon Eisenhower remembered, and it "contributed to the feeling of vulnerability in the White House and the determination to prevent future breaches of security." Nixon was particularly concerned about Yeoman Radford. "The P[resident]'s been doing a lot of thinking since this blew on the Anderson papers," White House chief of staff H. R. Haldeman wrote in his diary. "Anderson's guy also has the dope on" secret negotiations in Paris that Henry Kissinger had been conducting for the past two and a half years with the North Vietnamese. "It's a time bomb," Nixon believed, and the "worst way for this to come out is via Anderson with his distorted view."

To head off Anderson, the President decided to publicize the talks himself. In January 1972, in a speech televised live to the nation, Nixon dramatically revealed the clandestine meetings even while acknowledging that they had been unsuccessful. "There was never a leak," the Chief Executive declared proudly, "because we were determined not to jeopardize the secret negotiations." As usual, the news media swallowed the White House line—Nixon's "amazingly well-kept secret," *The Phoenix Gazette* reported, "should surprise Jack Anderson"—but some administration officials were baffled about why the President suddenly decided to make the failed talks public. "I wouldn't do it," Nixon confided privately, "except for the . . . Anderson Papers." In the words of one administration official: "They were afraid that Jack Anderson was going to scoop them."

At the same time, White House officials began a charm offensive to try to put the Anderson revelations behind them. The President's PR advisors urged Kissinger to trot out gags from comedian Bob Hope at an upcoming Washington Press Club dinner. Kissinger agreed and duly amused reporters with what he called "Teutonic jokes" and satirical yarns "on [the] Anderson papers." Nixon himself put in a cameo at the banquet and made fun of Kissinger over the Anderson leak. It went over so well that the President repeated the trick two weeks later at a news conference, although he ruined his joke by awkwardly explaining it afterward—and then immodestly congratulated himself for having kept his "good humor."

Privately, however, Nixon and his men were as humorless and vindictive as ever. "I would like to get ahold of this Anderson and hang him," Attorney General Mitchell said.

"Goddammit, yes," the President replied. "So listen, the day after the election, win or lose, we've got to do something with this son of a bitch."

"I would," Mitchell agreed.

"The statute of limitations [for prosecuting Anderson] won't have run [out], will it?" Nixon pressed.

"Won't have run [out] at all," the attorney general advised.

"He's guilty as hell, isn't he?" Haldeman asked.

"No question about it," the nation's chief law enforcement official answered.

Word of the President's decision quickly spread through the White House. "Lay off Anderson [for] now and tell all our people," Nixon instructed Ehrlichman. "We'll prosecute Anderson and the rest of them after the election."

But there was no need to wait until after the election to begin gathering evidence against the columnist. Administration aides explored setting up a covert operation to open Anderson's mail, but FBI officials convinced the White House that such a move would be "too risky." Attorney General Mitchell suggested wiretapping the newsman's phone but the President refused to approve that plan either. According to journalist Seymour Hersh, "Nixon apparently feared that Anderson's contacts inside the FBI were so extensive that he would be tipped off about a legally authorized wiretap" and might learn of additional illegal taps ordered on others: "Nixon's fear of Anderson—of what he knew, or could learn, about the workings of the White House—was acute." So the President and his advisors instead decided to monitor Anderson indirectly through his source, Yeoman Radford. "Nixon was really very interested in pinning the whole thing on Anderson," Ehrlichman explained.

The attorney general contacted Deputy FBI Director W. Mark Felt, the source later immortalized as "Deep Throat," who had investigated bogus allegations of White House homosexuality trumped up by Anderson two and a half years earlier. This time, Mitchell informed Felt that "Anderson had planted an informant" inside the White House and that "the President was gravely concerned over this . . . security breach." Because the leak "was unquestionably related to national security," Nixon wanted the FBI to spy on Radford. Felt warned Mitchell that physical surveillance of the yeoman "might be very dangerous because if Radford became aware of [it and told] Jack Anderson, even more damaging columns could result." Wiretaps, however, were less likely to be discovered and were soon installed at Radford's home and office and at his stepfather's house. At the same time, the Pentagon secretly planted an informant to work alongside the yeoman and spy on his activities.

No judge or court authorized the warrantless taps of Anderson's source—the attorney general was careful not to put his order in writing—but FBI memos justified this departure from the law based on "the necessity for maintaining the fewest possible records" because of the "obvious" risk that the bugging would be "leaked to Jack Anderson," a danger that was described as "very real and very great." To ensure that the President and attorney general were "advised on a day-to-day basis of developments in this case," agents hand-delivered daily summaries of the Radford taps to the White House and Justice Department inside sealed envelopes.

Haldeman was skeptical that this spying would be useful. Radford "would know that he'd be tapped and he would go use a [pay] phone [and] leave his phone off," the White House chief of staff cautioned. But the President wanted to proceed anyway. "You might get something," Nixon pointed out. "You never know if the guy's smart, and his wife may be dumb enough to make a call and you'll learn a few things."

Sure enough, FBI director J. Edgar Hoover soon discovered that "the first person [Radford] called following his arrival on the [West] coast was Jack Anderson." Ehrlichman reported the preliminary results of the FBI's investigation: "On the telephone Radford had sounded very worried" and "got a little code worked out" with Anderson using pseudonyms and trusted intermediaries to signal when to speak on a safe, predesignated line. "And so they hang up and [Radford] goes off and uses a pay phone and calls Anderson." The wiretaps, one investigator concluded, "did, in fact, reveal a rather close and somewhat surreptitious relationship between Radford and Jack Anderson."

Still, this was circumstantial evidence only, not enough to convict either the troublesome columnist or his source in court. Nixon's men never uncovered the one action that might have led to successful prosecution of Anderson: his secret payment to Radford of several thousand dollars. The administration did know that the yeoman was pressed for money and that to supplement his income he worked part-time at other jobs, including as a newspaper deliveryman, a drugstore clerk, and a $2.10-an-hour security guard. Radford's "checking account has never been over $100" and was frequently overdrawn, federal investigators found, and he owed several thousand dollars to various creditors, including the J. C. Penney department store. Yet the yeoman suddenly acquired money and a new car, according to his commanding officer. "The only place Radford could have gotten the cash," his navy supervisor believed, "is from Anderson." But the federal government, with all its investigative might, was never able to prove it.

Decades later, Anderson confided what happened: the sailor called Anderson's parents and told them about his financial difficulties. In turn, Orlando and Agnes Anderson relayed the conversation to their son. The columnist already felt guilty about Radford's troubles. "He was naïve and I took advantage of him," Anderson confessed. So the newsman phoned the yeoman. "I'd like to help you but I can't give you any money because it would be misinterpreted and it would hurt you more than me," Anderson explained. The navy clerk mentioned that he owned some undeveloped land in California located on a cliff over-looking the Pacific Ocean. Anderson had no interest in purchasing the property but to help Radford agreed to buy it anyway, sight unseen, for nine thousand dollars. To avoid the appearance of bribing a source, Anderson used his best friend from high school as a middleman to keep the newsman's name off the property deed and thus hide the deal from prying eyes. "It was really a payoff," the columnist admitted a few months before he died. "I could argue it wasn't a payoff but it really was."

President Nixon and his men never uncovered Anderson's "payoff" even though they maintained their tap on Radford's phones for more than five months. Had they discovered the secret transaction, they might have tried to indict Anderson for bribery and conspiracy. Instead, hapless government investigators were forced to listen in on the Radford family's phone conversations, day after day, week after week—and still they came up empty-handed. The administration finally discontinued this eavesdropping two days after Nixon's men were caught bugging the Watergate office building. "At that point," John Ehrlichman recalled, "Nixon decided to hang it up . . . The thing was just too touchy."

In early 1972, the Nixon administration escalated its war on Jack Anderson. Besides warrantless wiretapping and homosexual smears, the President's men also dispatched CIA operatives to spy on the columnist. Under the law, the CIA was explicitly prohibited from domestic spying. Yet that is exactly what it did in a massive and illegal covert operation against Anderson code-named "Project Mudhen," named for the swamp bird that digs in the dirt and squawks when it's angry.

CIA officials began the operation by dusting off their old files on the newsman. A 1967 CIA report described him as "opinionated, self-righteous, ambitious and highly envious (therefore belligerent) toward anyone in a position of power, especially 'Establishment' types." Another memo stated that "ANDERSON's politics are not known; however, it is generally conceded from most sources that he is a 'first-class liar.'" To update its findings, analysts put together a new twenty-five-page study of the journalist, gathered from public records by officers using "assumed names" because of "the extreme sensitivity of this case and the requirement that under no circumstances" should Anderson "be alerted to this inquiry." This CIA profile did not improve on earlier ones, mixing factual inaccuracies with unverified gossip in an unintentional parody of semiliterate bureaucratic nomenclature. Anderson "exhibits a flamboyant attitude and personal appearance" and "conducts his professional activities in an overt manner," CIA spooks wrote:

> [His] column and writings are of the exposé, sensationalistic, muckraking variety . . . He readily admits to being a publicity seeker and is apparently basking in the focus of attention which has come his way as a result of his recent disclosures . . . He eludes [sic] to a network of informants which he says he does not pay . . . [who] will conceivably continue to provide him with classified material when they (sources) feel so inclined.

Much of this "intelligence" was patently ludicrous. For example, operatives reported that "it is thought" that Anderson has "connections with unidentified officials of the *New York Times*," a wholly unsurprising fact given his twenty-five-year career as a Washington journalist. "That must have been my paper boy," Anderson later laughed.

In January 1972, the CIA began physical surveillance of Anderson. The agency dispatched a team of sixteen undercover officers in eight different vehicles—equipped with two-way radios, binoculars, and telephoto lenses—to conduct their spying around-the-clock. Intel-

ligence analysts assigned "operational cryptonyms"—aliases—to refer
to the "Merry-Go-Round" staff. Thus teetotaling Anderson's CIA code
name was "BRANDY," secretary Opal Ginn was dubbed "SHERRY,"
and young legman Brit Hume was called "EGGNOG." The spies put
together black briefing binders filled with photos, neighborhood maps,
and auto license plate numbers of their targets. In February, the CIA
rented a room high up in the Statler Hilton Hotel, across the street
from Anderson's office, to watch and photograph the comings and go-
ings of the newsman and his informants; ironically, it was located just
around the corner from the Sheraton-Carlton Hotel, where Anderson
had conducted his own electronic eavesdropping fourteen years earlier.
The mudhens had come home to roost.

Over a period of three months, operatives recorded the movements
of the Anderson family and staff in voluminous detail:

- January 13: "On most days, BRANDY goes to bed at approximately 0200 hours and awakes at approximately 0730 hours."
- March 4: "12:05, Subject and spouse enter the RENWICK
  Art Museum . . . 13:06, Subject and spouse depart gallery . . .
  Spouse goes to a newspaper dispensing machine. She apparently has trouble and spouse assists."
- March 20: "08:45, Subject's spouse and two children depart
  house in Plymouth [auto], heading in direction of school.
  17:00, Two unidentified Negroes depart office of subject."

What did the CIA learn from its surveillance? That Anderson is a
"somewhat careless driver and often violates speed limits and related
traffic procedures." Meanwhile, his reporter Les Whitten "operates his
personal automobile in a fast, impatient manner and will deviate from
normal routes in order to avoid minor traffic delays," while his legman
Joe Spear was "maintaining a rather routine pattern of professional
activities." ("In other words, we were boring as hell," Spear complained
upon reading his file. "I kind of felt bad about that. How do you explain
to your buddies that your own CIA spied on you . . . and concluded you
were boring?") The government operatives stalked the columnist to
restaurants where he ate lunch, radio and television studios where he

taped broadcasts, and universities where he delivered speeches. The spies sat and listened to the columnist's lectures on the First Amendment, duly noting in one surveillance report that their nefarious target "concluded his discourse by declaring that our government is the best in the world."

At one point, CIA officers followed and filmed Anderson as he was being followed and filmed by a television crew from the CBS program *60 Minutes*. The undercover spies shadowed the muckraker and his entourage while Anderson was interviewed in front of a range of visual backdrops at the White House, Pentagon, Justice Department, and U.S. Capitol. "The caravan of cars going from place to place must have made quite a ring-around-the-rosy," Anderson realized later, "with me in the lead, the CBS crew tailing me, and the CIA bringing up the rear."

In one particularly madcap scene, CIA spooks bugged their own boss, Director Richard Helms, as he lunched with Anderson and asked the columnist not to publish details about U.S. eavesdropping on Kremlin telephones. The meeting was Helms's idea, not Anderson's, but paranoid CIA operatives decided that the muckraker might secretly record it: "There is documented evidence (e.g., the . . . Sherman Adams case) that BRANDY has previously engaged in audio operations" and had recently been spotted "in possession of portable recording equipment." Why the newsman would even want to tape Helms in the first place was never spelled out. After all, a conversation in which the notoriously taciturn intelligence chief urged Anderson not to publish government secrets did not promise significant newsworthy disclosures. Nevertheless, the overactive CIA posted two teams of undercover operatives in a restaurant while other agents spied on Anderson's reporters to make sure they didn't engage in "counter-surveillance." "There was no explanation as to why [my staff] might spend their lunch hour taking pictures of me eating with Richard Helms," Anderson later wrote, but "Helms was rigged with sophisticated electronic equipment capable either of detecting or neutralizing my non-existent recording device. A CIA technician, I understand, manned the dials in a nearby mobile unit or hotel room." Afterward, the spies congratulated themselves on preventing any possible mishaps. But none of it helped the

CIA with its ostensible objective: shutting down the journalist's access to classified documents.

For more than a month, Anderson and his staff were oblivious to the surveillance, but in late March, one of the newsman's neighbors noticed some suspicious "loitering" in the parking lot of a church on a nearby hilltop. "Men in heavy coats carrying binoculars and cameras would emerge from their cars and study something off in the distance," Anderson learned. "My friend naturally [became] curious about what they were watching. After they had driven off one evening, he strolled over to the parking lot and looked out across the landscape. Below, in full view, was my house. He hurried back home and gave me a call." Suitably warned, Anderson "began keeping an eye on the rearview mirror. Sure enough, I noticed my car being tailed, awkwardly and conspicuously, by a series of other cars." Anderson experimented with speeding up and slowing down, but the autos—especially a distinctive yellow sedan—always reappeared.

Who was doing the spying? Anderson had irritated so many different branches of the government—the White House, the Pentagon, the FBI, the IRS—that the reporter had trouble narrowing the list of possible suspects. Indeed, it did not even occur to Anderson that the CIA was behind the surveillance because he naïvely believed it was following the law that restricted the agency only to foreign operations. Instead, Anderson focused on Assistant Attorney General Robert Mardian, who was conducting his own investigation of the columnist, separate from the CIA probe. Anderson decided to give Mardian "a taste of his own medicine." The muckraker assigned a college intern to track the prosecutor the same way Anderson was being shadowed. "This junior reporter tailgated Mardian wherever he went, staying conspicuously at his heels, occasionally whipping out a notebook and dramatically scrawling notes in full view of his prey," Anderson recalled. "If there is garbage on the doorstep," the intern was told, "make sure Mardian sees you going through the garbage." The assistant attorney general contacted the FBI and the ubiquitous Mark Felt quickly discovered that the culprit was Jack Anderson. It was the "same as going through [FBI director J. Edgar Hoover's] trash," Felt told Mardian. The columnist explained his strategy to another reporter: "If Mardian's investigating me, I'm going to investigate him."

Eventually, Anderson traced the license plates of the vehicles that had been tailing him and discovered that he was being tracked by the CIA, not the Justice Department. So the muckraker decided to turn the tables on the intelligence agency in a similar manner. "What the CIA didn't know," Anderson said, "was that I had my own trained spooks at home, nine of them"—Anderson's children—"plus their sundry teenage friends, all with time on their hands and spring fever."

Anderson turned his "Katzenjammer Kids" loose on the CIA operatives. "We drove around to where they were," Anderson's son Kevin, then fifteen years old, remembered. "We pulled up behind them and blocked them in" with our cars. "We started taking pictures and they put on their sunglasses and pulled up newspapers to block their faces." Twelve-year-old Tanya Anderson went "right up to the window" of a CIA surveillance van to take photos. "They called in another car," she said, and it came "screeching behind us, trying to pin us in." So her sister, eighteen-year-old Laurie, drove "over the lawn and jumped the curb and the next thing you know we're in a high-speed chase through the neighborhood." Tanya then climbed in the backseat and started taking more photos of the CIA spies with her 35-millimeter camera. "When they saw me taking the pictures, they screeched off," she said. "They'd been totally busted," Kevin recalled gleefully.

The Anderson children reveled in the excitement. They dressed up to look like their father—complete with overcoat, hat, and briefcase—to lead the CIA agents on wild-goose chases. On one occasion, the teenagers all gathered together and suddenly climbed into several different parked cars and "took off in a hurry in different directions" all at once for no reason "other than to harass these guys," Kevin remembered. Even Anderson's wife, Olivia, joined in. "It got to the point where sometimes you just flashed your lights" at the spies, "and we'd all go by and wave at them," she said. "I was having as much fun as the kids were."

The CIA operatives were not amused. "On 27 March 1972 at 0915 hours, an unidentified female . . . approached two of the surveillance vehicles . . . [and] took photographs from her vehicle of both surveillance vehicles," officers reported. "All units were withdrawn from the area." Six days later, while following the Anderson family to church, the undercover spies noticed that "two young females seemed to be staring at the surveillance vehicles and one surveillance unit reported that the two females waved at them." The operatives deduced that this was "a further indicator" that the Anderson family "may be becoming 'surveillance conscious.'" The next day, CIA spooks observed a woman "copying down the license number of the surveillance vehicle." Intelligence officials decided to end the operation in Anderson's neighborhood but continue spying on his downtown office. The columnist now "appeared extremely 'tail conscious,'" agents noted. "He kept looking around, sideways, behind his shoulder, and his gait was slower than usual."

By April, the CIA gave up: "The surveillance operation failed to establish the existence and/or identity of any individual who might have been supplying Anderson with classified government data," analysts concluded.

Anderson lampooned the "CIA farce" in his column. "Trained to skulk around the bazaars of the Middle East or the backstreets of Moscow snooping for intelligence to make the world safe for democracy," he wrote, "my CIA shadows were dunking donuts and sipping coffee in a church parking lot in suburban Washington and taking pictures of my yard full of bicycles." Anderson joked that "all those cops back there, tripping over their night sticks but gaining on me," had succeeded in keeping his "menopausal quirks and temptations . . . on the straight and narrow." The muckraker delighted in recounting how his children "outclassed" the CIA "in style and stealth, if not in electronics . . . The CIA could no longer stand this game of cat and mouse, especially when the mice were having so much fun." His taunt to the intelligence agency: "Watch out, CIA! The kids on my block are ready for you."

"It was high, mocking theater, and Anderson won the publicity war hands down," a *Washington Post* journalist wrote. "But at the time, there was no guarantee he would win his battles with the Powers That Be, and Anderson showed real nerve, even bravery, in his zealous crusades against the outrages of Nixon and his minions."

In truth, Anderson actually took the CIA surveillance quite seriously, and filed a lawsuit against the government for violating his privacy. As a result, the CIA was ordered to release many of its files and allow Anderson's lawyers to question intelligence operatives under oath. In turn, CIA director Richard Helms was forced to testify that he had personally authorized the spying even though it was "not general policy" for the CIA to investigate reporters. Helms stated that "so many" classified documents had "fallen into the hands of Mr. Anderson's office" that he "felt it incumbent" to try to plug the leaks. Indeed, according to the CIA's security director, Helms requested that surveillance reports on Anderson "be brought to his attention immediately on a daily basis." Who was behind such a high-level decision to have the CIA violate the law? "I *don't recall* any instructions or injunctions from the White House" to target Anderson, Helms testified. "I *don't recall* ever having discussed [it] with President Nixon." "Bullshit!" Anderson later exclaimed in an uncharacteristic burst of profanity. "It was clear he was lying," said the columnist, who sat in on the Helms deposition.

The muckraker was not alone in his belief that the Nixon White House was behind the illegal spying. Such surveillance, one author observed, was "the sort of operation that would have been anathema to the usually cautious Richard Helms." Certainly President Nixon had a stronger motive to stalk his longtime nemesis than did the CIA director, who had a reputation for prudence and aversion to publicity. To those who knew Helms, it was unthinkable that he would take the risk of such a politically dangerous and unlawful assignment without the President's personal authorization.

In any case, the CIA surveillance was more effective than the government realized. Years later, when Anderson reporter Les Whitten obtained a copy of his CIA file under the Freedom of Information Act, he was shocked to see a surveillance photo of himself with one of his best sources. Yet administration sleuths never understood what their own files revealed. "These guys were nothing but a bunch of cheap, lousy, unimaginative, dumb thugs!" Whitten exclaimed. Indeed, the fact that Anderson's teenage children were so easily able to thwart the covert operatives charged with protecting American interests only underscored the larger incompetence of the CIA, whose repeated intelligence failures would continue into the twenty-first century.

In the meantime, President Nixon's fury over his failure to stop Anderson intensified. And as the muckraker continued his exposés, the White House escalated its plans for retaliation.

II

BROTHERS

Richard Nixon and Jack Anderson shared more than mutual contempt, hardscrabble childhoods, and slash-and-burn histories. Both were also shadowed by jealous ne'er-do-well younger brothers who created embarrassment trying to cash in on the reflected glory of their siblings' fame and power.

Donald Nixon first came to public attention during the disastrous Howard Hughes loan scandal of 1960. Nearly a decade later, with his brother at last in the White House, Don boasted that he would "make a million in the next four years." He began his quest even before Richard took office when he checked into a luxury Washington hotel and forwarded the bill to the government. Yet as White House aide John Ehrlichman acidly noted, although Don "surely tried," he "lacked the wit to reap the benefits of being a Presidential brother." In an earlier era, Ehrlichman realized, Don "might have been a patent-medicine salesman or a carnival barker." Instead, "he was the modern equivalent, a 'consultant.'" Not that Don had any true expertise to offer, but as the President's brother, he was suddenly presented with a multitude of lucrative business opportunities. "Don could not admit to himself that the reason people were cultivating him, giving him cars and money, was that he was Richard Nixon's brother," Ehrlichman observed. "When Don's abilities were taken into account, whatever they gave him to do would be nothing but a sham." What Don lacked in ability, however, he made up in his unbridled sense of entitlement. He "clearly resented" Richard's success, Ehrlichman believed, and "would often complain to me about the countless hardships he suffered" as a result; his open "bitterness at his lot in life" was obviously because he "had spent a lifetime in the shadow of Richard the superachiever."

So the President's brother once again turned to the one patron who never let him down: Howard Hughes. The opportunistic billionaire, ever eager to sink his tentacles deeper into the Nixon family, did not disappoint, and dispatched an aide to befriend the needy presidential sibling. "Having gone through the Donald Nixon loan scandal during the 1960 presidential campaign," Hughes aide Robert Maheu recalled wearily, "I thought I had seen the last of" the President's brother. But soon Don Nixon and Hughes became involved in bogus mining claims, stock deals with mobsters, and vacation junkets paid for with Hughes money. Addicted to "playing the big shot," Ehrlichman wrote, "Don could not stay away from the flame . . . often to Richard's acute private embarrassment."

The President tried to keep an eye on his brother by assigning Ehrlichman to be his handler. Don was summoned to the White House for questioning about whether he was once again pocketing money from Hughes. "His denial to me was so loud and red-faced that I felt intuitively he was lying," Ehrlichman said. He delivered a "sermon" to Don to "get off the gravy train at once, leave [Hughes] alone and lead a life of quiet rectitude" by dropping all "phony consulting jobs having business with the Government."

The President didn't believe his brother's denials any more than Ehrlichman did and decided to have federal agents tail Don to find out what he was up to. "I don't want to use Hoover," Nixon told Ehrlichman, because "he can use it against me. See if the CIA will do it." But, unlike with Jack Anderson, where a national security rationale, however implausible, could at least be asserted, the CIA refused to undertake such a patently illegal personal errand as spying on the President's brother. Nixon turned instead to the Secret Service. Under the guise of protecting the President, his bodyguards tapped Don's phones and conducted surveillance on him.

Twice a week, the White House received written reports on Don's activities and quickly ascertained that he was indeed lying about his involvement with Hughes. Secret Service wiretaps disclosed that Don, once again in financial trouble, was plotting some "really big deals" with Hughes and other government contractors. The electronic bugs also revealed that the President's brother tried to use his connections to promote a Las Vegas casino. Most troubling of all, the dreaded Jack Anderson apparently knew about these machinations: federal agents observed the newsman dining with a top Hughes aide, who turned out to be a secret source of Anderson's. The columnist also bribed a hotel bellman to supply copies of Donald's phone messages during his visits to Washington.

The President was understandably worried about a scandal. "Nixon never forgot that I was the one who had uncovered the [1960 Hughes loan] story," Anderson said. "He also never forgot that his brother could get him into trouble." White House tapes show repeated conversations between the President and his staff about his brother's chicanery— and Nixon's fear that Anderson would once again expose it. "Don must not get any money" from Hughes or any other government contractors, the President told his aides; the risk of Anderson once again uncovering such impropriety was simply too great.

To try to keep Don out of trouble, the White House embarked on a search to find the President's brother a job, something safely lucrative with low visibility. Nixon instructed Ehrlichman to approach Republican businessman J. Willard Marriott, founder of the world's largest hotel chain, and explain the delicate problem. To "protect the President's interests," Nixon told Ehrlichman, "Marriott should be asked to hire Don" to keep him from trying to peddle his influence elsewhere. The hotel magnate agreed to "carry Don on the Marriott payroll," Ehrlichman reported back, but only "if the President personally asked him to." Nixon complied with the request and Marriott took on the Chief Executive's hapless brother as a corporate vice president.

But Anderson soon learned about this make-work job because he and Marriott were both part of Washington's tight-knit Mormon community. Soon, the columnist persuaded Marriott that his new employee should grant Anderson an interview. Ehrlichman rushed to the Oval Office to inform the President that his brother had agreed to talk to the muckraker the very next day.

"Jesus Christ," Nixon exclaimed, Don was just "so stupid." The President understood what his naïve brother and Marriott did not: that the scandal-prone Don could be dangerously malleable in the reporter's experienced hands.

"These Mormons are all nuts," the President declared. Ehrlichman didn't disagree, but pointed out that "Marriott claims to have some kind of influence on Anderson."

"Bullshit!" Nixon exclaimed; the newsman was obviously feigning sympathy to get access to Nixon's unsophisticated brother. "See, Anderson is a smart son of a bitch," the President added.

White House chief of staff H. R. Haldeman concurred: "Anderson plays both sides."

"That's right," Ehrlichman now echoed. "He's very opportunistic." Clearly, the dim-witted Don would be no match for Anderson's wiles.

The President pondered it all. "That poor Don," Nixon muttered. He pounded his fist on his desk, then lowered his voice to a near whisper: "Son of a bitch." Don "knew that, after all, Anderson and [Drew] Pearson were partners," Nixon marveled. More than that, they "were snakes! You don't talk to 'em!" the President repeated, incredulous at his brother's foolishness.

After consulting with Attorney General Mitchell, the President concluded firmly that we "cannot allow Don to see Anderson under any circumstances." Nixon's men had their marching orders. But the White House soon learned of what Haldeman called "the latest horror story" involving the President's brother. "E[hrlichman] discovered that Don had *already* talked to an Anderson reporter who he thought was just a personal friend" of a Hughes advisor, Haldeman wrote in his diary. "So [Don] spilled a whole bundle of stuff to him, which Anderson is going to run in a series of three columns starting later this week. Don now knows this and that's why he feels he has to see Anderson."

Indeed, after Anderson found out that the President's brother was "again sniffing around the Hughes trough," as the columnist put it, he dispatched one of his anonymous legmen to infiltrate Don's circle in California. Posing as a potential investor, Anderson's reporter George Clifford cultivated the President's brother and successfully maneuvered himself into position to overhear Don informing Hughes's staff that they "owe me" a lucrative contract. Ehrlichman hurried to the President's Executive Office Building hideaway office to brief him on the alarming news.

"Jack Anderson . . . sent a reporter out to the [West] coast and Don had talked to the reporter [that] Anderson had [dispatched]," Ehrlichman told Nixon.

"Oh shit," the President replied. "I just wonder how Don could be that dumb," Nixon added. "I try to keep the son of a bitch out of all kinds of trouble, but he had an unerring ability to "go out and make an ass of himself."

The President pondered the ramifications. "Doesn't this make it imperative that I not see him?" Nixon asked. "Yeah," Ehrlichman concluded; damage control now trumped familial obligations. The President sighed. "Anderson has it all," Nixon realized, and that meant "Anderson can use it" in his column.

Well, perhaps it might not be as bad as they feared. According to Ehrlichman, Marriott told Anderson that the White House had carefully "admonished Don not to have anything to do with any piece of business that involves the government" and that "anything Don did that was improper was on his own."

"That could be the solution," the President decided. "You know, to be fair," he added, "that's a legitimate story. Goddamn Don." Nixon had to admit that Don was indeed "throwing [my] name around." Perhaps a negative "Merry-Go-Round" column would force the presidential brother to behave.

Donald didn't see it that way. "I'm gonna sue the bastards," he vowed. "They keep writing about the Hughes loan [so] I'm gonna sue them."

"Don, you're not gonna sue anybody," Ehrlichman lectured the President's brother. "You're gonna keep your head down and lie low."

The strategy worked. In February 1972, newspapers around the country published Anderson's article about President Nixon's "irrepressible brother" and his "weakness for fattening foods and easy money." After yet another reprisal of Don's 1960 financial scandal with Hughes, Anderson wrote that Nixon's brother had once again "incorporated himself and [begun] selling shares to citizens who might have an interest in his blood line." But the columnist ended with an unexpected conclusion: this time, the President was determined to keep his brother "out of hot water" and prevent "any new embarrassments" by making sure that Don "avoid deals that might reflect unfavorably" on the White House. "I want to be sure that Don has no dealings with the federal government" and "is never asked to do anything that would embarrass this office," the Chief Executive was quoted as saying.

The White House was pleasantly surprised to find itself vindicated by its journalistic enemy. Marriott's personal connection to Anderson seemed to have made the difference after all. For once, Richard Nixon was portrayed in the "Merry-Go-Round" as the victim rather than the villain.

Jack Anderson's uncharacteristic empathy for President Nixon's brotherly difficulties was rooted in one of the most painful and little-known parts of the columnist's life: his own problems with an envious younger sibling who also tried to capitalize on his older brother's influence and celebrity. Gordon Anderson was seven years younger than Jack, the baby of the family and the favorite of their volatile father, with whom Jack had so often clashed. In the early 1950s, the youngest Anderson son followed Jack to Washington and unsuccessfully tried to imitate his success by becoming a reporter. Jack suggested that Gordon try another, more suitable line of work, but Gordon resented what he regarded as his older brother's patronizing advice. One night, Gordon called Jack on the phone, drunk and cursing. For the first time, Jack said, "I realized that this kid hates my guts." It was the beginning of a fraternal feud that would last the rest of the brothers' lives.

Over the years, as Jack became more famous and feared, some of his targets put Gordon on their payrolls in the hope of neutralizing his brother's exposés. Gordon actively solicited these offers by promising favorable treatment in the "Merry-Go-Round" in exchange. "Jack was very upset that Gordon was trying to use his name to make a buck, just like Donald Nixon," Anderson's legman Jack Mitchell recalled. "Jack feared that his enemies would use it to attack and destroy him." Anderson resorted to warning employers that they would receive no investigative immunity by hiring his brother. In fact, he said, it was just the opposite: "Merry-Go-Round" coverage would become more critical just to demonstrate that Jack couldn't be compromised. Gordon was inevitably fired when his bosses learned the unpleasant truth. He accused Jack of brotherly betrayal.

Gordon turned into the black sheep of the Anderson family, a thrice-divorced gambler and alcoholic who was jailed for vagrancy, stole money from his parents, and became estranged from his children. At one point, the FBI investigated Gordon for extortion after he allegedly made "threatening telephone calls" to a boss "indicating he would be written up in the newspaper" in his brother's syndicated column. Eventually, Gordon grew so jealous of Jack that he threatened to hire a hit man to assassinate him and openly talked of kidnapping and killing Jack's children and grandchildren. When the columnist visited Utah, where Gordon had returned to live, police had to provide armed protection. Jack called his hateful relationship with his brother "the saddest part of my life." It was one of the few subjects that could reduce the hardened newsman to tears.

Although Jack Anderson had sympathy for the President's brotherly woes, the columnist remained distrustful as ever of Nixon's relationship with Howard Hughes. After "a flurry of Administration favors" for the billionaire, Anderson wrote in an unpublished manuscript, "I had established to my own satisfaction, though not yet to my lawyer's," that the President was once again "on the take" from Hughes. To try to get more information, the newsman published what he later admitted were "puff items for the column that praised Hughes," designed "to keep the channels greased" so that Anderson could acquire more important and incriminating information about the President himself.

Sure enough, the reporter soon learned the identity of Nixon's secret "personal emissary" to Hughes: Charles G. "Bebe" Rebozo, the President's best friend, a taciturn Florida banker who had been a Nixon confidant for more than two decades. Anderson was excited by this discovery because he recognized that Rebozo—"known for his closed mouth and his handling of . . . private matters for Nixon"—was "just the man to handle money, personal money, money that no one would ever find out about." To the muckraker schooled in the corrupt ways of Washington, the President's best friend had obviously been designated as Nixon's bagman to collect cash from Hughes.

In August 1971, Anderson revealed that Hughes had "siphoned off" $100,000 from his Silver Slipper casino in Las Vegas and had the cash delivered to the President through his "close crony" Rebozo. Although the Hughes gambling money was supposedly intended "for Nixon's campaign," Anderson wrote, none of it was spent for political purposes or disclosed in public records as required by law. "Everyone called it a 'campaign contribution,' but there was no campaign" when the money was delivered, a Hughes biographer later noted, "and Rebozo made it clear that the contribution should be delivered directly to him—in cash—rather than to any campaign committee." The secret transaction, in other words, seemed to be evidence of a crime: at best an illegal campaign donation or untaxed gift, at worst an outright bribe.

Anderson was amazed by Nixon's brazen hypocrisy. By once again covertly taking funds from Hughes, the President was not only "doing what he wouldn't tolerate his brother doing," but also risking yet another financial scandal with the infamous billionaire. This would turn out to be the most important Nixonian slush fund ever, one whose path would ultimately lead to Watergate and resignation in disgrace.

The Hughes cash, one thousand hundred-dollar bills, was stuffed into unmarked manila envelopes and hand-delivered to Rebozo. Nixon's best friend counted the money, then marked the package with the initials *HH*—Howard Hughes—and locked it in a safety-deposit box in his bank. Despite the President's busy schedule, he made time to visit with Hughes's trusted courier right after the money was delivered.

The fact that Anderson learned of Nixon's clandestine payment from Hughes was stunning because both the President and the tycoon shared an obsession for secrecy that bordered on the pathological. But Anderson's network of informants was extensive, his timing impeccable. A few months earlier, Hughes had fired the newsman's longtime source Robert Maheu, who now wanted revenge on his former boss. Maheu would admit that the Nixon cash was indeed designed to "insure favorable treatment by the Administration" and that Hughes "decided to camouflage" the payments by funneling them through Rebozo. Anderson received additional confirmation from Maheu's attorney, another veteran Anderson informant. In addition, Hughes's sensitive handwritten notes were stored in the locked vault of yet another Anderson mole, who shared the incriminating paperwork with the reporter over dinner. "I am willing to go beyond all limitations on this," Hughes wrote, because Nixon would "be deeply indebted" and "recognize his indebtedness." Anderson now had tangible proof for his column.

The revelation of the secret $100,000 Hughes payment would turn out to be Anderson's most significant and far-reaching Nixon exposé ever. Yet, as with so many "Merry-Go-Round" stories, it initially landed with a thud. The muckraker's column "appeared to receive little notice," Senate investigator Sam Dash later remarked, "except at the White House." At first, even Anderson didn't fully appreciate the magnitude of his disclosure. After his one unnoticed column about it in the summer of 1971, he abandoned it for other subjects. Only five months later, when Hughes was back in the news, did the reporter revisit the topic; afraid of being scooped on his own story, Anderson fell back on a familiar tactic: recycling an earlier, unnoticed column by dressing it up with more sensational language to make it appear fresh.

On January 24, 1972, Anderson reported that "we have documentary evidence" that Hughes delivered $100,000 to the President through Rebozo—cash that "was siphoned like a sip of champagne from the Silver Slipper, one of Hughes' Las Vegas casinos," as the columnist later put it. Nixon's "cozy relationship" with Hughes, Anderson declared, "has revived our decade-old revelations about the $205,000 that he loaned to Nixon's brother Don" and does not "make good political advertising in an election year."

This time, Anderson's story produced immediate alarm in the White House, where Chief of Staff H. R. Haldeman closely guarded a file on Hughes that was marked "Top Secret—CONFIDENTIAL." Hours after Anderson's column was published, the President privately cursed "that goddamned Hughes thing." The next day, John Ehrlichman asked the White House counsel, John Dean, to "very discreetly" look into the matter. The President's men also tried to plug the leaks to Anderson. Rebozo phoned the courier who had delivered the manila envelopes filled with Hughes cash, only to discover in horror that the newsman not only knew the go-between's identity but had already called him with a stern warning: "Don't deny it, because I have seen the memo describing this in detail."

In subsequent columns, Anderson expanded his attack and suggested that the Hughes money was nothing less than an outright bribe. "The payments coincided closely with two government decisions favorable to Hughes," the muckraker charged. "President Nixon approved the sale of Air West [airlines] to Hughes" and "the Justice Department reversed an antitrust action which had barred Hughes from expanding his hotel-casino empire in Las Vegas." Anderson's columns "aroused something approaching panic in the White House," one author wrote, and presidential advisors carefully tracked Anderson's investigation to "anticipate any new allegations which might be forthcoming." The Hughes camp was equally concerned. Anderson has "hammered the $100,000 question to death," an aide warned the billionaire, "and there is no sign of a let-up."

The President had special reason to worry. He and his family had already spent tens of thousands of dollars of the illicit money. Senate investigators later determined that Rebozo had paid at least $50,000 of the President's private expenses with cash collected from Hughes and other wealthy patrons: more than $45,000 in improvements on Nixon's two vacation homes, including a swimming pool, golf putting green, and billiard table; and another $5,000 for platinum earrings studded with eighteen pear-shaped diamonds, a birthday present for the First Lady from her husband. In addition, Rebozo confided that he also passed out wads of Hughes's hundred-dollar bills as gifts to the President's brothers and to Nixon's faithful secretary, Rose Mary Woods.

White House aides euphemistically referred to the President's slush fund as the "tin box." "There was much more money in Bebe's 'tin box' than the Hughes $100,000," which was "only part of a much larger cash kitty kept in [Rebozo's] safety deposit box," Haldeman later admitted. "Rebozo, in effect, maintained a private fund for Nixon to use as he wished."

Once again, it was Jack Anderson who exposed the latest Nixon slush fund. Eventually, the President's men would use it to try to cover up their Watergate burglary. But before that happened, Anderson struck again.

12

"DESTROY THIS"

Despite Jack Anderson's pounding attacks, by early 1972 Richard Nixon appeared on his way to a second term in the White House. Indeed, with historic summits scheduled in Peking and Moscow, the President seemed destined to overwhelm his divided Democratic opponents in the upcoming November election. Nixon, however, took nothing for granted. "Remember 1960," he warned intimates. "I never want to be outspent again." He would not be. His Committee to Reelect the President—known by its eerily apt acronym CREEP—raised a staggering $60 million, the largest amount of money that had ever been spent in a political campaign.

Awash in cash, CREEP's full-time squad of "pickup men" who traveled across the country collecting donations were so overwhelmed by the torrent that they were physically unable to gather all the contributions offered. The cash was delivered in envelopes, sacks, and suitcases, and often laundered to hide fund-raising illegalities. Contributors ranged from shady entrepreneurs like Howard Hughes and Robert Vesco to foreign dictators from Iran, Greece, Nicaragua, and the Philippines. Right-wing businessmen such as Richard Mellon Scaife and H. Ross Perot gave large sums to CREEP; so did corporate titans who ran America's Fortune 500 companies. "Anybody who wants to be an ambassador must give at least $250,000," the President told aides. Donations were motivated less by political ideology than business investment, a kind of commercial tithe to grease the machinery of government. Corporations reported brazen White House pressure to pony up for the Nixon "kitty." Those that complied were rewarded; those that did not were punished. Subtlety was not allowed to interfere with success.

One of the most generous donors to the Nixon campaign was the International Telephone and Telegraph Company (ITT), a telecommunications conglomerate whose fortunes were especially dependent on administration decision-making. Under the aggressive leadership of its chairman, Harold Geneen, ITT had become one of the biggest and most powerful multinationals in the world by swallowing up other corporations, including the Sheraton hotel chain, Avis Rent a Car, and various food, building, and parking operations. By 1971, in the largest proposed merger in American history, ITT sought to grow even greater by acquiring Hartford Fire Insurance, although the Justice Department's antitrust division was fighting the move in court. Fortunately for ITT, the President himself personally tracked ITT's business fortunes—and its potential to help his reelection campaign.

"Does ITT have money?" White House chief of staff H. R. Haldeman asked Nixon during one discussion of the conglomerate's antitrust problems.

"Oh God, yes," the President replied. "That's part of this ball game."

Indeed, Nixon met privately with ITT's chairman during a dinner aboard the presidential yacht, the *Sequoia*. Afterward, the President confided to Haldeman that he had overruled his antitrust prosecutors and secretly "cut a deal with ITT" to "give them Hartford, which they badly need . . . Now this is very, very hush-hush and it has to be engineered very delicately." In return, ITT could be counted on to show its financial gratitude. "But it should be done later" to conceal the connection, Nixon ordered. "It should not be right now . . . Nothing done until the deal is over."

Haldeman obediently instructed the President's reelection campaign to "hit Geneen hard" for cash once ITT's takeover was complete. Given "how much benefit Geneen had reaped from the settlement," said White House counsel John Dean, CREEP would not "hesitate to milk" the decision "for all it was worth." Haldeman advised Nixon fundraisers to "work through" Deputy Attorney General Richard Kleindienst, a former Nixon campaign operative, because, as Dean explained,

"Kleindienst would be well acquainted with how much benefit Geneen had reaped from the settlement" and therefore how much money to demand in return.

On May 1, 1971, the Nixon Justice Department began reversing its position so as to allow ITT to acquire Hartford Insurance. On the very same day, Geneen found a way to thank the President for his help: by having ITT donate up to $400,000 to underwrite the upcoming Republican convention, where Nixon would once again be nominated for the presidency by his party. Understandably, the White House and ITT tried to keep the company's donation quiet, but the secret eventually leaked out and a few suspicious minds began raising questions. By the fall, Democratic Party chairman Lawrence O'Brien wondered aloud whether there was any connection "between ITT's sudden largesse to the Republican Party and the nearly simultaneous out-of-court settlement of one of the biggest merger cases in corporate history." Two months later, Jack Anderson wrote pointedly in his column that "the aura of a possible scandal continues to hang over the transaction." But neither the columnist nor the Democrats had any proof to back up their doubts. Anderson later acknowledged that his column was "more rumination than news," written primarily as a "lure" to solicit information from any insiders who might have an urge to talk.

In February 1972, Anderson's lure reeled in a whale of a story—a secret memo from ITT's chief political fixer in Washington explicitly stating that the conglomerate's $400,000 pledge led the Nixon Justice Department to change its mind and approve the ITT takeover. In a "personal and confidential" note typed on ITT letterhead, lobbyist Dita Beard informed her boss that "our noble commitment" of $400,000 "has gone a long way toward our negotiations on the merger eventually coming out as [ITT chairman] Hal [Geneen] wants." Beard added that Attorney General John Mitchell, Nixon's past and future campaign manager, "is definitely helping us, but cannot let it be known . . . If it gets too much publicity, you can believe our negotiations with [the] Justice [Department] will wind up shot down . . . Please destroy this, huh?"

The ITT memo "was the single most incriminating piece of paper I had ever seen," marveled Anderson's legman Brit Hume. The document appeared to offer proof of a corporate bribe, concrete evidence that was extraordinarily rare because such illegal quid pro quos were almost never put in writing. The fact that the memo was dated just four days after ITT secretly sent its check to the Republican Party—eight days after the Justice Department officially agreed to settle ITT's anti-trust case and weeks before either decision was announced publicly—seemed additional corroboration of a clandestine political payoff. "Emerging eight months before the election," one author wrote, the memo "could hardly have been more inflammatory." It was, Anderson said later, "the smoking gun—or, more accurately, a smoking memo, for it was a scorcher."

The scorching memo came to Anderson anonymously through the mail, which was opened by his secretary Opal Ginn, who in turn passed it on to twenty-eight-year-old Hume to investigate. "Holy shit!" Hume exclaimed when he read the document. "It was just unbeliev-able! I showed it to Jack and he said, 'Wow!'" Still, because Anderson did not know who had supplied the memo, he could not be certain that it was genuine; perhaps it was a forgery, a dirty trick designed to en-snare and discredit him. There seemed to be only one way to authenti-cate the document: by getting its author to admit that she wrote it. But Dita Beard, at age fifty-three, was a crusty and suspicious Washington insider whom Anderson feared would never let her guard down around the notoriously dangerous muckraker. However, young Hume's "un-lined, guileless face" and "transparently idealistic and sympathetic na-ture," Anderson believed, might "disarm Dita's fears, arouse her motherly instincts, and encourage the sly old tro[u]per to believe that here was a callow youth she could con." Hume was given the delicate task of get-ting Beard to verify that the memo was genuine and flush out addi-tional details of the story.

Hume carefully planned his approach to the ITT lobbyist. "I ruled out asking her directly if the memo were real," the legman later wrote. "This would make it clear that I didn't know. I also decided against saying I knew it was real, because this might seem an obvious bluff. After all, if I knew it was real, I would have no reason to say so. I didn't want to raise the question of authenticity at all. I knew that if the memo was a fake, she would immediately say so, no matter what I said, and that would probably be the end of it."

Hume met Beard in a conference room at ITT's office in downtown Washington. She was surrounded by public relations officials who were wary of anything having to do with Jack Anderson. Hume reached into the inside of his coat pocket, unfolded his copy of Beard's memo, and slid it to her across the table. She was flabbergasted to see it. Beard didn't deny writing it but stalled for time and excused herself. She went to her office and opened a cabinet, searching for a pink carbon copy of her memo. She returned empty-handed. "My files are a mess," she told Hume. "I can't find anything." Her face filled with apprehension, Beard nonetheless plunged ahead. "All right," she sighed, "what do you want to know about it?" Hume tried to reassure the lobbyist by minimizing the memo's significance, suggesting that he was merely making a routine inquiry and only wanted guidance about the memo's "proper context" so that he didn't write a "misleading" story. The legman went over the document line by line with Beard while she attempted to put it all in the best light possible. But she acknowledged that the handwritten initial at the top of the memo was "my own little 'D.'" "I had to resist the temptation to dance a jig on the table," Hume recalled, "because they had now authenticated the document." Hume made sympathetic noises suggesting that Anderson might not find the story worthy of publication and then departed, trying to hide his elation.

The next day, Beard phoned Hume. "I want to tell you the truth about all this," she said emotionally, and invited him to visit her that evening at home. Hume raced over to her red-brick house in suburban Washington. In an extraordinary two-hour interview filled with alcohol and tobacco smoke, Beard tearfully played "the poor girl role," as she later called it, and begged Hume for mercy. She said that ITT had "ordered" her to either leave town or claim that she "made up" the incriminating passages in her memo. But Beard realized there was no point trying to fool Hume about the authenticity of the document. "I wrote it," she told him once again. "Of course I wrote it." The lobbyist unpersuasively claimed that despite her written words, there was no linkage between ITT's donation and its antitrust settlement. But she admitted that soon after pledging to underwrite the Republican convention, Attorney General Mitchell told her that the corporation could go ahead with its Hartford takeover—and that President Nixon personally ordered his prosecutors to "lay off" ITT.

On February 29, 1972, in what one author called "another Jack Anderson special," the columnist began a four-part series exposing the ITT scandal. Beard's "highly incriminating memo," Anderson wrote, "not only indicates that the antitrust case had been fixed but that the fix was a payoff" for the company's donation. The next day, the muckraker publicly charged Richard Kleindienst, the Nixon administration's nominee to replace John Mitchell as attorney general, with telling "an outright lie" about his role in the case. Kleindienst claimed he had nothing to do with the settlement, which he maintained was "handled and negotiated exclusively" by his underlings in the antitrust division of the Justice Department. But Anderson reported that the attorney general–designate personally held "a half dozen secret meetings" with ITT officials before the litigation was "abruptly settled" on terms "highly favorable to ITT."

A day later, Anderson accused Mitchell himself of "trying to lie [his] way out" of the scandal. Nixon's longtime counselor, who had just resigned as attorney general to run the President's reelection campaign, claimed that he had not known of ITT's contribution while his Justice Department negotiated the antitrust settlement. But the "Merry-Go-Round" quoted two Republican officials who contradicted Mitchell's claim. "Anderson and Hume were aiming their blows at the very heart of the Nixon administration," an author noted, "attacking the integrity of two attorney generals. Both Mitchell and Kleindienst were headstrong political animals: Mitchell, from Nixon's old law firm, had been Nixon's campaign manager" four years earlier as well, while Kleindienst also was "a key organizer for Nixon in 1968."

Kleindienst was horrified by the Anderson columns. "I've got to see Mitchell right now!" he shouted. The older Mitchell was unperturbed. "Nobody is going to believe a bunch of trash like that from Anderson," he said reassuringly. "Forget it." Kleindienst was unmoved and warned that "it's going to develop into the biggest headline scandal you ever heard of—mark my words!"

It was a prophetic forecast. Anderson "lobbed" one ITT "bombshell" after another that "exploded in the Administration's face," White House counsel John Dean recalled. The heart of the problem, presidential aide Charles Colson realized, was the Beard memo, "because it was obviously very damaging on its face." As one writer observed, "Anderson's cluster bomb" not only unleashed "a major public relations disaster" but also exposed "the special treatment government afforded rich, powerful corporations." As a result, said White House communications director Herb Klein, "the news herd was now dashing everywhere."

The journalistic pack was enthusiastically led by Anderson, who helpfully made himself available for media interviews and handed out copies of his astonishing document, which newspapers around the country now published in full. The memo sent "shock waves through the Nixon White House," wrote Bob Woodward of *The Washington Post*, and cast "suspicion over the entire Administration," in the words of Hugh Sidey of *Life* magazine. *Newsweek* declared that Nixon's journalistic "nemesis" had unleashed a controversy that "ballooned into the most far-flung investigatory extravaganza of recent years," with both the White House and ITT "hip-deep together in a bog of political embarrassment." More than one commentator compared it to the Sherman Adams bribery scandal that Anderson had uncovered fourteen years earlier. The "blustery syndicated columnist" who uncovered "skulduggery in high places," *New York Times* reporter Fred Graham wrote, "has had so many big news breaks lately that he has become a newsmaker himself." Indeed, *Time* noted, journalism's "well-known dealer in secret memos" had once again "set Washington buzzing with rumor and speculation," while the "Nixon administration found itself laboring under the shadow of what could be a major image-damaging scandal," leaving Republican officials with "red-faced outrage."

Most outraged of all was attorney general–designate Kleindienst, who believed Anderson had portrayed him as a "liar" and conspirator "in a bribery scheme." Although the Senate Judiciary Committee had just unanimously approved Kleindienst's nomination, he publicly demanded that the committee reopen its hearings. Kleindienst explained privately that "if the record isn't made straight at once, this matter will make the Tea Pot Dome scandal look like a tea party by comparison!" Because he considered himself "very close" to the conservative chairman of the panel, Senator James Eastland, Kleindienst believed his nomination would once again quickly sail through. He "had full confidence that [Eastland] would pat him on the head and say he'd been a good boy, and it's been terrible what these nasty people say about you," Anderson recalled. The Mississippi senator tried to persuade Kleindienst to leave well enough alone, but as Colson put it, Kleindienst "charged off after his honor like Sir Galahad."

Hume worried that Kleindienst might "have an ace up his sleeve" that would undercut the Beard memo and embarrass Anderson during public hearings. The more experienced columnist told his legman to relax. "This is the stupidest thing Kleindienst could have done," Anderson laughed. "It's the best thing that could have happened to us." Indeed, President Nixon himself would later call Kleindienst's decision a "tactical disaster."

That was an understatement. The ITT testimony would turn into what was then the most protracted confirmation hearing in the history of the Senate, twenty-four days of questioning spread out over two months. It would, for the first time, unmask the Nixon campaign's fund-raising crimes and eventually lead to the criminal convictions of the President's senior advisors. Far more than Anderson's previous national security revelations, his exposure of political scandal threatened Nixon where he was most vulnerable. In the end, the columnist realized, the ITT scandal turned out to be "a dress rehearsal for Watergate— same cast, same tactics, same dirty tricks."

At first, Senator Eastland tried to help Kleindienst by stacking the hearings so that only the attorney general–designate and his allies would testify. But Anderson phoned Eastland and asked to be called as a witness as well. "I know you'll want to be fair," the newsman told the Senate chairman respectfully. "I know you don't want to have a one-sided hearing. So I hope you'll let us come and give our side." Beneath his politeness, Anderson acknowledged, was a warning: "What this meant, in translation, was that I was threatening to create a public nuisance and holler 'Foul' if we were refused." Eastland, equally courteous, thanked Anderson for his veiled threat: "Jack, now you understand that I want your testimony. I want you to tell the committee whatever you wish to tell them. Feel free and comfortable and at ease. We're not going to try to block you. But, you understand, we have to follow protocol. We're going to have to hear the government witnesses first."

Anderson "knew immediately" what that meant: Eastland would "save my testimony until the hearings had become back-page news" and the muckraker posed no danger to Kleindienst's confirmation. "Measuring in his wise old way the disruption we could cause as witnesses against the righteous breast-beating we would do if excluded," Anderson wrote, "Eastland decided to let us in the door while reserving the right to seat us at the least conspicuous place at the table and serve us last, after everyone had gone home." Anderson responded to the courtly senator with "an equal dose of saccharine," thanking him for his time and assuring him, "I know you're a fair man." After hanging up the phone, the columnist turned to Hume and pronounced the verdict: "They're going to screw us! But we'll screw them in return because it doesn't matter what they say in the hearing room. What matters is what we say on television and to the reporters."

Anderson began lobbying other senators. Not only did the columnist want to make sure that Eastland kept his promise to allow Anderson's testimony, he also wanted to deliver the same polite threat to Eastland's colleagues to make sure that they would conduct a thorough investigation: "I told senators what I knew, offered assistance, assured them of the growing public indignation my mail revealed, and let them know I had other documents I would make public at the proper time. This was a friendly warning not to jump too quickly to the ITT-G.O.P. side lest they be burned by subsequent revelations." Like his mentor Drew Pearson, Anderson now unabashedly injected himself as an advocate into the political fray.

The hearings began with ringing denials of wrongdoing from both ITT and the Justice Department. But testimony soon revealed that immediately after Anderson's inquiries, the conglomerate destroyed "many sacks" of internal documents in what an ITT manager later admitted was "a goddamn paper-shredding ceremony of monumental proportion[s]." One corporate executive justified the sudden purge of records because "there might have been a lot of others in there like that" Beard memo. Democrats were incredulous. Senator Sam Ervin called ITT's testimony "the worst presentation I have ever heard" in nearly two decades in Congress. "It looks very suspicious and bad," Senator John Tunney agreed. "Brit Hume comes in with an incriminating memo on one day . . . and the next day the documents are destroyed."

ITT's cover-up seemed perfectly reasonable to the Nixon White House. "Hell," Colson told the President, "anybody would go in and tear their files up . . . protecting against Jack Anderson or a leak in their office." But that wasn't how the mainstream media viewed it. "It is perhaps understandable for a company to be nervous at the prospect of having Jack Anderson rooting through its files," *Time* observed, but the testimony by ITT's administrators "left the impression of a beleaguered foreign embassy destroying secret papers on the eve of war." Still, the magazine added, "security precautions in many offices are being tightened because no one knows where [Anderson] will strike next." For his part, Anderson made a show of phoning ITT to offer his assistance. "I told [them] that if they had shredded all their copies of these documents, we'd be glad to let them look at ours," the columnist announced grandly.

To try to help the administration and minimize the impact of the scandal, Chairman Eastland banned television cameras from the proceedings. But this move also backfired. Anderson seized on the captive TV crews waiting outside in the hallway to give interviews filled with righteous indignation about the corrupt Nixon White House. Meanwhile, administration officials and ITT executives who were given an open forum by Senator Eastland brushed past the broadcast journalists. The predictable effect was television coverage as one-sided against the administration as the hearings were one-sided in its favor. "This was a political public relations contest in which Jack and I had no choice but to compete," Hume understood. "Each side struggled to come out ahead in the daily tally provided by the morning headlines."

The Senate hallway was the "perfect stage for Brit of the honest face and innocent eyes," Anderson later wrote of his young legman, whose performance was carefully coached ahead of time by his boss: "I wanted him to appear awed by the process of democracy at work, respectful of the statesmen on the committee, eager to put the truth on the public record. 'Don't give in to your natural temptation to snarl,' I advised him. 'I'll do the snarling. I'm the columnist. You're just a young reporter, concerned about the facts. Stop and reword your statements to find the most correct phrase. You should come across as someone who is so concerned about getting the story straight that you correct yourself as you go. You're simply telling what you saw and heard.'"

White House news summaries recorded the dismal results: on March 3, CBS anchorman Walter Cronkite "said what could be the 'biggest political scandal of an election year' may be developing . . . Reporter added Anderson felt vindicated." ABC described an "election year powder keg . . . Anderson got most of the film." On March 6, a PBS commentator stated that "if the truth of Dita Beard's memo is established, it would be a 'fantastic scandal'—perhaps the worst in 100 years . . . If a link to Mitchell is proven, it will amount to a bribe." On March 7, "All net[work]s led with ITT hearings." The next day, "Anderson, on CBS, said again that Kleindienst lied" while "Kleindienst said Anderson's charges aren't fair." Journalists "were playing us up more than they were playing the hearing up," the columnist remembered gleefully, "which was exactly what I had hoped."

The White House followed the scandal with growing anxiety. "It's an explosion," Haldeman informed the President, one that was unlikely to go away anytime soon.

Nixon wondered if he should return ITT's donation, as suggested by California governor Ronald Reagan. "Giving it back doesn't admit guilt," Haldeman replied, and might end the current crisis. "But the problem is each time you lift up another one of these rocks, some other things are going to start squirting around." There was simply "too much in the record to risk having it come out."

The President wanted prying reporters kept away from him: "I do not want to have to answer any questions on this thing." Especially from Jack Anderson.

"Goddammit," Nixon fumed, "why do people read that shit-ass Anderson?"

The more immediate difficulty, Haldeman informed the President, was that "Dita Beard had [a] three-hour interview with Jack Anderson's man."

"Why the Christ did she do that?" Nixon asked incredulously.

"I don't know, but she did it," Haldeman replied.

The President decided that Hume must have "just harassed her until she finally broke down." Nixon added, "I'd love to get him."

The President and his men returned to this theme—and their old, familiar refrain of homosexuality—days later in the Oval Office.

"Do we have anything on Hume?" Haldeman inquired. "I thought there was some taint on him."

"We're doing a check on him," Colson replied. "We don't have it yet."

"It would be great if we could get him on a homosexual thing," Haldeman suggested.

"Is he married?" Nixon asked.

They should check to be sure Hume was gay, Colson said. "He sure looks it."

"He sure does," Haldeman agreed.

"He just has the appearance of it," Colson continued.

He's pretty," Haldeman pointed out, "and he's—"

"—and the way he handled his demeanor is curious," Colson said.

"He acts funny," Haldeman added.

The President concurred: "Anderson, I remember from years ago: he's got a strange, strange habit out of—I think Pearson was [homosexual], too. I think he and Anderson [both were.]"

In fact, Anderson, Hume, and Pearson were all heterosexual and shared the antigay prejudices of their day. But such distinctions were lost on the Nixon White House, for whom all adversaries were automatically suspect—sexually as well as politically.

Meanwhile, administration anxiety over ITT deepened. "The President's men regarded Anderson's revelations as the most serious threat yet to Nixon's re-election," one author observed, and they "responded with all the single-minded determination that they had brought to such threats in the past." A special high-level task force was created to plot damage control, led by Charles Colson, the unabashedly ruthless and increasingly powerful forty-year-old presidential advisor who described himself as "a flag-waving, kick-'em-in-the-nuts, anti-press, anti-liberal Nixon fanatic." One of Colson's first goals, White House counsel Dean said, was to "nail Anderson" by planting "a few hundred" hostile questions for the columnist during his upcoming Senate testimony. Republican members of Congress were supplied with written talking points to interrogate Anderson under oath about how he "stole" the Beard memo, used "devious reasoning," and waged "a campaign of smear and innuendo" with "half truths and fourth-removed hearsay evidence." The President's advisors wanted to make Anderson, rather than ITT, the focus of the hearings.

On March 9, the investigative reporter testified before the Senate committee. Despite Eastland's plan to try to bury Anderson's appearance, public interest had only grown during the delay of the previous week as the hearings generated increasing attention in Washington and around the nation. Even the columnist's presence while waiting in the front row of the caucus room to testify generated press notice; journalist Mary McGrory wrote that Anderson looked eager to "finish Kleindienst off." Indeed, the muckraker's strategy was deliberately provocative. "What the hearings needed now," Anderson decided, "was a troublemaker, someone to stir things up and sharpen the issues. If the tactic of the other side was in part to put the spectators to sleep with obfuscation, ours must be to wake them up with accusations . . . What was needed was a disrupting influence, someone to contradict the smooth, coordinated alibis; someone to shout 'Liar'" and "bait pro-ITT senators . . . to foul up the whitewash machinery."

Anderson did not disappoint. After introducing his "Merry-Go-Round" columns into the record, he went on the attack. "The public record on this episode is blotted with falsehood," he declared, shaking his finger. "The aura of scandal hangs over the whole matter." He laid out the contradictions in the testimony of administration and ITT officials, especially by Kleindienst. "This country needs as its top law enforcement officer a man who understands the law and respects the truth," Anderson proclaimed. "Richard Kleindienst is not such a man. He is unfit to be attorney general." The commotion in response led Eastland to bang his gavel and demand order. "The sedate hearing room of the Senate Judiciary Committee had rarely rung with such harsh language," *Time* reported.

Because the facts seemed so powerfully on Anderson's side, Republicans instead challenged the columnist's credentials. "Are you a lawyer, Mr. Anderson?" asked Senator Roman Hruska. "No, but I understand the English language," Anderson retorted. "Now, let us make no mistake about it. The contribution of $400,000 by a corporation to support a political convention is a crime. It directly and clearly violates the Corrupt Practices Act." Hruska, a dim-witted conservative who had unintentionally helped defeat Nixon's Supreme Court nominee two years earlier by arguing that "mediocre" people deserved a place on the nation's highest court, was equal to the occasion once again. "Conventions all over America are bought all the time by business communities," the Nebraska Republican argued. The hearing exploded with incredulous laughter, including that of other senators. "I subscribe to that," Anderson agreed. Hruska, not knowing when to stop, added stubbornly that "everyone in this room knows it."

The Republican senator's animus was understandable: he had nearly been defeated for reelection two years earlier when Anderson exposed his ownership in a chain of movie theaters that played pornographic films. (For that matter, ten of the fifteen senators on the committee had at one time been skewered by the "Merry-Go-Round.") In any case, Anderson and Hruska now descended into a shouting match over ITT. The senator accused the columnist of engaging in a "political diatribe." Anderson in turn lectured Hruska that "one of the biggest merger cases in all history was being settled . . . at the same time that discussions were going on involving a contribution to the Republican Convention. Now, if there are people in the Senate who cannot see that this is wrong, there is something wrong with their eyesight."

Other GOP senators were equally unsuccessful challenging Anderson. Kentucky's Marlow Cook questioned the "irresponsible" journalist about previous inaccuracies in his column, including his false report of lavish spending by Nixon aide Donald Rumsfeld, but the reporter defused the issue by taking "full responsibility" for what he admitted was "the most glaring error the column has ever made." Another Republican, Senator Edward Gurney of Florida, tried to force the columnist to reveal who leaked him the ITT memo.

"What is the name of [your] inside source?" Gurney asked.

"I can't divulge it," Anderson replied.

"I am requesting that you do give the name," the senator pressed.

"I am refusing to give it," the newsman responded.

"Did you receive it from an employee of ITT?"

"It came from an inside source and, Senator, with all due respect, I am not going to identify [anyone] further than that."

"Inside ITT?"

"I am not going to identify beyond that."

Even Chairman Eastland sided with Anderson on this issue: "He has a right not to divulge it."

Of course, the fact that Anderson had been leaked the memo anonymously was lost on the Senate panel. "Jack said he couldn't reveal his source," Hume laughed. "Well, that was literally true—because he didn't know who the source was!" It was more than professional pride that kept the newsman from reporting this fact at the time: he did not want to give his critics any opening to challenge the authenticity of the Beard memo and preferred to have his enemies fear that his informant might still be lurking near them. Indeed, to scare his adversaries further, Anderson falsely announced that he "remained in contact" with his inside source, who might leak additional incriminating documents in the future.

Meanwhile, Republicans tried their best to implicate Anderson in impropriety.

"Did you pay for this document?" Senator Gurney asked.

"No," Anderson answered.

"It was given to you freely?"

"Yes."

"Have you ever paid for any sources of information?"

"Never," Anderson fudged. "When they ask for money I sen[d] them on to some other reporter. I am also a tightwad, Senator." When the laughter subsided, the newsman's interrogator was forced to conclude that however he did it, "you have one of the best means of acquiring information in Washington."

Anderson's testimony "drew sharp rebukes and bitter denunciations from Republican members of the committee," *The Washington Post* reported, but the attacks bounced harmlessly off the columnist's thick hide. "It's only in retrospect that you can appreciate how immense the foe was," Anderson's legman Joe Spear recalled. "Jack was scared of nobody. Somehow, with his bravado, he marched up there and shouted down the Senate."

White House aides carefully tracked Anderson's testimony and media appearances.

"Was Anderson an effective witness?" the President asked his chief of staff.

"Yes, he was," Haldeman had to admit. In fact, the Democrats "want to keep Anderson's testimony going" longer because it was so badly damaging Republicans.

The evening after Anderson's first day at the witness table, Kleindienst called Haldeman at home to bemoan the muckraker's "wild
charges" and urge a "massive W[hite] H[ouse] effort using [govern-
ment] facilities to respond." The hearings started out as a "lovefest,"
the embattled nominee complained, but "then [Anderson's] columns
came out."

The next day, Colson proposed to the President that Kleindienst
issue a statement denouncing the hearings as "an outrageous witch-hunt
reminiscent of the McCarthy years [instigated by] one of the most discredited and irresponsible reporters in Washington, a reporter known
for his unsubstantiated sensationalism and innuendo." Nixon liked the
idea and suggested that Kleindienst also attack Anderson and Hume
for "character assassination of the most despicable sort—assassination
of the character of the President of the United States." But Kleindienst
evidently didn't want to provoke Anderson further and never issued the
inflammatory statement that Colson drafted.

Anderson relished the furor. After two days of contentious testimony, he had landed some powerful blows against his foes but was
himself unscathed. We were "just skunking them," the columnist recalled happily.

The White House was forced to agree. "That fellow's slick," Colson
told the President. Still, Colson thought Anderson might have lied under oath by denying that he ever paid any of his sources for information: "He got right up to the line, just very, very close . . . We've got to
go back and study the transcript and see if indeed we can nail him on
perjury."

Haldeman was skeptical: "He's damn smart, the way he plays it.
We're gonna have a tough time. He knows exactly how to [say] what he
wants to say without being [legally] actionable."

"He's been at this for years," Nixon pointed out.

"And he leaves the committee room at just the time when he wants
to go out and say something to the reporters," Colson echoed. "Compared to the way he operates and our guys, it's just pitiful."

Most news outlets reached a similar verdict. Anderson and Hume
"proved to be strong witnesses," *The Wall Street Journal* reported, the
architects of "a major political headache for the Nixon administration"

in an election year. CBS News concluded that "whatever reputations are saved or lost" by the scandal, "one man's will remain intact: Jack Anderson, the crusading investigative reporter who has an extraordinary knack for obtaining other people's secret documents."

To be sure, Anderson was not the only vocal Nixon critic during the ITT scandal. Consumer advocate Ralph Nader and Democratic Party chairman Lawrence O'Brien also assailed the White House while several Democratic senators, led by Edward Kennedy, aggressively questioned witnesses from ITT. But Anderson and Hume carefully briefed these administration opponents, sharing their confidential reporters' notes, focusing the direction of questioning, and explaining the intricacies of the complicated affair. One cartoonist drew Anderson as a sniffing hound dog straining at his leash to pull Kennedy, who was wearing a deerstalker cap like Sherlock Holmes.

Predictably, the President focused on Anderson's connection with Kennedy. The last surviving Kennedy brother continued to be mentioned as a possible presidential candidate, and Nixon was unable to overlook how the Kennedys had planted the Hughes loan story with Anderson on the eve of the 1960 election. Now, a dozen years later, with ITT, "Kennedy and Anderson are preparing the leaks," the President noted. "They're all working together." Nixon's men echoed their boss: "Kennedy and Anderson had been conspiring," Colson agreed. It was "clearly . . . a Kennedy-Anderson conspiracy," Haldeman affirmed.

Even while complaining about a Democratic conspiracy, however, the President engineered a Republican one in response. Aides summoned Senator Marlow Cook to the White House and the GOP senator then dutifully attacked Anderson and Kennedy for engaging in a "political conspiracy." Nixon's advisors and the Republican National Committee also drafted speeches attacking Anderson to be delivered by other GOP congressmen. Senator Paul Fannin denounced Anderson's "yellow journalism"; Senator Barry Goldwater charged that the "gossip-monger" and his "irresponsible muckraking" were "producing a national crisis." The daily barrage began to trouble the columnist. "Coming from the Senate, a quarter not implicated in my recent run of exposés, they had the surface appearance of coming from detached statesmen who had no personal axe to grind," Anderson worried.

In fact, it was the President himself who was shaping his surrogates' message: "You got to use the word *smear*, I tell you, every day . . . This is a smear-a-day Congress rather than a law-a-day Congress, see?" "*A smear-a-day Congress*, that's a great phrase," Colson enthused. "We'll start using that one." Two days later, the pliable Senator Hruska publicly labeled the ITT hearings a "smear-a-day campaign masquerading as a Senate confirmation hearing."

Nixon repeated his refrain a week later: "Just continue to hit *smear, smear, smear, smear*." "Well," Colson replied, "Hruska last week . . . got picked up in *Time* and *Newsweek* . . . [saying] that this is 'a smear-a-day Congress.' . . . And he keeps saying it." "Get the word to a hundred congressmen and senators on the Republican side to start talking about *smear a day*, the President reiterated. "We write it in everything we send to them," Colson assured Nixon. But the President was insistent: "Just get the [congressional] whips to pass the word out . . . 'smear, smear, smear.'"

To plot their own smears, White House aides secretly huddled with ITT lawyers and CREEP operatives. Nixon's campaign manager, John Mitchell, contacted a federal prosecutor he once supervised about "programming" a pro-ITT witness for "appearing on T.V.," while a top Justice Department official "agreed that I.T.T. or Geneen should issue [a] press release" to combat the scandal. Meanwhile, the FBI "prepared a number of items for use by a friendly Senator to attack the credibility of Anderson." The abuse of law enforcement authorities for such nakedly political purposes did not seem to bother government officials.

Democrats returned the fire. Senator Edmund Muskie, Nixon's leading presidential competitor, made front-page headlines warning that the scandal had "shaken the confidence of Americans in the integrity of the political process." Another White House rival, Democratic senator George McGovern, drew cheers along the campaign trail by declaring: "I want an America with such a passion for justice that not even $400,000 will buy special privileges for a big corporation!" California's ambitious secretary of state, Jerry Brown, the future Democratic governor and presidential candidate, even filed a lawsuit to stop ITT's underwriting of the Republican convention on the grounds that it was an "egregious" violation of federal corruption laws. White House aides condescendingly referred to thirty-three-year-old Brown, son of the California politician who had defeated Nixon for governor a decade earlier, as "little Pat Brown." But that did not stop him from garnering national headlines by denouncing ITT's "political payoff."

The President and his advisors were appalled to find themselves embroiled in such a media circus. "Day after day, the White House staff raced around trying to minimize the political damage and keep any embarrassing material from the committee's partisan clutches," Nixon wrote in his memoirs. The President even had to "cancel his press conference idea for tomorrow," Haldeman noted in his diary, "because there's no way he can adequately handle the ITT question."

Nixon received conflicting advice about what to do. "Rumsfeld argued we should take our losses and get out," Haldeman noted, but the President feared that withdrawing Kleindienst's nomination would not stop the bloodletting. Treasury Secretary John Connally, a tough-talking Texan whom Nixon admired, urged the President to "hit 'em, hit 'em, hit 'em, that's the only way you can do it."

"Just go on the attack?" Nixon asked.

"Go on the attack," Connally repeated. "You have to go on the attack."

The President liked the advice. "Attack the goddamn media!" Nixon barked to his staff. "The press corps is anti-us" anyway, Nixon believed. "They were all for Hiss. Half of 'em were goddamn near Communists."

But although the President wanted to "attack the attackers," Haldeman wrote in his diary, Nixon "was concerned that we don't seem to have any dirt to throw back at the Democrats." So, to try to besmirch the opposition, the White House compiled a list of Democratic politicians who had received campaign contributions from ITT.

In addition, the President suggested that "now is the time to surface [embarrassing classified documents] on Kennedy and Vietnam in a more vicious way, and get some of that going as we counter-fire, so we're doing something on our own initiative instead of just reacting to the Democrats." In any event, Nixon told his staff, "I should be one step removed now . . . from this whole goddamn controversy."

Colson's task force began holding what one presidential aide called "panic sessions" several times a day. "As we kicked 'scenarios' around the room," White House lawyer Dean said, "a public-relations strategy emerged around two central themes: hide the facts and discredit the opposition."

The first to be discredited was Dita Beard, whose incriminating memo had caused the scandal in the first place. A onetime Washington debutante who had worked for Nixon's presidential campaign, Beard now endured withering attacks by her former allies, who suddenly discovered that she was an unstable alcoholic. A retired Republican governor publicly announced that he'd seen Beard get drunk at a party and pass out on the floor. Beard's doctor, who had worked for an ITT subsidiary and faced possible indictment for Medicare fraud by Kleindienst's Justice Department, overcame his objections to violating patient-client privilege and testified that Beard sometimes suffered from "distorted and irrational behavior" and therefore "could have written an inaccurate memo." The physician even quoted his patient as supposedly saying, "I was mad and disturbed when I wrote it." As for Kleindienst, he told reporters that Beard was "a poor soul, a rather sick person" and added that "it's just a sad situation."

At the same time, the White House focused on the notion that Beard and Anderson had somehow conspired to concoct the lobbyist's infamous memo in the first place. This idea was first floated by an unlikely source: President Nixon's barber, whom Anderson had opportunistically cultivated as his barber as well. "The chatty hairstylist turned out to be a two-way information channel, passing tidbits to each of us about the other," the columnist recalled. The double-agent barber claimed that Anderson's secretary, Opal Ginn, was a drinking buddy of Dita Beard, and that this was probably the origin of the leaked memo. "The implication," Anderson wrote, "was that they were a pair of souses who, in their degeneracy, had formed a conspiracy to 'get' the Administration." Worse, Opal later told friends, the White House "tried to make it out that she had a lesbian affair with Dita Beard." Once again, Nixon's men turned to homophobia as their last, best defense against their enemies. (Actually, both Beard and Ginn, though unmarried, were resolutely heterosexual—as well as equally hard-drinking and hard-bitten.) In any case, Dean interviewed the barber who had passed on the gossip "to see if we could discredit Anderson's testimony." But the results were disappointing: the information was all secondhand; "the barber had nothing."

Nonetheless, Colson believed that the rumor might finally allow the White House to wiggle out of the scandal and hurried to tell the President about the "Anderson vulnerability." Assistant Attorney General Robert Mardian assigned a federal prosecutor, who normally specialized in sensitive national security cases, to investigate. With help from ITT, authorities seemed to corroborate the allegation when they located a group photo that included Beard and Ginn at a local bar. "It was so vivid," Colson said, "actually having the photograph." The picture, Colson told the President, was "dynamite."

The White House rushed the photo to Republican senator Marlow Cook and other allies on the Judiciary Committee. "Tell Cook . . . [to] call Anderson's secretary [as a witness] and ask her about her association with Dita Beard," Nixon instructed his staff. "If you get the secretary up [on the witness stand], you scare them to death."

The President was right about that. "I don't want to get dragged into this fucking scandal!" Opal exclaimed. The very idea of testifying "makes me damn mad."

"Are they going to call the Ginnis [*sic*] girl?" Nixon pressed.

"Well, we're trying like hell to get them to," Colson replied.

"And put her under oath," the President added.

Colson believed that "there is a possibility of impeaching Anderson's testimony or holding him in contempt" of Congress. But Nixon seemed reluctant to get his hopes up. "Do you really think we have a chance to prove [that Anderson forged the Beard memo]?" the President wondered. "What [is the] evidence?" A White House aide speculated that Beard might have been afraid of being fired by ITT and that her friend Opal suggested writing the memo to "help you and help ourselves at the same time." Nixon still wasn't persuaded but decided there was nothing to lose: "Put on Anderson's secretary . . . she can't do any harm" and "might be a bad witness."

The next day, Senator Cook interrupted the hearings "to share some facts that just came to my attention." The senator dramatically informed the committee that "Dita Beard and another woman quite often met for drinks in the afternoon" at a cocktail lounge near the White House. The other woman, the lawmaker announced gravely, was her "drinking companion and her close friend Opal Ginn," who just "happens to be a long-time member of Jack Anderson's staff." Cook expressed "outrage" that this "close relationship" was not disclosed earlier and suggested that Anderson had "been less than candid with the committee." Furthermore, the senator said, it "casts doubt on the veracity of Anderson's account of how he obtained the memorandum and perhaps even on the origin and content of the memorandum itself." Cook's statement, according to a White House lawyer who helped prepare it, "all but said Jack Anderson was a liar."

The President was delighted. "You know, this thing could turn [around]," he said hopefully. Colson concurred and informed his boss that the Senate panel had now decided to summon Anderson's secretary as a witness. "She may break," Colson predicted. At the very least, "she'll have to break down in the sense [of admitting] that she knew Dita Beard well. I don't think she can dare get off the hook on that one." Perhaps feeling nostalgic for his days investigating Alger Hiss, Nixon imagined taking on a similar role now with Jack Anderson. "I wish I were a member of the Senate on that committee," the President said wistfully.

"Oh! Ach! Oh!" Colson exclaimed. I just wake up in the middle of the night, wishing I could get behind that bench and go after him."

"It's a golden opportunity [for] a fishing expedition," Nixon observed, "[to] go after him and bring in everything else he said: 'Well, now you're testifying on this, Mr. Anderson, let me ask you about some of the other stories you've written,' 'Now, Mr. Chairman, we're just testing the credibility of this witness.' Then you'd tackle him: 'Is that true, Mr. Anderson?' 'No, it's false.' . . . It is relevant, always, to attack the credibility of a witness."

"Oh, absolutely," Colson echoed. "You'd [take] them out of there in nothing flat. Of course, he's slippery, he's a very clever guy, I must say . . . He's a very slick fellow. So is Hume."

In the end, however, what mattered was not slickness but truth. And the truth was that Beard and Ginn were not even remotely close.

Although Anderson's secretary and ITT's lobbyist both frequented the same cocktail lounge, they had apparently conversed only once, at a retirement party for their bartender attended by about thirty-five people; that was when the group photograph that included the two women was taken. In fact, at that very party Beard had denounced Anderson as "a son of a bitch and I wouldn't touch him with a ten-foot pole." The columnist compiled affidavits from the bartender and other witnesses that shot down Senator Cook's story. Anderson sent it to the Republican lawmaker along with a demand that he eat his crow publicly by introducing the evidence into the hearing record. "I don't particularly look forward to [this]," the senator was forced to announce the next day, "but I really ought to ask that it be put in the record . . . In all fairness, if I owe Mr. Anderson an apology, I certainly would extend it to him." According to Dean, "Senator Cook was furious. He had been made a fool of by Colson," who never bothered to verify the thirdhand rumor before passing it on and putting Cook "on the end of a fragile limb" that quickly snapped.

Afterward, the President once again warned his staff to make sure that he was insulated from the scandal. "It's very important to keep ITT away from the White House," Nixon told Haldeman. "I'm not going to comment publicly on Dita Beard's testimony or Jack Anderson's charges."

But the President soon returned to directing damage control behind the scenes. For example, when one witness, a waiter at their cocktail lounge, insisted that Beard and Ginn were not friends, Nixon had a simple if illegal suggestion: "The waiter can be bought off."

To discredit Anderson further, according to Assistant Attorney General Mardian, Colson actually had the photo of Beard and Ginn doctored to insert Anderson's face to make it appear that the muckraker was partying with the lobbyist. "He wasn't in the picture so Colson figured he'd put him in the picture," Mardian recalled. "He actually got [it] manufactured . . . I tried desperately, when I found out what the hell was going on, to keep it out of evidence" in the Senate probe, "and I kept it" from being introduced as an exhibit in the hearing. (It was not Colson's first dirty trick on behalf of Nixon, or his last; it was not even Colson's only White House forgery, since he also helped concoct fraudulent government cables to falsely implicate President Kennedy in a foreign assassination.)

The ITT scandal had now escalated to the point of political sabotage. And it wasn't over yet.

Dita Beard had mysteriously vanished.

13

FROM BURLESQUE
TO GROTESQUE

After Jack Anderson published his columns about her, Dita Beard told a friend that she feared she would end up "going to jail." The ITT lobbyist then disappeared from Washington without a trace. The Senate issued a subpoena for Beard's testimony, but twenty-four FBI agents searching in five states were unable to locate her. "Where I am going," she confided to an intimate, "they won't be able to find me, and I won't be able to talk to them."

But Beard's whereabouts were no mystery to President Nixon's men, who helped hide her in the first place. G. Gordon Liddy, the former White House operative now employed at the Nixon reelection campaign, had whisked Beard on an airplane to Denver, where the lobbyist checked into a local hospital complaining of chest pains and waited for the heat to die down in Washington. "The fact that a White House undercover man had helped—or forced—Mrs. Beard to flee, ducking a congressional subpoena and trying to elude the FBI, meant that her memo and what she had told me in my two interviews with her were considered extremely explosive," Brit Hume later wrote.

White House aides briefed the President about their strategy for covering up the scandal.

"What they want to do is get Dita Beard to . . . disavow the memo," Chief of Staff H. R. Haldeman said, "and then they can blow Jack Anderson out of the water."

"How would she do it?" Nixon wondered. "Would she admit something?"

"They think so," Haldeman replied.

The President was skeptical: "How could she admit it's a fake memo . . . without destroying herself?"

"She thinks she's destroying *them*," Haldeman answered.

Nixon was not persuaded. "My view is that she wrote it," he told his staff, although she probably "did the typical thing" and exaggerated in the memo to impress her bosses; still, she might be willing to lie and deny that she wrote it just to get herself out of this jam.

"Does she hate Anderson?" the President asked.

"With a passion," Colson responded. "If we could prove this one a hoax," the White House aide told Nixon on another occasion, "it would discourage the hell out of them on others, you know, Anderson particularly, because he'll be after us all year long" otherwise.

The President's men decided to dispatch E. Howard Hunt, the ex–CIA agent working for the White House Plumbers, on a clandestine mission to persuade Beard to repudiate her memo. Colson carefully instructed Hunt on how to approach the lobbyist: he was to "assure her that her friends wouldn't reject her" and that "she would be forgiven" if she would just change her story to "admit" that she had fabricated the document and given it to Anderson. "We wanted to establish her complicity" in having "perpetrated [a] hoax," Colson said.

Hunt was warned to approach Beard in a physical disguise with a phony ID because "we don't want you traced back to the White House." To pay for his expenses, he was handed an envelope filled with cash from Nixon's reelection campaign; his flight to Denver was booked by a White House secretary. Hunt arrived at Beard's hospital room near midnight wearing makeup and an ill-fitting reddish brown wig, his voice disguised by an electronic alteration device provided by the CIA. The not-so-covert operative looked "very eerie," Beard's son remembered, with his hairpiece on "cockeyed, like he put it on in a dark car."

Hunt found Beard lying in her hospital bed, "her hair disheveled, her face bloated." He gave her a box of roses but she was not fooled by any pretense of sentimentality: she checked to be sure he hadn't hidden electronic bugs inside the flowers. Hunt then urged Beard to sign a statement denying her "involvement in the preparation and/or release of the memorandum" that Anderson had published. He promised that "her job at ITT was waiting for her as soon as she could return" and that "she and her family would be well taken care of for life." He added that "the most useful action" now would be for Beard to "return to Washington as soon as possible, making a brief statement, denying authorship of the memorandum . . . and then collapse" in public to garner sympathy. "Whether she was to collapse in front of the microphones," Haldeman said, "or while riding in a cab, was not made explicit."

But the cantankerous Beard refused to return to Washington to disavow her memo, let alone hold a press conference and collapse on cue. She insisted that she truly didn't know Anderson's secretary and hadn't concocted the memo for the columnist. Her main concern was making sure that she would receive a "Christmas bonus," which Hunt realized "was obviously a code for hush money."

Hunt called Colson late that night from a pay phone to pass on the bad news. Colson told Hunt to reassure Beard that her "Christmas bonus" would soon be delivered. But the President's advisor refused to believe her denial about Jack Anderson. "She's lying," Colson insisted to Hunt: "Bear down on her and get her to tell the truth." Hunt tried, but there was no budging Beard. She "wouldn't admit that she had faked" the memo, Colson reported unhappily. Hunt returned to Washington empty-handed.

In the Oval Office, aides informed the President about Hunt's secret approach to Beard.

"She's in bad shape physically," Colson said. "The best thing that could happen is if she bought the farm right now . . . There's a chance of that any day of the week."

"That she'll die?" Nixon asked.

"She might well, Mr. President."

Meanwhile, the FBI tracked Beard to her Denver hospital. Her doctors claimed that she was too ill to be questioned because of a possible "impending coronary." But senators, skeptical, asked for an independent investigation by the Denver Medical Association, whose cardiologists found no evidence that Beard had any kind of heart disease. A Senate panel made plans to fly to Colorado to interview the lobbyist at her bedside.

Colson came up with a modified "ploy" for minimizing the fallout: Beard "will say this is a goddamn smear, dirtiest politics I've seen anywhere," the White House aide told Nixon, "and then when they start getting into questions, she'll pass out. And that'll make one hell of an emotional scene . . . She calls for oxygen, the doctors rush oxygen to her. The senators are standing there feeling awful ghoulish. God!"

Colson laughed out loud at the prospect, especially because Beard's questioners would include Senator Edward Kennedy, whose recent accident at Chappaquiddick had led to the drowning of his female passenger. "Here's Teddy Kennedy," Colson chortled, and "he doesn't want to risk a woman dying, he's scared to death of it."

The President warmed to the plan. If Beard broke down under Kennedy's questioning, Nixon suggested, Colson should send the senator untraceable telegrams demanding: "Isn't one woman on your hands enough?"

The Chief Executive also proposed another dirty trick to play on Kennedy. "I have an idea," Nixon declared, "in terms of an anonymous letter. Why not one to Kennedy—it might scare the living bejesus out of him—saying 'Senator, get off of this . . . I work for ITT. I'm scared to death that the memo is a fake. You'd better protect yourself fast: within the next few days, it's going to come out.'"

"That's a damn good idea," Colson affirmed.

At the end of March, Kennedy and the rest of his Senate subcommittee traveled to Denver to interview Beard under oath from her hospital room. "She'll collapse at the right time," Colson assured the President. "Mrs. Beard is well programmed for her testimony," Colson later added. She's also ready to grab the oxygen mask when Teddy Kennedy starts burrowing in on her."

"Is she programmed to die at the right time?" Haldeman joked.

"I haven't figured out how to do it," Colson replied. "She might. She's in a very hysterical mood."

In Denver, Beard posed for photographers with the senators who had come to question her. She lay in bed, dressed in a cotton nightgown, with an oxygen tube attached to her nose and wires connecting her to a heart-monitoring machine. Beard "alternately sucked on cigarettes and gulped from her oxygen mask" while members of Congress "stood awkwardly around her bed," Kennedy remembered. "It makes you feel like some sort of ghoul," another senator commented self-consciously, just as Colson had predicted.

Beard now capitulated to the forces arrayed against her. "I want this committee and the world to know that the Anderson memorandum is not my memorandum," she announced, "and that I shall spend the rest of my life, for however long that might be, in an unceasing effort to find out who did this to me." Anderson's memo was a "hoax," Beard insisted, her initials on it "a forgery." Although she admitted that parts of the memo sounded familiar, she was certain that the most damaging portions had been fabricated.

As the White House had planned, after an hour of questioning, Beard clutched her chest, fell back on her pillows, and began moaning. Beard's doctors rushed to her side; the senators were abruptly ushered out of the room. "They all thought they'd have her blood on their hands," one reporter at the scene recalled, "but she was obviously faking it." Humorist Art Buchwald wrote that the "salty woman lobbyist" deserved an Oscar "for her dramatic role in 'The Jack Anderson Papers'" melodrama because Beard "won the hearts of America in the famous hospital scene."

Still, Beard's doctor declared the incident "a harbinger of possible" cardiac distress; she "will probably never be able to testify as long as she lives." Beard's lawyer, a Republican activist paid by ITT, claimed that her "near" heart attack was a "direct result of Anderson and Hume's cruel harassment and persecution of this lady." Reading from a previously prepared statement, Beard's attorney blamed the "irresponsible . . . ruthless . . . vicious" columnist who uncovered the scandal:

> That a sick and distraught woman responsible for the upbringing of five children has been driven to the point that she would risk her life to ensure that the truth be made public is a sad and disgusting commentary on the almost untrammeled power of Jack Anderson, an arrogant and brazen journalist, and his pathetic muckraking investigator Brit Hume . . . Sadly the alleged journalist Jack Anderson doesn't want to report the news—he wants to get someone.

"At last we've turned the corner," Colson exulted. "We've started to reverse the bad news." Soon, the scandal would be "all over."

But Beard's belated disavowal faced a skeptical audience. Four other witnesses, including Republicans who were close to the lobbyist, publicly testified that she had acknowledged writing the memo; even ITT officials admitted privately that the "memo was hers." Beard's sudden new denial "seemed at best peculiar," *Time* pointed out, "since Anderson's assistant had showed her the memo three weeks before, giving her plenty of time to denounce it," which she had notably failed to do. "If the memo was a fake," the magazine asked, "why did ITT go to the trouble of shredding its documents?" Besides, "ITT's defenders went to some lengths to portray Mrs. Beard as a sometimes irrational incompetent. Having first tried to discredit her, they are hard pressed to defend what she says now."

In response, Colson "scrambled to rehabilitate her image in the media, an image he himself had sought to discredit by leaking stories that she was a sad old drunkard," White House counsel John Dean wrote. "Suddenly, stories appeared concerning her distinguished career at ITT." As Anderson put it, "ITT's transformation of Beard from boozy perpetrator to stricken victim had begun."

Less than a week after senators were told that Beard was too sick to answer their questions, she sneaked out of the hospital to a nearby apartment for an interview with the CBS program *60 Minutes*. To emphasize her infirmity, Beard put a medical gown over her clothes while her lawyer monitored her TV performance. "The ground rules she established," correspondent Mike Wallace told viewers, were that "we would not press her, because of her heart condition, on matters that she or her attorney might find sensitive." Congressional Republicans were even more pliant. "The pro-ITT senators, who two weeks before had been setting up Mrs. Beard as a zombie, now embraced her as the sole repository of truth," Anderson wrote. "Democrats smelled a rodent." Even Haldeman conceded that Beard's newly minted denial was "greeted with general derision." Commentator Nicholas von Hoffman thought that the "case has long since passed from scandal to vaudeville." The headline over a *Washington Post* editorial suggested another evolution: FROM BURLESQUE TO GROTESQUE.

For his part, at least in public, Anderson was charitable about Beard's sudden change in position. "The only explanation I can give is that she is fifty-three, divorced, and has five children and hospital bills to pay," the columnist told reporters. "She is at ITT's economic mercy." Privately, Anderson expressed a different view. "This is the stupidest thing they could have done," he said to Hume. "They'll never get away with this." If the other side was going to engage in such obvious flim-flam, Anderson decided to try some himself. He had Hume hooked up to a polygraph machine to test whether his legman was telling the truth that Beard had admitted writing the memo. Not surprisingly, Hume passed the exam. "We had fun brandishing those tests and demanding that the other witnesses follow suit," Anderson recalled, "but none of them, patriots that they were, wanted any part of that revolution."

In the Oval Office, the President and his aides worried less about the columnist's promotional theatrics than about his continued digging into the administration's cover-up.

"Now, Anderson is an unscrupulous son of a bitch," Colson told Nixon, so "we had Secret Service [checking] on our phones all week just because we're concerned about Anderson."

"You mean maybe he's got an operative in your office?" the President asked.

"I don't think in mine," Colson replied.

"Does he have a tap?" Nixon wondered. "Does he have a tap on the White House phones?"

"Well, Secret Service checked and said no."

In fact, the only taps were the ones the White House itself was se-cretly making at the President's direction. But Anderson's history of bugging still worried Nixon and his men.

The President and his aides plotted what to do next. "The plan," Haldeman wrote in his diary, was to get Senate "Republicans [to] say they won't go any further, this is a fraud" and "we should investigate Anderson" instead of ITT. A White House advisor revived the idea of prosecuting Anderson for receiving stolen property, since the ITT memos were "pilfered documents." The legal "proof is not difficult" to establish, the aide noted, though Anderson's "martyrdom might not be worth it."

Ultimately, the Chief Executive decided that the only possible way to wiggle out of the scandal would be to produce an independent scientific analysis concluding that the Beard memo was fake. The lobbyist's self-interested statement "discrediting Anderson," the President recognized, "of course won't do it, you've got to have the hard thing." Nixon recommended that the FBI's well-regarded laboratory investigate whether the font and ink on Beard's memo matched that of her office typewriter. "It's so reminiscent of the Hiss case, where the typewriter broke the case," the President mused.

Colson was enthusiastic. "Oh, God!" he exclaimed to Nixon, the FBI director hated Anderson "with a passion." Clearly, his lab would produce the results the White House wanted. "I don't think J. Edgar Hoover has any scruples at all, when it comes to getting Anderson," Colson added. "If the memo is proven a fraud, then [Senator] Eastland will close the hearings down and then—"

"Well, he's got to do more than that," the President interrupted. "He's got to go after Anderson."

"Well, that's right," Colson agreed. "That's what I want to do. But we've got to prove it's a fraud first . . . and then let's go after Anderson."

Because Hoover disliked the abrasive Colson, White House counsel Dean said, "I was sent to enlist the director's cooperation, a delicate mission." Hoover—"immaculately dressed [and] perfumed"—welcomed the young lawyer to his Justice Department office. "Mr. Hoover," Dean told the director, we "have good reason to believe the so-called Dita Beard memorandum is a phony, and we'd like to have your lab test it because we are sure that your test will confirm that it is a forgery." Dean added that "Jack Anderson started it all with the memo, and if we can show it's a forgery—"

"I understand exactly, Mr. Dean, what you need," Hoover interrupted, "and I'm delighted to be of service. Jack Anderson is the lowest form of human being to walk the earth. He's a muckraker who lies, steals, and let me tell you this, Mr. Dean, he'll go lower than dog shit for a story." The FBI director was not being metaphorical. It turned out that when Anderson's staff went through Hoover's trash the year before, he had retaliated by instructing his butler to put his dog's feces in the garbage to soil the reporter's hands. "Lower than dog shit," Hoover repeated, his jowls shaking with anger.

Dean suppressed a chuckle because it was obviously no laughing matter to Hoover.

"Mr. Dean," the FBI director added, "if you'd like some material from our files on Jack Anderson, I'd be pleased to send it over."

The President's counsel returned triumphantly to the White House, "confident Hoover would supply the report" that Nixon needed to discredit Anderson and his memo.

Anderson did not know that the FBI offered to forward his dossier to the White House, but he was understandably alarmed when he learned that Hoover's laboratory would conduct tests to determine the authenticity of his memo. "I thought we were sunk," the usually cheerful columnist said. "Hoover would surely be delighted to get his hands on evidence that he could turn against me." The fact that Anderson had received the memo anonymously in the mail meant that he could not be certain it was genuine. Indeed, he had taken a substantial risk by publishing his story and distributing the explosive document to Congress and the media when he had no idea who sent it to him in the first place.

But Anderson had learned long ago to bluff his way to victory. He announced that he would not "drag" his (unknown) source in to testify publicly and asked reporters: "Do you think we would give the committee a document we didn't know was authentic?" In truth, Anderson was more rattled than he let on. "In the past, I had tended to laugh off attacks by high officials as a kind of public validation of my prowess, a sign I was really getting to 'em," he later wrote, "but as the barrage kept up, my bravado was wilting. In public relations as in physics, there is such a thing as the accumulation of a critical mass that, once formed, will blow all before it." Nevertheless, Anderson's account seemed more believable than the ever-changing White House dodges. "Is it seriously contended that columnist Jack Anderson forged the memo," New York Times columnist Tom Wicker inquired incredulously, "and if so, why and how?"

Still, Anderson had only himself to blame for the FBI probe. Why? Because he had voluntarily given his memo to Senator Eastland in the first place as part of his early effort to gin up congressional hearings to publicize his story. But without notifying Anderson or even other senators on his committee, Eastland had then passed the memo to top Justice Department officials, who delivered it to the White House. "The principal piece of evidence in the case, submitted formally by

Jack and myself, had, in effect, been slipped secretly to the defendant,"
Hume realized, and the slipshod chain of custody "left open the possibility it could be tampered with along the way." Anderson publicly
denounced "the extreme impropriety of allowing a party in interest in
a congressional investigation to take possession of a vital piece of evidence." He also complained that Eastland had not asked his permission before doing so.

"His permission," Nixon snorted in response. "That's the most arrogant thing I've ever heard of . . . Well, I would certainly think, though,
that Eastland would get stirred up about that goddamn remark of Anderson's."

"Isn't that outrageous?" Colson agreed.

Despite their bluster, Anderson and Hume recognized all too well
that they now had no real power to stop the administration from doing
whatever it wanted with the memo, although they hoped their public
protests "would discourage any funny business" from the FBI lab and
"prepare the way" for them to "denounce a dishonest report, if one were
made."

Perhaps because of his own history of dirty-trick forgeries, Colson
truly believed that the Beard memo had been faked. "It's more than a
gut feeling, damn it," he told the President. There are "too many things
that just don't add up and we're going to find, somewhere, a nigger in
the woodpile."

The next day, Colson told Nixon that he feared the FBI was conducting only a "cursory analysis" of the memo. "Kick them in the ass,
the President instructed."

Nixon's men did what they were told and exerted pressure to prevent FBI scientists from reaching unwanted results. With White House
approval, ITT "flooded the FBI with documents" arguing that Beard's
memo was fake. Dean also suggested that FBI lab technicians meet
with ITT's document experts for guidance. "They are persistent, aren't
they?" Hoover marveled. With the help of Justice Department prosecutors, an ITT representative even sneaked into the FBI to see how its
laboratory was analyzing the memo.

Meanwhile, ITT demanded physical possession of the document so
that the corporation's not-so-independent experts could conduct their

own tests on the document. This request made Dean "nervous," the White House counsel said, because "the FBI never touched evidence analyzed by anyone else. Hoover had an iron rule against competition [to prevent] the possibility of contradiction. I was afraid of what Hoover might do if he found out we had sent the original to an outside expert." But Colson decided "it was vital" for ITT to analyze the memo and "assured" Dean that "no one would know" about it. With the aid of Assistant Attorney General L. Patrick Gray, Dean smuggled the document out of the FBI laboratory. ITT's analyst removed two small corners of the original Beard memo to perform chemical tests and then, unsurprisingly, once again announced that the memo was phony.

Nonetheless, on March 18, Hoover's deputy, W. Mark Felt, informed Dean that the FBI concluded that the Beard memo was "probably authentic." Dean read the draft of the Bureau's report with "dismay. It was worse than I had expected." Dean tried to argue that the FBI's verdict should be "modified" so it wouldn't conflict with ITT's. But Felt replied that such a change was "completely out of the question." Dean insisted that Felt "check with Hoover. Tell him the request comes from the White House." Hoover exploded at the demand. "Call Dean right back and tell him I said for him to go jump in the lake!" the FBI director told his underling. "I want to cooperate when I can, but this request is completely improper!" Felt "would not budge," Dean said, "because the director would not budge."

The President was irate. "At least they could say 'We can't tell,'" Nixon fumed. That, at least, would establish enough doubt for the White House to keep insisting that the document was forged. Colson said he "had never before seen the President so furious."

And so—"oblivious to unfavorable developments and undaunted by failure," Dean said—Colson "kept coming back again like a battering ram." He even went behind Hoover's back to try to get FBI lab technicians to "falsify their findings," Assistant Attorney General Robert Mardian recalled. Colson's "machinations" were so "unbelievable," Mardian said, that he "had to go to [presidential confidant John] Mitchell and get him to go to Nixon to tell Colson to stop it."

On March 21, the President received more bad news. "We need your help with J. Edgar Hoover," Ehrlichman told Nixon. White House aides had made "a bad judgment call" and given the original Beard memo to ITT without informing the FBI. "This could be very, very embarrassing all the way around," Ehrlichman feared, "because this damn document was floating around [ITT's corporate headquarters] with no government people anywhere near it." Ehrlichman recommended trying "to cover that" by getting Hoover's retroactive permission to forward the memo to ITT. "This is an extraordinary thing for the Bureau to have to do," Ehrlichman realized, and it would require the President's personal intervention to pull off.

Nixon was skeptical that Hoover would go along: "I just got to say, this is a long shot." Ehrlichman didn't disagree but asked the President to "call Hoover and simply say he will be getting a call from me and that you would personally appreciate his cooperation in the request that will be made. You don't even have to use the words *ITT*."

"Oh, I won't," Nixon assured his aide.

Ehrlichman thought the argument most likely to persuade Hoover would be that "this is in his best interests because it'll be in the direction of getting Anderson." The next day, Ehrlichman informed the President that he had talked to Hoover and explained that it would be to their "mutual advantage" to discredit Anderson. "Yeah," Hoover replied, "I'd do anything to get that son of a bitch."

But as much as the FBI director disliked Anderson, he hated even more being played for a fool. Hoover was livid when he learned that the White House had sneaked the Beard memo from the FBI lab to ITT without his knowledge or approval. "Ehrlichman could not budge the director an inch," a discouraged Dean reported. Indeed, instead of helping the White House cover its tracks, Hoover threatened to have ITT's document expert indicted for "tampering with FBI evidence."

As the final coup de grâce, the FBI sent the White House its promised dossier on Anderson. "Chuck, you are going to be amazed what's in Hoover's famous files," Dean told Colson. "Well?" Colson asked. "Newspaper and magazine clippings," Dean replied. "Shit!" Colson exclaimed. In fact, the FBI had amassed more than fifty bulging files on Anderson that were filled with unsubstantiated allegations of impropriety that went back decades and totaled thousands of pages. But Hoover now decided not to share them with the Nixon White House. "I don't understand Edgar sometimes," the President told his staff. "He hates Anderson."

On March 23, the FBI director sent Senator Eastland a letter stating that the font and ink on Beard's memo were "substantially similar" to other documents from her typewriter and that the margins and indentations of her memo were "closely similar" to others that the lobbyist wrote at the time. Hoover concluded that there was "nothing . . . to suggest" that the document was faked or that Anderson had manufactured it.

"In other words," the President asked, "it supports Anderson, right?"

"It supports Anderson," Colson had to concede.

The story was front-page news around the country. The FBI was "unable to prove" that the memo "published by columnist Jack Anderson is a phony," the Associated Press reported. Senator Edward Kennedy issued a triumphant statement proclaiming that the FBI report "confirms unequivocally" that the document "submitted by Jack Anderson" was genuine. Not even the President's fiercest loyalists dared challenge the FBI findings.

By the end of March, the White House was forced to give up all further efforts to discredit Anderson's memo. Pollster Louis Harris found that more Americans believed the columnist than the Nixon administration.

The President's men moved to put the scandal behind them. In June, the Senate finally confirmed Richard Kleindienst as attorney general, but not before he and a host of Justice Department and ITT officials committed perjury trying to cover up their misconduct. Their "bald deceptions and outright falsehoods" in Senate testimony "registered a new low," a prosecution spokesman later said.

Kleindienst's lies were the most flagrant and shameless of all. "I was not interfered with by anybody at the White House" about ITT, he swore under oath. "I was not importuned; I was not pressured; I was not directed. I did not have conferences with respect to what I should or should not do . . . I would have had a vivid recollection if someone at the White House had called me up and said, 'Look, Kleindienst, this is the way we are going to handle that case.'" In fact, however, Kleindienst had had exactly that conversation, with the President himself, as White House tapes later revealed. "The IT & T thing—stay the hell out of it!" Nixon barked at Kleindienst. "Is that clear? That's an order . . . leave the goddamned thing alone." When Kleindienst explained that such a sudden reversal might prove awkward, the President exploded: "You son of a bitch, don't you understand the English language? . . . Drop the goddamn thing. Is that clear?"

It was Nixon himself, in other words, who rigged the ITT settlement in the first place—and then concealed the perjury of his top law enforcement officer when he tried to cover it all up. Additional evidence revealed other incriminating evidence that, in Colson's words, would "lay this case on the president's doorstep" and "directly involve" him in the scandal. Two years later, Kleindienst became the first attorney general in American history to plead guilty to breaking the federal laws he was sworn to enforce. Prosecutors wanted to file indictments against others for what they called the "extraordinarily numerous" crimes in the case, including bribery, perjury, and obstruction of justice; but no additional charges were ever brought. ITT effectively bought off Dita Beard by continuing to pay her salary and purchasing a ten-acre farm to which she retired in West Virginia. Despite her well-publicized medical woes, Jack Anderson wrote a year later, "our sources reported seeing her in Las Vegas. She was whooping it up just like she used to do in the backrooms of Washington. She looked quite healthy, the sources said, and she appeared to have overcome her delicate heart condition."

In the end, FBI Deputy Director W. Mark Felt realized, the White House cover-up of ITT proved to be "a prelude to Watergate." Both scandals included the same players: Liddy, Hunt, Dean, Mitchell, Ehrlichman, Haldeman, Nixon. And both involved similar crimes: perjury, conspiracy, obstruction of justice. The President would repeatedly compare the two scandals in private, minimizing both because "nobody stole anything." Nixon firmly believed that each was just the result of partisan politics and that the White House should simply "cut our losses and get out of this damn thing."

But Jack Anderson's assessment was more accurate. "The Watergate crimes and their prolonged cover-up were but an elaboration of the basic approach used during the ITT preliminaries," the columnist wrote. "By the time of the Watergate cover-up the techniques of conspiracy, fraud and perjury had been systematized into an automatic Administration response . . . In dozens of particulars, large and small, the tactics used by the Nixon men to wriggle out of Watergate were imitations, albeit refined by practice, of those used in ITT."

Jack Anderson now expanded his anti-Nixon crusade beyond his "Merry-Go-Round" column. In interviews with other journalists, the muckraker attacked the President as "a Dogpatch-style politician who always aims his knee at the groin, who scratches the eyes of his opponents and karate chops them in the neck." Anderson was equally scathing during a nationwide lecture tour. "What contempt they have for the public!" he shouted to his audiences. "To preach law and order while they violate the law!" The columnist "bellowed" his sermons, *The New York Times Magazine* reported, "arms flailing, fingers pointing, eyes rolling, in a menacing hellfire-and-brimstone tone." He "did more pacing, finger jabbing and eye rolling than Oral Roberts in full cry," *Newsweek* observed, "his rich baritone voice" booming like an evangelist's as he reached "new heights of righteous outrage" and "climaxed his pyrotechnics with a ringing call to action."

Meanwhile, under the banner "Jack Anderson, Supersnoop," *Time* put the columnist's scowling visage on its cover. "The Square Scourge of Washington," the newsweekly stated, had become a "household name" and achieved "a reporter's daydream: his revelations rock the nation, and he shifts from merely writing news to making it. Newspapers front-page his exposés, he stars at televised hearings and on talk shows, fellow newsmen want to interview him, and the reigning powers that he assaults seem powerless before him."

In the White House, the President and his aides expressed disgust at the celebrity of their old enemy.

"Anderson's got the cover on *Time* and [he's in] *Newsweek*," Colson marveled. "It's incredible how they're building that son of a bitch up, just incredible."

"Building him up on stuff, none of which has yet been proved," the President interrupted. True, there were "the Anderson Papers" on Nixon's secret arms deal with Pakistan, the President conceded: "Of course he's got that leak, those are proven more or less, but as far as this [ITT] stuff is concerned, not a goddamn thing has been proven, [not] one stinking goddamn thing."

The President continued to brood about Anderson's positive publicity. "Have somebody attack *Time* for having him on the cover," Nixon ordered his staff the next day. "Let Agnew do that" by denouncing the magazine for being "taken in by Anderson."

Two days later, the CBS News correspondent Morley Safer broadcast a glowing profile of Anderson on the prime-time television program *60 Minutes*. "You can hardly pass a Washington landmark these days without recalling a reputation that Jack Anderson destroyed, a scandal exposed, a revelation of the big lie in high places," Safer reported. Anderson then popped up in front of a variety of Washington backdrops: at the Pentagon, the columnist bragged that the "security boys are investigating us here all the time." Outside FBI headquarters, Anderson declared, "We got evidence from inside the FBI that J. Edgar Hoover's been using FBI employees to write his book." And in front of the Executive Office Building, Anderson boasted, "We've gotten quite a few secrets out of the White House . . . that prove that President Nixon and his foreign policy czar Henry Kissinger were lying about the India-Pakistan crisis." Safer described Anderson as

> The nosiest man in Washington . . . [with] an extraordinary record of news beats. Always on the attack . . . He prints all the news that most Government agencies regard as unfit to print . . . No other reporter prods quite so regularly at Washington's soft underbelly as Jack Anderson. No other reporter gets his hands on secret documents quite so often . . . He's become a Washington fixture—loved and feared and hated.

"It's very important to have a needle and stuff it in some of these windbags and let the hot air out," Anderson told *60 Minutes*. Informants who turned to Anderson, his legman Les Whitten added, did so to get "the hardest, toughest, meanest, most ornery" reporting possible: "When the story comes out, they want to see it hit hard and get right down to the absolute bone of the story. They don't want to see a minuet dance around it, they want to see some hot rock 'n' roll."

The President was outraged. "*60 Minutes,* the news magazines," he exclaimed. It's "absolute madness, glorifying" Anderson like this.

"It's gone to his head, too," Haldeman agreed. "He looks like a madman. Wild eyes."

Even so, the President realized, when it came to public relations, "we've been buried" by him.

Meanwhile, satirists aimed their humor at Nixon's nemesis. "Jack Anderson is a big know-ITT all," one cartoonist punned. Another sketched a Washington desk with a stack of three document-filled trays: "In," "Out," and "To be leaked to Jack Anderson." "I don't want to criticize the way he gets his news," Bob Hope told crowds, "but putting on a blond wig and a miniskirt and sitting on Kissinger's lap" was going too far.

Not all the attention Anderson received was laudatory. A writer from *The New Yorker* mocked Anderson's polyester cinnamon-and-mustard suits, purchased at a factory warehouse, and the orange and green colors of his family's living room: "There is no combination of words in the English language that Jack Anderson regards as a cliché—not 'boon companion,' not 'wine-dark seas,' not 'the story can now be told' . . . There is no lead paragraph Anderson considers too melodramatic." At the same time, many of the hundreds of letters Anderson received in his office each week were filled with vituperative denunciations. One envelope contained two pieces of paper separated by a slab of manure. Another was addressed only to "Jack Anderson, liar, louse, ring-tailed rat and yellow-bellied skunk." The U.S. Postal Service somehow figured out which of America's fourteen thousand Jack Andersons was the intended recipient.

In May, Anderson received the Pulitzer Prize in national reporting for his exposé of the Nixon administration's secret tilt to Pakistan. "The Anderson Papers brought to light facts that would not have been available through any other channels," the judges declared. "It is this kind of exposure to the sunlight of public opinion that contributes to the integrity and ultimate success of the democratic process."

"Horrible," the President grumbled. Anderson and his sources were nothing less than "thieves who took the stuff out of Kissinger's office."

Colson agreed, though he had to admit that Anderson had "achieved what Drew Pearson never achieved" and "become a kind of public personality." Indeed, less than three years after Pearson's death, Anderson had added another three hundred newspapers to his client base, an increase of nearly 50 percent.

Nixon allies were appalled by it all. "When they begin giving the Pulitzer Prize to Jack Anderson," Senator Barry Goldwater said, "it is time to call it the Benedict Arnold Award." Indeed, "it's encouraging to every damn crook in the country" to honor a "columnist who's a fence." In a televised interview, White House speechwriter Patrick Buchanan condemned Anderson's award as "atrocious" and "appalling . . . if you can get ahold of some secret documents, if you can seduce some miserable government employee to give you a National Security Council memorandum and then you run it in your column, you can get a Pulitzer Prize."

The President's men were not alone. Trustees of Columbia University, which awarded the Pulitzer, publicly voiced "deep reservations" about the "suitability" of giving the honor to Anderson. "If you crib documents and then put them in the paper," one said, "that's just not good journalism. If someone steals or robs, you can't throw holy water on it by claiming it was done in the public interest."

Anderson replied by blasting "those who believe in the Kremlin system of government control over information" and called the award "recognition of the public's right to get behind the phony security stands of government." In private, he admitted feeling "contemptuous" of the prize. "We had earned it many times over" in the past without receiving it, he said, so "when I finally got it, I was awfully tempted to throw it back in their face." But the columnist controlled his tongue and accepted the thorny laurel with outward modesty.

In truth, most Washington journalists recognized that Anderson had long deserved the accolade. "My friends are not always in accord with Jack's techniques," one Beltway pundit wrote, "but most do give him credit for at least two things: his enterprise in digging out facts that others are trying to hide, and his courage in printing stories that will make powerful men and organizations his implacable enemies." According to *Life* magazine, despite his "pristinely ascetic personal life," the muckraker had become an "improbable new folk hero of the young . . . an unlikely Pied Piper."

For the first time in his career, Anderson received widespread acclaim—and a sudden rash of social invitations—from the capital insiders who had so often ignored or ridiculed him in the past. He was feted for lunch at columnist Joseph Alsop's Georgetown mansion. Publisher Katharine Graham hosted him in her *Washington Post* office, where she "fawned all over him," urging him to join her newspaper's board of directors and allow his column to be moved from its exile alongside the comics to the more prestigious op-ed page. But Anderson turned her down. "He always stayed outside the doors of power," a journalist who knew him explained. "He was always the Mormon boy looking in."

Just like the Quaker president with whom he battled, Anderson could not bring himself to make peace with the Washington establishment that had scorned him for so long. "It was much more important to Jack to be respected in his church than in elite media circles," Anderson's longtime reporter, Les Whitten, realized. "So that clannishness kept him insulated from those gutless trained seals of the Washington press corps."

Anderson himself put it more diplomatically. "Don't worry," he reassured his staff presciently, "sooner or later we're bound to do something they think is outrageous" and then "they'll be giving us hell again."

14

"KILL HIM"

Jack Anderson's secretary was unfazed by the caller's urgent tone. After all, hundreds of insistent strangers now contacted the columnist's office each week to pass on story tips or seek help for personal problems. So, as usual, the phone call was transferred to one of Anderson's unpaid college interns, whose lowly work included screening out the crackpots. But this time, in March 1972, Lehigh University undergraduate Jeff Brindle was surprised to find himself talking with a senior government official who possessed highly sensitive documents about a plot by the Nixon administration to overthrow a democratically elected government in South America.

Less than an hour later, the anxious informant showed up at Anderson's door and handed the long-haired intern a brown manila envelope filled with twenty-six internal memos—stamped "Personal & Confidential"—written on the letterhead of ITT, the politically powerful conglomerate at the heart of Senate hearings that Anderson had instigated earlier that month. "Holy shit," Brindle remembers thinking, "there's a lot of top secret stuff in here about the CIA!"

The memos revealed a conspiracy between the CIA and ITT to overthrow Salvador Allende, the Marxist president of Chile who would fall victim to a coup d'état a year later. "Approaches continue to be made to select members of the [Chilean] Armed Forces in an attempt to have them lead some sort of uprising" against Allende, one ITT memo stated. Other documents reported that the anti-Allende rebellion had "full material and financial assistance by the U.S. military establishment" and that Chile's insurgents had received a "green light to move in the name of President Nixon."

The President's motive to stop Allende was primarily ideological anticommunism. "Chile could end up being the worst failure in our administration—our Cuba," White House national security advisor Henry Kissinger warned Nixon. ITT's motive, on the other hand, was economic: the multinational company owned Chile's telephone company and feared that Allende's new socialist government would confiscate up to $200 million of its assets. Together, the Nixon administration and ITT shared similar goals and discussed them in unvarnished terms. CIA officials urged ITT to help destabilize Allende by "inducing economic collapse" in Chile. ITT executives agreed and promised to "assist financially in sums up to seven figures." The secret memos, Anderson's legman Brit Hume marveled, "painted an extraordinary picture of a corporation utterly convinced of its right to interfere in the affairs of a foreign state in whatever fashion it chose in order to advance its own interests." They also portrayed U.S. foreign policy as a brutal tool of the President's corporate benefactors.

Anderson and Hume quickly authenticated the documents and drafted two columns about the secret regime-change plot. They saved their final phone calls, seeking comment from the CIA and ITT, for a Friday, when the upcoming weekend could be counted on to distract other reporters who might get wind of the story—and make it more difficult for their targets to leak a sanitized version of events to a journalistic competitor. According to the flurry of CIA memos generated that day, Hume told the intelligence agency that he had obtained "Personal/Confidential material that ties [the CIA] with IT & T" in "stopping" Allende and warned "it would be better if the Agency were not stuffy" about answering his "urgent" questions.

The "Merry-Go-Round" inquiries immediately set off alarms inside the Nixon administration and ITT. Dita Beard's boss called "to warn us that Jack Anderson has some documents," a CIA official wrote in a memo, although ITT "didn't know what Anderson will write." In turn, the CIA "discussed the problem with General [Alexander] Haig," Kissinger's deputy, to be sure that the White House was "advised about these developments." Within two hours of Hume's phone call to the

CIA, its director crossed the Potomac River from his Virginia headquarters for an emergency lunch with Anderson in downtown Washington. Not surprisingly, Richard Helms failed to persuade the newsman to spike his scoop. That evening, a CIA administrator drove to the Washington home of a top ITT executive to get copies of the documents leaked to Anderson. "ITT is not going to have any comment on these memos," the intelligence operative informed his superiors afterward. "They will neither confirm nor deny; no comment at all. ITT tried earlier to be gentlemen with Anderson and it didn't work."

But refusing comment didn't work, either. On March 21, the "Merry-Go-Round" hit newsstands across the country like an exploding mortar. "Secret documents which escaped shredding" by ITT "show that the company maneuvered at the highest levels" to sabotage Allende, Anderson reported. John McCone, a former CIA director who was now on the board of ITT, served as matchmaker in the "bizarre plot" between the intelligence agency and the conglomerate, while ITT also lobbied the White House and State Department to bring down the socialist leader. "Attorney General John Mitchell was even buttonholed at a wedding reception by a zealous ITT man," Anderson wrote. "These documents portray ITT as a virtual corporate nation in itself" that actually "considered triggering a military coup to head off Allende's election."

The next day, Anderson continued his barrage with a second column quoting directly from his cache of secret documents. "Everything should be done quietly but effectively to see that Allende does not get through the crucial next six months," one ITT memo advised; to "bring on economic chaos," the CIA advocated that ITT and other U.S. companies "drag their feet in sending money, in making deliveries, [and] in shipping spare parts" to Chile. "Undercover efforts are being made to bring about the bankruptcy of one or two of [Chile's] major savings and loan[s]," another confidential document stated. "This is expected to trigger a run on banks and the closure of some factories resulting in more unemployment," which "might produce enough violence to force the military to move."

Anderson's columns ignited a firestorm, enthusiastically fueled as usual by the muckraker himself, who selectively parceled out advance copies of his secret memos to *The New York Times* and *The Washington Post* for prominent play. The columnist fanned his own flames by making himself available for interviews with other journalists; after-ward, *Time* reported, "he flaunted a sheaf of stolen ITT documents" for television cameras, then dribbled out to the rest of the Washington press corps the last remnants of his Chile papers. "Unprecedented in their detail," one analyst wrote, the Anderson documents "candidly charted the intrigue of covert corporate collaboration" between ITT and the Nixon administration. On the *CBS Morning News*, the news-man hammered home the "fantastic" story of how the CIA and ITT plotted to "interfere in the domestic affairs of Chile."

As journalists jumped on the story, those implicated in the scandal retreated into silence. "Neither I.T.T. nor the Nixon Administration was willing to discuss the Anderson papers even to the extent of saying whether they were authentic," *The New York Times* reported. "The White House referred all inquiries to the State Department," whose spokesman "cut off questioning with the statement that 'I have nothing on that for you now.'" The CIA informed journalists, "We do not com-ment on anything that has been printed about the Agency." ITT issued a press release claiming that Anderson's columns were "without foun-dation" but refused to elaborate. "As more [Anderson] papers were published," *The New York Times* reported, "I.T.T. clammed up" com-pletely. The suspicious evasions seemed to confirm Anderson's incen-diary charges.

News outlets filled the vacuum with scathing editorials. *The Washing-ton Post* called the Anderson disclosures "astonishing . . . outrageous . . . dismal . . . [and] grave." Indeed, "President Nixon stands charged" with "personally approving" covert action "to prevent the democratically elected president of a supposedly friendly country from taking office," while "ITT is now accused of manipulating not only key aspects of domestic policy but of foreign policy as well." *The New York Times* de-clared that "special interests [should] not be allowed to meddle secretly in this nation's relations with other countries," adding that Anderson's memos demonstrated "a classic example of how a giant international corporation should never behave, particularly in a democratic coun-try with every right to work out its political destiny without outside interference."

In Congress, Democrats seized on the Anderson disclosures to con-demn the Nixon administration. Senator Frank Church called the columnist's revelations "very disturbing" and Senator Fred Harris demanded that the Justice Department investigate whether ITT broke any federal laws. Three days after Anderson's first column, the Senate Foreign Relations Committee announced that it would conduct a "major," "detailed," and "wide-ranging" investigation. White House aide Charles Colson warned the President that congressional Democrats were now trying to expand their probe of ITT's funding of the Republican Party to "bring in the Chile thing" as well. Secretary of State William Rogers was dispatched to a closed hearing to assure senators that the administration "did not engage in improper activities in Chile." But Chairman J. William Fulbright told reporters that Anderson's exposé had disclosed "very bad business" and his committee voted to subpoena ITT's documents on Allende.

Meanwhile, in Chile, Anderson's "revelations set off an explosion of nationalist indignation," author Peter Kornbluh wrote. "The leaked documents bolstered a long-standing belief among the Chilean left of U.S. economic imperialism, and confirmed widespread suspicions of Washington's covert efforts to thwart the Chilean socialist experiment." Facing fierce domestic opposition, Allende's government viewed the Anderson exposé as a "political windfall." Leftist publications thunderously denounced the *gringos*' "right-wing conspiracy" and declared that ITT stood for "Imperialism, Treason and Terror." The day after Anderson's series was published, protesters descended on the Chilean capital; organizers quoted extensively from the Anderson memos in angry speeches, and crowds burned banners on which the letters *ITT* were written. Chile's Senate held a special session to authorize an investigation, and diplomatic emissaries cited the "Anderson papers" to accuse the U.S. of violating international law. President Allende told cheering crowds that Anderson's columns were proof of the "seditious plan" of the Yankees and announced that ITT's holdings in Chile would be confiscated by his government. In a speech to the United Nations, Allende explained that ITT had "driven its tentacles deep into my country" and was attempting to "bring about civil war."

The scandal overwhelmed all other events in Chile. "The Government press and television are now devoting most of their space and time" to the Anderson documents, *The New York Times* reported. ALL NEWSPAPERS carried STORIES ON JACK ANDERSON EXPOSÉ SECRET

DOCUMENTS "DEMONSTRATING THAT ITT AND CIA HAD ENCOURAGED A COUP D'ETAT IN CHILE," CIA agents cabled headquarters in alarm. Anderson gave a lengthy interview to Chilean television assailing the CIA-ITT "campaign to ruin Chile's economy, goad the military to act, and to establish a dictatorship." The columnist "became an instant hero" in Chile, *The Washington Post* reported, and his memos were rushed by Chilean ambassador Orlando Letelier from the U.S. capital to his home country, where a team of government translators helped produce tens of thousands of copies of a ninety-three-page Spanish-language booklet—*Documents Secretos de la ITT*—that were immediately snapped up on the streets of Santiago. "News vendors declared the government volume an instant best-seller," the *Post* added, "competing well against the girlie magazines and screaming-headline newspapers that are the kiosks' standard fare."

Anderson's latest scoop brought yet another round of publicity to the columnist who had uncovered the scandal. "For a while at least," *Newsweek* reported, "ITT's Chilean imbroglio overshadowed the Dita Beard episode with which the whole ruckus had begun. And once again the man who broke the story was columnist Jack Anderson, whose uncanny access to Washington's secret filing cabinets has very nearly earned him the status of an independent branch of government." CBS commentator Nicholas von Hoffman was amused that

> Anderson, the rascal, has more memos! For next we find that in addition to trying to fix its case with the Justice Department, America's best-known conglomerate has also been passing the time trying to overthrow the government of Chile! Would you believe it? These machinations are too complicated to bear summarizing, but suffice it to say there is pussyfooting with CIA agents, plots to destroy the Chilean economy, and connivances with forlorn plans for coups d'etat, all thumbs, all clumsy, all like a burlesque of a Russian propaganda description of how an American, capitalist, international conglomerate is supposed to operate. And by God, ITT does! It does. It lives up to its Marxist stereotype.

Clearly, the administration's silence had failed to quell the international uproar. The President's men realized that they needed to change tactics, but they were in a difficult spot. For one thing, a top U.S. diplomat confided, "there was not much doubt about the authenticity" of Anderson's memos, which even White House aides privately admitted were genuine. Worse, the muckraker had uncovered only a fraction of the administration's much larger conspiracy to subvert Allende. As presidential counsel John Dean warned, exposing the full extent of American culpability in Chile could truly be "explosive."

To try to calm the furor, State Department officials privately debated how to word some sort of public denial. An early draft admitted that the U.S. had "weighed various contingencies" for stopping Allende, but the statement was deemed too candid and suppressed. Instead, a State Department spokesman announced—falsely—that the administration "firmly rejected . . . any ideas of thwarting" Allende that might or might not have been suggested and argued that Anderson's memos were merely "opinion and hearsay." The administration's reaction "ranged from evasion, to disinformation, to simply false information," Kornbluh wrote; this "initial Orwellian response to the CIA-ITT scandal set the stage for a protracted cover-up, made possible by a display of official mendacity virtually unparalleled in the annals of foreign policy. Outright deception—of the public, of Congress, and even other sectors of the U.S. government—permeated the administration's efforts to contain and conceal the facts."

ITT was equally duplicitous. A press release asserted that the conglomerate "has been and continues to be a good corporate citizen in Chile, as well as in all other countries where it has operations." ITT's denial was so unpersuasive that *New York Times* columnist Russell Baker suggested the company would be better off claiming that it was "only joking" about overthrowing Allende and that "nobody [in Washington] has a sense of humor anymore."

The administration wasn't amused. Typically, the President's first thoughts were about public relations. "Have you said anything, Ron, with regard to ITT and Chile?" Nixon asked Press Secretary Ronald Ziegler. "Well," the spokesman replied, "the State Department dealt with that." "What did they do," the President inquired, "deny it?" "They denied it," Ziegler said, "but they were cautious" because "they were afraid it might backfire." "Why?" Nixon asked. Ziegler explained that reporters had learned that the U.S. ambassador "received instructions to do anything short of" military intervention to overthrow Allende. "How the hell did that get out?" the President demanded. "Well," the White House aide responded, "Anderson got that from some source." Nixon was angry: the U.S. ambassador to Chile *"was* instructed to" stop Allende, "but he just failed, the son of a bitch. That was his main problem. He should have kept Allende from getting in."

As usual, the President and his advisors wanted to know how Anderson acquired his latest batch of incriminating documents. A right-wing Chilean newspaper, funded by the CIA, stated that the columnist—known for "printing whatever rumor or scandal reaches his ears"—received a bribe to publish the memos. Soon after, Nixon's secretary, Rose Mary Woods, received an "urgent" missive from an anti-Allende activist who alleged that Anderson collected a $70,000 payoff from Chilean ambassador Orlando Letelier for "aiding [and] abetting a Marxist government." Nixon's secretary was rightly skeptical of the charge but nonetheless passed it on to White House lawyer Fred Fielding. Five days later, the unfounded rumor was publicized on the libelproof House floor by Congressman John Rarick, a right-wing segregationist from Louisiana, but the fanciful claim gained little attention, perhaps because even the anti-Allende propagandists who had spread it did not seem to believe the rumor.

In fact, the ITT memos were leaked to Anderson by a senior aide to Senate Foreign Relations Committee chairman J. William Fulbright. The senator's role in the affair was complicated. A paragon of Washington's foreign policy establishment, Fulbright had been preoccupied by his opposition to the Vietnam War when he first received the Chile documents seventeen months earlier, courtesy of an ITT whistleblower. Fulbright's source recognized that the memos were "explosive" and over time became "disgusted" that the senator's staff did nothing with "all these ITT papers stacked up somewhere in its filing cabinets." Indeed, Fulbright did worse than nothing: he alerted CIA director Richard Helms that there was a leak and then suppressed the documents. Now, in the wake of Anderson's publication of the Dita Beard memo, Fulbright's advisors worried that their complicity might be exposed. The Arkansas Democrat's solution was to rush the documents to Anderson, whose own, separate pipeline into ITT would help conceal Fulbright's role in the scandal.

Days later, Senator Frank Church launched an official probe of CIA-ITT attempts to oust the Allende government. Anderson turned over his files to the Idaho Democrat and began working with his investigators as they embarked upon what would eventually turn into extensive public hearings about foreign assassinations and other crimes by U.S. intelligence agencies. Among those summoned to testify under oath was the man who had implemented the President's covert operation to sabotage Allende, CIA director Helms.

"Did you try in the Central Intelligence Agency to overthrow the government of Chile?" Senator Stuart Symington asked.

"No, sir," Helms lied.

"Did you have any money passed to opponents of Allende?"

"No, sir"—a second lie.

"So the stories you were in that war are wrong?"

"Yes, sir"—yet another lie.

Four years later, Helms's perjury led to federal court and a nolo contendere plea to deceiving Congress. After Attorney General Richard Kleindienst, Helms became the second high-level Nixon official convicted of a crime as a result of Anderson's ITT stories. For Helms, the irony was as palpable as it was painful: while his undercover operatives spied on Anderson, the columnist retaliated by exposing Helms's secret interference in Chile. As a result, Helms became the only CIA director in history forced to admit his crimes in court, thanks to one of the many Anderson sources whose identity Helms was unable to uncover.

The CIA director blamed his commander in chief. "President Nixon had ordered me to instigate a military coup in Chile," Helms later explained. Nixon "came down very hard . . . that he wanted something done and he didn't much care how." Indeed, once-classified government cables document the American conspiracy to crush Allende in irrefutable detail: ITT director McCone met with Helms and Kissinger to offer $1 million of corporate funds to depose the leftist leader; at least half that amount was channeled by ITT through the CIA to its anti-Allende operation. Records show that on more than three dozen separate occasions, senior CIA and ITT officials secretly conferred on how to bring down the socialist government. Two ITT executives in Chile even turned out to be clandestine CIA assets, given special code names in encrypted intelligence communications.

The decision to overthrow Allende was made at the very top of the Nixon White House. "I don't see why we need to stand by and watch a country go Communist due to the irresponsibility of its own people," Kissinger declared. The President's aides described Nixon as "furious" and "hysterical" at the prospect of Allende's election and "beside himself" once it happened. Nixon secretly ordered the CIA to "play a direct role in organizing a military coup," complete with a sabotage campaign to "make the economy scream." The President and his national security advisor issued instructions to put "pressure on every Allende weak spot in sight" to trigger a "military takeover." The CIA complied by secretly supplying weapons to dissident Chilean officers and channeling more than $8 million to covert anti-Allende operations. "It is firm and continuing policy," the administration cabled Santiago, "that Allende be overthrown by a coup."

He was. In September 1973, Chile's military bombed the presidential palace while Allende was inside and then stormed the building. Rather than be taken alive, Allende put a gun to his head and pulled the trigger. Chile's new military junta suspended the constitution and dissolved Congress. General Augusto Pinochet assumed dictatorial control for the next sixteen years and rounded up more than a hundred thousand people; thousands were summarily executed and tens of thousands tortured in a program of state-sponsored terror. "Of course, the newspapers [are] bleeding because a pro-Communist government has been overthrown," Kissinger told Nixon a few days after Allende's violent death. "Isn't that something," the President marveled. "I mean, instead of celebrating—in the Eisenhower period we would be heroes," Kissinger continued. "Well, we didn't—as you know—our hand doesn't show on this one," the President pointed out. "We didn't do it," Kissinger replied. "I mean, we helped them—created the conditions as great as possible." Nixon agreed: "That is right. And that is the way it is going to be played."

But no matter how it was played in the press, the role of the Nixon White House in trying to destabilize Allende's government was undeniable. Indeed, Jack Anderson's well-placed Pentagon source, Yeoman

Charles Radford, examined classified U.S. documents that spelled out specific methods for physically eliminating Allende. One options paper "discussed various ways of doing it," Radford said. "Either we have somebody in the country do it or we do it ourselves . . . I don't know if they used the word *assassinate*, but it was to get rid of him, to terminate him."

President Nixon also wanted to be rid of Jack Anderson. After all, in just the first three months of 1972, the reporter had exposed many of the administration's most embarrassing scandals: Nixon's clandestine tilt toward Pakistan, his secret cash from Howard Hughes, his fixing of ITT's antitrust case, and his sabotage of Allende. But to date, none of the President's efforts to stop Anderson had been successful. Not threats to file criminal charges. Not surveillance or wiretapping. Not even the President's order to smear Anderson as a homosexual. Instead, the columnist only seemed to grow bolder and more dangerous with his every revelation.

The White House decided to launch a formal campaign against its journalistic bête noire. "To take us off the defensive," presidential counsel John Dean declared in a memo, the administration must start "impeaching Jack Anderson." It was not enough just to react to each of his stories one at a time, after the fact, by "discrediting the allegations in his column," White House Plumber E. Howard Hunt realized; rather, Nixon's men had to become proactive by portraying Anderson as unreliable *before* his next attack. The goal, Hunt said, was to "diminish his reputation . . . personally and professionally."

To do so, the White House once again began trying to dig up dirt on the newsman. An informant promised "considerable derogatory information concerning Anderson," but it proved to be a disappointment—merely pages copied from a five-year-old book. Chief of Staff H. R. Haldeman dispatched investigator Jack Caulfield to interview Anderson's family and friends "under a subterfuge," but the results were equally meager. "Neighbors of the Anderson's [sic] advised that family was of good repute," Caulfield wrote in a memo. Another White House private eye, Tony Ulasewicz, began "asking questions about some scam" in which Anderson's troublesome brother Gordon was supposedly involved, but once again, Nixon's men came up empty-handed.

Still, the White House pressed on. A "Merry-Go-Round" fan from rural Maryland called Anderson to warn that "a man with a black bushy moustache was out there poking around for confirmation that I had obtained valuable shorefront property from the University of Maryland at a sweetheart price," the columnist recalled, "in return for exerting political influence to get the university a grant of some kind." The mustachioed man turned out to be Nixon operative G. Gordon Liddy, who later confirmed that he was ordered to "check out a rumor—which proved impossible to substantiate—that Anderson had been involved in a land fraud." At the behest of Nixon's campaign deputy Jeb Magruder, Liddy was also assigned to investigate rumors that Anderson was involved in a "kickback scheme" with the Democratic Party. That probe, too, went nowhere. In addition, Liddy said that he tried and failed to prove that Anderson "sent someone to break into our [campaign] headquarters but was thwarted by our security."

Frustrated by its inability to uncover wrongdoing by Anderson, the White House turned to investigators working for the private security firm Intertel, which was staffed by former prosecutors and retired agents from the FBI and the CIA. Intertel had already been hired by ITT to dig into the columnist's background, and the White House now piggybacked on its work, ordering up additional "specific assignments" for investigation. Intertel forwarded its reports on Anderson to the White House and the Justice Department, which in turn passed them to the Nixon reelection campaign and Republican Party headquarters. The impropriety of federal prosecutors and presidential aides conspiring with private political and corporate interests to undermine a newsman did not even faze those involved.

The President's men tried to plant derogatory stories about Anderson in the media, but the move backfired when journalists reported not the baseless charges but the heavy-handed government retaliation. The White House "is directing a major effort to discredit columnist Jack Anderson," *The Washington Post* reported in a front-page story; the administration's "extensive search for facts" about the muckraker also "includes feeding negative material about Anderson . . . to the press" and using "the resources of the Republican National Committee, the Committee for the Re-election of the President, and the Justice Department." The *Post* concluded dismissively that the only accurate information provided by the administration "deals with already known and generally uncontroversial details about Anderson" and was nothing more than a "panicky—and exceedingly clumsy—campaign" against him.

In the White House, Chief of Staff Haldeman informed the President that "unfortunately," instead of exposing Anderson, the press reported that Nixon's men were targeting him. "Who the hell put that [out]?" the President demanded. One of Nixon's own public relations aides, Haldeman acknowledged, who became "overly excited about some of these things." The President sighed in frustration: "You forget that sometimes people talk."

Still, Nixon's desire to go after Anderson remained undiminished. "I would like to get him," the Chief Executive reiterated to his staff, "get Anderson discredited."

The President's men escalated their efforts and infiltrated undercover operatives into Anderson's office. The Nixon campaign hired Lou Russell—an investigator for Congressman Nixon in the late 1940s who remained friendly with the President's secretary, Rose Mary Woods—to spy on the columnist. Russell successfully ingratiated himself with Anderson by passing on story tips and the newsman took pity on the "down-on-his-luck" gumshoe, giving him "odd jobs" to do and allowing him to "hang around" the "Merry-Go-Round" office. Russell began filing secret reports on Anderson with the Nixon campaign's security director, James McCord, the future Watergate burglar. But Anderson's eagle-eyed secretary, Opal Ginn, soon "surprised Russell poking around my desk," the muckraker recalled. Opal began watching more closely and noticed Russell "in unaccustomed parts of our suite, not lolling about as usual but with a kind of furtive alertness, ears cocked for conversations, eyes peeled for desk-top papers." Anderson got rid of Russell but soon agreed to take on a young intern who turned out to be the son of another spy hired by the Nixon campaign. To this day, it is unclear what Nixon's men learned from their infiltration of Anderson's office.

Meanwhile, the President personally proposed other undercover tactics to ensnare the muckraker. Why couldn't the White House "find someone to rifle [through] Anderson's files—the way [he] seemed to be doing with ITT and the government"? Nixon demanded. Better still, campaign operatives could plant fraudulent documents with the columnist to undermine his credibility. "Don't we have some spurious stuff that we can give to Jack Anderson?" Haldeman asked. "Let's play on Anderson's notoriety now. Let that out. He's a big man" now. Colson replied that he was already working on such a trap. "We got a whole plot concocted," he said eagerly. "I got just the scheme for that." Haldeman was skeptical that Anderson would fall for it: "He won't. He always checks it out." But Colson suggested a diabolical way to make the plan work: "We can get into his office and type some documents in his office—on his typewriter, on [official] stationery—that are explosive. And then get them back and feed them to him and let him publish them." Afterward, the White House could "prove they were typed in his office" and destroy Anderson once and for all. "Well," Haldeman replied, "that's screwing Jack Anderson."

It was not just idle talk. According to an FBI memo, the Nixon campaign faked a letter on Democratic National Committee stationery and mailed it to Anderson in an effort to discredit both the opposition party and the investigative columnist. In addition, Anderson said he received several government documents that were sent anonymously in the mail filled with "explosive" allegations. One was typed on White House letterhead. Anderson showed it to a trusted source who worked in the President's office. "He said, 'Yeah, this has got all the right signatures on it but let me check it and I'll call you back,'" Anderson recalled. After investigating, Anderson's source was startled to discover that no such document had been written: "It's a perfect forgery. It's got all the right signatures, the right routings, everything. But it doesn't exist!" Anderson realized that only someone with extraordinary sophistication and inside knowledge of White House procedures could have produced such convincing forgeries.

What other forms of retaliation did Nixon's men plan? "I don't know whether my doctor's office was broken into, my phone tapped, my mail intercepted, my files photostatted," the columnist told one of his reporters, "or what other White House routines were invoked." He certainly had no idea that Nixon's men had already come up with a plot to silence him by the one method guaranteed to be permanent: murder.

In the middle of March, in the midst of the ITT scandal, Charles Colson summoned his top clandestine operative to the Old Executive Office Building, across the street from the White House. According to E. Howard Hunt, Colson had apparently "just come from a meeting with President Nixon," whose hideaway office was next door, and seemed uncharacteristically "nervous" and "agitated" about the message he had to deliver. Colson told Hunt that Nixon "was incensed over Jack Anderson's frequent publication of leaks," that the "son of a bitch" columnist "had become a great thorn in the side of the President," and that it was imperative to "stop Anderson at all costs." Hunt stated that Colson proposed assassinating Anderson in a manner that would appear accidental, perhaps by using a special poison that could not be detected during an autopsy. Colson suggested various specific ways to get rid of Anderson, Hunt said, and "asked me if I could explore the matter with the CIA," where Hunt had previously worked as a spy. According to Hunt, Colson explained that neutralizing Anderson was "very important" to the White House and Hunt was "authorized to do whatever was necessary" to eliminate the investigative reporter.

The Nixon operative knew exactly who to contact to get the job done. He began with his sidekick G. Gordon Liddy, who had just been transferred to the Nixon campaign's intelligence operation and was "forever volunteering to rub people out," as Hunt put it. Liddy wasted little time before expounding on the obvious solution to his latest White House assignment: "They charged us with the task: 'Come up with ways of stopping Anderson.' We examined all of the alternatives and very quickly came to the conclusion [that] the only way you're going to be able to stop him is to kill him."

To lay the groundwork, Hunt and Liddy conducted physical surveillance of Anderson, tailing the columnist in Liddy's green Jeep as Anderson drove from a parking garage in downtown Washington to his residence in the Maryland suburbs. "The purpose was to locate Anderson's home and examine it from the outside for vulnerabilities," Hunt recalled. It turned out to be "just an ordinary house" with "no pits around it," so "if housebreakers wanted to get in they would have very little difficulty." Hunt concluded that he and Liddy could easily sneak into Anderson's home and "get rid of the pesky journalist" by putting "a drug-laden pill" in whatever medicine bottles Anderson used.

But what kind of poison should be slipped to the muckraker? This was a question beyond the expertise of the White House operatives. After all, while Hunt had plotted at the CIA to overthrow leftist leaders in Central America, he had no personal hands-on experience in murder; and while Liddy boasted that he "could kill a man with a pencil in a matter of seconds" by jamming it into a victim's neck, he was not an expert in the toxicology of poisons. So Hunt reached out to a former intelligence colleague who had been part of a CIA team that tried to poison Fidel Castro a decade earlier with botulism toxin—a plot, ironically, that had recently been exposed by Jack Anderson.

Hunt turned to the aptly named Dr. Edward Gunn, a CIA physician involved in the conspiracy to murder Castro, who was known as an expert in the "unorthodox application of medical and chemical knowledge"—which, Liddy knew, was "just a euphemism for assassination." Hunt telephoned Dr. Gunn at his home in suburban Washington and explained that he was now working for President Nixon.

"Oh," the poison expert responded. "Sure, I'll cooperate."

The men set up a lunch date across the street from the White House at the venerable Hay-Adams Hotel. On March 24, Hunt and Liddy walked the short distance from their offices to meet their lunch guest and plot Anderson's assassination.

"Well," Hunt told Liddy during their stroll along Pennsylvania Avenue, "Colson has just laid another one on me here. He wants me to find out" whether any particular "hallucinogenic drugs"—especially LSD—could be slipped to Anderson. LSD was the CIA's drug of choice during the 1960s, a synthetic psychedelic acid that sometimes led unsuspecting targets to go berserk and commit suicide. Dr. Gunn could provide details of the CIA's previous LSD experiments and explain which hallucinogens to avoid because they would leave behind traces that could be detected in Anderson's body. Hunt took care to emphasize that Dr. Gunn had recently retired from the CIA. "I took 'retired' to be in quotes," Liddy recalled, "since that is a standard technique" used to give the intelligence agency deniability in clandestine operations.

Nixon's aspiring assassins entered the Hay-Adams. The weather was too chilly to lunch on the rooftop, with its spectacular view overlooking the White House. So instead, Hunt and Liddy headed downstairs to the subterranean old grill, whose darkness could better cloak their plotting.

Hunt warmly greeted "Manny," the nickname preferred by Dr. Gunn, and introduced the toxicologist to Liddy, who was using the name of George Leonard as his "operational alias."

Hunt and Liddy explained that "they had an individual who was giving them trouble," Dr. Gunn recalled, and "they wanted something that would get him out of the way" without leaving any visible traces behind. Dr. Gunn's response was not what the Nixon operatives wanted to hear: that "there was nothing undetectable" that could be used on Anderson because any drug could eventually be discovered in a thorough medical test such as an autopsy. Perhaps Dr. Gunn was uncomfortable with such an explicit discussion of murder. Hunt shifted the conversation to the more neutral topic of prior CIA experience with poisons. Dr. Gunn seemed to relax a bit as he recounted his previous scientific exploits with LSD. "We painted the steering wheel of a car for absorption through the palms of the hand," Dr. Gunn recalled, and also "put it on a car door handle." Indeed, he advised, "there are many" kinds of hallucinogens besides LSD that could be administered surreptitiously to a target like Anderson. Still, Dr. Gunn cautioned that the CIA had encountered considerable "unpredictability of individual reaction" to such poisoning.

Hunt asked whether a "massive dose" of LSD would "cause such disruption of motor function that the driver of a car would lose control of it and crash." Dr. Gunn reiterated that individual reactions varied. Besides, in cold weather, Anderson might be protected from absorbing the drug by wearing gloves; and in warm weather, sweaty palms could have a similar effect. In addition, regardless of the weather, such a plot would be thwarted if Anderson didn't touch the contaminated steering wheel because his wife or children drove his car instead.

Liddy, a man of action, grew impatient with the inconclusive discussion. Uncertain "halfway measures were not appropriate," he declared. The only "logical and just solution" was that Anderson "be killed. Quickly. My solution was received with immediate acceptance, almost relief, as if they were just waiting for someone else to say for them what was really on their minds."

If the White House wanted to kill Anderson while he was in his car, there were simpler ways to do so than by poisoning him with LSD. Dr. Gunn pointed out that in other countries, the CIA had success ramming autos into a targeted vehicle during "a turn or sharp curve" to make it "flip over, crash, and, usually, burn." According to Liddy, Dr. Gunn suggested a specific street intersection that Anderson routinely drove through on his way to work whose "configuration [was] ideal" for such a crash, in part because it was already "notorious as the scene of fatal auto accidents" in Washington.

But Liddy feared that assassinating Anderson in this fashion was just "too chancy." Besides, there were also bureaucratic obstacles. "Dr. Gunn's method would require the services of an expert to ensure success," Liddy pointed out, and such a trained operative "might not be available to us" if the CIA refused to supply the experienced personnel to carry out Anderson's execution. Even if the intelligence agency agreed to take part in the muckraker's murder, the White House would be vulnerable to CIA blackmail afterward.

Hunt returned to the idea of poisoning Anderson and requested "an LSD-type drug" from the CIA. "Hunt always wanted to give LSD to people," Liddy later explained. But Dr. Gunn begged off on the grounds that he had retired from the intelligence agency a few months earlier and no longer had access to such hallucinogens. Although the CIA "refused to cooperate," Hunt later said, he didn't "press because he thought Liddy could get the drug" from his own contacts "if the time came when any controlled substance were needed."

No matter where Hunt obtained the hallucinogen, however, the question remained: how could it be slipped to Anderson without his knowledge?

"Of course, there's always the old simple method of simply dropping a pill in a guy's cocktail," Dr. Gunn offered. But Hunt realized that wouldn't work because "Anderson was a Mormon" with nine children and "they were very abstemious, they wouldn't even touch Coca-Cola."

"Aspirin roulette" seemed more plausible. Anderson might swallow a deadly dose, Liddy said, if "a poisoned replica of the appropriate brand of headache tablet [was slipped] into the bottle usually found in [his] medicine cabinet."

Anderson's house seemed easy enough to break into, as Hunt and Liddy had discovered during their surveillance of the columnist. But "to perform an entry operation simply to put one or two pills in a bottle seemed highly impractical," Hunt decided. After all, "how would you go clandestinely into a medicine cabinet with a household full of people and pore over all of the drugs and the pharmacopoeia assortments there until you found the one that Jack Anderson normally administered to himself?"

Liddy agreed: "Too iffy again. It would be only one out of 50 or even 100 tablets" that would be poisoned, "and months could go by before [Anderson] swallowed it." Not to mention the "danger that an innocent member of his family might take the pill" instead. So, Liddy said, like LSD on Anderson's steering wheel, aspirin roulette was "discussed and discarded" as well.

Finally, Liddy had enough pussyfooting around. Anderson "should just become a fatal victim of the notorious Washington street-crime rate," Liddy declared. "He would be assaulted, his wallet and watch removed" to make it appear that the motive was robbery. No one disagreed. "Drastic problems," Liddy later explained, "sometimes demand drastic solutions."

On this happy note, the men ended their lengthy lunch at the Hay-Adams. "I gave Dr. Gunn a hundred-dollar bill, from the Committee to Re-elect the President intelligence funds, as a fee for his services," Liddy recalled. The payment was made "at Hunt's suggestion . . . to protect Dr. Gunn's image as 'retired'" from the CIA.

But who would actually do the dirty deed and fatally mug Anderson?

Hunt decided to subcontract the job to soldiers he had previously signed up for the CIA invasion of Cuba's Bay of Pigs, men who were now working for the Nixon campaign. So "the assassination of Jack Anderson," Liddy said, would "be carried out by Cubans already recruited for the intelligence arm of the Committee to Re-elect the President."

But there was a gigantic problem: the ubiquitous Anderson was so well connected in the netherworld of covert operations that he actually knew two of the Cubans selected to execute him. More astonishing still, one of these intended assassins actually turned out to be a longtime friend and source of the columnist who had even stayed in the Anderson home as a houseguest. Nixon's operatives pondered their dilemma. What should have been a simple task—bumping off Anderson—was turning into a colossal headache.

Hunt explained the problem to Liddy: the White House might not "think it wise to entrust so sensitive a matter" as killing Anderson to his Cuban friends.

Liddy's response was unhesitating: "If necessary, I'll do it" myself. After all, Liddy said, "if the Cubans were ruled out, I was the best man for the job, considering my own FBI and martial arts training. We didn't want to make it look like anything more than another Washington street-crime statistic, remember, so no sophisticated weaponry could be employed" anyway.

Although Liddy owned an untraceable 9-millimeter pistol designed for use "when White House superiors tasked me with an assassination," he decided instead on a low-tech approach: to "knife" Anderson or break his neck. It would be "justifiable homicide," Liddy believed, because Anderson was "one of those mutant strains of columnist" whose "systematic leaking of top-secret information rendered the effective conduct of American foreign policy virtually impossible." Simply put, the columnist had "gone too far and he had to be stopped."

"I know it violates the sensibilities of the innocent and tender-minded," Liddy explained, "but in the real world, you sometimes have to employ extreme and extralegal methods to preserve the very system whose laws you're violating."

Did the White House really plot to assassinate Jack Anderson? The story seems almost too outlandish to be true and several Nixon aides questioned whether it ever occurred. But both G. Gordon Liddy and E. Howard Hunt admitted their involvement in the conspiracy. To be sure, Liddy was an outrageous character, a flamboyantly mustachioed macho man who thrilled to the radio speeches of Adolf Hitler and enjoyed showing off his testosterone-addled manliness with such feats of daring as eating a wild rat and holding his hand over a candle flame until his "flesh turned black" and the air filled with "the scent of burning meat." Still, as Nixon aide Leonard Garment acknowledged, "Liddy has been one of the truth-tellers among the Watergate survivors." No less a critic than Bob Woodward of *The Washington Post* called Liddy both "credible" and "meticulous."

Hunt had a more devious reputation but no obvious incentive to implicate himself needlessly in a murder conspiracy. His testimony about Jack Anderson, like Liddy's, seems consistent with the rest of the available evidence. "I was a little astonished to think that they were focusing on a correspondent, however unpopular he might be," Hunt later said of the Anderson plot. But in the Nixon White House, Anderson "was regarded as the enemy," Hunt explained. "Colson just *hated* him . . . And the more that Colson knew about Anderson, the more resolved he was to put an end to it by whatever means." Still, any order to murder Anderson, Hunt believed, must have come "directly from the President . . . If Nixon said 'Chuck, I want you to do this,' he would do it or he would find people to do it for him."

Indeed, Colson's blind allegiance to his president was as legendary as his ruthlessness. Haldeman called Colson "the President's personal 'hit man'" who "encouraged the dark impulses in Nixon's mind and *acted* on those impulses instead of ignoring them and letting them die." At Nixon's behest, Colson had already ordered subordinates to firebomb a Washington think tank and forge documents to implicate President Kennedy in the assassination of a foreign leader. "I would do anything Richard Nixon asks me to do—period," Colson said. "I had always followed Nixon's order . . . whatever the cost." According to Ehrlichman, Colson was the one aide the President could count on to "do this or that dastardly deed. Someone who would salute him and say, 'Yes, Mr. President, sir,' and get it done." Nixon agreed: "He'll do anything," the Chief Executive marveled, "I mean anything."

The exact role of President Nixon in the Anderson assassination plot may never be known. So far, no White House tapes have emerged to demonstrate that Nixon himself ordered the murder of his longtime journalistic enemy. But in the past, the President had shown no hesitation to sacrifice innocent lives abroad, from Vietnam to Pakistan to Chile, or to order numerous illegal acts at home in explosions of fury that his staff could disregard only at their peril.

In short, it is difficult to imagine Nixon's closest advisors plotting to execute America's leading investigative reporter without at least the tacit approval of their president. Hunt, for one, believed that Colson simply didn't have the "balls" to order Anderson's assassination without Nixon's prior authorization. Historian Stanley Kutler described Colson's role in the Nixon White House in similar, if more tactful, terms. "Colson rarely acted on his own initiative," Kutler wrote. "His deeds, like Haldeman's and Ehrlichman's, correlate with his notes of his regular meetings with the President." Nixon was a micromanager who hired zealous younger subordinates to ensure that they would carry out his will. The chain of command was clearly established, Haldeman said: "Nixon tells Colson, Colson orders Hunt, Hunt executes." Thus "Colson only fed off Nixon," Haldeman realized, for "if there were no Nixon, there would have been no Colson in the White House." Ultimately, Kutler concluded, when it came to the darkest crimes of his Praetorian Guard, "Richard Nixon commanded the patrol and dictated its missions."

At the end of March, after meeting with the CIA's poison expert, Hunt and Liddy reviewed the strengths and weakness of various methods of bumping off Anderson. A paper outlining the full range of deadly options "was written up in a memo and sent to the White House," Liddy said.

A few days later, at lunch with Hunt, Liddy again "brought up the matter of killing Jack Anderson" but this time Hunt "told me to forget it," Liddy recalled. Hunt explained that he had delivered his report briefing Colson on their recommendations for getting rid of the columnist, but that the White House decided it would be "unproductive" to do so at that time. The worst of the ITT scandal was at last starting to blow over and Hunt thought that Colson "was by now involved in other far more important matters." Liddy, accustomed to following orders, inquired no further. "That was the end of the affair," Hunt concluded.

No matter. Liddy and Hunt now had a more urgent assignment: bugging the Democratic Party headquarters in the Watergate office building.

15

WATERGATE

As the Senate wrapped up its hearings on the ITT scandal, President Nixon's men decided to break into the Democratic National Committee at the Watergate complex in Washington. This secret bugging was just part of a much larger espionage and sabotage operation instigated by the President himself against his adversaries that included burglary, forgery, surveillance, infiltration, and hate-filled anonymous letters and phone calls. The "true beginning of Watergate," Senator Edward Kennedy believed, was the ITT scandal that had just preceded it; and Jack Anderson's incriminating memo proved to be "the first 'smoking gun' of the long Watergate affair."

Nixon decided to target Democratic Party chairman Lawrence O'Brien, who had been attacking the White House about ITT in what the President feared was "only the beginning of a much greater assault" before the election: "I told my staff that we should come up with the kind of imaginative dirty tricks that our Democratic opponents used against us and others so effectively in previous campaigns." Nixon regarded O'Brien as the Democrats' "grand master" of political wizardry, "a partisan in the most extreme and effective sense" who had been "tutored in the Kennedy political machine" and would "hit hard" against Republicans in the upcoming race. Indeed, said White House counsel John Dean, O'Brien was "second only to Jack Anderson as a target of ugly thoughts—bitterly resented, even feared."

Nixon's obsession with O'Brien had festered for the past dozen years. According to a White House operative, the President's advisors "blamed O'Brien for leaking the story" of the Howard Hughes loan scandal to Anderson on the eve of the 1960 presidential election. Now Nixon learned that the hated O'Brien was himself secretly on Hughes's payroll. The President was outraged at what he felt was the Democrat's double standard. "We're going to nail O'Brien on this, one way or the other," Nixon vowed. "O'Brien's not going to get away with it [because] we're going to get proof of his relationship with Hughes." According to John Ehrlichman, the President pounded his desk in the Oval Office and announced, "I want to put O'Brien in jail. And I want to do it before the election."

In truth, the motive for bugging O'Brien was as much defensive as offensive. The President also feared that O'Brien's link to Hughes would enable the Democratic strategist to learn about the billionaire's most recent $100,000 gift to Nixon, which the President had already partially spent and desperately wanted to keep hidden. "Having been badly burned by my exposé of the Hughes loan," Anderson recalled, "Nixon was particularly sensitive about [his] Hughes connection. He didn't want to be burned again." Yet the muckraker had once again discovered—and reported—the President's latest Hughes payment, writing in his column that there was "documentary evidence" of the cash transaction and suggesting it was a bribe for favorable administration decisions. "That goddamned Hughes thing," Nixon exclaimed a few hours after Anderson's revelation was published. Well, "Larry O'Brien—he was on the payroll," too.

On March 30, 1972, Nixon's campaign manager, John Mitchell, approved the plan to break into the Democratic National Committee and bug O'Brien's phone. According to Mitchell's deputy, Jeb Magruder, the President personally authorized the spying, telling Mitchell, "You need to do that." The "primary purpose of the break-in," Magruder said, was to discover what O'Brien knew about the Hughes cash that Nixon had received—and to make sure that the secret was kept "under wraps" so it wouldn't interfere with his reelection. White House chief of staff H. R. Haldeman thought it was "absurd" to "take such a risk" as burglary. "But on matters pertaining to Hughes," Haldeman knew, "Nixon sometimes seemed to lose touch with reality."

Amazingly, just two weeks later, while Nixon's men were still planning the Watergate break-in, Anderson found out *in advance* about the bugging scheme. A New York journalist who sometimes collaborated with Anderson passed on a thirdhand rumor about a Republican espionage operation against O'Brien. The columnist made a few phone calls but was unable to confirm the allegation. He assigned a legman to investigate further, but suspected that it was a "bum tip" because his source's information was vague and in parts garbled. Besides, Anderson figured that anyone who eavesdropped on O'Brien's telephone calls would merely get "an ear full of bullshit" because O'Brien was "too smart to talk strategy on the phone." In the end, Anderson wrote, "unable to score a breakthrough and too busy to spend more time chasing phantoms, we let the thing drop." If he had pursued the lead more aggressively, perhaps the Nixon campaign would have postponed or canceled its ill-fated break-in. Anderson's investigative failure would prove more effective in destroying his longtime political enemy than all his exposés from the previous two decades.

Just days after plotting Anderson's assassination, Nixon operatives E. Howard Hunt and G. Gordon Liddy took charge of the Watergate operation. Hunt used four Cuban American undercover men from Miami—the same intended to execute Anderson—to carry out the bugging. Coincidentally, Anderson had long ago befriended one of them, a swarthy soldier of fortune named Frank Sturgis, whose unsuccessful efforts to topple Fidel Castro had been sympathetically portrayed by the reporter in the early 1960s. The gun-toting, muscular Sturgis once even spent several nights in Anderson's guest room during a visit to Washington.

In an even more remarkable coincidence, just a few hours before Sturgis and his gang broke into O'Brien's office, Anderson stumbled upon them at Washington's National Airport, where they had flown in from Florida for the operation. The chance meeting occurred as Anderson was racing to catch a plane to Cleveland to speak to a college journalism fraternity. The burglars, eavesdropping equipment in tow, were on their way to the Watergate and their rendezvous with infamy. "Frankie," Anderson called out to his old friend, who turned his back in an unsuccessful effort to hide from the prying newsman. Anderson went up to Sturgis and extended his hand, forcing him to reluctantly introduce his co-conspirator, Virgilio Gonzalez, who was carrying luggage filled with the tools he would soon use to pick the lock of the Democrats' office door. "What are you doing in town?" Anderson asked. "Well," Sturgis stammered, "I'm going to visit friends." Anderson realized that Sturgis was "chagrined to meet me, so I suspected something was up. 'Private business. Top secret. Top secret,' he explained tersely, with a conspiratorial smile." The columnist did not have time to chat further—he was running late as usual—but he "made a mental note to check up" when he returned to Washington.

Eight hours later, Sturgis and his felonious Cuban compadres were arrested at gunpoint by police inside the Democratic Party headquarters. Their equipment for wiretapping, lock-picking, and surreptitious photography was confiscated as evidence, along with their walkie-talkies, canisters of Mace, and cache of sequentially numbered hundred-dollar bills. The scandal that would become known as Watergate had begun.

The next morning, Anderson read about the burglary in the newspaper and realized "what Frankie's 'private business' had been." The columnist rushed to D.C.'s old red-brick jailhouse, where he gained entrance by signing a prison logbook claiming that he was a "Friend" on a "Social Visit" to see one of the inmates. Although the burglars had given aliases to police, Anderson asked to speak to the men arrested at the Democratic National Committee and eventually found himself talking to Sturgis through the jail's glass partition.

"Frank," Anderson asked solicitously, "what happened?"

"Jack, I'm sorry, I can't tell you," Sturgis replied.

Anderson figured he would have better luck if he could get Sturgis out of the jailhouse and away from his partners in crime. "Frankie, you're always getting into trouble when I'm not around to watch over you," Anderson gently chided. "Why don't you come home and stay with us?" The muckraker offered to post bond for Sturgis and put him up once again as a guest in the Anderson home. Sturgis was amenable, Anderson remembered, if only to avoid the jail's "disagreeable bugs and cockroaches." But the Cuban soldier of fortune warned his friend that he would not talk about Watergate because "we swore not to discuss this" and "we're sticking together." Anderson "didn't push it," he said, because "I figured I'd get him in my house [and] work him over. I'm smarter than he is and I'll know all he knows about it before he leaves, probably before breakfast" the next morning.

The columnist filed a motion in court to have Sturgis released into his custody. "Sitting in front of the judge, I could barely keep a straight face," Anderson later confessed. He testified that Sturgis posed no risk to the community and would not flee while staying at his home. "It was only a cheap burglary," Anderson argued. "I hate to see him in jail." "[An] audible groan of cynicism rolled through the press ranks," the muckraker later wrote. "The Justice Department, distrusting my charitable intentions, suspected I might pump him for more answers and vigorously objected to releasing Sturgis in my care." The presiding judge decided that "it wouldn't be a good idea for Frankie to waltz out of jail on the arm of Jack Anderson," and denied his motion. The newsman left the courtroom empty-handed.

Meanwhile, the President and his men quickly moved to suppress the scandal. In the hours after the Watergate arrests, Liddy rushed to Nixon's campaign headquarters and began shredding documents. Hunt destroyed incriminating materials at his home and fled town. The Plumbers' White House safe, filled with extensive evidence of their criminality—including a "large volume of material" about their various plots against Jack Anderson—was emptied out, its sensitive paperwork burned. The burglars' remaining eavesdropping equipment was thrown in the Potomac River.

At the same time, Press Secretary Ronald Ziegler dismissed it all as a "third-rate burglary" and cautioned reporters that "certain elements may try to stretch this beyond what it is." The President told television cameras that the "White House has had no involvement whatever" in the crime. "We never set out to construct a planned, conscious cover-up," Haldeman later wrote. "We reacted to Watergate just as we had to the Pentagon Papers, ITT, and the [Vietnam] operations. We were highly sensitive to any negative PR, and our natural reaction was to contain, or minimize, any potential political damage."

But Nixon and his advisors soon crossed the line from spin control to criminal conspiracy. They deliberately obstructed the FBI's investigation of the break-in and pressured prosecutors to limit their probe. They also paid hush money to the burglars and lied under oath to hide their complicity. White House tapes captured the President's crimes in explicit orders to his staff: "I don't give a shit what happens. I want you all to stonewall it, let them plead the Fifth Amendment, cover up or anything else if it'll save it, save this plan. That's the whole point."

Nixon believed that the Watergate break-in was a "chicken shit thing," no worse than misconduct by the President's political and journalistic enemies. "Somebody should say the arrested men were just trying to win a Pulitzer" like Jack Anderson, the President told aides. "I mean, they won Pulitzer Prizes for [what they got from] the thieves who took the stuff out of Kissinger's office . . . Now what the hell is the difference?" After all, "they praised Jack Anderson and made him a national hero" for similar behavior. Nixon could not bring himself to admit wrongdoing in Watergate, Ehrlichman said, because he was "emotionally and constitutionally unable to deliver himself to his enemies to any degree. He will fight, bleed and die before he will admit to Jack Anderson that he's wrong or that he's made a mistake."

Anderson had a similar inability to acknowledge error, and he now began making plenty of them. His first column on Watergate, right after the break-in, tried to link the burglary to "President Nixon's favorite Cuban, Bebe Rebozo" by stating that "Rebozo has been associated . . . with the Cuban bugging crew" from Watergate. In fact, the President's best friend had nothing to do with the crime and even *The Washington Post*, which was aggressively reporting on Watergate, spiked Anderson's ethnic guilt by association. "Jack Anderson said Rebozo was involved in it with the Cubans," Nixon fumed to his staff. Rebozo has "been so abused" by that "son of a bitch" columnist: "Goddammit, he can sue . . . because he knows goddamn well he's not involved with it. See what I mean? Jack Anderson, what they would like to do is they'd like to tie him in order to tie us into it."

So the White House tried to retaliate—and advance its cover-up—by blaming Anderson for the Watergate break-in. "We started a rumor yesterday morning" on Capitol Hill, Haldeman told the President, "that this whole thing is a Jack Anderson thing, that Jack Anderson did it . . . That Jack Anderson has put all of this together, he was bugging the Democratic offices." It was not completely far-fetched. In addition to Anderson's known history of bugging Washington hotel rooms, Haldeman explained, the muckraker was also "tied" to some of the Watergate burglars through his friendship with Frank Sturgis. "The great thing about this," Haldeman added, is that the burglary "is so totally fucked up and so badly done that nobody believes"—Nixon interrupted—"that we could have done it."

Nevertheless, the President's cover-up was already beginning to fray. Law enforcement authorities quickly linked Hunt and Liddy to the break-in and traced the burglars' cash to the Nixon reelection campaign—and then revealed these incriminating facts to *The Washington Post* and *The New York Times*. Democrats filed a lawsuit against CREEP and called upon Congress to investigate. The White House watched with growing alarm. "The problem that you've got," Nixon complained to his staff, "is that some lower echelon shit-ass at the Justice Department or the FBI will try to leak out stuff about this." But the President was being targeted not only by low-level law enforcement agents but also by a top FBI official who would eventually become known to the world as "Deep Throat."

Six weeks before the Watergate break-in, FBI director J. Edgar Hoover died unexpectedly at the age of seventy-seven. Some FBI agents blamed their boss's death on Jack Anderson. The day before, the columnist had begun a series of exposés about how Hoover—who "appears to have a hangup [about] sex"—had ordered his agents to "snoop into the sex habits" of famous Americans who "aren't even remotely involved in illegal activity." Anderson quoted "titillating tidbits" from the FBI's secret files. Hollywood actor Rock Hudson "was suspected of having homosexual tendencies," the FBI reported. Novelist James Baldwin "was evicted by [his] landlord for having homosexual parties." Football quarterback Joe Namath was "intoxicated on several occasions and also reportedly had an affair with an airline stewardess" that led to an abortion. Boxers Muhammad Ali and Joe Louis, actors Marlon Brando and Jane Fonda, civil rights leaders Martin Luther King and Ralph Abernathy, physician Benjamin Spock, entertainer Harry Belafonte— all were victims of the FBI's "incorrigible gossips," Anderson reported. The same day, Anderson testified to Congress that Hoover's "sex reports" showed an "intense interest in who is sleeping with whom in Washington."

That night, Hoover suffered a fatal heart attack. Two days later, the President named Hoover's successor: L. Patrick Gray, a staunch Nixon loyalist who first befriended the young Congressman in the 1940s, served as an advisor for Vice President Nixon, and worked in his 1960 presidential campaign. More recently, as assistant attorney general, Gray participated in the White House cover-up of the ITT scandal while his wife worked for Nixon's reelection campaign. In short, Nixon chose a man he believed would execute his directives without question. Hoover's men were outraged. W. Mark Felt, the FBI's second-in-command, believed he had earned the top job for himself and was angered by the White House move to politicize the Bureau. To retaliate, Felt began leaking about Watergate to two journalists: Sandy Smith of *Time* and Bob Woodward of *The Washington Post*, who referred to his anonymous source as "Deep Throat." The liberal *Post* was bolder and more aggressive following Felt's leads than the cautiously conservative weekly magazine. Woodward and his partner Carl Bernstein were also younger and hungrier than Smith, and knocked on numerous doors to cultivate low-level sources in Nixon's campaign as well. The *Post* reporters dominated early coverage of Watergate, piecing together the story bit by bit, one new fact at a time.

By October, the identity of Woodward's secret FBI source was slipped to the White House. *Time*'s Smith confided the information to his magazine's general counsel, who informed Nixon's campaign manager, John Mitchell. Felt "vehemently denied" leaking about Watergate, but the President wasn't fooled. According to acting FBI director Gray, Nixon went on a "rampage," his face "flushed" and "wild," stuttering "almost beyond coherence," a "rush of words [leaving] flecks of spittle at the corners of his mouth." The President told Hoover's replacement that the FBI was "crawling" with "at best, unloyal people and at worst treasonable people. We have to get them, break them." The Chief Executive ordered Gray to "tail" Felt and polygraph him. But Felt outmaneuvered the White House by putting himself in charge of the FBI's leak investigation and taking care to meet Woodward only at night in an out-of-the-way parking garage.

The Watergate leaks continued. But not to Jack Anderson. "Failing like almost everyone else to recognize the true significance of the break-in," one author wrote, "Anderson lost interest" in the story. As the columnist later admitted, he "couldn't foresee how big Watergate was going to become." Paradoxically, despite its legendary status, Watergate was not a story that lent itself to original investigative reporting. Because the political figures implicated in the scandal faced significant legal jeopardy, the evidence of wrongdoing they possessed was generally too dangerous to entrust to reporters and could be confided safely only to their own attorneys or law enforcement officials. In the end, all mythmaking to the contrary, Watergate journalism was largely derivative, reporting on investigations by authorities that were already under way before news outlets began covering them. "Television and newspapers publicized the story and, perhaps, even encouraged more diligent investigation," historian Stanley Kutler wrote; but "carefully timed leaks, not media investigations, provided the first news of Watergate."

Anderson was now at a particular disadvantage. Larger, establishment news outlets that once shunned investigative reporting were jumping on the Watergate story, taking advantage of resources and respectability that the columnist could only envy. In addition, *The Washington Post* and *The New York Times* had far more space to report in-depth while Anderson was limited to a 750-word newshole. Most of all, in an era before the fax machine or the Internet, the "Merry-Go-Round" was hobbled by a four-day delay sending out its stories to client newspapers by postal mail in the midst of a fast-breaking scandal where scoops rarely held for long. To try to stay on top of events, Anderson waited until the last minute to file his occasional exclusives, but his syndicate warned that continuing to push the deadline would "kill the column." So instead the column effectively killed Anderson's scoops.

Ultimately, Watergate destroyed Anderson's muckraking monopoly in Washington. The irony was palpable: Anderson had hunted Nixon for two decades and risen to the top of his enemies list; he'd been targeted for surveillance, sexual smears, and even an aborted assassination plot. But other, younger reporters—not Anderson—would reap the glory for harpooning the presidential whale. Nixon's dramatic fall "should have belonged to Jack and made him a revered American icon" for decades, his legman James Grady believed. "If your heroism is measured by the anger of your enemies, remember, the Plumbers never tried to harm Woodward and Bernstein but they were primed and dispatched to kill Jack."

In utterly different ways and for utterly different reasons, Watergate would prove catastrophic for both Richard Nixon and Jack Anderson. In the end, their most lethal enemy proved to be not each other but themselves.

Four weeks after the Watergate arrests, the Democratic Party nominated its candidate to oppose President Nixon in November: South Dakota senator George McGovern, a former preacher and prairie populist running on a staunch antiwar platform. Although McGovern trailed in public opinion polls, Republicans nevertheless unleashed a vicious sabotage squad against him. Nixon operatives plotted to bug McGovern's Washington headquarters and use prostitutes to compromise his top advisors. The President's men also planted undercover spies to work alongside McGovern's staff. One mole, Lucianne Goldberg—who later achieved fame for her role in President Bill Clinton's impeachment—reported that Nixon "loved" reading her memos about "who was sleeping with who" on the campaign trail. At the same time, the White House had Secret Service bodyguards spy on McGovern and leaked rumors to the press that he was having an adulterous affair.

On July 14, McGovern chose his vice presidential running mate, Senator Thomas Eagleton of Missouri. Three days later, a nervous caller phoned the Knight newspaper chain to report that Eagleton had a history of mental illness that included hospitalizations for electric shock therapy. The anonymous informant, who evidently had access to Eagleton's psychiatric records, supplied specific locations and dates where Eagleton had been treated and a devastating medical diagnosis: "severe manic-depressive psychosis with suicidal tendencies." Reporter Clark Hoyt tracked down one of the physicians involved in Eagleton's shock treatment. "I can't talk to you about that," the doctor exclaimed, turning pale and slamming the door in the journalist's face. Hoyt viewed the panicked response as confirmation of his story and confronted the McGovern campaign about it. The candidate's press secretary stalled for time to respond; because Hoyt lacked sufficient evidence to prove the allegation, he agreed to delay publication in an effort to get corroboration—or at least comment—from the Democrats. In fact, it turned out that Eagleton had concealed his psychiatric past not only from the press and public but also from McGovern, who now learned for the first time that his running mate had suffered three nervous breakdowns, two requiring electric shock therapy. McGovern quickly called a news conference to disclose Eagleton's medical condition, hoping to give the appearance of forthrightness and minimize the damage.

President Nixon moved immediately to exploit the scandal and ordered his staff to "destroy" Eagleton. Soon after, a Republican spokesman, cloaked in anonymity, told the press that "people simply aren't going to want to put a mental patient in charge of the nuclear arsenal." At the same time, Nixon called an unexpected news conference and declared, "I have given the strictest instructions that there are to be no comments" about Eagleton from his administration. "I am not going to interject myself into that problem." The President then went on to do just that, boasting that he had "never missed an appointment because of health. Considering what I have been through, some fairly stern crises and rather extensive travel, I don't think anybody would question the state of my health."

Democrats tried to fight back by reviving Jack Anderson's story about Nixon's own psychotherapy treatments with Dr. Arnold Hutschnecker, but that effort went nowhere. Meanwhile, Eagleton's desperate efforts to salvage his vice presidential nomination resembled nothing so much as Nixon's struggle two decades earlier to do the same. The embattled candidate considered giving a "Checkers"-like speech on prime-time television but decided instead to make his case through the many reporters who now swarmed to his beleaguered campaign. Instead of invoking his pet dog, Eagleton mawkishly told voters about his thirteen-year-old son: "Terry is an impressionable boy at an impressionable age. And other kids can be terribly cruel about this kind of thing. I never, never would do anything to hurt or embarrass my boy . . . I've got to win. I've got to do it for Terry."

Jack Anderson watched all of this from the sidelines, frustrated at his own irrelevance. A scandal involving the mental health of a prominent politician was exactly the kind of story that had been the muckraker's trademark for a quarter century, but he was conspicuously absent from the current coverage. *The Washington Post* was scooping him on Watergate, and now even the humble Knight newspaper chain was beating him on another scandal of national import. Anderson resolved to find a way to get back in the game.

Like many journalists, Anderson was aware of rumors that Eagleton had a problem with alcohol. Four years earlier, one of the newsman's sources told him that Missouri police had arrested Eagleton on multiple occasions for drunk driving. But at the time, Eagleton was just an obscure state politician and Anderson hadn't bothered to pursue the lead. Now that Eagleton was the Democratic Party's vice presidential nominee, Anderson decided to investigate further. The columnist contacted his original source, a Missouri Democrat named True Davis who had unsuccessfully run against Eagleton for the Senate in 1968. Davis told Anderson that he had seen paperwork showing that Eagleton had been arrested for drunk driving but that Eagleton somehow managed to cover up the charges. However, Davis had nothing to back up his rumor: no hard copies of tickets issued to Eagleton or names of any officers who allegedly arrested him. Davis himself refused to go public with the unproven accusation, not only because he had no concrete evidence but also because he had made peace with his former opponent and supported the McGovern-Eagleton ticket.

Anderson and his reporters began making phone calls to try to verify the drunk-driving allegations, but they came up empty-handed. Many Missouri politicians and police had heard the rumors, too, but none had any proof to substantiate them. Still, Anderson decided to go ahead anyway. "When a guy like True Davis says he saw those photostats," the muckraker told his staff, "there's obviously something to it. Someone's going to get this story, so I'm inclined to move ahead with something so we don't lose it." Legman Mike Kiernan helped draft a story that journalists were "streaming into St. Louis" to check out "rumors" that Eagleton had been "stopped for drunken driving" but had discovered only one arrest for speeding. Repeating this unverified gossip was arguably defensible in the heat of the campaign. But then Anderson crossed out the speeding-ticket line with his black felt-tipped pen and added a sentence that would haunt him for the rest of his career: "Eagleton has steadfastly denied any alcoholism in his past but *we have now located photostats* of half-a-dozen arrests for drunken and reckless driving." It wasn't true—Anderson possessed no paperwork whatsoever—but he felt "confident that the documents existed and that I would soon lay my hands on them." Because such an explosive scoop would not hold for his column's four-day postal delay, Anderson aired the report that morning on his Mutual Broadcasting radio program.

Before Anderson even had time to walk back from the nearby radio studio, journalists began besieging his office. "The phones were ringing off the hook," Kiernan recalled. "Reporters were lined up in the halls to get copies of the Eagleton tickets—but we didn't have any tickets!" In fact, Anderson didn't even know for sure whether such drunk-driving citations even existed. So he issued a disingenuous clarification stating that while he had not personally seen Eagleton's arrest records, he had "traced" them thanks to a "former high official from Missouri whose reliability is beyond question but who has asked us not to identify him." According to Brit Hume, "Jack seemed to have no doubt that the story would be vindicated, even if he had exaggerated it originally." Anderson held court with numerous print and broadcast journalists, Hume recalled, and "gave each interviewer the most ringing assurances of the reliability of his source."

But on the campaign trail, Eagleton called Anderson's bluff. "He doesn't have the documents," the Missouri senator declared, because "they do not exist." Eagleton categorically denied ever being arrested for drunken or reckless driving: "Anderson's statement to that effect in blunt and direct English is a damnable lie." Eagleton heatedly vowed that "Jack Anderson is not going to run me out of town or run me off this Democratic ticket." In private, the vice presidential nominee confided that "the Anderson thing was the best thing that could have happened, a blessing in disguise." Indeed, "the Anderson accusations gave Eagleton an opportunity to seize the offensive and capture the public's sympathy . . . as an embattled candidate fighting for his political life against false and perhaps even malicious accusations," McGovern later wrote. His campaign manager believed that "Anderson had changed the entire picture. While campaigning against the phony charges, Eagleton could somehow lump all the accusations together and present himself as the wronged man, the besieged man, the man against the system."

Just as Richard Nixon had done during his "Checkers" speech, as the President himself realized better than anyone. Anderson's "shockingly false story" reminded Nixon of "how Anderson's mentor, Drew Pearson, had done a similar thing to me" twenty years earlier, Nixon wrote in his memoirs. "I could empathize with Eagleton's frustration, and I admired his aplomb. He was as courageous as Anderson was contemptible." However, the President's sympathy for Eagleton didn't temper his desire to exploit the obvious political opportunity that presented itself. Nixon wants to "make McGovern look bad out of this," Haldeman wrote in his diary, and the President issued instructions to "hit him again while he's down to keep him down." Nixon also told Haldeman to have the White House take "a crack at Anderson" now that he was vulnerable: "I think hitting Anderson is very important, Bob, it's very, very important to discredit" him.

Anderson made it easier for his enemies by brushing off Eagleton's protestations of innocence. The investigative reporter's long and successful history of bluffing his way through controversy reinforced his "gut feeling" that his broadcast was accurate and that Eagleton's denial was simply a lie. "Are you worried about this?" Hume asked his boss anxiously. "No problem," the columnist replied with a smile. "Look, True Davis is a reliable guy. If he says he saw the photostats, then they existed. In a situation like this, the truth has a way of coming out . . . Besides, this shows we're willing to go after liberal Democrats" as well as conservative Republicans.

Still, Anderson now began a frantic effort to locate the evidence that he had already pretended to have. No such drunk-driving records ever turned up. Anderson tried to acquire a copy of Eagleton's FBI file in the hope that it might document the allegations, but the senator's dossier "already had been pulled and was in the hands of the Justice Department high command," the muckraker discovered. Anderson even reached out to his old source Murray Chotiner, the longtime Nixon advisor who had leaked George Wallace's sensitive tax returns two years earlier. But because of subsequent "Merry-Go-Round" attacks on the President, the columnist said, Chotiner replied with "the scorn due one who had not requited its love: 'Why should we bail Anderson out?'"

The newsman acknowledged to an interviewer that he "probably should have withheld" his report until obtaining paperwork to substantiate it. A page-one headline followed: ANDERSON BACKS OFF. The columnist hurriedly convened a meeting of his reporters to figure out how to handle the escalating crisis. Most of his staff urged him to admit that he had made a mistake and disavow his broadcast. "I just don't want you to act like Drew [Pearson] used to," Anderson's secretary, Opal Ginn, argued. "He refused to ever apologize, even if he was wrong." But Les Whitten believed a retraction was unnecessary. "Why do you have to make any statement at all?" Anderson's chief legman asked: "Just sit tight" and ride out the controversy.

As his reporters heatedly debated what to do, it became clear that Anderson was looking for support, not criticism. "Jack didn't want to back off when he thought the story might be vindicated at any moment," Hume recalled. "After an extraordinary streak of major stories, Jack didn't want the humiliation of announcing he had blundered when events might still bail him out." So instead, he issued a second "clarification" that only made matters worse. "In retrospect," Anderson announced, "I believe I broadcast the story prematurely and should have waited until I could authenticate the citations personally. Nevertheless, I have faith in my sources and stand by the story. If this faith should ever turn out to be unwarranted, I will issue a full retraction and apology."

Anderson's refusal to admit that he was wrong now transformed him, rather than Eagleton, into the media's prime investigative target. It did not help that True Davis had passed on the same unverified rumors about Eagleton to other Washington journalists, who realized, as one put it, that Anderson's source had only "very vague" secondhand information that "did not stand up under the sort of reexamination that any responsible news reporter would be obliged to give it before making it public." Davis himself announced that he was "quite embarrassed" and "sorry" that his remarks were "made public without verification." Still, while Anderson grudgingly conceded that his reporting had not been up to "prizewinning standards," he stubbornly refused to recant. His admission that he felt "the hot breath of other newsmen on my back" and "wanted to score a scoop" only reinforced the belief that he was driven by personal ambition, not principle. Anderson's "wholly unsubstantiated" report, *The New York Times* editorialized, was "irresponsible journalism." The muckraker "aired the story without supporting evidence, managed to do an incredible disservice to Senator Eagleton, and now seems to be backing off with a series of lame excuses," *The Washington Post* pronounced. "Metaphorically speaking, it is Mr. Anderson, not Senator Eagleton, who should be charged with reckless driving."

In response, Anderson defiantly vowed to "go after" Eagleton even more aggressively. The columnist's worried staff now descended on his home in suburban Washington to try to persuade him to change his mind. The "longer it continued without some acknowledgment of major error on Jack's part," Hume believed, "the more it would look as if he didn't know when a story was proved and when it wasn't. Far from being America's number one investigative reporter, Jack would appear a dimwit with no conscience." But a quarter century of pugnacious crusading had conditioned Anderson to launch automatic retaliatory strikes when attacked; self-reflection could always wait until later and be contemplated in private. The brave imperviousness to criticism that had long been Anderson's greatest investigative strength now became a crippling weakness.

As he consulted with his staff, Anderson "looked drawn and the muscles in the back of his jaw were working visibly," Hume recalled. "I had never seen him as tense." His hands trembled. Still, Anderson doggedly argued that his story was "technically true." "No, it wasn't," Hume shot back. "You said you'd located the documents when you hadn't located them." Anderson blamed other reporters for his woes; they had inaccurately characterized his clarifications and were jealous of his many scoops over the years. Jack "was so heavy into denial" that it was easy to miss how "horrible" he was feeling, Whitten remembered. "He knew he'd been had but he prayed that somehow his story was going to turn out to be true." Anderson told his staff he would think about issuing a public apology but made no firm commitment.

The next day, Anderson and Eagleton appeared together on the CBS News program *Face the Nation*. "This is the first time I've had a chance to face you," the columnist told the senator, "and I do owe you an apology." Anderson admitted that he "did not authenticate whether or not these tickets were genuine" and "went ahead with a story that I should not have gone ahead with, and that was unfair to you, and you have my apology." Eagleton was gracious in victory: "Well, let me say, Mr. Anderson, that the true test of moral character is, I guess, to admit when one makes a mistake . . . It takes quite a man to get on nationwide television to say he made a mistake, and I commend you for your courage." But unable to leave it at that, Anderson went on to declare, "I wish that I could now retract the story completely [but] I cannot do that yet" because it "still hasn't been pursued to a final end." Anderson said he had unanswered questions he wanted to investigate further and so his "conscience won't allow me" to issue a retraction. Eagleton was flabbergasted. The "story has been so thoroughly discredited," he replied, "that I just—it leaves me in a puzzlement as to why you can't retract a story that you say shouldn't have [been aired] in the first place."

Anderson's "apology" generated yet another wave of indignant press coverage. His "performance has been a reckless and wholly regrettable excursion into the worst kind of 'journalism,'" *The Washington Post* judged. "What exactly was Mr. Anderson refusing to 'retract' if not the allegations which, by his own account, it had been irresponsible to broadcast?" Anderson's "astonishing hedge," wrote columnist Charles Bartlett, "left Eagleton still impaled on the hearsay." Even the muckraker's staff was appalled and joked darkly that their boss's television platform should be renamed *Disgrace the Nation*. "Jack had acted terribly on the show," Hume believed. "Invoking conscience as justification for clinging to this discredited story was outrageous."

Two days later, Anderson finally bowed to the inevitable and issued an "unqualified" and "total" retraction. After meeting in private with Eagleton in his Senate office, Anderson told journalists that he had gone over "every scrap of evidence" he possessed and was now "totally" convinced that Eagleton was never arrested for drunk driving and that it was "inexcusable" for him to have reported otherwise. "I think the story did damage to the senator and I owe him a great and humble apology," Anderson admitted. He followed up with a half-hour mea culpa on NBC's *Today* show, acknowledging that he deserved to be "raked over the coals" for his mistake.

But it was too late to undo the damage. The day before Anderson's belated retraction, Eagleton had been forced to resign as McGovern's running mate. "Any chance, however slim, of salvaging the ticket was destroyed by Jack Anderson's erroneous charges," McGovern's campaign manager later wrote. Anderson's broadcast was "the straw that broke the Eagleton back," the Missouri senator agreed. "I might have remained on the ticket but for that."

The affair proved equally destructive to Anderson. Mainstream media outlets that had long disdained the newsman now seized the opening and publicly denounced him in scathing terms. Anderson was "mean and unreliable," one journalist opined; a "liar," declared another. His performance had been "scurrilous," a third reporter announced; "shameful," proclaimed a fourth; a "national disgrace," concluded a fifth. "Unethical? Unconscionable? Despicable? Pick your own adjective and feel free to apply it to Jack Anderson," a sixth newsman wrote. "The Anderson tactics are now clearly visible through the veneer of respectability his Pulitzer Prize afforded him earlier this year . . . Too bad the Pulitzer itself can't be ripped away." Mail from readers was overwhelmingly—often vituperatively—negative. Several newspaper clients canceled the "Merry-Go-Round" column. More than one urged him to give up journalism completely.

To his family and friends, Anderson seemed on the edge of emotional collapse. "He had been deflated, reminded of his proper place," one writer observed. "And he had done it to himself . . . made prideful and overly certain by his rise." It was the classic Washington story of reckless ambition undone by hubris, of opportunism punished by the kind of righteous retribution that Anderson himself had so often meted out to others for the past twenty-five years. "He had risen to a position of fame and credibility never before achieved by a muckraking journalist and, almost overnight, he had lost it," Hume wrote. "It seemed that Jack had had an upside-down reaction to his own success. Instead of feeling more secure, he felt more compelled. And once he had slipped, it was more difficult than ever to accept the humiliation of admitting error."

Just like his adversary Richard Nixon. The parallel, and the irony, was inescapable: after decades of successfully dodging so many hazards—from private lawsuits and public vilification to government spying and death threats—Anderson now managed to damage himself as none of his antagonists ever could. A lifetime of taking shots at others had finally backfired, and the greatest victim of Anderson's reporting became his own reputation. His lesion was as grave as it was preventable, caused not by his enemies but himself. And the number one beneficiary was of course his implacable foe in the White House. "No human hand could have devised the utterly satisfactory situation in which Nixon finds himself," columnist Mary McGrory noted, for the "next time Anderson uncovers a skeleton in Nixon's closet—a Dita Beard memo for instance, or inside papers about a 'tilt towards Pakistan'—Nixon need only loftily recall" Anderson's "second-hand charges about Eagleton's drinking habits" to make the exposé vanish.

The scandal also inflicted a mortal wound on Nixon's chief political adversary. The "Eagleton affair destroyed any chance I had of being elected President," McGovern said, and "became the number one news and editorial development of that campaign. It overshadowed the Watergate scandal as a subject of journalistic concern. It—not Watergate, not Vietnam, not the American economy—was *the* political story of 1972."

Indeed, media coverage of Watergate during the rest of the campaign was both paltry and reflexively supportive of the White House. Barely a dozen reporters out of approximately 1,200 domestic Washington correspondents were assigned to the story full-time. One third of the most important Watergate developments were not carried at all by the nation's largest newspapers; and the remaining two thirds were primarily cursory items buried in the back pages. Television coverage was equally scanty. In the ten months after the bungled break-in, reporters failed to ask even a single question about Watergate in nearly 90 percent of all White House news briefings.

The Watergate cover-up was working.

•

In November 1972, President Nixon was reelected in a landslide, carrying forty-nine states and winning 520 out of 538 electoral votes. But he did not savor his triumph. "It was as if victory was not an occasion for reconciliation," Henry Kissinger remembered, "but an opportunity to settle the scores of a lifetime." The President's advisors should not have been surprised. "Just remember all the trouble they gave us," Nixon said of his enemies a few weeks earlier. "We'll have a chance to get back at them one day." Now that day was at hand. "I want the most comprehensive notes on all of those that have tried to do us in," the President ordered; "they are going to get it . . . We haven't used the [FBI] and we haven't used the Justice Department, but things are going to change now."

In particular, Nixon wanted federal prosecutors to bring criminal charges against Jack Anderson: "I certainly don't intend to let that son of a bitch get away with" publishing the India-Pakistan documents. "I think we've got to prosecute that son of a bitch" and just "let the heads roll," the President told his advisors.

Ten days after the President's reelection, White House aides once again began searching for specific ways to go after Anderson. Charles Colson passed on a fanciful claim that Anderson received a $100,000 bribe fourteen years earlier to write favorably about Cuba's dictator. "You know my personal feelings about Jack Anderson," Colson added in a memo to presidential counsel John Dean. "After his incredibly sloppy and malicious reporting on Eagleton, his credibility has diminished. It now appears as if we have the opportunity to destroy it. Do you agree that we should pursue this actively?"

But before the White House could destroy its enemies in the press, it had to contain the damage from Watergate. So far, the burglars had kept silent, but they were unhappy with the amount of hush money they were receiving from the President's men. Frank Sturgis confided some of this to Anderson, who traveled to Miami to see what he could learn from his old friend. The day after Christmas, in a little-noticed column, Anderson reported that "the mystery deepens over who is paying the legal expenses" for the "high-powered, high-priced attorneys" defending the burglars. Anderson quoted Sturgis—shielded by anonymity—as saying, "We were told when we took the job that we would be taken care of." But the columnist was unable to flush out further details.

Two weeks later, the trial of the Watergate conspirators began in Judge John Sirica's Washington courtroom. In January 1973, the group's ringleader, E. Howard Hunt, pled guilty to all charges and falsely claimed that no higher-ups from the Nixon administration had been involved. Judge Sirica didn't believe him. "Who started this?" the judge demanded to know. "Who hired" the burglars in the first place?

Like everyone else, Anderson had the same questions. He treated Sturgis to lunch at a Chinese restaurant to try to get some answers. Sturgis told Anderson that his crew was following orders as part of a secret government operation. "We're having a meeting tonight," Sturgis added. "A White House representative wants to talk to us." "If I were nearby, would you come and tell me what happens?" Anderson asked. "Okay," Sturgis replied.

That evening, Anderson bought dinner for the burglars' defense attorney, Henry Rothblatt, a flamboyant litigator who sported a bow tie, black toupee, and waxed pencil mustache. Rothblatt was upset that he had not been fully paid for his legal work and that the White House was pressuring his clients to take sole responsibility for the break-in. Anderson offered to try to help persuade Sturgis to put aside his loyalty to Nixon. After dinner, the newsman accompanied Rothblatt to the Arlington Towers, an apartment complex across the Potomac River where the burglars and their attorney were staying. Rothblatt let Anderson camp out in his sixth-floor suite while the burglars met in another room downstairs. Sturgis secretly shuttled back and forth between floors, briefing Anderson on the conspirators' ongoing meeting. It turned out that Hunt was urging them to follow his lead and stay silent by pleading guilty to the charges against them. "They've offered to pay all our legal expenses if we keep our mouths shut," Sturgis told the columnist. "And they said they would take care of our families while we were in jail" by paying them $1,000 a month. Anderson realized it was hush money and that "they were being bribed" to obstruct justice.

The muckraker tried to persuade Sturgis not to become further involved in White House criminality. He warned that Nixon's men were "trying to protect themselves at your expense"—that Sturgis was "being taken for a ride"—and that he had a "duty to his country, [a] duty to his family," not to go silently to jail. The burglar was shaken by Anderson's plea but also realized that "Jack was looking for a scoop." Sturgis returned to his meeting downstairs. For hours, the conspirators argued passionately about what to do. After midnight, Hunt finally persuaded them "to follow orders like good soldiers" and stick together, "one for all and all for one."

Four days later, the Watergate burglars pled guilty to the charges against them. Like Hunt, they falsely testified that no higher-ups had been involved in the break-in, that they had operated entirely on their own and were not being pressured or paid for their silence.

Jack Anderson knew better. But he had promised Sturgis that he would protect this secret and did not publish it. On January 14, *New York Times* reporter Seymour Hersh broke the story: the burglars were being regularly paid in laundered funds that apparently came from Nixon's campaign. The article freed Anderson to report that Hunt was funneling one thousand dollars a month to the conspirators as hush money.

Judge Sirica was incensed. It was embarrassingly clear that the burglars were taking the blame to protect those above them, committing perjury to cover up an ongoing criminal conspiracy. But for now, the judge was powerless to stop the obvious farce taking place in his courtroom. The Watergate cover-up was continuing to hold.

16

DISGRACE

On January 20, 1973, Richard Nixon took the presidential oath for the last time, smiling broadly and giving crowds his familiar V-for-victory salute. Without irony, the President pledged to "restore respect for law" and, in an obvious echo of his late rival John F. Kennedy, proclaimed: "Ask not just what will government do for me, but what can I do for myself?"

Four days later, the Nixon administration launched its long-awaited plan to prosecute Jack Anderson. It was triggered by an FBI informant who passed on an outlandish rumor that the columnist was about to pay $100,000 to $200,000 for stolen government records about federal mistreatment of Native Americans. In fact, the "Merry-Go-Round" had been reporting about this subject for weeks, thanks to leaks from militants who had filched thousands of files from the Bureau of Indian Affairs during a takeover of its Washington headquarters two months earlier. "Day after day we published stories pieced together from these documents," Anderson wrote, and "I occasionally yielded to the temptation to make sport of the tribulations of the FBI, whose agents were tripping over their nightsticks in a dozen states, and had gotten no closer to the Indian documents than the quotations they read in our column." The administration was not amused and soon set a trap to try to catch Anderson as he received more classified records.

On the morning of January 31, barely a mile from the White House, a squad of FBI agents surprised Anderson's reporter Les Whitten as he helped his Indian sources load three boxes of documents into his yellow

Vega hatchback. "Oh my God," Whitten exclaimed, "police!" The agents "came swarming out of neighboring cars and doorways like ants from a rotten log," Whitten recalled. "I was scared totally and completely shit-less." He was arrested and handcuffed—his pen and reporter's pad confiscated—and driven downtown to be fingerprinted and booked.

The Nixon Justice Department charged Whitten with possession of stolen government documents, the felony indictment that the President had long wanted to file against Anderson himself. If convicted, Whitten could be behind bars for a decade. "They were out to get Jack in their net," Anderson's legman realized, "but instead of getting the big fish, they got the little fish: me." For five hours, in a suit and trench coat, Whitten sat in jail on a hard bench. His two Indian informants were also locked up on the same charges.

Anderson hurried to the federal courthouse in downtown Washington. As Whitten was arraigned, Anderson became so angry that he stood up to address the presiding magistrate. "Be quiet," his lawyer whispered, "you'll get us in more trouble." The columnist silently sat down. Afterward, on the steps of the courthouse, Anderson was less restrained and thunderously denounced the arrest as an "outrageous violation of the First Amendment . . . Never in my 25 years in Washington has the government gone to such lengths to block the free flow of information to the public . . . All of us on my staff are ready to join Les Whitten in jail, if we must, before we will stop digging out and reporting the news."

The media naturally swarmed to a story about the jailing of one of its own. U.S. ARRESTS AIDE OF JACK ANDERSON, the *New York Post* blared in a banner headline that filled nearly half of its front page. One Chicago editor condemned Whitten's arrest as "awful," another as "very dangerous." The "FBI is conducting a vendetta against Anderson," a Wisconsin newspaper warned. Journalists began wearing "Free Les Whitten" buttons. Herblock, the syndicated cartoonist, drew a sketch of Whitten in handcuffs surrounded by FBI agents who reported to their boss: "Great news, chief! We've got the cuffs on one of Jack Anderson's men."

The criminal charges were undeniably newsworthy. After all, the federal government was prosecuting the press not for *publishing* confidential documents but merely for *receiving* them, a new and far more draconian method of going after media critics. Even in the Pentagon Papers case—which involved serious questions of national security—criminal charges were filed only against those who leaked the documents, not the reporters who received them. In effect, Nixon's men were moving to criminalize unauthorized disclosures to journalists.

On Capitol Hill, Democrats denounced the arrest. Senator Edmund Muskie warned that the "administration has opened up a new front in its campaign against the First Amendment." Another lawmaker stated that the Nixon Justice Department "has achieved the censor's dream: it has found the means to strike at the dynasty of muckrakers." Anderson and Whitten were invited to testify at congressional hearings.

Meanwhile, the columnist decided to pursue a novel legal strategy. He made a lunch date with Interior Secretary Rogers Morton, whose department oversaw the Bureau of Indian Affairs, and turned on the charm. "You've done more for the Indians than any Interior secretary in history," Anderson crooned. "If you could slip me some confidential memos on what you've done, I could write a credible story." Morton fell for the flattery and handed over a government document containing the same low-level classification as the files Whitten was holding when he was arrested. "Rogers Morton is going to make a great witness for the defense," Anderson told his staff after the luncheon. The muckraker's strategy was to undercut the administration by making any prosecution for receiving confidential documents seem selective and arbitrary.

But before Anderson could even make this argument in court, the facts in the government's case started to unravel. Whitten's source, a mild-mannered Sioux lawyer with horn-rimmed glasses named Hank Adams, had always insisted that he was on his way to return the stolen papers when FBI agents arrested him and that he had invited Whitten along simply to cover the event as a news story. FBI officials had dismissed this "lame story," but the government was now forced to admit that Adams had indeed scheduled an appointment with federal officials for the very morning he was arrested with Whitten. Furthermore, the boxes of documents turned out to have been marked with the name and phone number of the FBI agent to whom they were to be delivered and Adams produced a receipt signed by the same FBI agent for other stolen records that he had recently returned to the government.

This new evidence destroyed the FBI's case and seemed proof that Whitten's arrest was a setup. "Would one of the most sophisticated reporters in town be carting around stolen documents in the street in broad daylight if he were engaged in some clandestine activity?" *The Washington Post* asked. The FBI's "undercover agent knew the documents were in Mr. Adams' apartment" the night before the arrest, the *Post* pointed out, so "why did the FBI wait until Mr. Whitten was there to spring the trap?" Because the FBI's real objective was to arrest the legman during the short window when the records were in his presence before being returned to the government. "If they really thought they had a case," Anderson observed, "obviously they would have followed [Whitten] and waited until he put [the papers] in his house or brought them to my office, but they knew" the documents were already "on the way" back to the government, "so they arrested" him first while they still could.

On February 14, Anderson testified before a federal grand jury and swore under oath that he never paid money for the leaked files. The irascible columnist astonished the panel with a little reverse psychology by begging the grand jurors to prosecute his legman: "He was just doing his job, I said, and we were prepared to go to trial. The government doesn't own the news, I told them, adding that I didn't think any jury in the United States would disagree with that. I was ready to win a court fight that would set a precedent and make sure no one ever did this to a reporter again."

The next day, the grand jurors took the unusual step of throwing out the FBI arrests. Prosecutors had to drop all charges against Whitten and his sources. A "Merry-Go-Round" party celebrating the legal triumph was covered in the society pages of the press. FBI officials were disgusted. Anderson had "manipulated the situation beautifully," Deputy Director Mark Felt complained, "wrapping himself in a cloak of martyrdom" as he "played his 'injured innocence' role to the hilt."

But the Nixon administration found a way to exploit its bungled case by secretly subpoenaing Anderson's telephone records, which then made it possible for the government to trace his confidential informants.

In all, the FBI obtained paperwork of more than three thousand calls made from Anderson's office and home and rushed them by Telex to twenty-three field offices around the country; agents then contacted the newsman's sources demanding to know why they were talking to him. Anderson soon found out and denounced the government for using his legman's "false arrest" as a "pretext" to "get a court order to pry into our telephone calls" in a "massive FBI investigation into our operations." Anderson also filed a motion in federal court, where Judge John Sirica—already suspicious of the Nixon administration's Watergate cover-up—expressed incredulity that the FBI insisted on holding on to Anderson's phone records when Whitten's arrest had already been dropped. The judge ordered the government to destroy the Anderson phone logs.

The columnist was convinced that the White House was to blame for his legal difficulties. Anderson accused White House chief of staff H. R. Haldeman of issuing a secret order to "nail" him by having federal prosecutors "make a case against us." Nixon press secretary Ronald Ziegler adamantly denied the charge, calling it "wrong, wrong, wrong." But the newsman insisted that one of his sources had witnessed Haldeman picking up the phone and instructing authorities to "pin a crime on Anderson. When asked what crime," the reporter wrote, "Haldeman asked the FBI to find one."

Anderson held acting FBI director L. Patrick Gray personally responsible and decided to make an example of Nixon's nominee. Abandoning any pretense of objectivity, the muckraker lobbied senators to oppose Gray's confirmation as permanent FBI director. Anderson invited himself to testify before the Senate Judiciary Committee, where he denounced Gray as "a political hatchetman for Richard Nixon" whose "prime interest" was not law enforcement but "pleasing the President."

Anderson even blackmailed a key legislator, Senate Majority Whip Robert Byrd, when he initially expressed reluctance to oppose Gray. "Bobby," Anderson told the West Virginia senator, "I've got more newspapers in West Virginia than Pat Gray has." The "message was clear; if I ever found any dirt on him, I had an audience in his home state that would love to read about it. There was a pause and then he said, 'All right. What do you want me to do?'" The influential Byrd agreed to lead the opposition to Gray. Armed with questions supplied by Anderson, Byrd exposed Gray's complicity in the Watergate cover-up. Nixon's nominee for FBI director had to resign.

Anderson was not gracious in victory. "Pat," he told Gray, "do your successor a favor. Tell him that the reason you were never confirmed as head of the FBI was because you sent one of Jack Anderson's reporters to jail."

In March 1973, Judge John Sirica handed down maximum prison sentences for the Watergate conspirators: twenty years for Gordon Liddy, thirty-five for Howard Hunt, and forty for each of the individual burglars. Faced with such lengthy confinement, wiretapper James Mc-Cord broke his silence and implicated higher-ups, who in turn did the same, one by one connecting top officials of the Nixon White House to the criminal conspiracy. The appointment of a special prosecutor and aggressive hearings by the Democratic Congress, armed with subpoena power, eventually overwhelmed the President and his men. A news frenzy ensued, fueled by leaks from all sides as the media became Washington's unofficial back channel for communication. Journalists passed on intelligence to government investigators, who reciprocated in turn. "I leaked all the time," Senate counsel Sam Dash later acknowledged. "Everybody did." The drama played out in the nation's daily newspapers and broadcasts.

It was a heady time for the handful of reporters who had focused on Watergate when the rest of the media had dismissed it. Once hunted by the Nixon administration, they were now the hunters, and it was the President's men who had become the prey. Jack Anderson received "jubilant" calls from *Washington Post* reporters Bob Woodward and Carl Bernstein, who met separately with Seymour Hersh of *The New York Times* to exchange encouragement and gossip. During an animated dinner of Chinese food punctuated by marijuana smoke, the three young newsmen made a pact to build on, rather than ignore, each others' Watergate stories. After one "Woodstein" scoop, the *Times* reporter phoned to offer sarcastic kudos to his *Post* competitors: "You fucker," Hersh yelled at Woodward, "you fucker!"

Pushed off his perch by his new rivals, Anderson unsuccessfully tried to reach back to old-fashioned investigative techniques from his past. He had his staff rifle through the trash of Watergate prosecutors, but it yielded nothing of value, despite painstaking efforts to piece together the shredded paperwork. At the same time, an Anderson legman tried to eavesdrop on the secret testimony of a Nixon aide by pressing a stethoscope to an adjacent wall, but even boring a hole through the barrier was not enough to make the muffled sounds audible. Anderson's staff also dispatched a handsome college intern to a well-placed bar to "try romancing" potential female sources who "like to drink a lot and screw." That failed as well. When a Watergate conspirator sought money from Anderson to tell his story, the columnist turned him down, but he got sucked in by another Nixon advisor who successfully peddled disinformation exonerating himself while heaping blame on his White House rivals. Eventually, Anderson even published a column suggesting that the President had a secret Swiss bank account where he received "mysterious" cash payments, although no credible evidence ever emerged to back up the allegation.

In any event, the bank that most interested Senate investigators was not in Switzerland but in Florida: the Key Biscayne Bank, run by Nixon's best friend, Bebe Rebozo. Anderson had already disclosed that Rebozo had squirreled away $100,000 in cash there for the President from Howard Hughes. Now Anderson learned that portions of the money had been secretly funneled to Nixon's brothers and secretary. This sensitive information came from a longtime informant, a lawyer who was now representing one of the President's fund-raisers. But the columnist couldn't report the story without burning his source, who was bound to secrecy by attorney-client privilege. What to do? Anderson passed the intelligence to the Senate Watergate Committee, which subpoenaed Nixon's fund-raiser and confirmed that the Hughes cash was spent on diamond earrings for the First Lady and on improvements at the Nixon family's Florida vacation home. But before Anderson could publish the blockbuster story in his column, Bob Woodward reported it in *The Washington Post*.

Meanwhile, in a desperate effort to contain the growing Watergate scandal, the President offered to share some of this secret cash with his top advisors, to help pay their legal bills. Once again, Nixon turned to hush money, using the very same slush fund that had gotten him in trouble in the first place. "It was not the amount of money" that was the main problem, one writer realized. "It wasn't even that it was dirty money. It was the very fact that it was *Hughes* money, the kind of money Nixon had been caught with before, the kind of money that had once cost him the White House. In a desperate effort to keep it from happening again, he had made it happen again." The President's paranoia had become self-fulfilling.

For a quarter century, Jack Anderson had fueled Richard Nixon's fury more than any other journalist. But as Nixon's presidency crumbled, the crusading columnist struggled to break news about his longtime enemy. "Jack's column in these months had some important Watergate stories," Brit Hume said, "but he did not lead the way, as he had on so many other stories about government misdeeds. All at once, though, Jack caught up. And in so doing, he got himself into a jam far more ominous than any he had ever been in before."

In April 1973, Anderson published a series of columns that quoted extensively from transcripts of secret testimony before the Watergate grand jury. Although Anderson trumpeted his "revelations" as "startling," their substance was comparatively unimportant because most of the key facts had already been reported elsewhere through verbal leaks to other journalists. Still, the fact that Anderson had obtained a copy of the closely guarded transcripts *was* startling, because these minutes were so sensitive that authorities kept them locked under tight security. Extraordinarily few people had access to the documents—only prosecutors and the clerks who recorded the minutes in the first place—and under the law, it was a crime to divulge them. Court personnel rushed to compare their transcripts with what was published in the "Merry-Go-Round," the FBI reported, and "determined they were identical, even down to the punctuation"—from ungrammatical questions posed by grand jurors to stammering answers from witnesses. The government was forced to acknowledge publicly that the Anderson minutes were indeed authentic.

The President was appalled. It was "shocking" to read the grand jury testimony in the newspaper, Nixon told his staff, but "Jack Anderson has them—ugh—verbatim" and "it is a major story." The President's men were equally dismayed. "Such leaking was normally a criminal offense," Howard Hunt complained. "Anderson, never one to miss the fun when human blood might be drawn," had even displayed the transcripts "boastingly to other reporters," Nixon fund-raiser Maurice Stans fumed. "Prosecutors were going crazy because they couldn't figure it out," Anderson's legman Mike Kiernan said. "Jack was a fast typist and took marvelous shorthand so everybody wondered if somebody was dictating the transcripts to him." Given his history of electronic eavesdropping, the FBI decided to conduct an electronic sweep of the grand jury room to uncover any hidden bugs that Anderson might have planted inside. But nothing turned up and Anderson's disclosures continued unabated. His columns were "incredible . . . devastating . . . unheard of," prosecutor Earl Silbert wrote in his diary; the foreman of the grand jury "was screaming about summoning Anderson" and forcing him to testify under oath to reveal his source. Silbert proposed a more draconian measure: suppressing Anderson's reporting in advance by having the court issue a restraining order to prohibit him from publishing additional transcripts.

On April 23, all fifteen federal judges in Washington met in a special executive session to decide what to do about the "Merry-Go-Round" leaks. An hour later, Judge Sirica directed prosecutors to conduct a criminal investigation of Anderson. "All hell broke loose," the columnist remembered happily. "Someone had broken the law, and the Justice Department and the judges damn well wanted to know who." Prosecutors faced a daunting task. "I am not to[o] optimistic" about uncovering Anderson's informant, Silbert wrote in his diary, and "just deploring" the leak without also gagging Anderson was a "wishy-washy result." One federal judge suggested granting the columnist immunity from prosecution to force him to reveal his source; if, as expected, Anderson refused, he could then be jailed for contempt of court and charged with obstruction of justice. "We thought we were about to be clapped behind bars," Anderson's legman Jack Cloherty recalled.

Defiant as always, Anderson publicly announced that he would not divulge his sources even if ordered to by the court. "Under our Constitution," he insisted, "we are free to publish any and all news." Anderson argued that the public had a right to know about the Watergate cover-up and pointed out that other journalists had already published grand jury testimony based on anonymous sources: "The government is upset, apparently, because we nailed down the testimony precisely rather than relying on hearsay." Hume worried that "Jack was not only saying publicly that he was being singled out for his accuracy" but was also preaching "a little civics lecture. I winced at the thought of how Jack's statement must have been received by those fifteen judges who had voted to have him investigated."

Anderson's defense may not have been humble but it was accurate, at least about grand jury secrets published by other reporters; however, those were verbal, not written, leaks, unlike Anderson's hundreds of pages of verbatim transcripts. Indeed, the columnist received not merely a leak but a veritable flood, one that continued day after day on the pages of hundreds of newspapers across the nation, making a public mockery of the grand jury's purportedly confidential deliberations. Anderson's glaring breach of secrecy posed a public challenge that was impossible for the judiciary to ignore.

"You've got to get off this collision course you're on with this court," Hume warned Anderson, or "you'll wind up in jail."

"I know what the risks are," Anderson retorted. "I'll put the column out from a jail cell if I have to."

The President would have been delighted to oblige. The leaks to "Jack Anderson's column," Nixon told a top Justice Department official, "the way the leaks are coming out, I mean, it gives the impression that we really aren't getting at it"—investigating the scandal. Which, of course, was precisely Anderson's point. "I didn't trust Nixon to prosecute his own wayward aides," the columnist said, and the President "looked upon the grand jury as a safe rug to sweep the Watergate scandal under. His intention, my sources said, was to lift a corner of the rug just enough to quiet the public clamor. He believed that as president he could control the prosecutors." Indeed, as White House tapes later demonstrated, that was exactly what Nixon was doing.

The President was convinced that Anderson had obtained the secret transcripts from dissident prosecutors trying to thwart the White House cover-up. "I think there's terrible significance to . . . these continuing leaks," Nixon told his staff, because they suggested a deliberate effort to keep the investigation alive by publicizing Watergate evidence. The President ordered his assistant attorney general to "take the three members of the prosecuting team and put them to a lie-detector test."

Actually, however, the Anderson transcripts came not from prosecutors but from the trash. Decades later, the columnist admitted that a man he had never met before simply walked in off the street and offered to sell the carbon paper used to make copies of the transcripts. "We were so excited we didn't know what to do," Les Whitten recalled. Anderson delicately finessed the request for a bribe because "we had a fish on the line and I didn't want to lose him." Anderson's staff assiduously lobbied the source, trying to persuade him that he had a moral duty to give them the paperwork gratis. To make sure they weren't being set up, Whitten drove the informant around Washington while legman Cloherty, a burly, bearded ex-quarterback in a leather trench coat, acted as a "third-rate Mob lookout in a cloak-and-dagger operation whose job was to make sure nobody saw us." Eventually, the reporters persuaded their source to dig through the courthouse trash bins for no charge and raced back to the "Merry-Go-Round" office with hundreds of carbon pages. "We all had dirty hands," Cloherty remembered. "I had to scrub mine several times to get the ink off." Opal Ginn, Anderson's devoted secretary, taped the carbon paper to a lampshade to illuminate it and then retyped it all at her desk. Anderson's staff worked round the clock putting together a complete set of nearly five hundred pages of transcripts.

To try to uncover Anderson's source, the FBI interrogated stenographers who had transcribed the testimony, but the typists denied leaking it. Agents also investigated a private company that hauled away trash from the district court. Slowly but steadily, the FBI seemed to be zeroing in on the columnist's secret informant. In response, to protect their source's identity, Anderson and Whitten devised a contingency plan to keep the FBI from confiscating their notes by locking themselves in their office and throwing their paperwork out the window. "I know it sounds romantic and crazy, these two overweight middle-aged people . . . physically trying to keep them from getting into our files," Whitten recalled, "but we were determined to do this" as a "tribute to the First Amendment." Anderson fully expected to go to prison: "When you've got all the judges in the District of Columbia and the U.S. attorney on your tail, and you know that the White House is using every arm-twisting method it knows, you're not too sure you're gonna win."

But the Nixon administration decided not to make a martyr out of the columnist. "I don't want to go too far there, because I don't want to get into a diversionary battle with Jack Anderson," Assistant Attorney General Henry Petersen told the President. Nixon agreed: "Oh, hell, no." That would give it "too much attention. I agree. I agree. Well, what I mean is, do [your] best to control it." The best way to control Anderson, prosecutors decided, was with honey, not vinegar. Assistant U.S. Attorney Seymour Glanzer believed that any criminal charges filed against the newsman would ultimately be thrown out of court, anyway. More important, Glanzer said, "we didn't want to prosecute the crime, we wanted to prevent it." So he proposed a face-saving solution that would get Anderson to stop publishing the transcripts by appealing to his "patriotic" desire to help the Watergate probe: instead of trying to force Anderson to reveal his source, he could return the documents directly to Judge Sirica rather than the Nixon Justice Department.

On April 25, the columnist and his attorneys gathered at the federal courthouse in Washington for a conference with Watergate prosecutors. "Jack had been warned repeatedly by both his lawyers before going into the meeting that the law was against him and that he must take a penitent approach," Hume recalled. One attorney explained that "Jack really doesn't have much to bargain with." Another emphasized that "we are coming in as supplicants, not as aggressors." According to Hume, Anderson—"one leg already in the jailhouse door"—was unconcerned. "Don't worry," he told his lawyers, "you let me handle it."

For nearly two hours, the muckraker and the Justice Department attorneys argued back and forth. Prosecutors explained that they had been instructed by a judicial panel to bring charges against Anderson's source and had to comply with that order. Anderson refused to reveal the identity of his informant and invoked the First Amendment's protection of religion as well as the press: "The Mormon faith holds that the Constitution of the United States is divinely inspired," Anderson pointed out. "So I could never consent to identifying a confidential source, no matter what." The newsman then bluffed prosecutors, pretending that he had obtained

all of the Watergate grand jury transcripts and was on the verge of publishing additional columns about them: "I have requests right now from
the *New York Times*, the *Los Angeles Times* and the wire services for the
full transcripts. My inclination is to give them to them. But before I do,
I wanted to hear your case." According to Hume, "Jack was playing boldly
with a weak hand, but I have watched him intimidate other formidable
people with that booming voice, ringing with certainty, and that stern
expression of his." Justice Department attorneys repeated their familiar
arguments about the importance of grand jury secrecy. "They were reasons well known to Jack," Hume said, "as they are to any experienced
reporter. But he listened most attentively." At the end of the lecture, Anderson surprised his audience. "You've convinced me," he said. "I have no
desire to interfere with the investigation of the case."

Anderson agreed to stop publishing the transcripts and turn them
over to Judge Sirica. But to try to keep prosecutors from coming after
him, he added, "I will never tell you any more before a grand jury than
I am telling you here today. So if you now call me before the grand jury
[to try to force him to reveal his source] I can only conclude that the
reason is that you want to put me in jail." Anderson warned that such
a move would turn him into a journalistic hero. He emerged from the
meeting and announced to reporters that he had voluntarily decided to
stop publishing the grand jury transcripts. Anderson explained that the
prosecutors had persuaded him that his column was scaring witnesses
from testifying about Watergate. "I don't want to hamper their investigation," the columnist added. "They made such a passionate point of
it." Naturally, he did not volunteer that he had already milked all of his
documents for everything that was newsworthy in them. But he did
emphasize that he had not been cowed: "There was no intimidation, no
threats, no coercion of any kind. If there had been, I'd have walked out
and handed the transcripts to everybody" in the press. In a more formal written statement, Anderson declared that "as a journalist, I have
an obligation and a right to continue to report any and all pertinent
information on this sordid scandal that so many people in high places
have worked so hard to keep from the public."

The compromise was widely praised. Former Nixon speechwriter
William Safire, a newly minted columnist for *The New York Times*,

called Anderson's move "gallant"—an adjective not normally applied to the muckraker, especially by Nixon loyalists. "Jack ended up gaining recognition for breaking the story," Hume marveled, "and nearly as much for stopping it . . . It was one of the most remarkable Houdini acts anyone in trouble with the government has ever made."

What did Anderson's publication of grand jury transcripts ultimately accomplish? The investigative reporter claimed that it helped foil the President's Watergate cover-up, but that was a gross exaggeration. In fact, Anderson's scoop came late in the rapidly accelerating scandal, after the White House was already well on its way to self-destruction. In the end, Anderson's legal showdown had less impact on Nixon than on the columnist himself, and then only as a symbol of his decline as a new generation of younger investigative reporters pushed him aside. The story proved to be Anderson's last real blast at the politician he had stalked for a generation.

In any case, as promised, the newsman turned over his documents to Judge Sirica, who locked them in his office safe. Nine months later, the judge announced that the FBI's investigation failed to turn up Anderson's source. By then, the Nixon White House, in its final death throes, had more important problems than plugging leaks to Anderson.

In the spring of 1973, the Watergate cover-up imploded. White House counsel John Dean warned the President that the burglars' increasing demands for hush money had reached the point of blackmail and were bound to be exposed. "We have a cancer within, close to the Presidency, that is growing," Nixon's lawyer told him. "It is growing daily. It's compounded, growing geometrically now." But the President directed Dean to continue their conspiracy: "If you need [more] money, I mean, you could get the money . . . you could get a million dollars. And you could get it in cash. I know where." Afraid of his escalating criminal liability, Dean began cooperating with prosecutors and directly implicated Nixon and his top aides. The President was both terrified and enraged by his lawyer's betrayal. "It isn't like a little goddamn yeoman [Charles Radford] that did that horrible thing," Nixon shouted. *"This son of a bitch was [my] counsel."* To try to limit his exposure, the President fired Dean and forced other top advisors to resign. White House press secretary Ronald Ziegler tried to repair the public relations damage by apologizing to the press and announcing that his previous false statements about Watergate were "inoperative." But none of it stopped the hemorrhaging.

In the summer of 1973, the Senate Watergate Committee held hearings, televised live, that riveted the nation. Nixon aides testified in what became a public morality play starring North Carolina's folksy Democratic senator Sam Ervin and Tennessee's smooth Republican senator Howard Baker, who said the scandal boiled down to one key question: "What did the President know and when did he know it?" The answer, it turned out, was that Nixon knew virtually everything about the Watergate cover-up right from the start. And, as the panel soon discovered, it was all documented in hundreds of hours of secret White House recordings. The Nixon tapes transformed Watergate from a political scandal to a constitutional crisis. The recordings offered proof not merely of corruption by White House aides but of criminal conduct by the President himself. Nixon's initial refusal to hand over the audio evidence also put him in direct conflict with Congress and the courts and suggested that he believed the President was above the law. That impression only deepened when he fired the special prosecutor who was investigating him, Archibald Cox (the "Coxsucker," as he was indelicately called in the White House). The new attorney general, Elliot Richardson, quit in protest, as did his second-in-command, in what became known as the "Saturday Night Massacre." The resignation of Vice President Spiro Agnew amid unrelated bribery charges— and his replacement by the popular congressional leader Gerald Ford—further emboldened House Democrats to introduce resolutions to impeach the President.

By the fall of 1973, Nixon's struggle for survival was primarily a legal one, fighting subpoenas from Congress and the new special prosecutor, Leon Jaworski. But as always, public relations remained a top presidential priority and diversion a favorite presidential tactic. White House veteran H. R. Haldeman, who had first planted the rumor that Jack Anderson had orchestrated the Watergate bugging, continued to peddle this yarn to prosecutors and Republican allies on Capitol Hill.

Haldeman made much of the fact that "Anderson just happened to be" at the Washington airport when the Watergate burglars arrived there a few hours before the break-in and that the columnist was the first person to visit the conspirators in jail after they were caught. Haldeman claimed to find it "incredible" and "astonishing" that the muckraker heard rumors of the crime before it was even carried out: "Jack Anderson, of all people in Washington, knew the Watergate break-in was going to take place. Why didn't he publish this fantastic scoop?" Because it was all a setup, Haldeman maintained: "If he had published his information, Watergate would never have taken place."

The White House conspiracy theories about Anderson were forwarded to the Senate Watergate Committee. Aides to Republican counsel Fred Thompson, the future senator and presidential candidate, began investigating Anderson and soon became "convinced they were onto something." Thompson's staff located a witness who claimed that Anderson had recently given Watergate burglar Frank Sturgis "a stack of fifty-dollar bills" in a Miami hotel. Senator Baker, who was trying to defend the President, sensed an opportunity and decided that "we ought to have a talk with Mr. Anderson."

In November 1973, the Watergate Committee questioned Anderson under oath. Senators decided not to have the muckraker testify in public because they were nervous that he would be "a loose cannon" and embarrass them. Anderson swore that he did not pay Frank Sturgis any money, that their airport meeting was just a chance encounter, and that his attempt to have the Watergate burglar released from jail into his custody was simply a tactic to try to get a scoop. Senate Republicans did not believe him. One committee counsel "proceeded to bore in on Anderson," Thompson said, "giving the interview the appearance of the old Mutt 'n' Jeff police interrogation." Anderson's claim that he was unable to corroborate rumors of the Nixon campaign's bugging—and had misplaced two sets of paperwork informing him about it—met with skepticism. "The man who made his living exposing the frailties of others had somehow managed to lose two files dealing with the same subject matter," Thompson scoffed. "All of us found the story hard to accept." In addition, Thompson doubted Anderson's explanation that he was on his way to a speaking engagement in Cleveland when he inadvertently encountered Sturgis at the Washington airport: "There was nothing in the Cleveland newspapers at the time that had any reference to an Anderson appearance," Thompson charged.

Anderson complained that the Republicans' "investigation of us . . . seemed almost as intensive as its investigation of Watergate" because they "were sure the break-in wasn't by accident" but "was my diabolical work." In fact, however, the conspiracy theories about Anderson were deliberate disinformation planted by the White House, one last Nixonian attempt to punish Anderson and cover up Watergate. Further investigation confirmed that Anderson was indeed on his way to a college journalism fraternity outside Cleveland when he ran into Sturgis at the Washington airport, and the newsman's notes about the Nixon campaign's bugging operation eventually turned up as well. (Thompson "couldn't believe that the legendary Jack Anderson would misplace something," Anderson laughed. "He had obviously never seen my desk.") Sturgis also corroborated Anderson's account that their airport meeting was strictly accidental: "It is a coincidence and it is a big coincidence, but I'm willing to take sodium pentothal [to prove it]," the burglar testified. Sturgis also swore under oath that he never received a wad of cash from Anderson. "Aside from the fact that I have never seen a big stack of $50 bills and would never be foolish enough to give one away," the columnist said, "the bigger question was why I would sit on the Watergate story. Even Thompson couldn't figure out the answer to that one." In the end, the attempt to frame Anderson for the Watergate break-in failed.

But Republicans soon came up with another way to try to help the President. "Why don't we distract attention from the White House," Senator Howard Baker suggested, "by getting the story out in public" about the navy yeoman who "leaked all this information to Jack Anderson?" A few weeks later, the previously secret story of Pentagon spying on Henry Kissinger was leaked to the press. The timing was no coincidence. Top Nixon advisors were now facing trial for burglarizing the office of Daniel Ellsberg's psychiatrist, and their defense rested on the dubious proposition that they had done so to protect national security. To buttress their case that they had been trying to ward off grave dangers to the Republic, they now exposed—and exaggerated—the actions of Anderson's source, Yeoman Charles Radford. In truth, his spying for the Defense Department was not a classic case of espionage; after all, Radford passed information not to a hostile foreign government but to another branch of the administration's national security team. Indeed, although the incident understandably alarmed the Nixon White House, such covert intelligence-sharing took place in both previous and subsequent administrations.

Still, in the paranoid atmosphere of Watergate, the revelations created a furor, and the Senate Armed Services Committee began holding hearings in February 1974. Admiral Thomas Moorer, chairman of the Joint Chiefs of Staff, testified that he didn't know the documents Radford gave him were stolen from the White House and insisted that he was authorized to have them anyway. Henry Kissinger, who two years earlier had called for Moorer's firing because of the spying, now took the witness stand to defend the admiral who had targeted him. The real culprit, Kissinger said, was not Moorer but Jack Anderson, who published the documents that embarrassed Kissinger. For his part, Yeoman Radford swore that his theft of White House paperwork was authorized by the Pentagon high command but steadfastly denied leaking classified documents to Anderson. Senators tried to shake Radford's story.

"Yeoman Radford, do you consider it a coincidence that you had dinner with Mr. Anderson the day before these leaks appeared in his column?" Senator Strom Thurmond asked. "Yes, sir, I do; most definitely I do," Radford replied. "Do you say again that you passed no material to Mr. Anderson and you passed no material to anyone else who passed it to him?" Thurmond repeated. "Yes, sir, I do say that," Radford reiterated. Chairman John Stennis pressed further: "You had no connection, telephone calls or connections with him in any way through other people?" "No, sir," Radford replied. "You did not write to him, you did not use the mail or anything like that?" "No, sir." But in fact, the FBI traced both mail and phone calls between Anderson and Radford, including a conversation in which the yeoman "expressed pride in the fact that Anderson's columns had won the Pulitzer" and relished the "triumphal moment" with him.

The Senate panel convened in secret session to decide what to do. Democrat Sam Nunn declared that Radford "very likely" gave "perjured testimony" to the committee and recommended that the Justice Department conduct a criminal investigation. Senator Thurmond wanted

Anderson to testify under oath but Senator John Tower believed that the panel was "not going to get anywhere" doing that. Chairman Stennis sought legal advice on how to punish the muckraker but White House counsel Fred Buzhardt advised that it would be virtually impossible to prove that "Anderson had an intent to harm this country or to give aid to another country by publishing the material," as required under the federal Espionage Act. Senator Barry Goldwater thought Anderson might be vulnerable for making an "offer [of] money to Radford" in exchange for classified documents but that "we should not bother with" such a prosecution. Senator Hugh Scott, a longtime Anderson source, agreed that "we ought to drop the matter."

In the end, the Senate committee issued a report absolving the Pentagon for spying on the White House and attacked Anderson for publishing "at least 70 highly sensitive, classified documents" in "a serious compromise to national security." The panel concluded that Anderson's "lack of prosecution" was "deeply regrettable."

At long last, filing criminal charges against Anderson had bipartisan support. But President Nixon was now too politically wounded to take advantage of the opportunity.

By 1974, investigations by prosecutors and Congress had expanded beyond Watergate to include a broad range of criminal activity by the President and his aides. These "White House horrors," as former attorney general John Mitchell characterized them, ranged from burglary and forgery to warrantless wiretaps and bombing plots. Nixon's financial propriety was also, once again, at issue. Besides his receipt of cash from Howard Hughes, the President was accused of spending more than $1 million in public funds for personal improvements on his vacation houses in Florida and California, and had to pay $284,000 in taxes amid allegations that he had backdated paperwork to finagle improper deductions. The shadow of financial chicanery that first attached itself during Nixon's slush fund scandal more than two decades earlier haunted him to the end, even as he vigorously defended his integrity. "I earned everything I got," the President told an audience of newspaper editors. "I am not a crook."

As always, Nixon blamed his troubles on his enemies—especially in the media—rather than himself. "These assholes are out to destroy us," the President raged. "Screw them, screw them . . . we're going to treat them with the contempt they deserve." In public, Nixon denounced what he called the most "outrageous, vicious, distorted" reporting he had ever seen. "Don't get the impression that you arouse my anger," he told journalists bitterly. "You see, one can only be angry with those he respects." (The President's acolytes followed his lead; one of them, Karl Rove, used a phony grassroots organization to rally supporters against the "lynch mob atmosphere created [by] the Nixon-hating media.")

But attacking the press did little to salvage the President's mounting legal and political woes. His continued refusal to turn over subpoenaed tapes aroused further suspicion when one turned out to have a mysterious "gap" of eighteen and a half minutes. Nixon's loyal secretary publicly took the blame for what experts said were at least five deliberate erasures during a key conversation between the President and his chief of staff three days after the Watergate break-in. But although Rose Mary Woods claimed that she accidentally obliterated the tape while trying to transcribe it, not even her coworkers in the White House believed that. More likely, the President himself erased it in a deliberate attempt to destroy evidence that implicated him.

To combat prosecutors' subpoenas, Nixon released written transcripts of his conversations, which he personally edited to remove the most embarrassing sections, including voluminous explosions of presidential profanity that were sanitized with the notation "expletive deleted." Still, even these cleaned-up transcripts produced a wave of public revulsion. Senate Republican leader Hugh Scott called them "shabby, disgusting, immoral." The *Los Angeles Times*, once Nixon's most ardent booster in the press, joined the growing chorus urging Congress to impeach the President.

In May 1974, the House Judiciary Committee began impeachment hearings. After months of gathering evidence, the panel voted to charge Nixon with obstructing justice and abusing his presidential power. Lawmakers twice cited Jack Anderson's reporting in their final impeachment report: first, because Nixon "knew or had reason to know" that

Attorney General Kleindienst had "testified falsely" about ITT during Senate hearings instigated by the "columns [of] Jack Anderson"; second, because Nixon had violated "the constitutional rights of citizens" by "misusing IRS information," including the "sensitive" tax records of Alabama governor George Wallace that were "transmitted to columnist Jack Anderson" and published in the "Merry-Go-Round." In these and other instances, the committee found, "Richard M. Nixon acted in a manner contrary to his trust as President and subversive of constitutional government" and "by such conduct, warrants impeachment and trial, and removal from office."

Any doubt that Nixon would be forced from the White House was removed when the Supreme Court unanimously ruled that he must turn over all subpoenaed tapes. Among them was a so-called smoking gun recording in which the President clearly conspired to cover up Watergate by halting the FBI's investigation of the break-in. The damning recording led every single Republican on the House Judiciary Committee—even the President's most diehard stalwarts—to support impeachment.

Nixon's final days in office were filled with depression and rage. He slurred his words in drunken late-night phone calls. Aides worried that he would commit suicide. But his cover-up continued to the very end. Presidential staff worked overtime shredding sacks of incriminating documents; according to one witness, the Oval Office was "heavy with the acrid smell of paper recently burned in the fireplace." In his last hours in the Executive Office Building, Nixon broke down and sobbed uncontrollably in the arms of Henry Kissinger. "What have I done?" the President cried. "What has happened?"

In August 1974, Richard Nixon became the only president in American history to resign from office. In a tearful farewell speech to his White House staff, televised live, he finally seemed to realize what led to his disgrace: "Never be petty," he said. "Always remember, others may hate you, but those who hate you don't win unless you hate them, and then you destroy yourself."

PART IV

ENDINGS

17

FINAL YEARS

Richard Nixon waved goodbye from the helicopter that picked him up one last time from the White House lawn. Soon after, as Air Force One took him into exile, the former president sat in his cabin, silent and alone. A quarter century after he first arrived in the nation's capital, he was heading home to California. "Our long national nightmare," declared the new president, Gerald Ford, "is over."

Not for the disgraced ex-president. In San Clemente, Nixon alternated between shock and grief, anger and self-pity. "Fiercely proud, he could neither admit his emotional dependence on approbation nor transcend it," Henry Kissinger wrote. "Deeply insecure, he first acted as if a cruel fate had singled him out for rejection and then he contrived to make sure that his premonition came to pass." Nixon needed to believe that he was the victim of a partisan witch hunt, the unfair and unfortunate target of a conspiracy between his many enemies in politics and the press. In fact, however, Watergate was not some inexplicable aberration but, in the context of his caustic career, a predictable if not preordained consequence.

In the end, more than seventy people were convicted of Watergate-related crimes. Nineteen went to prison, from the burglars themselves to the top echelon of the Nixon White House: H. R. Haldeman, John Ehrlichman, John Mitchell, Charles Colson, John Dean. But Richard Nixon was spared. Just a month after his resignation, President Ford pardoned him for all crimes he committed while in office. Nixon never had to face indictment or trial. He had "suffered enough," Ford declared, and it was time to end the "ugly passions" of Watergate. Nixon thanked his successor for his compassion and acknowledged that he should have acted "more decisively and more forthrightly" during Watergate. But his limited contrition did little to stem the furious public reaction. Ford's popularity plummeted, his pardon widely blamed for the loss of his presidency two years later.

Jack Anderson thought it wrong that Nixon's "co-conspirators wound up in jail when he retreated into wealthy retirement," costing taxpayers "a whopping" $1 million a year for Secret Service protection, office space and staff, and an annual federal pension. After such protracted public combat, Anderson viewed Nixon's downfall as a kind of crowning victory and could not resist gloating from the moment it happened. Indeed, on the very day the President announced his resignation, the muckraker bragged in his column that he had "been in the forefront of those who have accused President Nixon of condoning lawlessness while he preached law and order." Anderson then summarized his greatest anti-Nixon hits, "not to boast but to encourage public officials to tell the truth." A *Washington Post* editor publicly described Anderson's parting shot as a "tasteless column that amounted to an ill-timed advertisement for himself."

But Anderson's self-congratulation could not mask the fact that history was now leaving him behind. "Jack was overtaken by events," Brit Hume understood. "He had been one of a handful of investigative reporters in America and then Watergate made it all the rage. Every newspaper and television network began an investigative team. It took away Jack's competitive advantage. He no longer had the field to himself." The rise of television, and the dwindling influence of the syndicated column, further eroded Anderson's clout. Our "column continues," his secretary, Opal Ginn, wrote a friend. "But between you and me, hasn't it been rather dull lately? We can't get a handle on anything since Watergate."

The newfound celebrity of Anderson's young rivals—especially Bob Woodward and Carl Bernstein, who were lionized in the popular film *All the President's Men*—seemed like a cruel trick played on the old muckraker. "The man who had kept the torch burning, sometimes singlehandedly, always on the outside of the 'in' crowd, was ignored," Anderson's legman James Grady recalled, "even while the kind of investigative reporting that Jack had been doing became fashionable and defined that era in the history of journalism." Anderson's promoters tried to make up for it in advertisements: "Investigative journalism didn't start with Watergate. Jack Anderson has been at it for years." But his PR campaign was unable to overshadow Watergate or its media mythology. Richard Nixon himself could not have come up with a more fitting way to deflate Anderson's outsized ego.

A year after Nixon's resignation, Bob Woodward of *The Washington Post* revealed the White House plot to assassinate Jack Anderson. Based on anonymous sources, Woodward's account was greeted with denials from Nixon acolytes. A quick and cursory internal CIA probe "found nothing" to the assassination allegations and cleared itself of wrongdoing. A congressional committee led by Senator Frank Church also began an investigation. Howard Hunt told the panel that he did not try to murder Anderson but did plot to drug him, a distinction he hoped would minimize his legal exposure. Poisoning Anderson might seem "hair-raising to an outsider," Hunt testified, but "there were a lot of creative people, not only in the CIA, but also in the White House, and ideas were a penny a dozen." For his part, Colson denied even Hunt's limited confession, calling it "totally off the wall." Beyond that, Colson's memory was otherwise remarkably hazy: he acknowledged that Nixon asked him "many times" to discredit Anderson and that he "probably" did so in response; but he maintained that he could not re-call what action if any he took against the dastardly journalist.

Federal authorities never really attempted to get beyond the conve-nient memory loss and self-interested claims of the suspects. Ultimately, congressional investigators questioned only three people—Colson, Hunt, and Dr. Edward Gunn, the CIA toxicologist—all of whom had themselves been linked to the murder plot. The Senate panel failed to interview any disinterested witnesses or compel testimony under oath, while Gordon Liddy avoided all questioning by invoking his Fifth Amendment right against self-incrimination. Without issuing subpoe-nas or offering immunity from prosecution, authorities provided no incentive to any of the conspirators to provide truthful testimony. As a result, none of the government investigations ever got to the bottom of what happened. In the end, Senator Church's committee uncharacteristically took the easy way out, issuing a four-and-a-half page report concluding that Nixon's men had plotted to poison but not murder Anderson.

Years later, after the threat of additional prison time no longer hung over their heads, Hunt and Liddy would both admit their role in the White House plot to assassinate Anderson. Hunt said that he and Liddy had secretly staked out Anderson's home to see how to break into it, and tailed Anderson in his car to observe his driving route. Their motive, Liddy asserted, was patriotism: "As the direct result of an Anderson story, a top U.S. intelligence source abroad had been so compromised that, if not already dead, he would be in a matter of days. That was too much. Something had to be done." In fact, there was no evidence that Anderson's reporting ever led to the death of any American intelligence asset and neither Liddy nor anyone else ever provided any such proof. Still, to the very end, Liddy was prepared to carry out the Anderson hit, if necessary all by himself: "I would have knifed him or broken his neck, probably. One of us would have died, no doubt about it."

To be sure, the White House plot to assassinate Anderson was ultimately aborted and the conspirators were soon caught breaking into the Watergate building. But the final outcome could easily have been very different. Anderson, for one, believed that it was just a fluke that he wasn't murdered, and then only because the CIA failed to trust Nixon's men with the necessary toxins. As always, the moral responsibility went back to the man at the top. "One day we'll get them," President Nixon had told Colson, "we'll get them on the ground where we want them. And we'll stick our heels in, step on them hard and twist." If not for bad luck at the Watergate complex, Nixon's second term might well have contained the kind of lethal revenge his men plotted against Jack Anderson—and no one but the conspirators themselves might ever have known about it.

After his resignation, Richard Nixon struggled for the remaining twenty years of his life to rehabilitate his tarnished reputation. A year after being forced from the presidency, he made his first public appearance at a Teamsters Union golf tournament that was attended by several well-known mobsters. This inauspicious beginning was followed by a more respectable stop along the comeback trail: a trip to China, the first in a series of international travels designed to remind the public of his foreign policy achievements. In 1977, Nixon advanced his revisionist narrative—and received more than half a million dollars—by sitting down for a lengthy interview with television personality David Frost. A worldwide audience of fifty million watched as Nixon denounced the news media and argued that he broke no laws because "when the President does it, that means it is not illegal." Ever defiant, Nixon refused "to get down and grovel," seeking forgiveness. Watergate, he insisted, was the result of his enemies seizing on his mistakes: "I gave them a sword. And they stuck it in. And they twisted it with relish. And, I guess, if I'd been in their position, I'd have done the same thing."

The next year, Nixon collected $2.5 million for a lengthy, self-serving memoir. He went on to write six more books, filled mostly with windy platitudes about foreign policy. He also moved back to Manhattan and cultivated the mien of a senior statesman by inviting elite journalists and politicos to dinner parties at his East Side townhouse. By the mid-1980s, media outlets once again embraced the latest incarnation of a New Nixon. *The New York Times* called him "an elder statesman, commentator on foreign and domestic affairs, adviser to world leaders, a multimillionaire and a successful author and lecturer honored by audiences at home and abroad." *Newsweek* put the former president on its cover under the headline: HE'S BACK: THE REHABILITATION OF RICHARD NIXON.

In 1990, this historical revisionism achieved its apotheosis in the Richard M. Nixon Library and Birthplace, complete with a 52,000--square-foot museum and interactive video theaters. Funded by wealthy Nixon supporters, hagiographic exhibits depicted Watergate as a coup engineered by Nixon's enemies; "irresponsible journalists" were banned from the library's premises. But Nixon's final cover-up could not alter reality and his propaganda efforts could only achieve so much before the bar of history. "Watergate proved fatal to his political life and undoubtedly will haunt his historical reputation," the scandal's leading historian concluded. "History will record a fair share of the significant achievements of Nixon's presidency, but Watergate will be the spot that will not out."

In June 1993, Pat Nixon died following a battle with lung cancer. Her husband was inconsolable. The former president broke down in public at her funeral and clutched the hand of his longtime psychotherapist, Dr. Arnold Hutschnecker, who was seated with the Nixon family. Ten months later, Nixon himself died of a stroke at the age of eighty-one. His funeral was attended by the five presidents who succeeded him in office. "He made mistakes," Bill Clinton eulogized. "But the enduring lesson of Richard Nixon is that he never gave up." Rose Mary Woods, Bebe Rebozo, Spiro Agnew, and even George McGovern attended the funeral. So did two men who went to prison in service of their leader: Charles Colson wept, while Gordon Liddy gave Nixon's coffin a brisk military salute.

Unlike Richard Nixon, Jack Anderson did not seek rehabilitation after Watergate; he sought restoration, as America's leading investigative reporter. But it was not to be. Anderson never made his own comeback. Instead, his career plummeted over the next thirty years as he became embroiled in scandals of his own making and marginalized as a figure of scorn.

Without Nixon to kick around anymore, Anderson focused his attention on Jimmy Carter. The new president "was an introvert in an extrovert's job, just like Richard Nixon," Anderson believed, and "I came to understand that no two presidents were more alike," each "burdened with insecurities, eager for acceptance, [and] disdainful of critics." In truth, Carter bore little resemblance to Nixon; but like a general fighting the last war, Anderson persuaded himself that Nixon's ghost had returned to the White House disguised as a former peanut farmer from Georgia. The muckraker began what presidential press secretary Jody Powell called a four-year "vendetta" against Carter. "I was just doing the same thing that I did to Nixon," Anderson insisted, but his legman Joe Spear thought Anderson's underlying motive was hunger for the kind of notoriety that had escaped him during Watergate.

During Carter's second year in office, Anderson accused White House chief of staff Hamilton Jordan of participating in a "political fix" by blocking the capture of the fugitive Robert Vesco after a childhood friend of Jordan's received stock from the crooked financier. But the story wasn't true: Anderson had relied on a swindler who turned out to have manufactured bogus paperwork to falsely implicate the President's closest aide. Still, Anderson testified in court on behalf of his unsavory source, who had forged the fraudulent documents to try to get pending embezzlement charges dropped. Undaunted, Anderson then used his influence to provoke a Senate investigation and helped ghostwrite its one-sided findings, which he then quoted in his column without revealing his own behind-the-scenes role. President Carter publicly blasted Anderson as "the one columnist in this nation who habitually lies." Similarly harsh judgments were "shared by a large number of the more respected journalists in Washington," Carter's press secretary said, because Anderson's "*modus operandi* is to take care of those who will feed him dirt on others, and flail away at everyone else." That indictment reflected a growing sentiment in the nation's capital that was rapidly becoming conventional wisdom.

Anderson reinforced this harsh verdict following the seizure of fifty-three U.S. hostages by Iranian militants in the fall of 1979. Nine months later, with the Americans still languishing in captivity after a botched rescue effort, Anderson charged that President Carter was planning a larger military invasion to free them in a forthcoming "October Surprise" designed to ensure his reelection the following month. Although this "startling, top-secret plan" was opposed by the Pentagon, Anderson reported, Carter was "rushing ahead" anyway "to save himself from almost certain defeat" in the upcoming election. The White House denounced the Anderson columns as "absolutely false . . . grotesque and totally irresponsible." The muckraker hadn't even bothered to call the Defense Department or White House for comment. Numerous newspapers, including *The Washington Post*, spiked the "Merry-Go-Round" after being unable to verify the incendiary allegation. "Had [the story] been true, Anderson would have had the scoop of the century," Carter's press secretary admitted. "But the allegation was totally false, a fabrication from start to finish, and a particularly vicious one" because Anderson portrayed the President "as a man who would send thousands of Americans to die in combat . . . simply because he wanted to improve his political prospects."

Anderson's October Surprise story was planted by a group of conservative Republican strategists whose mission, according to former Nixon aide William Safire, was to "embarrass, bedevil and defeat" Carter in the upcoming election and replace him with Ronald Reagan. Operatives even fabricated bogus CIA documents criticizing the President and leaked them to Washington journalists. But only Anderson fell for the disinformation campaign. The muckraker who had made his reputation exposing Nixonian lies was now feeding at the propaganda trough put out by Nixon's successors.

Anderson's credibility eroded further in the 1980s, when he was seduced and coopted by President Reagan. "There was an all-American quality" about Reagan, the columnist wrote unabashedly, that was "reflected in his amiable, open face, which compelled trust and confidence. It was also his easiness of manner, his engaging sincerity, the way his whole personality smiled every time his face lit up in a grin." Anderson's toadying earned him frequent visits to the White House, where he dispensed advice and chatted with the President. Although Reagan did not disclose newsworthy information in these meetings, Anderson publicly bragged about his "exclusive" interviews, which he milked for many columns. During one get-together, the newsman suggested that Reagan create a "Young Astronauts" program to stoke student enthusiasm for science. The President was encouraging and asked Anderson to chair the group; he happily obliged. Anderson then used his column to tout Reagan's "dramatic bid to keep America ahead" in the space race and quoted from his memos to the White House on the subject. Two of Anderson's children were put on the Young Astronauts' payroll while their father and the President solicited financial donations for the organization, including from Richard Nixon's old corporate benefactors whom Anderson had investigated just a few years earlier. The obvious conflict of interest seemed to escape the newsman.

In addition, President Reagan appointed Anderson to co-chair a presidential commission designed to root out wasteful government spending. Once more, Anderson promoted the Reagan initiative in his column and personally lobbied wealthy business executives to support it financially. Again, the columnist seemed oblivious to the journalistic impropriety of soliciting money from potential investigative targets or openly shilling for the President. "Jack decided to sell his soul to Ronald Reagan," one of Anderson's reporters said sadly. Another explained that "what Jack craves even more than fame is acceptance."

In fact, Anderson became so compromised by his coziness with Reagan that he helped cover up the biggest White House conspiracy since Watergate. In 1985, in exchange for the release of yet another group of American hostages captured in the Middle East, the President approved clandestine arms shipments to the militant Islamic regime of Iran's Ayatollah Khomeini, whose theocracy had supported the first seizure of U.S. prisoners five years earlier. Reagan's secret arms-for-hostages pact violated both an international embargo and his bellicose antiterrorism policy against rewarding kidnappers. So, to hide its arming of Iran, the Reagan White House established a covert off-the-shelf operation that resembled Nixon's Plumbers. The scandal was exposed a year later, not by investigative reporters in Washington, but by an obscure Beirut magazine that learned of the scheme from feuding extremist factions in Iran. However, it turned out that Anderson and his partner Dale Van Atta had known of the disastrous deal almost from the very beginning. But administration officials warned Anderson that publishing the story would be "irresponsible, even traitorous" because it might endanger the hostages and leave the columnist with "blood on your hands." After a personal appeal from Reagan, Anderson censored his blockbuster story. The crusading reporter who refused to be intimidated by President Nixon's bogus national security claims helped conceal the worst presidential scandal since Watergate. It was, Van Atta believed, "the lowest point for Jack as a journalist" during his entire career. In old age, the once-hardened muckraker had grown soft.

Anderson's final years were marred by careless factual errors, self-promotional stunts, and embarrassing financial conflicts of interest that generated widespread ridicule from his peers in the press. It did not help that he had to fire several of his reporters for fabricating information. One staffer, Ron McRae, invented a "top-secret" Pentagon program that was supposedly conducting research on the "transmission of nuclear bombs instantaneously around the world through the power of positive thinking." The bogus story was published in nearly a thousand newspapers in January 1981, unencumbered by any subsequent retraction. Nine months later, an academic survey of editors around the nation ranked Anderson as Washington's worst columnist for both accuracy and integrity. Within a few years, even his client newspapers complained that Anderson's image had become "tarnished," his stories "beaten to death" and filled with nonstop self-congratulation about past scoops. "Jack got passed off as an entertaining crank," Brit Hume recognized. "He pressed ahead and kept going for another twenty years, but it was never the same. Once you lose your reputation for reliability, it diminishes your impact tremendously."

As his influence shrank, Anderson's ego ballooned. Dazzled by the fame and money television generated, he signed a multimillion-dollar contract to appear daily on ABC's *Good Morning America* program, where he wore a girdle under his suit to hide his pot belly. "He fell in love with being a celebrity," his daughter Laurie recalled, and it "inevitably went to his head. He was just full of himself." Anderson publicly complained, "I have to do almost daily what Woodward and Bernstein did once." But with his daily column and television broadcasts, plus regular radio reports, newsletters, and lectures, he no longer had time to uncover original investigative stories himself. "Jack spread himself thinner and thinner," one of his legmen recalled. "The column began to slip because the same amount of material had to be spread over a lot more outlets." To compensate, Anderson expanded his staff by hiring young, low-salaried assistants, but they were mostly too inexperienced to dig up important stories. One reporter bought a rubber stamp with the word CONFIDENTIAL on it to make leaked memos sound more important. "That was our currency," another Anderson legman, Howard Rosenberg, explained, "so the more secret documents you could get, the better, even if they were filled with official self-serving bullshit." The column's downward spiral would prove irreversible.

The problem was greater than just Anderson's idiosyncratic personality. As elite media outlets began practicing the kind of investigative reporting that Anderson helped pioneer, he found himself pushed further to the fringes of mainstream journalism. The ever-entrepreneurial columnist adapted by focusing on sensational theatrics rather than substantive newsgathering. He began writing a column for *The National Star*, a supermarket scandal sheet, joined the staff of the tabloid TV show *Inside Edition*, and hosted syndicated entertainment programs that his own staff compared to a Barnum & Bailey act. In a cheesy television series called *Truth*, Anderson grilled disreputable characters hooked up to polygraph machines to see whether they were lying. In another program, *Target: USA!*, he smuggled a handgun into the Capitol building and, with cameras rolling, whipped it out on a senator to demonstrate lax congressional security procedures. Anderson also negotiated to have Hollywood produce a film and then a TV sitcom about his life, but the idea never got off the drawing board. "He was always looking for the big score," his agent Lucianne Goldberg remembered. "He wanted me to market a 'Jack Anderson Board Game' to Parker Brothers, but the idea never went anywhere."

Anderson was more successful generating public notice with stories about hanky-panky in the nation's capital. He helped expose several members of Congress for using cocaine and marijuana. He also reported that Senator Harry Byrd, Jr., seduced a distraught but "voluptuous" female constituent—"her measurements are 40-26-36"—who sought federal help locating her missing husband. Byrd admitted inviting the woman to his apartment but denied taking advantage of her, so Anderson suggested that the senator submit to an independent medical exam to verify the accuser's "intimate physical description" of his anatomy. The lawmaker declined the proposal.

Homosexuality also returned to the "Merry-Go-Round" as a subject of investigation. The columnist who in earlier decades only hinted at rumors about Joe McCarthy and J. Edgar Hoover now engaged in explicit gay "outings." In 1986, Anderson's old enemy Roy Cohn, McCarthy's onetime Senate counsel who had become a politically connected superlawyer, became gravely ill with what he claimed was liver cancer. In fact, the closeted Cohn was dying of AIDS and Anderson exposed this fact in his column, along with an account of how Cohn used his influence to get special medical treatment from the government. Afterward, Anderson outed Defense Secretary Dick Cheney's spokesman, Pete Williams. "Here you have more than 10,000 people discharged from the military" because of homosexuality, Anderson declared, while Pentagon civilians like Williams, who "held the same security clearances and were privy to the same secrets as uniformed personnel," faced no such penalty. This "double standard and outdated piety" made Williams's sexual orientation newsworthy, Anderson insisted. Cheney, the future vice president who was also the father of a lesbian daughter, "was very angry," Anderson recalled, and Cheney's wife "snapped at me" when they next met at a Washington party.

Many of Anderson's sexposés were watered down or suppressed by the largest newspapers that subscribed to his column. "By the end," Anderson's partner Van Atta recalled, "we got more notice for the columns that were killed than for the ones that ran. The only attention we got was for the salacious stories." ABC scaled back Anderson's on-air commentaries. "He hasn't had a hot scoop in some time," a network executive complained. Anderson tried to compensate for his weak material by increasing the decibel level of his delivery. But his melodramatic bombast—honed during the fire-and-brimstone missionary sermons he delivered on street corners of the rural South a generation earlier—was a poor match for the cool medium of television. ABC fired him from its morning show. *Washington Post* editors, too, viewed Anderson as a vaudevillian relic and discussed canceling his column; instead, they decided to run the "Merry-Go-Round" less often and edit it more carefully.

Despite it all, Anderson reveled in his notoriety. He became close with a beautiful jet-setting Persian oil heiress, Lilly Fallah Lawrence, who fed him inside information about corruption in Iran—and lavished the columnist's inner circle with caviar and truffles. To house his growing staff, Anderson bought an elegant nineteenth-century Victorian mansion six blocks from the White House. With "corner turrets and imposing stone steps, finely carved wood trim and huge office fireplaces inside," one journalist wrote, it "is eerily reminiscent of the stately surroundings favored by the powerful Washington lawyers and lobbyists Anderson has often derided." The twenty-three-room "Castle," as his employees called their new office, had once been a tony Washington bordello. Anderson used its bidet to store government documents and reporters' notes.

Anderson's expanding journalistic franchise was legally registered under the name "Muckrakers, Incorporated," an oxymoron that symbolized the contradiction between the newsman's old public-service idealism and his new role shilling for corporate sponsors. His "buckraking"—collecting $250,000 a year in speaking fees from the kinds of special interest groups he targeted for investigation—was publicly compared to bribery. Worse was Anderson's choice of business associates. One was accused of fraud and lying to the federal government. Another, a former Reagan campaign aide and high-level CIA spy, was allegedly involved in improper stock trading. A third had been implicated in a notorious television quiz-show scandal and produced teen "sexploitation" films. A fourth was the publisher of a pornographic magazine. A fifth was the reputed leader of a bizarre cult that claimed to communicate with space aliens. "There was always some marginal character buzzing around Jack, promising to make him a millionaire, supposedly with little effort on his part," legman Jack Mitchell remembered. "Jack always listened, no matter what those around him said or how many times they warned him. He wanted the money."

In another deal that sounded like the kind of scam that Anderson himself once exposed, an ad designed to look like a news article asked: "Want To Become A Millionaire? . . . Jack Anderson, the famous Washington Investigative Reporter, will participate in a multi-million-dollar program to work with a select group of individuals to show them how to make money." Anderson offered to "teach people how to be successful in real estate investing or some other entrepreneurial business . . . and market that great idea they have always dreamed about"—for a price, of course. Anderson's employees were so appalled, they banded together to sign a joint letter informing their boss that they had been "flooded with calls" from potential customers who "are clearly naïve about business decisions and are willing to make an investment based solely on your good name." These "cheap advertising tricks and high-pressure sales tactics smack of a con," Anderson's reporters warned. "We are seriously concerned for your reputation and the reputation of the column."

But Anderson's dubious moneymaking schemes continued unabated. He proposed selling classified government documents that whistleblowers had leaked to him over the years by loading them into a computer database and charging hefty fees for access to the records. Besides potentially jeopardizing the identities of his confidential sources, the venture also risked forfeiting Anderson's protected status as a journalist and leaving him legally vulnerable to criminal prosecution if he profited from selling national secrets to foreign agents who signed up for his service. "It boggled the imagination how he could be so smart on some things and so dumb on others," Van Atta marveled. At the same time, Anderson kept accepting money under the table from Irv Davidson, even after the shady Washington lobbyist was indicted in a Mafia bribery case and pled guilty to federal fraud charges. Anderson "feels his reputation is so golden that no one could ever believe he had done anything wrong," one of his reporters explained.

The columnist was also compromised by a Washington businessman and socialite named Tongsun Park, who turned out to be a corrupt bagman in a scandal that became known as "Koreagate." On behalf of the government of South Korea, Park was secretly bribing members of Congress with cash-filled envelopes and sex with attractive Asian women. He was also a silent partner in the Diplomat National Bank, whose founding director and executive committee chairman was Jack Anderson. The newsman hadn't known about Park's involvement, or the fact that associates of South Korean evangelist Sun Myung Moon secretly and illegally owned the majority of the bank. But Anderson attacked federal investigators who uncovered this damning information and reportedly threatened to use his column to stop a burgeoning congressional probe of his business partners. The journalist's heavy-handed tactics became page-one news across the country. Anderson "has finally been caught with his pants down," *The Washington Star* declared, "and with some very strange bedmates." The columnist escalated the scandal by vowing to sue his media critics and file charges against investigators who leaked information about his bank. The *National Observer* mocked the "awkward position—for an investigative journalist—of condemning congressional leaks and threatening libel suits . . . It's the kind of story that columnist Jack Anderson ordinarily thrives on." He was ultimately forced to sever his ties with the bank, but it was too late to salvage his credibility in the affair.

Anderson's far-flung outside business connections inescapably tainted his journalism. According to one of his reporters, he killed a story about Frank Sinatra's organized-crime ties because the two men had become partners in a Nevada company. Anderson allegedly spiked another article because it might have angered a potential investor in his expensive bimonthly newsletter, *Jack Anderson Confidential.* The columnist even wrote a puff piece in *Parade* magazine about an "innovative" martial arts instructor named Jhoon Rhee who had "transformed" the "spectacular sport" by designing special safety equipment—without disclosing his own financial interest in Rhee's company or that Anderson and some members of his family and staff received free karate lessons from Rhee. It was "not corruption in the classic, conscious sense," Anderson's legman James Grady believed, "just the kind of mindless cheapness that Jack would have loved to expose in others."

More disturbing was Anderson's receipt of $10,000 from Exxon to produce a television documentary minimizing its notorious *Valdez* supertanker oil spill in Alaska. Although more than ten million gallons of crude had been discharged into Prudhoe Bay in one of the most devastating man-made environmental disasters in history, Anderson breezily declared that "no species affected by the spill is in danger of extinction" and the "food chain is very much intact" because wildlife had "made a strong rebound" and "returned to their natural habitat." Most damning of all, Anderson concealed Exxon's underwriting of the broadcast because the corporation insisted on being a "stealth sponsor." Anderson pulled out of the deal only after an internal revolt by his staff, who leaked the story to *Washington Post* media reporter Howard Kurtz, himself a former "Merry-Go-Round" legman. "I always had a hard time understanding why a man of Jack's talent and track record kept getting into jams with unsavory characters or questionable sources of funds," Kurtz later said. "But he ran his operation like a mom-and-pop store and always had a Depression-era mentality that he might get caught short and fold up shop."

These endless disasters demoralized Anderson's staff. We "had made a long climb up a slippery slope to achieve the credibility and impact the column had," Brit Hume wrote. "Now, it seemed, we had slid near the bottom of the greasy pole again and would have to start all over." Bickering divided Anderson's newsroom. Les Whitten, who did more of the column's reporting than anyone, resented the rapid rise of the younger Hume, whom Whitten considered a lazy glamour boy.

"After each story Brit did, he spent a week on the phone talking to all his friends about how great he was," Whitten complained. "I yelled at him about it and said he should see a psychiatrist. He cried and said, 'You're right, I don't know why I do that, I guess I'm insecure. I do need a psychiatrist.'" The problem, Hume wrote, was that his work for Anderson "was not as exciting as it had been" and he found it "hard to crank out" the endless copy the column required: "I got into a rut. The feeling that it was time to move on became irresistible." By 1973, Hume left the column; he eventually became famous in his own right as the leading anchorman for Fox News. In the years that followed, Whitten and other reporters also departed, many disillusioned by the boss they had once so admired.

Throughout it all, the aging columnist resisted naming a permanent successor to replace him. Anderson had worked too long and hard to get to the top to turn it all over now, even though he was increasingly removed from day-to-day reporting and began referring to himself grandiloquently as the "publisher" of his multimedia franchise. Under duress, Anderson agreed to share the "Merry-Go-Round" byline with a rotating cast of employees who were temporarily groomed to inherit his mantle. But for one reason or another, none ever seemed to work out; the old newsman evidently didn't want to contemplate his own mortality. Behind his back, staffers began mocking him.

This derision obscured the positive deeds that Anderson still accomplished—the occasional scoop that others overlooked, the mentoring of young journalists, the backing of a new nationwide organization to train the next generation of muckrakers. More significantly, Anderson also spent millions of dollars in legal fees defending freedom of the press. His most expensive case was against Liberty Lobby, a right-wing hate group that Anderson accurately characterized as racist, neo-Nazi, and anti-Semitic. "They dragged Jack through ten years of litigation," Anderson's lawyer Michael Sullivan recalled with admiration, "but he wouldn't pay those bastards a dime even if it bankrupted him." Yet he received little support in Washington media circles for waging these lonely legal battles. Anderson eventually won his court battle against Liberty Lobby— a significant victory in communications law—but he lost the larger war: no insurance company would ever indemnify him again. "Jack was con-

sidered too hot to handle," Sullivan said, "even though he never lost a libel case and his most dangerous stories were behind him." Without insurance coverage to protect him, Anderson's reporting necessarily grew
more cautious. "I took a lot of chances," the old muckraker sighed, "but
it became riskier and riskier and I had to back off."

As Anderson's column declined, so did its circulation. By the early
1990s, the number of newspapers that published the "Merry-Go-
Round" was barely half that of its peak two decades earlier; those that
remained were mostly smaller newspapers, often in rural areas with
relatively few readers. In a devastating blow, Anderson's longtime flag-
ship paper, *The Washington Post*, canceled the column. "No one seemed
to notice," the paper's executive editor said acidly, and readers were told
only that the newspaper "is reorganizing the features that appear in the
comics pages." Anderson's diminishing audience led to shrinking revenue and staff layoffs. From a high of nearly two dozen reporters, his
staff dwindled to just four. Financing was kept afloat by a home equity
line and personal credit card debt.

In 1991, Anderson laid off sixty-five-year-old Opal Ginn, his secretary of nearly four decades, with just three weeks' notice and no sev-
erance. "I wasn't even given time to apply for Social Security," she
said. Perhaps the parting was inevitable: "I've been wanting to do it for
years," Anderson confided to an intimate. Opal's alcoholism had grown
out of control. She mixed daily Bloody Marys in the kitchen of the
"Merry-Go-Round" office and drank at her desk from a bottle of scotch
stashed in a drawer. At home, she downed so much liquor that she
regularly passed out at night in front of her television set. Once, Opal
returned to the office after a liquid lunch "six sheets to the wind," legman Marc Smolonsky recalled, and then "lay down on Jack's desk,
hiked up her skirt and spread her legs"—while a visiting television
crew recorded her antics. "I grabbed her and hustled her out," Smolonsky recalled, and the footage never aired. But Opal's alcoholic anger
was harder to suppress. She inspired fear among the rest of the staff,
fomenting fights, spreading malicious gossip, playing employees off
against each other.

Opal's outward venom seemed to be the result of her inner, thwarted
love for her boss. "He was her whole life and she had to protect every

bit of that at all costs," a coworker said. "As Jack's influence diminished, Opal just tightened her grip to cling on to whatever she could."
Opal's abrupt dismissal "broke her heart," Whitten recalled, and was
fraught with peril because "she knew *everything* about Jack." For years,
Opal had threatened to write a kiss-and-tell exposé of Anderson and
claimed she had been offered $250,000 to do so but had turned it
down out of loyalty to her boss. Now her allegiance was broken, devotion replaced by rage as her office husband of more than thirty years
was "putting her out to pasture." On her way out the door, Opal stuffed
incriminating paperwork from her desk into several large garbage bags.
She "knew every source he made up, every story he exaggerated, every
place where he crossed the line," a staffer realized. Anderson turned
his ex-secretary into the kind of informant he had cultivated so successfully to ruin the careers of others: a woman scorned.

Opal began writing her kiss-and-tell book. She also contacted an
attorney, who sent the columnist a letter charging that Anderson was
using Opal's "abrupt, unwarranted dismissal" to stop paying her $10,000
annual pension. "Where others have agreed to 'tell all,' she steadfastly
refused," the lawyer noted pointedly. "Now, apparently you expect her to
fade silently away . . . It is not going to be so easy." Opal threatened to sue
Anderson and reached out for help to other former "Merry-Go-Round"
employees. Whitten wrote Anderson about Opal's "dire straits," which
he said left her "near penury." Her health had worsened from years of
drinking and smoking: "She's probably too proud to tell you how infirm
she is and how she is already even pinching on medicine, but she told
me." Another former legman, Jack Mitchell, reminded his ex-boss of "a
lifetime of loyalty to you by Opal," whose "decades of dedicated selfless
professional service" were "more instrumental over a period of many
years for the successful operation of your office and column" than the
work of any other staff member. Anderson replied that while he "share[d]
your concern for Opal," he never agreed to pay a pension to her or any
other employee. Whatever the truth of the matter, one friend recalled,
"after she was fired by Jack, Opal stayed home for weeks and just got
drunk every night until she passed out."

In 1993, unable to afford Washington's high cost of living, Opal
decided to move back to her native Georgia. Her friends gathered to
toast her farewell. Anderson was not among them. Over the next five

years, in a bedroom of her sister's house, Opal wrote her book-length exposé. "She wouldn't let me read it," her sister said. "She didn't show it to anyone. She didn't want anyone to read it." Opal was profoundly ambivalent about her work: on the one hand, she wanted to get even for her humiliating rejection; on the other hand, she was more despondent than angry after her break with the only man she had ever truly loved. "After that," Opal said, "I don't care whether I live or die." On her seventy-third birthday, she decided to destroy her book manuscript, and the diary on which it was based. "Don't do it," her sister begged. But Opal replied, "I can't do it—stab him in the back." She fed the written contents of her life's work into a paper shredder and wept.

Seven months later, Opal died in a nursing home in rural Georgia. "She kept drinking and smoking even after she had emphysema real bad," a friend remembered. "Opal basically committed suicide." When Anderson called to express condolences, he revealed that he had been in touch with Opal by telephone in the weeks before her death—and now wanted to know what happened to her manuscript pages. He was relieved to learn that they had been destroyed. On the day of Opal's funeral, surviving family members looked hopefully to see if Anderson would attend the ceremony. He did not.

Anderson never reconciled with his brother Gordon, who continued to fight with other members of the family but not with Jack, who had cut off all contact and never saw or spoke with him for the rest of his life. Jack did reach an accommodation of sorts with his disapproving father. At a birthday party in a Salt Lake City nursing home, Orlando Anderson, feeble and wheelchair-bound at age ninety-two, was overcome with emotion.

"We're proud of you, Jack," he told his son. "You know that." It was the first time his father had ever said those words.

"I guess you get to be ninety and you repent," Anderson joked. But his father turned serious and began sobbing.

"You're the most generous son a father could have," Orlando cried.

It was the only time Jack ever saw his dad weep. And, as it turned out, it was the last time he would ever see him alive again. Jack hugged Orlando and gently patted him on the back.

"It's all right," he told his father soothingly, eyes moist with his own tears. "It's all right."

In the summer of 2004, the last of America's old-fashioned muckrakers finally decided to call it quits and announced the demise of what was the longest-running syndicated column in the nation. Jack Anderson's retirement was not so much the end of an era—after all, that had long since passed—as it was a reminder of a kind of journalism that had already faded into history. "Jack understood the folks out there," Anderson legman–turned–media critic Tom Rosenstiel pointed out. "That's what print journalism lost over the years as it focused on demographics and advertising while Jack focused on his readers." But now, the column that had once championed the proverbial Kansas City milkman had become as archaic as the milkman himself, as obsolete as door-to-door dairy delivery in an Internet age. Even the "Merry-Go-Round" name was a throwback to a time when children rode carousels with innocent abandon, before computer chips and video games supplanted such old-fashioned pastimes. And yet the imagery of Washington's merry-go-round, with its predictable circularity of scandal and exposure, remained as timeless as ever.

Anderson's health would not have allowed him to keep the column going even if he had wanted to. Since 1986, he had been suffering from Parkinson's disease. His symptoms were mild at first but would eventually include tremors, rigid muscles, drooling, and occasional hallucinations. It was a painfully debilitating condition made more wrenching because Anderson's mind remained sharp even while his body left him bedridden. At the same time, he developed prostate cancer, which ultimately spread throughout his body. Anderson's family gave him expensive and loving care throughout, retrofitting a bedroom to accommodate his wheelchair, hanging framed magazine profiles about his journalistic crusades to remind him of his glory years. His illness managed to achieve what none of his political adversaries ever could: it humbled him. The modest and unassuming nature that had first endeared Jack to friends when he arrived in Washington more than a half century earlier returned at last, accompanied by a sweetness of disposition rarely associated with his thundering public persona. As his prognosis worsened, he found comfort in impish humor and in rereading the Book of Mormon. By the end, he had to be outfitted with an oxygen mask and, unable to swallow, received food and morphine intravenously.

Anderson died in December 2005, in his bed at home in suburban Washington, at the age of eighty-three. His funeral in the chapel of the local Mormon temple was filled with three hundred people—congregants, former staff, friends, and a family brood that included several dozen grandchildren. A frail Irv Davidson, the eighty-four-year-old Mafia lobbyist and longtime Anderson financial angel, nodded off as a choir sang a Christian hymn on virtue:

> *Do what is right*
> *Let the consequences follow*
> *Battle for freedom in spirit and might*
> *And with stout hearts look ye forth till tomorrow*
> *God will protect you*
> *Then do what is right.*

Not everyone believed the columnist had lived his life by that lofty spirit. "Jack Anderson had feet of clay," his onetime reporter Sally Denton wrote in an obituary essay. "He entered into business partnerships with nefarious characters, squandered an empire that by all rights belonged to the public trust, protected sources who were manipulating him, allowed his ego to dictate his judgment, and abandoned those who were most devoted to him." Les Whitten believed that Anderson "betrayed the ideal" when he "stopped being a reporter and started being a celebrity. He was really corrupted by his ego." And yet, as Whitten understood, for decades Anderson "exposed things that nobody else had the guts to expose." In an era when other journalists automatically deferred to those in power, Anderson and his mentor Drew Pearson were the only mainstream newsmen who vigorously challenged political leaders, who demanded an equal place at the table on behalf of the public. They were imperfect tribunes, sometimes reckless ones. But almost single-handedly, they kept muckraking alive when it was needed most, until a new generation could extend and improve on it. Unlike the professional class of investigative reporters who followed—well educated and paid, backed by powerful media companies—Anderson did it on his own. "Jack had no network to back him up," Brit Hume observed, "no institutional body to take care of him and fight for him." His victories, like his defeats, rested squarely on his own shoulders.

Mistakes were inherent in such reportorial combat. "Look," a rival columnist said, "when you are in the front lines the way he is, you sometimes shoot your own men." Anderson's strengths, like his flaws, were glaring; both were rooted in the stony soil of his Utah upbringing and stemmed from his rigid resolve to influence events as well as chronicle them, an unyielding insistence that the First Amendment was more than just a stenographer's license. "Power is Washington's main marketable product," the reporter knew, "seldom permanent, shifting with the pressures of the times and the advantages of the moment." Above all, his career was about power—political, governmental, journalistic— about how to use it, how to abuse it, and how to expose it. He understood all too well the inherent and inevitable cost of power's dirty compromises.

That wasn't how Anderson liked to think of himself, of course. He held himself up as a crusader on a mission, a righteous preacher against wickedness and venality. "His readers were his flock," one of his legmen wrote, "his reporters his evangelists and disciples" as he "walked among the heathen with the Constitution as [his] Bible," exposing sinners, and condemning them "to hell or purgatory . . . His ethics were to use his column-pulpit to make the world more ethical. Even if it meant turning into a thief to expose a thief."

He was buried in a family plot in Virginia. His tombstone described him with three words: "Husband—Father—Muckraker."

EPILOGUE

The ghosts of Richard Nixon and Jack Anderson continue to haunt Washington long after their departure from the nation's capital. The poisoning of politics and the press that marked their careers has tainted governance and public discourse ever since.

Of course, the rise of Washington's modern scandal culture is the product of larger forces and deeper institutional changes beyond these two men. The spread of cable, satellite, and the Internet has transformed the media into an instantaneous cacophony of infotainment delivered by profit-chasing conglomerates whose commodification of the news all too often manufactures political scandal where none exists, while ignoring substantive policy problems of far deeper significance. At the same time, government secrecy, special-interest money, political polarization, and corrosive cynicism have become ever-present features of public life, reinforcing Washington's media-driven scandal mania.

In the immediate aftermath of Watergate, journalists and public officials vowed to do better. Congress passed legislation to strengthen ethics codes, open up official records, and reform campaign financing. But politicians quickly found ways to circumvent these changes. Similarly, Watergate initially led to a flourishing of investigative reporting at both local and national levels, as well as nonprofit organizations to support it. But in Washington, the zeal for muckraking soon began to fade. "In learning from Watergate," one historian observed, journalists "too often emulated not the trailblazers whose skepticism had produced fruitful inquiries but the latecomers who jumped on Watergate only as it was becoming a media spectacle." Such "cynicism fed easy opinion-mongering and bandwagon journalism [that] was bound to be superficial and fickle—and could easily revert to its mirror image, an equally shallow pose of credulous appreciation."

The lessons of Watergate had a different meaning for two young Nixon aides, Dick Cheney and Donald Rumsfeld. They feared the presidency had been gravely weakened by Nixon's ouster—and the news media dangerously empowered—and would spend the rest of their years in public life trying to change that dynamic. The problem, they believed, was not President Nixon's conduct but the failure of his aides to protect their boss from harm. Cheney and Rumsfeld were determined it would not happen to them again. Three decades later, they would succeed during the presidency of George W. Bush in what Cheney called "a restoration" of the pre-Watergate "power and authority of the president."

This transformation took a generation to achieve. Nixon's loyalists started their long march under President Gerald Ford, who appointed Rumsfeld—"a ruthless little bastard," Nixon had said admiringly—to be the new White House chief of staff. Rumsfeld in turn tapped Cheney as his deputy. The two men engineered a takeover that stripped power from moderate Republicans in favor of hard-line conservatives. Their reign was briefly cut short by Jimmy Carter's presidency, but the true post-Nixon "restoration" that Cheney sought began four years later with Ronald Reagan's rise to the White House.

With his handsome looks, melodious voice, and aw-shucks demeanor, President Reagan was a media manipulator's dream. Decades of coaching in Hollywood had trained the "Great Communicator" for the role of a lifetime. His success, one Reagan aide explained, was simple: "He's an actor. He's used to being directed and produced. He stands where he is supposed to and delivers his lines." Reagan was "the ultimate presidential commodity," his campaign press secretary realized, "the right product" to market to the American public. And the White House admen were some of the best in the business. Reagan's PR team built on Nixon's, using the same line-of-the-day message, advertising gimmicks, and mass-marketing techniques but expanding them with detailed polling and focus groups as well. They also played to the media's institutional weaknesses—especially television's need for compelling visuals—by positioning Reagan with picturesque back-drops to reinforce whatever image they were trying to promote. "The idea was to divert people's attention away from substantive issues," one scholar wrote, "by creating a world of myths and symbols that made people feel good about themselves and their country." Press Secretary Larry Speakes, a veteran of the Nixon White House, was open about the administration's strategy. "You don't tell us how to stage the news," a sign on his desk declared, "and we don't tell you how to cover it."

Reagan's men played hardball, ruthlessly staying on message by tightly restricting presidential access, punishing dissident journalists, increasing government secrecy, and administering lie detector tests to suspected leakers. Except, of course, when the leaks were sanctioned from on high, in which case news organizations lapped up what they were fed. Jimmy Carter's staff could only shake their heads in wonder at it all. The lesson, said Carter's press secretary, Jody Powell, was that "the press's bark is much worse than its bite. They'll huff and puff around, but in the end you can severely cut into the flow of information and manage it with a much firmer hand than we were able or willing to do." The Nixon veterans who peopled Reagan's media apparatus learned to camouflage their contempt for the press. Reagan's men were "slicker and smarter and therefore more dangerous and more effective" than Nixon's, said CBS News anchorman Dan Rather, who covered both administrations.

Reagan's transformation of the relationship between the president and the press went beyond merely the stagecraft of the moment. More lastingly, his administration began deregulating broadcasting, stimu-lating media mergers and expanding corporate profits. This windfall to communications conglomerates advanced the rise of right-wing talk radio, which further promoted the conservative agenda. Rush Lim-baugh was the most famous of the broadcasters to saturate the air-waves in the wake of Reagan's radio revolution. Another was Gordon Liddy, the Watergate burglar who conspired to assassinate Jack Ander-son but nonetheless became a right-wing folk hero, easily recognizable by his distinctive shaved head and bushy mustache. As a bestselling author, actor, and lecture-circuit staple, Liddy used his syndicated radio show to attack "fulminating feminists, proselytizing poofters, the environmentally ill, these multilateralist UN one-world government worshippers and other politically correct castrati."

In 1988, George H. W. Bush was elected president after a nasty campaign run with the assistance of Nixon's media consultant Roger Ailes. Afterward, Bush's Republican National Committee suggested that leading Democratic opponents in Congress were homosexuals. If Defense Secretary Dick Cheney—whose daughter and press spokesman were gay—objected to this homophobic vitriol, he never expressed it publicly. Instead, Cheney seemed focused on what he had learned from Watergate: "You don't let the press set the agenda" because "if you let them do that, they're going to trash your presidency."

Four years later, Democrats finally learned from their mistakes and produced their party's first successful two-term president in half a century. Bill Clinton's charisma was matched by such hard-boiled tactics as "opposition research" into rivals' vulnerabilities and a "rapid response" team run out of a "War Room" to shoot down attacks from the other side, but he would need all that help and more, thanks to an outsized libido and persistent corner-cutting that led to a series of self-inflicted mini-scandals. "Travelgate," "Filegate," and "Whitewatergate" were minor controversies inflated to Watergate-like proportions by the appellation of the now-overused suffix. These pseudo-scandals were relentlessly hyped by the right-wing radio industry that Reagan had unleashed a few years earlier and by the new conservative Fox News Channel run by Roger Ailes, the former Nixon spinmeister. At the same time, Richard Mellon Scaife, a billionaire who once funneled money to Nixon's presidential campaign, spent nearly $2 million to dig up dirt on the Clintons. Also secretly investigating Clinton's sex life were conservative activists, including Lucianne Goldberg, the former Nixon spy turned literary agent provocateur. Eventually, Clinton's enemies—with the help of Fox News commentator Tony Snow, the future White House press secretary—discovered the President's affair with White House intern Monica Lewinsky and leaked the news to two reliable conservative allies: Independent Counsel Kenneth Starr and Internet gossip Matt Drudge.

The result was a kind of faux-Watergate—complete with aggressive prosecutors, congressional hearings, and a media orgy—but this time it was a cover-up without an underlying crime. Clinton's attempt to hide his adultery simply couldn't compare to the massive and systemic abuses of governmental power exercised by Nixon. Yet the structural apparatus that led to Clinton's impeachment owed its origins to Watergate. "Richard Nixon's downfall served as the touchstone for the scandal machine that followed," Clinton's attorney Lanny Davis recognized. "The cycle of 'gotcha' politics—with each side justifying their shock-and-awe attacks based on the other side's last 'gotcha'—became endless and systemic." A poisonous press fueled Washington's modern scandal culture, stoking sensationalism and partisanship to attract attention and profits. "Food fights masquerading as policy discussions on cable news networks, ravers and haters on talk radio, and the criminalization of political differences," Davis observed, "generated a level of vicious and personally destructive power unlike anything seen in America before."

The flip side to this fevered frenzy was journalism's abdication of its watchdog role on issues of substance, from the savings-and-loan scandals of the 1980s to accounting, banking, and investment fraud in the decades that followed. During the presidency of George W. Bush, news outlets enthusiastically beat their war drums to support the invasion of Iraq, eagerly regurgitating administration propaganda about the menace posed by Saddam Hussein. But such manipulation did not change reality; as in Vietnam, Iraq turned into a quagmire in which the administration was reduced to bromides about staying the course while denouncing opponents as appeasers. The Nixonian echoes were impossible to escape: Henry Kissinger advised President Bush and Vice President Cheney, and Vietnamization morphed into Iraqization.

Bush's policies may have been no wiser than Nixon's but his PR efforts were more ambitious. The administration spent an estimated $1.6 billion on propaganda, outsourcing much of the work to independent firms to conceal the government's role. To tout the success of the U.S. occupation, the Pentagon bribed Iraqi newspapers, undermining the very democratic freedoms America was supposedly fighting to promote. Defense Secretary Rumsfeld, the Nixon veteran known for operating on the "Haldeman model" of management, deployed a phalanx of propagandists—misleadingly billed as independent "military analysts"—to boost the war on network television; these supposedly unbiased experts were covertly paid and coached by the Pentagon. At the same time, the Bush administration secretly funneled hundreds of thousands of taxpayer dollars to right-wing commentators to tout the domestic agenda of the White House. One conservative columnist on the government payroll interviewed Vice President Cheney on television about supposed liberal media bias, never revealing his own receipt of payola. In addition, at least twenty federal agencies produced hundreds of fake TV news reports that deliberately obscured the fact that this pro-Bush material was manufactured by the administration. Spinmeisters even posed as reporters to lob softball questions at government news conferences.

Bush's inner circle could also play rough when necessary. After *The New York Times* exposed the administration's warrantless spying on Americans—another throwback to the Nixon era—the President personally denounced the revelation as "a shameful act" that was "helping the enemy." Like Nixon, Bush considered seeking an injunction prohibiting the *Times* from publishing its story. Yet the White House was perfectly willing to leak classified information to buttress its policies, and unhesitatingly revealed the identity of an undercover CIA agent to retaliate against a leading government whistleblower. In an echo of the Nixon White House's "enemies list," a Bush appointee also secretly ordered a study of alleged bias in the media, categorizing coverage by whether it was pro- or anti-Bush. Public broadcasting's Bill Moyers was singled out for opprobrium, complete with threats to halt federal funding. The administration "turned its hit men loose on us," Moyers said. "I always knew Nixon would be back."

So did Karl Rove, Bush's political mastermind who first got his start as a young Nixon operative and briefly came to the attention of Watergate prosecutors investigating campaign dirty tricks. Rove's reputation for scurrilous tactics—particularly for impugning his opponents' sexual orientation—would follow him throughout his career, although his direct culpability was never proved. But his pandering to homophobia by exploiting the issue of gay marriage was just one of many "wedge issues" used to divide the public. In the White House, said an old Nixon hand, Rove operated with the ruthless authority of "Haldeman and Ehrlichman all in one."

President Bush also turned to another Nixon veteran, Charles Colson. The Watergate felon emerged from prison as a born-again Christian and bonded with the President over their evangelical beliefs. Colson was invited to the White House and became a "confidant" of Bush and Rove, Colson's biographer wrote, exerting "considerable influence" on the "Christian direction" of the President's policies. Colson also received $2 million from the administration to support his "faith-based initiatives." In 2004, Nixon's old hatchet man campaigned against Bush's Democratic opponent at anti–gay marriage rallies, where he publicly suggested that homosexuals are "lower than the animal species." Colson was Rove's "spiritual ancestor," said Howard Hunt, the Watergate burglar who had been Colson's partner in crime, and his resurrection by the Bush White House seemed fitting. The Watergate criminal who allegedly ordered the assassination of Jack Anderson was respectfully feted in television interviews, where deferential hosts identified him only as a "former White House counsel" and made no mention of the felonies that had made him infamous.

In all, the post-Watergate turnaround was breathtaking. Three decades after Nixon's resignation, his acolytes had completed a stunning reversal, expanding executive power while taming the news media. After the "erosion" that followed Watergate, Vice President Cheney said proudly, "we've been able to restore the legitimate authority of the presidency." Thanks to sophisticated propaganda, hardball intimidation, sensationalist distractions, and deregulatory bribery, Nixon's men had poisoned the press in a way their mentor never dreamed possible. Richard Nixon would have been proud.

Washington's merry-go-round had once again come full circle. But the author of the column that bore that name was too ravaged by disease to fully appreciate how Nixon's men had returned to power. It was just as well. Jack Anderson would not have wanted to believe his life's work was in vain.

Still, the old reporter never stopped wondering about the White House plot to assassinate him. Charles Colson had always denied that he or President Nixon was culpable, but Anderson didn't believe it. In the columnist's final years, while hospitalized for Parkinson's disease, he hatched one last sting to try to link Nixon to the plot. The newsman passed word to Colson that he was dying and asked him to call out of Christian compassion. Colson did. "I told him I'd been at the hospital and was having a hard time," Anderson said, and that "no recovery was possible." The two men exchanged pleasantries and flattery, and talked about old times. Anderson had once offered to loan Colson money before he went to prison and Colson remembered the gesture with gratitude. Nixon's evil genius had even autographed one of his books for his old foe: "Jack," the inscription said, "Bless you—you are a good man in every sense." Finally, with their chat flowing warmly, as casually as he could, Anderson brought up the White House murder plot. "There's one thing I'd like to know," the old newsman said. "After all these years, what really happened?" The conversation's tone changed completely, Anderson recalled, and Nixon's aide once again denied complicity "almost word-for-word" in the same language as he had in years past. Anderson believed the answer was "contrived" because Colson was "too cavalier" about such a serious subject, that the Watergate felon was "cordially lying" one last time to protect Nixon.

Anderson took it all in stride. In the last months of his life, as he withered away in his sickbed, he jokingly suggested that a visitor try to "blame this"—his cancer and Parkinson's disease—"on Nixon."

Six weeks after Anderson died, the FBI contacted his seventy-eight-year-old widow and demanded to inspect all of the personal papers the newsman had left behind. Authorities asserted that Anderson's archives—some two hundred boxes in all—might contain classified documents that could jeopardize national security. A young female FBI agent deftly befriended Olivia Anderson the way her late husband had with so many reluctant informants. In this case, the federal investigator bonded with the trusting housewife over their shared roots in West Virginia and convinced Olivia that they might be distant cousins; soon,

Anderson's widow was persuaded to sign a form granting the FBI access to her husband's records. Olivia's children were outraged when they discovered what had happened and insisted that the FBI had duped their grieving mother. The family banded together: they refused to cooperate with the government and went public about the incident.

The news generated front-page headlines around the world. *USA Today* criticized the administration's "dubious-sounding excuses to paw through" Anderson's archives. *The Salt Lake Tribune* pointed out that the FBI "waited until Jack Anderson was dead before going after what the muckraking columnist would never have given the agency in life" in "the sort of government excess that Jack Anderson spent his life exposing." *The Kansas City Star* thought the "attempted raid on Anderson's files looks like a poorly veiled effort to remove material that could be embarrassing to federal agencies and perhaps enable them to punish people who once shared information with Anderson." *Time* observed puckishly that "Anderson has now performed a feat of Mau-Mauing perhaps unique among all muckrakers: he is irritating the government from the grave."

In a post–September 11 world, the misplaced priorities of the government seemed glaring. "Is the public really best served in the age of high-tech terrorism by having F.B.I. agents rifling through a dead reporter's files?" *The New York Times* wondered. The ghoulish overtones were equally inescapable. The *Austin American-Statesman* complained that the administration was "rifling Anderson's corpse" and "picking his bones," while the *Chicago Tribune* scolded that "the FBI won't let his work rest in peace." Columnist Molly Ivins joked that "Anderson is still under investigation, although seriously dead." Perhaps the FBI was "worried he might have photos of J. Edgar Hoover in a dress after all these years," she added.

The Senate Judiciary Committee held hearings on the affair. "Is there any truth to the fact that some of these papers were looked at because it goes into the personal life of J. Edgar Hoover?" Senator Patrick Leahy wanted to know. Senator Arlen Specter wondered why the government hadn't sought Anderson's files during his lifetime if they were so important. Senator Charles Grassley accused the FBI of "tricking" Olivia Anderson by getting her away from her skeptical children and pressuring her into "signing a consent form that she didn't understand." In the end, the withering criticism forced the administration to back off. Meanwhile, the Senate panel that had so often clashed with Anderson while he was alive now treated his memory with a reverence the newsman would scarcely have recognized. Chairman Specter enthusiastically asked the "wonderful" Anderson family to stand and be publicly recognized: "Congratulations to you, Mrs. Anderson, and all the Andersons."

Gordon Liddy was disgusted. The loyal Nixon apparatchik still believed the old canard that Anderson had betrayed his country by publishing state secrets. Now the late columnist was being lionized by Republicans as well as Democrats. Liddy's e-mailed reaction was ungrammatical but unmistakable:

> too bad the plumbers didn't get to that anti american traitor jackoff anderson, good riddence

Anderson would have relished all of it. Media outlets resurrected film footage of the newsman in his prime: pecking away on his manual typewriter, taunting the Nixon administration by waving classified documents in the air, posing for photos with his would-be White House assassins. *The New York Times* published lengthy excerpts from Anderson's memoir while other publications offered primers on his career for those too young to remember it. "Back in the day, Jack Anderson was a one-man truth squad who wrote a ripsaw column," the *San Francisco Chronicle* explained. "In today's blogosphere and news channel cycles, there's no equivalent—and maybe even less memory of Anderson's stature." The *Deseret Morning News* noted the historical irony: "Richard Nixon and Jack Anderson may both be dead, but their fight continues."

The old muckraker's antagonists managed to achieve what Anderson tried in vain to accomplish during the last quarter century of his life: get him back on the front page as a journalistic hero standing up to the government. In death as in life, Jack Anderson—just like his old adversary Richard Nixon—would forever be defined by his enemies.

NOTES

A NOTE ON SOURCES

Richard Nixon and Jack Anderson left behind an extensive if not unprecedented paper trail, one that makes them ideal case studies of the relationship between politics and the press in Washington. Nixon's presidency was the best-documented in American history, primarily because his White House surreptitiously recorded nearly four thousand hours of conversations, using automatic voice-activated technology that captured embarrassingly frank discussions in real time. In addition, Nixon's advisor Henry Kissinger secretly preserved twenty thousand transcript pages of his own contemporaneous phone conversations; multiple government investigations of Watergate led to voluminous subpoenaed documents and testimony; and officials implicated in the scandal published an unusual number of tell-all memoirs to help pay their legal bills. At the same time, Anderson's journalistic output during his fifty-year career in Washington produced literally millions of words in twenty books, more than ten thousand syndicated columns, and thousands more magazine and newsletter articles, radio and television broadcasts, speeches, and interviews, which are preserved along with his correspondence, internal memos, and reporter's notes in some two hundred storage boxes at George Washington University.

For my research, I consulted hundreds of books and articles and thousands of primary source records housed in dozens of archival collections around the country. I filed Freedom of Information Act requests with fifty different agencies of the federal government, followed by numerous appeals to gain access to withheld documents—sometimes with the help of legal counsel—with varying degrees of success. In addition, I conducted more than two hundred oral history interviews and tracked down dozens of hours of taped interviews conducted by others, which I had transcribed. Specifics about all of this are detailed below. Unfortunately, several key surviving figures from the Nixon administration, including Charles Colson and G. Gordon Liddy, declined my repeated requests to be interviewed.

Two caveats: First, this book does not purport to be a biography of Richard Nixon or a full chronicle of his administration's successes and failures; other works have amply covered this ground. Nor is this a comprehensive biography of Jack Anderson's personal and professional life. Rather, this is an account of the interaction between these two men that illustrates larger issues about government and the media—and the rise of investigative scandal coverage—during their time. Second, although the book's narrative is presented largely in chronological order, I have on occasion deviated from a strict time line to avoid confusing the reader. In particular, a minute-by-minute rendering of Nixon's meandering White House conversations proves repetitive and tedious, so I have in places combined and condensed material to avoid bogging down the reader even while painstakingly attributing distinct quotations and other source information in the endnotes.

The Nixon tapes posed the greatest single challenge—and opportunity—of my research. They proved to be the most honest record of the President's battles with Anderson and the press, but they are often muffled or scratchy, making them difficult to hear clearly. With the help of several student research assistants I transcribed dozens of previously unpublicized White House tapes and hired an audio engineer to try to make the words more comprehensible. I was also careful to have at least two sets of ears listen to each recording quoted in this book to try to ensure accuracy as much as is humanly possible. Audio excerpts from these new, enhanced tapes have been streamed online and are available on the book's website.

Surprisingly, much of this primary source material—which offers a fascinating window on our political history—is still unknown to the public. The time-consuming nature of transcription has deterred historians and journalists from going through all the Nixon tapes released so far; and the Nixon estate and various federal agencies continue to resist full declassification, citing national security and personal privacy even though virtually all individuals involved died long ago. For example, the FBI heavily redacted eight thousand pages of files it released on Jack Anderson and his boss Drew Pearson, who died in 1969; and the CIA's response to my Freedom of Information Act request on Anderson consisted mostly of news articles or other material already available to the public—with internal memos often so heavily censored as to be worthless. In addition, both agencies, and other parts of the federal bureaucracy, withheld documents that Anderson himself publicly disseminated more than three decades earlier, raising questions about what else the government is still holding back. Still, I will continue to file legal appeals for additional material.

Meanwhile, I encourage interested readers to view additional photos, read supplementary material, and listen to selected excerpts of the Nixon White House tapes at www .poisoningthepress.com.

LIST OF ABBREVIATIONS

AP	Associated Press
CCP	Charles Colson papers, Billy Graham Center, Wheaton College, Wheaton, IL
Chp.	Chapter
CIAFOIA	Central Intelligence Agency subject files on Jack Anderson obtained by the author under the Freedom of Information Act
DOJFOIA	Department of Justice civil division files from *Anderson v. Nixon* lawsuit obtained by the author under the Freedom of Information Act
DP	Drew Pearson
DPP	Drew Pearson papers, LBJ Library, University of Texas, Austin, TX
DVAP	Dale Van Atta private paper collection, Ashburn, VA
EZP	Adm. Elmo R. Zumwalt papers, Texas Tech University, Lubbock, TX
FBIFOIA	Federal Bureau of Investigation subject files obtained by the author under the Freedom of Information Act

HBP	Sen. Howard Baker papers, Hoskins Library, University of Tennessee, Knoxville, TN
Intv.	Interview
JA	Jack Anderson
JAP	Jack Anderson papers, Gelman Library, George Washington University, Washington, D.C.
JA v. RN	civil suit #76-1794, *Jack Anderson v. Richard Nixon*, Washington, D.C.
JEP	John Ehrlichman papers, Hoover Institution, Stanford University, Palo Alto, CA
JFKAA	John F. Kennedy assassination archives, National Archives, College Park, MD
LBJL	Lyndon B. Johnson Library, Austin, TX
LCP	Len Colodny private paper collection, Tampa, FL
LWP	Les Whitten papers, Lehigh University, Bethlehem, PA
MCP	Sen. Marlow W. Cook papers, Ekstrom Library, University of Louisville, Louisville, KY
MGR	Washington "Merry-Go-Round" column; originals housed with Jack Anderson papers, Gelman Library, George Washington University, Washington, D.C.
MLKP	Martin Luther King papers, Martin Luther King Library, Atlanta, GA
ND	Not dated or date unknown
NARA	Richard Nixon presidential papers, National Archives, College Park, MD
NSA	National Security Archive, Gelman Library, George Washington University, Washington, D.C.
NISI	News Items of Special Interest, the Pentagon's daily internal summary of media coverage of the Defense Department
NYRB	*The New York Review of Books*
NYT	*The New York Times*
PCP	Public Citizen Papers, Washington, D.C. (ITT hearings)
PPP	Pulitzer Prize Papers, Columbia University, New York, NY
RMP	Robert C. Mardian papers, Hoover Institution, Stanford University, Palo Alto, CA
RNL	Richard Nixon Library and Museum, Yorba Linda, CA
RNVPP	Richard Nixon vice presidential papers, National Archives, Laguna Nigel, CA
SASC	Senate Armed Services Committee files, Center for Legislative Affairs, National Archives, Washington, D.C. (1974 Joint Chiefs of Staff–National Security Council document transmittal hearings)
SFRC	Senate Foreign Relations Committee files, Center for Legislative Affairs, National Archives, Washington, D.C. (1963 hearings on foreign lobbying)
SWC	Senate Watergate Committee files, Center for Legislative Affairs, National Archives, Washington, D.C.
Telecon	Transcripts of telephone conversations secretly made by Henry Kissinger's stenographer assistants
UPI	United Press International
WHT	Richard Nixon White House tapes, National Archives, College Park, MD
WP	*The Washington Post*
WS	*The Washington Star*
WSJ	*The Wall Street Journal*

WSPF   Watergate Special Prosecution Force files, National Archives, College
            Park, MD

PROLOGUE

3   Hay-Adams: www.hayadams.com; chilly afternoon: "Weather," *WP* (March 25,
     1972), E5; "thorn in [his] side": testimony, E. Howard Hunt (Jan. 10, 1976), 10,
     JFKAA; "got to do something": WHT #643-13 (Jan. 3, 1972).
4   assassination plot: Church Report, 133–37; Bob Woodward, "Hunt Told Associates
     of Orders to Kill Jack Anderson," *WP* (Sept. 21, 1975), A1ff.; Liddy, 207–10.
5   Paul Revere: Douglas Martin, "Jack Anderson, Investigative Journalist Who An-
     gered the Powerful," *NYT* (Dec. 18, 2005), 38; seventy million: Sheehan, 10; sui-
     cide: Tricia Drevets, "A Man Who Digs Up What's Covered Up," *Editor and Publisher*
     (July 18, 1987), 32, and "Abscam Figure Sues Writer," *NYT* (Feb. 4, 1982), B19.
7   Nixon kept his distance: Greenberg, 150; "ugly thoughts": Dean, *Blind*, 88; "arch
     nemesis": Colson, *Born Again*, 242.
7   "fight, bleed": Wicker, 685.
8   "Few reach": JA and Clifford, 3.
8–9 "much inflamed": Tebbel and Watts, 13; "concubine": Newton, 7; "putrid state":
     Spear, 35.
9   press corruption: Ritchie, *Press*, chps. 3–5.

1: THE QUAKER AND THE MORMON

13–14 "wasn't a town": Ambrose, *Education*, 19; Quaker background: Chuck Fager, "The
       Quaker President," *Washington City Paper* (June 10, 1994), 21–27.
14   "ground into me": Morris, 128; eschewed the more familiar "Dick": Morris, 9; "never
       had a meal without grace": Nixon, *RN*, 95; "commitment to Christ": Morris, 87.
14   talk to men on the street: Ambrose, *Education*, 19; "unquestioned tribal closeness,"
       "plain, exacting life": Morris, 25, 47; "honest lawyer": Morris, 83; "be of some good":
       Morris, 85; "wonderful missionary": Morris, 108.
15   bounced from job to job: Gellman, 9; "playing was daydreaming": Morris, 34;
       "scrappy, belligerent": R. Dallek, 5; Frank's temper: Morris, 34, 50, 64–65; "beat-
       ing": Brodie, 40.
15   "cultured, refined": Morris, 54; "mother's favorite": Morris, 139; "saint": Lukas, 568.
15   "hard," "cranky and puritanical": Brodie, 54; "switch in her hand": Morris, 62.
15   "In her whole life": Summers, *Arrogance*, 9, 13.
16   "sank into a deep impenetrable silence": Morris, 147; "taking charity": Ambrose,
       Education, 51; "three sons in one": Ambrose, *Education*, 57.
16   "very strict parents": Morris, 50; "Just don't argue": Morris, 78.
16   "offended some of his Quaker teachers": Morris, 102; polio student: Morris, 167.
17   "very serious child": Morris, 42; "kept mostly to himself": Morris, 60; "Gloomy
       Gus," grind: Ambrose, *Education*, 36, 46, 75; "didn't smell good": Ambrose, *Educa-
       tion*, 27; "oddball": Morris, 176; "stuffy!": Ambrose, *Education*, 66; starched shirt:
       Morris, 59.
17   "very tense": Morris, 140; "nasty temper," "slightly paranoid": Volkan et al., 45;
       "something mean": R. Dallek, 7.

17   "never could get up the nerve": Morris, 93; "didn't know how to be personable": Ambrose, *Education*, 50; "be harsh and I'd cry": Ambrose, *Education*, 67.

17–18 "any pay": Ambrose, *Education*, 37–38; mock radio shows: Morris, 76; "far-off places": Ambrose, *Education*, 26.

18   Harvard or Yale: Morris, 110; speakeasy: Gellman, 15; "sixteen weeks of misery," "twelve long hard hours": Morris, 66.

18   "clapboard shack": Gellman, 16; "What starts the process": Ambrose, *Education*, 39.

18–19 "fifteen colors of the rainbow": Gellman, 18; "love at first sight," "Don't laugh!": Volkan et al., 46–47.

19   Nixon in the navy: Ambrose, *Education*, chp. 7.

19   1946 campaign: Ambrose, *Education*, chp. 8.

20   Mormon beliefs/polygamy: Ostling and Ostling, xix, 72; Nils Anderson: Gibbons, 4–5; JA intv. Gibson; Loveless intv.

20   Orlando Anderson: Gibbons, 7–8; Chambless, "Muckraker," 3–4; JA, W. Anderson intv., Chambless; "patient and persevering": JA and Gibson, 24.

20   religiosity: Gibbons, 11–12; tithing, homeless man: JA intv.

21   bike trip: JA and Gibson, 26; Tudor house, "martyr complex": Harrington, 21, 23; "craps in the outhouse," JA intv.; "better for my health": JA, essay, "Good Night" (Nov. 12, 1940), JAP.

21   "smoldering volcano," Alaska, "spinning the whole day": JA intv.; "opened his fingers": Knudsen intv.

21   "rock-hard Utah soil": JA and Gibson, 23.

22   "Jack psychologically escaped": Harrington, 40.

22   cub reporter: Harrington, 23; "Jack rode his bicycle": Omer intv.

22   "Informant 42": JA FBIFOIA (Dec. 18, 1940); "big black madam": Bailey intv.

22   "cute girls": Bagley intv.; "uppity-up": Harrington, 23; "too many honors": JA intv.

23   Warren believed: W. Anderson intv.; "All these high ambitions," "trying to restrain": Harrington, 40.

23   "waste of time": JA intv. Gibson; going undercover, "towering rage": JA and Gibson, 26–30; "steam, fire, brimstone!": Harrington, 40.

23   "wanted me out": JA intv. Gibson; taxicab: JA and Gibson, 30; throng of girls: W. Anderson intv.

24   missionary experience, "grab an audience": Gibbons, 16, 34, 38; speaking style: Chambless, "Secular Evangelist," v, 27; wooden soapbox: K. Anderson intv.; "moss-covered woods": letter, JA to Cousin Axel (Dec. 14, 1943), JAP; "pluck, faith": Dowling, 96.

24   spartan: Gibbons, 38; "Suddenly I am asked": JA intv.

25   "hauled me up," "hard-headed": JA intv.

25   "missionary experience": JA and Boyd, 42.

25   five feet, ten inches: JA seaman's ID certificate (Sept. 13, 1944), JAP; Senator Thomas: JA and Gibson, 33; "didn't relish," "boondoggle": JA intv.

25   safeguard lifeboats: letter, JA to parents (Oct. 1, 1944), JAP.

26   "serve my country": letter, JA to parents (May 29, 1945), JAP; "possibility of his indictment": letter, George M. McMillan to O. N. Anderson (Aug. 6, 1945), JAP.

26   "My father worked": Harrington, 40.

26–27 "only white man": JA, autobiographical essay, F174, 1 of 2, DPP; "greased brown paper": JA and Gibson, 45; "Soviet activity," "Communist influence": letter, JA to parents (Aug. 24, 1947), JAP.

27 "It is hardly": letter, JA to parents (Sept. 25, 1945), JAP; "chiefly to avoid trouble": letter, JA to parents (Nov. 9, 1945), JAP.

27 "Working for *Stars*": letter, JA to Frowso (March 25, 1946), JAP; "VD ward": letter, JA to parents (June 1, 1946), JAP; "chatted breezily": letter, JA to parents (May 17, 1946), JAP; "minor celebrity": letter, JA to parents (July 9, 1946), JAP.

27–28 "hates newsmen," "reminded him firmly": letter, JA to parents (Oct. 14, 1945), JAP; "wired a terse message": letter, JA to parents (March 16, 1946), JAP; "steadfastly refused": letter, JA to Frowso (March 25, 1946), JAP.

28 military discharge: JA and Gibson, 52.

28 "calling": JA intv.; Mormon influence: Chambless, "Muckraker," 7–11.

28 "On numerous occasions": JA and Gibson, 18.

29 "Over the years": Harrington, 22–23.

29 *Lives of great men*: Morris, 77.

2: WASHINGTON WHIRL

33 "white linen suits," "spats," trolley cars, pressrooms: Brinkley, 23, 186, 107, 232, 281.

33 1946 election: Morris, 341–42; Ambrose, *Education*, 141.

34 "news center of the world," "narrow hospital trundle bed": letters, JA to parents (March 27, 1947, and April 11, 1947), JAP.

34 "fusty, old-fogey": letter, JA to parents (Oct. 12, 1947), JAP.

34–35 "million other," "simple expendient": letter, JA to father (Feb. 14, 1947), JAP; renounced, ashamed: JA intv.

35 "The name Drew Pearson": JA and Boyd, 8; "most intensely feared": *Time*, "Querulous Quaker" (Dec. 13, 1948); "career spanning": Pilat, 2.

35 "trivial, reactionary": DP, *Washington*, 321.

36 "Scorpion," Patton: Pilat, 5, 11.

36 Coughlin, MacArthur, stroke: Pilat, 141–46, 191, and "Bankhead Services Set for Today," *WP* (June 14, 1946), 6.

36 "polecat": JA and Boyd, 10; paid tipsters: Kluckhohn and Franklin, 67, 71, and Frederick C. Klein, "Writer Drew Pearson Stirs New Storms," *WSJ* (May 25, 1966), A1, 9; bribery and burglary: Pilat, 33, 166; censors: Sweeney, 157, 138–39; eavesdroppers: JA and Boyd, 6; "extract": FBI memo (March 21, 1951), DP FBIFOIA.

37 "man of great principle": JA intv. Gibson.

37 "not compatible": JA and Gibson, 59.

37 "overly impressed": JA intv.; "fresh-faced youth": Dowling, 96.

37 Pearson's mansion: Pilat, 200–201; "combination newsroom": JA and Boyd, 5–6.

38 Ku Klux Klan: JA and Boyd, 35–53; "Snooping for scoops," "fox hunts": letters, JA to parents (June 9, 1947, and June 23, 1947), JAP.

38 "laughably naïve," "what to make of all this," "brought up to regard": JA and Boyd, 25, 49, 34.

39 "won the Hiss case in the papers": Kutler, *Abuse*, 7; "Nixon entered": Morris, 349.

40 "admitted pervert," "spurned homosexual": Weinstein, 359, 497; Chambers gay: Tanenhaus, 345, 579; Rosetta stone: Weinstein, 493–94; Tanenhaus, 244; WHT #640-5 (Dec. 22, 1971).

41 Thomas: Gellman, 203; JA and Boyd, 133; JA and Gibson, 67–69; JA, "The Scorned Secretary Did Him In," *Parade* (June 3, 1979), 13; kickbacks, "The man at the

head," "amazing capabilities," "premixed martinis": DP, MGR (Aug. 7, 1948, Dec. 9, 1949, Sept. 7, 1948, and Aug. 13, 1948), JAP.

41 behind the scenes: DP, *Diaries*, 94; "get the job done": JA and Boyd, 168, 341.

42 plagiarism: Greenberg, 55; "Here I was": TV transcript, JA intv. Deke DeLoach (Feb. 22, 1995), JAP; Hoover leaked: Sullivan, 45, 267.

42 "pal of mine": JA and Boyd, 115; "I don't have a thing": JA intv. Gibson.

42 "For one thing," "across-the-board": JA and Boyd, 210, 124.

42–43 "For ten minutes": JA and Boyd, 215; "You will be": Mazo and Hess, 128.

43 "pink down to her underwear": Ambrose, *Education*, 218; "Don't vote the Red": R. Dallek, 21.

43 "castrate": Arnold, 13; "lousy cunt," "stupid fucking bitch": McCulloch intv.

44 "see that Dick," "needed a larger home": Morris, 759, 768; equivalent of $160,000: www.bls.gov/data/inflation_calculator.htm; corporate interests: Morris, 636–37.

44–45 "needed time," "considerable care": JA and Boyd, 379; "Dick tells me": JA intv.; "Bill, are you sure": JA and Gibson, 82.

45 scooped by Nixon: Morris, 758–61; "kids love the dog": R. Dallek, 24.

45 "from beginning to end": memo, JA to DP, "Nixon Record" (Sept. 20, 1952), G281, 2 of 3, DPP.

45–46 "unearthed a slew": Greenberg, 50; false story: Eisenhower, 127; "seldom gave": JA and Boyd, 14.

46 "interceded," "tax reduction": DP, MGR (Sept. 29, 1952), JAP; Malaxa background: Morris, 648–49; Summers, *Arrogance*, 130–31; bribe allegation: Hersh, *Camelot*, 158–61; Summers, *Arrogance*, 132–34; $900,000 contemporary equivalent: www.bls.gov/data/inflation_calculator.htm.

47 election-eve attacks: DP, MGR (Oct. 6, 8, 10, 1952), JAP; "characteristically teeming": Nixon, *RN*, 109; twenty years later: Ambrose, *Triumph*, 588.

47 "never pulled any wires": transcript, DP broadcast (Nov. 2, 1952), #SM 63, RNL; telegrams: Carter Products to RN (Nov. 3, 1952) and RN to Robert E. Kitner (Nov. 3, 1952), vice presidential correspondence, DP file, Box 583, RNVPP.

47 "premature exposure": JA and Boyd, 380–81.

48 "once powerful": Greenberg, 50; "half-truth" and "smear": Nixon, *Crises*, 126; "character assassination" and "permanently and powerfully": Nixon, *RN*, 108; "deep scar": Nixon, *Crises*, 128; press reaction: DP and JA, *Congress*, 433; DP, *Diaries*, 263; Rowse, 3–4, 8–9.

48 "largely admiring": Morris, 737, 768.

48 "Washington is buzzing": DP broadcast (Dec. 7, 1952) cited in letter, Franklyn Waltman to John Moore (Dec. 9, 1952), #120, RNL; "dug up": letter, JA to parents (Nov. 5, 1952), 2, JAP; "more than $52,000": letter, H. W. Sanders to Franklyn Waltman (April 10, 1950), #120, RNL; equivalent of $500,000: www.bls.gov/data/inflation_calculator.htm.

49 "libel," "forgery": Nixon, *RN*, 109; "highly unlikely": letter, JA to parents (Nov. 5, 1952), 2, JAP; circulated a copy: DP, *Diaries*, 239.

49 Senate probe: Nixon, *RN*, 109; "purported letter": letter, Franklyn Waltman to John Moore (Dec. 9, 1952), JAP; forgery: W. H. Lawrence, "Forgeries Charged to Nixon Accusers," *NYT* (Feb. 10, 1953), 1, 17.

49–50 "You wait": JA and Gibson, 72; "big, thick hands": Nixon, *RN*, 138; "Moscow-directed": "M'Carthy Accuses Pearson and Aide," *NYT* (March 25, 1954), 15.

50   sexual liaisons: Gentry, 433–34; DP, *Diaries*, 188–89, 250; Oshinsky, 222–23, 310; JA FBIFOIA (May 17, 1954); "disreputable pervert": DP, MGR (April 22, 1954), JAP; "unusually preoccupied": DP, MGR (June 5, 1954), JAP; "pint-sized": DP, MGR (April 1, 1954), JAP; rest of the media: Joseph and Stewart Alsop, "McCarthy-Cohn-Schine Tale Was Half Told," *WP* (March 15, 1954), 11; Bayley, chp. 7.

50   "almost certain," "wage their entire campaign": DP, MGR (Oct. 17, 1955), JAP.

50–51 Chotiner background: Morris, 292–93; Kennedy subpoenaed: Warren Unna, "Probers Call Nixon's '52 Manager," *WP* (April 26, 1956), A1ff., and C. P. Trussel, "Nixon's Aide in '52 Denies Trying to Sway Contracts," *NYT* (May 4, 1956), A1ff.; leaked to Anderson: memo, JA to DP (May 23, 1956), "Chotiner, Murray #4," G230, 1 of 2, DPP; influence-peddler: DP, MGR (Sept. 4, 1956), JAP; "communist smear": memo, "Re: Murray Chotiner" (May 1, 1956), "Chotiner, Murray #1," G230, 1 of 2, DPP.

51   "contact man": DP radio broadcast (May 12, 1956), cited in memo, A. H. Belmont to L. V. Boardman (May 14, 1956), DP FBIFOIA; Cohen background, "I've killed no one": Martin Weil, "Retired Racketeer Mickey Cohen Dies at 62," *WP* (July 30, 1976), C10; $25,000: Cohen and Nugent, 232–33; quarter million dollars: www.bls .gov/data/inflation_calculator.htm; "slanderous": letter, Murray Chotiner to WTSP-TV (May 23, 1956), Chotiner #3, G230, 1 of 2, DPP; lobbied Robert Kennedy: memo, "Suggested Questions of Chotiner" (ND), Chotiner #1, G230, 1 of 2, DPP; "flatly refused": memo, JA to DP (June 20, 1956), Chotiner #5, G230, 2 of 2, DPP.

52   youngest vice president: Volkan et al., 57.

52   "When I saw": JA intv. Gibson; "dirty trick": JA intv.; "After he stopped": Harrington, 43.

52   maternal inspection: Olivia Anderson intv.; "only news": JA to father (April 24, 1949), JAP; wedding ceremony: Fritsch intv.; supervisors now kept a close watch: JA and Gibson, 68.

53   "We have had children": Frank Farmer, "New Ride on Old Merry-Go-Round," Springfield (MO) *Sunday News and Leader* (Feb. 7, 1971), B-5ff.; $130-a-week: memo, Washington Field Office to J. Edgar Hoover, "John Mitchell Henshaw" (March 20, 1951), 7, JA FBIFOIA; "hand-me-downs": Bruch intv.; hundred-dollar bonuses: JA intv.; slave quarters: JA and Boyd, 5.

53   "wouldn't say anything": JA intv.; "very unsophisticated": Abell intv.

53–54 Anderson promotion: JA and Gibson, 80–81; JA intv. Gibson.

54   party animal: Reynolds, Bruch intvs.; disguise: Mayfield intv.; "obvious to everyone": Smolonsky intv.; surrogate husband: Mayfield intv.; "madly in love": Bruch intv.;

54   Opal's lovers: intvs., Denton, Mitchell, Whitten.

    Opal's lovers included a mobbed-up Washington lobbyist named Fred Black, who reportedly supplied call girls to members of Congress from a "hospitality suite" he rented in the Sheraton-Carlton Hotel, three blocks from the White House. Among the politicians who allegedly took advantage of Black's generosity in the early 1960s was then-congressman Gerald Ford, who had a room key to the suite. According to Bobby Baker, a business associate and friend of Black, "Ford on several occasions got oral sex" there from a high-priced call girl whom Baker befriended, Ellen Rometsch. A beautiful young brunette, Rometsch had sex with several dozen of Baker's powerful friends, most famously President Kennedy. As Baker put it, "She spread a lot of joy in Washington." Eventually, the FBI bugged Black's hotel room as part of a federal corruption probe and Jack Anderson reported that the government's "hidden listening device picked up bedroom scenes," including that of a "prominent Washington figure [who] brought a girl into Black's suite" and "utilized the bedroom." But Anderson didn't name names, perhaps because of his secretary's own affair with the lobbyist at the heart of the scandal. At least one of Ford's encounters with Rometsch was recorded by the FBI, Baker said, adding that J. Edgar Hoover used the incriminating evidence to blackmail Ford for political support.

Bruce Lambert, "Fred B. Black, 80," *NYT* (Jan. 25, 1993), B7; mobbed-up: Wallace Turner, "F.B.I. Use of Listening Devices Prompts Charges and Inquiries," *NYT* (July 3, 1966), A25; Lawrence Feinberg, "Ex-Lobbyist Sentenced in Cocaine Scheme," *WP* (July 23, 1985), C1; "hospitality suite": Baker and King, 169; Ford room key, "got oral sex": Baker intv.; Rometsch: Hersh, *Camelot*, 388–90; "spread a lot of joy": Baker intv.; FBI bugs: John P. MacKenzie, "Use of 'Bug' Is Admitted by Justice," *WP* (May 25, 1966), A1, 4; "hidden listening device"; JA, MGR (Dec. 4, 1970), JAP; secretary's affair: Denton and Morris, 309, Denton intv.; Hoover blackmail: Baker intv. and Joe Stephens, "Ford Told FBI of Skeptics on Warren Commission," *WP* (Aug. 8, 2008), A5.

55 deliberately scheduled: Neider, Olivia Anderson intvs.; "I used to think": Grady intv.; country girls: Mayfield, Olivia Anderson intvs.

55 Rose Mary Woods: Morris, 640; Ambrose, *Education*, 247; Patricia Sullivan, "Rose Mary Woods Dies," *WP* (Jan. 24, 2005), B4; "thick-ankled babes": L. Goldberg intv.; dated important men: McCord, 60; Mitchell, Denton, Whitten intvs.

3: BUGGING AND BURGLARY

56 "New Nixon": Cabell Phillips, "Nixon in '58—and Nixon in '60," *NYT Magazine* (Oct. 24, 1958), 11, 68; "more human," duck social events, dig up dirt: DP, *Diaries*, 419, 402, 442, 384; Nixon house: Amy Argetsinger and Roxanne Roberts, "Surreal Estate," *WP* (July 12, 2007), C2, and Kirstin Downey, "Nixon . . . Slept Here," *WP* (Sept. 16, 2007), C11; Nixon reportedly confided: Costello, 111.

56–57 Anderson revealed: JA, "Harris Quashes Probe of Adams," *WP* (May 13, 1958), B21; collected bribes: JA, "The Vicuna Coat Cover-up," *WP* (May 20, 1973), C7, and William Safire, "Abominable No-Man," *NYT* (Nov. 3, 1986), A23; dominated the news: Ambrose, *Education*, 490–92; Nixon counterattack: memo, Richard Nixon to Bill Key (June 19, 1958) and memo from "LGG" (June 2, 1958), "DP," Box 583, RNVPP; "potent questions": DP, *Diaries*, 455.

57 "mighty blow": JA and Boyd, 350–51; "studded with gifts," "indirectly from the American taxpayers": DP, "Presents to Ike Are Most Lavish," *WP* (June 20, 1958), B15.

57 caught with bugging: JA and Boyd, 356–60; "revulsion": "The Goldfine Bug," *WP* (July 8, 1958), A12; "grotesque": "A Very Bad Bug," *New York Journal American* (July 8, 1958), 14; "very embarrassing situation": DP, *Diaries*, 462.

58 "get a congressman," "raise question of violation of federal law": memo, William Key to Richard Nixon, "Take Two Goldfine" (ND), DP, Box 583, RNVPP; "disgraceful," "snooper": Tom Nelson, "Fire Goldfine 'Snooper,'" *New York Daily Mirror* (July 8, 1958), 2; "Peeping Tom": R. P. Kennard, Jr., letter to editor, *WP* (July 12, 1958), A6.

58 White House pressure, Anderson grand jury subpoena: DP, *Diaries*, 466, 484, 487; "greatest morass": Pack, 276; "Everybody knew": JA intv. Gibson; confidential FBI informant: FBI memo, 139-727-14, "I. Irving Davidson," 5 (Oct. 1, 1958), JFKAA.

58 "uneven-handed justice": DP, "Different Types of Justice Seen," *WP* (Oct. 8, 1958), C15; "political investigation": letter, DP to Robert V. Murray (June 5, 1959), Sherman Adams G225, 1 of 3, DPP; dropped their investigation: James Clayton, "D.C. Hotel Cashier Is Exonerated," *WP* (Oct. 24, 1958), A1.

59 "embarrassing," "keyhole": Sheehan, 10; "greatest pungency": JA and Boyd, 5; quoted and publicity: JA and Boyd, 358; James J. Butler, "Jack Anderson, Investigative Reporter," *Editor and Publisher* (July 26, 1958), 15, 68; and "Stop the Merry-Go-Round," *WP Magazine* (Dec. 18, 1977), 5 (reprint of 1958 article [ND]); "pariahs": JA intv. Gibson.

59 Nixon's conclusion: Nixon, *RN*, 194; Eisenhower, 127.

60 "Since we were both": JA manuscript, "Chappaquiddick," 7–8, JAP.

60 photographic evidence, "no intention of tattling": JA and Gibson, 391.
    Anderson said that the photos he saw did not show Kennedy in a "compromising position" and so he told his source that "I can't prove anything with that." Kennedy's playboy senatorial friend George Smathers confirmed to Anderson that the stories of JFK's womanizing were true but Anderson believed they were not newsworthy because it hadn't "affected his public conduct." Smathers told Anderson that JFK "made the great mistake of confessing everything to his wife before his marriage" in "a compulsion to tell her everything." The result, Smathers said, was that whenever he visited the White House, the First Lady viewed Smathers with hostility; thereafter, according to Anderson, Smathers advised JFK "not to be so candid" about his sexual affairs. JA manuscript, "Chappaquiddick," 7–8, JAP; JA intv. Gibson.

60 "energized him," "soon discovering": JA and Boyd, 362, 378.

61 "manipulative recluse": JA and Boyd, 382.

61 "really for Richard": Summers, *Arrogance*, 157.

62 "needs some cash": Summers, *Arrogance*, 155; "whistle of astonishment": Dietrich and Thomas, 281; $1.6 million: www.bls.gov/data/inflation_calculator.htm.

62 "don't give a darn": Summers, *Arrogance*, 155; "going too far," "fishy," "I want the Nixons": Dietrich and Thomas, 281–83.

62 unorthodox loan: Phelan, "Nixon Family," 21–24; Phelan, *Scandals*, 84, 88; North-Broome, 88, 93.

62 secrecy: Phelan, *Scandals*, 88; "Eastern division": Phelan, *Scandals*, 87; "only instance": Phelan, "Nixon Family," 22.

62 What Hughes received: JA and Boyd, 384–85.

63 "impossible to verify": Phelan, *Scandals*, 92.

63 "definitely not a philanthropist": Summers, *Arrogance*, 158.

63 falling-out: Phelan, *Scandals*, 89; "clandestine investigative arm": JA and Boyd, 381.

63–64 accident or burglary: Phelan, "Nixon Family," 24; "purloined": Summers, *Arrogance*, 508; Kennedys, who did indeed pay: Phelan, *Scandals*, 89; equivalent of more than $100,000: www.bls.gov/data/inflation_calculator.htm.

64 something "hot": Phelan, "Nixon Family," 25; "I and my father": North-Broome, 116–17.

64 "I don't know," "I never heard": Phelan, "Nixon Family," 25; more than one secret meeting: North-Broome, 114.

64–65 "bowled me over," photographic studio: Phelan, "Nixon Family," 25; "terrific scoop": Dudman intv.

65 "a large sum": Phelan, "Nixon Family," 25; Dietrich role: McCulloch intv.

65 "save Nixon's neck," "came out in public," "Fortunately, those were the days": Maheu and Hack, 83–84; "I pushed for it": McCulloch intv.; none dared run the story: Drosnin, 312, and JA manuscript, "Prologue: Remaining Segments," 5, JAP.

65–66 "Jack, this time," "On the face of it": JA manuscript, "Prologue: October 1960," 2, 3, JAP; "If the public": JA and Boyd, 382.

66 public records carefully concealed, "The trouble with," "I've called Jim," "On my way," "helping the Kennedy campaign": Boyd manuscript, "Prologue: October 1960," 5–9, JAP; "evocative of semisleeping": JA and Boyd, 383.

66 "reluctance to reveal," "a pride that only": JA manuscript, "Prologue: October 1960," 12–13, JAP; internal documents: letters, James J. Arditto to Frank J. Waters (Jan. 30, 1959), Phillip Reiner to F. J. Strickland (April 24, 1957), James J. Arditto to Thomas W. Bewley (June 18, 1957), James J. Arditto to Nadine Henley (July 7, 1958), Eleanor Rohrbeck intv. notes (ND)—all in "Nixon-Hughes Loan 15," G281, 3 of 3, DPP.

67 "It's late" conversation: JA manuscript, "Prologue: October 1960," 14–16, JAP.

67–68 "onus of starting," "agitate the Nixon antennae," "If Nixon bites": JA manuscript, "Outline of Remaining Segments of Prologue," 9–10, JAP; "might yet [try to] lie": JA and Boyd, 383.

68 "about to unload," "protect our side": Klein, 416.

68–69 VP BARES, "In an attempt," "panicked," "cock-and-bull": Phelan, "Nixon Family," 26; "lost their heads": Phelan, *Scandals*, 91; ignored the two most important names: JA and Boyd, 384; "To call it unbelievable": Maheu and Hack, 85.

69 "hesitated to write," approval and knowledge, dummy owner, "no evidence that the Hughes loan was connected": DP, MGR (Oct. 25, 1960), JAP; "reason for conflict of interest laws": JA and Boyd, 385; headlines: "Pearson Bares $205,000 Loan to Nixon Kin by Hughes Lawyer," *Los Angeles Examiner* (Oct. 27, 1960), 1, 2.

69–70 refused to allow, could not be located, "Drew did not want": JA and Boyd, 385–86; "smear": "Nixon Aide Accuses Columnist of 'Smear' over Story of Loan," *NYT* (Oct. 27, 1960), 30.

70 "not make a flat statement," "all the documents together": Anthony Lewis, "An Aide to Nixon to Explain Loan," *NYT* (Oct. 28, 1952), 16; "Now fearing the worst": JA and Boyd, 386.

70–71 "deeply grieved" to "influence outcome": AP, "Donald Nixon Admits He Got Hughes Loan," *WP* (Oct. 31, 1960), 12, and "Brother of Nixon Got Hughes Loan," *NYT* (Oct. 31, 1960), 23.

71 News accounts: AP, LOAN ADMITTED BY NIXON KIN, Madison (WI) *Capital Times* (Oct. 31, 1960), 1, 4; citing documents: DP, MGR (Oct. 25, 1960), JAP; "sucker": Phelan, "Nixon Family," 26.

71 Reiner went public, "all major decisions," "fantastic attempt": Robert G. Spivack, "Code Name Hid Dick Nixon's Role," *New York Post* (Nov. 1, 1960), 1, 2, 4.

71 "You're going to lose": Philip Benjamin, "Throngs Hail G.O.P. Leaders," *NYT* (Nov. 3, 1960), 25; "Henceforth": JA and Boyd, 387.

72 "Mr. Nixon has been talking": script (ND), "Nixon the Candidate," G281, 1 of 3, DPP.

72 special Senate committee: DP, "Proposed Speech for Lyndon Johnson," "Nixon—Hughes Loan," G281, 3 of 3, DPP; SUGGEST PRESS STATEMENT: DP, "Press Collect, Cong. Jack Brooks," "Nixon, Donald—clips," G282, 2 of 3, DPP; "integrity of our government": AP, "Conflict of Interest Inquiry Asked by Kefauver," *St. Louis Post-Dispatch* (Oct. 28, 1956), 2.

72 "Because Pearson": Phelan, *Scandals*, 81; Republican publishers: New England Society of Newspaper Editors, "News Coverage of Two 1960 Presidential Campaign Stories in Forty-Three New England Daily Newspapers" (ND), 5–16, 28–30, "Nixon—Hughes Loan," G281, DPP.

73 "came too late": Ambrose, *Education*, 603.

73 "I hope": Nixon, *Crises*, 698; cost them the White House: Lukas, 364, Drosnin, 466, Ulasewicz and McKeever, 184, Eisenhower, 198, JA and Gibson, 272, Wolfgang Saxon, "Donald Nixon, 72, Dies," *NYT* (June 30, 1987), B8; "decisive factor": Drosnin, 513.

73 "most ruthless group of political operators": Nixon, *RN*, 225.

74 "What lost Nixon": Phelan, *Scandals*, 96, 97.

4: COMEBACK

75 all smiles: James Clayton, "'Superb' Nixon Is Quick to Congratulate Kennedy," *WP* (Jan. 21, 1961), B3; "What if I": Nixon, *RN*, 224.

75 fewer journalists were persuaded, "Red appeaser," bowing to Khrushchev, "Is Brown Pink?": Ambrose, *Education*, 653, 660–61.

76 "fucking local yokels," "sweat off my balls": Summers, *Arrogance*, 226.

76 twenty-five negative columns: DP, MGR (March 5, March 10, March 11, March 12, March 27, March 29, April 15, April 21, May 16, May 17, May 24, May 28, June 15, June 23, July 8, July 28, Sept. 17, Sept. 27, Oct. 8, Oct. 9, Oct. 18, Oct. 29, Oct. 31, Nov. 2, and Nov. 3, 1962), JAP.

76 campaign to persuade Cohen: DP, MGR (June 17, 1959), JAP; "Candy Barr Gets Bail" (ND) and "Cohen Pops Out on the Diamond," *Los Angeles Examiner* (June 3, 1961); letters, DP to Mickey Cohen (May 28, 1959), DP to Carl Backman (May 28, 1959), DP to John Metcalf (May 28, 1959), DP to Thomas J. Brown (June 17, 1960), DP to Hon. Price Daniel (May 28, 1959), A. L. Wirin to DP (Sept. 13, 1960), and Jack A. Dahlstrum to DP (Sept. 19, 1960)—all in Mickey Cohen, #267, DPP; "I'm inclined": DP, *Diaries*, 549.

76 "dynamite-laden," "family skeleton": DP, MGR (March 5 and Sept. 27, 1962), JAP; "I must have answered": Nixon, *RN*, 243.

76–77 Nixon body language: Ambrose, *Education*, 669–71; last press conference: "Transcript of Nixon's News Conference," *NYT* (Nov. 8, 1962), 18.

77 "press mainly reported": Klein, 63; "Political Obituary": Ambrose, *Education*, 673; "No public figure": James Reston, "Richard Nixon's Farewell," *NYT* (Nov. 9, 1962), A34.

77 "right in the ass": Summers, *Arrogance*, 231–32; right-wing fury: Ambrose, *Education*, 673.

77 Anderson moonlighted: Pilat, 25; free stock: Don Digilio, "Columnist Has Interest in *Sun*," *Las Vegas Review-Journal* (Oct. 27, 1970); "loans": memo, "Jack Anderson," (Oct. 21, 1957), 2, JA FBIFOIA; complimentary airplane travel: Hoyt and Leighton, 205; plugging these benefactors: JA, MGR (Dec. 21, 1961), JAP, I. Davidson intv.

78 Davidson background: I. Davidson intv.; memo, "DAVIDSON: Arms," 1–2 (March 6, 1963), Fulbright hearings, SFRC; FBI "CORRELATION SUMMARY: I. Irving Davidson" (Dec. 11, 1968), JFKAA; "Handy Andy": Gordon Chaplin, "The Fantastic Deals of I. Irving Davidson," *WP* (March 21, 1976), 246ff.; prostitutes: FBI memo, A. Rosen to G. H. Scatterday, "Isadore Irving Davidson" (Nov. 29, 1961), JFKAA.

78 "wardrobe featured": Hume, 41; office rental: I. Davidson intv. and FBI memo, "Jack Anderson" (May 12, 1967), 15, "I. Irving Davidson, Haiti," JFKAA; free hotel bills: Fulbright hearings, SFRC, 1616–23; stock tips: FBI memo (Jan. 15, 1955), JA FBIFOIA; paid news source: FBI memo (Oct. 1, 1958), JA FBIFOIA.

78 "The only thing": I. Davidson intv.; "writing articles": FBI memo, "Jack Anderson" (May 12, 1967), 15, "I. Irving Davidson, Haiti," JFKAA.

Anderson repaid Davidson's generosity in many ways. "Anderson and Davidson frequently worked together in pushing foreign clients of Davidson," the lobbyist's secretary told the FBI. Records indicate that Anderson promised to introduce Davidson to Attorney General Robert Kennedy, who was prosecuting the lobbyist's clients, and pass on messages to RFK on behalf of the Indonesian dictator Suharto, whom Davidson represented. Anderson also signed an extraordinary confidential letter to Davidson that deputized him to be a reporter for the "Merry-Go-Round" column. "This will authorize you to use my name and facilities in whatever way is necessary to help you gather news," Anderson wrote. "Remuneration and expenses will be worked out between us on the merits of each case." The letter served to create a cover for financial transactions between the two men. "Pushing foreign clients": FBI memo, "Jack Anderson" (May 12, 1967), 15, "I. Irving Davidson, Haiti," JFKAA; RFK intermediary: memo, I. Irving Davidson to JA (Jan. 8, 1962); FBI memo, A. Rosen to G. H. Scatterday, "Isadore Irving Davidson" (Nov. 29, 1961), and FBI memo, "I. Irving Davidson" (Oct. 26, 1961)—all in JFKAA; "authorize you to use my name": letter, JA to Davidson (Jan. 5, 1960), DVAP.

79 "Remember, God": Grady intv.

79 Senate probe: Fulbright hearings, SFRC passim.

79 Checks, hotel expenses: memos, "DAVIDSON: Press" (March 6, 1963) and "Press—3," Fulbright hearings, SFRC; "expedient": letter, Irv Davidson to Michael Koll-Nescher and Avraham Simner (July 19, 1962), Fulbright hearings, SFRC.

79 "facts relating to the 'loans'": memo, "Anderson phone call to the Chairman" (ND), Fulbright hearings, SFRC; "out to get him": Walter Pincus, "Telephone Call from Jack Anderson" (March 8, 1963), Fulbright hearings, SFRC.

80 Davidson testimony, hotel bill: Fulbright hearings, 1524–1688 and 1617–23; "influence-peddler": Bernard L. Collier, "Morse Charges U.S. Uses Lobbyist for Domingo Deals," *New York Herald Tribune* (June 11, 1960); investigator later explained: Pincus intv.

80 Davidson confided: JA intv. Gibson, JA intv.; "Not long ago": JA, *Washington Exposé*, 191.

Nixon "dismissed everybody from the room," Anderson quoted Davidson as saying, "and I handed him the $5,000, and he grinned sheepishly." The cash "probably came from the American taxpayers via foreign aid," the newsman wrote. "Prosecution would be almost impossible in this case, since the only two witnesses would never incriminate themselves." Anderson added that Davidson recounted the bribe story in a casual manner and only then because he was amused by Nixon's "sticky fingers" comment: Davidson "thought it was incredible that [Nixon] would make a remark like that." Davidson later confirmed the story in an interview with the author. Sources for the above: "dismissed everybody": JA intv. Gibson; "probably came": JA, *Washington Exposé*, 191; "incredible": JA intv. Gibson; confirmed the story: JA intv. See also JA, "How Foreign Agents Operate in the U.S.," *Parade* (Feb. 3, 1963), 12–13, and "Press-6," SFRC.

81 "senile old bastard": Ambrose, *Triumph*, 27; "sad, depressed man," hit wife, divorce, "There was a sadness": Summers, *Arrogance*, 240, 235–36.

81 1964 positioning, "My friends": Ambrose, *Triumph*, 39, 46.

82 four hundred Republican groups in forty states: Ambrose, *Triumph*, 60; "maturer, mellower man": Kutler, *Wars*, 34; "press, lulled": Garment, *Throat*, 28.

82 "Without a day": Ambrose, *Triumph*, 100.

82 "homosexual ring," "tape recording of a sex orgy," "zooming chances": DP and JA, MGR (Oct. 30, 1967), JAP.

82–83 "wasn't much," "Only two": JA and Gibson, 395; "natty dresser," "practicing homo-sexuals," "daisy chain": Cannon, *Governor*, 239, 241, 245; Reagan advisors, "Key-stone Cops," "queers": Nofziger, 76–78.

   Among the Reagan aides whispered about in the gay sex scandal was thirty-one-year-old Jack Kemp, a former all-star football quarterback who later became a Republican congressman, Cabinet member, presidential candidate, and GOP vice presidential nominee. The handsome and athletic Kemp was not gay, Nofziger said, but was the apparent object of a crush by Governor Reagan's chief of staff, Phil Battaglia, who "took Kemp under his wing, and had him accompany him whenever he left Sacramento, which was frequently." Battaglia and Kemp "became friends, but nothing more. At times Battaglia cried on his shoulder, disclosing his fears and frustrations, but not his desires, if he had any." Still, just to be sure, Nofziger's private detective spied on Kemp and Battaglia when they traveled out of town together. "We searched out their room arrangements in a hotel in San Francisco," Nofziger wrote, "and discovered they took separate, nonadjoining rooms and slept in them all night." Kemp was "naïve" and purchased a Lake Tahoe cabin with Battaglia but was not present during any gay orgies there, Nofziger added: "Despite his innocence, for more than twenty years Kemp was dogged by the rumors, but he . . . rode it out with courage and an absolute refusal to let it ruin him, his family, or his career." None-theless, the "Merry Go Round" story may have kept Kemp from the White House. "It was that homosexual thing," Nofziger told conservative columnist Robert Novak, that persuaded Reagan to choose George H. W. Bush instead of Kemp as his run-ning mate in 1980. Cannon, *Governor*, 239, 241, 243, 245, 248, 249, 251–52; Can-non, *Ronnie*, 183; Novak, 354.

83 Reagan news conference: Lawrence E. Davies, "Reagan Denies a Report by Drew Pearson of Homosexual Ring Involving Members of Governor's Staff," *NYT* (Nov. 1, 1967), 29; Julius Duscha, "Reagan Says 'There Is No Truth' to Report of Homo-sexual Aides," *WP* (Nov. 1, 1967), 1, 8; Charles Raudebaugh, "Reagan and Drew Pearson Trade Charges," *San Francisco Chronicle* (Nov. 1, 1967), 1, 7; "lie he did": Nofziger, 81.

83 REAGAN DENIES: Jack Welter, "Reagan Denies 'Homo' Rumor," *San Francisco Exam-iner* (Nov. 1, 1967), 1, 4; second Reagan press conference: Gladwin Hill, "Reagan Will 'Not Talk Further' About Report on Homosexuals," *NYT* (Nov. 15, 1967), 32; UPI, "Credibility Questions Irk Reagan," *WP* (Nov. 15, 1967), 7.

84 "greatly diminished," "deep national implications": Rowland Evans and Robert Novak, "Reagan's Denial," *WP* (Nov. 6, 1967), A21.

84 "aberrant sexual behavior," "talking too much," "scandalmongers": Nofziger, 74, 80, 81.

84 "It could be argued": JA and Gibson, 395.

85 "Mr. Nixon": letter, RN staff to Lyn Nofziger (Nov. 1, 1967), "REAGAN, GOV.," G212, 2 of 3, DPP.

85 "Reagan piece": Klurfeld, 265.
85 "Gentlemen" and 79 percent: Ambrose, *Triumph*, 135, 145.
86 Hilton incident: Ehrlichman, 41–42; Anderson "phobia": Hersh intv.
87 Hoover background: Gentry, 376; Garrow, *FBI,* 165, 286; R. Powers, 69–70.
87 wiretaps: Garrow, *FBI,* 92–99; Branch, *Parting,* 907–09; Sullivan and Brown, 137.
88 a dozen large tape reels, group sex, "tom cat," "burrhead": Garrow, *FBI,* 104–08.
88 distributed throughout Washington: Oates, 266; "Fucking is a form": Garrow, *Bearing,* 275; "piece of tail": Heymann, 302; "making it with," "best pussy-eater," "loaded," "running naked": memo, Les Whitten to JA, "Re: M. L. King" (Aug. 27, 1975), LWP, 007.070.06; "I'm fucking for God!": Branch, *Pillar,* 207.

 Hoover's deputy William Sullivan later told Jack Anderson's legman Les Whitten that it may have been one of King's associates, not the famous orator himself, whose similar-sounding voice was recorded making the most profane comments on FBI wiretaps. Similarly, a later FBI investigation concluded that it was "someone in King's party other than King" who "was involved with some prostitutes in the hotel in Oslo." (According to one version of the event, two civil rights workers were seen running down the hallway "stark naked" after being robbed by prostitutes; according to another account, the hookers performed sexual favors for King's associates on condition of getting to sleep with King himself, only to be deprived of that honor.) King associate: Whitten intv.; Oslo incident: FBI memo, W. R. Wannall to J. G. Deegan, "Article by Jack Anderson" (Oct. 20, 1975), 7, MLKP.
88 embellished: Whitten intv. and FBI memo, W. R. Wannall to J. G. Deegan, "Article by Jack Anderson" (Oct. 20, 1975), 7, MLKP; evidence sealed: Theoharis and Cox, 358, and "F.B.I. Ordered to Send King Tapes to Archives," *NYT* (Feb. 1, 1977), A12; press corps self-censorship: Oates, 315; Garrow, *FBI,* 127, 128, 130–31, 172; chauffeur's fellatio: Gentry, 388.
89 "go down in history": memo, Deke DeLoach to John Mohr (Feb. 4, 1964), 2, DP FBIFOIA; "have the story exclusively": JA intv.; "so I caught the first plane": Dowling, 98–99.
89 "King was not superhuman": Sherrill, 14.
89 Kennedy signed paperwork: Navasky, 157–58, 165.
90 "illicit love affair": DP and JA, MGR (May 24, 1968), JAP.
90 created a furor: Witcover, *85 Days,* 212; Fred P. Graham, "Drew Pearson Says Robert Kennedy Ordered Wiretap on Phone of Dr. King," *NYT* (May 25, 1968), 17; DP and JA, "Wiretap Column Sparks Charges," *WP* (June 4, 1968), D13; R. W. Apple, Jr., "Kennedy Disputes M'Carthy," *NYT* (June 2, 1968), 64; David S. Broder, "3 Stump Oregon to Windup," *WP* (May 26, 1968), 12.
90 column would be passed out to voters, duck televised debates, rehearsed his answer: Thomas, *Kennedy,* 380–81.
90–91 "Of course it was timed," LBJ personally met with Pearson: Thomas, *Kennedy,* 378–79; "deeply troubled": memo, Ramsey Clark to J. Edgar Hoover (May 27, 1968), DP FBIFOIA.
91 Georgetown lunch: DeLoach intv; transcript, DeLoach intv. JA, JAP; spoke directly with President Johnson: Thomas, *Kennedy,* 379.
91 Hoover insults: memos, J. Edgar Hoover (Jan. 8, 1957, Jan. 30, 1970, and April 30, 1951), JA FBIFOIA, and (July 1, 1969), JAP.

91–92 "Jack Anderson called": memo, C. D. DeLoach to Clyde Tolson (May 21, 1968), DP FBIFOIA; "How did Jack," "excellent investigative reporter": transcript, De-Loach intv. JA, JAP.

92 "did not originate": memo, J. Edgar Hoover to Ramsey Clark (May 28, 1968), DP FBIFOIA.

92 "deliberate bum steer": JA intv. Gibson; correct the record: JA and Les Whitten, "Hoover Floated Hoax Story on King," *WP* (Dec. 17, 1975), C18.

92 RFK assassination: Moldea, 13, 83.

92–93 Chicago convention, "peace with honor," Operation Candor, "perfectly clear": Ambrose, *Triumph*, 183, 195, 181, 121–22.

93 ducked television appearances, Southern strategy: Ambrose, *Triumph*, 137, 155; "Let's face it," "niggers": McGinnis, 63, 101–03; Madison Avenue: Garment, *Crazy*, 136–38; "guilt complex": Kutler, *Wars*, 166; "enemy": Spear, 56.

93–94 "For eight years," "upheld Humphrey": JA and Boyd, 388; recycled Nixon skeletons: DP and JA, MGR (March 26, April 6, April 11, July 4, Aug. 4, Aug. 7, Aug. 12, Aug. 17, Oct. 15, Oct. 18, Oct. 25, Oct. 28, and Nov. 2, 1968), JAP; "revert," "dossiers," "purge," "goons": Greenberg, 68.

94 signed statement, "I invited," "did not meet the quota": DP and JA, MGR (Oct. 31, 1968), JAP; medical parole, "all gamblers," "considerable piece of money": Cohen and Nugent, 233–37; quarter of a million dollars equivalent: www.bls.gov/data/inflation_calculator.htm.

94–95 "secured a statement," "putting the squeeze," "something in return": DP and JA, MGR (Oct. 31, 1968), JAP.

95 "Nixon's press secretary": letter, DP to Michael Cohen (Nov. 1, 1968), "Cohen, Mickey," Box 267, 3 of 3, DPP.

95 "very odd man": R. Dallek, 91; "never really healed," "even the score": Garment, *Throat*, 49, 60; "third person": JA and Gibson, 176.

96 Hutschnecker visits: Erica Goode, "Arnold Hutschnecker, 102, Therapist to Nixon," *NYT* (Jan. 3, 2001), C15; correspondence between RN and Arnold Hutschnecker (1955 to 1962), general correspondence, Box 364, RNVPP; "It is safer": Jean M. White, "The Dance with Nixon," *WP* (Nov. 20, 1973), B2.

96 "Nixon's shrink": Greenberg, 242; spotted by neighbors: Harriet Van Horne, "Nixon and the Doctor," *New York Post* (Nov. 15, 1968, 54); less than discreet: Winger-Berger, 249–51, and letter, Peter Blake to DP (Oct. 23, 1968), "Nixon Health," G281, 1 of 3, DPP; dossier and Winchell: Summers, *Arrogance*, 520, 89; Sinatra: Thomas, *Kennedy*, 107.

96–97 antianxiety medication: Summers, *Arrogance*, 317–18; "pseudo-ulcers," "deep depression": Leonard Garment intv. Bill Kauffman and John Meroney (Nov./Dec. 1998), www.aei.org; "neurotic symptoms," "less manly," "cuckoo": Summers, *Arrogance*, 92–97, 9.

97 "urgent & confidential": letters, Peter Blake to DP (Oct. 23 and Oct. 29, 1968), "Nixon Health," G281, 1 of 3, DPP.

97 "psychiatric treatment" to "reluctant to talk": DP, "Deciding on the Nixon Treatment," *WP* (Nov. 23, 1968), D11.

97 drafted a special column: DP and JA (Oct. 29, 1968), "Nixon Health," G281, 1 of 3, DPP.

97–98 "Given the history": Klein, 413; "only for problems": Summers, *Arrogance*, 319.

98 "changed his story": Sherrill, 8; "It seemed to me strange": DP, "Deciding on the Nixon Treatment," *WP* (Nov. 23, 1968), D11; "could not be expected": JA and Boyd, 389.

98 "Our position was": Klein, 413.

98–99 "KILL NIXON STORY": draft column, DP and JA (Oct. 29, 1968), "Nixon Health," G281, 1 of 3, DPP; "seemed torn": JA and Boyd, 389; "deserve credit," "changed the results": Klein, 415, 412.

99 final election margin: Ambrose, *Triumph*, 219.

99 "psychiatric problems," "standing up under great pressure": William M. Blair, "Psychiatric Aid to Nixon Denied," *NYT* (Nov. 14, 1968), 34; "Correspondents who": Greenberg, 243.

99–100 "I simply will not comment," "absolutely false": William M. Blair, "Psychiatric Aid to Nixon Denied," *NYT* (Nov. 14, 1968), 34; "decision to bring the report": "Vaporous Rumor," *WP* (Nov. 15, 1968), editorial page; "Personally I sympathize": DP, "Deciding on the Nixon Treatment," *WP* (Nov. 23, 1968), D11.

100 Klein sent telegrams, "Pearson had volunteered": Klein, 415.

100 "legitimate story": JA and Gibson, 389–90; quacks: JA intv.

100 "I wonder if": letter, Mickey Cohen to DP (Nov. 6, 1968), "Cohen, Mickey," Box 267, 3 of 3, DPP.

100–101 "This was an ego": Perlstein, 26.

101 "smears": Kutler, *Wars*, 161; "see that someone": Oudes, xxviii; "Enemies": Halberstam, 606.

5: THE PRESIDENT AND THE COLUMNIST

105 inaugural weather, heckling: Ambrose, *Triumph*, 245.

105–6 Watergate building: Ambrose, *Triumph*, 246; "Berlin Wall," "Go fuck yourself!": Wicker, 400; "too old": JA manuscript, "Wallace II," 6, JAP.

106 Davidson background: Gordon Chaplin, "The Fantastic Deals of I. Irving Davidson," *WP* (March 21, 1976), 246ff.; Chotiner background: Vera Glaser, "Murray Chotiner," North American Newspaper Alliance (Nov. 12, 1968), DPP, and Chotiner calendar, "Misuse of IRS," Box 17, WSPF.

106–7 "drop by" to "using whom": JA manuscript, "Wallace II," 2, 6–9, JAP.

107 "engaged in," "Naval officer," Mustang: FBI memo, C. D. DeLoach to Clyde Tolson (June 11, 1969), 1–2, JAP.

107–8 surveillance routine, "insane" to "Nazi crowd": Trento intv.

108 "very damaging" to "kept out of it": FBI memo, C. D. DeLoach to Clyde Tolson (June 11, 1969), 1–2, JAP.

108 Hoover role, "Nothing could grab": Ehrlichman, 159; "homosexualists," "deviates": Gentry, 624.

108–9 "Mitchell got out" and "good alibis": Ehrlichman, 159; "villas" to "gay cell": Chapin intv.

109–10 "misinformed," "gratitude": Ehrlichman, 160; "lay a threat," "show his claws": Summers, *Official*, 375–76.

110 "didn't believe for a minute": JA and Gibson, 163; "Anderson stated": FBI memo, C. D. DeLoach to Clyde Tolson (June 11, 1969), 2, JAP.

110 "the way they work" to "everybody they don't like": J. Edgar Hoover, "Memorandum for Personal Files" (July 1, 1969), 1–3, JAP.

111 "stirred up a minor panic": JA and Gibson, 163.

111 "Other presidents": JA and Gibson, 152.

111 "Merry-Go-Round" references: MGR card index (Jan. 20, 1969–Sept. 1, 1969), JAP; "During the first": JA and Boyd, 390.

111   DP death: "Drew Pearson, Columnist, Dies," NYT (Sept. 2, 1969), A1.

112   "descendant of the tradition": "Drew Pearson," NYT (Sept. 2, 1969), 46; "conscience of a Quaker": "Drew Pearson," WP (Sept. 3, 1969), 22; memorial service: "Pearson Eulogized as Great Statesman," WP (Sept. 5, 1969), C6; ashes: Abell intv.

112   blur: JA intv.; "overwhelmed with grief": JA and Gibson, 136; "Jack really resented": Trento intv.; $255 a week: letter, Warren Woods to Tyler Abell (Sept. 22, 1969), DVAP.

112   twice as many newspapers: "Columnists: The Tenacious Muckraker," Time (Sept. 12, 1969), 82; canceled columns: J. Trento, 23.

112–13   Pearson had promised: JA and Gibson: 81; "served notice on me": JA intv. Gibson; Abell qualifications: Abell intv.; "absolute panic": F. Cohen intv.; byline had been added: Douglas Martin, "Jack Anderson," NYT (Dec. 18, 2005), 38; "pastel character": Hume, 9.

113   signed the syndicate's legal contract: JA intv. Gibson; "inappropriate": letter, Tyler Abell to Warren Woods (Sept. 18, 1969), DVAP; Pearson's widow: letter, JA to Luvie Pearson (Sept. 25, 1969), DVAP.

114   staff turnover: Pilat, 312; Dowling, 96; JA intv. Gibson; bills and commitments: JA and Gibson, 137, and letter, Warren Woods to Tyler Abell (Sept. 22, 1969), DVAP; Freidin: JA intv.; "Reporter Is Termed a Spy in McGovern Camp," NYT (Aug. 28, 1973), 21; "Freidin Cheerfully Acknowledges Getting Paid by GOP," WP (Sept. 5, 1973), 11; "Varying Ties to C.I.A. Confirmed in Inquiry," NYT (Dec. 27, 1977), 41; "boyish movie star": Dowling, 96; "swashbuckler": Whitten intv.

114   "Jack was afraid": Whitten intv.; "fighting for his journalistic life": Dowling, 96.

115   McCormack case: Ben-Veniste, chp. 2; undercover intern: JA, "Speaker Never Took Money," WP (Oct. 30, 1969), G11, and JA, "McCormack Probe," WP (Jan. 7, 1971), B7; "mimicry" fooled LBJ: JA, "McCormack's Aide Held Potent Spot," WP (Oct. 20, 1970), B11.

115   "wanted to be rid," "hard to hush this one up": Ambrose, Triumph, 284, 283; "marks the end of Teddy": Haldeman, Diaries, 72.

115–16   sealed deposition transcripts: JA and Gibson, 139–40; filch Time magazine's in-house memos: JA intv. Gibson; playing off Kennedy intimates, "perversities of the informant": JA manuscript, "Chappaquiddick," 9–11, 16, 17, 21–24, JAP.

116   "didn't tell the whole truth," "too late": JA, MGR (Aug. 8 and 13, 1969), JAP.

116   "innuendoes and falsehoods": "Columnist and Kennedy," Newsweek (Aug. 1969); "wouldn't make any comment": "Kennedy Denies Story He Tried to Shift Blame," WP (Aug. 9, 1969), 4.

116   "Anderson reconstruction . . . largely fictional": "Anderson's Brass Ring," Time (Jan. 17, 1972), 34; later corroboration: Kappel, 230; Hume, 20; Greene intv.

116   National Enquirer, "Drew's death": JA and Gibson, 140–41.

116   Hume background, comments on JA: Hume, 18, 14, 48.

117   "rather go to a movie": Douglas Martin, "Jack Anderson," NYT (Dec. 18, 2005), 38; Pearson's widow, "like being a janitor": Hume intv.

117   "style is a trifle primitive": Dowling, 93.

118   "In the 'Merry-Go-Round'": Hume, 7, 43, 86, 87.

118   thirty-two additional newspapers: Dowling, 96; "Just what other": "Jack Anderson Column Wins Praise of A-N Readers," Aberdeen (SD) American News (Feb. 22, 1970), 5.

118–19 "I had no intention": JA and Gibson, 177; "out of pacifist," "be the first": memos, Ken Cole to John Ehrlichman (Oct. 21, 1969) and John R. Brown III to John Ehrlichman (Jan. 20, 1970), Ehrlichman #18, NARA.

119 "wielded an economic ax": JA, "Anti-Poverty Czar Embellishes Office," WP (Sept. 22, 1969), B13; "head of the poverty program": Dowling, 101.

Cheney said that Anderson refused to run a retraction but Anderson claimed Rumsfeld asked him not to as a "favor," to avoid giving the story additional publicity. "Merry-Go-Round" corrections were notoriously rare and grudging, often deliberately rehashing the worst facts about a target to discourage others from making similar requests. "The only thing worse than a Jack Anderson story," a spokesman for a federal agency laughed, "is a Jack Anderson correction." John Carmody, "Jack Anderson: His Code of Ethics," WP (April 3, 1972), B1; Susan Sheehan, "The Case of the O.E.O. Office," NYT Magazine (Aug. 13, 1972), 80; Byrne intv.

119–20 "You call up": Hendrick Hertzberg, "Getting the Goods," The New Yorker (Jan. 22, 1972), 23; "in best sense," "fear kept them honest": Whitten intv.; "like he was the Pope": Smolonsky intv.

120 "cannot win": Ambrose, Triumph, 500; "Alabama Project": Carter, Politics of Rage, 400.

121 "$400,000": Carter, Politics of Rage, 388–99, 392.

121 "kickbacks," "misused": JA, MGR (Nov. 26, 1968), JAP; "weasel-like": Carter, Politics of Rage, 404; "bundle of cancelled checks": JA manuscript, "Wallace I," 9, JAP; "We will be happy": JA, MGR (Nov. 29, 1968), JAP.

121 "I laid before" to "these matters": JA manuscript, "Wallace I," 15–16, JAP.

121–22 "squatters' rights," "go higher": JA manuscript, "Wallace I," 16–17; "After months," "but will do": JA manuscript, "Wallace II," 13, 14, JAP.

122 felony: IRS impeachment hearings, 35.

122 "You went," "brass monkey": JA manuscript, "Wallace II," 10, JAP.

122 "I remembered": Nixon, RN, 676.

122 Chotiner role in tax audits, Wallace: Adam Clymer and Thomas Pepper, "IRS Chief Quit over Tampering," Baltimore Sun (June 13, 1974), 1, and Eileen Shanahan, "Nixon Asked Data on Wallace Tax," NYT (July 17, 1974), 17.

122 "scoundrel," "request of the President": Mollenhoff, 109–10.

122–23 "spread out on a table": JA and Gibson, 177; "directed me" to "movements": JA manuscript, "Wallace II," 15, JAP.

123 SWARM to "attendant," campaign kickbacks: JA, MGR (April 13, 1970), JAP.

123 "trying to convict," "politics of the dirtiest sort": "Wallace Brother Assails Newsman," NYT (April 16, 1970), 25; "peck of trouble," "good news": Carter, Politics of Rage, 405; "edge of political extinction": JA manuscript, "Wallace II," 19, JAP.

123 UNLESS WHITES VOTE: JA manuscript, "Wallace II," 20, JAP.

124 "niggers beat us": Carter, Politics, 394.

124 "screaming": memo, untitled (ND), 9, "Misuse of IRS," Box 24, WSPF; "clearly the source": IRS impeachment hearings, 41; "furious and noisy" to "Number One suspect": Mollenhoff, 114–15.

124 Haldeman and Ehrlichman, "cautioning not to leak": memo, Henry L. Hecht, "Interview of K. Martin Worthy" (Oct. 17, 1973), 3, Box 24, WSPF.

124 "constituted a criminal act": IRS impeachment hearings, 35–42.

125 "We owe" to "cause him": JA, MGR (April 26, 1971), JAP.

125–26 grand jury probe, quid pro quo, "explicit agreement": Carter, *Politics of Rage*, 408–14; "pyromaniac": Carter, *Wallace*, 423.

126 "back in the early mists" to "exposure": JA manuscript, "Tailfins," 8, and "Wallace II," 9, JAP.

126 "plaintive," "What arrangement?" "olive branch": JA and Gibson, 177; "Jeez": JA manuscript, "Tailfins," 8, JAP; "use[d] our column," "pressure on him" to "eliminate": JA, MGR (June 26, 1974, and June 28, 1973), JAP.

127 "unspoken hope" to "inform the public": JA manuscript, "Tailfins," 8, and "Wallace II," 9, JAP.

6: REVENGE

128 "Truth": Maltese, 27; dozens if not hundreds: Ambrose, *Triumph*, 250; the word *enemy*: Safire, 343, 121–22.

128 news summaries, "Nixon spent": Ambrose, *Triumph*, 370, 251.

129 "program Ziegler" (emphasis in original), "line-of-the-day": Maltese, 24, 94.

129 "attack group": Maltese, 94; "small and unelected elite," "The day when the network": Porter, 47, 50; "flicks the scab": Spear, 39; FCC challenge: Porter, 53–54.

129–30 "good politics," "just can't stand": Aitken, *Colson*, 143, 140; "anti-Nixon": "CBS, ABC Claim Coercion": *WP* (April 30, 1974), A12; "bring you to your knees": Spear, 150.

130 felony legislation: Spear, 161; antitrust charges, "Almost every president": Porter, 154–59, 3.

130 homosexuals: memo, J. Edgar Hoover to Clyde Tolson (Nov. 25, 1970), Rowland Evans FBIFOIA; "urgent" and "out to get us": Ambrose, *Triumph*, 251; "nut cutters" and "brutal": R. Dallek, 381; "vicious" and "sons of bitches": Kutler, *Abuse*, 135; "screw our political enemies": Kutler, *Wars*, 104; Anderson first: JA and Gibson, 216.

　　In particular, Nixon told aides that *The Washington Post* should be given "damnable, damnable, problems" getting its broadcast licenses renewed: "There ain't going to be no forgetting and there'll be goddamn little forgiving." Nixon also ordered the White House chief of staff, H. R. Haldeman, to "go after" *Post* publisher Katharine Graham and vowed to "screw" the newspaper by targeting its real estate holdings and inciting shareholders against the company: "They don't realize how rough I can play. But when I start, I will kill them. There's no question about it." "Damnable": Porter, 169; "no forgetting" to "kill": Kutler, *Abuse*, 174, 177, 173.

130 illegal wiretaps: Ambrose, *Triumph*, 273.

130 burglaries: Jackson, Rather intvs.

130 "his ascension": Halberstam, 606.

131 cultivate the columnist: Gold intv.; "the words": Victor Gold, "Last of the Muckrakers," *Washingtonian* (Oct. 1997), 37; "let me know" to "transgressions": Dowling, 95.

131–32 "fag" to "drugs being used": Hume, 49–54.

132 "deeply troubled" to "beauty parlor": JA, MGR (Sept. 8, 1970), JAP; "double entendre": JA and Gibson, 181.

132 "implications": "Son of Agnew Says He Has Left Wife," *NYT* (Sept. 6, 1970), 26; spiked, "surprised and disappointed": Hume, 58–59; "no idea": Howard Kurtz, "Moving to the Right," *WP* (April 19, 2006), C1; "I jumped": JA and Gibson, 180; "went after the kid": Brit Hume, "Now It Can Be Told," *More* (April 1975), 12.

　　Tragically, Hume's own son later committed suicide amid reports that he was about to be "outted" by the media for allegedly having a homosexual affair with a married congressman. Like Hume's story suggesting that Randy Agnew was gay, rumors of Sandy Hume's homosexuality were never proved. But in 1998, the allegation produced a media feeding frenzy. The twenty-eight-year-old journalist put a gun to his head and pulled the trigger. "The proximate cause," said his grieving father, was Sandy's arrest on drunk driving charges the night before: "He was manifestly depressed about it" and "believed, for reasons that are not entirely clear, [that it] was going to be ruinous." Scarborough, 133–34; David Fiderer, "When Joe Scarborough Dragged Dick Armey Out of a Closet of Shame," *Huffington Post* (Aug. 11, 2009); Howard Kurtz, "Moving to the Right," *WP* (April 19, 2006), C1ff.

132 "difficult to define": JA, MGR (Oct. 4, 1973), JAP.
    Federal prosecutors uncovered Vice President Agnew's marital infidelity while investigating his financial corruption; his abrupt decision to resign from office as part of a plea bargain was triggered in part by his desire to avoid public disclosure of his adultery, which otherwise would have become public at his trial. According to one account, "Agnew would not stay in hotels overnight unless the Secret Service arranged for [his favorite mistress] to be given an adjoining room." One federal agent later complained: "We were facilitating his adultery. We felt like pimps." Witcover, *Bedfellows*, 351; Witcover intv; Kessler, 36.

133 "freebies": Richard M. Cohen, "Chain Sent Free Food to VIPs," *WP* (Sept. 15, 1973), A4; "media had a field day" to "sanctimony": Agnew, 138.

133 "private memos" to "fired tomorrow": memo, John R. Brown III to H. R. Haldeman, "Re: Jack Anderson Comments" (Feb. 2, 1971), Haldeman #297, NARA; "I believe": WH news digest (Jan. 29, 1971), 10, NARA.

133 "Anderson does": memo, Jack Caulfield to H. R. Haldeman, "Subject: Anderson Leaks" (Feb. 11, 1971), Haldeman #297, NARA.

134 "intimidate our sources": JA, "News Leaks," *WP* (Feb. 13, 1971), D21.

134 "confidential comments" to "more meetings": JA, "Sshh! It's Secret," *WP* (March 2, 1971), B11; "the latest" to "bugged???": memo, William E. Timmons to H. R. Haldeman, "Leadership Leaks" (March 2, 1971), Haldeman #297, NARA.

134 stream of directives: Pentagon NISIs (April 3, April 22, Dec. 10, and Dec. 18, 1970; Feb. 8 and Feb. 17, 1971; May 15, 1972), DVAP, memos, Gordon Strachan to Fred Malek and John Dean (July 1, July 13, July 15, Sept. 27, and Sept. 28, 1971), Haldeman #297, NARA; "Anyone who was caught": JA and Gibson, 178.

134–35 "most chauffeured" to "big cheese himself": JA, "AF Staff Car Used for Columnist," *WP* (April 18, 1972), B15; "big boobs": Van Atta intv. Jack Mills, DVAP; "Dear Jack": Van Atta, 319; "rarely wrote": Eagleburger intv. Van Atta, DVAP.

135 "I have done" to "Get High on Life": Krogh, 12, 11, 60, 22.

136 "tight-fitting velvet pants" to "brittle from hair spray": Krogh, 18, 19.

136 "good to meet you" to "tie clasps": Krogh, 33, 35, 34, 39; "deliciously bizarre": Greenberg, 339.

136 Elvis badge: Krogh, 45.

136–37 "given the nature" and "Top Secret": Krogh, 49, 48; "presidential dictum": JA, "Presley Gets Narcotics Bureau Badge," *WP* (Jan. 27, 1972), D23.

137 "mincing": Gentry, 159; "spousal": R. Powers, 171–73.

137 "holding hands": transcript, Bill Kurtis documentary, "Jack Anderson: The Fall of J. Edgar Hoover" (June 20, 1995), 17, JAP.

137–38 "dog" to "nice looking fellow": J. Edgar Hoover, FBI memos (Jan. 8, 1957; April 30, 1951; Jan. 30, 1970), JA FBIFOIA, and (July 1, 1969), JAP.

138 "So different": JA and Gibson, 168.

138 "time someone pried": JA intv. Gibson.

138 Whitten tailing Hoover: JA and Gibson, 168–69; "couldn't get any evidence": JA
     intv. Gibson; "Edgar and Clyde": JA, MGR (Jan. 1, 1971), JAP.

138 "Chuck was relentless": JA and Gibson, 169; "You can get arrested": Dowling, 95.

139 Hoover menu: Gentry, 669; "Gelusil": Dowling, 95.

139 "It's unsettling": JA, "Hoover's Trash Shows He's Human," WP (March 27, 1971), C11.

139 "tireless guardian": JA, "Hoover Books Ghostwritten at FBI," WP (May 11, 1971),
     B15; "venomous" to "carrion": memos, J. Edgar Hoover (Jan. 11, 1971; Sept. 28, 1971;
     Sept. 2, 1971), JA FBIFOIA.

139 "faithful companion" to "picked up": JA, "$100-a-Day Suites Free to Hoover," WP
     (May 12, 1971), B21; "startling evidence" to "high and mighty": JA, "Hoover Neither
     Hero nor Ogre," WP (Feb. 4, 1971), E23; "very paranoid": Summers, Official, 391, 95.

139–40 "explode": Roy Cohn, "Could He Walk on Water?" Esquire (Nov. 1972), 117, 251;
     "not a reporter": Christopher Lydon, "Hoover Praises Mrs. Mitchell and Comments
     on Critics," NYT (May 25, 1971), 19; "virulent critics" to "trash he writes": JA, "FBI's
     Bulldog Bites Critic Again," WP (Nov. 24, 1971), B11.

140 "straight face": DeLoach, 103.

140 "The tougher the attacks": Ambrose, Triumph, 473; Hoover cautious: Kutler, Wars,
     99, 120.

7: VIETNAM

141–42 Vietnam War background: Ambrose, Triumph, 223; R. Dallek, 134, 619–20;
     Ellsberg, 354–55.

141–42 Vietnamization: Ambrose, Triumph: 309, 319, 349, 387, 407, 419, and Hersh, Price,
     119, 121; Korean War: Ambrose, Triumph, 224, and Hersh, Price, 51; "two-faced":
     Zumwalt, 413.

142 Cambodia bombing: Hersh, Price, 193.

142 "cock-sucking story," "fire him": Isaacson, 217; wiretaps: Hersh, Price, chp. 7.

142 Cambodia invasion, Nixon's war, student strikes: R. Dallek, 191, 619, 202; "peace
     with power": Wills, 183.

143 "bums": Ambrose, Triumph, 348; "revolutionary terrorism": R. Dallek, 208; Lincoln
     Memorial: Ambrose, Triumph, 355–57; Hutschnecker: Adam Clymer, "Most Presi-
     dents Had a Counselor," NYT (Sept. 3, 2000), WK3; Patton, "level that goddamn
     country": R. Dallek, 202, 308.

143 "bedeviling": Laird intv. Van Atta, DVAP; confided in his diary: Curtis Tarr journal,
     DVAP; Jack Anderson dartboard: J. Trento, 19.

143–44 Linger: Hersh, Price, 182–83; "stunned": letter, Stephen Linger to Fred Linger,
     "Personal & Confidential," 6–7, JAP; "only guy": Linger intv.; "spilled my guts": Hersh
     intv.

144 "top secret," "until now": JA, "Air Force Turns Rainmaker in Laos," WP (March 18,
     1971), F7; first known: John Noble Wilford, "Scientists Are Critical of Rainmaking
     in War," NYT (July 3, 1972), 2; "very sensitive": report, "Unauthorized Disclosure of
     Classified Defense Information" (April 13, 1971), 1–2, 4, Young #19, NARA.

144 peace talks: JA, "Scant Data Cramps Paris Negotiators," WP (March 22, 1971), D11.

144 "most explosive story": Hersh, Price, 182; Hanoi/Haiphong: JA, "Plan to Bomb
     Haiphong Kept Ready," WP (March 24, 1971), E11.

144–45 Laos/Cambodia/code names: JA, "Pentagon's Messages Beg Denial," *WP* (March 30, 1971), B13.
145 "intelligence," "communiqués": JA, "Victory Talk Smacks of a 1966 Rerun," *WP* (March 6, 1971), D27.
145 "attracted little attention," "extensive investigation," "interrogations": Hersh, *Price*, 182; "bad leak": minutes, Laird staff meeting (April 5, 1971), 12, DVAP; Kissinger staff: JA columns (March/April, 1971), NSC #807, NARA.
145 "intercepted enemy messages": JA, "Intelligence Ills Have Fatal Results," *WP* (April 9, 1971), D15.
145–46 "private messages" to "White House": JA, "U.S. Is Forced to Spy on Saigon," *WP* (April 30, 1971), D19; "distressing" to "tightly held": memo, Dave McManis to Gen. Alexander Haig, "Subject: Jack Anderson" (May 4, 1971), NSC #807, NARA.
146 "really hurt," "enemies abroad": memo, W. Donald Stewart to Martin Hoffman (Jan. 21, 1974), 2, HBP, and statement, W. Donald Stewart (March 17, 1974), 4, HBP; "intelligence goofs": JA, "Intelligence Ills Have Fatal Results," *WP* (April 9, 1971), D15.
146 "cocksuckers" to "goddamn war": R. Dallek, 261; "JACK ANDERSON is a perjurer": CIA note (April 8, 1971), DDA doc. #74, CIAFOIA.
146 "Although" to "source": memo, Dave McManis to Gen. Alexander Haig, "Subject: Jack Anderson" (May 4, 1971), NSC #807, NARA.
146–47 nearly two hundred, "no direct knowledge" to suspicious candidates: report, "Unauthorized Disclosure of Classified Defense Information" (June 21, 1971), 2, 57–58, Young #19, NARA; "crazy" to "hysteria": Sheila Hershow, "To Chase Leaks," *Federal Times* (Oct. 25, 1976), 5.
147 "Anderson's information" to "terminated": report, "Unauthorized Disclosure of Classified Defense Information" (June 21, 1971), 1, 4–5, 108, Young #19, NARA.
148 "bloodhounds": JA, "Pentagon Is Hunting for Leaks Again," *WP* (March 24, 1971), D17; "Keystone Kops": Sheila Hershow, "To Chase Leaks," *Federal Times* (Oct. 25, 1976), 5.
148 "Anderson's columns": Hersh, *Price*, 182, 183.
148–49 "ahead of everybody": JA intv.; "In retrospect": Hersh, *Price*, 183.
149 Pentagon Papers: Rudenstine, *passim*.
149 "made no effort": Dale Van Atta, "The Column Jack Wrote," *Daily Universe* (April 4, 1972), 5, emphasis in original; Ellsberg-Sheehan leak: Rudenstine, 46–47.
149–50 four entire pages: Neil Sheehan, "Vietnam Archive: Pentagon Study Traces 3 Decades of Growing U.S. Involvement," *NYT* (June 13, 1971), 1, 35–38; "doesn't hurt," "*keep out*" (emphasis in original): Rudenstine, 71; Haig, "unconscionable" to "this sort of thing": Prados and Porter, 90, 97, 99, 98.
150 page-one article: Neil Sheehan, "Vietnam Archive: A Consensus to Bomb Developed Before '64 Election, Study Says," *NYT* (June 14, 1971), 1, 30; "bastards": Prados and Porter, 101; "cocksucker," "son of a bitch": WHT #521-9 (June 15, 1971); microfilmed the classified documents: Wells, 398; "gets back" to "goddamn left-wingers": Prados and Porter, 102, 103.
150 "launch an attack": Haldeman, *Diaries*, 365; "statute of limitations" to "our enemies": Prados and Porter, 102, 106; "old man" to "in jail": Dean, *Rehnquist*, 267.
150–51 "immediate and irreparable," "any trace": Prados and Porter, 157, 147; "For the first time": Rudenstine, 106.
151 "indicate the importance": Haldeman, *Diaries*, 366; "one of those fights" to "aid and comfort to the enemy" (emphasis in original): Prados and Porter, 112, 110; "destroy the *Times*": Rudenstine, 121.

151 "A newspaper industry": Ellsberg, 398–99.

151 "energized": Kutler, *Wars*, 111.

Just hours after losing the Pentagon Papers case, the President summoned FBI director J. Edgar Hoover to the Oval Office and instructed him to gather ammunition to prosecute "some of the other people around" Ellsberg. "Well," Hoover replied, "that skunk [Jack Anderson] was at the *Post* and had copies made" of the classified documents. Hoover added that the publisher of *The Washington Post*, fifty-four-year-old Katharine Graham, had "aged terribly" and looked "about 85 years old." "She's a terrible old bag," Nixon replied. Hoover agreed: "She's an old bitch in my opinion." WHT #6-84 (July 1, 1971).

152 "Those sons of bitches" (emphasis in original): Kutler, *Abuse*, 8.

152 "Kill him" to "*That's the way it's done*" (emphasis in original): Kutler, *Abuse*, 9, 10; "our man": Wells, 465.

152–53 bisexual drug-user: Michael Young, "The Devil and Daniel Ellsberg," *Reason* (June 2002), and Hersh, *Price*, 384–85; "Henry had a problem": Haldeman and DiMona, 110; "Every one": Kutler, *Abuse*, 35; "my Jew boy": R. Dallek, 93; "the Jew": Rosen, *Strong Man*, 161; "Jews are born spies": WHT #537-004 (July 5, 1971); "disloyalty": Prados and Porter, 103.

Nixon told aides that "most Jews are disloyal . . . you can't trust the bastards" and that "there's this strange malignancy that seems to creep among them . . . radicalism." As a result, the President believed, Daniel Ellsberg presented "a *marvelous opportunity*" for his old House Un-American Activities Committee to win public acclaim: "Going after all these Jews [is] what's going to charge up an audience. Jesus Christ, they'll be hanging from the rafters." Emphasis in original. Sources for the above: "most Jews": WHT #536-016 (July 3, 1971); "strange malignancy": WHT #537-004 (July 5, 1971); "*marvelous opportunity*": Kutler, *Abuse*, 20.

153 "paranoiac": Kutler, *Wars*, 78; "not going after": Kutler, *Abuse*, 15; "If we can't": Kutler, *Wars*, 78; red-faced desk-pounding: Aitken, *Colson*, 154; "I don't give a damn": Kutler, *Wars*, 108.

153 "horrible things" to "tiger": Kutler, *Abuse*, 15, 8, 14, 13; "beauty of this": www.white housetapes.net/transcript/nixon/you-need-team; Liddy and Hunt: Wells, 8, 16, 474, and Szulc, 134–35.

8: THE ANDERSON PAPERS

155 two million: Christopher Hitchens, "The Case Against Henry Kissinger," *Harper's* (March 2001), 59; "nuclear showdown," "brought the United States": JA and Clifford, 205, 208.

155–56 "Kill three million": Ben Kiernan, "Cost of a Genocide Ignored," *The Australian* (Dec. 5, 2007), 5; a hundred thousand: memo, Harold H. Saunders to Henry Kissinger, "Lunch Ambassador Jha" (May 18, 1971), NSA; ten million: Hitchens, op. cit., 59.

156 "old witch": R. Dallek, 340; that "that bitch, that whore": Reeves, 391.

156 "we don't really have any choice": Hersh, *Price*, 457.

156 U.S.-supplied tanks and aircraft: Van Hollen, 342.

156 "absolute neutrality": Carroll Kilpatarick, "Nixon Vows 'Absolute Neutrality,'" *WP* (Dec. 7, 1971), A12.

156 ban: Van Hollen, 344; "I like the idea": telecon, Nixon/Kissinger (Dec. 4, 1971), NSA; officials warned: Capt. H. N. Kay, Pentagon minutes (Dec. 6, 1971), 6, JAP;

"directive": memo, Al Haig to Henry Kissinger (Jan. 19, 1972), NSA; "We are standing alone": telecon, Bhutto/Kissinger (Dec. 11, 1971), NSA.

157 "no longer abide": JA and Gibson, 179; "nuclear powder keg": JA and Clifford, 211.

157 Seventh Fleet: Zumwalt, 367; "possible rescue": Craig R. Whitney, "Carrier Leaves Vietnam, May Sail to Dacca Area," *NYT* (Dec. 13, 1971), 1, 16; "transparently false": Van Hollen, 356; "pure power play": telecon, Nixon/Kissinger (Dec. 11, 1971), NSA; "put a little pressure": WHT #308-13 (Dec. 22, 1971); "brazen," "bluff": telecon, Laird/Kissinger (Dec. 11, 1971), NSA; "coming off like men," "tough": R. Dallek, 346.

157–58 "as much . . . in daylight": Zumwalt, 367; prominent coverage: Pentagon news summary (Dec. 15, 1971), DVAP; "Pentagon sources": Szulc, 443.

158 "needled," "soul searching," "reluctantly": JA and Gibson, 182; "can't even run": JA intv.; cited in Ellsberg intv. Amy Goodman (April 26, 2006), DemocracyNow.org; "got to decide": Robert Sherrill, "Leaks Follow the Course of Greatest Impact," *NYT* (Jan. 9, 1972), D1.

158–59 first in a series: JA, "Pearson Foresaw U.N. Failures," *WP* (Dec. 13, 1971), C23; "cautious, timid": Jack Rosenthal, "Anderson Ready for Battle with Government," *NYT* (Jan. 6, 1972), 17; "held so closely" to "horoscope": JA and Gibson, 182, 183.

159 "It's very important": WHT #308-13 (Dec. 22, 1971).

159 "I never saw": Whitten intv.; Ziegler deal: Robert Walters, "Anderson Makes It to the Top," *WS* (Jan. 6, 1972), A8.

159–60 "more sensational": JA intv. Gibson; "bore the Kansas city milkman," "baptism by fire": Hume, 95, 92; "censorship curtain" to "*tilt*" (emphasis added): JA, "U.S., Soviet Vessels in Bay of Bengal," *WP* (Dec. 14, 1971), B15; JA, "U.S. Moves Give Soviets Hold on India," *WP* (Dec. 16, 1971), G15.

Privately, Kissinger made other injudicious remarks. He characterized Pakistanis as "sometimes extremely stupid" although "straightforward," unlike Indians, who "are more devious." And he encouraged President Nixon to treat Pakistan's genocidal dictator "with love rather than brutality." Behind his back, Kissinger also complained that U.N. ambassador George H. W. Bush was "an idiot" and berated him to his face for not being more critical of India: "Don't screw it up the way you usually do." The future president replied: "I want a transfer when this is over" to "a nice quiet place like Rwanda." Memos, Harold H. Saunders (Aug. 11 and July 31, 1971), NSA; R. Dallek, 350; telecon, Bush/Kissinger (Dec. 16, 1971), NSA.

160 "secret diplomatic dispatches" to "diversionary action": JA, "U.S. Task Force Didn't Frighten India," *WP* (Dec. 21, 1971), E15; "world stood on the edge": JA, "Why I Blew the Whistle," *Parade* (Feb. 13, 1972), 8.

160 "What do we do": R. Dallek, 347.

160 "The papers": JA, MGR (Dec. 30, 1971), JAP.

161 "that I couldn't possibly": JA and Gibson, 183.

161 "Officials conceded": Benjamin Welles, "U.S. Effort to Aid Pakistan Is Cited," *NYT* (Dec. 31, 1971), A1, 7; ANDERSON STRIKES: "New White House Leaks," *WS* (Jan. 1, 1972), A5.

161 prominent front-page coverage: Sanford J. Ungar, "Secret U.S. Papers Bared," *WP* (Jan. 5, 1972), 1, 8; White House news summary (Jan. 5, 1972), NARA; Hume, 101.

162 "take either my word": AP, "Leak Investigation," Young #19, NARA; "held up several of the documents," "stay on the attack": Hume, 101, 100.

162 news outlets around the world: "White House Papers on Page 1 in London," *WP* (Jan. 6, 1972); Pentagon news summary (Jan. 5–6, 1972), DVAP.

162 "Mocking headlines": Isaacson, 379; "turned Washington," "shock waves": Mark R. Arnold, "Anderson Jars 'Striped-Pants Set,'" *National Observer* (Jan. 15, 1972); ADVISERS LIED, "starker headlines": *Charlotte Observer* (Jan. 7, 1972), cited in Young #18, NARA; "major challenge": Sanford J. Ungar, "Secret U.S. Papers Bared," *WP* (Jan. 5, 1972), 1; "unguided journalistic missile": White, 283; tied up phone lines, "again completely accurate": Young Report, 70, 62; "jolted": Richard Helms, "State of the Agency Address" (June 30, 1972), 7, NSA.

163 "If the Administration": Hume, 92, 99.

163 "very serious-leaks": Stennis hearings (Feb. 6, 1974), 48; "one of the most": Nixon, *RN*, 531.

163 "fun" to "failures": Zumwalt, 366, 365; "even more vivid": Max Frankel, "Official-dom in Action," *NYT* (Jan. 6, 1972), 18; "officials concede": William McGaffin, "U.S. Court Attack on Writer Doubted," *Chicago Daily News* (Jan. 6, 1972), 1.

163 "no security": Orr Kelly and Jeremiah O'Leary, "Anderson Releases Papers," *WS* (Jan. 5, 1972), 1ff.

164 opened up his briefcase, "just in case": Sanford J. Ungar, "Secret U.S. Papers Bared," *WP* (Jan. 5, 1972), A8.

164 "silence the press": JA, *Parade* manuscript draft (ND), 6–7, JAP.

164 "If we had": Mark R. Arnold, "Anderson Jars 'Striped-Pants Set,'" *National Observer* (Jan. 15, 1972).

164–65 "damaging decisions": James Reston, "The Anderson Papers," *NYT* (Jan. 9, 1972), D1; "San Andreas fault": White House news summary (Jan. 6, 1972), 5, NARA; "remarkable series": Tom Wicker, "Laudable Job by Jack Anderson," *NYT* (Jan. 4, 1972), 3; "striking revelations": "South Asian Irony," *NYT* (Jan. 12, 1972), 42; "cynicism": "Tilt," *WP* (Jan. 6, 1972), A16.

165 "stolen our dollars": WH news summary (Jan. 24, 1972), 8, NARA; "Secrecy": cartoon, Pat Oliphant, Los Angeles Times Syndicate (Jan. 19, 1972).

165 "move is part": Paul Scott, "Fulbright May Foster 'Credibility' Challenge," *San Diego Union* (Jan. 14, 1972), B11; "major charge": Haldeman, CD Diaries (Jan. 13, 1972); "really kill": WHT #647-9 (Jan. 13, 1972); "my good friend Joe McCarthy": WHT #314-1 (Jan. 13, 1972).

166 "reliable sources": Robert M. Smith, "White House Took Steps to Stop Leaks Months Before Anderson Disclosures," *NYT* (Jan. 9, 1972), 18; "sources close": Sydney H. Schanberg, "Keating Held Not Unhappy over Pakistan Cable 'Leak,'": *NYT* (Jan. 7, 1972), A3.

166 blame game: Kenneth J. Freed, "Leak Investigation," AP (Jan. 5, 1972); in Young #18, NARA; and Sanford J. Ungar, "House Committee Will Probe Classification of Documents," *WP* (Jan. 6, 1972), A1ff. At the Justice Department, Assistant Attorney General Robert Mardian complained that he "was being beaten over the head for comments on the Anderson leaks" and issued a statement declaring that prosecutors would have "no comment on matters under investigation." "Bob," White House aide David Young pointed out, "that's obviously implying that you *are* investigating it and we have tried to low-key it and avoid saying that. In fact we have had a very straight line all around that we do not comment on Anderson articles . . . We don't want Anderson to get the advantage of saying 'somebody's investigating me.'" Young then informed the President that Mardian had "blown it" by confirming "in a backhanded way" that "Jack Anderson was under investigation by the Justice Depart-

ment," which was "exactly what we didn't want to happen." Young Report, 67–69, NARA.

166 Bush: White House news summary (Jan. 31, 1972), NARA; "vandals": "Ashbrook Asks Probe of Leak of 'State Secrets,'" WS (Jan. 9, 1972), A32; "matter of great concern": "Nixon Acts to End Security Leaks," NYT (Jan. 18, 1972), 12; "don't want to heighten": WHT #648-4 (Jan. 17, 1972); "story is not dying": White House news summary (Jan. 19, 1972), NARA.

166–67 "personal standing": Hersh, Price, 465; "devastated": Ehrlichman, 307, 302; "stop the meetings": memo, Stennis hearings (March 7, 1974), 41; "minutes . . . in German": memo, Jeanne W. Davis to Henry Kissinger, "Minutes of the SRG Meeting" (Jan. 17, 1972), NSA; "it is best": memo, Harold H. Saunders to Henry Kissinger, "Material for Dealing with Jack Anderson" (Jan. 5, 1972), NSC, NARA.

167 "credibility as a briefer is destroyed": WHT #314-1 (Jan. 13, 1972); "moral integrity": telecon, Bill Safire/Kissinger (Jan. 12, 1972), 4, NSA; "staff got him all cranked up": Haldeman, CD Diaries (Dec. 22, 1971).

168 "Nixon palace guard": Kalb and Kalb, 263; "Presidential connivance": telecon, Ehrlichman/Kissinger (Jan. 6, 1972), NSA; "lion-tamer": telecon, Bill Safire/Kissinger (Jan. 12, 1972), 4, NSA; "cut off [the] head": telecon, McNamara/Kissinger (Jan. 4, 1972), NSA; "hang them by their thumbs": telecon, John Roche/Kissinger (Jan. 10, 1972), NSA.

168 "deceitful": Reeves, 98; "out of favor": R. Dallek, 351.

168 "tri-weekly": WHT #643-13 (Jan. 3, 1972).

168–69 "mood swings," "very insecure": Ehrlichman, 307–08; "obsequious excess" to "drunken friend": R. Dallek, 432, 47, 318, 92–93; "maniac": Kalb intv.

169 "ranted," "suicidal," Hutschnecker: R. Dallek, 350, 443–44; "I could think": Ehrlichman, 308.

169 "He's personalizing": WHT #17-28 (Dec. 24, 1971); "warped" to "bullshit": WHT #310-30 (Dec. 26, 1971).

169 "childish tantrums": R. Dallek, 351; "full of the usual charges": Haldeman, Diaries, 393; "overreacting": notes, H. R. Haldeman (Jan. 5 and 10, 1972), Haldeman #45, NARA; "take the press on": Young Report, 75.

170 "Henry started calling": Hersh, Price, 475; "Henry massaged": Ehrlichman, 310.

170 Annenberg's exchange: telecon, Annenberg/Kissinger (Jan. 8, 1972), NSA.

170 "horrible beating": WHT #660-8 (Jan. 29, 1972); "put Henry": WHT #640-3 (Dec. 22, 1971).

To bolster his position in the White House, Kissinger lobbied his former boss, New York governor Nelson Rockefeller, who remained a potent force in Republican politics. In a series of "traumatic" phone calls, Kissinger threatened to resign and complained that the President was not coming to his defense after Anderson's attacks. Rockefeller tried to buck up his protégé: "Henry, you are fabulous. I have been praying night and day that steps are taken to keep your" position in the White House. Rockefeller offered to issue "a strong statement" in support of Kissinger, or to call Nixon directly, but Kissinger vetoed the idea: "If you talk to him, he will think I put you up to it." Instead, Rockefeller contacted Attorney General John Mitchell to suggest that the President "find some excuse to call" Kissinger and reassure him, which Mitchell realized was just a scheme "to use him for leverage." Consumed by self-pity, Kissinger told Rockefeller that "it is a disgrace" that such maneuvers were necessary but allowed, "If I should feel the national interest would be affected by my leaving, I might stay."

Evidently sharing Nixon's belief that Kissinger needed psychological counseling, Rockefeller gingerly brought up the idea with his protégé: "Between you and me, there is a very eminent psychiatrist—a very able one and a friend." But Kissinger ignored the remark and Rockefeller didn't pursue it. (Nixon signaled his decision to forgive Kissinger by suggesting that as a reward for his hard work, the President's bachelor friend Bebe Rebozo should "give Henry all of his phone numbers of girls that are not over thirty.")

Sources for the above quotes: "traumatic": notes, H. R. Haldeman (Jan. 10, 1972), Haldeman #45, NARA; "fabulous" to "eminent psychiatrist": telecon, Rockefeller/Kissinger (Jan. 14, 1972), NSA; "numbers of girls": Haldeman, CD Diaries (Feb. 28, 1972).

171 "it was a good time": note, White House news summary (Jan. 12, 1972), NARA; Kissinger friend: Merry, 475; "positive authority": Joseph Alsop, "U.S. Role in South Asia," *WP* (Jan. 14, 1972), A23; "unchallengeable": Joseph Alsop, "Indian Aims on Pakistan," *WP* (Dec. 27, 1971), A17.

171 Desai: Hersh, *Price*, 450; Wicker, 666; Van Hollen, 346–47, 351; Huque, 189.

171 "one of the few": T. Powers, 263; "these reports": Kissinger, *White House*, 90.

171–72 "intelligence fitted": Hersh, *Price*, 460; "no indication": Benjamin Welles, "Anti-India Remark Is Laid to Kissinger," *NYT* (Jan. 1, 1972), 2.

172 war's aftermath: Blood, 336.

172 "decision to risk": Hersh, *Price*, 462, 457.

172 "Through their misreading": Kux, 307; "From any standpoint": Bundy, 288–89, 291.

172–73 "Indians will": telecon, Nixon/Kissinger (Jan. 11, 1972), 3, NSA; "American decision": Dhar, 184; "Anderson Papers": Kux, 306–07.

173 "function of a secrecy system": Arthur M. Schlesinger, Jr., "The Secrecy Dilemma," *NYT Magazine* (Feb. 6, 1972), 38.

173 celebrity: Hume, 104; William M. Blair, "Man in the News: Modern Muckraker Jack Northman Anderson," *NYT* (Jan. 6, 1972), A17; *Parade* (Feb. 13, 1972), cover; "Jack Anderson Starting in the Press Today," *Cleveland Press* (Jan. 10, 1972), 1; "like the Pentagon": Hendrik Hertzberg, "Getting the Goods," *The New Yorker* (Jan. 22, 1972), 21–23; "skunk": WHT #648-4 (Jan. 17, 1972); "varied network": "A Peek Behind the Scenes," *Newsweek* (Jan. 17, 1972), 14; "networks are vying": Robert Walters, "Anderson Makes It to the Top," *WS* (Jan. 6, 1972), A8.

174 "breach of trust": James J. Kilpatrick, "Leak of Papers to Anderson a Grave Breach," *WP* (Jan. 13, 1972), A9; "not a journalist": WHT #313-22 (Jan. 10, 1972); "persistent sensationalist": "Anderson's Brass Ring," *Time* (Jan. 17, 1972), 34; "bombastic": Phil Casey, "The Mormon Muckraker: Another Side," *WP* (Jan. 16, 1972), G1ff.

Columnist James J. Kilpatrick was in no position to make moral judgments. A decade before attacking Anderson, the rabidly segregationist journalist criticized *The New York Times* for "Negrophilia" and wrote that "the Negro race, as a race, is in fact an inferior race." But despite Kilpatrick's unapologetic belief in white supremacy, he was considered a respectable conservative commentator and his syndicated column was published in *The Washington Post* and other newspapers across the country. Roberts and Klibanoff, 236, 350.

174 "surpassed detractors": Mary McGrory, "The Scribes Turn on Anderson," *WS* (Jan. 16, 1972), C1; "savoring what must be": Mark R. Arnold, "Anderson Jars 'Striped-Pants Set,'" *National Observer* (Jan. 15, 1972).

174 "I didn't get": Robert Sherrill, "Leaks Follow the Course of Greatest Impact," *NYT* (Jan. 9, 1972), D1.

9: SEX, SPIES, BLACKMAIL

175 "beside themselves": Zumwalt, 370; "full-scale investigation": Ehrlichman, 302.

175–76 "hounding": memo, Fred Malek to John Dean (Dec. 15, 1971), "Jack Anderson Article," Haldeman #297, NARA; "Anderson article": memo, Fred Malek to H. R. Haldeman (Dec. 15, 1971), "Progress Report on Leaks Project," Haldeman #297, NARA; "access to the documents": memo, G. Marvin Gentile to David R. Young, "Jack Anderson's Column" (Jan. 4, 1972), Plumbers #18, NARA; freeze-frame images: Robert Gehrke, "CIA Materials Give Look into Attempt to Snuff Out Castro," *Salt Lake Tribune* (June 27, 2007), A4.

176 five copies: memo, David R. Young, "Distribution of Welander Memo" (Dec. 15, 1971), Young #23, NARA; chief suspect: Hersh, *Price*, 470–71, Colodny and Gettlin, 3, 15–20; "no newsman": memo, Donald G. Sanders to Fred Thompson (Dec. 5, 1973), HBP.

177 "easy access": JA and Gibson, 188; befriended: JA intv.; "animus": Radford intv.

177 Empress: JA intv. Gibson; Isaacson, 380.

177 "shit hit the fan": Radford intv.; "If people": Fred Buzhardt, "Report of Investigation" (Jan. 10, 1972), 10, LCP; "did you give": Colodny and Gettlin, 19.

178 "ten times": testimony, Robert Welander, Stennis hearings (Feb. 20–21, 1974), 124–52, 164; "became a crusader": manuscript draft, Elmo Zumwalt, "The Radford Story," 9, EZP.

178 "We decided": Young Report, 12; "very suspicious": Radford intv.; "extreme amount": Fred Buzhardt, "Report of Investigation" (Jan. 10, 1972), 30, 12, LCP; "polygraph makes clear": Haldeman, *Diaries*, 386.

178–79 "son of a bitch" to "hope to do": memo, W. Donald Stewart to Martin Hoffman (Jan. 21, 1974), 1, 3, LCP; statement, W. Donald Stewart, Senate Watergate Committee (Feb. 19, 1974), 68, 40, HBP; statement, W. Donald Stewart (March 14, 1974), 3, 4, LCP.

179–80 "I was afraid": Richard Lamb, "Tale of the Shadow Chaser," *George* (Oct. 1998), 132; "I felt like": Radford intv.; "We can't talk here": Radford intv. Gettlin; "under the seats" to "I won't tell": JA intv.; "Because of my talking": Radford intv.

180–81 "could not recall": Fred Buzhardt, "Report of Investigation" (Jan. 10, 1972), 22–23, LCP; "You are going": Young Report, 16, 27, 26; "undoubtedly": statement, W. Donald Stewart (March 14, 1974), 2, LCP; "out con": statement, W. Donald Stewart (Dec. 31, 1974), 6, LCP; "if he 'confessed'": memo, W. Donald Stewart to Martin Hoffman (Jan. 21, 1974), 3, LCP.

181 "able to pinpoint" to "storehouse of information": WHT #639-30 (Dec. 21, 1971).

181 "If you can't trust": WHT #309-1 (Dec. 24, 1971).

181–82 "the yeoman served" to "exactly the same": WHT #639-30 (Dec. 21, 1971).

182 "He's another Ellsberg" to "didn't do it!": WHT #640-3 (Dec. 22, 1971). Emphasis in original.

182 "This son of a bitch" to "we've got to root out": WHT #640-5 (Dec. 22, 1971).

182 "That Radford" to "has to be shot!": WHT #308-13 (Dec. 22, 1971).

183 try to extract a confession to "or paying him": WHT #641-10 (Dec. 23, 1971); "gross": statement, Colonel Allen Rozsa (Dec. 19, 1971), Young #23, NARA; "bunch of scabs": WHT #648-4 (Jan. 17, 1972).

183 "no apparent motive," "comical": Colodny and Gettlin, 50; "puritanical": JA and Gibson, 225.

183 "Is the yeoman": Ehrlichman calendar (Dec. 21, 1971), Ehrlichman #2, JEP.

183–84 "if there was": Young Report, 38; "after sleeping" to "a lot of these things": WHT #640-5 (Dec. 22, 1971).

184 "Homosexuality destroyed" to "fags": WHT (May 13, 1972) as cited in James Warren, "Nixon on Tape Expounds," *Chicago Tribune* (Nov. 7, 1999).
   The President also opined that "the Catholic church went to hell three or four centuries ago" because of homosexuality. "You know what happened to the popes?" Nixon added. "They were layin' the nuns." In the same conversation, the President complained that "the upper class in San Francisco . . . is the most faggy goddamned thing you could ever imagine . . . I can't shake hands with anybody from San Francisco." Ibid.

184 "Now I think" to "going to find": WHT #640-5 (Dec. 22, 1971).

184 "establish": Hersh, *Price*, 477; "at once" to "Radford": Bob Woodward, "Anderson Slur Said Ordered," *WP* (Oct. 13, 1975), A1, A14.

184–85 "traitor": W. Donald Stewart, "Statement to Senate Armed Services Committee" (March 14, 1974), 3, LCP; "bastard": Radford intv.; "not to see" to "president's order": Bob Woodward, "Anderson Slur Said Ordered," *WP* (Oct. 13, 1975), A1, A14; "homosexual tendencies": memo, David Young to John Ehrlichman, "Interview with Adm. Rembrandt Robinson" (Dec. 27, 1971), 2, Young #24, NARA.

185 "nothing to indicate" to "with the President": transcript, Ehrlichman-Laird phone conversation (Dec. 23, 1971), 1–4, Young #24, NARA.

185 "to check on": Young Report, 44; "tailing Anderson": WHT #308-13 (Dec. 22, 1971); "keeping [Radford] under surveillance": WHT #309-1 (Dec. 24, 1971).

185–86 "obsessive line": Hougan, 69; "best friend," "effeminate," "big manly": Colodny and Gettlin, 468–69; "I could spot": Ehrlichman-Young intv. Adm. Rembrant Robinson (Dec. 27, 1971), 11, Young #24, NARA; "one more polygraph": notes, Fred Buzhardt intv. (Nov. 6, 1975), WSPF; "bullshit": Laird intv.
   The White House ordered a tap on Radford's "effeminate" friend based on the suspicion that he was having an "intimate relationship" with the yeoman. The Nixon aide who directed the investigation, David Young, later suggested to prosecutors that "Anderson was blackmailing Radford because he had learned that Radford was homosexual." Young speculated that "Radford was involved in a homosexual relationship with another military officer—not with Jack Anderson." But no evidence ever surfaced to support that sexual smear, either. Sources for the above: "intimate relationship": statement, W. Donald Stewart (March 14, 1974), 7, LCP; "blackmailing": memo, Carl B. Feldbaum to File, "Subject: Plot Against Jack Anderson" (Oct. 8, 1975), Jaworski/Ruth #1, WSPF, NARA.

186 bulletin board: JA and Gibson, 226, and Seymour M. Hersh, "Nixon's Active Role on Plumbers," *NYT* (Dec. 10, 1973), 30.

187 five thousand pages, "burn bags": Hersh, *Price*, 466–67.

187 "Be careful": Radford intv.

187 "turned out" to "Joint Chiefs": WHT #639-30 (Dec. 21, 1971).

188 "extraordinary account": Ehrlichman, 303; "surreptitiously" to "Admiral Moorer": Colodny and Gettlin, 33 and Appendix B.

188 hard-liner: William F. Jasper, "Admirals Sound the Alarm," *The New American* (March 29, 1999); Adam Bernstein, "Adm. Thomas Moorer Dies," *WP* (Feb. 7, 2004), B7.

188 "confirms": WHT #308-13 (Dec. 22, 1971).

188–89 "And they knew" to "Jesus Christ!": WHT #640-5 (Dec. 22, 1971).

189 "I've got" to "Oh my God": WHT #308-13 (Dec. 22, 1971).

189 "Can him" to "out of here": WHT #639-30 (Dec. 21, 1971).

189 "was the recipient" to "was involved": WHT #639-30 (Dec. 21, 1971).

189 "bunch of shits": Ambrose, *Ruin*, 367.

189 Pentagon's man: Bundy, 581; Colodny and Gettlin, 42–43; Ehrlichman, 304.

189 "I am afraid" to "I would do that": WHT #639-30 (Dec. 21, 1971).

"Is Haig aware of this?" Nixon asked about the military spy ring. The President noted suspiciously that "Haig seems to be the only one who hasn't expressed concern about the spying." White House aide Young added to Nixon's mistrust by informing him that "Haig called in a rage" and threatened that "if there is any way you are suspecting me, I'll have both of your asses before the President tomorrow morning!" Young told the President that Haig slammed down the phone "obviously simmering and pretty uptight on whether [anyone] had said anything which implicated him" in the military spying. According to Ehrlichman, Young was convinced that "Haig constantly sold Henry out to the military" and "probably planted Radford to help the military spy on" Kissinger in the first place. WHT #639-30 (Dec. 21, 1971); Young Report, 48; Ehrlichman, 304. See also Rosen, *Strong Man*, 399.

189 "knows damn well" to "Just let it rot": WHT #308-13 (Dec. 22, 1971).

189–90 "federal offense" to "wouldn't believe it": WHT #639-30 (Dec. 21, 1971) and WHT #308-13 (Dec. 22, 1971).

190 They "*knew*" to "poor substitute": WHT #639-30 (Dec. 21, 1971).

190 "trained" to "out of control": WHT #308-13 (Dec. 22, 1971); "didn't feel too badly": Colodny and Gettlin, 467; "cultivation" to "wastebaskets": Ehrlichman, 304, 310.

191 "get his ass": Mitchell intv. Colodny, LCP.

191 "up to his eyeballs": Mary Gore Dean intv. Colodny, LCP.

191 "use this": WHT #640-5 (Dec. 22, 1971).

191 "Prosecuting is" to "We certainly have Anderson": WHT #639-30 (Dec. 21, 1971).

191–92 "inculpate": memo, David Young to John Ehrlichman, "Items to Discuss with Attorney General" (Dec. 21, 1971), 2, Young #23, NARA; "For obvious": memo, David R. Young to John D. Ehrlichman, "BASIS FOR PROSECUTION OF OUR FAVORITE COLUMNIST" (Jan. 18, 1972), Young #18, NARA; "only two guys" to "bring a newsman in": WHT #314-1 (Jan. 13, 1972).

192 "nail" to "Anderson papers": WHT #647-9 (Jan. 13, 1972); "he's gonna confess" to "gotta be a witness": WHT #648-4 (Jan. 17, 1972); "find something . . . invent something": WHT #647-9 (Jan. 13, 1972).

192 "One piece": WHT #646-2 (Jan. 12, 1972).

In a suggestion of dubious propriety, Nixon urged Agnew to hold a private meeting with Supreme Court justice William Rehnquist, a conservative ally whom the President had recently appointed to the bench, to explore the administration's legal options against journalists like Anderson. "Even though Rehnquist is on the court, there's no reason you can't talk to him," Nixon told his vice president. "You can say that I had asked [and] you're concerned about this and what is his opinion." Nixon added that "Rehnquist may have some damn good ideas" because "he's a first-class brain [and] a level-headed guy." Agnew told the President that he would talk to the justice but it is not known whether such a meeting ever took place. WHT #646-2 (Jan. 12, 1972).

192   welcomed prosecution: WH news summary (Jan. 6, 1972), NARA; WHT #648-4 (Jan. 17, 1972).

192–93 "that bastard" to "find some others": WHT #308-13 (Dec. 22, 1971).

193   "I can see" to "bottle him up?": WHT #640-3 (Dec. 22, 1971).

193   "under wraps" to "death!": WHT #640-5 (Dec. 22, 1971).

193   "gotten to Radford": WHT #643-13 (Jan. 3, 1972).

193   "If my sources": Mark Arnold, "Anderson Jars 'Striped-Pants Set,'" *National Observer* (Jan. 15, 1972); similarly unmistakable: WH news summary (Jan. 6, 1972), 4, NARA; "If the Government": Sanford J. Ungar, "Secret U.S. Papers Bared," *WP* (Jan. 5, 1972), A8; "If they want": Jack Rosenthal, "Anderson Ready for Battle with Government, but Appears Unlikely to Get One," *NYT* (Jan. 6, 1972), 17.

193   "Anderson would obviously": WHT #639-30 (Dec. 21, 1971).

194   "The real sad thing" to "blackmail me" (emphasis in original): WHT #641-10 (Dec. 23, 1971).

194   "out of the water": Thomas B. Ross, "Admiral's Threat Linked to Nixon Closing Spy Case," *Chicago Sun-Times* (Feb. 24, 1974), 1.

194   Moorer: Hersh, *Price*, 473.

195   "if you pursued" to "Hmmph!": WHT #639-30 (Dec. 21, 1971).

195   "If you go after Radford": Laird intv.

195   "I lost more sleep" to "We cannot have it": WHT #639-30 (Dec. 21, 1971).

195   "can't let it get out": WHT #308-13 (Dec. 22, 1971).

195   "See" to "damn thing to do": WHT #640-5 (Dec. 22, 1971).

195   "monumental" to "sweep it under the rug": Haldeman, *Diaries*, 386, 385.

195   "circumstantial evidence": "Transcript of the President's News Conference," *NYT* (Feb. 11, 1972), 16.

196   "beside myself" to "enraged": Kissinger testimony, Stennis hearings (Feb. 6, 1974), 61, 51; "Moorer should be in jail": WHT #310-19 (Dec. 23, 1971); *"ridiculous"* to "keep the lid on it": WHT #17-37 (Dec. 24, 1971), emphasis in original.

196   "You see" to *"what you want"*: WHT #309-1 (Dec. 24, 1971), emphasis added.

196   "had the goods" to "preshrunk": Hersh, *Price*, 476.

196–97 "get counsel" to "we were through": Young Report, 58, 25; "cockier than hell" to "send you up forever": transcript, Laird/Ehrlichman call (Jan. 3, 1972), Ehrlichman #37, NARA.

197   burn any remaining: Radford intv.

197   "time bomb": Nixon, *RN*, 532; "by the balls": letter, W. Donald Stewart to Len Colodny (July 2, 1986), LCP.

197   "Finding out": Radford intv.

197   "Damn" to "Unbelievable": WHT #640-11 (Dec. 22, 1971).

197   "back-channel games": WHT #308-13 (Dec. 22, 1971).

198   "The thing" to "yup": WHT #639-30 (Dec. 21, 1971).

198   "the worst thing about it": WHT #640-3 (Dec. 22, 1971).

10: CAT AND MOUSE

199   "no further leaks": Nixon, *RN*, 532.

199   Japanese rearmament: JA, "Sato Steering Away from the U.S.," *WP* (Jan. 6, 1972), D11; HAVE CHECKED: cables, U.S. Embassy to Secretary of State (Tokyo: Jan. 6 and 7, 1972), NSC #807, NARA.

199 Cambodia: JA, "U.S. Deception on Role in Cambodia," *WP* (Jan. 11, 1972), B11; Israel: JA, "And in Other Secret Memos," *WP* (Jan. 16, 1972), B11; Europe: JA, "Europe First, Laird Tells NATO," *WP* (Jan. 17, 1972), B11; "Congress and the American people": Murray Marder, "State Department Defends Coaching Cambodia on Aid," *WP* (Jan. 12, 1972) A16.

199–200 Saigon: JA, "Cables Show Doubletalk on VC," *WP* (Jan. 21, 1972), D15; "suppressed study": JA, "Millions Wasted in Viet Pacification," *WP* (Jan. 22, 1972), D31; "classified reports": JA, "U.S. Troops Warned on Viet Civilians," *WP* (Jan. 28, 1972), F11; "intelligence reports": JA, "U.S. Losing War, Hanoi Said to Feel," *WP* (Feb. 1, 1972), B11; "I continue": UPI (Jan. 5, 1972).

200 "muddy the waters": JA intv.; "great volume": Young Report, 98; "publish data": W. Donald Stewart, "Memorandum for the Record" (April 30, 1974), LCP; "milked these leaks": Zumwalt, manuscript draft, "The Radford Story," 9, EZP.

200 seventy-three of his columns: R. Powers, 263; "cauterized": Richard Helms, "Director's State of the Agency Address" (June 30, 1972), 7, NSA.

200 Kremlin bugs: JA, "CIA Eavesdrops on Kremlin Chiefs," *WP* (Sept. 16, 1971), F7, and JA and Gibson, 238–39.

201 "blew our best intelligence source": Laurence Stern, "U.S. Tapped Top Russians' Car Phones," *WP* (Dec. 5, 1973), A1, 16; muckraker insisted: JA and Gibson, 238–39.

201 "As the direct result": Liddy, 207.

201 "had been shaken": Eisenhower, 326, 325; "doing a lot of thinking," "dope, "distorted view": Haldeman, CD Diaries (Jan. 14, 1972); "Anderson's guy," "time bomb": Haldeman notes (Jan. 14, 1972), Haldeman #45, NARA.

201–02 "never a leak": "Transcript of the President's Address," *NYT* (Jan. 26, 1972), 10; "amazingly well-kept secret": WHT #19-89 (Jan. 25, 1972); "I wouldn't do it": WHT #19-40 (Jan. 23, 1972); "afraid that Jack Anderson": Bob Woodward, "Hunt Told Associates of Orders to Kill Jack Anderson," *WP* (Sept. 21, 1975), 14.

202 Bob Hope, "Teutonic jokes": telecons, Herbert Klein/Kissinger (Jan. 20, 1972) and Ray Price/Kissinger (Jan. 26, 1972), NSA; Nixon cameo: Hoyt and Leighton, 156; "good humor": transcript, Nixon press conference (Feb. 10, 1972), 13–14, Young #18, NARA.

The President eventually decided that "these Anderson papers" are "a Washington story primarily" and that while "we've taken some heat," ultimately "nobody gives a goddamn about India and Pakistan" because they are so far away and filled with "such miserable people." WHT #644-14 (Jan. 10, 1972).

202 "I would like" to "about it": WHT #643-13 (Jan. 3, 1972); "Lay off": Ehrlichman, 309.

203 "too risky": Young Report, 99; Mitchell suggested: Ehrlichman, 306; "Nixon apparently feared": Hersh, *Price*, 478.

203 "pinning the whole thing on Anderson": Ehrlichman intv. Colodny, LCP.

203 "Anderson had planted an informant": deposition, W. Mark Felt (Nov. 14, 1977), 19, *JA v. RN*; "President was gravely concerned" and other details of Radford bugging: FBI memo, T. J. Smith to E. S. Miller (June 14, 1973), "Charles Edward Radford II," JAP.

204 "would know" to "learn a few things": WHT #639-30 (Dec. 21, 1971).

204 "first person [Radford] called": FBI memo, Tom Bishop to M. A. Jones (Jan. 26, 1972), "Meeting with the Director," 6, JAP; "Radford had sounded very worried": Ehrlichman, 308; "got a little code worked out": WHT #317-6 (Jan. 24, 1972).

204 Radford finances: Young Report, 15, and Fred Buzhardt, "Report of Investigation" (Jan. 10, 1972), 9, 11, 20, LCP; "only place Radford": Welander intv. Gettlin, LCP.

205 Anderson confided: JA intv. Gibson; "naïve," "payoff": JA intv.; nine thousand dollars: Oliva Anderson intv.

205 discontinued this eavesdropping: FBI memo, T. J. Smith to E. S. Miller (June 14, 1973), "Charles Edward Radford II," JAP; "At that point": Ehrlichman intv. Colodny, LCP.

206 Mudhen: JA and Gibson, 236.

206 "opinionated, self-righteous": memo, Joseph C. Goodwin to CIA Director (July 10, 1967), 2, CIAFOIA; "first-class liar": memo to Chief, Security Research Staff (July 25, 1967); memo to Chief, Security Research Staff (Sept. 7, 1967)—all in CIAFOIA.

206 twenty-five-page study, "extreme sensitivity": "Project Mudhen Briefing Folder" (ND), 2, 23, JAP; "assumed names": memo, "At Washington, D.C." (Jan. 5, 1972), JAP; "flamboyant attitude": memo, "Project MUD HEN" (Feb. 24, 1972), JAP.

206 "connections with the *New York Times*": memo to Special Agent in Charge, "Subject: Project Celotex II" (March 9, 1972), 1, JAP; "my paper boy": JA and Gibson, 237.

      Upon learning that Anderson had landed a book contract, the CIA spooks reached an equally obvious conclusion: "It is believed that this work is to be published by a New York City concern, further identity unknown." Memo to Special Agent in Charge, "Subject: Project Celotex II" (March 9, 1972), 1, JAP.

206–07 sixteen operatives: memo, "Project Mud Hen" (March 9, 1972), 1, JAP; telephoto lenses: deposition, Howard Osborn (Nov. 16, 1977), 114, *JA v. RN*.

207 "operational cryptonyms": memo to Special Agent in Charge, "Project MUD HEN" (March 3, 1972), JAP; "BRANDY," photos, maps: "Project Mudhen Briefing Folder" (ND), JAP.

207 Statler Hilton: memo, "SURVEILLANCES," 2, CIAFOIA.

207 Jack Anderson's bedtime: "Project Mudhen Briefing Folder," 6–7; art museum, "two unidentified Negroes": CIA Operations Log, "Celotex/Phase II" (March 4 and March 20, 1972), JAP.

207 "careless driver": memo, "Project MUD HEN" (Feb. 24, 1972); "routine pattern": CIA memo, "Joseph Carroll Spear" (Nov. 24, 1972), JAP; "boring as hell": Spear intv. Gibson.

208 "our government is the best in the world": memo, "Project MUD HEN" (March 30, 1972), 4, JAP.

208 *60 Minutes*: memo, "Project MUD HEN" (March 30, 1972), JAP; "caravan of cars": JA and Gibson, 237.

208 "documented evidence": memo, "BRANDY Audio Capabilities" (ND), JAP; "in possession," "counter-surveillance": memo, "Project MUD HEN" (March 15, 1972), JAP.

208 "no explanation": JA and Gibson, 240.

209 "loitering" and "taste of his own medicine": JA and Gibson, 233, 235, 236; "garbage on the doorstep": Brindle intv.

209–10 "same as going": notes, Robert Mardian (April 5, 1972), RMP; "If Mardian's investigating": Sanford J. Ungar, "Bare U.S. Papers on Pakistan War," *New York Post* (Jan. 5, 1972), 5.

210 "What the CIA didn't know": JA and Gibson, 236.

210 "We drove around": K. Anderson, Neider, Bruch, Oliva Anderson. intvs.
210 "On 27 March": memo, "Project MUD HEN Summary of Significant Activities from 27 March–2 April 1972," JAP.

  Actually, the "two young females" who waved at the CIA operatives were Anderson's teenage son Kevin and another long-haired male friend. K. Anderson intv.
211 "copying down the license": memo, "Project MUD HEN Summary of Significant Activities from 3 April–9 April 1972," JAP; "failed to establish": memo, CIA summary of Project Mudhen for Church Committee (ND), JAP.
211 "CIA farce": JA, MGR (Nov. 19, 1975), JAP; "skulk around the bazaars": JA, "Being Spied on Has Benefits of Sorts," WP (Jan. 31, 1975), E17; "high, mocking theater": Harringon, 44.
212 Jack Anderson lawsuit: D. Anderson, 238–40, 255; release many files: Timothy S. Robinson, "CIA Elaborately Tracked Columnist," WP (May 4, 1977), A1.
212 "not general policy" to "don't recall" (emphasis added): deposition, Richard Helms (Dec. 6, 1977), 99, 46, 106, 47, 72, JA v. RN; "daily basis": deposition, Howard Osborne (Nov. 16, 1977), 93, JA v. RN.
212 "Bullshit!": JA intv.; "anathema": Hougan, 87.
212 "These guys": Whitten intv.

11: BROTHERS

214–15 "make a million" to "super-achiever": Ehrlichman, 170–74, 179.
215 "Having gone": Maheu and Hack, 215; shady financial deals: Drosnin, 439; "playing the big shot": Ehrlichman, 171, 173.
215 "His denial" to "the Government": Ehrlichman, 174.
215 "I don't want to use Hoover": Gentry, 625; "really big deals": Ehrlichman, 176–77.
216 newsman dining: Terry Lenzner, "Gemstone Plan" (ND), 6, SWC; bribed a hotel bellman: Trento intv.
216 "Nixon never forgot": JA and Gibson, 219.
216 "Don must not get": WHT #661-1 (Jan. 31, 1972); "protect the President's interests": Ehrlichman, 183, 185.
216–17 "Jesus Christ" to "You don't talk to 'em": WHT #661-1 (Jan. 31, 1972).
217 "cannot allow": Haldeman notes (Feb. 7, 1972), Haldeman #45, NARA.
217 "latest horror story" (emphasis added): Haldeman, Diaries, 407.
217 "sniffing around the Hughes trough": JA manuscript, untitled chp., 10, JAP.
218 "sent a reporter out to the coast" to "Goddamn Don": WHT #319-11 (Feb. 7, 1972).
218 "throwing [my] name" to "mak[ing] an ass": WHT #321-8 (Feb. 9, 1972).
218 "I'm gonna" to "lie low": WHT #661-1 (Jan. 31, 1972).
218 "irrepressible": JA, "Nixon Puts an Eye on His Brother," WP (Feb. 16, 1972), D7.
219 "I realized": JA intv.
219 Gordon on their payroll: G. Anderson intv.; Gordon actively solicited, fired: JA and Whitten intvs.; Maxine Cheshire, "The Muckraker and the Entrepreneur," WP (May 25, 1972), C1; "Jack was very upset": Mitchell intv.
220 black sheep: JA, G. Anderson, K. Anderson, T. Anderson, W. Anderson, Bruch, Jorgensen, Fritsch intvs.
220 "threatening telephone calls": FBI memo (June 7, 1966), JA FBIFOIA; death threats: JA, G. Anderson, K. Anderson intvs.; "saddest part": JA intv.

220 "a flurry of Administration favors": JA manuscript, "Tailfins," 2–3, 7, JAP.
221 "known for his closed mouth": JA manuscript, untitled chp., 10, 11, and "Tailfins," 3, JAP.
221 "siphoned off": JA, MGR (Aug. 6, 1971), JAP; not spent or disclosed: Morton Mintz, "Nixon, Testimony in Conflict," WP (Oct. 28, 1973), A3; "Everyone called it": Drosnin, 323; illegal donation or gift: John Herbers, "Nixon Backs Move by Rebozo on Gift," NYT (Oct. 18, 1973), 32.
221 "wouldn't tolerate his brother": JA intv. Gibson.
221 hundred-dollar bills, manila envelopes: Drosnin, 366, 398.
222 "insure favorable treatment": memo, Terry Lenzner to Sen. Sam Ervin, "Hughes-Rebozo Summary" (ND), 3, SWC "camouflage": Maheu and Hack, 205; Maheu's attorney: Maheu intv.; paperwork over dinner: Howard Kohn, "Strange Bedfellows," Rolling Stone (May 20, 1976), 84; "I am willing": Drosnin, 47, 309.
222 "appeared to receive": Dash, 203.
222 "documentary evidence": JA, MGR (Jan. 24, 1972), JAP; "siphoned": JA and Gibson, 218.
222–23 "Top Secret": memo, H. R. Haldeman (ND), Hughes-Rebozo #804, WSPF; "goddamned Hughes thing": WHT #317-6 (Jan. 24, 1972); "very discreetly": memo, John Ehrlichman to John Dean (Jan. 25, 1972), Hughes-Rebozo #460, NARA; "Don't deny it": Drosnin, 438.
223 "payments coincided": JA, "Senators Eye Hughes-Rebozo Dealings," WP (Oct. 9, 1973), B15.
223 "aroused . . . panic": Lukas, 179; "anticipate new allegations": Ouedes, 360; "hammered": memo, Dick Hannah to Howard R. Hughes (Feb. 15, 1974), 2, JAP.
223 President's private expenses: Lukas, 367–68.
　　As early as 1971, "a troubled White House source" told Anderson that "Rebozo was collecting cash contributions as 'walking around money' for the President." According to Anderson's informant, "no written records were kept" but Nixon "sometimes would acknowledge the contributions by telephoning the donors." Unable to corroborate the allegation, the columnist forwarded it to Senate Democrats, whose investigators issued subpoenas and eventually nailed down documentation. JA, MGR (May 16, 1974), JAP.
223 "tin box": Haldeman and DiMona, 21–22.

12: "DESTROY THIS"
225 "Remember 1960": Lukas, 112, 139, 143.
225 Contributors: Lukas, 126–27, 129, 140; Diederich, 89; Summers, Arrogance, 395–97. "Anybody who": Reeves, 462–63.
226 ITT background: Sampson, passim; Schoenberg, passim; largest proposed merger: Curt Matthews, "Giant ITT Merger Spawns Election-Year Controversy," WP (March 2, 1972), A4.
226 "Does ITT" to "deal is over": Reeves, 324; Sequoia: Rosen, Strong Man, 187.
226 "hit Geneen:" Dean, Blind, 53.
227 "sudden largesse," "lure": JA and Clifford, 40; "aura of a possible scandal": JA, "Aura of Scandal," WP (Dec. 9, 1971), L15; "more rumination": JA and Gibson, 195.

227 "personal and confidential": memo, D. D. Beard to W. R. Merriam, "San Diego Convention" (June 15, 1971), Ehrlichman #15, NARA.

227–28 "single most incriminating": Hume, 107; "Emerging eight months": Sampson, 202; "smoking gun": JA and Gibson, 195.

228 "Holy shit!": Hume intv.; "unlined, guileless": JA and Clifford, 49.

228 "I ruled out": Hume, 113.

229 "My files": Hume, 114–16; "dance a jig": Hume intv.; two-hour interview, "poor girl": notes, Robert Mardian, "Dr. Liszka" (March 3, 1972), Kleindienst #14, RMP; "ordered" to "lay off": Hume, 118–23.

230 "another Anderson special": Reeves, 460; "highly incriminating": JA, "Secret Memo Bares Mitchell-ITT Move," WP (Feb. 29, 1972), B11; "outright lie": JA, "Kleindienst Accused in ITT Case," WP (March 1, 1972), B15; "abruptly settled": JA, MGR (March 2, 1972), JAP.

230 "lie [his] way out": JA, MGR (March 3, 1972), JAP; "aiming their blows": Sampson, 213–41.

230 "I've got to": Kleindienst, 102.

230–31 "lobbed": Dean, Blind, 52; "obviously very damaging": memo, Charles Colson to David Shapiro, "Howard Hunt Work Assignments" (April 18, 1973), 3, CCP; "cluster bomb": Cohan, 122; "news herd": Klein, 231.

231 handed out copies: "Columnist Releases ITT Memo," WP (March 2, 1972), A5, and "Text of Memorandum," NYT (March 3, 1972), 20; "shock waves": Woodward, 8; "suspicion": Hugh Sidey, "The Presidency," Life (March 31, 1972), 12; "nemesis": WH news summary (March 14, 1972), 9, #39, NARA; Sherman Adams: Clark Mollenhoff, "Watch on Washington" (March 19, 1972); "blustery": Fred P. Graham, "Maybe So, but Who Will Believe It?" NYT (March 5, 1972), E2; "well-known dealer": "The ITT Affair," Time (March 13, 1972).

231–32 "liar," "Tea Pot Dome": Kleindienst, 103; reopen: Spencer Rich, "Kleindienst Is Seeking New Hearing," WP (March 1, 1972), A1; "very close": Kleindienst intv. Rosen; "full confidence": memo, "Anderson Talk at Georgetown" (March 24, 1972), Kleindienst #14, RMP; "Sir Galahad": Dean, Blind, 52.

232 "ace up his sleeve": Hume, 136; "tactical disaster": Nixon, RN, 582.

232 protracted: Kleindienst, 104; "dress rehearsal": JA and Gibson, 193.

232–33 "want to be fair": Hume, 134; "What this meant": JA and Clifford, 70; "Jack, now" to "back-page news": JA and Gibson, 199; "Measuring," JA and Clifford, 70; "saccharine": JA intv. Gibson; "fair man": JA and Gibson, 199.

233 "I told senators": JA and Clifford, 69.

233 "many sacks," "looks very suspicious": Sanford J. Ungar, "ITT Shredded Files," WP (March 17, 1972), A1; "goddamn paper-shredding": Burns, 240–42; "might have been a lot of others": Sanford J. Ungar, "ITT Executive Denies He Got Beard Memo," WP (April 11, 1972), A7; "worst presentation": JA and Clifford, 97.

233 "Hell": WHT #688-18 (March 18, 1972).

234 "perhaps understandable": "The Thickening ITT Imbroglio," Time (March 27, 1972); "security precautions": Time, "The Square Scourge of Washington" (April 3, 1972).

234 "I told [them]": Hume, 196.

234 "public relations contest": Hume, 158.

234 "perfect stage": JA and Gibson, 199.

235 "Cronkite said": White House news summaries (March 3–8, 1972), Dean #43, NARA; "playing us up": JA intv. Gibson.

235 "explosion": WHT #321-31 (March 8, 1972).

235 "But the problem": WHT #677-5 (March 6, 1972).

235 "too much": Haldeman, *Diaries*, 437.

235 "I do not want": WHT #678-4 (March 6, 1972).

235 "Goddammit": WHT #685-3 (March 14, 1972).

235 "Dita Beard had": WHT #677-5 (March 6, 1972).

235 "just harassed": WHT #679-1 (March 7, 1972).

235 "Do we have anything": WHT #692-7 (March 23, 1972).

236 "The President's men": Lukas, 183; "flag-waving": Brodie, 476.

236 "nail Anderson": Dean, *Blind*, 320; "stole": memo, "Questions and Answers for Jack Anderson," Dean #43, NARA, and memo, "Kleindienst Nomination—ITT hearings," Kleindienst #14, RMP.

237 "finish Kleindienst off": Hume, 176; "hearings needed now": JA and Clifford, 94, 69.

237 "blotted with falsehood": JA testimony, ITT hearings, 392, 396, 403; "sedate hearing room": "Slugging It Out over the ITT Affair," *Time* (March 20, 1972).

237 "Are you a lawyer": JA testimony, ITT hearings, 404, 402; "mediocre": Kutler, *Wars*, 147.

238 "Conventions" to "eyesight": JA testimony, ITT hearings, 405, 406; laughter, pornographic: Hume, 173, 167; skewered: Gibbons, 140.

238 "irresponsible": Fred P. Graham, "Witness Disputes Mitchell Denial," *NYT* (March 11, 1972), 13; "full responsibility": JA testimony, ITT hearings, 428.

238 "What is the name": JA testimony, ITT hearings, 449.

239 "Jack said": Hume intv.; "remained in contact": "Jack Anderson Looks at Muskie, ITT, U.S. Secrets," *Philadelphia Bulletin* (April 30, 1972), 3.

239 "Did you pay": JA testimony, ITT hearings, 449–50.

239 "sharp rebukes": Sanford J. Ungar, "No Nixon Role in ITT Case," *WP* (March 10, 1972), 12; "only in retrospect": Spear intv. Gibson.

239 "Was Anderson an effective": WHT #321-31 (March 8, 1972).

239 "keep Anderson's testimony going": WHT #682-9 (March 10, 1972).

240 Kleindienst called: Haldeman, *Diaries*, 428; "wild charges": notes, H. R. Haldeman, "Kldst" (March 9, 1972), Haldeman #45, NARA.

240 "outrageous witch-hunt": WHT #682-9 (March 10, 1972) and Kleindienst statement draft (ND), Kleindienst #14, RMP.

240 "just skunking them": JA intv.

240 "That fellow's": WHT #682-9 (March 10, 1972).
   Anderson "was awfully jumpy" when denying under oath that he paid informants, Colson told the President, so "my suspicion" is that "a fellow who overhears conversations and feeds them to Anderson, gives him leads, could have been on his payroll." Colson was correct, but the Nixon administration never proved it. Anderson also apparently committed perjury during his Senate testimony by denying that he surreptitiously recorded conversations, which his legman Joe Trento said he had observed two years earlier. But Nixon's men never discovered this compromising fact, either. WHT #688-18 (March 18, 1972) and Trento intv.

240–41 "proved to be": Louis M. Kohlmeier, "Testimony in Deepening ITT Antitrust Case Links Controversy Directly with Nixon," *WSJ* (March 10, 1972), A1; "whatever reputations": Morley Safer, transcript, *60 Minutes* (March 12, 1972), 8.

241   Sherlock Holmes: Cartoon, Jeff MacNeely, *Charlotte Observer* (March 18, 1972), editorial page.

241   "Kennedy and Anderson": WHT #688-18 (March 18, 1972); "conspiring," "conspiracy": WHT #682-9 (March 10, 1972).

241   "political conspiracy": letter, Sen. Marlow Cook to Sen. James Eastland (March 11, 1972), MCP, and Sanford J. Ungar, "White House Runs ITT Counterattack," *WP* (March 18, 1972), A10; RNC drafted speeches: JA, "Investigators Trailing Columnist," *WP* (March 23, 1972), G13; "yellow journalism," "gossip-monger": WH news summaries (March 10 and 15, 1972), #39, NARA; "Coming from": JA manuscript, "1972," 9–10, JAP.

241   "You got to": WHT #21-68 (March 14, 1972).

241   "smear-a-day campaign": Sanford J. Ungar, "ITT Shredded Files," *WP* (March 17, 1972), A16.

241   "Just continue": WHT #22-13 (March 24, 1972).

241   secretly huddled: memo, Paul Hoeber, "Office Interview with Fred Fielding" (Sept. 27, 1973), 2, WSPF.

241   "programming," "press release": Mardian diary (March 30 and 12, 1972), Kleindienst #14, RMP.

241   "prepared a number of items": FBI letter, E. S. Miller to Mr. Baker (March 5, 1973), 2, "Confirmation-Gray" #27, WSPF; statement, Charles Colson, "Given to FBI" (May 16, 1973), CCP.

241–42   "shaken the confidence": "Muskie to Disclose Donors," *WP* (March 12, 1972), A1; "passion for justice": WH news summary (March 14, 1972), 20, #39, NARA; "egregious": Steven V. Roberts, "Official Sues I.T.T.," *NYT* (March 21, 1972), 22; Sanford J. Ungar, "New Note Revealed by ITT," *WP* (March 21, 1972), A7; "little Pat," WH news summary (March 21, 1972), 9, #39, NARA.

243   "Day after day": Nixon, *RN*, 582; "cancel his press conference": Haldeman, *Diaries*, 427.

243   "Rumsfeld argued": Haldeman, CD Diaries (March 13, 1972).

243   "hit 'em" to "on the attack": WHT #682-2 (March 10, 1972).
        Treasury Secretary Connally, who had already shaken down the dairy industry for a seven-figure donation to Nixon's reelection campaign, told the President that the ITT case was surprising—not because of the bribery allegations but because Nixon's point men didn't demand more money from ITT: "I was thinking, 'why'd he settle the case for a [six-figure] contribution?'" Connally asked Nixon. Connally was subsequently indicted but acquitted of taking a bribe in the dairy industry case. Richard Severo, "John Connally of Texas, a Power in 2 Political Parties, Dies at 76," *NYT* (June 16, 1993), A1, and WHT #682-2 (March 10, 1972).

243   "goddamn media!": WHT #685-10 (March 14, 1972).

243   "anti-us": WHT #682-9 (March 10, 1972).

243   "attack the attackers": Haldeman, *Diaries*, 427.

243   White House list: memo, L. Higby to John Dean (March 30, 1972), Dean #41, NARA; "now is the time": Haldeman, *Diaries*, 429–30.

244   "panic sessions": Hume, 151; "As we": Dean, *Blind*, 53.

244   Beard background: Michael Kernan and Dorothy McCardle, "Dita Beard," *WP* (March 14, 1972), B1, 6; Kentucky's ex-governor: Hume, 159–61; "distorted" to "sad situation": JA and Clifford, 98–99.

244–45 "chatty hairstylist": JA and Gibson, 200; "implication": JA and Clifford, 122; lesbian affair: Warren intv.; "see if we could": Dean, *Blind*, 56.

245 "Anderson vulnerability," "dynamite": Haldeman notes (March 14 and 16, 1972), Haldeman #45, NARA; Mardian assigned, "so vivid": memo, John L. Martin to Robert C. Mardian (March 14 and 17, 1972), Kleindienst #14, RMP, and Colson deposition, *JA v. RN* (Nov. 22, 1977), 72, 95–96, CCP.

245 "I don't want": Hume, 186; Hume intv.

245 "Are they" to "under oath": WHT #688-18 (March 18, 1972).

245 "possibility of impeaching" to "bad witness": WHT #683-20/#684-1 (March 13, 1972).

245–46 "share some facts": statement, Sen. Marlow W. Cook (March 14, 1972), Dean #43, NARA; "all but said": Dean, *Blind*, 56.

246 "You know" to "that one": WHT #21-68 (March 14, 1972).

In the midst of discussing ITT—apropos of nothing except evidently the homosexuality that Nixon always associated with the Hiss case—the President said to Colson out of the blue, "We oughtta call on some State Department people and see if they're homosexual. Get into that." "Sir?" Colson asked in seeming disbelief. "Maybe we ought to have a committee, then, to open that up on some State Department career people and see whether they're homosexual," Nixon repeated. "I can tell you that [many] are," the President added. "I wouldn't be surprised," Colson agreed, recovering his footing: "Many people [there] certainly seem that way." WHT #688-18 (March 18, 1972).

246 "I wish" to "so is Hume": WHT #688-18 (March 18, 1972).

246–47 Beard and Ginn, "ten-foot pole," Cook apology: Hume, 185–88; witnesses: affidavits, JA, Opal Ginn, Milton Pitts, and Barbara E. Higgins (March 17, 1972), Dean #41 and #43, NARA; "Cook was furious": Dean, *Blind*, 56.

247 "very important" to "bought off": WHT #323-33 (March 17, 1972).

247 "He wasn't": Mardian intv. Rosen; other Colson forgeries: Lukas, 84–85.

13: FROM BURLESQUE TO GROTESQUE

249 "going to jail": note, Robert Mardian "Conversation with Louie Nunn" (March 6, 1972), Kleindienst #14, RMP; subpoena: JA and Clifford, 97; "Where I am going": Fred P. Graham, "I.T.T. Lobbyist in Hospital," *NYT* (March 5, 1972), 26; "The fact": Hume, 150–51.

249–50 "What they want" to "destroying them": WHT #682-9 (March 10, 1972).

250 "My view" to "typical thing": WHT #678-4 (March 6, 1972).

250 "Does she hate": WHT #688-18 (March 18, 1972); "If we could": WHT #682-9 (March 10, 1972).

250 "friends wouldn't reject" to "complicity": note, Charles Colson, "Reasons for Suspicion re: Dita Beard Memo" (ND), CCP; "perpetrated [a] hoax": memo, Charles Colson, "Circumstances Surrounding Howard Hunt's Interview of Dita Beard" (June 13, 1972), 2, CCP.

250 "we don't want you traced": Hunt, *Undercover*, 199.

250 "very eerie": Bob Woodward and Carl Bernstein, "Hunt Linked to Dita Beard Challenge," *WP* (Feb. 21, 1973), A1, 21.

250–51 "disheveled": Hunt, *Undercover*, 201, 204; "involvement" to "then collapse": memo, E. Howard Hunt, "Meetings with Mrs. Dita Beard" (March 17, 1972), CCP; "Whether she": Haldeman and DiMona, 152.

251 "Christmas bonus": Hunt, *Spy*, 199; "She's lying": Dean, *Blind*, 56.

251 "She's in bad shape" to "Mr. President": WHT #688-18 (March 18, 1972).

251 "impending coronary": JA and Clifford, 97; no evidence: "2 Question Dita Beard Heart Ills," *WP* (April 19, 1972), A6.

251–52 "ploy" to "scared to death of it": WHT #688-18 (March 18, 1972).

252 "Isn't one woman": Clymer, 191.

252 "I have" to "damn good idea": WHT #21-68 (March 14, 1972).

252 "She'll collapse": WHT #688-18 (March 18, 1972).

252 "Mrs. Beard" to "how to do it": WHT #692-7 (March 23, 1972).

252–53 posed in a nightgown: Anthony Ripley, "Senators Laughing Before Mrs. Beard's Attack," *WP* (March 27, 1972), A22; "alternately sucked": Kennedy, 326–27; "I want this committee": Sanford J. Ungar, "Collapse Ends Quiz by Panel," *WP* (March 27, 1972), A18; "hoax," "forgery": statement, Dita Beard (ND), Kleindienst #14, RMP.

253 "They all thought": Shanahan intv.; "salty": Art Buchwald, "Awards for Some Other Performances of the Year," *WP* (April 13, 1972), C1; "harbinger": Fred P. Graham, "Lobbyist Suffers a Heart Seizure," *NYT* (March 27, 1972), 22; Republican activist: Fred P. Graham, "Lobbyist's Lawyer Accused Anderson," *NYT* (March 28, 1972), A24; "near" to "get someone": statement, David W. Fleming (March 27, 1972), Dean #43, NARA.

The original draft of Beard's rebuttal was stored in the files of White House counsel Dean, along with a cover note from its author asking "the P[resident]—is this inclusive enough?" In other words, Beard's statement repudiating her memo was submitted ahead of time to President Nixon, who evidently approved her denial word for word despite his stated conviction that Beard did indeed write the memo herself. Note to the President from Robert F. Bennett (ND), Dean #41 & 43, NARA.

253 "At last": Dean, *Blind*, 58.

254 Four other witnesses: Fred P. Graham, "No Final Verdict," *NYT* (April 23, 1972), E1; "memo was hers": note, Robert Mardian (March 26, 1972), Kleindienst #14, RMP; "seemed at best peculiar": "The Thickening ITT Imbroglio," *Time* (March 27, 1972).

254 "scrambled": Dean, *Blind*, 57; "ITT's transformation": JA and Gibson, 205.

254 medical gown: Hume, 237; "ground rules": transcript, *60 Minutes* (April 2, 1972), 2, 4–5.

254 "pro-ITT": JA and Clifford, 102; "general derision": Haldeman and DiMona, 152; "vaudeville": script, Nicholas von Hoffman, "Spectrum," CBS Radio (April 1, 1972); FROM BURLESQUE: "The ITT Affair," *WP* (March 28, 1972), A18.

254–55 "only explanation": Sampson, 226; "stupidest thing": Hume, 199; "fun brandishing": JA and Clifford, 107.

255 "Now, Anderson" to "said no": WHT #688-18 (March 18, 1972).

255 "The plan": Haldeman, CD Diaries (March 17, 1972).

255 "pilfered": memo, Ken Khachigian to Fred Fielding (March 30, 1972), Dean #43, NARA.

256 "discrediting Anderson" to "after Anderson": WHT #688-18 (March 18, 1972).

256 "sent to enlist": Dean, *Blind*, 54, 55.

256 feces: V. Stewart intv.

256–57 "Lower than" to "send it over": Dean, *Blind*, 55.

257 "sunk": JA and Gibson, 206.

257 "drag," "authentic?": WH news summaries (March 18 and 27, 1972), #40, NARA; "In the past": JA manuscript, "1972," 10, JAP; "seriously contended": Tom Wicker, "More Equal Protection," *NYT* (March 28, 1972), 43.

257–58 voluntarily given: JA and Clifford, 125; "principal piece," "discourage funny business": Hume, 204, 205; "His permission" to "outrageous": WHT #21-128 (March 21, 1972).

258 "more than a gut" to "nigger in the woodpile": WHT #21-62 (March 13, 1972).

258 "cursory" to "ass": WHT #21-68 (March 14, 1972).

258 "flooded": Dean, *Blind*, 57; "persistent": Felt, 173; sneaked: memo, Charles Colson, "Circumstances Surrounding Howard Hunt's Interview of Dita Beard" (June 13, 1972), 4, CCP.

259 "nervous": Dean, *Blind*, 57; phony: Walter C. McCrone Associates, "Microanalytical Study of Beard Memorandum" (March 27, 1972) and Pearl L. Tytell, "Report on Questioned Document" (March 27, 1972), Box B26, PCP.

259 "probably authentic": deposition, W. Mark Felt (Nov. 14, 1977), *JA v. RN*, 72; "dismay": Dean, *Blind*, 58.

259 "modified" to "improper!": Felt, 170; "would not budge": Dean, *Blind*, 58.

259 "At least": WHT #688-18 (March 18, 1972); "never before seen": Dean, *Blind*, 173.

259 "oblivious": Dean, *Blind*, 53; "falsify": Mardian intv. Rosen.

259–60 "We need" to "getting Anderson": WHT #691-7 (March 21, 1972).

260 "mutual advantage" to "son of a bitch": WHT #324–43 (March 22, 1972).

260 "budge," "tampering": Dean, *Blind*, 58, 59.

260–61 "Chuck" to "hates Anderson": Dean, *Blind*, 56, 58.

261 "substantially similar": letter, J. Edgar Hoover to Sen. James Eastland (March 23, 1972), Dean #43, NARA.

261 "In other words": WHT #22-11 (March 24, 1972).

261 "unable to prove": Mike Shanahan, "Kleindienst," AP (March 24, 1972); "confirms unequivocally": Richard Halloran, "President Defends Kleindienst," *NYT* (March 25, 1972), 13.

261 more Americans: Louis Harris, "Anderson Believed," *WP* (May 1, 1972), A3.

261 Kleindienst confirmed: Spencer Rich, "64–19 Ends Bitter Hill Conflict," *WP* (June 9, 1972), A1; "bald deceptions": Doyle, 397.

261–62 "not interfered" to "Is that clear?": Schoenberg, 266–67.

262 "president's doorstep": Jules Witcover, "Memo Links President to ITT Antitrust Settlement," *WP* (Aug. 2, 1973), A1.

262 "extraordinarily numerous": memo, ITT prosecutors (ND), exhibit 7, *JA v. RN*; Beard retirement: Fleming intv. Rosen and Betsy Carter, "Dita on the Farm," *Newsweek* (Sept. 25, 1978), 18; "whooping it up": JA MGR (Dec. 17, 1973), JAP.

262 "prelude": Felt, 174; "nobody stole": Kutler, *Abuse*, 608, 59.

262 "Watergate crimes": JA and Clifford, 123.

263 "Dogpatch-style": Larry DuBois, "Interview: Jack Anderson," *Playboy* (Nov. 1972), 87ff.; "What contempt": Chambless, "Secular Evangelist," 173.

263 "bellowed": Sheehan, 78; "pacing, finger jabbing": "A Muckraker with a Mission," *Newsweek* (April 3, 1972), 53.

263 "Supersnoop": "The Square Scourge of Washington," *Time* (April 3, 1972), 40–44.
263 "Anderson's got": WHT #692–97 (March 23, 1972).
264 "Have somebody": WHT #22-13 (March 24, 1972).
264–65 "hardly pass" to "rock 'n' roll": transcript, Morley Safer, CBS News *60 Minutes* (March 26, 1972), 1–8.
265 "*60 Minutes*" to "buried": WHT #327-5 (March 27, 1972).
265 "know-ITT": cartoon, Gene Mora, "Graffiti," *Salt Lake City Tribune* (June 15, 1972); "don't want to criticize": WHT #714-22 (April 20, 1972).
265 "no combination": Sheehan, 80, 82, 78; hundreds of letters: William M. Blair, "Modern Muckraker," *NYT* (Jan. 6, 1972), A17; manure: Spear intv. Gibson; "liar, louse": Hume, 37.
265 "Anderson Papers": statement, Pulitzer prize jurors, "Report of the National Jury" (March 10, 1972), PPP.
265 "Horrible": WHT #720-19 (May 5, 1972); "thieves": Kutler, *Abuse*, 169.
266 "achieved": WHT #682-9 (March 10, 1972); three hundred newspapers: Sheehan, 10.
266 "Benedict Arnold": Dean and Goldwater, 277; "encouraging": "Dole Scores Media," *NYT* (May 14, 1972), 66.
266 "atrocious": Henry Mitchell, "Attack on Media," *WP* (May 5, 1972), B1.
266 "deep reservations," "public interest": "The Pulitzer Controversy," *Newsweek* (May 15, 1972), 58.
266 "Kremlin system," "phony security": Ronald Sarro, "Times, Anderson Win Pulitzers," *WS* (May 2, 1972), A9; "contemptuous": JA intv. Gibson.
266–67 "My friends": Bill Gold, "The Human Side of Those 'Inhuman' Reporters," *WP* (May 3, 1972), B14; "pristinely ascetic": John Neary, "Parting Shots," *Life* (April 21, 1972), 93; "fawned," "Mormon boy": Clifford intv.
267 "gutless trained seals": Whitten intv.; "Don't worry": Hume, 104, 105.

14: "KILL HIM"
268 "Holy shit": Brindle intv.
268–69 "Approaches" to "green light": *Documentos*, 32, 12, 10.
269 "our Cuba": R. Dallek, 239; "inducing," "assist financially": *Documentos*, 21, 8; "painted": Hume, 192.
269 "Personal/Confidential": CIA memo, "Daily Notes" (March 17, 1972), CIAFOIA.
269 "warn us": CIA memo, Kenneth E. Greer, "Call from W. R. Merriam of ITT" (March 17, 1972), CIAFOIA; "discussed . . . with General [Alexander] Haig": redacted CIA document (ND), CIAFOIA.
269 "ITT is not going to have any comment," "tried earlier": CIA memo, Kenneth E. Greer, "Call from W. R. Merriam of ITT" (March 17, 1972), CIAFOIA.
269 "Secret documents": JA, MGR (March 21, 1972), JAP; "wedding reception": JA, MGR (March 22, 1972), JAP.
269 "Everything should be done" to "force the military to move": ITT documents, JAP.
270–71 parceled out: "Anderson Charges Plot Against Allende by I.T.T. and C.I.A.," *NYT* (March 21, 1972), A23, and William Greider, "ITT Memos Bare Anti-Allende Plotting," *WP* (March 22, 1972), A10; "flaunted a sheaf": "The Square Scourge of Washington," *Time* (April 3, 1972); "Unprecedented in their detail": Kornbluh, 97; "fantastic": Connie Chung, "Interview with Jack Anderson," *CBS Morning News* (March 21, 1972), CIAFOIA.

271 "Neither I.T.T.": "I.T.T. Is Accused of Having Tried to Influence U.S. Policies in Latin America," *NYT* (March 23, 1972), 16; "White House referred": "ITT Said to Seek Chile Coup in '70," *NYT* (March 22, 1972), 25; "do not comment": CIA memo, "Daily Notes" (March 22, 1972), CIAFOIA; "without foundation": William Greider, "ITT Memos Bare Anti-Allende Plotting," *WP* (March 22, 1972), A10; "As more [Anderson] papers": Tad Szulc, "I.T.T.: A Private Little Foreign Policy," *NYT* (March 26, 1972), E4.

271 "astonishing . . . outrageous": "ITT: And Now Chile," *WP* (March 22, 1972), A22; "special interests": "The I.T.T. and Chile," *NYT* (March 26, 1972), E12.

272 "very disturbing," "wide-ranging," "very bad business": WH news summary (March 23, 1972), 5, NARA; demanded that the Justice Department: letter, Robert C. Mardian to Sen. Fred Harris (April 18, 1972), Kleindienst #14, RMP; "major": John W. Finney, "Fulbright Panel Sets I.T.T. Inquiry," *NYT* (March 25, 1972), 1; "detailed": Stanley Karnow, "ITT's Chile Caper," *WP* (March 27, 1972), 14; "bring in the Chile thing": WHT #21-131 (March 22, 1972); "did not engage": Murrey Marder, "State Denies Interference in Chile Vote," *WP* (March 24, 1972), A18.

272 "revelations set off": Kornbluh, 98; "political windfall": Juan de Onis, "I.T.T. Dispute Helps Allende Politically," *NYT* (March 24, 1972), 6; "Imperialism, Treason and Terror": Lewis H. Diuguid, "Chile Puts ITT Documents on Sale," *WP* (April 5, 1972), A6; protesters: Lewis H. Diuguid, "Workers Rally in Support of Chile's Allende," *WP* (March 24, 1972), A20; Chile's Senate: Terri Shaw, "Chilean Party Urges Takeover of ITT," *WP* (March 30, 1972), A5; "Anderson papers": WH news summary (April 11, 1972), 18, NARA; "seditious plan": "ITT Papers to Be Sent to Allende," *WP* (March 24, 1972), A19; "driven its tentacles": Sampson, 265.

272–73 "The Government press": Juan de Onis, "I.T.T. Dispute Helps Allende Politically," *NYT* (March 24, 1972), 6; ALL NEWSPAPERS: CIA cable (March 1972), CIAFOIA; "campaign to ruin": transcript, *Havana Prensa Latina* (March 25, 1972), NSC #807, NARA; "instant hero": Lewis H. Diuguid, "ITT Just One Hot Topic of Debate in Chile," *WP* (March 26, 1972), A26; "News vendors": Lewis H. Diuguid, "Chile Puts ITT Documents on Sale," *WP* (April 5, 1972), A6.

273 "For a while": "ITT: Now, the Chile Papers," *Newsweek* (April 3, 1972); "Anderson, the rascal": transcript, Nicholas von Hoffman, "Spectrum," CBS Radio (April 1, 1972).

274 "not much doubt": Tad Szulc, "State Department Denies Any Move to Block Allende," *NYT* (March 24, 1972), 7; "explosive": Kornbluh, 98.

274 "weighed various contingencies" to "conceal the facts": Kornbluh, 99, 100; "opinion and hearsay": Murrey Marder, "State Denies Interference in Chile Vote," *WP* (March 24, 1972), A18.

274 "good corporate citizen": Stanley Karnow, "ITT's Chile Caper," *WP* (March 27, 1972), 14.

274 "only joking": Russell Baker, "Sagas of April," *NYT* (April 2, 1972), E13.

274 "Have you said": WHT #22-6 (March 23, 1972); "What did they do": Kornbluh, 99–100.

275 funded by the CIA: Kornbluh, 91–94; "printing whatever rumor": Lewis H. Diuguid, "ITT Just One Hot Topic of Debate in Chile," *WP* (March 26, 1972), A26; "urgent": memo, Rose Mary Woods to Fred Fielding (April 5, 1972), Dean #42, NARA; rumor was publicized: John R. Rarick, "Chile, Jack Anderson, and ITT,"

Congressional Record (April 10, 1972); segregationist: David Maraniss, "A Publisher's Moral Compass," *WP* (July 5, 1990), A3; did not seem to believe the rumor: redacted CIA memo (Sept. 12, 1972), CIAFOIA.

275 leaked to Anderson: Levinson, 8, and Levinson intv.; "explosive," Fulbright alerted: Warren W. Unna, "Senate Guilt on CIA," *WP* (Nov. 13, 1977), C1–2 and Unna intv.

276 Anderson turned over his files: JA and Clifford, 118; eventual hearings: Levinson intv.

276 "Did you try" to "Yes, sir": Helms and Hood, 414.

276 "President Nixon had ordered me," "came down very hard": Helms and Hood, 405, 404.

276 American conspiracy: R. Dallek, 515; Kornbluh, 18; Sampson, 260, 266; Hersh, *Price*, 265–69, 272–73, 276.

277 "I don't see" to "beside himself": Hersh, *Price*, 265, 277, 269; "economy scream" to "firm and continuing policy": R. Dallek, 234–37.

277 Pinochet dictatorship: Kornbluh, 349–63.

277 "newspapers [are] bleeding": R. Dallek, 511–12.

278 "discussed various ways": Hersh, *Price*, 259.

278 "impeaching Jack Anderson": memo, John Dean to John Ehrlichman, "Suggestions" (March 8, 1972), Ehrlichman #15, NARA.

278 "discrediting the allegations": affidavit, E. Howard Hunt (March 21, 1978), 8, *JA v. RN.*

278 "considerable derogatory information": memo, "Mention of Jack Anderson" (ND), Dean #43, NARA; "under a subterfuge": memo, Jack Caulfield to John Dean (May 15, 1972), JAP; "asking questions": JA manuscript, "1972," 5, JAP, and plaintiff's answers to interrogatories (Jan. 21, 1977), 11, *JA v. RN.*

279 "black bushy moustache": JA manuscript, "1972," 5, JAP; "check out a rumor," "thwarted by our security": Liddy, 213; "kickback scheme": WSPF memo, Charles F. C. Ruff to Rex E. Lee (Nov. 1, 1976), DOJFOIA, and Magruder, 190.

279 Intertel "specific assignments": JA, MGR (March 1 and May 10, 1973), JAP.

279–80 "directing a major effort": Sanford J. Ungar, "White House Runs ITT Counterattack," *WP* (March 18, 1972), A1, 10; "extensive search": Don Oberdorfer, "Mrs. Beard, Anderson Aide in Photo," *WP* (March 17, 1972), A16; "deals with already known": Bob Woodward and Carl Bernstein, "Bugging Suspect Investigated Writer," *WP* (Sept. 27, 1972), A1; "panicky—and exceedingly clumsy": "The ITT Affair," *WP* (March 19, 1972), B6.

280 "unfortunately": WHT #323-33 (March 17, 1972).

280 "get him": WHT #688-12 (March 18, 1972).

280 Lou Russell: Morris, 348–49, and FBI memo, Rodney C. Kicklighter and James M. Hopper (June 29, 1972), 2, NSA; "down-on-his-luck": JA manuscript, "1972," 10, JAP; spy's son: JA and Gibson, 232–33.

281 "rifle [through] Anderson's files": Reeves, 464.

281 "Don't we have": WHT #692-7 (March 23, 1972).

281 faked a letter: FBI memo, Daniel C. Mahan and Angelo J. Lano, "Victoria L. Chern interview" (May 15, 1973), 6, NSA.

281 "explosive": JA intv. Gibson.

281 "I don't know": George Clifford, "The Plumbers' Plot to 'Get' Jack Anderson," *Argosy* (Jan. 1975), 23.

282 "just come from a meeting" to "whatever was necessary": affidavit, E. Howard Hunt (March 21, 1978), 4, 7, 5, *JA v. RN*; testimony, E. Howard Hunt (Jan. 10, 1976), 4, 10, JFKAA; Bob Woodward, "Hunt Told Associates of Orders to Kill Jack Anderson," *WP* (Sept. 21, 1975), A1; Hunt, *Spy*, 199.
282 "forever volunteering": "Murder, Incorporated?" *Newsweek* (April 28, 1980), 28; "They charged us": Summers, *Arrogance*, 407.
282–83 surveillance, "vulnerabilities": Hunt intv.; "pesky": Hunt, *Spy*, 199.
283 Central America: Patricia Sullivan, "Ex-Spy Crafted Watergate," *WP* (Jan. 24, 2007), A1; "kill a man with a pencil": Wells, 16.
283 botulism: Bryan Smith, "How the CIA Enlisted the Chicago Mob to Put a Hit on Castro," *Chicago* (Nov. 2007).
283 "unorthodox application" Liddy, 207; "euphemism": Paula Zahn, "G. Gordon Liddy Discusses New Book," *CBS This Morning* (June 14, 1991).
283 "I'll cooperate": Hunt intv.
283 "Colson has just laid another one": testimony, E. Howard Hunt (Jan. 10, 1976), 12–13, JFKAA.
284 "I took 'retired'": Liddy, 207.
284 grill, "Manny": testimony, E. Howard Hunt (Jan. 10, 1976), 5, 32, JFKAA.
284 "operational alias": Liddy, 207.
284 "individual who was giving them trouble": memo, John P. Lydick to Jack Anderson File, "Interview of Dr. Edward M. Gunn" (Oct. 21, 1975), Ruff #1, WSPF; "nothing undetectable": notes, John Lydick and Michael Lehr, "Dr. E. M. Gunn" (Oct. 17, 1975), Ruff #1, WSPF.
284 "We painted": testimony, E. Howard Hunt (Jan. 10, 1976), 6, JFKAA; "unpredictability": Liddy, 208.
284 "massive dose": Liddy, 208, and testimony, E. Howard Hunt (Jan. 10, 1976), 7, JFKAA.
285 "halfway measures" to "fatal auto accidents": Liddy, 208.
285 "too chancy": Eric Norden, "Interview: G. Gordon Liddy," *Playboy* (Oct. 1980), 67; "require the services of an expert": Liddy, 208.
285 "LSD-type drug": notes, John Lydick and Michael Lehr, "Dr. E. M. Gunn" (Oct. 17, 1975), Ruff #1, WSPF.
285 "Hunt always wanted": Wells, 509; begged off: Church Report, 136; "refused to cooperate": memo, John Matheny to William Hyland, "SSC 'Final' Reports" (June 1976), 4, JFKAA; "if the time came": testimony, E. Howard Hunt (Jan. 10, 1976), 7, JFKAA.
286 "Of course": testimony, E. Howard Hunt (Jan. 10, 1976), 6, 8, JFKAA.
286 "Aspirin roulette": Liddy, 208.
286 "perform an entry": testimony, E. Howard Hunt (Jan. 10, 1976), 7, 8, JFKAA.
286 "Too iffy," "drastic problems": Eric Norden, "Interview: G. Gordon Liddy," *Playboy* (Oct. 1980), 67–68; "discussed and discarded" to "Re-elect the President": Liddy, 208, 209.
286–87 Anderson and Cubans: JA and Gibson, 242–43; Barker intv.
287 "think it wise": Liddy, 209, 210; "if the Cubans were ruled out": Eric Norden, "Interview: G. Gordon Liddy," *Playboy* (Oct. 1980), 70; "tasked me with an assassination": Liddy, 225; "knife" to "laws you're violating": Eric Norden, "Interview: G. Gordon Liddy," *Playboy* (Oct. 1980), 70, 67.
288 Nixon aides questioned: Price, 184–85; Chapin intv.

288 Hitler, rat-eating, "flesh turned black": Liddy, 11, 24, 190; "truth-tellers": Garment, *Throat*, 194; "credible": Bob Woodward, "Gordon Liddy Spills His Guts," *WP Book World* (May 18, 1980), 2.

288 "astonished": Jack White and Randall Richard, "Hunt: MD Told Me of CIA's Druggings," *Providence Journal-Bulletin* (Oct. 24, 1975), A8; "regarded as the enemy": Hunt intv., emphasis in original.

288 "hit man," *"acted"* (emphasis in original): Haldeman and DiMona, 5, 59; "period," "dastardly deed": Aitken, *Colson*, 164, 161; "always followed": Kleindienst, 199; "I mean anything": Kutler, *Abuse*, 38.

289 "balls": Hunt intv.; "Nixon tells Colson": Haldeman and DiMona, 218, 61; "rarely acted," "commanded the patrol": Kutler, *Wars*, 179, 81.

289–90 "written up": "Spin Surgeon," *NYT* (June 16, 1991), D7; "brought up": Liddy, 213; "unproductive": affidavit, E. Howard Hunt (March 21, 1978), 6, 7, *JA v. RN*; "end of the affair": Church Report, 137.

15: WATERGATE

291 "true beginning": Kennedy, 328, 325.

291 "only the beginning": Nixon, *RN*, 583, 496, 677, 734; "second only": Dean, *Blind*, 88.

291–92 "blamed O'Brien": Ulasewicz and McKeever, 184; "nail O'Brien": Ambrose, *Triumph*, 422; "put O'Brien in jail": Drosnin, 455.

292 "badly burned": JA and Gibson, 222; "documentary evidence": JA, MGR (Jan. 24, 1972), JAP; "goddamned Hughes thing": WHT #317-6 (Jan. 24, 1972).

292 "You need": David Von Drehle, "30 Years Later, a Watergate Allegation," *WP* (July 27, 2003), A5; "primary purpose": J. Anthony Lukas, "Why the Watergate Break-in?" *NYT* (Nov. 30, 1987), A10; Haldeman and DiMona, 19.

293 "bum tip" to "let the thing drop": Chambless, "Muckraker," 176–78.

293 befriended one of them: JA and Gibson, 242–44.

293 journalism fraternity: Hougan, 180–81.

293–94 "Frankie" to "in town": deposition, JA (Nov. 12, 1973), 13, SWC; "visit friends": deposition, Frank Sturgis (July 26, 1973), 36, 37, 42, SWC; "chagrined": JA and Gibson, 244.

294 Watergate arrests: Ambrose, *Triumph*, 558.

294 "what Frankie's": JA and Gibson, 244; "Social Visit": FBI memo, "Francis Anthony Sturgis" (June 19, 1972), #139-166, NSA; "what happened?": deposition, Frank Sturgis (July 26, 1973), 105, SWC.

294–95 "Frankie" to "before breakfast": JA intv.; "straight face": JA and Gibson, 244.

295 destroyed incriminating materials: Lukas, 211, 213, 226; Kutler, *Wars*, 317; "large volume": memo, Frank Martin to Henry Ruth, "Plot Against JA" (Oct. 14, 1975), WSPF.

"Because she read that Jack Anderson ploughed through the trash cans of J. Edgar Hoover's home," Watergate burglar James McCord later told authorities, "my wife threw personal letters, newspapers and [typewriter] ribbons into the fireplace" and burned them in the hours after Nixon's men were arrested. Nonetheless, prosecutors found that the conspirators' White House safe still "contained between one-half and a full file drawer of material pertaining to Jack Anderson." Memo, James McCord to Senate Judiciary Committee (March 29, 1974), NSA, and memo, Michael Lehr to File (Oct. 21, 1975), Ruff #1, WSPF.

295 "third-rate burglary," "no involvement whatever": Kutler, *Wars*, 189, 191; "We re-acted": Haldeman, *Diaries*, 472.

295–96 criminal conspiracy: Kutler, *Wars*, chps. ix–xi; "stonewall": Kutler, *Wars*, 287.

296 "chicken shit," "I mean": Kutler, *Abuse*, 497, 169; "Somebody should say": Nixon, *RN*, 639; "they praised": WHT #801-24 (Oct. 17, 1972); "emotionally and constitutionally": Wicker, 685.

296 "Nixon's favorite Cuban": Chambless, "Muckraker," 193–94; "Jack Anderson said": Kutler, *Abuse*, 52, 57.

296 "We started a rumor": Kutler, *Abuse*, 64.

297 Law enforcement authorities: Kutler, *Wars*, 190; Carl Bernstein and Bob Woodward, "Bug Suspect Got Campaign Funds," *WP* (Aug. 1, 1972), A1; Walter Rugaber, "Calls to G.O.P. Unit Linked to Raid on the Democrats," *NYT* (July 25, 1972), A1; "lower echelon shit-ass": Kutler, *Abuse*, 108.

297–98 blamed their boss's death: Gentry, 719–20; "snoop into the sex habits" to "incorrigible gossips": JA, MGR (May 1 and 17, 1972), JAP; "sex reports": "Columnist Urges Secret-Data Curb," *NYT* (May 2, 1972), 29.

298 Gray: Ambrose, *Triumph*, 543; Gentry, 30–31; Gray, xx.

298 Felt: Gray, 125, 160; media coverage: Feldstein, "Watergate Revisited," 66; Halberstam, 629–31, 644, 667–78; and Liebovich, Appendix C.

298 "vehemently denied" to "tail": Gray, 129, 163, 160, 170, 173, 174.

299 "Failing . . . to recognize": Dygart, 98.

299 "Television and newspapers": Kutler, *Wars*, viii.

299 "kill the column": letter, William C. Payette to JA (Dec. 13, 1973), JAP.

300 "belonged to Jack": Grady intv.

300 McGovern sabotage: Kutler, *Wars*, 212, 253; Hougan, 119–20; Cheshire and Greenya, 161; "Reporter Is Termed a Spy in McGovern Camp," *NYT* (Aug. 28, 1973), A21; "sleeping with who": George Lardner, "Goldberg a Veteran at Recording Gossip," *WP* (Feb. 4, 1998), A12.

Nixon aide Donald Rumsfeld cautioned that McGovern will call "for an end to 'senseless killing'" in Vietnam, so the administration should "associate McGovern with his unpopular extreme supporters and positions." In the same memo, Rumsfeld used flattery to butter up his boss: "Thank God" we have a president who is "tough, pragmatic, courageous."

Charles Colson also offered campaign advice. "McGovern will do well with the blacks, the poor and now the fags," he wrote. "I hope there aren't more around than we think."

Memo, Donald Rumsfeld to H. R. Haldeman, "Response to Your Memo" (June 16, 1972), 3–4, NSA, and letter, Charles Colson to Bebe Rebozo (Sept. 30, 1972), CCP.

300 "severe manic-depressive psychosis": Perry, 195.

300 "I can't talk": Davis W. Merritt, "Eagleton Health Story Broken by Anonymous Tip," *Editor and Publisher* (July 29, 1972), 13; Hoyt intv.

301 "destroy": Walter Pincus, "Democrat Endorsed Cambodia Invasion," *WP* (June 24, 2009), A3; "mental patient": Lou Cannon, "Nixon Asks for Silence on Eagleton," *WP* (July 27, 1972), A16; "strictest instructions": "Transcript of President's News Conference," *NYT* (July 28, 1972), 10.

301 Nixon psychotherapy: James M. Naughton, "Nixon Disclosure on Health Asked," *NYT* (July 27, 1972), A1, 32.

301 "Checkers"-like: John W. Finney, "Defense Recalls 'Checkers' Speech by Nixon," *NYT* (July 31, 1972), 12, and Laurence Stern, "Eagleton Race Assumes Aura of Surrealism," *WP* (July 30, 1972), A10; "Terry is an impressionable boy": JA and Clifford, 144.

302 True Davis: JA and Gibson, 209–11; JA and Clifford, 138–41, 145–48.

302–03 "When a guy": Hume, 264; "streaming into St. Louis" to *"located"* (emphasis added): JA, radio script and clarification (July 27, 1972), JAP; "confident that the documents existed": JA and Gibson, 211.

303 "phones were ringing": Kiernan intv.; "traced" to "his source": Hume, 265–66.

303 "damnable lie": Christopher Lydon, "Assails Radio Report by Jack Anderson," *NYT* (July 28, 1972), A1, 12; "run me out of town": Robert Adams, "Looking into Procedure for Replacing Nominee," *St. Louis Post-Dispatch* (July 28, 1972), 5.

303–04 "best thing that could have happened": Dougherty, 197; "seize the offensive": McGovern, 209; "changed the entire picture": Hart, 261.

304 "shockingly false": Nixon, *RN*, 664.

304 "McGovern look bad": Haldeman, CD Diaries (July 30, 1972); "hit him again while he's down": Haldeman, *Diaries*, 490; "hitting Anderson": WHT #756-3 (July 28, 1972).

304 "gut feeling": JA and Gibson, 212; "Are you worried?": Hume, 266.

304–05 "already had been pulled" to "bail Anderson out": JA and Clifford, 148, 161.

305 "should have withheld": Robert Walters and Michael Satchell, "Anderson Backs Off," *WS* (July 28, 1972), A1; "act like Drew" to "full retraction and apology": Hume, 268–70.

305–06 "very vague": Maxine Cheshire, "Anderson on Eagleton," *WP* (July 29, 1972), A16; "quite embarrassed": Sally Quinn, "William True Davis," *WP* (Aug. 1, 1972), B1; "prizewinning standards," "score a scoop": James M. Naughton, "Data on Eagleton Reported Lacking," *NYT* (July 29, 1972), A10; "hot breath": "Davis Was Anderson Source," *St. Louis Post-Dispatch* (July 30, 1972), 31; "wholly unsubstantiated": "The Anderson Charges," *NYT* (July 29, 1972), 24; "without supporting evidence": "The Eagleton Affair (Cont'd)," *WP* (July 29, 1972), A16.

306 "go after" to "you hadn't located them": Hume, 272, 273, 275; "heavy into denial": Les Whitten, "Eulogy for a Muckraker," *Huffington Post* (Dec. 27, 2005); "horrible," "prayed": Whitten intv.

307 "first time" to "first place": "Excerpts from the Eagleton-Anderson Exchange," *WP* (Aug. 1, 1972), A18.

307 Anderson's "apology": "Jack Anderson's 'Apology,'" *WP* (Aug. 1, 1972), A18; "astonishing hedge": Charles Bartlett, "Anderson Takes Prize in Parade of Inhumanity," *Chicago Daily News*; "*Disgrace the Nation*": Kiernan intv.; "acted terribly": Hume, 278–79.

307–08 "unqualified" to "humble apology": "Anderson Makes Full Retraction," *WP* (Aug. 2, 1972), A4; "raked over the coals": WH news summary (Aug. 3, 1972), 14, NARA.

308 "Any chance": Hart, 260; "straw that broke the Eagleton back": "Eagleton: Anderson 'Last Straw,'" *WP* (Aug. 13, 1972), A2.

308 "mean": Edwin A. Roberts, Jr., "The Eagleton Affair," *National Observer* (Aug. 12, 1972); "liar": "Does Jack Anderson?" Fulton (MO) *Daily Star* (July 28, 1972), 1; "scurrilous": Perry, 184; "shameful": WH news summary (July 31, 1972), 22, NARA; "national disgrace": WH news summaries (Aug. 4, 1972), 16, #42, NARA; "Unethical?": Roscoe C. Born, "Reporters, Prizes, and Retribution," *National Observer* (Aug. 10,

1972), 10; mail from readers: Stan Rose, "Place for Muckraking," Shawnee Mission (KS) *Scout-Sun* (Aug. 23, 1972); "canceled" to "give up journalism": "Newspaper Drops Anderson Column," *WP* (Aug. 6, 1972), D3, and "Anderson Apologizes," *Editor and Publisher* (Aug. 5, 1972), 10.

308 edge of emotional collapse: Whitten intv.; "deflated," "prideful": Harrington, 46, 44; "risen to a position": Hume, 281.

309 "No human hand": Mary McGrory, "Eagleton Affair Making Nixon's Cup Run Over," *WS* (July 31, 1972), A5.

309 "Eagleton affair" to "*the* political story" (emphasis in original): McGovern, 191, 192.

309 coverage of Watergate: Lubars and Wicklein, 5; Halberstam, 651; Leibovich, 88.

310 "as if victory": Kissinger, *White House*, 1406.

310 "Just remember": Kutler, *Abuse*, 146, 149–50; "I certainly don't intend": WHT #763-15 (Aug. 7, 1972).

310 "I think we've got": WHT #780-15 (Sept. 16, 1972).

310 $100,000 bribe, "You know my personal feelings": memo, Charles Colson to John Dean (Nov. 17, 1972), Hughes-Rebozo #86, WSPF.

310 traveled to Miami: FBI memo, JA intv. (July 31, 1973), 4, WSPF; "mystery deepens": JA, MGR (Dec. 26, 1972), JAP.

311 "Who started this?": Woodward and Bernstein, *All the President's Men*, 230. Carl Bernstein and Bob Woodward, "Hunt Declares No Higher-ups in Plot," *WP* (Jan. 12, 1973), A1, and Bob Woodward and Carl Bernstein, "Watergate Trial Judge Wants 'Exploration,'" *WP* (Jan. 10, 1973), A15.

311 treated Sturgis to lunch: memo, R. Ben-Veniste and G. Goldman to File, "Interview of JA" (Oct. 3, 1973), 5, USA Witness File #1, WSPF; "We're having a meeting": JA intv. Gibson; "If I were nearby": JA and Gibson, 250.

311 flamboyant litigator: Eric Pace, "Henry B. Rothblatt, Watergate Burglars' Attorney," *NYT* (Sept. 3, 1985), D21, and Clifford A. Rieders, "Deep Throat and Me," www .riederstravis.com/op_ed/june/deep_throat.pdf.

311 Rothblatt was upset, Arlington Towers: memo, R. Ben-Veniste and G. Goldman to File, "Interview of JA" (Oct. 3, 1973), 5–6, USA Witness File #1, WSPF, and deposition, Frank Sturgis (July 26, 1973), 116–17, SWC.

311–12 "They've offered": JA and Gibson, 250; "being bribed" to "[a] duty to his family": deposition, JA (Nov. 12, 1973), 73, 38, SWC.

312 "looking for a scoop": deposition, Frank Sturgis (July 27, 1973), 124; "follow orders": memo, R. Ben-Veniste and G. Goldman to File, "Interview of JA" (Oct. 3, 1973), 6, USA Witness File #1, WSPF.

312 pled guilty: Kutler, *Wars*, 254.

312 Hersh and Anderson stories: Seymour M. Hersh, "4 Watergate Defendants Reported Still Being Paid," *NYT* (Jan. 14, 1973), A1, 44, and JA, MGR (Jan. 15, 1973), JAP.

312 Sirica was incensed: Halberstam, 682.

16: DISGRACE

313 V-for-victory salute: Haynes Johnson, "Inaugural Smooth," *WP* (Jan. 21, 1973), A14; "Ask not": "A Transcript of President Nixon's Second Inaugural Address to the Nation," *NYT* (Jan. 21, 1973), 40.

313 $100,000 to $200,000: deposition, L. Patrick Gray (Dec. 15, 1977), 88, *JA v. RN*; "Day after day": JA and Clifford, 178.

314 "Oh my God": Collins intv.; "shitless": Whitten intv. Gibson; "swarming": Les Whitten, "Whispering Avengers and Other Sources," *WP* (Aug. 4, 1974), 214ff.

314 charged Whitten: John P. MacKenzie and Donald P. Baker, "FBI Arrests Reporter in Stolen Data," *WP* (Feb. 1, 1973), A1; "get Jack": Whitten intv.

314 "Be quiet": Murphy intv.; "outrageous violation": statement, JA (ND), #00707603, LWP.

314 blared: Helen Dudar and Andrew Porte, "U.S. Arrests Aide of Jack Anderson," *New York Post* (Jan. 31, 1973), A1; "awful": AP, "Arrest of Reporter Viewed with Misgivings by Editors," *Chicago Tribune* (Feb. 2, 1973), B28; "vendetta": "Outrage Against Whitten," Madison (WI) *Capital-Times* (Feb. 6, 1973); "Free Les Whitten": JA and Gibson, 253; Whitten in handcuffs: Herblock cartoon, *WP* (Feb. 7, 1973).

315 criminalize unauthorized disclosures: Feldstein, "Jailing a Journalist," 157.

315 "new front": JA, MGR (Feb. 15, 1973), JAP.

315 "You've done more": JA and Gibson, 254.

315–16 always insisted: Donald P. Baker, "Indian Explains Actions," *WP* (Feb. 2, 1973), C1, and Adams intv.; "lame story": Felt, 265; receipt: JA and Clifford, 181.

316 "Would one": "The Arrest of Les Whitten," *WP* (Feb. 12, 1973), A20; "If they really": transcript, "Interview with JA," WTTG-TV *Panorama* (Feb. 3, 1973), 14, JAP.

316 Anderson testified: Paul Ramirez, "Grand Jury Queries 4 on BIA Papers," *WP* (Feb. 15, 1973), D1; "He was just": JA and Gibson, 254.

316 grand jurors: Lawrence Meyer, "U.S. Drops Charges in BIA Thefts," *WP* (Feb. 16, 1973), B1, 10; party: Judith Martin, "Celebrating with Toasts and Empathy," *WP* (Feb. 16, 1973), B3.

316 "manipulated the situation": Felt, 265.

316–17 secretly subpoenaing: Barry Kalb, "Anderson Phone Data Seized, U.S. Indicates," *WS* (Feb. 27, 1973), A4; three thousand calls: James P. Capitanio, "Certificate Setting Forth Compliance with Court's Order of 6 July 1973" (July 31, 1973), File 97, Box 1, LWP; twenty-three field offices and Sirica incredulity: Timothy S. Robinson, "Use of Anderson Telephone Records by FBI Blocked," *WP* (April 17, 1973), A17; demanding to know: Murphy intv.; "false arrest": JA, "FBI Used Arrest to Probe Anderson," *WP* (Feb. 23, 1973), D17; destroy the Anderson phone logs: "Anderson's Records Destroyed by Court," *WP* (July 7, 1973), E2.

317 "nail" to "wrong": JA, MGR (July 4, 1973), JAP; "pin a crime" to "find one": memo, JA, "Chronology of a Conspiracy" (ND), JAP; JA intv.

317 "hatchetman": Gray hearings (March 9, 1973), 476.

317 "Bobby": JA and Gibson, 257.

318 "I leaked": Stanley Kutler, "Watergate Misremembered," *Slate* (June 18, 2002).

318 "jubilant": JA intv. Gibson; marijuana, "you fucker!": Downie, 85, 87.

"We were all sitting around getting high and putting down everybody," Hersh said, but Woodward was careful not to indulge in the marijuana joints shared by Bernstein and Hersh. Ibid., Hersh intv.

319 trash: Doyle, 70; tried to eavesdrop: Cloherty intv.; "romancing": memo, Mark Frazier to JA (ND), JAP; sought money: Fleming intv. Colodny, LCP; McQuaid, 211; Swiss bank account: John M. Crewdson, "Rebozo Denies Shifting Funds to Swiss Banks for President," *NYT* (March 21, 1974), 32, and Nixon, *RN*, 953.

319 Rebozo money: Dash, 234; Carl Bernstein and Bob Woodward, "Hughes Gift Tied to Miss Woods, Nixon Kin," *WP* (April 6, 1974), A1; Armstrong intv.

320 "*Hughes* money" (emphasis in original): Drosnin, 462, 473–74.

The Senate Watergate Committee suppressed evidence documenting the Hughes connection to the scandal reportedly because prominent Democrats—including Hubert Humphrey, Lyndon Johnson, and Robert Kennedy—were also recipients of Hughes cash. "Everybody was feeding at the same trough," said Republican senator Lowell Weicker. According to Senate investigator Scott Armstrong, Democratic lobbyist Thomas Corcoran personally persuaded Senator Sam Ervin to delete the Hughes findings from the committee's final report. Armstrong intv.

320 "Jack's column": Hume, 284.

320 series of columns: JA, MGR (April 16–26, 1973), JAP; "startling": JA and Gibson, 259; access, authentic: "Column's Quotes Termed Authentic," WP (April 20, 1973), A14.

320 "shocking": notes, John Ehrlichman (April 20, 1973), Ehrlichman #7, NARA.

321 "ugh—verbatim": WHT #38-111 (April 19, 1973).

321 "major story": WHT #38-137 (April 25, 1973).

321 "Such leaking": Hunt, Spy, 295; "human blood": Stans, 419, 428.

321 "going crazy": Kiernan intv.; electronic sweep: FBI memo, R. J. Gallagher to Gebhardt, "Watergate" (April 17, 1973), NSA; "incredible": diary, Earl Silbert (April 23, 1973), 2, and (April 24, 1973), 2, WSPF; JA intv. Gibson.

321 executive session: Lawrence Meyer and Timothy S. Robinson, "Jury Leaks Probed," WP (April 24, 1973), A1; Sirica directed: statement, Judge John Sirica (April 23, 1973), Silbert #51, WSPF; "All hell": JA intv. Gibson; "not to[o] optimistic": diary, Earl Silbert (April 23, 1973), 2, and (April 24, 1973), 2, WSPF; immunity: Glanzer intv.; "clapped behind bars": Cloherty intv.

321–22 "Under our Constitution": Lawrence Meyer and Timothy S. Robinson, "Jury Leaks Probed," WP (April 24, 1973), A10; "singled out": Hume, 289.

322 "You've got" to "jail cell": Hume, 290.

322 "Jack Anderson's column": Kutler, Abuse, 328.

322 "I didn't trust": JA and Gibson, 259.

322 "terrible significance": Kutler, Abuse, 328.

323 "so excited," "Mob lookout": Whitten intv.; "fish on the line": JA and Gibson, 257; "dirty hands": Cloherty intv.

323 interrogated stenographer, hauled away trash: FBI memos, Edward R. Leary, Daniel C. Mahan, and Robert E. Lill intv. Doris F. Hoover (April 23, 1973), and Robert E. Lill and John W. Hinderman intv. Elizabeth Ann Tipton (April 30, 1973), NSA.

Prosecutor Earl Silbert wrote in his diary that Anderson's "bizarre" leak must have come from one of the male stenographers who transcribed the minutes: "a number of the people in the office where copies had been turned in [are] kind of homosexual, etc. they were clearly the kind that might [be] leaking the information." Diary, Earl Silbert (April 23, 1973), 1–2, NARA.

323–24 "romantic and crazy": Whitten intv. Gibson; "on your tail": JA intv. Gibson.

324 "diversionary battle": WHT #38-101 (April 18, 1973).

324 "we didn't want": Glanzer intv.

324–25 "Jack had been warned" to "passionate point of it": Hume, 292–95.

325 "no intimidation": John M. Crewdson, "Anderson Won't Print More Jury Testimony," NYT (April 26, 1973), 34; "sordid scandal": statement, JA, United Feature Syndicate release (April 25, 1973), JAP.

326 "gallant," "Houdini": Hume, 295–96.

326 foil cover-up: Chambless, "Muckraker," 325–27.

326 locked them in his office safe: Murphy intv.; investigation failed: Timothy Robin-
    son, "Watergate Jury Leak Probe Fails," *WP* (Jan. 25, 1974), A13.
326–27 "cancer," "million dollars," "inoperative": Kutler, *Wars*, 266, 276, 309; *"son of a
    bitch"*: Kutler, *Abuse*, 419 (emphasis in original).
327 "What did," "Coxsucker," "Saturday Night Massacre": Kutler, *Wars*, 345, 333, 406.
328 "Anderson just happened": Haldeman and DiMona, 129, 131.
328 "convinced" to "Mr. Anderson": F. Thompson, 215, 217.
328–29 "loose cannon": JA intv.; Anderson swore: deposition, JA (Nov. 12, 1973), pas-
    sim, SWC; "bore in" to "Anderson appearance": F. Thompson, 219–23.
329 "almost as intensive": JA, "My Journal on Watergate," *Parade* (July 22, 1973), 7; "dia-
    bolical": JA intv.
329 journalism fraternity: Hougan, 180–81; "never seen my desk," "figure out the an-
    swer": JA and Gibson, 247; "big coincidence": deposition, Frank Sturgis (July 26, 1973),
    58, SWC.
329 "distract attention": cable, Richard Helms (Dec. 1973), CIAFOIA.
329–30 leaked to the press: Colodny and Gettlin, 379–80; exaggerated: Zumwalt, 373–
    74; took place in previous and subsequent administrations: Gentry, 153; JA, "How
    Our Services Spy on Each Other," *Parade* (Dec. 15, 1957); Hersh, *Price*, 208; Van
    Atta, 244; Rosen, *Strong Man*, 166; Welander intv. Gettlin, LCP; Bumiller, 203–04.
330 Moorer and Kissinger testimony: Stennis hearings (Feb. 6, 1974), passim.
330 Radford swore: Radford testimony, Stennis hearings (Feb. 20, 1974), 9, 15–17, 23;
    Radford cross-examination by Thurmond and Stennis, "Yeoman Radford" to "No,
    sir": Radford testimony, Stennis hearings (Feb. 21, 1974), 231, 229.
330 FBI traced, "expressed pride": Ehrlichman, 309, and Ehrlichman intv. Colodny, LCP.
330–31 secret session, "very likely" to "drop the matter": transcript, Stennis hearings (Feb. 6,
    1974), 62 (March 7, 1974), and 42 (May 7, 1974), 4, 6–8.
331 "at least 70" to "deeply regrettable": Stennis hearings (Dec. 19, 1974), 4–6.
331 "White House horrors," pay back $284,000 in taxes, "I am not a crook": Kutler,
    Wars, 81, 433–34.
332 "These assholes": Kutler, *Abuse*, 489; "outrageous": Kutler, *Wars*, 408–09; "lynch
    mob atmosphere": David Greenberg, "In Nixon's Tricks, Rove's Roots" *NYT* (May 1,
    2007).
332 "gap" of eighteen and a half minutes: Kutler, *Wars*, 429–31; President himself: David
    Greenberg, "Unsolved Mysteries," *NYT* (June 5, 2005), WK4.
332 "expletive deleted," "shabby," growing chorus: Kutler, *Wars*, 452–55.
332–33 cited Jack Anderson's reporting, "contrary to his trust": House Impeachment
    Report, 174–76, 141–42, 4.
333 smoking gun: Kutler, *Wars*, 534–38.
333 slurred his words, drunken late-night phone calls: R. Dallek, 497, 524; suicide:
    Woodward and Bernstein, *Final Days*, 447–48.
333 shredding, "acrid smell": Ambrose, *Ruin*, 449–50.
333 "What have I done?": Woodward and Bernstein, *Final Days*, 471.
333 "Never be petty": Ambrose, *Ruin*, 444.

17: FINAL YEARS
337 sat alone, "national nightmare": Ambrose, *Ruin*, 445–46.
337 shock, "Fiercely proud": Ambrose, *Ruin*, 450, 452, 588.

337–38 more than seventy people were convicted: Kutler, *Wars,* 620; "Statement by the President," *NYT* (Sept 9, 1974), A24; "suffered enough," "more decisively": Ambrose, *Ruin,* 461.

338 "co-conspirators": JA and Gibson, 263; "whopping": JA, "Nixon Costs U.S. $1 Million a Year," *WP* (Sept. 25, 1974), D35.

338 "been in the forefront": JA, "Score Is Kept on Games Played Here," *WP* (Aug. 8, 1974), G7; "tasteless": Downie, 163.

338 "Jack was overtaken": Hume intv.; dwindling influence: Jonathan Alter, "Beam Me Up, Scotty," *Washington Monthly* (Dec. 2002); "column continues": letter, Opal Ginn to author (Nov. 25, 1974), JAP.

338–39 "kept the torch burning": Grady intv.; "didn't start with Watergate": JA and Boyd, book jacket.

339 assassination plot: Bob Woodward, "Hunt Told Associates of Orders to Kill Jack Anderson," *WP* (Sept. 21, 1975), A1; denials: Price, 184–85; "found nothing": memo, Henry Ruth to Carl B. Feldbaum, "Alleged Plot Against Jack Anderson" (Oct. 3, 1975), Jaworski/Ruth #1, WSPF.

339 Howard Hunt told the panel, "many times," "probably": Church Report, 134–37; "hair-raising": testimony, E. Howard Hunt (Jan. 10, 1976), 19, 15, JFKAA; "totally off the wall": Bob Woodward, "Watergate Unit to Probe Plot on Columnist," *WP* (Sept. 30, 1975), A14.

339–40 authorities never really attempted, poison but not murder: Church Report, 133–37.

340 staked out Anderson's home: Hunt intv.

340 "if not already dead": Liddy, 207; "knifed him": Eric Norden, "Interview: G. Gordon Liddy," *Playboy* (Oct. 1980), 70.

340 fluke: deposition, JA (Jan. 3, 1978), 36–37, *JA v. RN.*

340 "stick our heels in": Ambrose, *Triumph,* 660; Kutler, *Wars,* 252.

341 Teamsters, China, "gave them a sword": Ambrose, *Ruin,* 487, 491, 506–12.

341 memoir . . . HE'S BACK: Ambrose, *Ruin,* 468, 516, 530, 550, 558–59, 565, 570, 574, 538–40, 554, 561.

341–42 Nixon Library: David Greenberg, "Another Nixon Pardon," *Slate* (Jan. 24, 2006); "irresponsible journalists": Ambrose, *Ruin,* 577; "spot that will not out": Kutler, *Wars,* xiv.

342 Hutschnecker: Greenberg, 242.

342 Nixon funeral, "made mistakes": Maureen Dowd, "Clinton Asks Nation to Judge Ex-President on His Entire Life," *NYT* (April 28, 1994), A1, 21; Summers, *Arrogance,* xii–xiii.

342 "introvert": JA and Gibson, 286; "vendetta": James M. Perry, "Multimedia Maven," *WSJ* (April 25, 1979), A1; "just doing": JA intv. Gibson; notoriety: Spear intv. Gibson.

343 "political fix," forged documents: Charles R. Babcock and Fred Barbash, "Vesco Evidence Not Authentic, Anderson Says," *WP* (Sept. 26, 1978), A1; Anderson testified: Charles R. Babcock and Fred Barbash, "Columnist and Confidant Feud," *WP* (Nov. 5, 1978), A3; provoke a Senate investigation: Morton Mintz and Art Harris, "Columnist Is Go-between for Senator, Swindler," *WP* (Aug. 3, 1980), A3; "habitually lies": JA and Gibson, 289; "*modus operandi*": Powell, 41.

343 "October Surprise" to "grotesque and irresponsible": "Post Withholds Jack Anderson 'Invasion' Column," *WP* (Aug. 17, 1980), A3; Richard Burt, "U.S. Rebutting Columnist," *NYT* (Aug. 26, 1980), A5.

343–44 hadn't even bothered, spiked the "Merry-Go-Round," "scoop of the century," "embarrass, bedevil," disinformation campaign: Powell, 252–55, and George C. Wilson, "Is the Press Being Duped?" *WP* (Sept. 25, 1983), C5.

Anderson's junior partner, Dale Van Atta, later acknowledged that the Pentagon proposal for invading Iran was only a "contingency plan" leaked by anti-Carter members of the military. Nonetheless, Van Atta said, "Jack hyped" the information and "leaned on me to tell [*Washington Post* editors] that we had more evidence than we had." According to another Anderson legman who investigated the October Surprise allegation, Ron McRae, "Nobody I talked to knew anything about it. Still, I felt certain pressure to come through for Anderson, who I knew wanted this story intensely. And so . . . I did a horrible thing: I [falsely] told Anderson that my sources had confirmed the story." Van Atta intv., Ron McRae, "Beyond Gonzo," *Spy* (June 1992), 52.

344 "all-American quality": JA and Gibson, 341; "exclusive" interviews: JA and Dale Van Atta, MGR (March 3, 5, 19, 30, April 13 and 23, 1986), JAP.

344 "Young Astronauts": JA and Gibson, 361–62; "dramatic bid": JA, "President Hopes to Spur Youths into Space Age," *WP* (July 6, 1984), B8; Anderson's children on the Young Astronauts' payroll: Corn, 560; solicited financial donations: letter, JA to Don Kendall (Jan. 18, 1985), JAP.

344–45 presidential commission: JA and Joseph Spear, "A Reagan Promise Pays Off," *WP* (Sept. 10, 1987), DC11; letter, JA to Jay Van Andel (Oct. 25, 1984), JAP; "sell his soul": Van Atta intv.; "what Jack craves": Harrington, 49.

345 Iran scandal: JA and Dale Van Atta, "Iran-Contra Affair," *The World Almanac* (New York: Pharos Books, 1988); Draper, 120; Patricia Sullivan, "David Kimche, 82," *WP* (March 10, 2010), B7; resembled Nixon's Plumbers: Hertsgaard, 303; "irresponsible, even traitorous": Dale Van Atta, "Giving Up the Scoop of the '80s," *Boston Globe* (June 28, 1987), F1ff; "lowest point": Van Atta intv.

345–46 reporters fabricating information: Spear intv. Gibson and Fred Vallejo, "Anderson Goes It Alone," *Washington Journalism Review* (Jan. 1982); "top-secret" to "positive thinking": JA, "Pentagon Invades Buck Rogers' Turf," *WP* (Jan. 9, 1981), D16, and Ron McRae, "Beyond Gonzo," *Spy* (June 1992), 53–54; worst columnist: Wendy Swallow, "Rating Washington Columnists," *Washingtonian* (Oct. 1981), 87–88; "tarnished": letter, David Hendin to JA (Jan. 26, 1988), JAP; "entertaining crank": Hume intv.

346 girdle: Loveless intv.; "went to his head": Harrington, 47; "do almost daily," "thinner and thinner": Kornheiser, F6; low-salaried assistants: Whitten intv.; rubber stamp: Newman intv.; "self-serving bullshit": Rosenberg intv.

347 *National Star*: Novak, 297; *Inside Edition*: Margo Hammond, "Merry-Go-Round Is Slowing Down," *St. Petersburg Times* (Feb. 16, 1997), D7ff; "Barnum & Bailey": Capaccio intv.; *Truth*: JA and Gibson, 406; *Target: USA!*: Matt Roush, "Jack Anderson: On 'Target,' or Tabloid TV?" *USA Today* (May 31, 1989), 30; Hollywood: "Hollywood's Love Affair with Anderson," *WP* (March 23, 1980), SM5, and "A Jack Anderson Sitcom," *NYT* (Aug. 11, 1983), A18; "big score": L. Goldberg intv.

347 cocaine: JA, "Dornan Presses Probe of Hill Cocaine Use," *WP* (Aug. 4, 1982), VA13; JA, "Clearing Up Atmosphere on Drug Story," *WP* (May 11, 1983), VA15; Robert J. McCloskey, "The Anderson Allegations," *WP* (May 4, 1983), A26.

347 "voluptuous" to "intimate physical description": Benjamin C. Bradlee, "Why The Post Killed That Anderson Column," *WP* (June 21, 1976), A23, and JA, "The Senator Byrd Story," *WP* (June 24, 1976), A31.

347–48 Roy Cohn: JA and Dale Van Atta, "NIH Treated Roy Cohn for AIDS," *WP* (July 25, 1986), C19.

348 "Here you have": David Astor, "Controversial Piece on Pentagon Official," *Editor and Publisher* (Aug. 17, 1991), 40; "outdated piety": JA and Gibson, 394; Cheney: JA intv. Gibson.

348 sexposés suppressed: Alwood, 280; "only attention . . . salacious stories": Van Atta intv.; "hot scoop": George Maksian, "Anderson May Be Jumping Jack," New York *Daily News* (Nov. 29, 1982); edit it more carefully: Armstrong intv.

348–49 Persian oil heiress: Bruch, Lawrence intvs.; JA and Gibson, 105, 328; "corner turrets": Todd Smith, "Old Mansions Give Businesses New Ambience," *Washington Times* (July 17, 1990), C1; "eerily reminiscent," "Muckrakers, Incorporated": Downie, 138; "Castle," bidet: Newman intv.

349 "buck-raking": Richard Harwood, "Honoraria for Journalists," *WP* (Jan. 29, 1989), D6; fraud and lying: Maxine Cheshire, "The Muckraker and the Entrepreneur," *WP* (May 25, 1972), C1; improper stock trading: Corn, 559; "sexploitation": Welles, "Business Deals," F11; publisher of a pornographic magazine: letter, JA to Bob Guccione (Oct. 27, 1983), JAP; bizarre cult: Elissa Silverman, "You Don't Know Jack," *Washington City Paper* (March 2–8, 2001), 20–25; "marginal character": Mitchell intv.

349 "Become A Millionaire?" to "reputation of the column": letter and ad, Dale Van Atta, Joe Spear, Daryl Gibson, Michael Binstein, and Opal Ginn to JA (July 25, 1988), JAP.

349–50 selling classified, "boggled the imagination": Van Atta intv.

350 Davidson money: Davidson intv.; Davidson indictment, pleas, and "reputation so golden": Welles, "Tarnishing," 22.

350 "Koreagate": S. Trento, 110; Charles R. Babcock, "The Envelope, Please, Mr. Park," *WP* (April 5, 1978), A2; Michael Dobbs, "'Koreagate' Figure Tied to Oil-for-Food Scandal," *WP* (April 15, 2005), A19; Diplomat National Bank: Welles, "Business Deals," F1, 3; Scott Armstrong and Maxine Cheshire, "Bank Stock Owned by Park, Pak," *WP* (Nov. 14, 1976), A1; Scott Armstrong, "Columnist to Quit Role with Bank," *WP* (Nov. 22, 1976), A1; "pants down": Satchell, A1; "awkward position": Mark R. Arnold, "The Final Victim," *National Observer* (Dec. 4, 1976).

351 Sinatra: Denton intv.; angered a potential investor: Corn, 558; Jhoon Rhee "transformed" the "spectacular sport": JA, "The Big Bout in Congress," *Parade* (Aug. 3, 1975); Welles, "Business Deals," F1, F3; Bob Addie, "Allen, Anderson: Boosters of Karate," *WP* (May 15, 1975), C5; Steve Daley, "Rhee: The Art of Marshaling Influence," *WS* (Nov. 19, 1976); Smolonsky intv.; "mindless cheapness": Grady intv.

351 "no species affected" to "stealth sponsor": Howard Kurtz, "The Muckraker and the Oil Spill," *WP* (Dec. 22, 1992), C1; "Depression-era mentality": Kurtz intv.

351–52 "long climb": Hume, 283–84; lazy glamour boy: Whitten intv. Gibson; "see a psychiatrist": Whitten intv.; "got into a rut": Hume, 284; reporters also departed: Cloherty, Owens, Smolonsky, Van Atta intvs.

352 "publisher": Harrington, 22; rotating cast of employees: Chuck Conconi, "Personalities," *WP* (April 3, 1985), D3; Howard Kurtz, "New Muckraker for Jack Anderson," *WP* (Nov. 21, 1999), D1; mocking: Newman intv.

352 occasional scoop: JA and Dale Van Atta, "Buckley Is Dead," *WP* (Dec. 13, 1985), B21; mentoring journalists: JA and Gibson, 9–13; backing of a new nationwide organization: Aucoin, 123–29.

352–53 Liberty Lobby: Mintz, 5–8, 202; Al Kamen, "High Court Gives News Media Major Victory on Libel Law," *WP* (June 26, 1986), A1; "They dragged Jack" to "behind him": Sullivan intv.; "I took a lot of chances": JA intv. Gibson.

353 column declined, staff dwindled: Susan Hansen, "Jack, Be Nimble," *NewsInc.* (March 1992), 13–14; "No one seemed to notice": Margo Hammond, "Merry-Go-Round Is Slowing Down," *St. Petersburg Times* (Feb. 16, 1997), D7; "reorganizing the features": "Dear Readers," *WP* (Jan. 24, 1997), E1; Financing kept afloat, credit card debt: Howard Kurtz, "New Muckraker for Jack Anderson," *WP* (Nov. 21, 1991), D1.

353 laid off Opal, "I wasn't even given time": Howard Kurtz, "Jack Anderson Column in Jeopardy," *WP* (Oct. 15, 1991), E1; "wanting to do it": Van Atta intv.; alcoholism: JA, Reynolds, Van Atta intvs.; "six sheets to the wind": Smolonsky intv.; inspired fear: Denton, Rosenberg, Van Atta intvs., Spear intv. Gibson.

353–54 "her whole life," "knew every source": Gibson intv.; "broke her heart": Whitten intv.; kiss-and-tell book: JA, Muncy intvs.; "putting her out to pasture": Howard Kurtz, "Jack Anderson Column in Jeopardy," *WP* (Oct. 15, 1991), E1; incriminating paperwork: Van Atta intv.

354 "abrupt, unwarranted dismissal": letter, Richard Bolger to JA (April 21, 1998); "dire straits": letter, Les Whitten to JA (Aug. 4, 1998); "lifetime of loyalty": Jack Mitchell to JA (Aug. 5, 1998); "share[d] your concern": letter, JA to Jack Mitchell (Aug. 7, 1998)—all in JAP; "got drunk every night": Muncy intv.

354 toast her farewell: Gooding intv.

355 "wouldn't let me". . . Anderson funeral absence: Mayfield intv.; death: "Obituaries: Opal Ginn," *WP* (July 15, 1999), B6; "basically committed suicide": Muncy intv.

355–56 Gordon estrangement: JA, G. Anderson, K. Anderson intvs.; Salt Lake City nursing home, "We're proud" to "It's all right": Harrington, 44, 50.

356 Anderson's retirement: Howard Kurtz, "Curtain Call?" *WP* (Aug. 16, 2004), C7; "Jack understood": Rosenstiel intv.

356 Anderson's health, last days: JA, T. Neider, S. Neider, Whitten, Grady, Van Atta intvs.

357–58 Anderson died: Patricia Sullivan, "Investigative Columnist Jack Anderson Dies," *WP* (Dec. 18, 2005), C8; "feet of clay": Sally Denton, "Jack Anderson: An American Original," *Progressive Review* (Dec. 2005); "betrayed the ideal": Harrington, 47–48, and Whitten intv.; "no network": Hume intv.

358 "you sometimes shoot your own men": Les Whitten, "Eulogy for a Muckraker," *Huffington Post* (Dec. 27, 2005); "marketable product": JA and Clifford, 3.

358 "readers were his flock": Inderjit Badhwar, "Notes from the Washington Merry-Go-Round," *Indian Express* (Dec. 26, 2005), 9.

358 buried: Van Atta intv.; tombstone: photo, JAP.

EPILOGUE

359 post-Watergate reforms: Kutler, *Wars*, 574, 586, and Francine Kiefer, "Watergate Reforms Fade," *Christian Science Monitor* (June 17, 2002), A1; "learning from Watergate": Greenberg, 177.

360 Cheney and Rumsfeld: Anne E. Kornblut, "The News Media Is Still Recovering from Watergate," *NYT* (June 5, 2005), WK4; "restoration": Emily Bazelon, "All the President's Powers," *NYT* (Nov. 18, 2007), BR18.

360 "ruthless little bastard": Cockburn, 20; stripped power: Suskind, 24–25.

360 "actor," "ultimate presidential commodity": Hertsgaard, 46, 6.

360–61 PR team, advertising gimmicks: Hertsgaard, 38, 5; "divert people's attention": Maltese, 199; "stage the news": Tebbel and Watts, 552.

361 Reagan's men played hardball, leaks: Hertsgaard, 6, 41, 109–11, 233.

361 "bark is much worse than its bite": Hertsgaard, 7–8; "slicker and smarter": Tebbel and Watts, 545.

361 Reagan deregulation: Hertsgaard, 182; talk radio: Michael Massing, "The End of News?" *NYRB* (Dec. 1, 2005), 23–24; Johann Hari, "G. Gordon Liddy: Voice of Unreason," *The Independent* (Nov. 22, 2004).

362 homosexual smear: Margaret Carlson, "Getting Nasty," *Time* (June 24, 1989); "You don't let press set the agenda": Maltese, 2.

362 Clinton tactics: Maltese, 228–29; Scaife: Lukas, 112: Neil A. Lewis, "Almost $2 Million Spent in Magazine's Anti-Clinton Project," *NYT* (April 15, 1998), A20; pseudo-scandals: Lowry, 125, 131; Goldberg and Snow: David Streitfeld and Howard Kurtz, "Literary Agent Was Behind Secret Tapes," *WP* (Jan. 24, 1998), A1ff.

Ailes may have been the founder of Fox News, but it was his former boss, Richard Nixon, who first suggested "the creation of a 4th Network as a means of elevating the standard of all TV broadcasting." Nixon even approached his longtime financial angel, billionaire Howard Hughes, about starting such a conservative network, but it would take another three decades before it became a reality under Ailes. Drosnin, 162.

363 "Richard Nixon's downfall" to "America before": Davis, 6, 2, 1.

363 journalism's abdication: Martha M. Hamilton, "What We Learned in the Melt-down," *Columbia Journalism Review* (Jan./Feb. 2009), and Massing, passim; Nixo-nian echoes: R. Dallek, "Iraq Isn't Like Vietnam—Except When It Is," *WP* (May 20, 2007), B3, and Scott Shane, "Parsing the Nixon and Kissinger Pas de Deux," *NYT* (April 17, 2007), E1.

363–64 Bush propaganda: Christopher Lee, "Update: Prepackaged News," *WP* (Feb. 14, 2006), A13; Jacob Weisberg, "Beyond Spin," *Slate* (Dec. 7, 2005); Mark Mazzeretti and Borzou Daragahi, "U.S. Military Covertly Pays to Run Stories in Iraqi Press," *Los Angeles Times* (Nov. 30, 2005), A1, 12. "Haldeman model": William Hamilton, "Bush Says Top Aide Urged Bush to Fire Rumsfeld," *WP* (Sept. 30, 2006), A4; "mili-tary analysts": David Barstow, "Behind TV Analysts, Pentagon's Hidden Hand," *NYT* (April 20, 2008), A1, 24–25.

364 funneled taxpayer dollars: David Barstow and Robin Stein, "Under Bush, a New Age of Prepackaged News," *NYT* (March 13, 2005), A1, 18–19; Eric Alterman, "Bush's War on the Press," *The Nation* (May 9, 2005); Ian Buruma, "Theater of War," *NYT* (Sept. 17, 2006), BK 11; Spencer S. Hsu, "FEMA Official Apologizes for Staged Briefing with Fake Reporters," *WP* (Oct. 27, 2007), A3.

364 "shameful act," "helping the enemy": Peter Baker and Charles Babington, "Bush Ad-dresses Uproar over Spying," *WP* (Dec. 20, 2005), A1; injunction: Jeffrey Rosen, "Behind the Scenes of Secret Surveillance," *NYT* (April 3, 2008) 9.

364 leak classified information: Neil A. Lewis, "Libby, Ex-Cheney Aide, Guilty of Lying in C.I.A. Leak Case," *NYT* (March 7, 2007), A5; secretly ordered a study: David Folkenflik, "CPB Memos Indicate Level of Monitoring," *NPR Morning Edition* (June 30, 2005); "hit men": John Eggerton, "Moyers Has His Say," *Broadcasting and Cable* (Nov. 28, 2005), 16; "Nixon would be back": Paul Fahri, "A Different Recep-tion for Public Broadcasting," *WP* (March 20, 2005), A8.

364–65 Karl Rove, "Haldeman and Ehrlichman": Dean, *Worse*, 4, 11, and James Ridgeway, "Grime Pays," *Village Voice* (July 12, 2005), 20.
365 "confidant": Aitken, *Colson*, 13, 411; $2 million: Gary Wills, "A Country Ruled by Faith," *NYRB* (Nov. 16, 2006), 9; "lower than the animal species": Max Blumenthal, "Born Again, Again," *Washington Monthly* (July 1, 2005), 47ff.; "spiritual ancestor": Hunt, *Spy*, 173; "former White House counsel": Frank Rich, "Don't Follow the Money," *NYT* (June 12, 2005), D14.
365 "erosion": Weisberg, 178–79.
366 "I told him I'd been" to "blame this on Nixon": JA intv.; "Bless you": book inscription, Charles Colson, *Against the Night*, JAP.
366–67 FBI actions: K. Anderson, Olivia Anderson, Bruch intvs.; went public: Scott Carlson, "George Washington U. to Receive Jack Anderson's Papers," *Chronicle of Higher Education* (April 18, 2006), 1ff.
367 front-page headlines: Scott Shane, "F.B.I. Seeking Access to Dead Columnist's Papers," *NYT* (April 19, 2006), A1; Suzanne Goldenberg, "Family Refuses FBI Access to Columnist's 'Legacy,'" *The Guardian* (April 21, 2006), A21; Nathan Guttman, "FBI Wants Deceased Reporter's Notes on AIPAC Case," *Jerusalem Post* (April 20, 2006), A2; "dubious sounding": "Still a Target," *USA Today* (April 20, 2006), A11; "waited until Jack Anderson was dead": "Hands Off," *Salt Lake Tribune* (April 20, 2006), editorial page; "attempted raid": "FBI Needs to Back Off," *Kansas City Star* (April 20, 2006), editorial page; "Mau-Mauing": Brian Bennett and Mark Thompson, "A Reporter's Last Battle," *Time* (May 1, 2006), 29.
　　In an effort to obtain Anderson's files, two FBI agents even visited the author at home, flashing their badges and demanding access to twenty-five-year-old documents that were part of the research for this book. "We're not after [Anderson's] reporters," FBI agent Leslie Martell said. "Just their sources." Why did the Bush administration want to look through Anderson's dusty archives? The columnist's family believed it was revenge for Anderson's long feud with J. Edgar Hoover; others suspected surviving Nixon loyalists in Bush's administration, especially Vice President Cheney and Defense Secretary Rumsfeld, who had tangled with Anderson in the past. But the true reason appears to be more bizarre: a disgruntled former Anderson legman named Ron McRae told the FBI that Anderson's papers might contain evidence that his sources had committed espionage. McRae's reliability as an informant should have been suspect: not only did he write an article about how he "invented" stories for Anderson's column and by his own account became destitute and homeless, eating out of garbage cans; he also spent time in prison for sodomizing a young boy. Nonetheless, the FBI evidently believed his espionage allegation and used heavy-handed tactics to investigate it after Anderson's death. Sources for the above: FBI probe: Mark Feldstein, "A Chilling FBI Fishing Expedition," *WP* (April 29, 2006), A16; "invented," destitute: Ron McRae, "Beyond Gonzo," *Spy* (June 1992), 50–56; sodomizing: letter, Richard H. Black to JA, "Re: Ronald Michael McRae" (Aug. 21, 1987), JAP.
367 "public really best served": "The Anderson Files," *NYT* (April 24, 2006), A18; "rifling Anderson's corpse": "Secrecy Extends Beyond the Grave," *Austin American-Statesman* (April 22, 2006), A22; "rest in peace": "The FBI's Paper Chase," *Chicago Tribune* (May 11, 2006), editorial page; "although seriously dead": Molly Ivins, "Jack Anderson Investigation," *Portland Oregonian* (April 30, 2006), E6.

428 NOTES

367–68 "any truth" to "all the Andersons": transcript, Senate Judiciary Committee hearings (June 6, 2006); forced the administration to back off: Lara Jakes Jordan, "FBI No Longer Seeks Leaked Documents," AP (Jan. 4, 2007).
368 *anti american traitor*: e-mail, G. Gordon Liddy to James Grady (Nov. 20, 2006), JAP.
368 film footage: John Roberts, "Battle over Secrets," CNN (April 20, 2006) and Bob Orr, "FBI and Family," CBS Evening News (April 19, 2006); memoir excerpts: Peter Edidin, "One Man's Secret Is Another Man's Scoop," *NYT* (April 23, 2006), D5; "Back in the day": "The FBI's Fishing Trip," *San Francisco Chronicle* (April 25, 2006), B6; "their fight continues": "Release the Anderson Files," *Deseret Morning News* (April 22, 2006), editorial page.

BIBLIOGRAPHY

PRIMARY SOURCES

Oral history interviews with author

Tyler Abell, Dotti Ackerman, Hank Adams, Gordon Anderson, Jack Anderson, Jodi Anderson, Kevin Anderson, Olivia Anderson, Teri Anderson, Warren Anderson, Scott Armstrong, Inderjit Badhwar, David Bagley, F. Don Bailey, Robert G. "Bobby" Baker, Bernard Barker, Dick Bast, Mike Binstein, James Boyd, Benjamin C. Bradlee, Jeff Brindle, Laurie Bruch, John E. Byrne, Tony Capaccio, Dwight Chapin, Garry Clifford, Jack Cloherty, Faye Cohen, Sheldon Cohen, Anita Collins, I. Irving Davidson, Lynne Davidson, Cartha "Deke" DeLoach, Sally Denton, Richard Dudman, Thomas Eagleton, Daniel Ellsberg, Ray Fritsch, Frank Gibbons, Daryl Gibson, Seymour Glanzer, Barbara Godfrey, Victor Gold, Don Goldberg, Lucianne Goldberg, Peggy Gooding, James Grady, Bob Greene, Bill Gruver, Bill Haddad, Margaret Herring, Seymour Hersh, Stephen Hess, Clark Hoyt, Brit Hume, E. Howard Hunt, Dennis Hyten, Robert Jackson, Sanford Jorgensen, Marvin Kalb, Michael J. Kelley, Mike Kiernan, Darwin Knudsen, Howard Kurtz, Melvin Laird, Lilly Fallah Lawrence, George Lardner, Terry Lenzner, Lee Levine, Jerome Levinson, Ernest Linger, Cheri Loveless, Robert Maheu, Scott Maier, Frank Mankiewicz, Robert Mardian, Geneva Mayfield, Earl Mazo, Colman McCarthy, Frank McCulloch, George McGovern, Alan McSurely, James Mintz, Morton Mintz, Jack Mitchell, Linda Morgan, Alan B. Morrison, Alvin Moscow, Bill Moyers, Sarah Muncy, Samantha Neider, Tanya Neider, Jack Nelson, Joy Nelson, Barbara Newman, Robert Novak, Wayne Omer, Ronald Ostrow, Bob Owens, Walter Pincus, Kerry Plumer, Viola Pomponio, J. Stanley Pottinger, Charles Radford, Tonne Radford, Dan Rather, Robin Reynolds, Ira Rosen, Howard Rosenberg, Tom Rosenstiel, Gary Rubens, Morley Safer, Michael Satchell, Philip Scheffler, Mike Shanahan, David Shapiro, Earl Silbert, Marc Smolonsky, Linda Spear, Valerie Stewart, W. Donald Stewart, Betty Murphy Southard, Michael Sullivan, Joseph Trento, Wallace Turner, Warren Unna, Dale Van Atta, Vicki Warren, Les Whitten, Barbara Booke Whittle, Jules Witcover.

Oral history interviews conducted by others

Jack Anderson interview with Deke DeLoach
Timothy Chambless interview with Jack Anderson and Warren Anderson

Len Colodny interviews with Jack Anderson, Mary Gore Dean, John Ehrlichman, David Fleming, Melvin Laird, Robert Mardian, John Mitchell, Thomas Moorer
Joe B. Frantz interview with Drew Pearson
Robert Gettlin interviews with Charles Radford, Robert Welander
Daryl Gibson interviews with Jack Anderson, Joe Spear, Les Whitten
Cheri Loveless videotaped interview with Jack Anderson and Warren Anderson
James Rosen interviews with David Fleming, Alexander Haig, Richard Kleindienst, Robert Mardian
Dale Van Atta interviews with Lawrence Eagleburger, Melvin Laird, Jack Mills

Archives
American University, Washington, D.C.: digitized original online DP MGR columns, 1932–1959
Central Intelligence Agency, Langley, VA
Len Colodny private paper collection, Tampa, FL
Columbia University, New York, NY: Pulitzer Prize papers
Dartmouth College Library, Hanover, NH: Sherman Adams papers
Dwight D. Eisenhower Library, Abilene, KS: William Rogers papers
Federal Bureau of Investigation, Washington, D.C.
George Washington University, Washington, D.C.: Gelman Library, National Security Archive, and Jack Anderson papers
Justice Department, Washington, D.C.: civil division, *JA v. RN*
John F. Kennedy Presidential Library, Cambridge, MA
Lehigh University, Bethlehem, PA: Les Whitten papers
Library of Congress, Washington, D.C.: Leonard Garment papers; Howard Liebengood papers; John J. Sirica papers
Martin Luther King Library, Atlanta, GA: Martin Luther King papers
Mississippi State University, Mississippi State, MS: Sen. John C. Stennis papers
National Archives:
    John F. Kennedy assassination archives, College Park, MD
    Richard Nixon vice presidential papers, Laguna Niguel, CA
    Richard Nixon presidential papers and White House tapes, College Park, MD
    Center for Legislative Affairs archives (Senate Armed Services Committee, Foreign Relations Committee, Permanent Subcommittee on Investigations, and Watergate Committee), Washington, D.C.
    Watergate Special Prosecution Force files, College Park, MD
Public Citizen, Washington, D.C.: ITT papers
Richard Nixon Library and Museum, Yorba Linda, CA
Senate Historical Office, Washington, D.C.: oral history interview transcripts
Stanford University, Palo Alto, CA: Hoover Institution Archives, John Ehrlichman papers, Jeb Magruder papers, Robert Mardian papers
Texas Tech University, Lubbock, TX: Special Collections Library, Elmo Zumwalt papers
University of Iowa, Ames, IA: Sen. Harold Hughes papers
University of Louisville, Louisville, KY: Ekstrom Library, Sen. Marlow W. Cook papers
University of Mississippi, University, MS: Sen. James Eastland papers
University of North Carolina, Chapel Hill, NC: Wilson Library, Alan McSurely papers

University of Tennessee, Knoxville, TN: Hoskins Library, Sen. Howard Baker papers
University of Texas, Austin, TX: Lyndon B. Johnson Library, Drew Pearson papers, Bob
    Woodward and Carl Bernstein papers
Wheaton College, Wheaton, IL: Billy Graham Center Archives, Charles W. Colson papers
University of Wisconsin, Madison, WI: Robert S. Allen papers and Clark Mollenhoff
    papers
Dale Van Atta private paper collection, Ashburn, VA

Government reports
Activities of Nondiplomatic Representatives of Foreign Principals in the United States, Sen-
    ate Foreign Relations Committee hearing, 88th Cong., 1st session (March 8,
    1963)—referred to as "Fulbright hearings"
Documentos Secretos de la ITT (Santiago, Chile: Empresa Editora Nacional Quimantu,
    1972)—referred to as "*Documentos*"
Impeachment of Richard M. Nixon, President of the United States, House Judiciary Com-
    mittee Report, 93rd Congress, 2nd Session (Aug. 20, 1974)—referred to as "House
    Impeachment Report"
Memo, David R. Young to President Richard Nixon, "Chronology of Events Relating to
    Investigation into Disclosure by Jack Anderson" (ND), Young #23, NARA—referred
    to as "Young Report"
*Nomination of Louis Patrick Gray III, of Connecticut, to Be Director, Federal Bureau of
    Investigation*, Senate Judiciary Committee hearings, 93rd Congress, 1st Session
    (March 9, 1973)—referred to as "Gray hearings"
Nomination of Richard G. Kleindienst, of Arizona, to Be Attorney General, Senate Judi-
    ciary Committee hearings, 92nd Congress, 2nd Session (March 2, 3, 6, 7, 8, 9, 10,
    14, 15, 16, 26, 29, 1972)—referred to as "ITT hearings"
Statement of Information, House Judiciary Committee hearings, Nixon Impeachment
    (May–June 1974), Internal Revenue Service, Book VIII—referred to as "IRS Im-
    peachment Hearings"
"Supplementary Detailed Staff Reports on Foreign and Military Intelligence," Box IV,
    *Final Report of the Select Committee to Study Governmental Operations with Respect
    to Intelligence Activities*, United States Senate, 94th Cong., 2nd session (April 23,
    1976)—referred to as "Church Report"
*Transmittal of Documents from the National Security Council to the Chairman of the
    Joint Chiefs of Staff*, Senate Armed Services Committee hearings (Feb. 6, 1974;
    Feb. 20–21, 1974; March 7, 1974; May 7, 1974; Dec. 19, 1974)—referred to as "Stennis
    hearings"

SECONDARY SOURCES
Spiro T. Agnew. *Go Quietly . . . or Else* (New York: William Morrow, 1980).
Jonathan Aitken. *Charles W. Colson: A Life Redeemed* (New York: Doubleday, 2005).
———. *Nixon: A Life* (London: Weidenfeld and Nicolson, 1993).
Edward Alwood. *Straight News: Gays, Lesbians, and the News Media* (New York: Colum-
    bia University Press, 1996).
Stephen Ambrose. *Nixon: The Education of a Politician, 1913–1962*. Vol. I (New York:
    Simon and Schuster, 1987).

————. *Nixon: The Triumph of a Politician, 1962–1972.* Vol. II (New York: Simon and Schuster, 1989).

————. *Ruin and Recovery, 1973–1990.* Vol. III (New York: Simon and Schuster, 1991).

Douglas Anderson. *A Washington Merry-Go-Round of Libel Actions* (Chicago: Nelson-Hall, 1980).

Jack Anderson. *Washington Exposé* (Washington, D.C.: Public Affairs, 1967).

———— and Fred Blumenthal. *The Kefauver Story* (New York: Dial, 1956).

———— and James Boyd. *Confessions of a Muckraker* (New York: Ballantine, 1979).

———— and George Clifford. *The Anderson Papers* (New York: Random House, 1973).

———— and Daryl Gibson. *Peace, War and Politics* (New York: Forge, 1999).

———— and Ronald W. May. *McCarthy: The Man, the Senator, the "Ism"* (Boston: Beacon, 1952).

James L. Aucoin. *The Evolution of Investigative Journalism* (Columbia: University of Missouri Press, 2005).

Bobby Baker and Larry L. King, *Wheeling and Dealing: Confessions of a Capitol Hill Operator* (New York: Norton, 1978).

Stephen Bates. *If No News, Send Rumors: Anecdotes of American Journalism* (New York: Holt, 1991).

Edwin R. Bayley. *Joe McCarthy and the Press* (New York: Pantheon, 1981).

John C. Behrens. *Typewriter Guerrillas: Close-ups of Twenty Top Investigative Reporters* (Chicago: Nelson-Hall, 1977).

Richard Ben-Veniste. *The Emperor's New Clothes: Exposing the Truth from Watergate to 9/11* (New York: Thomas Dunne, 2009).

Michael R. Beschloss, ed. *Taking Charge: The Johnson White House Tapes, 1963–1964* (New York: Touchstone, 1997).

Archer K. Blood. *The Cruel Birth of Bangladesh: Memoirs of an American Diplomat* (Dhaka, Bangladesh: University Press, 2002).

Taylor Branch. *Parting the Waters* (New York: Simon and Schuster, 1988).

————. *Pillar of Fire* (New York: Simon and Schuster, 1998).

David Brinkley. *Washington Goes to War* (New York: Knopf, 1988).

Fawn M. Brodie. *Richard Nixon: The Shaping of His Character* (Cambridge, MA: Harvard University Press, 1983).

Elisabeth Bumiller. *Condoleezza Rice: An American Life* (New York: Random House, 2007).

William Bundy. *A Tangled Web: The Making of Foreign Policy in the Nixon Presidency* (New York: Hill and Wang, 1998).

Thomas S. Burns. *Tales of ITT: An Insider's Report* (Boston: Houghton Mifflin, 1974).

William Burr, ed. *The Kissinger Transcripts: The Top Secret Talks with Beijing and Moscow* (New York: New Press, 1998).

Lou Cannon. *Governor Reagan: His Rise to Power* (New York: Public Affairs, 2003).

————. *Reagan* (New York: Putnam, 1982).

————. *Ronnie and Jesse: A Political Odyssey* (Garden City, NY: Doubleday, 1969).

Dan T. Carter. *George Wallace, Richard Nixon and the Transformation of American Politics* (Waco, TX: Markham, 1992).

————. *The Politics of Rage* (Baton Rouge: Louisiana State University Press, 2000).

Timothy Chambless. "Columnist Jack Anderson, the Secular Evangelist: Five Speeches on Morality in Government Delivered in Utah, 1972–1975." Master's thesis (Salt Lake City: University of Utah Press, 1977).

———. "Muckraker at Work: Columnist Jack Anderson and the Watergate Scandal, 1972–1974." Ph.D. dissertation (Salt Lake City: University of Utah Press, 1987).

Maxine Cheshire and John Greenya. *Maxine Cheshire, Reporter* (Boston: Houghton Mifflin, 1978).

Paul Coe Clark, Jr. *The United States and Somoza, 1933–1956: A Revisionist Look* (Westport, CT: Praeger, 1992).

Adam Clymer. *Edward M. Kennedy: A Biography* (New York: William Morrow, 1999).

Andrew Cockburn. *Rumsfeld: His Rise, Fall, and Catastrophic Legacy* (New York: Scribner, 2007).

William D. Cohan. *The Last Tycoons: The Secret History of Lazard Frères & Co.* (New York: Doubleday, 2007).

Mickey Cohen and John Peer Nugent. *In My Own Words: The Underworld Autobiography of Michael Mickey Cohen* (Englewood Cliffs, NJ: Prentice-Hall, 1975).

Gail Collins. *Scorpion Tongues: The Irresistible History of Gossip in American Politics* (New York: Harcourt Brace, 1999).

Len Colodny and Robert Gettlin. *Silent Coup: The Removal of a President* (New York: St. Martin's, 1991).

Charles W. Colson. *Born Again* (Old Tappan, NJ: Chosen Books, 1976).

David Corn. "Mellowing of a Muckraker." *The Nation* (Nov. 14, 1987), 541ff.

William Costello. *The Facts About Nixon: An Unauthorized Biography* (New York: Viking, 1960).

Matthew Dallek. *The Right Moment* (New York: Oxford University Press, 2004).

Robert Dallek. *Kissinger and Nixon: Partners in Power* (New York: HarperCollins, 2007).

Samuel Dash. *Chief Counsel: Inside the Ervin Committee* (New York: Random House, 1976).

Lanny Davis. *Scandal: How "Gotcha" Politics Is Destroying America* (New York: Palgrave Macmillan, 2004).

John W. Dean. *Blind Ambition: The White House Years* (New York: Simon and Schuster, 1976).

———. *Worse than Watergate: The Secret Presidency of George W. Bush* (New York: Little, Brown, 2004).

———. *The Rehnquist Choice* (New York: Free Press, 2001).

——— and Barry M. Goldwater, Jr. *Pure Goldwater* (New York: Palgrave Macmillan, 2008).

Cartha "Deke" DeLoach. *Hoover's FBI: The Inside Story by Hoover's Trusted Lieutenant* (Lanham, MD: Regnery, 1995).

Sally Denton and Roger Morris. *The Money and the Power: The Making of Las Vegas and Its Hold on America, 1947–2000* (New York: Knopf, 2001).

P. N. Dhar. *Indira Gandhi, the "Emergency," and Indian Democracy* (Oxford: Oxford University Press, 2000).

Bernard Diederich. *Somoza* (New York: Dutton, 1981).

Noah Dietrich and Bob Thomas. *Howard: The Amazing Mr. Hughes* (Greenwich, CT: Fawcett, 1972).

John Dinges and Saul Landau. *Assassination on Embassy Row* (New York: McGraw-Hill, 1981).

Richard Dougherty. *Goodbye, Mr. Christian: A Personal Account of McGovern's Rise and Fall* (Garden City, NY: Doubleday, 1973).

Tom Dowling. "Who Knows What Evil Lurks in the Hearts of Men? Jack Anderson Knows." *Washingtonian* (May 1971), 90–101.

Leonard Downie. *The New Muckrakers* (Washington, D.C.: New Republic, 1976).

James Doyle. *Not Above the Law: The Battles of Watergate Prosecutors Cox and Jaworski* (New York: Morrow, 1977).

Theodore Draper. *A Very Thin Line: The Iran-Contra Affairs* (New York: Touchstone, 1991).

Elizabeth Drew. *Washington Journal: The Events of 1973–1974* (New York: Random House, 1975).

Michael Drosnin. *Citizen Hughes* (New York: Holt, Rinehart and Winston, 1985).

James H. Dygart. *The Investigative Journalist: Folk Heroes of a New Era* (Englewood Cliffs, NJ: Prentice-Hall, 1976).

John Ehrlichman. *Witness to Power* (New York: Simon and Schuster, 1982).

Julie Nixon Eisenhower. *Pat Nixon: The Untold Story* (New York: Simon and Schuster, 1986).

Daniel Ellsberg. *Secrets: A Memoir of Vietnam and the Pentagon Papers* (New York: Viking, 2002).

Fred Emery. *Watergate: The Corruption of American Politics and the Fall of Richard Nixon* (New York: Random House, 1994).

Mark Feldstein. "Blame It on Jack." *Washingtonian* (Aug. 2004), 33–36.

———. "Fighting Quakers: The 1950s Battle Between Richard Nixon and Columnist Drew Pearson." *Journalism History*, v. 30, no. 2 (Summer 2004), 76–90.

———. "The Jailing of a Journalist: Prosecuting the Press for Possession of Stolen Government Documents." *Communication Law and Policy*, v. 10, no. 2 (Spring 2005), 137–77.

———. "Media Coverage and a Federal Grand Jury: Publication of the Secret Watergate Transcripts (1973)." *American Journalism*, v. 24, no. 2 (Spring 2007), 7–33.

———. "Watergate Revisited." *American Journalism Review*, v. 26, no. 4 (Aug./Sept. 2004), 60–67.

———. "Watergate's Forgotten Investigative Reporter: The Battle Between Columnist Jack Anderson and President Richard Nixon." Ph.D. dissertation, University of North Carolina Press (Chapel Hill, NC: 2002).

Mark Felt. *The FBI Pyramid* (New York: Putnam, 1979).

——— and John O'Connor. *A G-Man's Life: The FBI, Being "Deep Throat," and the Struggle for Honor in Washington* (New York: Public Affairs, 2006).

Michael Friedly and David Gallen. *Martin Luther King, Jr.: The FBI File* (New York: Carroll and Graf, 1993).

Leonard Garment. *Crazy Rhythms* (New York: Times Books, 1997).

———. *In Search of Deep Throat* (New York: Basic Books, 2000).

David J. Garrow. *Bearing the Cross: Martin Luther King, Jr., and the Southern Christian Leadership Conference* (New York: Harper, 2004).

———. *The FBI and Martin Luther King, Jr.: From "Solo" to Memphis* (New York: Norton, 1981).

Irwin F. Gellman. *The Contender: Richard Nixon, the Congress Years, 1946–1952* (New York: Free Press, 1999).

Curt Gentry. *J. Edgar Hoover: The Man and the Secrets* (New York: Norton, 1991).

Francis M. Gibbons. *Jack Anderson: Mormon Crusader in Gomorrah* (New York: Writers Club, 2003).

L. Patrick Gray III. *In Nixon's Web: A Year in the Crosshairs of Watergate* (New York: Times, 2008).

David Greenberg. *Nixon's Shadow: The History of an Image* (New York: Norton, 2003).

Vinod Gupta. *Anderson Papers: A Study of Nixon's Blackmail of India* (New Delhi: Indian School Supply Depot, 1972).

Richard Hack. *Howard Hughes: The Private Diaries, Memos and Letters* (Beverly Hills, CA: New Millennium, 2001).

———. *Puppetmaster: The Secret Life of J. Edgar Hoover* (Beverly Hills, CA: New Millenium Press, 2004).

David Halberstam. *The Powers That Be* (New York: Knopf, 1979).

H. R. Haldeman. *The Haldeman Diaries: Inside the Nixon White House* (New York: Putnam, 1994). CD-ROM of same title released 1994 by Sony Electronic Publishing's Sony Imagesoft (Santa Monica, CA).

——— and Joseph DiMona. *The Ends of Power* (New York: Times, 1978).

Walt Harrington. "The Private Rebellion of Jack Anderson." *Washington Post Magazine* (June 10, 1990), 20–25, 40–50.

Gary Warren Hart. *Right from the Start: A Chronicle of the McGovern Campaign* (New York: Quadrangle, 1973).

Richard Helms and William Hood. *A Look over My Shoulder: A Life in the Central Intelligence Agency* (New York: Random House, 2003).

Seymour M. Hersh. *The Dark Side of Camelot* (New York: HarperCollins, 1998).

———. *The Price of Power: Kissinger in the Nixon White House* (New York: Summit, 1983).

Mark Hertsgaard. *On Bended Knee: The Press and the Reagan Presidency* (New York: Schocken, 1989).

Arthur Herzog, Jr. *Vesco: From Wall Street to Castro's Cuba* (Lincoln, NE: Writer's Club, 2003).

C. David Heymann. *RFK: A Candid Biography of Robert F. Kennedy* (New York: Dutton, 1998).

James W. Hilty. *Robert Kennedy: Brother Protector* (Philadelphia: Temple University Press, 1997).

Jim Hougan. *Secret Agenda: Watergate, Deep Throat and the CIA* (New York: Random House, 1984).

Ken Hoyt and Frances Spatz Leighton. *Drunk Before Noon: The Behind-the-Scenes Story of the Washington Press Corps* (Englewood Cliffs, NJ: Prentice-Hall, 1979).

Brit Hume. *Inside Story* (Garden City, NY: Doubleday, 1974).

E. Howard Hunt. *American Spy: My Secret History in the CIA* (New York: Wiley, 2007).

———. *Undercover: Memoirs of an American Secret Agent* (New York: Putnam, 1974).

Muhmudul Huque. *The Role of the United States in the India-Pakistan Conflict* (Dhaka, Bangladesh: Academic Publishers, 1992).

Arnold A. Hutschnecker. *The Drive for Power* (New York: Evans, 1974).

Walter Isaacson. *Kissinger* (New York: Simon and Schuster, 2005).

David K. Johnson. *The Lavender Scare: The Cold War Persecution of Gays and Lesbians in the Federal Government* (Chicago: University of Chicago Press, 2004).

Charles Kaiser. *The Gay Metropolis, 1940–1996* (New York: Houghton Mifflin, 1997).

Marvin Kalb and Bernard Kalb. *Kissinger* (Boston: Little, Brown, 1974).

Kenneth R. Kappel. *Chappaquiddick Revealed* (New York: Shapolsky, 1989).

Edward M. Kennedy. *True Compass: A Memoir* (New York: Twelve, 2009).

Ronald Kessler. *In the President's Secret Service: Behind the Scenes with Agents in the Line of Fire and the Presidents They Protect* (New York: Crown, 2009).

Henry Kissinger. *White House Years* (London: George Weidenfeld and Nicolson, 1979).

———. *Years of Upheaval* (Boston: Little, Brown, 1982).

Herbert G. Klein. *Making It Perfectly Clear* (Garden City, NY: Doubleday, 1980).

Richard Kleindienst. *Justice: The Memoirs of an Attorney General* (Ottawa, IL: Jameson, 1985).

Frank L. Kluckhohn and Jay Franklin. *The Drew Pearson Story* (Chicago: Hallberg, 1967).

Herman Klurfeld. *Behind the Lines: The World of Drew Pearson* (Englewood Cliffs, NJ: Prentice-Hall, 1968).

Edward W. Knappman. *Watergate and the White House* (New York: Facts on File, 1974).

Peter Kornbluh. *The Pinochet File* (New York: New Press, 2004).

Tony Kornheiser. "Jack Anderson & His Crusading Crew." *Washington Post* (Aug. 7, 1983), F1, 6.

Egil "Bud" Krogh. *The Day Elvis Met Nixon* (Bellevue, WA: Pejama, 1994).

Stanley I. Kutler. *Abuse of Power: The New Nixon Tapes* (New York: Free Press, 1997).

———. *The Wars of Watergate: The Last Crisis of Richard Nixon* (New York: Norton, 1990).

Bob Kuttner. "The One That Got Away." *More* (Oct. 1972), 3–5, 18–19.

Dennis Kux. *India and the United States: Estranged Democracies, 1941–1991* (Washington: National Defense University Press, 1992).

Victor Lasky. *It Didn't Start with Watergate* (New York: Dial, 1977).

Jerome I. Levinson. *Who Makes American Foreign Policy?* (Gaithersburg, MD: Signature, 2004).

G. Gordon Liddy. *Will: The Autobiography of G. Gordon Liddy* (New York: St. Martin's, 1980).

Louis W. Liebovich. *Richard Nixon, Watergate, and the Press* (Westport, CT: Praeger, 2003).

Richard Lowry. *Legacy: Paying the Price for the Clinton Years* (Washington, D.C.: Regnery, 2004).

Walter Lubars and John Wicklein. *Investigative Reporting: The Lessons of Watergate* (Boston: Boston University School of Public Communication, April 23–24, 1975).

J. Anthony Lukas. *Nightmare: The Underside of the Nixon Years* (New York: Viking, 1976).

Jeb Stuart Magruder. *An American Life: One Man's Road to Watergate* (New York: Atheneum, 1974).

Robert Maheu and Richard Hack. *Next to Hughes* (New York: HarperCollins, 1992).

John Anthony Maltese. *Spin Control: The White House Office of Communications and the Management of Presidential News* (Chapel Hill: University of North Carolina Press, 1994).

Victor Marchetti and John D. Marks. *The CIA and the Cult of Intelligence* (New York: Knopf, 1974).

Michael Massing. *Now They Tell Us: The American Press in Iraq* (New York: New York Review of Books, 2004).

Earl Mazo and Stephen Hess. *Nixon: A Political Portrait* (New York: Harper and Row, 1968).

James W. McCord, Jr. *A Piece of Tape: The Watergate Story, Fact and Fiction* (Rockville, MD: Washington Media Services, 1974).

Joseph McGinnis. *The Selling of the President 1968* (New York: Trident, 1969).

George McGovern. *Grassroots: The Autobiography of George McGovern* (New York: Random House, 1977).

Kim McQuaid. *The Anxious Years: America in the Vietnam-Watergate Era* (New York: Basic Books, 1989).

Robert W. Merry. *Taking on the World: Joseph and Stewart Alsop—Guardians of the American Century* (New York: Viking, 1996).

William "Fishbait" Miller and Frances Spatz Leighton. *Fishbait: The Memoirs of the Congressional Doorkeeper* (New York: Warner, 1977).

Frank P. Mintz. *The Liberty Lobby and the American Right: Race, Conspiracy, and Culture* (Westport, CT: Greenwood, 1985).

Dan E. Moldea. *The Killing of Robert F. Kennedy* (New York: Norton, 1995).

Clark R. Mollenhoff. *Game Plan for Disaster: An Ombudsman's Report on the Nixon Years* (New York: Norton, 1976).

Roger Morris. *Richard Milhous Nixon: The Rise of an American Politician* (New York: Holt, 1990).

Victor S. Navasky. *Kennedy Justice* (New York: Atheneum, 1971).

Eric Newton, ed. *Crusaders, Scoundrels, Journalists* (New York: Crown, 1999).

Richard M. Nixon. *RN: The Memoirs of Richard Nixon* (New York: Grosset and Dunlap, 1978).

———. *Six Crises* (Garden City, NY: Doubleday, 1962).

Lyn Nofziger. *Nofziger* (Washington, D.C.: Regnery, 1992).

Nicholas North-Broome. *The Nixon-Hughes "Loan"* (New York: American Public Affairs Institute, 1972).

Robert D. Novak. *The Prince of Darkness: 50 Years Reporting in Washington* (New York: Crown Forum, 2007).

Stephen B. Oates. *Let the Trumpet Sound: The Life of Martin Luther King, Jr.* (New York: New American Library, 1982).

Lawrence F. O'Brien. *No Final Victories* (Garden City, NY: Doubleday, 1974).

Kathryn S. Olmsted. *Challenging the Secret Government* (Chapel Hill: University of North Carolina Press, 1996).

David M. Oshinsky. *A Conspiracy So Immense: The World of Joe McCarthy* (New York: Free Press, 1983).

Richard N. Ostling and Joan K. Ostling. *Mormon America: The Power and the Promise* (New York: HarperCollins, 1999).

Bruce Oudes, ed. *Richard Nixon's Secret Files* (New York: Harper and Row, 1989).

Robert Pack. *Edward Bennett Williams for the Defense* (New York: Harper and Row, 1983).

Drew Pearson. *Diaries, 1949–1959.* Edited by Tyler Abbell (New York: Holt, Rinehart and Winston), 1974.

———. *Washington Merry-Go-Round* (New York: Blue Ribbon, 1931).

——— and Jack Anderson. *The Case Against Congress: A Compelling Indictment of Corruption on Capitol Hill* (New York: Simon and Schuster, 1968).

Rick Perlstein. *Nixonland: The Rise of a President and the Fracturing of America* (New York: Scribner, 2008).

James M. Perry. *Us and Them: How the Press Covered the 1972 Election* (New York: Potter, 1973).

James Phelan. "The Nixon Family and the Hughes Loan." *The Reporter* (Aug. 16, 1962), 20–26.

————. *Scandals, Scamps and Scoundrels: The Casebook of an Investigative Reporter* (New York: Random House, 1982).

Oliver Pilat. *Drew Pearson: An Unauthorized Biography* (New York: Harper's Magazine Press, 1973).

William E. Porter. *Assault on the Media: The Nixon Years* (Ann Arbor: University of Michigan Press, 1976).

Jody Powell. *The Other Side of the Story* (New York: Morrow, 1984).

Richard G. Powers. *Secrecy and Power: The Life of J. Edgar Hoover* (New York: Free Press, 1987).

Thomas Powers. *The Man Who Kept the Secrets: Richard Helms and the CIA* (New York: Pocket, 1979).

John Prados and Margaret Pratt Porter. *Inside the Pentagon Papers* (Lawrence: University Press of Kansas, 2004).

Raymond Price. *With Nixon* (New York: Viking, 1977).

Richard Reeves. *President Nixon: Alone in the White House* (New York: Simon and Schuster, 1991).

James Reston, Jr. *The Conviction of Richard Nixon* (New York: Harmony, 2007).

Jeffrey T. Richelson. *The U.S. Intelligence Community* (New York: Ballinger, 1989).

Donald A. Ritchie. *Press Gallery: Congress and the Washington Correspondents* (Cambridge, MA: Harvard University Press, 1991).

————. *Reporting from Washington: The History of the Washington Press Corps* (Oxford: Oxford University Press, 2005).

Gene Roberts and Hank Klibanoff. *The Race Beat: The Press, the Civil Rights Struggle, and the Awakening of a Nation* (New York: Knopf, 2006).

James Rosen. "Nixon and the Chiefs." *Atlantic Monthly* (April 2002), 53–59.

————. *The Strong Man: John Mitchell and the Secrets of Watergate* (New York: Doubleday, 2008).

Arthur Edward Rowse. *Slanted News: A Case Study of the Nixon and Stevenson Fund Stories* (Boston: Beacon, 1957).

David Rudenstine. *The Day the Presses Stopped: A History of the Pentagon Papers Case* (Berkeley: University of California Press, 1996).

William Safire. *Before the Fall: An Inside View of the Pre-Watergate White House* (New York: Da Capo, 1988).

Anthony Sampson. *The Sovereign State of ITT* (New York: Stein and Day, 1973).

Michael Satchell. "Jack Anderson Falls Victim to His Enormous Success," *Washington Star* (Nov. 28, 1976), A1, 9.

Joe Scarborough. *Rome Wasn't Burnt in a Day* (New York: HarperCollins, 2004).

Bob Schieffer. *This Just In: What I Couldn't Tell You on TV* (New York: Putnam, 2003).

Robert J. Schoenberg. *Geneen* (New York: Norton, 1985).

Michael Schudson. *Watergate in American Memory: How We Remember, Forget, and Reconstruct the Past* (New York: Basic Books, 1993).

Robert Sobel. *ITT: The Management of Opportunity* (New York: Times, 1982).

Tad Szulc. *The Illusion of Peace: Foreign Policy in the Nixon Years* (New York: Viking, 1978).

Susan Sheehan. "The Anderson Strategy." *The New York Times Magazine* (August 13, 1972), 10–11, 76–83.

Walter Sheridan. *The Fall and Rise of Jimmy Hoffa* (New York: Saturday Review, 1972).

Robert G. Sherrill. "Drew Pearson: An Interview." *The Nation* (July 7, 1969), 7–16.
Melvin Small. *The Presidency of Richard Nixon* (Lawrence: University Press of Kansas, 1999).
Anastasio Somoza and Jack Cox. *Nicaragua Betrayed* (Boston: Western Islands, 1980).
Joseph C. Spear. *Presidents and the Press: The Nixon Legacy* (Cambridge, MA: MIT Press, 1984).
Maurice Stans. *The Terrors of Justice: The Untold Side of Watergate* (New York: Everest House, 1978).
William C. Sullivan and Bill Brown. *The Bureau: My Thirty Years in Hoover's FBI* (New York: Norton, 1979).
Anthony Summers. *The Arrogance of Power: The Secret World of Richard Nixon* (New York: Viking, 2000).
———. *Official and Confidential: The Secret World of J. Edgar Hoover* (New York: Putnam, 1993).
Ron Suskind. *The One Percent Doctrine* (New York: Simon and Schuster, 2007).
Barry Sussman. *The Great Cover-up: Nixon and the Scandal of Watergate* (New York: Crowell, 1974).
Michael Sweeney. *Secrets of Victory: The Office of Censorship and the American Press and Radio in World War II* (Chapel Hill: University of North Carolina Press, 2001).
Sam Tanenhaus. *Whittaker Chambers: A Biography* (New York: Modern Library, 1998).
John Tebbel and Sarah Miles Watts. *The Press and the Presidency: From George Washington to Ronald Reagan* (New York: Oxford University Press, 1985).
Athan G. Theoharis. *J. Edgar Hoover, Sex and Crime: An Historical Antidote* (Chicago: Dee, 1995).
——— and John Stuart Cox. *The Boss: J. Edgar Hoover and the Great American Inquisition* (Philadelphia: Temple University Press, 1988).
Evan Thomas. *The Man to See: Edward Bennett Williams* (New York: Simon and Schuster, 1991).
———. *Robert Kennedy: His Life* (New York: Simon and Schuster, 2000).
Fred D. Thompson. *At That Point in Time: The Inside Story of the Senate Watergate Committee* (New York: Quadrangle, 1975).
Hunter S. Thompson. *Fear and Loathing: On the Campaign Trail '72* (New York: Popular Library, 1973).
Joseph John Trento. "Jack Anderson: The Terror of Official Washington." *Saga* (Sept. 1972), 18–23.
Susan Trento. *The Power House: Robert Keith Gray and the Selling of Access and Influence in Washington* (New York: St. Martin's, 1992).
Tony Ulasewicz and Stuart A. McKeever. *The President's Private Eye* (Westport, CT: Publishers Group West, 1990).
Dale Van Atta. *With Honor: Melvin Laird in War, Peace, and Politics* (Madison: University of Wisconsin Press, 2008).
Christopher Van Hollen. "The Tilt Policy Revisited: Nixon-Kissinger Geopolitics and South Asia." *Asian Survey*, vol. 20, no. 4 (April 1980), 339–61.
Vamik D. Volkan, Norman Itzkowitz, and Andrew W. Dod. *Richard Nixon: A Psychobiography* (New York: Columbia University Press, 1997).
Nicholas von Hoffman. *Citizen Cohn* (New York: Doubleday, 1988).
Mike Wallace and Gary Paul Gates. *Close Encounters* (New York: Morrow, 1984).

Steve Weinberg. "The Anderson File," *Columbia Journalism Review* (Nov./Dec. 1989), 35–39.

Richard Weiner. *Syndicated Columnists*. 3rd ed. (New York: Weiner, 1979).

Allen Weinstein. *Perjury: The Hiss-Chambers Case* (New York: Random House, 1997).

Jacob Weisberg. *The Bush Tragedy* (New York: Random House, 2008).

Chris Welles. "Jack Anderson's Business Deals," *Los Angeles Times* (Dec. 25, 1983), F1, F3, F11.

———. "Tarnishing of Muckraker Anderson." *Los Angeles Times* (Dec. 21, 1983), A1, A20–22.

Tom Wells. *Wild Man: The Life and Times of Daniel Ellsberg* (New York: Palgrave Macmillan, 2001).

Theodore H. White. *The Making of the President 1972* (New York: Atheneum, 1973).

Tom Wicker. *One of Us: Richard Nixon and the American Dream* (New York: Random House, 1991).

Garry Wills. *Nixon Agonistes: The Crisis of the Self-Made Man* (New York: Houghton Mifflin, 1969).

Robert N. Winter-Berger. *The Washington Pay-off: An Insider's View of Corruption in Government* (New York: Dell, 1972).

Jules Witcover. *85 Days: The Last Campaign of Robert Kennedy* (New York: Putnam, 1969).

———. *Very Strange Bedfellows: The Short and Unhappy Marriage of Richard Nixon and Spiro Agnew* (New York: Public Affairs, 2007).

Kristi Witker. *How to Lose Everything in Politics Except Massachusetts* (New York: Mason and Lipscomb, 1974).

Bob Woodward. *The Secret Man: The Story of Watergate's Deep Throat* (New York: Simon and Schuster, 2005).

——— and Carl Bernstein. *All the President's Men* (New York: Simon and Schuster, 1974).

——— and Carl Bernstein. *The Final Days* (New York: Avalon, 1976).

Elmo R. Zumwalt, Jr. *On Watch: A Memoir* (New York: Quadrangle, 1976).

ACKNOWLEDGMENTS

I am indebted to many people who helped make this book possible. The late Jack Anderson and his family provided extensive cooperation, granting lengthy interviews and sharing letters, diaries, and photos without preconditions. In addition, in the weeks after the columnist's death, the Andersons banded together to resist a sudden attempt by the FBI to seize his archives from my university library, a disturbing maneuver that made front-page headlines across the nation (and which is described in the Epilogue). I am grateful to the many writers who successfully rallied against this assault on academic and press freedom, including the PEN American Center, the Association of American Publishers, the American Library Association, and Investigative Reporters and Editors. The resulting publicity led the Senate Judiciary Committee to hold hearings—Anderson's son Kevin and I testified about the FBI's heavy-handed tactics—and bipartisan condemnation forced the Bush administration to back down, allowing my research to resume unimpeded. George Washington University librarian Jack Siggins was steadfast throughout, protecting the integrity of the two hundred boxes of documents that Anderson donated to the university.

Thanks also to the more than two hundred people who agreed to be interviewed for this book, including Bobby Baker, Bernard Barker, Ben Bradlee, Dwight Chapin, John Dean, Deke DeLoach, Tom Eagleton, Daniel Ellsberg, Lucianne Goldberg, Sy Hersh, Brit Hume, E. Howard Hunt, Marvin Kalb, Howard Kurtz, Melvin Laird, Robert Mahen, Frank Mankiewicz, Robert Mardian, George McGovern, Bill Moyers, Robert Novak, Dan Rather, and Earl Silbert.

Special appreciation goes to those who worked with me to unearth new primary source materials. Attorneys Meredith Fuchs and Kristin Adair of the nonprofit National Security Archive filed a lengthy legal petition on my behalf to declassify Justice Department records, one of dozens of formal appeals that I lodged with the federal government to release historical documents. Archivists Timothy Naftali, Martin Mc-Gann, Philip Metzger, Katherine Mollan, Mary Knill, Jean Kornblut, and Rob Reed cut through bureaucratic obstacles to expedite the release of paperwork. Michael Sweeney, Lara Jakes Jordan, and John Richards shared eight thousand pages of FBI files on Anderson and his boss Drew Pearson that they obtained under the Freedom of Information Act. Daryl Gibson copied several thousand additional pages of documents, and dubbed dozens of hours of audiotapes from oral history interviews with Anderson and his staff that she recorded for his memoirs in the early 1990s; Dave Lippman patiently transcribed them for me. Tim Chambless provided helpful research notes and photos from his master's thesis and doctoral dissertation on Anderson, and Tom Blanton, Bill Gaines, James Giglio, John Jenks, Corey G. Johnson, Mary Curry, and Donald Ritchie supplied other archival documents, most usefully Henry Kissinger's secret phone transcripts. Anderson's widow Olivia, son Kevin, and daughters Laurie Bruch, Cheri Loveless, and Tanya Neider—along with Anderson legmen Les Whitten, Dale Van Atta, James Grady, Jack Mitchell, Howard Rosenberg, and Marc Smolonsky—provided not only valuable paperwork but acute insight and analysis. And although I do not share their revisionist interpretation of Watergate, writers Len Colodny, Bob Gettlin, and James Rosen generously shared primary research documents, including their raw interview transcripts with key Nixon administration figures.

Transcribing Nixon's White House tapes proved to be a particular challenge, but I was greatly helped over the years by graduate students at George Washington University who worked as my research assistants: Becky Jorgensen Yeager, Elbert Ventura, Jeremy Holden, Gerard Matthews, Dionella Martinez, and Jillian Badanes, who also tracked down photos for this book. Other students also conducted interviews or research that proved useful: Jacqueline Donohue, Marcie Kohenak, Amy Smith, Erin McCann, Abra Belke, Molly Davis, Joy R. Wolf, Vanessa Maltin, Ariel Morrison, Arden Anilan, Joe Sangiorgio, Dan Fearey, Krista Gaffney, Jennifer Lee, Meghan Riley, Niki Dasarathy, Jane Byrne Bornhorst, Deena Altman, and Andrea Mandell. I am grateful to all, including any whose names I may have inadvertently omitted.

I have been been blessed with patient friends and colleagues who read various versions of the book and offered astute suggestions for improvement: Marc Miller, Susan Edwards, David Greenberg, Debby Leff, Chris Hanson, Michael Zuckerman, Tara Connell, Matthew Dallek, Jack Shafer, Chris Sterling, E. J. Levy, Belle Adler, Stanley Kutler, Tom Bowers, Peter Coclanis, Walter Jackson, Chuck Stone, Peter Kornbluh, Jimmy Potash, Sally Scott, Eric Mandelbaum, Paul Morrison, and the late Phyllis Zinicola, who is missed by the many people who loved her. Two of my readers deserve special mention: Mark Nykanen unflaggingly edited numerous manuscript drafts, combining nuanced criticism with unstinting encouragement to refine both substance and style; and historian Margaret Blanchard, my dissertation advisor and academic mentor, first persuaded me to write this book and nursed it along in its infancy but tragically did not live long enough to see its publication.

Other colleagues and friends have been supportive in a myriad of ways: David Abrahamson, Ed Alwood, Douglas Anderson, Maurine Beasley, Chris Callahan, Jack Cloherty, Allen Dale, Jean Folkerts, Mike Freedman, Amos Gelb, Ted Glasser, Tom Goldstein, James Grimaldi, Kim Gross, Jane Hall, Brant Houston, Mike Hubbard, Mike Isikoff, David Cay Johnston, Carolyn Kitch, Kevin Klose, Marty Koughan, Tom Kunkel, Don Lehman, Chuck Lewis, Jerry Manheim, Lynn Marvin, Al May, David Mindich, Dan Moldea, Pat Phalen, Paula Poindexter, Bill Regardie, Rem Rieder, Yvette Rivera, Steve Roberts, Ricki Seidman, Mike Shanahan, Linda Steiner, Carl Stern, Michael Sullivan, Lee Thornton, Susan Tifft, Pat Washburn, and Steve Weinberg.

The Freedom Forum provided a generous fellowship that enabled me to begin my research and earn a doctoral degree while supporting a family; thanks to Charles Overby, Jerry Sass, Richard Cole, and Mary Kay Blake for making this life-changing opportunity possible. The financial assistance of George Washington University's School of Media and Public Affairs, the Fund for Investigative Journalism, the Alicia Patterson Foundation, and the Lyndon Johnson Foundation provided necessary support, and I am appreciative to those who made it possible, including Margaret Engel, Lee Huebner, and the late John Hyde.

My literary agent, Alice Martell, has been a loyal champion of this book from the start, combining savvy pragmatism with uncompromising dedication and a wicked sense of humor. I have been equally lucky to have a renowned publisher. Farrar, Straus and Giroux's Sarah Crichton has been a perceptive editor, experienced and wise, and has made this a better book in large ways and small. Her editorial assistant, Dan Piepenbring, handled the tedious work of acquiring necessary legal rights and steering the manuscript through production. Attorney Henry Kaufman vetted the content, Jeff Seroy and Kathy Daneman directed publicity, Amanda Schoonmaker subsidiary rights, and Ryan Chapman online marketing. John Glusman deserves credit for first seeing the potential in my manuscript proposal. And engineer John O'Leary enhanced the audio quality of Nixon's White House tapes for the book's website.

On a personal note, deepest appreciation to my loving family: my father, Alan, who first introduced me to the "Washington Merry-Go-Round" column and taught me the importance of fighting injustice; my mother, Felice, who set an example of compassion for the underdog; my sisters, Rachel, Suzie, and Sarah, and their families, whose unwavering devotion comes wrapped in dark hilarity; my beloved Grandma Bess, whose stories about her childhood brought home the delight that is history; the Sessions family, especially Kathy, Bob, and Julia Sessions, Teresa Kramer, and Carl and Laura Sessions Stepp, who have been supportive for more than two decades; and my children, Beth and Robbie, whom I utterly adore and truly are my unconditional pride and everlasting joy. I love you all.

Finally, a statement of disclosure: I worked for Jack Anderson as a barely paid student intern during the summers of 1973 and 1976. My personal contact with the columnist was minimal—I was too inexperienced and he was too busy for it to be otherwise—but I absorbed the spirit of joyful muckraking that permeated his office, and went on afterward to an investigative reporting career of my own. I hope this familiarity has not compromised my fairness, but that ultimately will be up to the reader to decide.

INDEX

A NOTE ABOUT THE AUTHOR

Mark Feldstein is the Richard Eaton professor of journalism at the University of Maryland. For two decades, he worked as an investigative reporter for newspapers, magazines, and television, including as an on-air correspondent at CNN and ABC News. On assignment, Feldstein was beaten up in the U.S., censored in Egypt, and escorted out of Haiti under armed guard, earning dozens of journalism's top honors, including the Edward R. Murrow Broadcasting Award, a duPont-Columbia Award, and two George Foster Peabody medallions. A graduate of Harvard who received his doctorate at the University of North Carolina at Chapel Hill, Feldstein has also won awards for his scholarship from the American Journalism Historians Association and other academic organizations. He is widely quoted as a media analyst by leading news outlets in the United States and abroad, and has testified as an expert witness before Congress on First Amendment issues.